IT Essentials v6 Companion Guide

Cisco Networking Academy

Cisco Press

800 East 96th Street

Indianapolis, Indiana 46240 USA

IT Essentials v6 Companion Guide, Sixth Edition

Copyright © 2017 Cisco Systems, Inc.

Published by:
Cisco Press
800 East 96th Street
Indianapolis, IN 46240 USA

All rights reserved. No part of this book may be reproduced or transmitted in any form or by any means, electronic or mechanical, including photocopying, recording, or by any information storage and retrieval system, without written permission from the publisher, except for the inclusion of brief quotations in a review.

Printed in the United States of America

1 16

Library of Congress Control Number: 2016950551

ISBN-13: 978-1-58713-355-8

ISBN-10: 1-58713-355-5

Warning and Disclaimer

This book is designed to provide information about the Cisco Networking Academy IT Essentials course. Every effort has been made to make this book as complete and as accurate as possible, but no warranty or fitness is implied.

The information is provided on an "as is" basis. The authors, Cisco Press, and Cisco Systems, Inc. shall have neither liability nor responsibility to any person or entity with respect to any loss or damages arising from the information contained in this book or from the use of the discs or programs that may accompany it.

The opinions expressed in this book belong to the author and are not necessarily those of Cisco Systems, Inc.

This book is part of the Cisco Networking Academy® series from Cisco Press. The products in this series support and complement the Cisco Networking Academy curriculum. If you are using this book outside the Networking Academy, then you are not preparing with a Cisco trained and authorized Networking Academy provider.

CISCO

For more information on the Cisco Networking Academy or to locate a Networking Academy, Please visit www.cisco.com/edu.

Editor-In-Chief
Mark Taub

Product Line Manager
Brett Bartow

Business Operation Manager, Cisco Press
Ronald Fligge

Executive Editor
Mary Beth Ray

Managing Editor
Sandra Schroeder

Development Editor
Ellie C. Bru

Project Editor
Mandie Frank

Copy Editor
Christopher Morris

Composition
codeMantra

Indexer
Erika Millen

Proofreader
Sudhakaran

Trademark Acknowledgments

All terms mentioned in this book that are known to be trademarks or service marks have been appropriately capitalized. Cisco Press or Cisco Systems, Inc., cannot attest to the accuracy of this information. Use of a term in this book should not be regarded as affecting the validity of any trademark or service mark.

Special Sales

For information about buying this title in bulk quantities, or for special sales opportunities (which may include electronic versions; custom cover designs; and content particular to your business, training goals, marketing focus, or branding interests), please contact our corporate sales department at corpsales@pearsoned.com or (800) 382-3419.

For government sales inquiries, please contact governmentsales@pearsoned.com.

For questions about sales outside the U.S., please contact intlcs@pearson.com.

Feedback Information

At Cisco Press, our goal is to create in-depth technical books of the highest quality and value. Each book is crafted with care and precision, undergoing rigorous development that involves the unique expertise of members from the professional technical community.

Readers' feedback is a natural continuation of this process. If you have any comments regarding how we could improve the quality of this book, or otherwise alter it to better suit your needs, you can contact us through email at feedback@ciscopress.com. Please make sure to include the book title and ISBN in your message.

We greatly appreciate your assistance.

Americas Headquarters
Cisco Systems, Inc.
170 West Tasman Drive
San Jose, CA 95134-1706
USA
www.cisco.com
Tel: 408 526-4000
800 553-NETS (6387)
Fax: 408 527-0883

Asia Pacific Headquarters
Cisco Systems, Inc.
168 Robinson Road
#28-01 Capital Tower
Singapore 068912
www.cisco.com
Tel: +65 6317 7777
Fax: +65 6317 7799

Europe Headquarters
Cisco Systems International BV
Haarlerbergpark
Haarlerbergweg 13-19
1101 CH Amsterdam
The Netherlands
www-europe.cisco.com
Tel: +31 0 800 020 0791
Fax: +31 0 20 357 1100

Cisco has more than 200 offices worldwide. Addresses, phone numbers, and fax numbers are listed on the Cisco Website at **www.cisco.com/go/offices.**

©2007 Cisco Systems, Inc. All rights reserved. CCVP, the Cisco logo, and the Cisco Square Bridge logo are trademarks of Cisco Systems, Inc.; Changing the Way We Work, Live, Play, and Learn is a service mark of Cisco Systems, Inc.; and Access Registrar, Aironet, BPX, Catalyst, CCDA, CCDP, CCIE, CCIP, CCNA, CCNP, CCSP, Cisco, the Cisco Certified Internetwork Expert logo, Cisco IOS, Cisco Press, Cisco Systems, Cisco Systems Capital, the Cisco Systems logo, Cisco Unity, Enterprise/Solver, EtherChannel, EtherFast, EtherSwitch, Fast Step, Follow Me Browsing, FormShare, GigaDrive, GigaStack, HomeLink, Internet Quotient, IOS, IP/TV, iQ Expertise, the iQ logo, iQ Net Readiness Scorecard, iQuick Study, LightStream, Linksys, MeetingPlace, MGX, Networking Academy, Network Registrar, Packet, PIX, ProConnect, RateMUX, ScriptShare, SlideCast, SMARTnet, StackWise, The Fastest Way to Increase Your Internet Quotient, and TransPath are registered trademarks of Cisco Systems, Inc. and/or its affiliates in the United States and certain other countries.

All other trademarks mentioned in this document or Website are the property of their respective owners. The use of the word partner does not imply a partnership relationship between Cisco and any other company. (0609R)

About the Contributing Author

Kathleen Czurda-Page is the lead instructor for the Cisco Networking Academy at North Idaho College. She teaches IT Essentials and CCNA courses, along with introduction-to-computers-in-business courses and courses in business leadership. Kathleen has a degree in Computer Applications in Business from North Idaho College. She earned her bachelor's degree in Professional Technical Education, her master's degree in Adult and Organizational Learning, and education specialist degree in Adult/Organizational Learning and Leadership at the University of Idaho. She also holds Cisco and CompTIA certifications. Kathleen lives with her lovely family in Coeur d'Alene, Idaho.

Contents at a Glance

Introduction xxix

Chapter 1 Introduction to the Personal Computer System 1

Chapter 2 Introduction to Lab Procedures and Tool Use 73

Chapter 3 Computer Assembly 103

Chapter 4 Overview of Preventive Maintenance 157

Chapter 5 Windows Installation 185

Chapter 6 Windows Configuration and Management 245

Chapter 7 Networking Concepts 317

Chapter 8 Applied Networking 383

Chapter 9 Laptops and Mobile Devices 445

Chapter 10 Mobile, Linux, and OS X Operating Systems 517

Chapter 11 Printers 617

Chapter 12 Security 663

Chapter 13 The IT Professional 729

Chapter 14 Advanced Troubleshooting 761

Appendix A Answers to "Check Your Understanding" Questions 783

Glossary 805

Index 841

Contents

Introduction xxix

Chapter 1 **Introduction to the Personal Computer System** 1

Objectives 1

Key Terms 1

Introduction (1.0) 4

Welcome (1.0.1) 4

Introduction to the Personal Computer (1.0.1.1) 4

Personal Computer Systems (1.1) 4

Cases and Power Supplies (1.1.1) 5

Cases (1.1.1.1) 5
Power Supplies (1.1.1.2) 7
Power Supply Wattage (1.1.1.3) 10

Internal PC Components (1.1.2) 12

Motherboards (1.1.2.1) 12
CPU Architectures (1.1.2.2) 14
Enhancing CPU Operation (1.1.2.3) 15
Cooling Systems (1.1.2.4) 17
ROM (1.1.2.5) 20
RAM (1.1.2.6) 21
Memory Modules (1.1.2.7) 22
Adapter Cards and Expansion Slots (1.1.2.8) 23
Storage Devices (1.1.2.9) 26
Storage Device Interfaces and RAID (1.1.2.10) 28

External Ports and Cables (1.1.3) 33

Video Ports and Cables (1.1.3.1) 33
Other Ports and Cables (1.1.3.2) 36
Adapters and Converters (1.1.3.3) 40

Input and Output Devices (1.1.4) 41

Input Devices (1.1.4.1) 41
Output Devices (1.1.4.2) 45
Monitor Characteristics (1.1.4.3) 47

Select Computer Components (1.2) 49

Select PC Components (1.2.1) 49

Building a Computer (1.2.1.1) 49
Select the Motherboard (1.2.1.2) 50
Select the Case and Fans (1.2.1.3) 51
Select the Power Supply (1.2.1.4) 53
Select the CPU and CPU Cooling System (1.2.1.5) 53

Select RAM (1.2.1.6) 55
Select Adapter Cards (1.2.1.7) 56
Select Hard Drives (1.2.1.8) 57
Select a Media Reader (1.2.1.9) 59
Select Optical Drives (1.2.1.10) 61
Select External Storage (1.2.1.11) 61
Select Input and Output Devices (1.2.1.12) 62

Configurations for Specialized Computer Systems (1.3) 62

Specialized Computer Systems (1.3.1) 63
Thick and Thin Clients (1.3.1.1) 63
CAx Workstations (1.3.1.2) 64
Audio and Video Editing Workstations (1.3.1.3) 64
Virtualization Workstations (1.3.1.4) 65
Gaming PCs (1.3.1.5) 66
Home Theater PCs (1.3.1.6) 67

Summary (1.4) 69

Summary (1.4.1) 69

Summary of Exercises 69

Labs 70

Check your Understanding 70

Chapter 2 Introduction to Lab Procedures and Tool Use 73

Objectives 73

Key Terms 73

Introduction (2.0) 74

Welcome (2.0.1) 74
Introduction to Lab Procedures and Tool Use (2.0.1.1) 74

Safe Lab Procedures (2.1) 74

Procedures to Protect People (2.1.1) 74
General Safety (2.1.1.1) 74
Electrical Safety (2.1.1.2) 75
Fire Safety (2.1.1.3) 75

Procedures to Protect Equipment and Data (2.1.2) 76
ESD and EMI (2.1.2.1) 76
Power Fluctuation Types (2.1.2.2) 78
Power Protection Devices (2.1.2.3) 78

Procedures to Protect the Environment (2.1.3) 79
Safety Data Sheet (2.1.3.1) 79
Equipment Disposal (2.1.3.2) 80

Proper Use of Tools (2.2) 82
Hardware Tools (2.2.1) 82
General Tool Use (2.2.1.1) 82
ESD Tools (2.2.1.2) 83
Hand Tools (2.2.1.3) 84
Cable Tools (2.2.1.4) 85
Cleaning Tools (2.2.1.5) 85
Diagnostic Tools (2.2.1.6) 85
Software Tools (2.2.2) 88
Disk Management Tools (2.2.2.1) 88
Protection Software Tools (2.2.2.2) 88
Organizational Tools (2.2.3) 89
Reference Tools (2.2.3.1) 89
Miscellaneous Tools (2.2.3.2) 90
Demonstrate Proper Tool Use (2.2.4) 91
Antistatic Wrist Strap (2.2.4.1) 91
Antistatic Mat (2.2.4.2) 92
Hand Tools (2.2.4.3) 93
Cleaning Materials (2.2.4.5) 94
Video—Computer Disassembly (2.2.4.6) 97
Summary (2.3) 98
Summary (2.3.1) 98
Summary of Exercises 98
Lab 98
Check Your Understanding 99

Chapter 3 **Computer Assembly** 103
Objectives 103
Key Terms 103
Introduction (3.0) 104
Welcome (3.0.1) 104
Computer Assembly (3.0.1.1) 104
Assemble the Computer (3.1) 104
Open the Case and Connect the Power Supply (3.1.1) 104
Open the Case (3.1.1.1) 104
Install the Power Supply (3.1.1.2) 105
Install the Motherboard (3.1.2) 107
Install the CPU and the Heat Sink and Fan Assembly (3.1.2.1) 107
Install RAM (3.1.2.3) 112

Install Motherboard (3.1.2.4) *114*
Install Drives (3.1.3) 115
Install the Hard Drive (3.1.3.1) *115*
Install the Optical Drive (3.1.3.2) *116*
Install the Adapter Cards (3.1.4) 117
Types of Adapter Cards (3.1.4.1) *117*
Install a Wireless NIC (3.1.4.2) *118*
Install a Video Adapter Card (3.1.4.3) *120*
Install Cables (3.1.5) 120
Connect Power to the Motherboard (3.1.5.1) *121*
Connect Power to the Internal Drive and Case Fans (3.1.5.2) *123*
Connect the Internal Data Cables (3.1.5.4) *125*
Install the Front Panel Cables (3.1.5.6) *126*
Reassemble the Case Assembly (3.1.5.9) *130*
Install the External Cables (3.1.5.10) *130*

Boot the Computer (3.2) 132

POST, BIOS, UEFI (3.2.1) 132
BIOS Beep Codes and Setup (3.2.1.1) *132*
BIOS and CMOS (3.2.1.2) *133*
BIOS Setup Program (3.2.1.3) *136*
UEFI Setup Program (3.2.1.4) *137*
BIOS and UEFI Configuration (3.2.2) 137
BIOS Component Information (3.2.2.1) *137*
BIOS Configurations (3.2.2.2) *137*
BIOS Security Configurations (3.2.2.3) *139*
BIOS Hardware Diagnostics and Monitoring (3.2.2.4) *140*
UEFI EZ Mode (3.2.2.5) *141*
UEFI Advanced Mode (3.2.2.6) *143*

Upgrade and Configure a Computer (3.3) 144

Motherboard and Related Components (3.3.1) 144
Motherboard Component Upgrades (3.3.1.1) *144*
Upgrade the Motherboard (3.3.1.2) *145*
Upgrade the BIOS (3.3.1.3) *146*
Upgrade CPU and Heat Sink and Fan Assembly (3.3.1.4) *147*
Upgrade the Ram (3.3.1.5) *147*
Storage Devices (3.3.2) 148
Upgrade Hard Drives (3.3.2.1) *148*
Peripheral Devices (3.3.3) 149
Upgrade Input and Output Devices (3.3.3.1) *149*

Summary (3.4) 151
Summary (3.4.1) 151
Summary of Exercises 152
Labs 152
Check Your Understanding 152

Chapter 4 Overview of Preventive Maintenance 157
Objectives 157
Key Terms 157
Introduction (4.0) 158
Welcome (4.0.1) 158
Overview of Preventive Maintenance (4.0.1.1) 158
Preventive Maintenance (4.1) 158
PC Preventive Maintenance Overview (4.1.1) 158
Benefits of Preventive Maintenance (4.1.1.1) 159
Preventive Maintenance Tasks (4.1.1.2) 159
Clean the Case and Internal Components (4.1.1.3) 160
Inspect Internal Components (4.1.1.4) 161
Environmental Concerns (4.1.1.5) 162
Troubleshooting Process (4.2) 163
Troubleshooting Process Steps (4.2.1) 163
Introduction to Troubleshooting (4.2.1.1) 163
Identify the Problem (4.2.1.2) 164
Establish a Theory of Probable Cause (4.2.1.4) 168
Test the Theory to Determine Cause (4.2.1.5) 169
Establish a Plan of Action to Resolve the Problem and Implement the Solution (4.2.1.6) 170
Verify Full System Functionality and, If Applicable, Implement Preventive Measures (4.2.1.7) 171
Document Findings, Actions, and Outcomes (4.2.1.8) 172
Common Problems and Solutions (4.2.2) 172
PC Common Problems and Solutions (4.2.2.1) 172
Summary (4.3) 180
Summary (4.3.1) 180
Summary of Exercises 180
Check your Understanding 180

Chapter 5 Windows Installation 185
Objectives 185
Key Terms 185

Introduction (5.0) 188

Welcome (5.0.1) 188

Windows Installation (5.0.1.1) 188

Modern Operating Systems (5.1) 188

Operating System Terms and Characteristics (5.1.1) 188

Terms (5.1.1.1) 188

Basic Functions of an Operating System (5.1.1.2) 190

Processor Architecture (5.1.1.3) 192

Types of Operating Systems (5.1.2) 193

Desktop Operating Systems (5.1.2.1) 193

Network Operating Systems (5.1.2.2) 194

Customer Requirements for an Operating System (5.1.3) 194

OS Compatible Applications and Environments (5.1.3.1) 194

Minimum Hardware Requirements and Compatibility with OS Platform (5.1.3.2) 195

Operating Systems Upgrade (5.1.4) 196

Checking OS Compatibility (5.1.4.1) 196

Windows OS Upgrades (5.1.4.2) 197

Data Migration (5.1.4.3) 198

Operating System Installation (5.2) 199

Storage Device Setup Procedures (5.2.1) 200

Storage Device Types (5.2.1.1) 200

Hard Drive Partitioning (5.2.1.2) 203

File Systems (5.2.1.4) 206

OS Installation with Default Settings (5.2.1.6) 208

Account Creation (5.2.1.8) 210

Finalize the Installation (5.2.1.9) 212

Custom Installation Options (5.2.2) 214

Disk Cloning (5.2.2.1) 214

Other Installation Methods (5.2.2.2) 215

Network Installation (5.2.2.3) 217

Restore, Refresh, and Recover (5.2.2.4) 219

System Recovery Options (5.2.2.5) 220

Boot Sequence and Registry Files (5.2.3) 222

Windows Boot Process (5.2.3.1) 222

Startup Modes (5.2.3.3) 223

Windows Registry (5.2.3.4) 224

Multiboot (5.2.4) 226

Multiboot Procedures (5.2.4.1) 226

Disk Management Utility (5.2.4.2) 227

Partitions (5.2.4.3) 230

Drive Mapping or Drive Letter Assignment (5.2.4.4) 231

Disk Directories (5.2.5) 234
Directory Structures (5.2.5.1) 234
User and System File Locations (5.2.5.2) 236
File Extension and Attributes (5.2.5.3) 237
Application, File and Folder Properties (5.2.5.4) 239

Summary (5.3) 241

Summary (5.3.1) 241

Summary of Exercises 241

Labs 241

Check Your Understanding 242

Chapter 6 Windows Configuration and Management 245

Objectives 245

Key Terms 245

Introduction (6.0) 247

Welcome (6.0.1) 247
Windows Configuration and Management (6.0.1.1) 247

The Windows GUI and Control Panel (6.1) 247

Windows Desktop, Tools, and Applications (6.1.1) 247
Windows Desktop (6.1.1.1) 247
Desktop Properties (6.1.1.2) 250
Start Menu (6.1.1.3) 251
Task Manager (6.1.1.4) 253
Computer and Windows Explorer (6.1.1.6) 256
Windows Libraries (6.1.1.7) 258
Install and Uninstall Applications (6.1.1.8) 258
Control Panel Utilities (6.1.2) 260
Introduction to Control Panel Utilities (6.1.2.1) 260
User Accounts (6.1.2.2) 262
Internet Options (6.1.2.4) 264
Display Settings (6.1.2.6) 265
Folder Options (6.1.2.7) 266
Action Center (6.1.2.8) 267
Windows Firewall (6.1.2.9) 268
Power Options (6.1.2.10) 269
System Utility (6.1.2.11) 270
Device Manager, Devices and Printers, and Sound (6.1.2.13) 272
Region, Programs and Features, and Troubleshooting (6.1.2.15) 275
HomeGroup and Network and Sharing Center (6.1.2.17) 276

Administrative Tools (6.1.3) 277
Computer Management (6.1.3.1) 277
Event Viewer (6.1.3.2) 279
Services (6.1.3.3) 281
System Configuration (6.1.3.4) 281
Performance Monitor and Windows Memory Diagnostics (6.1.3.5) 282
Programming Tools (6.1.3.6) 283
Disk Defragmenter and Disk Error-Checking Tool (6.1.4) 284
Disk Defragmenter and Disk Error-Checking Tool (6.1.4.1) 284
System Information (6.1.4.3) 285
Command Line Tools (6.1.5) 286
Windows CLI Commands (6.1.5.1) 286
System Utilities (6.1.5.5) 289

Client-Side Virtualization (6.2) 290

Purpose and Requirements of Virtualization (6.2.1) 290
Purpose of Virtual Machines (6.2.1.1) 290
Hypervisor: Virtual Machine Manager (6.2.1.2) 291
Virtual Machine Requirements (6.2.1.3) 294

Common Preventive Maintenance Techniques for Operating Systems (6.3) 295

OS Preventive Maintenance Plan (6.3.1) 295
Preventive Maintenance Plan Contents (6.3.1.1) 295
Updates (6.3.1.3) 296
Scheduling Tasks (6.3.1.4) 297
Restore Points (6.3.1.6) 298
Hard Drive Backup (6.3.1.8) 299

Basic Troubleshooting Process for Operating Systems (6.4) 301

Applying the Troubleshooting Process for Operating Systems (6.4.1) 302
Identify the Problem (6.4.1.1) 302
Establish a Theory of Probable Cause (6.4.1.2) 302
Test the Theory to Determine Cause (6.4.1.3) 303
Establish a Plan of Action to Resolve the Problem and Implement the Solution (6.4.1.4) 304
Verify Full System Functionality and Implement Preventive Measures (6.4.1.5) 304
Document Findings, Actions, and Outcomes (6.4.1.6) 305
Common Problems and Solutions for Operating Systems (6.4.2) 305
Common Problems and Solutions (6.4.2.1) 305

Summary (6.5) 311

Summary (6.5.1) 311

Summary of Exercises 311

Labs 311

Check Your Understanding 312

Chapter 7 Networking Concepts 317

Objectives 317

Key Terms 317

Introduction (7.0) 320

Welcome (7.0.1) 320

Networking Concepts (7.0.1.1) 320

Principles of Networking (7.1) 320

Computer Networks (7.1.1) 320

Network Definition (7.1.1.1) 320
Host Devices (7.1.1.2) 321
Intermediary Devices (7.1.1.3) 322
Network Media (7.1.1.4) 323
Bandwidth and Latency (7.1.1.6) 325
Data Transmission (7.1.1.7) 325

Types of Networks (7.1.2) 326

LANs (7.1.2.1) 326
WLANs (7.1.2.2) 327
PANs (7.1.2.3) 328
MANs (7.1.2.4) 329
WANs (7.1.2.5) 329
Peer-to-Peer Networks (7.1.2.6) 330
Client-Server Networks (7.1.2.7) 331

Networking Standards (7.2) 332

Reference Models (7.2.1) 333

Open Standards (7.2.1.1) 333
Protocols (7.2.1.2) 334
OSI Reference Model (7.2.1.3) 335
TCP/IP Model (7.2.1.4) 335
Protocol Data Units (7.2.1.5) 338
Encapsulation Example (7.2.1.6) 339
De-Encapsulation Example (7.2.1.7) 340
Comparing the OSI and TCP/IP Models (7.2.1.8) 341

Wired and Wireless Ethernet Standards (7.2.2) 341

CSMA/CD (7.2.2.1) 341
Ethernet Cable Standards (7.2.2.2) 342

CSMA/CA (7.2.2.3) 343
Wireless Standards (7.2.2.4) 343
Wireless Security (7.2.2.5) 344

Physical Components of a Network (7.3) 345

Network Devices (7.3.1) 345
Modems (7.3.1.1) 345
Hubs, Bridges, and Switches (7.3.1.2) 345
Wireless Access Points and Routers (7.3.1.3) 347
Hardware Firewalls (7.3.1.4) 349
Other Devices (7.3.1.5) 350

Cables and Connectors (7.3.2) 351
Coaxial Cables (7.3.2.1) 351
Twisted-Pair Cables (7.3.2.2) 353
Twisted-Pair Category Ratings (7.3.2.3) 355
Twisted-Pair Wire Schemes (7.3.2.4) 356
Fiber-Optic Cables (7.3.2.8) 358
Types of Fiber Media (7.3.2.9) 359
Fiber-Optic Connectors (7.3.2.10) 359

Basic Networking Concepts and Technologies (7.4) 361

Networked Equipment Addressing (7.4.1) 361
Network Addressing (7.4.1.1) 361
IP Addresses (7.4.1.2) 362
IPv4 Address Format (7.4.1.3) 363
Classful and Classless IPv4 Addressing (7.4.1.4) 365
Number of IPv6 Addresses (7.4.1.5) 366
IPv6 Address Formats (7.4.1.6) 367
Static Addressing (7.4.1.8) 368
Dynamic Addressing (7.4.1.9) 370
ICMP (7.4.1.10) 371

Transport Layer Protocols (7.4.2) 373
Role of the Transport Layer (7.4.2.1) 373
Transport Layer Features (7.4.2.2) 373
Transport Layer Protocol (7.4.2.3) 374
TCP (7.4.2.4) 376
UDP (7.4.2.5) 376
Port Numbers (7.4.2.6) 376

Summary (7.5) 378

Summary (7.5.1) 378

Summary of Exercises 378

Labs 379

Packet Tracer Activities 379

Check Your Understanding 379

Chapter 8 Applied Networking 383

Objectives 383

Key Terms 383

Introduction (8.0) 385

Welcome (8.0.1) 385

Applied Networking (8.0.1.1) 385

Computer to Network Connection (8.1) 385

Networking Cards (8.1.1) 386

Network Installation Completion List (8.1.1.1) 386
Selecting a NIC (8.1.1.2) 387
Installing and Updating a NIC (8.1.1.3) 388
Configuring a NIC (8.1.1.4) 389
Advanced NIC Settings (8.1.1.5) 390

Wireless and Wired Router Configurations (8.1.2) 393

Connecting the NIC (8.1.2.1) 393
Connecting the Router to the Internet (8.1.2.2) 394
Setting the Network Location (8.1.2.3) 395
Logging in to the Router (8.1.2.4) 397
Basic Network Setup (8.1.2.5) 398
Basic Wireless Settings (8.1.2.6) 399
Testing Connectivity with the Windows GUI (8.1.2.7) 402
Testing Connectivity with the Windows CLI (8.1.2.8) 403

Network Sharing (8.1.3) 406

Domain and Workgroup (8.1.3.1) 406
Connecting to a Workgroup or Domain (8.1.3.2) 407
Windows Homegroup (8.1.3.3) 408
Sharing Resources in Windows Vista (8.1.3.4) 409
Network Shares and Mapping Drives (8.1.3.5) 410
Administrative Shares (8.1.3.6) 412
Network Drive Mapping (8.1.3.7) 414

Remote Connections (8.1.4) 415

VPN (8.1.4.1) 415
Remote Desktop and Remote Assistance (8.1.4.2) 416

ISP Connection Technologies (8.2) 418

Broadband Technologies (8.2.1) 418

Brief History of Connection Technologies (8.2.1.1) 419
DSL and ADSL (8.2.1.2) 419
Line of Sight Wireless Internet Service (8.2.1.3) 420
WiMAX (8.2.1.4) 420
Other Broadband Technologies (8.2.1.5) 421
Selecting an ISP for the Customer (8.2.1.6) 423

Internet Technologies (8.3) 424

Data Centers and Cloud Computing (8.3.1) 425

Data Center (8.3.1.1) 425

Cloud Computing versus Data Center (8.3.1.2) 425

Characteristics of Cloud Computing (8.3.1.3) 425

SaaS, IaaS and PaaS (8.3.1.4) 426

Cloud Types (8.3.1.5) 426

Networked Host Services (8.3.2) 427

DHCP Services (8.3.2.1) 427

DNS Services (8.3.2.2) 427

Web Services (8.3.2.3) 428

File Services (8.3.2.4) 428

Print Services (8.3.2.5) 429

Email Services (8.3.2.6) 430

Proxy Settings (8.3.2.7) 430

Authentication Services (8.3.2.8) 431

Intrusion Detection and Prevention Services (8.3.2.9) 431

Universal Threat Management (8.3.2.10) 431

Common Preventive Maintenance Techniques Used for Networks (8.4) 432

Network Maintenance (8.4.1) 432

Preventive Maintenance Procedures (8.4.1.1) 433

Basic Troubleshooting Process for Networks (8.5) 433

Applying the Troubleshooting Process to Networks (8.5.1) 433

Identify the Problem (8.5.1.1) 434

Establish a Theory of Probable Cause (8.5.1.2) 434

Test the Theory to Determine Cause (8.5.1.3) 435

Establish a Plan of Action to Resolve the Problem and Implement the Solution (8.5.1.4) 435

Verify Full System Functionality and Implement Preventive Measures (8.5.1.5) 436

Document Findings, Actions, and Outcomes (8.5.1.6) 436

Common Problems and Solutions for Networks (8.5.2) 437

Identify Common Problems and Solutions (8.5.2.1) 437

Summary (8.6) 439

Summary (8.6.1) 439

Summary of Exercises 439

Labs 439

Packet Tracer Activities 440

Check Your Understanding 440

Chapter 9 Laptops and Mobile Devices 445

Objectives 445

Key Terms 445

Introduction (9.0) 448

Welcome (9.0.1) 448

Laptops and Mobile Devices (9.0.1.1) 448

Laptop Components (9.1) 448

Features of Laptop Components (9.1.1) 449

External Features Unique to Laptops (9.1.1.1) 449
Common Input Devices and LEDs in Laptops (9.1.1.2) 453
Internal Components (9.1.1.3) 454
Special Function Keys (9.1.1.4) 456
Docking Station Versus Port Replicator (9.1.1.5) 457

Laptop Displays (9.1.2) 460

LCD, LED, and OLED Displays (9.1.2.1) 461
Backlights and Inverters (9.1.2.2) 461
WiFi Antenna Connectors (9.1.2.3) 462
Webcam and Microphone (9.1.2.4) 463

Laptop Configuration (9.2) 464

Power Settings Configuration (9.2.1) 464

Power Management (9.2.1.1) 464
Managing ACPI Settings in the BIOS (9.2.1.2) 465
Managing Laptop Power Options (9.2.1.4) 465

Wireless Configuration (9.2.2) 468

Bluetooth (9.2.2.1) 468
Cellular WAN (9.2.2.2) 471
WiFi (9.2.2.3) 471

Laptop Hardware and Component Installation and Configuration (9.3) 472

Expansion Slots (9.3.1) 472

Expansion Cards (9.3.1.1) 472
Flash Memory (9.3.1.2) 474
Smart Card Reader (9.3.1.3) 475
SODIMM Memory (9.3.1.4) 476

Replacing Hardware Devices (9.3.2) 478

Overview of Hardware Replacement (9.3.2.1) 478
Power (9.3.2.2) 480
Keyboard, Touchpad, and Screen (9.3.2.4) 482
Internal Storage Drive and Optical Drive (9.3.2.6) 485
Wireless Card (9.3.2.8) 487

Speakers (9.3.2.9) 488
CPU (9.3.2.10) 488
Motherboard (9.3.2.11) 490
Plastic Frames (9.3.2.12) 491

Mobile Device Hardware Overview (9.4) 492

Mobile Device Hardware (9.4.1) 492

Mobile Device Parts (9.4.1.1) 492
Non-Upgradeable Hardware (9.4.1.2) 492
Touchscreens (9.4.1.3) 493
Solid State Drives (9.4.1.4) 494
Connection Types (9.4.1.5) 495
Accessories (9.4.1.7) 496

Other Mobile Devices (9.4.2) 498

Wearable Devices (9.4.2.1) 498
Specialty Devices (9.4.2.2) 499

Common Preventive Maintenance Techniques for Laptops and Mobile Devices (9.5) 500

Scheduled Maintenance for Laptops and Mobile Devices (9.5.1) 500

Scheduling Maintenance (9.5.1.1) 500

Basic Troubleshooting Process for Laptops and Mobile Devices (9.6) 502

Applying (9.6.1) 502

Identify the Problem (9.6.1.1) 503
Establish a Theory of Probable Cause (9.6.1.2) 503
Test the Theory to Determine Cause (9.6.1.3) 504
Establish a Plan of Action to Resolve the Problem and Implement the Solution (9.6.1.4) 505
Verify Full System Functionality and Implement Preventive Measures (9.6.1.5) 505
Document Findings, Actions, and Outcomes (9.6.1.6) 506

Common Problems and Solutions for Laptops and Mobile Devices (9.6.2) 506

Identify Common Problems and Solutions (9.6.2.1) 506

Summary (9.7) 512

Summary (9.7.1) 512

Summary of Exercises 513

Labs 513

Check Your Understanding 514

Chapter 10 Mobile, Linux, and OS X Operating Systems 517

Objectives 517

Key Terms 517

Introduction (10.0) 520

Welcome (10.0.1) 520

Mobile, Linux, and OS X Operating Systems (10.0.1.1) 520

Mobile Operating Systems (10.1) 520

Android versus iOS (10.1.1) 520

Open Source versus Closed Source (10.1.1.1) 520
Mobile Application Development (10.1.1.2) 521
Application and Content Sources (10.1.1.3) 522

Android Touch Interface (10.1.2) 525

Home Screen Items (10.1.2.1) 525
Managing Apps, Widgets, and Folders (10.1.2.2) 527

iOS Touch Interface (10.1.3) 530

Home Screen Items (10.1.3.1) 530
Managing Apps and Folders (10.1.3.2) 533

Windows Phone Touch Interface (10.1.4) 535

Start Screen Items (10.1.4.1) 535
Managing Apps and Folders (10.1.4.2) 537

Common Mobile Device Features (10.1.5) 538

Screen Orientation and Calibration (10.1.5.1) 538
GPS (10.1.5.2) 540
Convenience Features (10.1.5.5) 541
Information Features (10.1.5.6) 543

Methods for Securing Mobile Devices (10.2) 545

Passcode Locks (10.2.1) 545

Overview of Passcode Locks (10.2.1.1) 545
Restrictions on Failed Login Attempts (10.2.1.3) 549

Cloud-Enabled Services for Mobile Devices (10.2.2) 550

Remote Backup (10.2.2.1) 551
Locator Applications (10.2.2.2) 551
Remote Lock and Remote Wipe (10.2.2.3) 552

Software Security (10.2.3) 553

Antivirus (10.2.3.1) 553
Patching and Updating Operating Systems (10.2.3.2) 556

Network Connectivity and Email (10.3) 557

Wireless and Cellular Data Network (10.3.1) 557

Wireless Data Network (10.3.1.1) 557
Cellular Communications (10.3.1.3) 559

Bluetooth (10.3.2) 563

Bluetooth for Mobile Devices (10.3.2.1) 563
Bluetooth Pairing (10.3.2.2) 564

Configuring Email (10.3.3) 566

Introduction to Email (10.3.3.1) 566
Android Email Configuration (10.3.3.3) 568
iOS Email Configuration (10.3.3.4) 570
Internet Email (10.3.3.5) 571

Mobile Device Synchronization (10.3.4) 572

Types of Data to Synchronize (10.3.4.1) 572
Synchronization Connection Types (10.3.4.2) 576

Linux and OS X Operating Systems (10.4) 577

Linux and OS X Tools and Features (10.4.1) 577

Introduction to Linux and OS X Operating Systems (10.4.1.1) 577
Overview of Linux and OS X GUI (10.4.1.2) 579
Overview of Linux and OS X CLI (10.4.1.3) 582
Overview of Backup and Recovery (10.4.1.5) 585
Overview of Disk Utilities (10.4.1.6) 589

Linux and OS X Best Practices (10.4.2) 592

Scheduled Tasks (10.4.2.1) 592
Security (10.4.2.2) 594

Basic CLI (10.4.3) 597

File and Folder Commands (10.4.3.1) 597
Administrative Commands (10.4.3.2) 598

Basic Troubleshooting Process for Mobile, Linux, and OS X Operating Systems (10.5) 599

Applying the Troubleshooting Process to Mobile, Linux, and OS X Operating Systems (10.5.1) 600

Identify the Problem (10.5.1.1) 600
Establish a Theory of Probably Cause (10.5.1.2) 601
Test the Theory to Determine Cause (10.5.1.3) 602
Establish a Plan of Action to Resolve the Problem and Implement the Solution (10.5.1.4) 602
Verify Full System Functionality and Implement Preventive Measures (10.5.1.5) 603
Document Findings, Actions, and Outcomes (10.5.1.6) 604

Common Problems and Solutions for Mobile, Linux, and OS X Operating Systems (10.5.2) 604

Identify Common Problems and Solutions (10.5.2.1) 604

Summary (10.6) 610
Summary (10.6.1) 610
Summary of Exercises 611
Labs 611
Check Your Understanding 611

Chapter 11 Printers 617
Objectives 617
Key Terms 617
Introduction (11.0) 619
Welcome (11.0.1) 619
Printers (11.0.1.1) 619
Common Printer Features (11.1) 619
Characteristics and Capabilities (11.1.1) 619
Characteristics and Capabilities of Printers (11.1.1.1) 620
Printer Connection Types (11.1.1.2) 622
Printer Types (11.1.2) 623
Inkjet Printers (11.1.2.1) 623
Laser Printers (11.1.2.2) 625
Laser Printing Process (11.1.2.3) 626
Thermal Printers (11.1.2.5) 628
Impact Printers (11.1.2.6) 629
Virtual Printers (11.1.2.7) 630
Installing and Configuring Printers (11.2) 631
Installing and Updating a Printer (11.2.1) 632
Installing a Printer (11.2.1.1) 632
Types of Print Drivers (11.2.1.2) 632
Updating and Installing Printer Drivers (11.2.1.3) 633
Printer Test Page (11.2.1.4) 634
Test Printer Functions (11.2.1.5) 635
Configuring Options and Default Settings (11.2.2) 636
Common Configuration Settings (11.2.2.1) 637
Global and Individual Document Options (11.2.2.2) 638
Optimizing Printer Performance (11.2.3) 640
Software Optimization (11.2.3.1) 640
Hardware Optimization (11.2.3.2) 640
Sharing Printers (11.3) 641
Operating System Settings for Sharing Printers (11.3.1) 641
Configuring Printer Sharing (11.3.1.1) 641
Connecting to a Shared Printer (11.3.1.2) 642
Wireless Printer Connections (11.3.1.3) 644

Print Servers (11.3.2) 644

Purposes of Print Servers (11.3.2.1) 644
Software Print Servers (11.3.2.2) 645
Hardware Print Servers (11.3.2.3) 645
Dedicated Printer Servers (11.3.2.4) 646

Maintaining and Troubleshooting Printers (11.4) 646

Printer Preventive Maintenance (11.4.1) 647

Vendor Guidelines (11.4.1.1) 647
Replacing Consumables (11.4.1.2) 648
Cleaning Methods (11.4.1.3) 649
Operational Environment (11.4.1.4) 651

Troubleshooting Printer Issues (11.4.2) 651

Identify the Problem (11.4.2.1) 652
Establish a Theory of Probable Cause (11.4.2.2) 652
Test the Theory to Determine Cause (11.4.2.3) 653
Establish a Plan of Action to Resolve the Problem and Implement the Solution (11.4.2.4) 653
Verify Full System Functionality and Implement Preventive Measures (11.4.2.5) 654
Document Findings, Actions, and Outcomes (11.4.2.6) 654

Common Problems and Solutions for Printers (11.4.3) 655

Identify Common Problems and Solutions (11.4.3.1) 655

Summary (11.5) 658

Summary (11.5.1) 658

Summary of Exercises 658

Labs 659

Check Your Understanding 659

Chapter 12 Security 663

Objectives 663

Key Terms 663

Introduction (12.0) 666

Welcome (12.0.1) 666

Security (12.0.1.1) 666

Security Threats (12.1) 666

Types of Security Threats (12.1.1) 666

Malware (12.1.1.1) 667
Phishing (12.1.1.3) 669
Spam (12.1.1.4) 670
TCP/IP Attacks (12.1.1.5) 670
Zero-Day Attacks (12.1.1.7) 672
Social Engineering (12.1.1.8) 673

Security Procedures (12.2) 674

Windows Local Security Policy (12.2.1) 674

What Is a Security Policy? (12.2.1.1) 674
Accessing Windows Local Security Policy (12.2.1.2) 675
Usernames and Passwords (12.2.1.3) 676
Security Settings for Account Policies (12.2.1.4) 677
Local Password Management (12.2.1.5) 678
Security Settings for Local Policies (12.2.1.6) 679
Exporting the Local Security Policy (12.2.1.7) 679

Securing Web Access (12.2.2) 679

Web Security (12.2.2.1) 680
ActiveX Filtering (12.2.2.2) 681
Pop-up Blocker (12.2.2.3) 681
SmartScreen Filter (12.2.2.4) 682
InPrivate Browsing (12.2.2.5) 682

Protecting Data (12.2.3) 683

Software Firewalls (12.2.3.1) 683
Biometrics and Smart Cards (12.2.3.2) 685
Data Backups (12.2.3.3) 686
File and Folder Permissions (12.2.3.4) 687
File and Folder Encryption (12.2.3.5) 689
Windows BitLocker (12.2.3.6) 689
Data Wiping (12.2.3.7) 691
Hard Drive Recycling and Destruction (12.2.3.8) 693

Protection Against Malicious Software (12.2.4) 694

Malicious Software Protection Programs (12.2.4.1) 694
Remediating Infected Systems (12.2.4.2) 695
Signature File Updates (12.2.4.3) 697

Security Techniques (12.2.5) 698

Common Communication Encryption Types (12.2.5.1) 698
Service Set Identifiers (12.2.5.2) 701
Wireless Security Modes (12.2.5.3) 702
Universal Plug and Play (12.2.5.4) 703
Firmware Updates (12.2.5.5) 703
Firewalls (12.2.5.6) 703
Port Forwarding and Port Triggering (12.2.5.7) 705

Protecting Physical Equipment (12.2.6) 706

Physical Equipment Protection Methods (12.2.6.1) 706
Security Hardware (12.2.6.2) 708

Common Preventive Maintenance Techniques for Security (12.3) 710

Security Maintenance (12.3.1) 710

Operating System Service Packs and Security Patches (12.3.1.1) 710

Data Backups (12.3.1.2) 711
Windows Firewall (12.3.1.4) 711
Maintaining Accounts (12.3.1.6) 713
Managing Users (12.3.1.7) 714
Managing Groups (12.3.1.8) 717

Basic Troubleshooting Process for Security (12.4) 718

Applying the Troubleshooting Process to Security (12.4.1) 718
Identify the Problem (12.4.1.1) 718
Establish a Theory of Probable Cause (12.4.1.2) 719
Test the Theory to Determine Cause (12.4.1.3) 719
Establish a Plan of Action to Resolve the Problem and Implement the Solution (12.4.1.4) 720
Verify Full System Functionality and, If Applicable, Implement Preventive Measures (12.4.1.5) 720
Document Findings, Actions, and Outcomes (12.4.1.6) 721

Common Problems and Solutions for Security (12.4.2) 721
Identify Common Problems and Solutions (12.4.2.1) 722

Summary (12.5) 724

Summary (12.5.1) 724

Summary of Exercises 724

Labs 724

Check Your Understanding 724

Chapter 13 The IT Professional 729

Objectives 729

Key Terms 729

Introduction (13.0) 730

Welcome (13.0.1) 730
The IT Professional (13.0.1.1) 730

Communication Skills and the IT Professional (13.1) 730

Communication Skills, Troubleshooting, and the IT Professional (13.1.1) 731
Relationship Between Communication Skills and Troubleshooting (13.1.1.1) 731
Relationship Between Communication Skills and Professional Behavior (13.1.1.2) 732

Working with a Customer (13.1.2) 732
Using Communication Skills to Determine Customer Problems (13.1.2.1) 732
Displaying Professional Behavior with Customers (13.1.2.2) 733

Keeping the Customer Focused on the Problem (13.1.2.4) 735
Using Proper Netiquette (13.1.2.5) 738
Employee Best Practices (13.1.3) 738
Time and Stress Management Techniques (13.1.3.1) 738
Observing Service-Level Agreements (13.1.3.2) 740
Following Business Policies (13.1.3.3) 741
Ethical and Legal Issues in the IT Industry (13.2) 743
Ethical and Legal Considerations (13.2.1) 743
Ethical Considerations in IT (13.2.1.1) 743
Legal Considerations in IT (13.2.1.2) 744
Licensing (13.2.1.3) 745
Legal Procedures Overview (13.2.2) 747
Computer Forensics (13.2.2.1) 747
Cyber Law and First Response (13.2.2.2) 748
Documentation and Chain of Custody (13.2.2.3) 749
Call Center Technicians (13.3) 750
Call Centers, Level One Technicians, and Level Two Technicians (13.3.1) 750
Call Centers (13.3.1.1) 750
Level One Technician Responsibilities (13.3.1.2) 752
Level Two Technician Responsibilities (13.3.1.3) 753
Summary (13.4) 754
Summary (13.4.1) 754
Summary of Exercises 755
Labs 755
Activity Professional Behaviors with Customers (13.1.2.3) 755
Check Your Understanding 756

Chapter 14 Advanced Troubleshooting 761
Objectives 761
Key Terms 761
Introduction (14.0) 762
Welcome (14.0.1) 762
Advanced Troubleshooting (14.0.1.1) 762
Six Steps for Troubleshooting Review (14.0.1.2) 762
Computer Components and Peripherals (14.1) 763
Apply Troubleshooting Process to Computer Components and Peripherals (14.1.1) 763
Advanced Problems and Solutions for Components and Peripherals (14.1.1.1) 763

Operating Systems (14.2) 766

Apply Troubleshooting Process to Operating Systems (14.2.1) 766

Advanced Problems and Solutions for Operating Systems (14.2.1.1) 766

Networks (14.3) 770

Apply Troubleshooting Process to Networks (14.3.1) 770

Advanced Problems and Solutions for Networks (14.3.1.1) 770

Security (14.4) 775

Apply Troubleshooting Process to Security (14.4.1) 775

Advanced Problems and Solutions for Security (14.4.1.1) 775

Summary (14.5) 779

Summary (14.5.1) 779

Summary of Exercises 779

Labs 779

Check Your Understanding 780

Appendix A Answers to "Check Your Understanding" Questions 783

Glossary 805

Index 841

Syntax Conventions

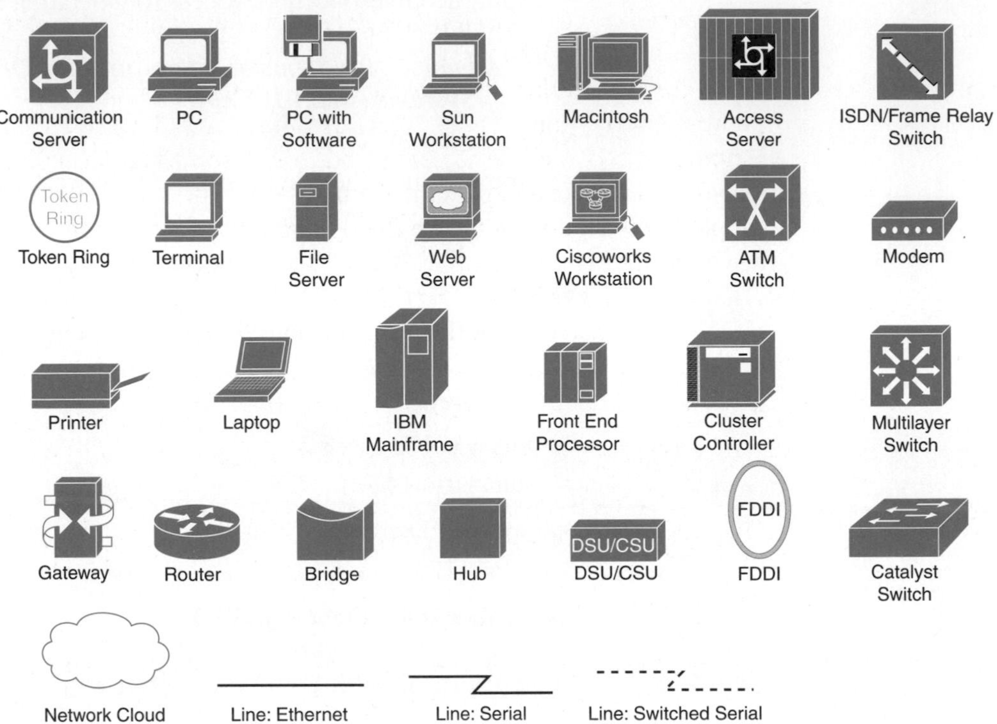

The conventions used to present command syntax in this book are the same conventions used in the *IOS Command Reference*. The *Command Reference* describes these conventions as follows:

- **Boldface** indicates commands and keywords that are entered literally as shown. In actual configuration examples and output (not general command syntax), boldface indicates commands that are manually input by the user (such as a **show** command).
- *Italic* indicates arguments for which you supply actual values.
- Vertical bars (|) separate alternative, mutually exclusive elements.
- Square brackets ([ ]) indicate an optional element.
- Braces ({ }) indicate a required choice.
- Braces within brackets ([{ }]) indicate a required choice within an optional element.

Introduction

IT Essentials v6 Companion Guide is a supplemental book to the Cisco Networking Academy IT Essentials: Version 6 course. The course includes information to allow you to develop working knowledge of how computers and mobile devices operate. It covers information security topics as well as providing practice experience in computer procedures, networking, and troubleshooting. The course is designed to prepare you to take and pass the CompTIA A+ 900 series exams. By reading and completing this book, you have the opportunity to review all key concepts that the CompTIA A+ exams cover. If you use this book along with its companion, *IT Essentials v6 Lab Manual* (ISBN 978-1-58713-354-1), you can reinforce those concepts with hands-on exercises and test that knowledge with review questions and exercises.

The IT Essentials: PC Hardware and Software course aligns with the CompTIA A+ (220-901) exam and CompTIA A+ (220-902) exam. You must pass both exams to earn the CompTIA A+ certification.

Who Should Read This Book

This book is intended for students in the Cisco Networking Academy IT Essentials v6 course. This student is usually pursuing a career in information technology (IT) or wants to have the knowledge of how a computer works, how to assemble a computer, and how to troubleshoot hardware and software issues.

Book Features

The features in this book facilitate an understanding of computer systems and troubleshooting system problems. The highlights of each chapter are as follows:

- **Objectives:** Each chapter starts with a list of objectives that should be mastered by the end of the chapter. The objectives are framed as focus questions addressing the concepts covered in the chapter.
- **Key terms:** Each chapter includes a list of the key terms identified in the chapter, listed in the order in which they appear in the chapter. These terms serve as a study aid and are defined in the book's Glossary. The key terms reinforce the concepts introduced in the chapter and help you understand the chapter material before you move on to new concepts. You can find the key terms highlighted in blue throughout the chapter, in the context in which they are most important.
- **Explanatory text, lists, figures, and tables:** This book contains figures, procedures, and tables to accompany the thorough text explanations of

the objective content and to help explain and visualize theories, concepts, commands, and setup sequences.

- **Chapter summaries:** At the end of each chapter is a summary of the concepts covered in the chapter. The summary provides a synopsis of the chapter and serves as a study aid.
- **Lab and class discussion references:** There are references to the labs and class discussion exercises that can be found in the accompanying *IT Essentials v6 Lab Manual* (ISBN 978-1-58713-354-1).
- **Packet Tracer activities:** Cisco Packet Tracer simulation-based learning activity files promote the exploration of networking and network security concepts and enable you to experiment with network behavior. How to access these activities is discussed in the following section, "Accessing Packet Tracer Activities."
- **"Check Your Understanding" review questions:** Review questions are presented at the end of each chapter to serve as an assessment. In addition, the questions reinforce the concepts introduced in the chapter and help test your understanding before you move on to subsequent chapters. Answers to the questions are available in the Appendix.

Accessing Packet Tracer Activities

All the Packet Tracer activities are available within your IT Essentials Version 6 course on Netacad.com.

Note that you need to have the Packet Tracer software to use these Packet Tracer activity files. Packet Tracer is available only through the Cisco Networking Academy. Ask your instructor for a copy of this software.

How This Book Is Organized

This book corresponds to the Cisco IT Essentials course and is divided into 14 chapters, one appendix, and a glossary of key terms:

- **Chapter 1, "Introduction to the Personal Computer":** Information technology (IT) is the design, development, implementation, support, and management of computer hardware and software applications. A computer is an electronic machine that performs calculations based on a set of instructions. A computer system consists of hardware and software components. This chapter discusses hardware components found in a computer system, selecting replacement computer components, and configurations for specialized computer systems.

- **Chapter 2, "Introduction to Lab Procedures and Tool Use":** This chapter covers basic safety practices for the workplace, hardware and software tools, and the disposal of hazardous materials. Safety guidelines help protect individuals from accidents and injury and protect equipment from damage. Some of these guidelines are designed to protect the environment from contamination by discarded materials. You also learn how to protect equipment and data and how to properly use hand and software tools.
- **Chapter 3, "Computer Assembly":** Assembling computers is a large part of a technician's job. As a technician, you must work in a logical, methodical manner when working with computer components. At times, you might have to determine whether a component for a customer's computer needs to be upgraded or replaced. It is important that you develop advanced skills in installation procedures, troubleshooting techniques, and diagnostic methods. This chapter discusses the importance of component compatibility across hardware and software.
- **Chapter 4, "Overview of Preventive Maintenance":** Troubleshooting is the systematic process used to locate the cause of a fault in a computer system and to correct the relevant hardware and software issues. In this chapter, you learn general guidelines for creating preventive maintenance programs and troubleshooting procedures. These guidelines are a starting point to help you develop your preventive maintenance and troubleshooting skills.
- **Chapter 5, "Windows Installation":** As a technician you will be required to install operating systems of many types using a variety of methods. This chapter examines components of Windows 8.x, Windows 7, and Windows Vista operating systems, the different Windows OS requirements, and the various installation methods.
- **Chapter 6, "Windows Configuration and Management":** In this chapter, you learn about the support and maintenance of the Windows operating system after it has been installed. You learn how to use the tools that optimize and maintain the operating system using applications within Windows. Windows 8.x, Windows 7, and Windows Vista all perform better with a good preventive maintenance plan, and this chapter describes preventive maintenance strategies and procedures. It also covers in detail problem-solving techniques; it provides you with a step-by-step troubleshooting process for operating systems and the knowledge to determine problems to provide solutions.
- **Chapter 7, "Networking Concepts":** This chapter provides an overview of network principles, standards, and purposes. The different types of networks, protocols, and reference models, in addition to the hardware needed to create a network, are also discussed in this chapter. You also learn about network software, communication methods, and hardware relationships used in supporting small wired and wireless networks.

- **Chapter 8, "Applied Networking":** In this chapter, you learn about different types of Internet technologies and how to set up a SOHO router and connect it to the Internet. You also learn about creating network users, sharing resources, and remote access methods using the Windows operating system. Technicians must be able to setup, configure and troubleshoot networks. This chapter also teaches you how to troubleshoot problems when networks and Internet connections fail.
- **Chapter 9, "Laptops and Mobile Devices":** A mobile device is any device that is handheld, is light, and typically uses a touchscreen for input. Like a desktop or laptop computer, mobile devices use an operating system to run applications (apps) and games and play movies and music. It is important to become familiar with as many different mobile devices as possible. You may be required to know how to configure, maintain, and repair various mobile devices. Mastering the skills necessary to work on mobile devices is important to your career advancement. This chapter focuses on the many features of mobile devices and their capabilities, including configuration, synchronization, and data backup. With the increase in demand for mobility, the popularity of mobile devices will continue to grow. During the course of your career, you will be expected to know how to configure, repair, and maintain these devices. The knowledge you acquire about desktop computers will help you service laptops and mobile devices. Laptops run the same operating systems as desktops computers with built-in WiFi, multimedia device, and ports to attach to external components. A mobile device is any device that is handheld, is light, and typically uses a touchscreen for input. Like a desktop or laptop computer, mobile devices use an operating system to run applications (apps) and games and play movies and music. Mobile device also have different CPU architecture, designed to have a reduced instruction set when compared to laptop and desktop processors. You may be required to know how to configure, maintain, and repair various mobile devices. Mastering the skills necessary to work on laptops and mobile devices is important to your career advancement. This chapter focuses on the many features of laptops, mobile devices and their capabilities.
- **Chapter 10, "Mobile, Linux, and OS X Operating Systems":** In the previous chapters Windows operating systems and desktop computers have been the primary focus. In this chapter you learn about different operating systems such as iOS, Android, OS X, and Ubuntu Linux and their characteristics. In this chapter you also learn about the main maintenance tasks and related tools in these operating systems. You learn how these tools are used on mobile devices, how to secure mobile devices, as well as the uses of cloud-enabled services for mobile devices, and the way that mobile devices connect to networks, devices, and peripherals.

- **Chapter 11, "Printers"**: This chapter provides essential information about printers. You learn how printers operate, what to consider when purchasing a printer, and how to connect printers to an individual computer or to a network.
- **Chapter 12, "Security"**: Technicians need to understand computer and network security. Failure to implement proper security procedures can have an impact on users, computers, and the general public. Private information, company secrets, financial data, computer equipment, and items of national security are placed at risk if proper security procedures are not followed. This chapter covers why security is important, security threats, security procedures, how to troubleshoot security issues, and how you can work with customers to ensure that the best possible protection is in place.
- **Chapter 13, "The IT Professional"**: As a computer technician, you not only fix computers, but also interact with people. In fact, troubleshooting is as much about communicating with the customer as it is about knowing how to fix a computer. In this chapter, you learn to use good communication skills as confidently as you use a screwdriver.
- **Chapter 14, "Advanced Troubleshooting"**: In your career as a technician, it is important that you develop advanced skills in troubleshooting techniques and diagnostic methods for computer components, operating systems, networks, laptops, printers, and security issues. Advanced troubleshooting can sometimes mean that the problem is unique or that the solution is difficult to perform. In this chapter, you learn how to apply a troubleshooting process to solve computer problems.
- **Appendix A, "Answers to 'Check Your Understanding' Questions"**: This appendix lists the answers to the "Check Your Understanding" review questions that are included at the end of each chapter.
- **Glossary**: The Glossary provides you with definitions for all the key terms identified in each chapter.

About the CompTIA A+ Certification

As a CompTIA Authorized Quality Curriculum, *IT Essentials: PC Hardware and Software v5* helps prepare you for the new CompTIA A+ Essentials and Practical Applications certification exams. To become A+ certified, you need to pass two exams to become certified in your chosen career area:

- CompTIA A+ (220-901)
- CompTIA A+ (220-902)

After becoming certified, you will be qualified to work as a computer support professional and technician in a variety of work environments and industries.

The CompTIA A+ exam is explained in detail, including a list of the objectives, at the following website:

http://www.comptia.org/certifications/listed/a.aspx

When you are ready to take the exam, you must purchase and schedule your two CompTIA A+ exams. You can find the necessary information to accomplish this at the following website:

https://certification.comptia.org/testing

CHAPTER 1

Introduction to the Personal Computer System

Objectives

Upon completion of this chapter, you will be able to answer the following questions:

- What is a computer system?
- How can I identify the names, purposes, and characteristics of cases and power supplies?
- What are the names, purposes, and characteristics of internal PC components?
- What are the names, purposes, and characteristics of ports and cables?
- How can I identify the names, purposes, and characteristics of input devices?
- How can I identify the names, purposes, and characteristics of output devices?
- What situations require replacement of computer components?
- How do I determine what purchases or upgrades are needed?
- How do I select replacement or upgrade components?
- What are some types of specialty computer systems?
- What are some of the hardware and software requirements for specialty computer systems?

Key Terms

This chapter uses the following key terms. You can find the definitions in the Glossary.

Advanced Technology (AT) power supply Page 7

Adapter Page 40

address bus Page 50

alternating current Page 7

Aspect ratio Page 47

audio and video editing workstation Page 64

AT Extended (ATX) Page 7

ATX12V Page 7

Basic input/output system (BIOS) Page 12

cache Page 15

Capture card Page 23

cathode ray tube (CRTs) Page 46

(CAx) workstation Page 64

Central processing unit (CPU) Page 12

Chipset Page 12

Complex instruction set computer (CISC) Page 15

Contrast ratio Page 47

Converter Page 40

CPU throttling Page 16

Current Page 10

data bus Page 50

data cable Page 39

direct current (DC) Page 7

DLP Page 46

Dot pitch Page 47

Double Data Rate 2 SDRAM (DDR2) Page 21

Double Data Rate 3 SDRAM (DDR3) Page 21

Double Data Rate 4 SDRAM(DDR4) Page 21

Double Data Rate SDRAM (DDR) Page 21

dual channel Page 22

dual in-line memory module (DIMM) Page 22

dual voltage power supply Page 11

Dynamic RAM (DRAM) Page 21

Electronic capacitors Page 11

electrically erasable programmable read-only memory (EEPROM) Page 20

EPS12V Page 7

erasable programmable read-only memory (EPROM) Page 20

error correcting code (ECC) Page 23

Expansion slots Page 12

external Serial ATA (eSATA) Page 31

FireWire Page 39

flash drive Page 27

form factor Page 5

Frame rate Page 47

front side bus (FSB) Page 16

hard drive Page 26

hardware Page 4

High Definition Multimedia Interface (HDMI) Page 34

Home Theater Personal Computer (HTPC) Page 67

Horizontal, vertical, and color resolution Page 47

Hyper-Threading Page 15

HyperTransport Page 16

input devices Page 41

input/output (I/O) cards Page 57

Interlace/non-interlace Page 47

keyed connectors Page 8

KVM switch Page 45

LCD Page 45

LED Page 46

L1 cache Page 23

L2 cache Page 23

L3 cache Page 23

Land grid array (LGA) Page 14

media reader Page 59

Memory modules Page 22

Mini-PCI Page 25

Monitor resolution Page 47

Mirroring Page 31

motherboard, system board, or the main board Page 12

multi rail Page 10

multicore CPU Page 16

Native resolution Page 47

Network interface card (NIC) Page 23

nonparity Page 23

nonvolatile memory Page 27

Northbridge Page 12

OLED Page 46

optical drive Page 27

optical media Page 27

output devices Page 41

Overclocking Page 16

Parity Page 23

PCI Express Page 26

PCI-Extended Page 25

Peripheral Component Interconnect (PCI) Page 25

Pin grid array (PGA) Page 14

Pixel Page 47

Plasma Page 46

Power Page 7

power supply Page 7

printed circuit board (PCB) Page 10

Programmable read-only memory (PROM) Page 20

rail Page 10

Random-access memory (RAM) Page 12

read-only memory (ROM) Page 20

Reduced instruction set computer (RISC) Page 15

redundant array of independent disks (RAID) Page 24

Refresh rate Page 47

Serial ATA (SATA) Page 28

Resistance Page 10

ROM Page 21

single channel Page 22

single rail Page 10

small outline DIMM (SODIMM) Page 22

Software Page 4

solid state drives (SSD) Page 26

Sound adapter Page 23

Southbridge Page 13

Static RAM (SRAM) Page 21

Striping Page 31

Thunderbolt card Page 24

TV tuner card Page 23

Unified Extensible Firmware Interface (UEFI) Page 12

Universal Serial Bus (USB) port Page 23

Video adapter Page 23

video port Page 33

virtual desktop infrastructure (VDI) Page 65

virtualization Page 65

volatile memory Page 21

Voltage Page 10

voltage selector switch Page 11

watts (W) Page 10

Wireless NIC Page 23

zero insertion force Page 14

Introduction (1.0)

Understanding the function of computer hardware and software, working hands-on with computer components, and learning about interacting with customers are all important to developing the knowledge and skills to work as a technician in the IT field.

Welcome (1.0.1)

It is necessary to understand the various computer components that comprise a personal computer system. It guides you on your first steps of the journey through the IT Essentials course and you will often encounter terms and concepts introduced here throughout the course.

Introduction to the Personal Computer (1.0.1.1)

A computer is an electronic machine that performs calculations based on a set of instructions. The first computers were huge, room-sized machines that took teams of people to build, manage, and maintain. The computer systems of today are both exponentially faster and only a fraction of the size of those original computers.

A computer system consists of hardware and software components. *Hardware* is the physical equipment. It includes the case, keyboard, monitor, cables, storage drives, speakers, and printers. *Software* includes the operating system and programs. The *operating system* manages computer operations such as identifying, accessing, and processing information. *Programs* or *applications* perform different functions. Programs vary widely depending on the type of information that is accessed or generated. For example, instructions for balancing a personal budget are different from instructions for simulating a virtual reality world on the Internet.

This chapter begins the journey of exploring and learning about computer hardware. It discusses the hardware components found in a computer system, replacement computer components, and configurations for specialized computer systems.

Personal Computer Systems (1.1)

Personal computer systems (PCs) are made up of hardware and software components that must be chosen with specific features in mind. All the components must be compatible to work as a system. PCs are built based on how a user works and what needs to be accomplished. They may require upgrading when work needs are not being met.

Cases and Power Supplies (1.1.1)

Computer *cases* are the enclosures that house the internal computer components including the power supply. They come in different sizes, also known as *form factor*.

Cases (1.1.1.1)

The case of a desktop computer houses the internal components such as the power supply, motherboard, central processing unit (CPU), memory, disk drives, and assorted adapter cards.

Cases are typically made of plastic, steel, or aluminum and provide the framework to support, protect, and cool the internal components.

A device *form factor* refers to its physical design and look. Desktop computers are available in a variety of form factors. These types include:

- **Horizontal case**—These were popular with early computer systems. The computer case was horizontally oriented on the user's desk with the monitor positioned on top. This form factor is no longer popular.
- **Full-size tower**—This is a computer case that is oriented vertically. It is typically located on the floor under or beside a desk or table. It provides room for expansion to accommodate additional components such as disk drives, adapter cards, and more. It requires an external keyboard, mouse, and monitor. (See Figure 1-1a.)
- **Compact tower**—This is a smaller version of the full-size tower and is commonly found in the corporate environment. It may also be called a *mini-tower or small form factor (SFF)* model. It can be located on the user's desk or on the floor. It provides limited room for expansion. It requires an external keyboard, mouse, and monitor. (See Figure 1-1b.)
- **All-in-one**—All of the computer system components are integrated into the display. They often include touchscreen input and built-in microphone and speakers. Depending on the model, all-in-one computers offer little to no expansion capabilities. It requires an external keyboard, mouse, and power source. (See Figure 1-1c.)

Figure 1-1a Types of Computer Cases—Full Tower

Figure 1-1b Types of Computer Cases—Compact Tower

Figure 1-1c Types of Computer Cases—All-in-One

Note

This list is not exhaustive because many case manufacturers have their own naming conventions. These may include *super tower*, *full tower*, *mid tower*, *mini tower*, *cube case*, and more.

Computer components tend to generate a lot of heat; therefore, computer cases contain fans that move air through the case. As the air passes warm components, it absorbs heat and then exits the case. This process keeps the computer components from overheating. Cases are also designed to protect against static electricity damage. The computer's internal components are grounded via attachment to the case.

Note

Computer cases are also referred to as the *computer chassis*, *cabinet*, *tower*, *housing*, or simply *box*.

Power Supplies (1.1.1.2)

Electricity from wall outlets is provided in *alternating current (AC)*. However, all components inside a computer require *direct current (DC)* power. To obtain DC power, computers use a *power supply*, as shown in Figure 1-2a, to convert AC power into a lower-voltage DC power.

The following describes the various computer desktop power supply form factors that have evolved over time:

- *Advanced Technology (AT)*—This is the original power supply for legacy computer systems now considered obsolete.
- *AT Extended (ATX)*—This is the updated version of the AT, but it is still considered to be obsolete.
- *ATX12V*—This is the most common power supply on the market today. It includes a second motherboard connector to provide dedicated power to the CPU. There are several versions of ATX12V available.
- *EPS12V*—This was originally designed for network servers but is now commonly used in high-end desktop models.

Figure 1-2a Power Supply

A power supply includes several different connectors, as shown in Figure 1-2b.

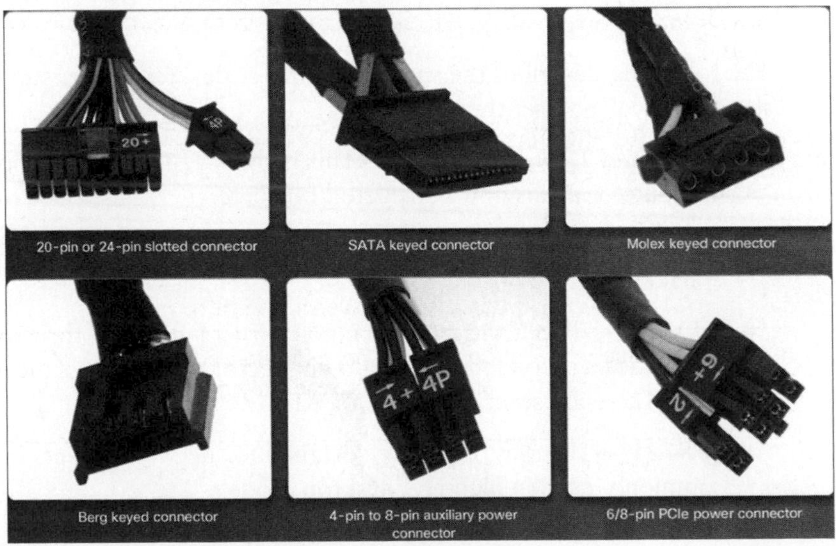

Figure 1-2b Computer Power Supply Connectors

These connectors are used to power various internal components such as the motherboard and disk drives. The connectors are *keyed* which means that they are designed to be inserted in only one orientation. Common power supply connectors include the following:

- A **Molex keyed connector**—connects to optical drives, hard drives, or other devices that use older technology.
- A **Berg keyed connector**—connects to a legacy floppy drive. A Berg connector is smaller than a Molex connector.
- A **SATA keyed connector**—connects to an optical drive or a hard drive. The SATA connector is wider and thinner than a Molex connector.
- A **20-pin or 24-pin slotted connector**—connects to the motherboard. The 24-pin connector has two rows of 12 pins each, and the 20-pin connector has two rows of 10 pins each.
- A **four-pin to eight-pin auxiliary power connector**—two rows of two or four pins; supplies power to all areas of the motherboard. The auxiliary power connector is the same shape as the main power connector but smaller. It can also power other devices within the computer.
- A **6/8-pin PCIe power connector**—two rows of three or four pins; supplies power to other internal components.

The different connectors also provide different voltages. The most common voltages supplied are 3.3 volts, 5 volts, and 12 volts. The 3.3 volt and 5 volt supplies are typically used by digital circuits, whereas the 12 volt supply is used to run motors in disk drives and fans. Table 1-1 highlights the different voltages provided by a power supply.

Table 1-1 Power Supply Voltages and Color Codes

Voltage	Wire Color	Use	Power Supply Form		
			AT	ATX	ATX12V
+12 V	Yellow	Disk drive motors, fans, cooling devices, and system bus slots	✓	✓	✓
–12 V	Blue	Some serial port circuits and early programmable read-only memory (PROM)	✓	✓	✓
+3.3 V	Orange	Most newer CPUs, some types of system memory, and AGP video cards		✓	✓
+5 V	Red	Motherboards, Baby AT early CPUs, many motherboard components	✓	✓	✓
–5 V	White	ISA bus cards and early PROMs	✓	✓	✓
0 V	Black	Ground; used to complete circuits with other voltages	✓	✓	✓

Power supplies can also be *single rail*, ***dual rail***, or *multi rail*. A *rail* is the *printed circuit board (PCB)* inside the power supply to which the external cables are connected. A single rail has all of the connectors connected to the same PCB whereas a multi rail PCB has separate PCBs for each connector.

A computer can tolerate slight fluctuations in power, but a significant deviation can cause the power supply to fail.

Power Supply Wattage (1.1.1.3)

To understand a watt and the other basic units of electricity that a computer technician must know, refer to the bulleted list below:

- *Voltage* is a measure of work required to move a charge from one location to another. Voltage is **measured in volts (V)**. A computer power supply usually produces several different voltages.
- *Current* is a measure of the amount of electrons moving through a circuit. Current is **measured in amperes, or amps (A)**. Computer power supplies deliver different amperages for each output voltage.
- *Resistance* refers to the opposition to the flow of current in a circuit. Lower resistance allows more current, and therefore more power, to flow through a circuit. A good fuse has low resistance or almost 0 ohms. Resistance is **measured in ohms**.
- *Power* is a measure of the pressure required to push electrons through a circuit (voltage), multiplied by the number of electrons going through that circuit (current). The **measurement is called watts (W)**. Computer power supplies are rated in watts.

Power supply specifications are typically expressed in *watts (W)*.

A basic equation, known as Ohm's Law, expresses how voltage is equal to the current multiplied by the resistance: **V = IR**. In an electrical system, power is equal to the voltage multiplied by the current: **P = VI**.

Computers normally use power supplies ranging from 250W to 800W output capacity. However, some computers need 1200W and higher capacity power supplies. When building a computer, select a power supply with sufficient wattage to power all components. Each component inside the computer uses a certain amount of power. Obtain the wattage information from the manufacturer's documentation. When deciding on a power supply, make sure to choose one that has more than enough power for the currently installed components. A power supply with a higher wattage rating has more capacity; therefore, it can handle more devices.

On the back of some power supplies is a small switch called the *voltage selector switch*, as shown in Figure 1-3. This switch sets the input voltage to the power supply to either 110V/115V or 220V/230V. A power supply with this switch is called a *dual voltage power supply*. The correct voltage setting is determined by the country in which the power supply is used. Setting the voltage switch to the incorrect input voltage could damage the power supply and other parts of your computer. If a power supply does not have this switch, it automatically detects and sets the correct voltage.

Figure 1-3 Dual Voltage Power Supply

Caution

Do not open a power supply. *Electronic capacitors* located inside of a power supply, shown in Figure 1-4, can hold a charge for extended periods of time.

Figure 1-4 Power Supply Capacitors

For more information about power supplies, go to the course to click the link on page 1.1.1.3.

Lab Ohm's Law 1.1.1.4

In this lab, you answer questions based on Electricity and Ohm's Law. Refer to the lab in *IT Essentials v6 Lab Manual*.

Internal PC Components (1.1.2)

This section discusses the names, purposes, and characteristics of the internal components of a computer.

Motherboards (1.1.2.1)

The *motherboard*, also known as the *system board* or the *main board*, is the backbone of the computer. A motherboard is a printed circuit board (PCB) that contains buses, or electrical pathways, that interconnect electronic components. These components may be soldered directly to the motherboard or added using sockets, expansion slots, and ports.

Some types of connections on the motherboard where computer components are located or can be added are:

- *Central Processing Unit (CPU)*—This is considered the brain of the computer.
- *Random Access Memory (RAM)*—This is a temporary location to store data and applications.
- *Expansion slots*—These provide locations to connect additional components.
- *Basic input/output system (BIOS)* **chip and** *Unified Extensible Firmware Interface (UEFI)* **chip**—BIOS is used to help boot the computer and to manage the flow of data between the hard drive, video card, keyboard, mouse, and more. Recently, the BIOS has been enhanced by UEFI. UEFI specifies a different software interface for boot and runtime services but still relies on the traditional BIOS for system configuration, power-on self-test (POST), and setup.
- *Chipset*—This consists of the integrated circuits on the motherboard that control how system hardware interacts with the CPU and motherboard. It also establishes how much memory can be added to a motherboard and the type of connectors on the motherboard.

Most chipsets consist of the following two types:

- *Northbridge*—Controls high speed access to the RAM and video card. It also controls the speed at which the CPU communicates with all of the other components in the computer. Video capability is sometimes integrated into the Northbridge.

- *Southbridge*—Allows the CPU to communicate with slower-speed devices including hard drives, Universal Serial Bus (USB) ports, and expansion slots.

Figure 1-5 illustrates how a motherboard connects various components.

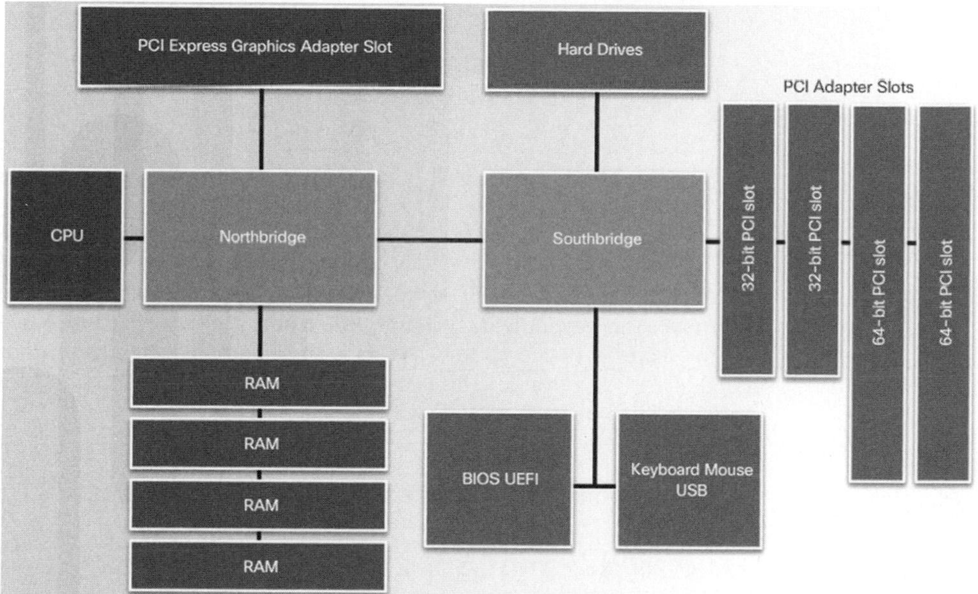

Figure 1-5 Motherboard Component Connections

The form factor of motherboards pertains to the size and shape of the board. It also describes the physical layout of the different components and devices on the motherboard.

There have been many variations of motherboards developed over the years. There are three common motherboard form factors:

- **Advanced Technology eXtended (ATX)**—This is the most common motherboard form factor. The ATX case accommodates the integrated I/O ports on the standard ATX motherboard. The ATX power supply connects to the motherboard via a single 20-pin connector. Dimensions—12 inches x 9.6 inches (30.5 cm x 24.4 cm)

- **Micro-ATX**—This is a smaller form factor that is designed to be backward-compatible with ATX. Micro-ATX boards often use the same Northbridge and Southbridge chipsets and power connectors as full-size ATX boards and therefore can use many of the same components. Generally, Micro-ATX boards can fit in standard ATX cases. However, Micro-ATX motherboards are much smaller than ATX motherboards and have fewer expansion slots. Dimensions—9.6 inches × 9.6 inches (24.4 cm × 24.4 cm)

- **ITX**—The ITX form factor has gained in popularity because of its very small size. There are many types of ITX motherboards; however, Mini-ITX is one of the most popular. The Mini-ITX form factor uses very little power, so fans are not needed to keep it cool. A Mini-ITX motherboard has only one PCI slot for expansion cards. A computer based on a Mini-ITX form factor can be used in places where it is inconvenient to have a large or noisy computer. Dimensions—8.5 × 7.5 (21.5 × 19.1)
- **Mini-ITX**—The Mini-ITX form factor is designed for small devices such as thin clients and set-top boxes. Dimensions—6.7 inches × 6.7 inches (17 cm × 17 cm)

Note

It is important to distinguish between form factors. The choice of motherboard form factor determines the way individual components attach to it, the type of power supply required, and the shape of the computer case. Some manufacturers also have proprietary form factors based on the ATX design. This causes some motherboards, power supplies, and other components to be incompatible with standard ATX cases.

For more information on motherboards, go to the course to click the link on page 1.1.2.1.

CPU Architectures (1.1.2.2)

Although the motherboard is considered to be the backbone of the computer, the *central processing unit (CPU)* is considered to be the brain. In terms of computing power, the CPU, sometimes referred to as the *processor*, is the most important element of a computer system. Most calculations take place in the CPU.

CPUs come in different form factors, each style requiring a particular slot or socket on the motherboard. Common CPU manufacturers include Intel and AMD.

The CPU socket or slot is the connection between the motherboard and the processor. Modern CPU sockets and processors are built around the following architectures:

- *Pin grid array (PGA)*—As shown in Figure 1-6, in PGA architecture, the pins are on the underside of the processor. The CPU is inserted into the motherboard CPU socket using *zero insertion force (ZIF)*. ZIF refers to the amount of force needed to install a CPU into the motherboard socket or slot.
- *Land grid array (LGA)*—Figure 1-7 shows that in LGA architecture, the pins are in the socket instead of on the processor.

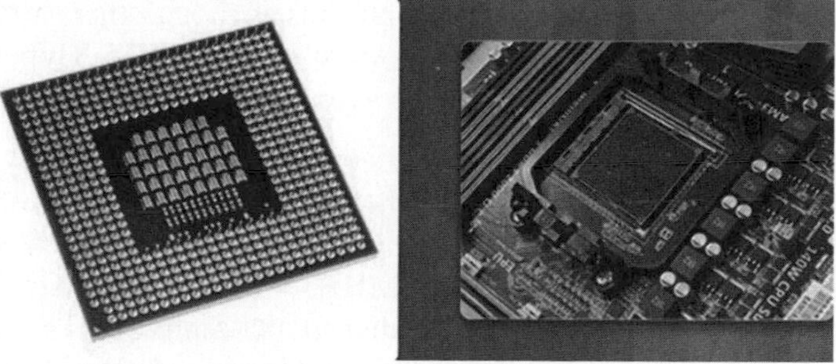

Figure 1-6 PGA CPU and Socket

Figure 1-7 LGA CPU and Socket

A program is a sequence of stored instructions. A CPU executes these instructions by following a specific instruction set.

There are two distinct types of instructions sets that CPUs may use:

- *Reduced instruction set computer (RISC)*—This architecture uses a relatively small set of instructions. RISC chips are designed to execute these instructions very rapidly.
- *Complex instruction set computer (CISC)*—This architecture uses a broad set of instructions, resulting in fewer steps per operation.

While the CPU is executing one step of the program, the remaining instructions and the data are stored nearby in a special, high-speed memory, called *cache*.

Enhancing CPU Operation (1.1.2.3)

Various CPU manufacturers complement their CPU with performance-enhancing features. For instance, Intel incorporates Hyper-Threading to enhance the performance of some of their CPUs. With *Hyper-Threading*, multiple pieces of code (threads) are executed simultaneously in the CPU. To an operating system, a single CPU with Hyper-Threading performs as though there are two CPUs when multiple threads are being processed. AMD processors use HyperTransport to enhance CPU performance. *HyperTransport* is a high-speed connection between the CPU and the Northbridge chip.

The power of a CPU is measured by the speed and the amount of data that it can process. The speed of a CPU is rated in cycles per second, such as millions of cycles per second, called megahertz (MHz), or billions of cycles per second, called gigahertz (GHz). The amount of data that a CPU can process at one time depends on the size of the *front side bus (FSB)*. This is also called the *CPU bus* or the *processor data bus*. Higher performance can be achieved when the width of the FSB increases. The width of the FSB is measured in bits. A bit is the smallest unit of data in a computer. Current processors use a 32-bit or 64-bit FSB. The front side bus is just one type of bus on a motherboard. *Busses* are the wires on the motherboard through which data is transmitted from one part of the computer to another.

Overclocking is a technique used to make a processor work at a faster speed than its original specification. Overclocking is not a recommended way to improve computer performance and can result in damage to the CPU. The opposite of overclocking is CPU throttling. *CPU throttling* is a technique used when the processor runs at less than the rated speed to conserve power or produce less heat. Throttling is commonly used on laptops and other mobile devices.

The latest processor technology has resulted in CPU manufacturers finding ways to incorporate more than one CPU core into a single chip. *Multicore processors* have two or more processors on the same integrated circuit. The list below shows descriptions of various types of multicore processors:

- **Single core CPU**—One core inside a single CPU that handles all the processing. A motherboard manufacturer might provide sockets for more than one single processor, providing the ability to build a powerful, multiprocessor computer.
- **Dual core CPU**—Two cores inside a single CPU in which both cores can process information at the same time.
- **Triple core CPU**—Three cores inside a single CPU that is actually a quad-core processor with one of the cores disabled.
- **Quad core CPU**—Four cores inside a single CPU.
- **Hexa-core CPU**—Six cores inside a single CPU.
- **Octa-core CPU**—Eight cores inside a single CPU.

Integrating the processors on the same chip creates a very fast connection between them. Multicore processors execute instructions more quickly than single-core processors. Instructions can be distributed to all the processors at the same time. RAM is shared between the processors because the cores reside on the same chip.

A multicore processor is recommended for applications such as video editing, gaming, and photo manipulation.

High-power consumption creates more heat in the computer case. Multicore processors conserve power and produce less heat than multiple single-core processors, thus increasing performance and efficiency.

CPUs have also been enhanced through the use of the *NX bit*, also called the *execute disable bit*. This feature, when supported and enabled in the operating system, is able to protect areas of memory that contain operating system files from malicious attacks by malware.

Cooling Systems (1.1.2.4)

The flow of current between electronic components generates heat. Computer components perform better when kept cool. If the heat is not removed, the computer may run more slowly. If too much heat builds up, the computer could crash or components can be damaged. Therefore, it is imperative that computers be kept cool.

Note

Computers are kept cool using active and passive cooling solutions. Active solutions require power whereas passive solutions do not.

Increasing the air flow in the computer case allows more heat to be removed. An active cooling solution uses fans inside of a computer case to blow out hot air. For increased air flow, some cases have multiple fans to bring in cool air while another fan blows out hot air. A case fan installed in the computer case, as shown in Figure 1-8, makes the cooling process more efficient.

Figure 1-8 Case Fan

Inside the case, the CPU generates a lot of heat. To draw heat away from the CPU core, a heat sink is installed on top of it, as shown in Figure 1-9. The heat sink has a large surface area with metal fins to dissipate heat into the surrounding air. This is known as *passive cooling*. Between the heat sink and the CPU is a special thermal compound. The thermal compound increases the efficiency of heat transfer from the CPU to the heat sink by filling any tiny gaps between the two.

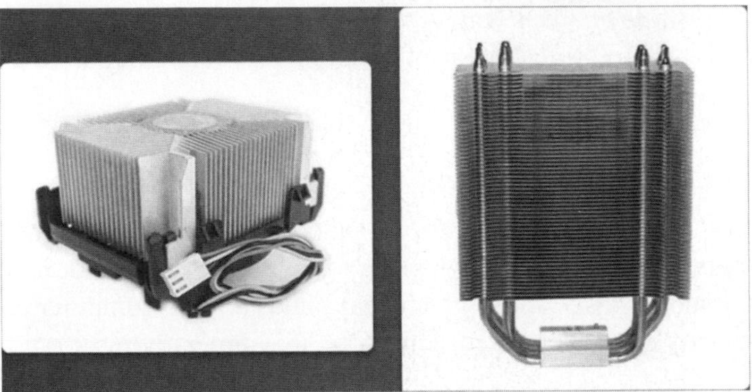

Figure 1-9 CPU Heat Sink

CPUs that are overclocked or running multiple cores tend to generate excessive heat. It is a very common practice to install a fan on top of the heat sink as shown in Figure 1-10. The fan moves heat away from the metal fins of the heatsink. This is known as *active cooling*.

Figure 1-10 CPU Fan

Other components are also susceptible to heat damage and are often equipped with fans. Many video adapter cards have processors called *graphics-processing units (GPU)* which generates excessive heat. Some video adapter cards come equipped with one or more fans, as shown in Figure 1-11.

Figure 1-11 Graphics Card Cooling System

Computers with extremely fast CPUs and GPUs might use a water-cooling system. Figure 1-12 is an example of a water cooling system. A metal plate is placed over the processor, and water is pumped over the top to collect the heat that the processor generates. The water is pumped to a radiator to disperse the heat into the air and the water is then recirculated.

Figure 1-12 Water Cooling System

CPU fans make noise and can be annoying at high speeds. An alternative to cooling a CPU with a fan is a method that uses heat pipes. The heat pipe contains liquid that is permanently sealed at the factory and uses a system of cyclic evaporation and condensation.

To view an animation on how to install a fanless cooling system, go to the course to click the link on page 1.1.2.4. You will need to scroll to mid-page to find the animation.

ROM (1.1.2.5)

A computer has different types of memory chips. However, all memory chips store data in the form of bytes. A *byte* is a grouping of digital information and represents information such as letters, numbers, and symbols. Specifically, a byte is a block of eight bits, each stored as either 0 or 1 in the memory chip.

An essential computer chip is the *read-only memory (ROM) chip*. ROM chips are located on the motherboard and other circuit boards and contain instructions that can be directly accessed by a CPU. The instructions stored in ROM include basic operation instructions such as booting the computer and loading the operating system.

Following is a list of details about the different types of ROM memory:

- *Read-only memory chips (ROM)*: Information is written to a ROM chip when it is manufactured. A ROM chip cannot be erased or rewritten. This type of ROM is obsolete.
- *Programmable read-only memory (PROM)*: Information is written to a PROM chip after it is manufactured. A PROM chip cannot be erased or rewritten.
- *Erasable programmable read-only memory (EPROM)*: Information is written to an EPROM chip after it is manufactured. An EPROM chip can be erased with exposure to UV light. Special equipment is required.
- *Electrically erasable programmable read-only memory (EEPROM)*: Information is written to an EEPROM chip after it is manufactured. EEPROM chips are also called *flash ROMs*. An EEPROM chip can be erased and rewritten without having to remove the chip from the computer.

It is important to note that ROM chips retain their contents even when the computer is powered down. The contents cannot be erased or changed easily.

Note

ROM is sometimes called *firmware*. This is misleading, because firmware is actually the software that is stored in a ROM chip.

RAM (1.1.2.6)

RAM is the temporary working storage for data and programs that are being accessed by the CPU.

As shown in the list below, there are different types of RAM that can be used by a computer:

- *Dynamic RAM (DRAM)*—is a memory chip that is used as main memory. DRAM must be constantly refreshed with pulses of electricity in order to maintain the data stored within the chip.
- *Static RAM (SRAM)*—is a memory chip that is used as cache memory. SRAM is much faster than DRAM and does not have to be refreshed as often. SRAM is much more expensive than DRAM.
- *Synchronous DRAM (SDRAM)*—is DRAM that operates in synchronization with the memory bus. The memory bus is the data path between the CPU and the main memory. Control signals are used to coordinate the exchange of data between SDRAM and the CPU.
- *Double Data Rate SDRAM (DDR SDRAM)*—is memory that transfers data twice as fast as SDRAM. DDR SDRAM increases performance by transferring data twice per clock cycle.
- *Double Data Rate 2 SDRAM (DDR2 SDRAM)*—is a faster than DDR-SDRAM memory. DDR2 SDRAM improves performance over DDR SDRAM by decreasing noise and crosstalk between the signal wires.
- *Double Data Rate 3 SDRAM (DDR3 SDRAM)*—expands memory bandwidth by doubling the clock rate of DDR2 SDRAM. DDR3 SDRAM consumes less power and generates less heat than DDR2 SDRAM.
- *Double Data Rate 4 SDRAM (DDR4 SDRAM)*—quadruples DDR3 maximum storage capacity, requires 40 percent less power due to it using a lower voltage and has advanced error-correction features.

Unlike ROM, RAM is *volatile memory*, which means that the contents are erased every time the computer is powered off.

Note

ROM is *nonvolatile*, which means that the contents are not erased when the computer is powered off.

Adding more RAM in a computer enhances the system performance. For instance, more RAM increases the memory capacity of the computer to hold and process programs and files. With less RAM, a computer must swap data between RAM and the much slower hard drive. The maximum amount of RAM that can be installed is limited by the motherboard.

Memory Modules (1.1.2.7)

Early computers had RAM installed on the motherboard as individual chips. The individual memory chips, called *dual inline package (DIP) chips*, were difficult to install and often became loose. To solve this problem, designers soldered the memory chips to a circuit board to create a memory module that would then be placed into a memory slot on the motherboard.

The different types of memory modules are described in Table 1-2.

Note

Memory modules can be single-sided or double-sided. Single-sided memory modules contain RAM only on one side of the module. Double-sided memory modules contain RAM on both sides.

Table 1-2 Memory Modules

DIP	Dual inline package is an individual memory chip. A DIP has dual rows of pins used to attach it to the motherboard.
SIMM	Single inline memory module is a small circuit board that holds several memory chips. SIMMs have 30-pin or 72-pin configurations.
DIMM Memory	*Dual inline memory module* is a circuit board that holds SDRAM, DDR SDRAM, DDR2 SDRAM, and DDR3 SDRAM chips. There are 168-pin SDRAM DIMMs, 184-pin DDR DIMMs, and 240-pin DDR2 and DDR3 DIMMs.
SODIMM	*Small outline DIMM* has a 72-pin and 100-pin configurations for support of 32-bit transfers or a 144-pin, 200-pin, and 204-pin configurations for support of 64-bit transfers. This smaller, more condensed version of DIMM provides random access data storage that is ideal for use in laptops, printers, and other devices where conserving space is desirable.

The speed of memory has a direct impact on how much data a processor can process in a given period of time. As processor speed increases, memory speed must also increase. Memory throughput has also been increased through multichannel technology. Standard RAM is *single channel*, meaning that all of the RAM slots are addressed at the same time. *Dual channel* RAM adds a second channel to be able to access a second module at the same time. *Triple channel* technology provides another channel so that three modules can be accessed at the same time.

The fastest memory is typically static RAM (SRAM), which is cache memory for storing the most recently used data and instructions by the CPU. SRAM provides the processor with faster access to the data than retrieving it from the slower dynamic RAM (DRAM), or main memory.

The three most common types of cache memory are described below:

- *L1 cache* is internal cache and is integrated into the CPU.
- *L2 cache* is external cache and was originally mounted on the motherboard near the CPU. L2 cache is now integrated into the CPU.
- *L3 cache* is used on some high-end workstations and server CPUs.

Memory errors occur when the data is not stored correctly in the chips. The computer uses different methods to detect and correct data errors in memory.

Different types of error-checking methods are described in the list below:

- *Nonparity* memory does not check for errors in memory.
- *Parity* memory contains eight bits for data and one bit for error checking. The error-checking bit is called a parity bit.
- *Error-correcting code* memory can detect multiple-bit errors in memory and correct single-bit errors in memory.

Adapter Cards and Expansion Slots (1.1.2.8)

Adapter cards increase the functionality of a computer by adding controllers for specific devices or by replacing malfunctioning ports.

A variety of adapter cards are available that are used to expand and customize the capability of a computer:

- *Sound adapter*—Sound adapters provide audio capability.
- *Network interface card (NIC)*—A NIC connects a computer to a network using a network cable.
- *Wireless NIC*—A wireless NIC connects a computer to a network using radio frequencies.
- *Video adapter*—Video adapters provide video capability.
- *Capture card*—Capture cards send a video signal to a computer so that the signal can be recorded to the computer hard drive with video-capture software.
- *TV tuner card*—These provide the ability to watch and record television signals on a PC by connecting a cable television, satellite, or antenna to the installed tuner card.
- *Universal Serial Bus (USB) port*—USB ports connect a computer to peripheral devices.

- *Thunderbolt card*—These connect a computer to peripheral devices.
- *Redundant array of independent disks (RAID)*—A RAID adapter connects to multiple hard disk drives (HDDs) or solid-state drives (SSDs), making them work as one logical unit.

Figure 1-13 shows some of these adapter cards. It should be noted that some of these adapter cards can be integrated on the motherboard.

Figure 1-13 Adapter Cards

Note

Older computers may also have a modem adapter, an accelerated graphics port (AGP), a small computer system interface (SCSI) adapter, and more.

Computers have expansion slots on the motherboard to install adapter cards. The type of adapter card connector must match the expansion slot. The different types of expansion slots are illustrated in Figures 1-14 to 1-17, which are collectively shown in Table 1-3.

Table 1-3 Expansion Slots

Figure 1-14 PCI

Peripheral component interconnect (PCI) is a 32-bit or 64-bit expansion slot. PCI is the standard slot currently used in most computers.

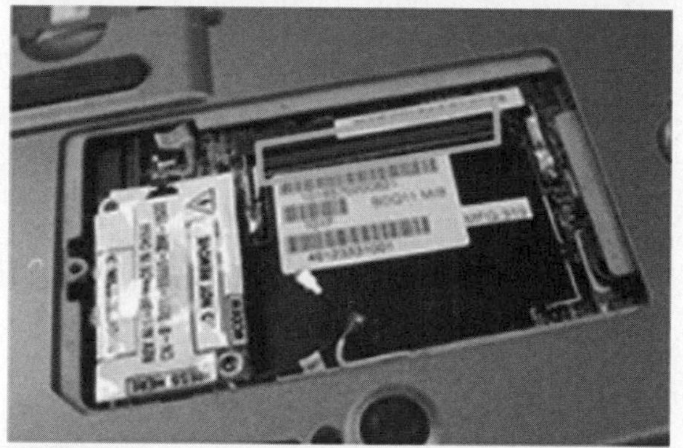

Figure 1-15 Mini PCI

Mini-PCI is a 32-bit bus used by laptops. Mini-PCI has three different form factors: Type 1, Type II, and Type III.

Figure 1-16 PCI-X

PCI-Extended is a 32-bit bus with higher bandwidth than the PCI bus. PCI-X can run up to four times faster than PCI.

(*Continued*)

Table 1-3 *Continued*

 **Figure 1-17** PCIe	*PCI Express* is a serial bus expansion slot. PCIe has x1, x4, x8, and x16 slots. PCIe is replacing AGP as an expansion slot for video adapters and can be used for other types of adapters.

Storage Devices (1.1.2.9)

Storage drives, as shown in Figure 1-18, read information from or write information to magnetic, optical, or semiconductor storage media. The drives can be used to store data permanently or to retrieve information from a media disk.

The following are common types of storage drives:

- *Hard disk drive (HDD)*—HDDs are the traditional magnetic disk devices that have been used for years. Their storage capacity ranges from gigabytes (GBs) to terabytes (TBs). Their speed is measured in revolutions per minute (RPM). This indicates how fast the spindle turns the platters that hold data. The faster the spindle speed, the faster a hard drive can find data on the platters. Common hard drive spindle speeds include 5400, 7200, and 10,000 RPM.
- *Solid state drive (SSD)*—SSDs use nonvolatile flash memory chips to store data. This means that they are faster than magnetic HDDs. Their storage capacity also ranges from GBs to TBs. SSDs have no moving parts and therefore make no noise, are more energy efficient, and produce less heat than HDDs. SSDs have the same form factor as HDDs and are increasingly being used in place of magnetic HDDs.
- **Hybrid drive**—Also called a *solid state hybrid drive (SSHD)*, these are a compromise between a magnetic HDD and an SSD. They are faster than an HDD but less expensive than an SSD. They are a magnetic HDD with an onboard SSD serving as cache. The SSHD drive automatically caches data that is frequently accessed.
- **Tape drive**—Magnetic tapes are most often used for archiving data. The tape drive uses a magnetic read/write head. Although data retrieval using a tape drive can be fast, locating specific data is slow because the tape must be wound on a reel until the data is found. Common tape storage capacities vary between a few GBs to TBs.

- *External flash drive*—An external flash drive, such as a USB thumb drive that connects to a USB port, uses the same type of *nonvolatile memory* chips as SSDs. It does not require power to maintain its data. Their storage capacity ranges from MBs to GBs.

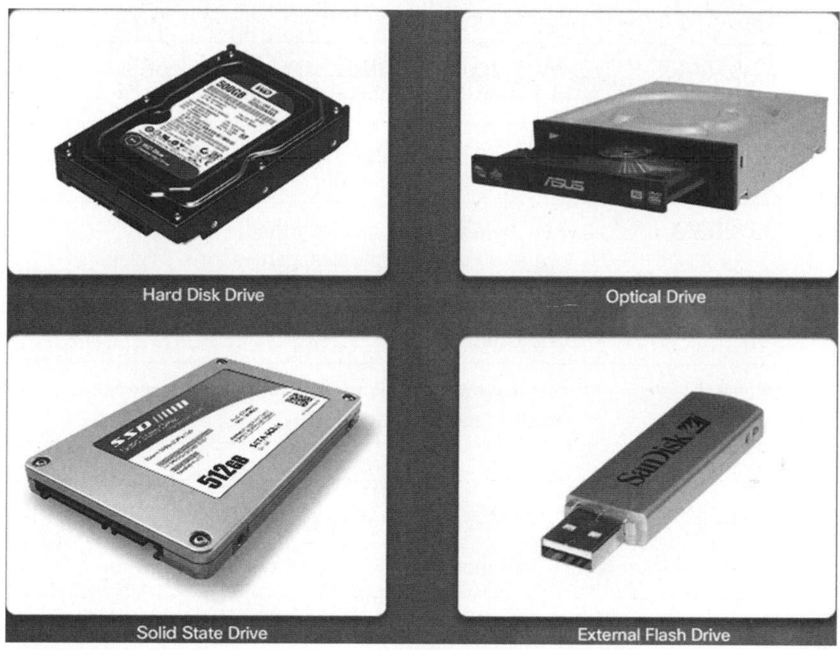

Figure 1-18 Storage Drives

An *optical drive*, another type of storage drive, uses lasers to read data on *optical media*. There are three types of optical drives, including *compact disc (CD)*, *digital versatile disc (DVD)*, and *Blu-ray disc (BD)*. CD, DVD, and BD media can be prerecorded (read-only), recordable (write once), or rewriteable (read and write multiple times). Table 1-4 describes the various types of optical media and their approximate storage capacities.

Table 1-4 Types of Optical Media

Optical Media	Description	Storage Capacity
CD-ROM	CD read-only memory media that is prerecorded	700 MB
CD-R	CD recordable media that can be recorded one time	
CD-RW	CD rewriteable media that can be recorded, erased, and recorded	

(Continued)

Table 1-4 *Continued*

Optical Media	Description	Storage Capacity
DVD-ROM	DVD read-only memory media that is prerecorded	4.7 GB (single layer) 8.5 GB (dual layer)
DVD-RAM	DVD rewriteable media that can be recorded, erased, and recorded	
DVD+/-R	DVD recordable media that can be recorded one time	
DVD+/-RW	DVD rewritable media that can be recorded, erased, and rerecorded	
BD-ROM	Blu-ray read-only memory media that is prerecorded with movies, games, or software	25 GB (single layer) 50 GB (dual layer)
BD-R	Blu-ray recordable media that can be recorded one time	
BD-RE	Blu-ray rewriteable media that can be recorded, erased, and recorded	

Note

Older computers may still incorporate legacy storage devices including floppy disk drives.

Storage Device Interfaces and RAID (1.1.2.10)

Internal HDDs, SSDs, and optical drives often connect to the motherboard using *Serial AT Attachment (SATA)* connections. SATA drives connect to the motherboard using a SATA seven-pin data connector.

At one end of the cable, the connector is keyed for the drive and the opposite end is keyed for the drive controller. Figure 1-19 shows a SATA cable.

There are three main versions of SATA: SATA 1, SATA 2, and SATA 3. The cables and connectors are the same, but the data transfer speeds are different. SATA 1 allows for a maximum data transfer rate of 1.5 Gb/s while SATA 2 can reach up to 3 Gb/s. SATA 3 is the fastest with speeds up to 6 Gb/s.

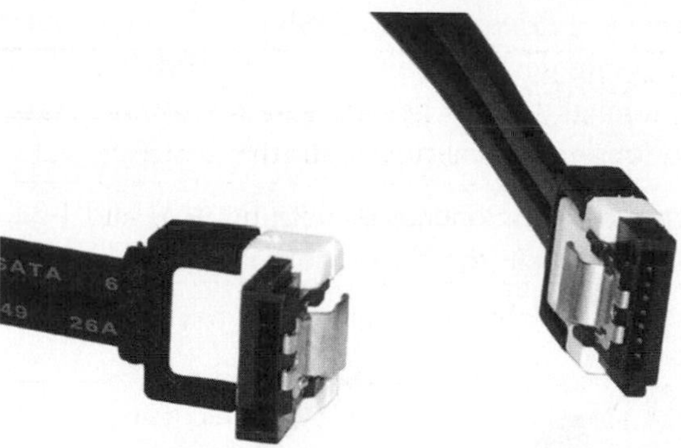

Figure 1-19 Sata Cable

> **Note**
>
> Legacy internal drive connection methods include *integrated drive electronics (IDE)*, *enhanced integrated drive electronics (EIDE)*, and *parallel ATA*.

Storage devices can also connect externally to the computer. Portable hard disk drives can be connected to a laptop using a USB cable. USB has become the most common way to connect external devices. External SATA (eSATA) is another way to connect external storage devices. eSATA cables and connectors have a different shape than SATA cables and connectors. Figure 1-20 shows a portable hard disk drive connected to a laptop using a USB cable.

Figure 1-20 Connecting a Portable USB Hard Drive

USB 3.0 and USB 3.1 are blue in color at the computer port or the plug at the end of the cable based on the USB 3.x specifications. Because of their fast transmission rates, they have become popular for connecting external storage devices. USB drives are also *hot-swappable*, which means that there is no need to reboot a computer when adding or removing a drive. A single USB port in a computer can theoretically support up to 127 separate devices with the use of USB hubs. A USB hub connects multiple USB devices. Finally, many devices can be powered through the USB port, eliminating the need for an external power source.

There are several types of USB connectors. Figures 1-21 and 1-22 display common USB connector types, including the USB-C (or USB Type C), which is the newest USB connector.

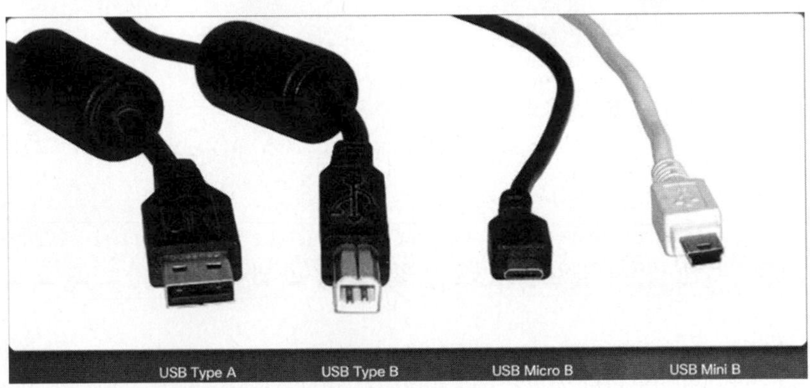

Figure 1-21 Types of USB Connectors

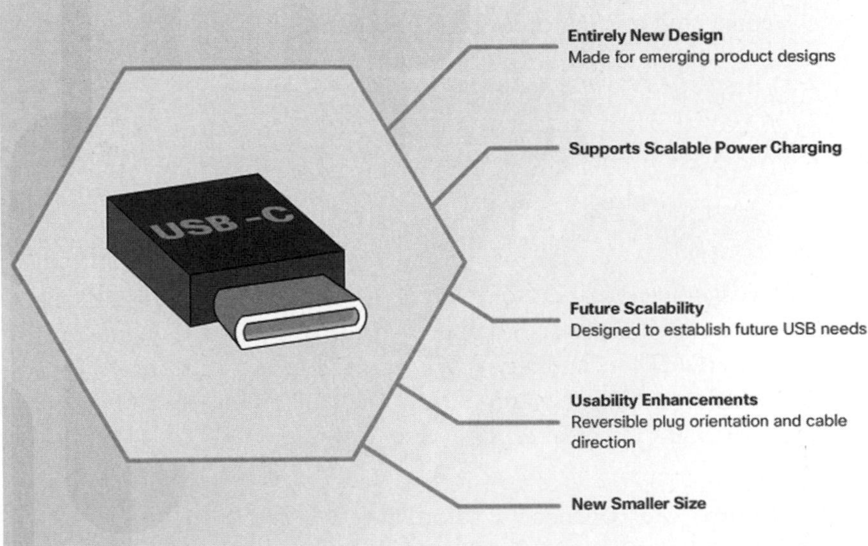

Figure 1-22 USB-C Connector

Methods of connecting external storage devices and bandwidths are described in Table 1-5.

Table 1-5 External Connection Types and Bandwidths

Connection Type	Description	Max Bandwidth	Max Cable Length
FireWire 400 (IEEE 1394a)	■ Supports hot-swappable drives ■ Port support up to 63 devices using hubs ■ Provides power	400 Mb/s	4.5 meters (15 ft.)
FireWire 800 (IEEE 1394b)	■ Backwards compatible with FireWire 400 ■ Can also connect using Ethernet cable	800 Mb/s	4.5 meters (15 ft.) 100 meters (328 ft.)
eSATA	■ Connects external SATA drives ■ External drives require a power cable ■ Not compatible with SATA	3 Gb/s	2 meters (6.6 ft.)
USB 2.0	■ Supports hot-swappable drives ■ Port support up to 127 devices using hubs ■ Provides power	480 Mb/s	5 meters (16.4 ft.)
USB 3.0	■ Backwards-compatible with USB 2.0	5 Gb/s	3 meters (9.8 ft.)
USB 3.1	■ Backwards-compatible with USB 2.0 and 3.0	10 Gb/s	3 meters (9.8 ft.)

Storage devices can also be grouped and managed to create large storage spaces with redundancy. To do so, computers can implement a redundant array of independent disks (RAID) technology. *RAID* provides a way to store data across multiple hard disks for redundancy and/or performance improvement. To the operating system, a RAID array appears as one disk.

The following terms describe how RAID stores data on the various disks:

- *Parity*—Detects data errors.
- *Striping*—Writes data across multiple drives.
- *Mirroring*—Stores duplicate data on a second drive.

There are several levels of RAID available. Table 1-6 compares these different RAID levels.

Table 1-6 RAID Level Comparison

RAID	Minimum Number of Drives	Description	Advantages	Disadvantages
0	2	Data striping without redundancy	High performance.	No data protection and failure of one drive results in loss of all data.
1	2	Disk mirroring	High-performance and high data protection because all data is duplicated.	Highest cost of implementation because an additional drive of equal or larger capacity is required.
2	2	Error-correcting code	This level is no longer used.	Same performance can be achieved at a lower cost using RAID 3.
3	3	Byte-level data striping with dedicated parity	For large sequential data requests.	Does not support multiple, simultaneous read and write requests.
4	3	Block-level data striping with dedicated parity	Supports multiple read requests, and if a disk fails the dedicated parity is used to create a replacement disk.	Write requests are bottlenecked due to the dedicated parity.
5	3	Combination of data striping and parity	Supports multiple simultaneous reads and writes, data is written across all drives with parity, and data can be rebuilt from information found on the other drives.	Write performance is slower than RAID 0 and 1.
6	4	Independent data disks with double parity	Block-level data striping with parity data distributed across all disks can handle two simultaneous drive failures.	Lower performance than RAID 5, and not supported on all disk controllers.
0+1	4	Combination of data striping and mirroring	High performance, highest data protection.	High cost overhead because duplication of data requires twice the storage capacity.
10	4 (must be an even number)	Mirrored set in a striped set	Provides fault tolerance and improved performance.	High cost overhead because duplication of data requires twice the storage capacity.

External Ports and Cables (1.1.3)

This section describes and identifies common cables and ports used for connecting peripherals inside and externally on computers.

Video Ports and Cables (1.1.3.1)

A *video port* connects a monitor to a computer using a cable. Video ports and monitor cables transfer analog signals, digital signals, or both. Computers are digital devices that create digital signals. The digital signals are sent to the graphics card where they are transmitted through a cable to a digital display. Digital signals can also be converted to analog signals by the graphics card and transferred to an analog display. Lower image quality is a result of converting a digital signal to an analog signal. A display and a monitor cable that support digital signals will provide higher image quality than those supporting only analog signals.

Figures 1-23 to 1-29 of Table 1-7 list several video ports and connector types.

Table 1-7 Video Ports and Connector Types

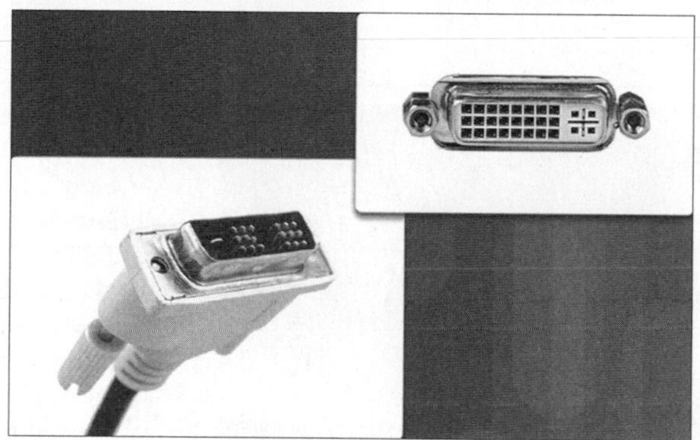 **Figure 1-23** DVI	**Digital Visual Interface (DVI)**—The DVI connector is usually white and consists of 24 pins (three rows of eight pins) for digital signals, four pins for analog signals, and a flat pin called a ground bar. Specifically, DVI-D handles digital signals only, whereas DVI-A handles only analog signals. DVI uses a dual-link interface that creates two groups of data channels that can carry more than 10 Gb/s of digital video information.

(Continued)

Table 1-7 *Continued*

 **Figure 1-24** DisplayPort	**DisplayPort connector**—DisplayPort is an interface technology that is designed to connect high-end graphics-capable PCs and displays, as well as home theater equipment and displays. The connector consists of 20 pins and can be used for audio, video, or both. DisplayPort supports video data rates up to 8.64 Gb/s.
	Mini DisplayPort—A smaller version of the DisplayPort connector is called a Mini DisplayPort. It is used in Thunderbolt 1 and Thunderbolt 2 implementations.
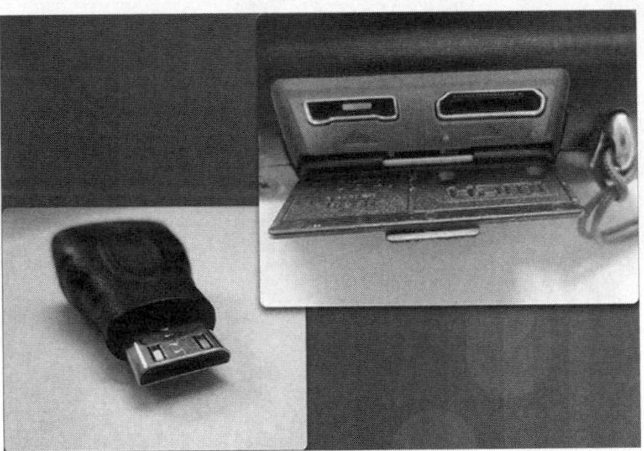 **Figure 1-25** miniHDMI	*HDMI*—High Definition Multimedia Interface was developed specifically for high-definition televisions. However, its digital features also make it a good candidate for computers. There are two common types of HDMI cables. **Full-size HDMI** Type A cable is the standard cable used to connect audio and video devices. **Mini-HDMI** Type C is used to connect laptops and portable devices such as tablets. The Type C connector shown in Figure 3 is smaller than the Type A connector and has 19 pins.

Figure 1-26 Thunderbolt and Thunderbolt 2 Connector

Thunderbolt—Thunderbolt 1 and Thunderbolt 2 use the Mini DisplayPort (MDP) adapter, whereas Thunderbolt 3 requires a USB-C connector.

Figure 1-27 VGA

VGA connector—This is a connector for analog video. It has three rows and 15 pins. It is also sometimes referred to as the DE-15 or HD-15 connector.

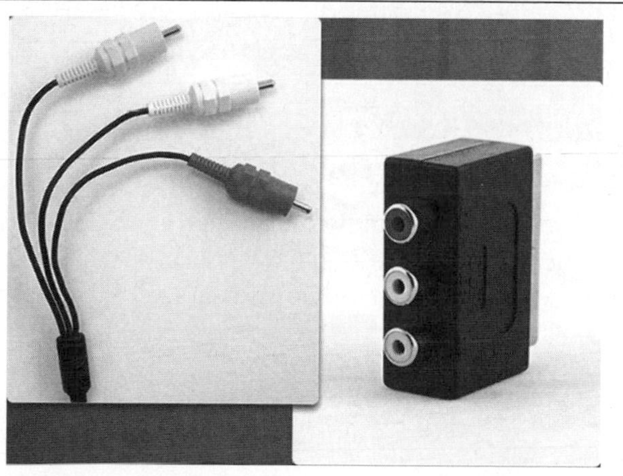

Figure 1-28 RCA

RCA connectors—RCA connectors have a central plug with a ring around it and are used to carry audio or video. RCA connectors are often found in groups of three, in which a yellow connector carries video and a pair of red and white connectors carries left and right audio channels.

(*Continued*)

Table 1-7 *Continued*

 **Figure 1-29** BNC	**BNC connector**—BNCs connect coaxial cables to devices using a quarter-turn connection scheme. BNC is used with digital or analog audio, or video.
	Din-6—This connector has six pins and is commonly used for analog audio, video, and power in security camera applications.
	Wireless—These typically have additional transmitters to be connected to an external monitor/TV.

Note

Legacy monitor connection methods include composite/RGB or S-Video.

Other Ports and Cables (1.1.3.2)

Input/output (I/O) ports on a computer connect peripheral devices, such as printers, scanners, and portable drives. In addition to the ports and interfaces previously discussed, a computer may also have other ports:

- **PS/2 ports**—PS/2 port connects a keyboard or a mouse to a computer. The PS/2 port is a six-pin mini-DIN female connector. The connectors for the keyboard and mouse are often colored differently. If the ports are not color-coded, look for a small figure of a mouse or keyboard next to each port. A PS/2 port is show in Figure 1-30.

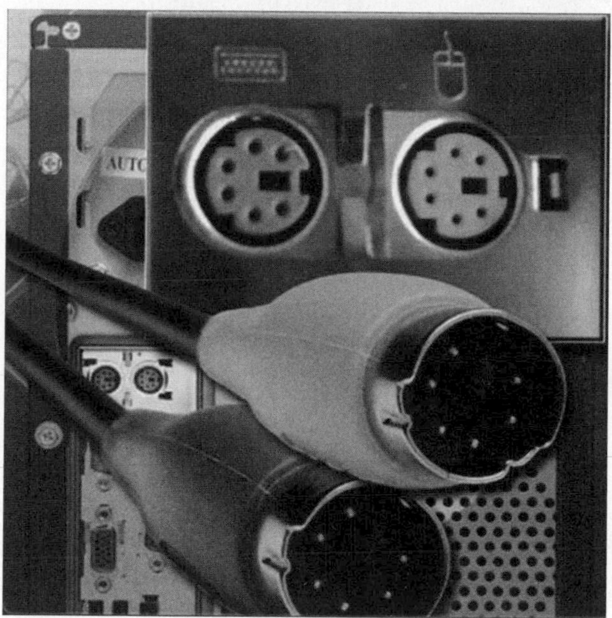

Figure 1-30 PS/2 Cable and Connector

- **Audio ports**—Audio ports connect audio devices to the computer. Analog ports typically include a line in port to connect to an external source (such as a stereo system), a microphone port, and line-out ports to connect speakers or headphones. Digital input and output ports are also available to connect digital sources and output devices. These connectors and cables transfer pulses of light over fiber-optic cables or copper.
- **Game port/MIDI**—Connects to a joystick or MIDI-interfaced device. In Figure 1-31 you can see examples of audio and gameport connectors.

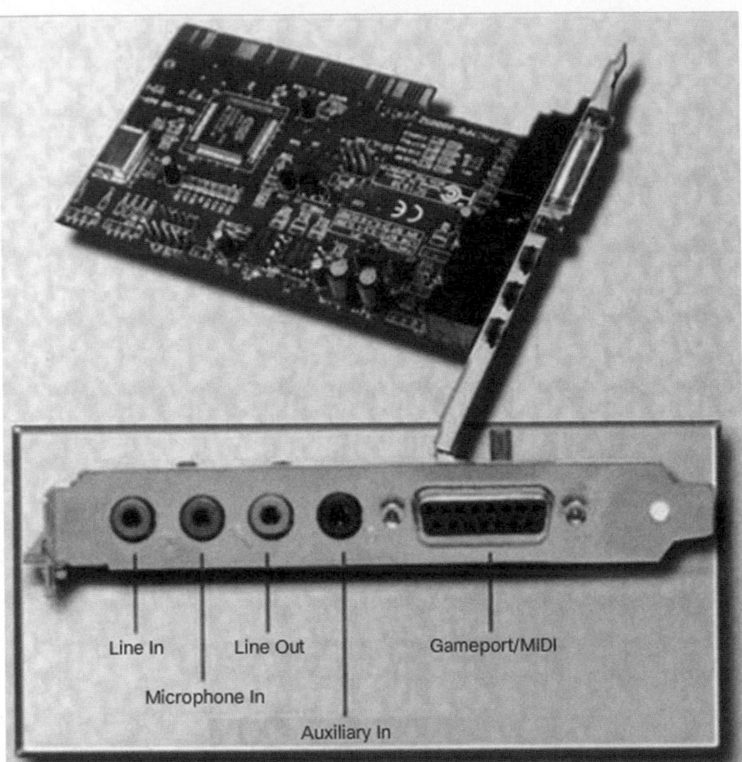

Figure 1-31 Audio and Gameport Connectors

- **Ethernet network port—**(Figure 1-32) displays a network cable and connector. A network port, this used to be known as an RJ-45 port. An Ethernet network port has eight pins and connects devices to a network. The connection speed depends on the type of network port. There a two common Ethernet standards being used. Specifically, Fast Ethernet (or 100BASE) can transmit up to 100 Mb/s, and Gigabit Ethernet (1000BASE) can transmit up to 1000 Mb/s. The maximum length of the Ethernet network cable is 100 m (328 ft).

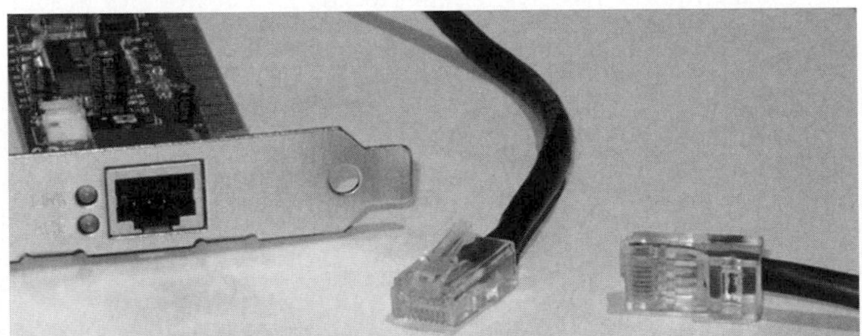

Figure 1-32 Network Cable and Connector

- **USB ports and cables**—The Universal Serial Bus (USB) is a standard interface that connects peripheral devices to a computer. USB devices are hot-swappable, which means that users can connect and disconnect the devices while the computer is powered on. USB connections can be found on computers, cameras, printers, scanners, storage devices, and many other electronic devices. A USB hub connects multiple USB devices. A single USB port in a computer can support up to 127 separate devices with the use of multiple USB hubs. Some devices can also be powered through the USB port, eliminating the need for an external power source.
  - USB 1.1 allowed transmission rates of up to 12 Mb/s in full-speed mode and 1.5 Mb/s in low-speed mode. A USB 1.1 cable has a maximum length of 9.8 ft (3 m).
  - USB 2.0 allows transmission speeds up to 480 Mb/s. A USB 2.0 cable has a maximum length of 16.4 ft (5 m). USB devices can only transfer data up to the maximum speed allowed by the specific port.
  - USB 3.0 allows transmission speeds up to 5 Gb/s. USB 3.0 is backward-compatible with previous versions of USB. A USB 3.0 cable does not have a maximum defined length, although a maximum length of 9.8 ft (3 m) is generally accepted.
- **FireWire ports and cables**—*FireWire* is a high-speed, hot-swappable interface that connects peripheral devices to a computer. A single FireWire port in a computer can support up to 63 devices. Some devices can also be powered through the FireWire port, eliminating the need for an external power source. FireWire uses the Institute of Electrical and Electronics Engineers (IEEE) 1394 standard and is also known as *i.Link*. The IEEE creates publications and standards for technology.
  - The IEEE 1394a standard supports data rates up to 400 Mb/s for cable lengths of 15 ft (4.5 m) or less. This standard uses a four-pin or six-pin connector.
  - The IEEE 1394b (Firewire 800) standard allows for a greater range of connections, including CAT5 UTP and optical fiber. Depending on the media used, data rates are supported up to 3.2 Gb/s for distances of 328 ft (100 m) or less.
- **eSATA Data Cables**—The eSATA cable connects SATA devices to the eSATA interface using a seven-pin *data cable*. This cable does not supply any power to the SATA device. A separate power cable provides power to the disk.

Note

Other ports include serial ports, parallel ports, and modem ports.

Adapters and Converters (1.1.3.3)

There are many connection standards in use today. Many are interoperable but require specialized components. These components are called adapters and converters:

- *Adapter*—This is a component that physically connects one technology to another. For example, a DVI to HDMI adapter. The adapter could be one component or a cable with different ends.
- *Converter*—This performs the same function as an adapter but also translates the signals from one technology to the other. For example, a USB 3.0 to SATA converter enables a hard disk drive to be used as a flash drive.

There are many types of adapters and converters available:

- **DVI to HDMI adapter**—The adapter is used to connect an HDMI monitor to a DVI port.
- **DVI to VGA adapter**—As shown in Figure 1-33, this adapter is used to connect a VGA cable to a DVI port.

Figure 1-33 DVI to VGA Adapter

- **USB A to USB B adapter**—This adapter is used to connect a USB A port to a USB B port.
- **USB to Ethernet adapter**—This adapter is used to connect a USB port to an Ethernet connector. Figure 1-34 shows the adapter.

Figure 1-34 USB to Ethernet adapter

- **USB to PS/2 adapter**—Figure 1-35 shows this adapter type. This adapter is used to connect a USB keyboard or mouse to a PS/2 port.

Figure 1-35 USB to PS/2 adapter

- **HDMI to VGA converter**—The converter translates the VGA output signal of a PC to an HDMI output signal so that an HDMI monitor can be used.
- **Thunderbolt to DVI converter**—The converter translates the Thunderbolt mini DisplayPort video signal to a DVI video signal so that a DVI monitor can be used.

Input and Output Devices (1.1.4)

Input and *output devices* are usually outside of the computer case, connected with cable to ports that allow communication to happen with components inside the computer.

Input Devices (1.1.4.1)

An *input device* enters data or instructions into a computer.

Figures 1-36 to 1-42 of Table 1-8 list examples of input devices.

Table 1-8 Examples of Input Devices

Figure 1-36 Mice, Keyboard and Touchpad

Mice and keyboards—These are the two most commonly used input devices. The keyboard is used to enter text whereas the mouse is used to navigate the graphical user interface (GUI). Laptops also have touchpads to provide built-in mouse features.

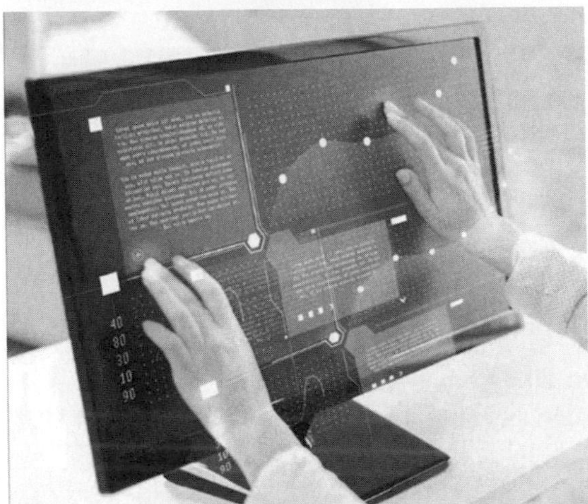

Figure 1-37 Touchscreen

Touchscreens—These input devices have touch- or pressure-sensitive screens. The computer receives instructions specific to the place on the screen that the user touches.

Figure 1-38 Joystick and Gamepad

Joysticks and gamepads—These are input devices for playing games. Gamepads allow the player to control movement and views with small sticks and multiple buttons. Many gamepads also have triggers that register the amount of pressure the player puts on them. Joysticks are often used to play flight simulation-style games.

Figure 1-39 Digital Camera

Digital cameras and digital video cameras—These input devices capture images that can be stored, displayed, printed, or altered. Stand-alone or integrated webcams capture images in real time.

Figure 1-40 Scanner

Scanners—These devices digitize an image or document. The digitization of the image is stored as a file that can be displayed, printed, or altered. A bar code reader is a type of scanner that reads Universal Product Code (UPC) bar codes. It is widely used for pricing and inventory information.

(Continued)

Table 1-8 *Continued*

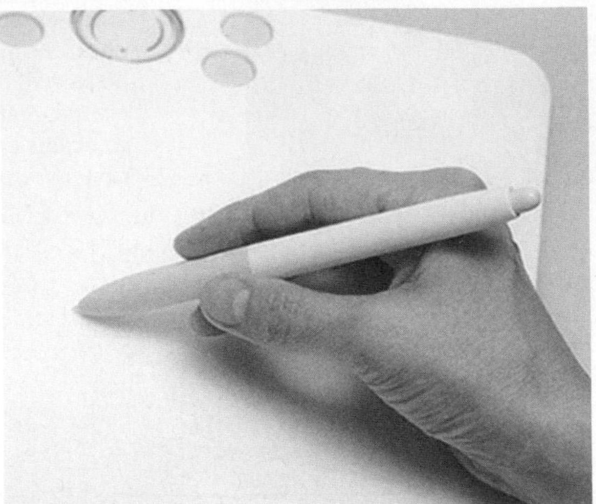 **Figure 1-41** Digitizer	**Digitizers**—This device allows a designer or artist to create blueprints, images, or other artwork by using a pen-like tool called a stylus on a surface that senses where the stylus tip touches it. Some digitizers have more than one surface, or sensor, and allow the user to create 3D models by performing actions with the stylus in midair.
 **Figure 1-42** Fingerprint Reader	**Biometric identification devices**—These input devices identify a user based on a unique physical feature such as their fingerprints or voice. Many laptops now have fingerprint readers to automate logging in to the device.
	Smart card readers—These input devices are typically used on a computer to authenticate the user. A smart card may be the size of a credit card with an embedded microprocessor that is typically under a gold contact pad on one side of the card.

A *keyboard, video, mouse (KVM) switch* is a hardware device that can be used to control more than one computer while using a single keyboard, monitor, and mouse. For businesses, KVM switches provide cost-efficient access to multiple servers. Home users can save space using a KVM switch to connect multiple computers to one keyboard, monitor, and mouse.

Newer KVM switches have the capability to share USB devices and speakers with multiple computers. Typically, by pressing a button on the KVM switch, the user can change the control from one connected computer to another connected computer. Some models of the switch transfer control from one computer to another using a specific key sequence on a keyboard, such to transfer control to the next computer.

Figure 1-43 shows an example of a KVM switch.

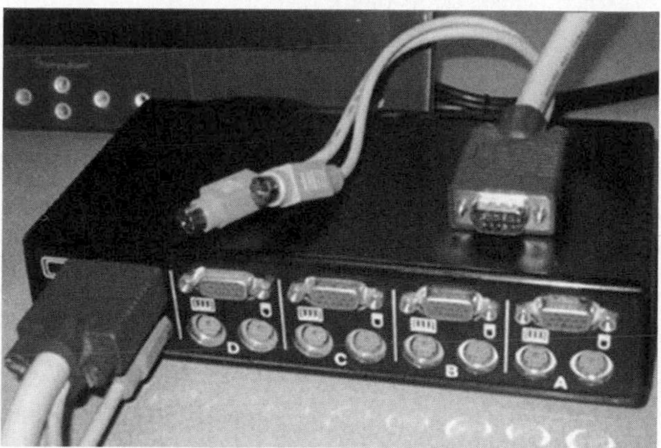

Figure 1-43 KVM Switch

Output Devices (1.1.4.2)

An output device presents information to the user from a computer.

Monitors and projectors are primary output devices for a computer. There are different types of monitors. The most important difference between these monitor types is the technology used to create an image:

- *LCD*—Liquid crystal display (LCD) is commonly used in flat panel monitors and laptops. It consists of two polarizing filters with a liquid crystal solution between them. An electronic current aligns the crystals so that light can either pass through or not pass through. The effect of light passing through in certain areas and not in others is what creates the image. LCD comes in two forms, active matrix and passive matrix. Active matrix is sometimes called thin film transistor (TFT). TFT allows each pixel to be controlled, which creates very sharp color images. Passive matrix is less expensive than active matrix but does not provide the same level of image control. Passive matrix is not commonly used in laptops.

- *LED*—A light-emitting diode (LED) display is an LCD display that uses LED backlighting to light the display. LED has lower power consumption than standard LCD backlighting, allows the panel to be thinner, lighter, brighter, and display better contrast.
- *OLED*—An organic LED display uses a layer of organic material that responds to electrical stimulus to emit light. This process allows each pixel to light individually, resulting in much deeper black levels than LED. OLED displays are also thinner and lighter than LED displays.
- *Plasma*—Plasma displays are another type of flat panel monitor that can achieve high levels of brightness, deep black levels, and a very wide range of colors. Plasma displays can be created in sizes of up to 150 inches (381 cm) or more. Plasma displays get their name from the use of tiny cells of ionized gas that light up when stimulated by electricity.
- *DLP*—Digital Light Processing (DLP) is a projection technology. DLP projectors use a spinning color wheel with a microprocessor-controlled array of mirrors called a digital micromirror device (DMD). Each mirror corresponds to a specific pixel. Each mirror reflects light toward or away from the projector optics. This creates a monochromatic image of up to 1024 shades of gray in between white and black. The color wheel then adds the color data to complete the projected color image.

Note

Legacy monitors include *cathode ray tubes (CRTs)*.

Printers are output devices that create hard copies of computer files. Some printers specialize in particular applications, such as printing color photographs. All-in-one printers are designed to provide multiple services, such as printing, scanning, faxing, and copying.

Speakers and *headphones* are output devices for audio signals. Most computers have audio support either integrated into the motherboard or on an adapter card. Audio support includes ports that allow input and output of audio signals. The audio card has an amplifier to power headphones and external speakers.

Televisions are also output devices, but they may also have input capabilities. A Smart TV runs an operating system that allows it to receive input from the user and connect to many content sources over the Internet and from smartphones, tablets, and other connected devices. Using a *Smart TV* virtually eliminates the need for a set-top box. A *set-top box* is a device which connects a standard TV to content sources such as a cable, satellite, or streaming.

Monitor Characteristics (1.1.4.3)

Monitor resolution refers to the level of image detail that can be reproduced. Higher resolution settings produce better image quality.

Several factors are involved in monitor resolution:

- *Pixel*—The term *pixel* is an abbreviation for *picture element*. Pixels are the tiny dots that comprise a screen. Each pixel consists of red, green, and blue (RGB).
- *Dot pitch*—*Dot pitch* is the distance between pixels on the screen. A lower dot pitch number produces a better image.
- *Contrast ratio*—The *contrast ratio* is a measurement of the difference in intensity of light between the brightest point (white) and the darkest point (black). A 10,000:1 contrast ratio shows dimmer whites and lighter blacks than a monitor with a contrast ratio of 1,000,000:1.
- *Refresh rate*—The *refresh rate* is expressed in Hertz (Hz) and refers to how often per second the image is rebuilt. A higher refresh rate produces a better image.
- *Frame rate*—The *frame rate* refers to how often a video source can feed an entire frame of new data to a display. A monitor's refresh rate in Hz directly equates to the maximum frame per second (FPS) of that monitor. For example, a monitor with a refresh rate of 144 Hz will display a maximum of 144 frames per second.
- *Interlace/non-interlace*—Interlaced monitors create the image by scanning the screen two times. The first scan covers the odd lines, top to bottom, and the second scan covers the even lines. Non-interlaced monitors create the image by scanning the screen, one line at a time from top to bottom.
- *Horizontal, vertical, and color resolution*—The number of pixels in a line is the *horizontal resolution*. The number of lines in a screen is the *vertical resolution*. The number of colors that can be reproduced is the *color resolution*.
- *Aspect ratio*—*Aspect ratio* is the horizontal to vertical measurement of the viewing area of a monitor. For example, QSXGA measures 2560 pixels horizontally by 2048 pixels vertically, which creates an aspect ratio of 5:4. If a viewing area was 16 inches wide by 12 inches high, then the aspect ratio would be 4:3. A viewing area that is 24 inches wide by 18 inches high also has an aspect ratio of 4:3.
- *Native resolution*—*Native resolution* is the number of pixels that a monitor has. A monitor with a resolution of 1280 x 1024 has 1280 horizontal pixels and 1024 vertical pixels. Native mode is when the image sent to the monitor matches the native resolution of the monitor.

Table 1-9 shows common monitor resolutions and their resolution and aspect ratios.

Table 1-9 Display Resolutions

Display Standard	Linear Pixels	Aspect Ration
VGA	640 × 480	4:3
SVGA	800 × 600	4:3
HD	1280 × 720	16:9
WXGA	1280 × 800	16:10
SXGA	1280 × 1024	5:4
QHD	1440 × 2560	16:9
UXGA	1600 × 1200	4:3
FHD	1920 × 1080	16:9
UHD	3840 × 2160	16:9
WQUXGA	3840 × 2400	16:10
FUHD	7680 × 4320	16:9
QUHD	15360 × 8640	16:9

Monitors have controls for adjusting the quality of the image. Here are some common monitor settings:

- **Brightness**—Intensity of the image
- **Contrast**—Ratio of light to dark
- **Position**—Vertical and horizontal location of the image on the screen
- **Reset**—Returns the monitor settings to factory settings

Adding monitors can increase work efficiency. The added monitors allow you to expand the size of or duplicate the desktop so you can view more open windows. Many computers have built-in support for multiple monitors.

Connecting Multiple Monitors to a Single Computer

Connecting multiple monitors requires multiple video cards or a video card with multiple ports.

NOTE

To use multiple monitors, you will need two or more video ports available and additional monitors.

1. Click **Start > Control Panel > Display.**
2. Click **Change display settings.** (The Screen Resolution window should show two monitor icons. If multiple monitors are not displayed on the screen, the monitor may not be supported.)
3. Click the monitor icon that represents your main display. If the monitor is not already the main display, check the box next to **Make this my main display.**
4. Choose **Extend these displays** from the **Multiple displays** drop-down box.
5. Click **Identify.** Windows 7 will display large numbers to identify the two monitors. Drag and drop the monitor icons to match the physical arrangement of the monitors.
6. Choose the desired **Resolution** and **Orientation** from the drop-down boxes.
7. Click **OK.**

There are several advantages to connecting Multiple monitors to a single computer:

- Extending the Windows desktop across two monitors is an inexpensive way to enhance a computer.
- Dualview can also be used to add a second monitor to laptops.
- Using multiple monitors increases productivity. For example, a user can use one screen to video conference while taking notes in an application displayed on the other monitor.

Select Computer Components (1.2)

In this section, you study how to make informed decisions on selecting computer components for building new systems or upgrading existing systems.

Select PC Components (1.2.1)

When upgrading or building a new computer, several factors must be considered.

Building a Computer (1.2.1.1)

Before making any purchases, determine what the purpose of the computer will be. What do you want to do with the computer? Are you buying or building a new home system for the family? Are you building a workstation for a client in an architectural firm who needs to run graphic-intensive applications such as AutoCAD? Or are you building a gaming machine that will give you an edge over competitors?

The next question is how many and what types of external devices will be connected to the computer? Do you require a RAID system? Does the client require older or proprietary components to be connected? Do you need to install a powerful graphics card?

The purpose of the computer and the types of external components you want to use initially influence the selection of the motherboard. The motherboard must accommodate the desired CPU and CPU cooling solution, the type and amount of RAM, and the types and number of expansion slots and ports.

Select the Motherboard (1.2.1.2)

New motherboards, as shown in Figure 1-44, often have new features or standards that may be incompatible with older components. When you select a replacement motherboard, make sure that it supports the CPU, RAM, video adapter, and other adapter cards. The socket and *chipset* on the motherboard must be compatible with the CPU. The motherboard must also accommodate the existing heat sink and fan assembly when reusing the CPU. Pay particular attention to the number and type of expansion slots. Make sure that they match the existing adapter cards and allow for new cards that will be used. The existing power supply must have connections that fit the new motherboard. Finally, the new motherboard must physically fit into the current computer case.

When building a computer, choose a chipset that provides the capabilities that you need. For example, you can purchase a motherboard with a chipset that enables multiple USB ports, eSATA connections, surround sound, and video.

The CPU package must match the motherboard socket type or CPU slot type. A CPU package contains the CPU, connection points, and materials that surround the CPU and dissipate heat.

Data travels from one part of a computer to another through a collection of wires known as the bus. The bus has two parts. The data portion of the bus, known as the *data bus*, carries data between the computer components. The address portion, known as the *address bus*, carries the memory addresses of the locations where data is read or written by the CPU.

The bus size determines how much data can be transmitted at one time. A 32-bit bus transmits 32 bits of data at one time from the processor to RAM, or to other motherboard components, whereas a 64-bit bus transmits 64 bits of data at one time. The speed at which data travels through the bus is determined by the clock speed, measured in MHz or GHz.

PCI expansion slots connect to a parallel bus, which sends multiple bits over multiple wires simultaneously. PCI expansion slots are being replaced with *PCIe expansion slots* that connect to a serial bus, which sends one bit at a time at a much faster rate.

When building a computer, choose a motherboard that has slots to meet your current and future needs.

Figure 1-44 Motherboard

Select the Case and Fans (1.2.1.3)

The choice of motherboard and external components then influences the selection of the case and power supply. The motherboard form factor must be matched with the correct type of computer case and power supply. For example, an ATX motherboard requires both an ATX-compatible case and power supply.

Cases often come with a power supply preinstalled. In this situation, you still need to verify that the power supply provides enough power to operate all the components that will be installed in the case.

You can select a larger computer case to accommodate additional components that may be required in the future. Or you might select a smaller case that requires minimal space. In general, the computer case should be durable, easy to service, and have enough room for expansion.

Various factors affecting the choice of a computer case are described in Table 1-10

Table 1-10 Choosing a Computer Case

Factor	Rational
Model type	The type of motherboard you choose determines the type of case that can be used. The size and shape must match exactly.
Size	If a computer has many components, it will need more room for airflow to keep the system cool.
Power supply (PSU)	You must match the power rating and connection type of the power supply to the type of motherboard you have chosen.
Appearance	For some people, the way the case looks does not matter at all. For others, it is critical. There are many case designs to choose from if it is necessary to have an attractive case.
Status display	What is going on inside the case can be very important. LED indicators that are mounted on the outside of the case can tell you if the system is receiving power, when the HHD is being used, and when the computer is in sleep or hibernate mode.
Vents	All cases have a vent on the PSU, and other vents to help draw into or out of the system.

A computer has many internal components that generate heat while the computer is running. Case fans should be installed to move cooler air into the computer case while moving heat out of the case. When choosing case fans, there are several factors to consider such as:

- **Case size**—Larger cases often require larger fans because smaller fans cannot create enough air flow.
- **Fan speed**—Noise can be an issue, and using larger fans that spin slower can reduce noise.
- **Number of components**—Multiple components can produce more heat requiring more fans.
- **Physical environment**—Case fans must be able to disperse enough heat to keep the case cool in various temperatures.
- **Number of mounting places**—The number of mounting places varies by design.
- **Location of mounting places**—Locations of mounting places vary by design.
- **Electrical connections**—Some case fans are connected directly to the motherboard, whereas others are connected directly to the power supply.

Note

The direction of air flow created by all the fans in the case must work together to bring the cooler air in while moving the hotter air out. Installing a fan backwards or using fans with the incorrect size or speed for the case can cause the air flows to work against each other.

Select the Power Supply (1.2.1.4)

Power supplies convert AC input to DC output voltages. Power supplies typically provide voltages of 3.3V, 5V, and 12V, and are measured in wattage. The power supply must provide enough power for the installed components and allow for other components that may be added at a later time. If you choose a power supply that powers only the current components, you might need to replace the power supply when other components are upgraded.

Table 1-11 describes various factors to consider when selecting a power supply.

Table 1-11 Choosing a Power Supply

Factors	Considerations
Type of motherboard	The power supply must be compatible with the motherboard.
Required wattage	Add the wattage for each component.
Number of components	Make sure the power supply provides enough wattage to support all the components in the system plus another 25% at minimum.
Type of components	Make sure the power supply has the right number and types of connectors for the components.
Type of case	The power supply must be compatible with the case in form factor and mounting.

Be careful when connecting the power supply cables to other components. If you have a difficult time inserting a connector, try repositioning it, or check to make sure that no bent pins or foreign objects are in the way. If it is difficult to plug in a cable or other part, something is wrong. Cables, connectors, and components are designed to fit together snugly. Never force a connector or component. If a connector is plugged in incorrectly, it can damage the plug and the connector. Take your time and make sure that you are connecting the hardware correctly.

Select the CPU and CPU Cooling System (1.2.1.5)

Before you buy a CPU, make sure that it is compatible with the existing motherboard. Manufacturers' websites are a good resource to investigate the compatibility between CPUs and other devices. Table 1-12 shows the list of the various sockets available by manufacturer and their supported processors.

Table 1-12 Intel and AMD sockets

Intel Socket	Architecture	AMD Socket	Architecture
775	Land grid array (LGA)	AM3	Pin grid array (PGA)
1155	LGA	AM3+	PGA
1156	LGA	FM	PGA
1150	LGA	FM	PGA
1366	LGA	FM	PGA
2011	LGA		

When upgrading the CPU, make sure the correct voltage is maintained. A *voltage regulator module (VRM)* is integrated into the motherboard. You can configure the CPU voltage settings in the BIOS or UEFI software. The speed of a modern processor is measured in GHz. A *maximum speed rating* refers to the maximum speed at which a processor can function without errors. Two primary factors can limit the speed of a processor:

- The processor chip is a collection of transistors interconnected by wires. Transmitting data through the transistors and wires creates delays.
- As the transistors change state from on to off or off to on, a small amount of heat is generated. The amount of heat generated increases as the speed of the processor increases. When the processor becomes too hot, it begins to produce errors.

The *front-side bus (FSB)* is the path between the CPU and the *Northbridge*. It is used to connect various components, such as the chipset and expansion cards, and RAM. Data can travel in both directions across the FSB. The frequency of the bus is measured in MHz. The frequency at which a CPU operates is determined by applying a clock multiplier to the FSB speed. For example, a processor running at 3200 MHz might be using a 400 MHz FSB. 3200 MHz divided by 400 MHz is 8, so the CPU is eight times faster than the FSB.

Processors are further classified as 32-bit and 64-bit. The primary difference is the number of instructions that can be handled by the processor at one time. A 64-bit processor processes more instructions per clock cycle than a 32-bit processor. A 64-bit processor can also support more memory. To utilize the 64-bit processor capabilities, ensure that the operating system and applications installed support a 64-bit processor.

The CPU is one of the most expensive and sensitive components in the computer case. The CPU can become very hot; therefore, most CPUs require a heat sink, combined with a fan for cooling.

The following list shows several factors to consider when choosing a CPU cooling system:

- Socket type
- Motherboard physical specifications
- Case size
- Physical environment

Select RAM (1.2.1.6)

New RAM may be needed when an application locks up or the computer displays frequent error messages. To determine if the problem is the RAM, execute the RAM test in the BIOS. If the test is not available, special RAM testing programs are available to download. Another method is to replace the old RAM module with a known good module. Restart the computer to see if the computer runs without error messages.

When selecting new RAM, you must ensure that it is compatible with the current motherboard. Also, the speed of the new RAM must be supported by the chipset. It may be helpful to take the original memory module with you when you shop for the replacement RAM. Figure 1-45 depicts an example of RAM.

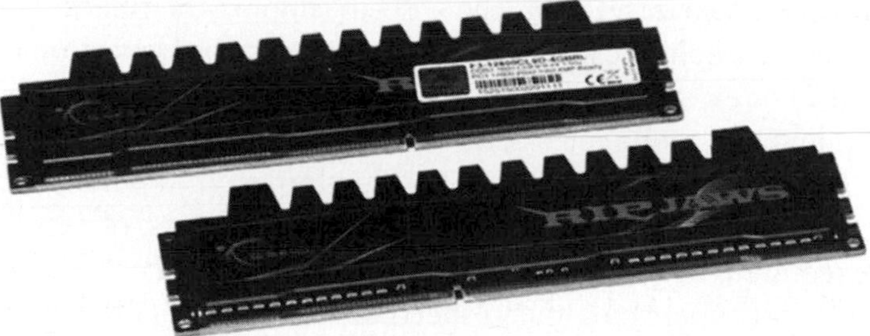

Figure 1-45 RAM

Memory may also be categorized as unbuffered or buffered:

- *Unbuffered memory*— This is regular memory for computers. The computer reads data directly from the memory banks making it faster than buffered memory. However, there is a limit on the amount of RAM that can be installed.
- *Buffered memory*— This is specialized memory for servers and high-end workstations that use a large amount of RAM. These memory chips have

a control chip built into the module. The control chip assists the memory controller in managing large quantities of RAM. Avoid buffered RAM for a gaming computer and the average workstation because the extra controller chip reduces RAM speed.

Select Adapter Cards (1.2.1.7)

Adapter cards, also called *expansion cards*, are designed for a specific task and add extra functionality to a computer. Before purchasing an adapter card, consider the following questions:

- Is there an open expansion slot?
- Is the adapter card compatible with the open slot?
- What are the customers current and future needs?
- What are the possible configuration options?

Note

If the motherboard does not have a compatible expansion slot, an external device may be an option.

The following is a list of possible expansion cards that may be upgraded:

- **Graphics card**—The type of graphics card installed affects the overall performance of a computer. For example, a graphics card that needs to support intensive graphics could be RAM intensive, CPU intensive, or both. The computer must have the slots, RAM, and CPU to support the full functionality of an upgraded graphics card. Choose the graphics card based on current and future needs. For example, to play 3D games, the graphics card must meet or exceed the minimum requirements. Some GPUs are integrated into the CPU. When the GPU is integrated into the CPU, there is no need to purchase a graphics card unless advanced video features, such as 3D graphics, or very high resolution are required. Factors to consider when purchasing a new graphics card are slot type, port type, amount and speed of video RAM (VRAM), GPU, and maximum resolution.
- **Sound cards**—The type of sound card installed determines the sound quality of your computer. A computer system must have quality speakers and a subwoofer to support the full functionality of an upgraded sound card. Choose the correct sound card based on your customer's current and future needs. For example, if a customer wants to hear a specific type of surround sound, the sound card must have the correct hardware decoder to reproduce it. In addition, the customer can get improved sound accuracy with a sound card that has a higher sample rate. Factors to consider when purchasing a new sound card are slot type; digital

signal processor (DSP), which improves the accuracy and reliability of the digital signal; sample rate; port and connection types; hardware decoder; and signal-to-noise ratio.

- **Storage controllers**—A *storage controller* is a chip that can be integrated into the motherboard or on an expansion card. Storage controllers allow for the expansion of internal and external drives for a computer system. Storage controllers, such as RAID controllers, can also provide fault tolerance or increased speed. The amount of data and the level of data protection needed for the customer influences the type of storage controller required. Choose the correct storage controller based on your customer's current and future needs. For example, if a customer wants to implement RAID 5, a RAID storage controller with at least three drives is needed. Factors to consider when purchasing a new storage controller card are slot type, connector quantity internal or external connectors, card size, controller card RAM, controller card processor, and RAID type.
- *I/O cards*—Installing an I/O card in a computer is a fast and easy way to add I/O ports. USB are some of the most common ports to install on a computer. Choose the correct I/O card based on your customer's current and future needs. For example, if a customer wants to add an internal card reader, and the motherboard has no internal USB connection, a USB I/O card with an internal USB connection is needed. Factors to consider when purchasing a new I/O card are slot type, I/O port type, I/O port quantity, and additional power requirements.
- **NICs**—Customers often upgrade a network interface card (NIC) to get faster speeds and more bandwidth. Factors to consider when purchasing a new network card are slot type, speed, connector type, wired or wireless connection, and standards compatibility.
- **Capture cards**—A *capture card* imports video into a computer and records it on a hard drive. The addition of a capture card with a television tuner allows you to view and record television programming. The computer system must have enough CPU power, adequate RAM, and a high-speed storage system to support the capture, recording, and editing demands of the customer. Choose the correct capture card based on your customer's current and future needs. For example, if a customer wants to record one program while watching another, either multiple capture cards or a capture card with multiple TV tuners must be installed. Factors to consider when purchasing a new capture card are slot type, resolution and frame rate, I/O port, and format standards.

Select Hard Drives (1.2.1.8)

You may need to replace an internal storage device when it no longer meets your customer's needs, or it fails. Signs that an internal storage device is failing might be unusual noises, unusual vibrations, error messages, or even corrupt data or applications that do not load.

Factors to consider when purchasing a new hard disk drive are internal or external, HDD or SSD or SSHD, hot-swappable, heat generation, noise generation, and power requirements.

Internal drives usually connect to the motherboard with SATA whereas external drives connect with USB, eSATA, or Thunderbolt.

Figure 1-46 shows a mechanical, magnetic HDD.

Figure 1-46 Hard Drive

Figure 1-47 shows the components of a solid state drive (SSD).

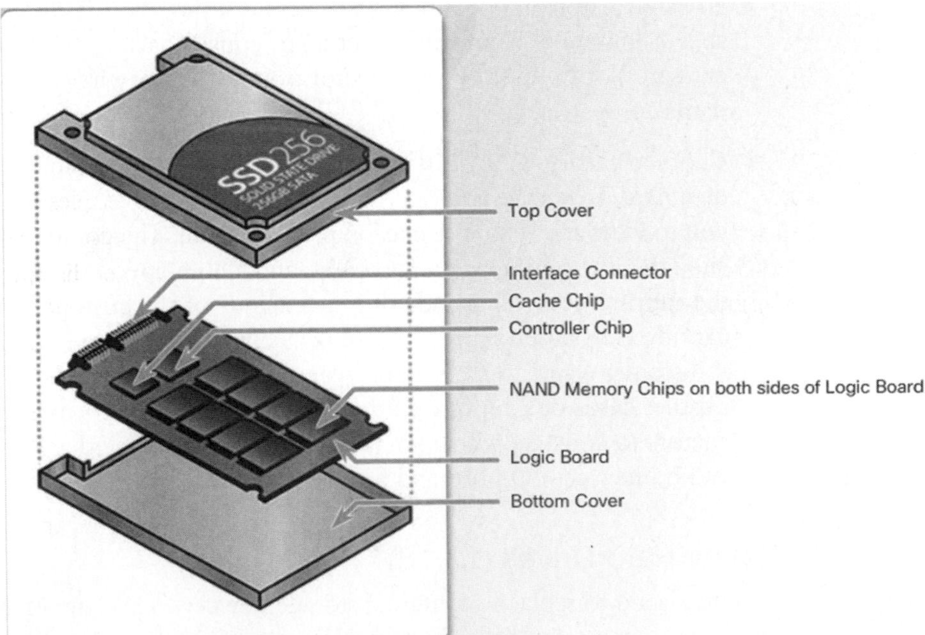

Figure 1-47 SSD Components

Note

SATA and eSATA cables are similar but they are not interchangeable.

Select a Media Reader (1.2.1.9)

A *media reader* is a device that reads and writes to different types of media cards, for example, those found in a digital camera, smart phone, or MP3 player. Figure 1-48 shows a media reader.

Figure 1-48 Media Reader

When replacing a media reader, ensure that it supports the type and storage capacity of cards that will be used.

Factors to consider when purchasing a media reader are media cards supported, internal or external, connector type.

Choose the correct media reader based on your customer's current and future needs. For example, if a customer needs to use multiple types of media cards, a multiple format media reader is needed. These are some common media cards, as shown in Figure 1-49.

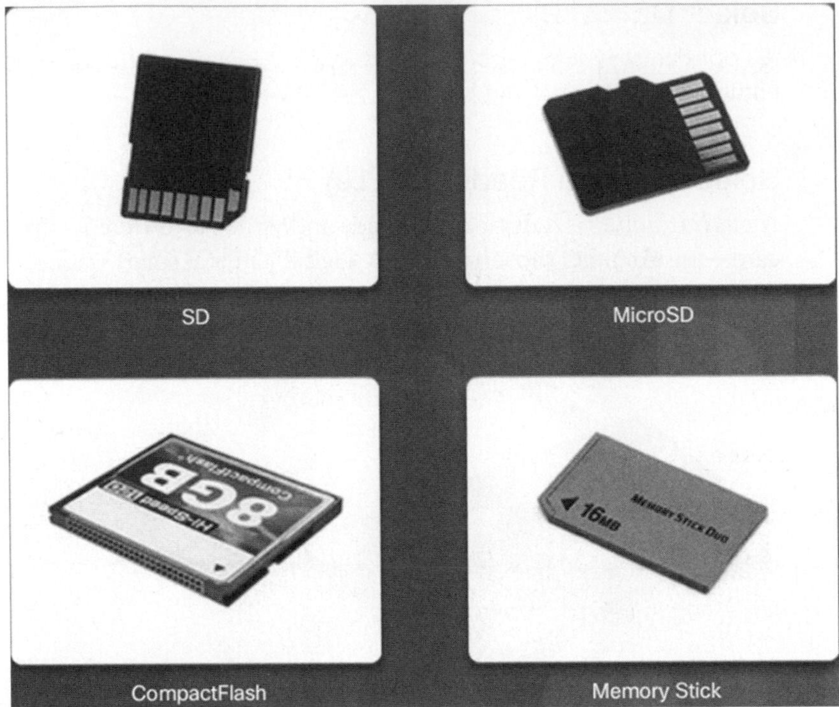

Figure 1-49 Common Media Cards

- **Secure digital (SD)**—SD cards were designed for use in portable devices such as cameras, MP3 players, and laptops. SD cards can hold as much as 2 GB. SD High Capacity (SDHC) cards can hold as much as 32 GB, whereas SD Extended Capacity (SDXC) cards can hold as much as 2 TB of data.
- *MicroSD*—A much smaller version of SD, commonly used in smartphones and tablets.
- *MiniSD*—A version of SD between the size of an SD card and a microSD card. The format was developed for mobile phones.
- **CompactFlash**—CompactFlash is an older format, but still in wide use because of its high speed and high capacity (up to 128 GB is common). CompactFlash is often used as storage for video cameras.
- **Memory Stick**—Created by Sony Corporation, Memory Stick is a proprietary flash memory used in cameras, MP3 players, handheld video game systems, mobile phones, cameras, and other portable electronics.
- *eMMC*—Embedded MultiMediaCard is popular with smartphones and some tablets.
- **xD**—Also known as Picture Card, it was used in some digital cameras.

Select Optical Drives (1.2.1.10)

An optical drive uses a laser to read data from and write data to optical media. Figure 1-50 is an example of an DVD-RW optical drive.

Figure 1-50 Optical Drive

Factors to consider when purchasing an optical drive are connector type, reading capability, writing capability, optical media type.

Table 1-13 summarizes optical drive capabilities.

Table 1-13 Purchasing a New Optical Drive

Optical Device	Read CD	Write CD	Read DVD	Write DVD	Read Blu-Ray	Write Blu-Ray	Rewrite Blu-ray
CD-ROM	X						
CD RW	X	X					
DVD-ROM	X		X				
DVD-RW	X	X	X	X			
BD-ROM	X		X		X		
BD-R	X	X	X	X	X	X	
BD-RE	X	X	X	X	X	X	X

DVDs hold significantly more data than CDs, and Blu-ray discs store significantly more data than DVDs. DVDs and BDs can also have dual layers for recording data, essentially doubling the amount of data that can be recorded on the media.

Select External Storage (1.2.1.11)

External storage offers portability and convenience when working with multiple computers. External storage connects to an external port, such as a USB, eSATA, or Thunderbolt. External flash drives, sometimes called *thumb drives*, connect to a USB port and are a type of removable storage.

Factors to consider when purchasing an external storage solution are port type, storage capacity, speed, portability, power requirements.

Choose the correct type of external storage for your customer's needs. For example, if your customer needs to transfer a small amount of data, such as a single presentation, an external flash drive is a good choice. If your customer needs to back up or transfer large amounts of data, choose an external hard drive.

Select Input and Output Devices (1.2.1.12)

Select the hardware and software based on customer requirements. After you determine which input or output device the customer needs, you must determine how to connect it to the computer.

Figure 1-51 displays the backplane of a computer and some common input and output connectors. Technicians should have a good understanding of these interfaces and ports.

Figure 1-51 Common Input and Output Connectors

Lab—Research Computer Components 1.2.1.13

In this Lab, you gather information about the components you need to complete your customer's computer. Information is provided for the components that your customer already has. Use these specifications to make sure that the components you research are compatible with the components your customer already owns.

Configurations for Specialized Computer Systems (1.3)

Most computers are general-purpose computers built to process a variety of tasks and operations. Specialized computers refer to computers built to perform specific tasks.

Specialized Computer Systems (1.3.1)

This section identifies and discusses some of these specialized computers.

Thick and Thin Clients (1.3.1.1)

Computers are sometimes referred to as:

- **Thick clients**—Sometimes called *fat clients*, these are standard computers that we have discussed in this chapter. The computers have their own operating system, multitude of applications, and local storage. They are standalone systems and do not require a network connection to operate. All of the processing is performed locally on the computer.
- **Thin clients**—These are typically low-end network computers that rely on remote servers to perform all data processing. Thin clients require a network connection to a server and usually access resources using a web browser. However, the client can be a computer running thin client software or a small, dedicated terminal consisting of a monitor, keyboard, and mouse. Typically, the clients do not have any internal storage and have very little local resources.

Table 1-14 describes the differences between thick and thin clients.

Table 1-14 Identifies Differences Between Thick and Thin Clients

	Thick Client	Thin Clients
Resources required	Monitor, mouse, keyboard, tower (with CPU and RAM), internal storage	Monitor, mouse, keyboard, small computer
Footprint	Large	Small
Network access	Optional	Required
Data processing performed	Locally on computer	Remotely on servers
Effort to deploy corporately	More	Less
Cost to deploy corporately	More	Less

Along with thick and thin clients, there are computers that are built for specific purposes. Part of the responsibilities of a computer technician is to evaluate, select appropriate components, and upgrade or custom-build specialized computers to meet the needs of customers.

CAx Workstations (1.3.1.2)

One example of a specialized computer is a workstation used to run computer-aided design (CAD) or computer-aided manufacturing (CAM) software.

A CAD or CAM *(CAx) workstation* is used to design products and control the manufacturing process. CAx workstations are used to create blueprints, design homes, cars, airplanes, computers, and many of the parts in the products that you use every day. A computer used to run CAx software must support the needs of the software and the I/O devices that the user needs to design and manufacture products. CAx software is often complex and requires robust hardware.

Consider the following hardware when you need to run CAx software:

- **Powerful processor—**CAx software must make enormous amounts of calculations very quickly. It should perform fast rendering of 2D and 3D graphics. Fast, multicore processors are recommended in CAD workstations.
- **High-end video card—**These high-resolution graphic cards perform fast rendering of 2D and 3D graphics using specialized GPU. Multiple monitors are desired, or even required, so that the user can work with code, 2D renderings, and 3D models all at the same time.
- **RAM—**Because of the high amount of data processed by a CAx workstation, RAM is very important. The more RAM that is installed, the more data the processor can calculate before needing to read from slower hard drives. Install the maximum amount memory supported by the motherboard and the operating system. The quantity and speed of the memory should exceed the minimums recommended by the CAx application.

Audio and Video Editing Workstations (1.3.1.3)

An *audio editing workstation* is used to record music, create music CDs, and CD labels. A *video editing workstation* can be used to create television commercials, primetime programming, and movies for the theater, or home movies.

Specialized hardware and software are combined to build a computer to perform audio and video editing. Audio software on an audio editing workstation is used to record audio, manipulate how the audio sounds through mixing and special effects, and finalize recordings for publication. Video software is used to cut, copy, combine, and change video clips. Special effects are also added to video using video software.

Consider the following hardware when you need to run audio and video editing software:

- **Specialized audio card—**When recording music to a computer in a studio, multiple inputs from microphones and many outputs to effects equipment may be needed. An audio card capable of handling all these inputs and outputs is needed. Research different audio card manufacturers and understand the needs of your customer to install an audio card that will meet all the needs of a modern recording or mastering studio.

- **Specialized video card**—A video card that can handle high resolutions and multiple displays is necessary to combine and edit different video feeds and special effects in real time. You must understand the needs of the customer and research video cards to install a card that can handle the large amounts of information that come from modern cameras and effects equipment.
- **Large, fast hard drives**—Modern video cameras record in high resolution at fast frame rates. This translates into a large amount of data. Small hard drives will fill up very quickly, and slow hard drives will not be able to keep up with demands, even dropping frames at times. A large, fast hard drive such as SDD or SSHD drives are recommended to record high-end video without errors or missed frames. RAID levels such as 0 or 5, where striping is used, can help to increase read or write speeds.
- **Dual monitors**—When working with audio and video, two, three, or even more monitors can be very helpful to keep track of everything that is going on with multiple tracks, scenes, equipment, and software. HDMI, DisplayPort, and Thunderbolt cards are recommended whereas DVI is acceptable. If multiple monitors are required, specialized video cards are necessary when building an audio or video workstation.

Virtualization Workstations (1.3.1.4)

You may need to build a computer for a customer who uses virtualization technologies. Simultaneously running two or more operating systems on one computer is called *virtualization*. Often, an operating system is installed, and virtualization software is used to install and manage additional installations of other operating systems. Different operating systems from multiple software companies may be used.

There is another type of virtualization called ***virtual desktop infrastructure (VDI)***. VDI allows users to log in to a server to access virtual computers. Input from the mouse and keyboard is sent to the server to manipulate the virtual computer. Output such as sound and video is sent back to the speakers and display of the client accessing the virtual computer.

Low-powered thin clients use a server that is much more powerful to perform difficult calculations. Laptops, smart phones, and tablets can also access the VDI to use virtual computers. These are some other functions of virtual computing:

- Test software or software upgrades in an environment that does not hurt your current operating system environment.
- Use more than one type of operating system on one computer, such as Linux or Mac OS X.

- Browse the Internet without harmful software hurting your main installation.
- Run old applications that are not compatible with modern operating systems.

Virtual computing requires more powerful hardware configurations because each installation needs its own resources. One or two virtual environments can be run on a modern computer with modest hardware, but a complete VDI installation may require fast, expensive hardware to support multiple users in many different environments.

This is some of the hardware required to run virtual computers:

- **Maximum RAM—**You need enough RAM to meet the requirements of each virtual environment and the host computer. A standard installation using only a few virtual machines might require as little as 1 GB of RAM to support a modern operating system such as Windows 8. With multiple users supporting many virtual computers for each user, you might need to install 64 GB of RAM or more.
- **CPU cores—**Although a single core CPU can perform virtual computing, a CPU with additional cores increases speed and responsiveness when hosting multiple users and virtual machines. Some VDI installations use computers that have many CPUs with multiple cores.

Gaming PCs (1.3.1.5)

Many people enjoy playing computer games. Each year, games become more advanced and require more powerful hardware, new hardware types, and additional resources to ensure a smooth and enjoyable gaming experience.

You may have a customer who wants you to design and build a computer used for playing video games. This is some of the hardware required when building a gaming computer:

- **Powerful processor—**Games require all the components in the computer to work together seamlessly. A powerful processor helps ensure that all the software and hardware data can be addressed in a timely fashion. A powerful processor can support high frame rates, 3D rendering, and high audio performance. Multicore processors help increase the responsiveness of hardware and software.
- **High-end video card—**Modern games use high resolutions and intricate detail. A video card that has a fast, specialized GPU and high amounts of fast video memory is necessary to ensure that the images displayed on the monitor are high quality, clear, and smooth. Some gaming machines use multiple video cards to produce high frame rates, or to be able to use multiple monitors.
- **High-end sound card—**Video games use multiple channels of high-quality sound to immerse the player in the games. A high-quality sound card increases

the quality of sound above that of built-in sound on a computer. A dedicated sound card also helps improve overall performance by taking some of the demand off of the processor. Gamers often use specialized headphones and microphones to interact with other online gamers.

- **High-end cooling**—High-end components often produce more heat than standard components. More robust cooling hardware is often needed to make sure that the computer stays cool under heavy loads while playing advanced games. Oversized fans, heat sinks, and liquid cooling devices are often used to keep CPUs, GPUs, and RAM cool.
- **Large amounts of fast RAM**—Computer games require large amounts of memory to function. Video data, sound data, and all the information needed to play the game are constantly being accessed. The more RAM that the computer has, the less often the computer needs to read from storage drives. Faster RAM helps the processor keep all the data in sync, because the data that it needs to calculate can be retrieved when it is needed.
- **Fast storage**—7200 RPM and 10,000 RPM drives can retrieve data at a much faster rate than 5400 RPM hard drives. SSD and SSHD drives are more expensive, but they improve the performance of games dramatically.
- **Gaming-specific hardware**—Some games involve communicating with other players. A microphone is required to talk to them, and speakers or headphones are required to hear them. Find out what type of games your customer plays to determine if a microphone or headset is needed. Some games can be played in 3D. Special glasses and specific video cards may be required to use this feature. Some games benefit from the use of more than one monitor. Flight simulators, for example, can be configured to display cockpit images across two, three, or even more monitors at the same time.

Home Theater PCs (1.3.1.6)

Building a *home theater personal computer (HTPC)* requires specialized hardware to deliver a high-quality viewing experience for the customer. Each piece of equipment must connect and properly provide the necessary services and resources to support the different demands required from an HTPC system.

A useful feature of an HTPC is the ability to record a video program to watch at a later time, known as *time shifting*. HTPC systems can be designed to display live television, stream movies and Internet content, display family photos and videos, and even surf the Internet on a television. Consider the following hardware when building an HTPC:

- **Specialized cases and power supplies**—Smaller motherboards can be used when building an HTPC so that the components can fit into a more compact form factor case. This small form factor looks like a component usually found in a home theater. Usually an HTPC case contains large fans that move more slowly and create less noise than those found in an average workstation. Power supplies that do not have fans can be used (depending on power requirements) to further reduce the amount of noise created by the HTPC. Some HTPC designs contain highly efficient components and require no fans for cooling.

- **Surround sound audio**—Surround sound helps to bring the viewer into the video program. An HTPC can use surround sound from the motherboard when the chipset supports it, or a dedicated sound card can be installed to output high-quality surround sound to speakers, or to an additional amplifier for even better sound.
- **HDMI output**—The HDMI standard allows for transmission of high-definition video, surround sound, and data to televisions, media receivers, and projectors. HDMI can also control the functions of many devices that support control.
- **TV tuners and cable cards**—A tuner must be used for the HTPC to display television signals. A TV tuner converts analog and digital television signals into audio and video signals that the computer can use and store. Cable cards can be used to receive television signals from a cable company. A cable card is required for access to premium cable channels. Some cable cards can receive as many as six channels simultaneously.
- **Specialized hard drive**—Hard drives that have low noise levels and have reduced power consumption are commonly known as *audio/video (A/V) drives*. These drives are specially designed for long, steady recording and long life.

Instead of building an HTPC, some customers may opt to build a home server PC instead. The home server PC can be placed anywhere in the home and be accessed by multiple devices at the same time. The home server shares files, provides printer sharing, and streams audio, video, and photos to computers, laptops, tablets, televisions, and other media devices over the network. A home server may have a RAID array to protect valuable data from a hard drive failure. To stream data to multiple devices without delays, install a gigabit NIC.

Lab—Build a Specialized Computer System—1.3.1.7

In this lab, you gather information about building a specialized computer system that supports hardware and software, allowing a user to perform tasks that an off-the-shelf system cannot perform.

Summary (1.4)

Information technology involves things related to computing such as hardware, software, networking used for managing and processing information. In this chapter you were introduced to many aspects of information technology.

Summary (1.4.1)

This chapter introduced the components that comprise a personal computer system and how to consider upgrade components. Much of the content in this chapter will help you throughout this course.

- Information technology encompasses the use of computers, network hardware, and software to process, store, transmit, and retrieve information.
- A personal computer system consists of hardware components and software applications.
- The computer case and power supply must be chosen carefully to support the hardware inside the case and allow for the addition of components.
- The internal components of a computer are selected for specific features and functions. All internal components must be compatible with the motherboard.
- Use the correct type of ports and cables when connecting devices.
- Typical input devices include the keyboard, mouse, touch screen, and digital cameras.
- Typical output devices include monitors, printers, and speakers.
- Cases, power supplies, the CPU and cooling system, RAM, hard drives, and adapter cards, must be upgraded when devices fail or no longer meet customer needs.

Specialized computers require hardware specific to their function. The type of hardware used in specialized computers is determined by how a customer works and what a customer wants to accomplish.

Summary of Exercises

This is a summary of the Lab activities associated with this chapter.

Labs

The following labs cover material from this chapter. Refer to the labs in the *IT Essentials v6 Lab Manual*.

Lab 1.1.1.4: Ohm's Law

Lab 1.2.1.13: Research Computer Components

Lab 1.3.1.7: Build a Specialized Computer System

Check your Understanding

You can find the answers to these questions in the appendix, "Answers to 'Check Your Understanding' Questions."

1. What is the purpose of the voltage selector switch?

   A. It sets the power supply voltage to accommodate the voltage needs of computer components.

   B. It sets the correct input voltage to the power supply, depending on the country where the power supply is used.

   C. It allows the user to increase the number of devices the power supply can support.

   D. It changes the voltage to match the type of motherboard used in the computer.

2. Which IEEE standard defines the FireWire technology?

   A. 1284

   B. 1394

   C. 1451

   D. 1539

3. What is the maximum data speed of high-speed USB 2.0?

   A. 1.5 Mbps

   B. 12 Mbps

   C. 380 Mbps

   D. 480 Mbps

   E. 480 Gbps

   F. 840 Gbps

4. A network administrator currently has three servers and needs to add a fourth, but does not have enough room for an additional monitor and keyboard. Which device allows the administrator to connect all the servers to a single monitor and keyboard?

   A. touch screen monitor

   B. PS/2 hub

   C. USB switch

   D. KVM switch

   E. UPS

5. What danger is posed to a technician by opening a power supply even after it has been unplugged for an extended period of time?

   A. shock from stored high voltage

   B. burns from hot components

   C. exposure to heavy metals

   D. poisoning from toxic fumes

6. Which term refers to the technique of increasing the speed of a processor from the specified value of its manufacturer?

   A. throttling

   B. multitasking

   C. overclocking

   D. hyperthreading

7. Which technology would be best to use for drive redundancy and data protection?

   A. CD

   B. DVD

   C. PATA

   D. RAID

   E. SCSI

8. What is a characteristic of a hot-swappable eSATA drive?

   A. The computer must be shut down in order for the drive to be connected.

   B. A hot-swappable eSATA drive produces less heat.

   C. It can be connected and disconnected to the computer without turning off the computer.

   D. It has a lower spin rate (RPM).

9. Which is a possible use for virtual computing?

   A. To allow users to browse the Internet without the risk of malware infecting the host software installation

   B. To allow computer hardware to be tested

   C. To allow computer hardware upgrades to be tested

   D. To allow ROM firmware upgrades to be tested

10. When a computer is being built, which three components must have the same form factor? (Choose three.)

    A. Case

    B. Power supply

    C. Monitor

    D. Video card

    E. Motherboard

    F. Keyboard

11. What is the function of the power supply?

    A. To convert AC power into a lower voltage DC power

    B. To convert AC power into a higher voltage DC power

    C. To convert DC power into a lower voltage AC power

    D. To convert DC power into a higher voltage AC power

CHAPTER 2

Introduction to Lab Procedures and Tool Use

Objectives

Upon completion of this chapter, you will be able to answer the following questions:

- What are safe working conditions and procedures?
- What procedures help protect equipment and data?
- What procedures help to properly dispose of hazardous computer components and related material? What tools and software are used with personal computer components and what is their purpose?
- What is proper tool use?

Key Terms

This chapter uses the following key terms. You can find the definitions in the Glossary.

Electrostatic discharge (ESD) *Page 76*

Electromagnetic interference (EMI) *Page 77*

Brownout *Page 78*

Spike *Page 78*

Noise *Page 78*

Blackout *Page 78*

Power surge *Page 78*

Surge suppressor *Page 78*

Standby power supply (SPS) *Page 78*

Uninterruptible power supply (UPS) *Page 78*

material safety and data sheet (MSDS) *Page 80*

tone generator and probe *Page 86*

History of repairs *Page 90*

antistatic wrist strap *Page 83*

antistatic mat *Page 83*

Power supply tester *Page 94*

Cable tester *Page 94*

Loopback plug *Page 94*

Multimeter *Page 94*

Disk Management *Page 88*

Format *Page 88*

CHKDSK *Page 88*

System File Checker (SFC) *Page 88*

Windows Action Center *Page 89*

Window Firewall *Page 89*

Introduction (2.0)

Safety is an important topic and exercise in the workplace. Safety guidelines help protect individuals from accidents and injury. They also help to protect equipment from damage.

Welcome (2.0.1)

The consequences of poor safety practices in the workplace can result in serious injury, increased equipment damage, harm to the environment, and other problems. Even a small incident will decrease productivity and increase costs. It is essential for all employees to understand safety at work.

Introduction to Lab Procedures and Tool Use (2.0.1.1)

This chapter covers basic safety practices for the workplace, hardware and software tools, and the disposal of hazardous materials. Safety guidelines help protect individuals from accidents and injury. They also help to protect equipment from damage. Some of these guidelines are designed to protect the environment from contamination caused by improperly discarded materials.

Safe Lab Procedures (2.1)

Everyone must understand and follow safety procedures.

Procedures to Protect People (2.1.1)

Safe working conditions help prevent injury to people and damage to computer equipment. A safe workspace is clean, organized, and properly lit.

General Safety (2.1.1.1)

Follow safety guidelines to prevent cuts, burns, electrical shock, and damage to eyesight. As a best practice, make sure that a fire extinguisher and first-aid kit are available. Poorly placed or unsecured cables can cause tripping hazards in a network installation. Cable management techniques such as installation of cables in conduit or cable trays help to prevent hazards.

This is a partial list of basic safety precautions to use when working on a computer:

- Remove your watch and jewelry and secure loose clothing.
- Turn off the power and unplug equipment before performing service.

- Cover sharp edges inside the computer case with tape.
- Never open a power supply or a monitor with a built-in power supply.
- Do not touch areas in printers that are hot or that use high voltage.
- Know where the fire extinguisher is located and how to use it.
- Keep food and drinks out of your workspace.
- Keep your workspace clean and free of clutter.
- Bend your knees when lifting heavy objects to avoid injuring your back.
- Wear safety goggles to prevent damage to eyesight.

Before cleaning or repairing equipment, make sure that your tools are in good condition. Clean, repair, or replace items that are not functioning adequately.

Electrical Safety (2.1.1.2)

Follow electrical safety guidelines to prevent electrical fires, injuries, and fatalities.

Some printer parts become hot during use, and other parts, such as power supplies, contain high voltage. Check the printer manual for the location of high-voltage components. Some components retain a high voltage even after the printer is turned off. Make sure that the printer has had time to cool before making the repair.

Electrical devices have certain power requirements. For example, AC adapters are manufactured for specific laptops. Exchanging AC adapters with a different type of laptop or device may cause damage to both the AC adapter and the laptop.

Fire Safety (2.1.1.3)

Follow fire safety guidelines to protect lives, structures, and equipment. To avoid an electrical shock and to prevent damage to the computer, turn off and unplug the computer before beginning a repair.

Fire can spread rapidly and be very costly. Proper use of a fire extinguisher can prevent a small fire from getting out of control. Use the memory aid P-A-S-S to remember the basic rules of fire extinguisher operation:

- **P:** Pull the pin.
- **A:** Aim at the base of the fire, not at the flames.
- **S:** Squeeze the lever.
- **S:** Sweep the nozzle from side to side.

Be familiar with the types of fire extinguishers used in your country or region. Each type of fire extinguisher has specific chemicals to fight different types of fires:

- Paper, wood, plastics, cardboard
- Gasoline, kerosene, organic solvents
- Electrical equipment
- Combustible metals

When working with computer components, be alert for odors emitting from computers and electronic devices. When electronic components overheat or short out, they emit a burning smell. If there is a fire, follow these safety procedures:

- Never fight a fire that is out of control or not contained.
- Always have a planned fire escape route before beginning any work.
- Get out of the building quickly.
- Contact emergency services for help.
- Locate and read the instructions on the fire extinguishers in your workplace before you have to use them.

Procedures to Protect Equipment and Data (2.1.2)

Replacing equipment and recovering data is expensive and time consuming. This section identifies potential threats to systems and descries procedures to help prevent loss and damage.

ESD and EMI (2.1.2.1)

Replacing equipment and recovering data is expensive and time consuming. This section identifies potential threats to systems and describes procedures to help prevent loss and damage.

Electrostatic Discharge

Electrostatic discharge (ESD) can occur when there is a buildup of an electric charge (static electricity) that exists on a surface which comes into contact with another, differently charged surface. ESD can cause damage to computer equipment if not discharged properly. Follow proper handling guidelines, be aware of environmental issues, and use equipment that stabilizes power to prevent equipment damage and data loss.

At least 3,000 volts of static electricity must build up before a person can feel ESD. For example, static electricity can build up on you as you walk across a carpeted floor. When you touch another person, you both receive a shock. If the discharge causes pain or makes a noise, the charge was probably above 10,000 volts. By comparison, less than 30 volts of static electricity can damage a computer component.

ESD can cause permanent damage to electrical components. Follow these recommendations to help prevent ESD damage:

- Keep all components in antistatic bags until you are ready to install them.
- Use grounded mats on workbenches.
- Use grounded floor mats in work areas.
- Use antistatic wrist straps when working on computers.

Electromagnetic Interference

Electromagnetic interference (EMI) is the intrusion of outside electromagnetic signals in a transmission media, such as copper cabling. In a network environment, EMI distorts the signals so that the receiving devices have difficulty interpreting them.

EMI does not always come from expected sources, such as cellular phones. Other types of electric equipment can emit a silent, invisible electromagnetic field that can extend for more than a mile.

There are many sources of EMI:

- Any source designed to generate electromagnetic energy
- Man-made sources like power lines or motors
- Natural events such as electrical storms, or solar and interstellar radiations

Wireless networks are affected by radio frequency interference (RFI). RFI is caused by radio transmitters and other devices transmitting in the same frequency. For example, a cordless telephone can cause problems with a wireless network when both devices use the same frequency. Microwaves can also cause interference when positioned in close proximity to wireless networking devices.

Climate

Climate affects computer equipment in a variety of ways:

- If the environment temperature is very high, equipment can overheat.
- If the humidity level is very low, the chance of ESD increases.
- If the humidity level is very high, equipment can suffer from moisture damage.

Power Fluctuation Types (2.1.2.2)

Voltage is a measure of energy required to move a charge from one location to another. The movement of electrons is called *current*. Computer circuits need voltage and current to operate electronic components. When the voltage in a computer is not accurate or steady, computer components might not operate correctly. Unsteady voltages are called power fluctuations.

The following types of AC power fluctuations can cause data loss or hardware failure:

- *Blackout*—Complete loss of AC power. A blown fuse, damaged transformer, or downed power line can cause a blackout.
- *Brownout*—Reduced voltage level of AC power that lasts for a period of time. Brownouts occur when the power line voltage drops below 80 percent of the normal voltage level and when electrical circuits are overloaded.
- *Noise*—Interference from generators and lightning. Noise results in poor quality power, which can cause errors in a computer system.
- *Spike*—Sudden increase in voltage that lasts for a short period and exceeds 100 percent of the normal voltage on a line. Spikes can be caused by lightning strikes, but can also occur when the electrical system comes back on after a blackout.
- *Power surge*—Dramatic increase in voltage above the normal flow of electrical current. A power surge lasts for a few nanoseconds, or one billionth of a second.

Power Protection Devices (2.1.2.3)

To help shield against power fluctuation problems, use devices to protect the data and computer equipment:

- *Surge suppressor*—Helps protect against damage from surges and spikes. A surge suppressor diverts extra electrical voltage that is on the line to the ground.
- *Uninterruptible power supply (UPS)*—Helps protect against potential electrical power problems by supplying a consistent level of electrical power to a computer or other device. The battery is constantly recharging while the UPS is in use. The UPS provides a consistent quality of power when brownouts and blackouts occur. Many UPS devices can communicate directly with the computer operating system. This communication allows the UPS to safely shut down the computer and save data prior to the UPS losing all battery power.
- *Standby power supply (SPS)*—Helps protect against potential electrical power problems by providing a backup battery to supply power when the incoming voltage drops below the normal level. The battery is on standby during normal operation. When the voltage decreases, the battery provides DC power to a

power inverter, which converts it to AC power for the computer. This device is not as reliable as a UPS because of the time it takes to switch over to the battery. If the switching device fails, the battery cannot supply power to the computer.

Figure 2-1 shows examples of devices to shield against power fluctuations.

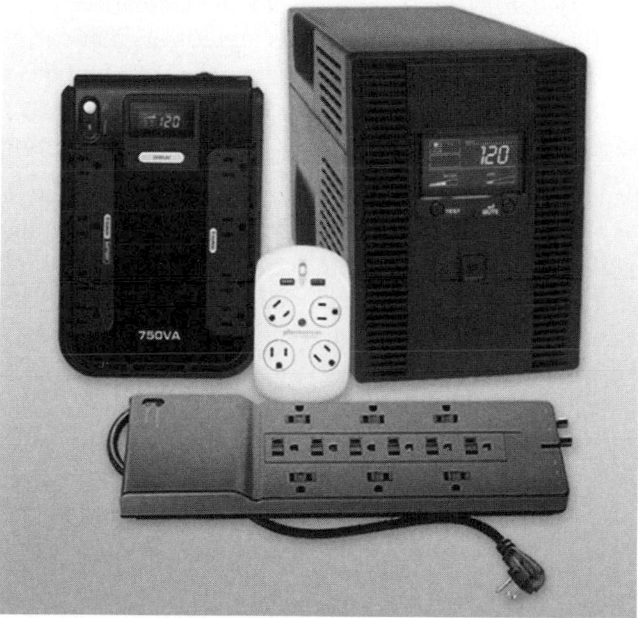

Figure 2-1 Types of Power Protection Equipment

Caution

UPS manufacturers suggest never plugging a laser printer into a UPS because the printer could overload the UPS.

Procedures to Protect the Environment (2.1.3)

Most computer and peripherals use and contain at least some materials that can be considered toxic to the environment. This section describes tools and procedures that help identify these materials and the steps for proper handling and disposal of the materials.

Safety Data Sheet (2.1.3.1)

Computers and peripherals contain materials that can be harmful to the environment. Hazardous materials are sometimes called toxic waste. These materials can contain high concentrations of heavy metals such as cadmium, lead, or mercury. The regulations for the disposal of hazardous materials vary by state or country. Contact the local recycling or waste removal authorities in your community for information about disposal procedures and services.

A safety data sheet (SDS) used to be known as a *material safety and data sheet (MSDS)*. A *safety data sheet* is a fact sheet that summarizes information about material identification, including hazardous ingredients that can affect personal health, fire hazards, and first-aid requirements. The SDS contains chemical reactivity and incompatibility information. It also includes protective measures for the safe handling and storage of materials and spill, leak, and disposal procedures.

To determine if a material is classified as hazardous, consult the manufacturer's SDS. In the United States, the Occupational Safety and Health Administration (OSHA) requires that all hazardous materials be accompanied by an SDS when transferred to a new owner. The SDS information included with products purchased for computer repairs or maintenance can be relevant to computer technicians. OSHA also requires that employees be informed about the materials that they are working with and be provided with material safety information.

The SDS explains how to dispose of potentially hazardous materials in the safest manner. Always check local regulations concerning acceptable disposal methods before disposing of any electronic equipment.

The SDS contains valuable information:

- Name of the material
- Physical properties of the material
- Hazardous ingredients contained in the material
- Reactivity data, such as fire and explosion data
- Procedures for spills and leaks
- Special precautions
- Health hazards
- Special protection requirements

In the European Union, the regulation Registration, Evaluation, Authorization and restriction of Chemicals (REACH) came into effect on June 1, 2007, replacing various directives and regulations with a single system.

Equipment Disposal (2.1.3.2)

The proper disposal or recycling of hazardous computer components is a global issue. Make sure to follow regulations that govern how to dispose of specific items.

Organizations that violate these regulations can be fined or face expensive legal battles. Regulations for the disposal of the items on this page vary from state to state and from country to country. Check your local environmental regulation agency.

Batteries

Batteries often contain rare earth metals that can be harmful to the environment. Batteries from portable computer systems can contain lead, cadmium, lithium, alkaline manganese, and mercury. These metals do not decay and remain in the environment for many years. Mercury is commonly used in the manufacturing of batteries and is extremely toxic and harmful to humans.

Recycling batteries should be a standard practice. All batteries, including lithium-ion, nickel-cadmium, nickel-metal hydride, and lead-acid, are subject to disposal procedures that comply with local environmental regulations.

Monitors

Handle CRT monitors with care. Extremely high voltage can be stored in CRT monitors, even after being disconnected from a power source.

Monitors contain glass, metal, plastics, lead, barium, and rare earth metals. According to the U.S. Environmental Protection Agency (EPA), monitors can contain approximately 4 pounds (1.8 kg) of lead. Monitors must be disposed of in compliance with environmental regulations.

Toner Kits, Cartridges, and Developers

Used printer toner kits and printer cartridges must be disposed of properly in compliance with environmental regulations. They can also be recycled. Some toner cartridge suppliers and manufacturers take empty cartridges for refilling. Some companies specialize in refilling empty cartridges. Kits to refill inkjet printer cartridges are available but are not recommended, because the ink might leak into the printer, causing irreparable damage. Using refilled inkjet cartridges might also void the inkjet printer warranty.

Chemical Solvents and Aerosol Cans

Contact the local sanitation company to learn how and where to dispose of the chemicals and solvents used to clean computers. Never dump chemicals or solvents down a sink or dispose of them in a drain that connects to public sewers.

The cans or bottles that contain solvents and other cleaning supplies must be handled carefully. Make sure that they are identified and treated as special hazardous waste. For example, some aerosol cans explode when exposed to heat if the contents are not completely used.

Figure 2-2 shows various types of hazardous computer components.

Figure 2-2 Hazardous Computer Components

Proper Use of Tools (2.2)

Using tools properly helps prevent accidents and damage to equipment and people. This section describes and covers the proper use of a variety of hardware, software, and organizational tools specific to working with computers and peripherals.

Hardware Tools (2.2.1)

For every job there is the right tool. Make sure that you are familiar with the correct use of each tool and that the correct tool is used for the current task. Skilled use of tools and software makes the job less difficult and ensures that tasks are performed properly and safely.

General Tool Use (2.2.1.1)

Computer repair requires some task-specific tools. Make sure that you are familiar with the correct use of each tool and that the correct tool is used for the task. Skilled use of tools and software makes the job less difficult and ensures that tasks are performed properly and safely.

A toolkit should contain all the tools necessary to complete hardware repairs. Figure 2-3 shows an example of a PC repair toolkit.

Figure 2-3 Toolkit

As you gain experience, you learn which tools to have available for different types of jobs. Hardware tools are grouped into four categories:

- ESD tools
- Hand tools
- Cleaning tools
- Diagnostic tools

ESD Tools (2.2.1.2)

There are two ESD tools: the antistatic wrist strap and the antistatic mat. The *antistatic wrist strap* protects computer equipment when grounded to a computer chassis. The *antistatic mat* protects computer equipment by preventing static electricity from accumulating on the hardware or on the technician. Figures 2-4 and 2-5 show the two types of ESD tools discussed above.

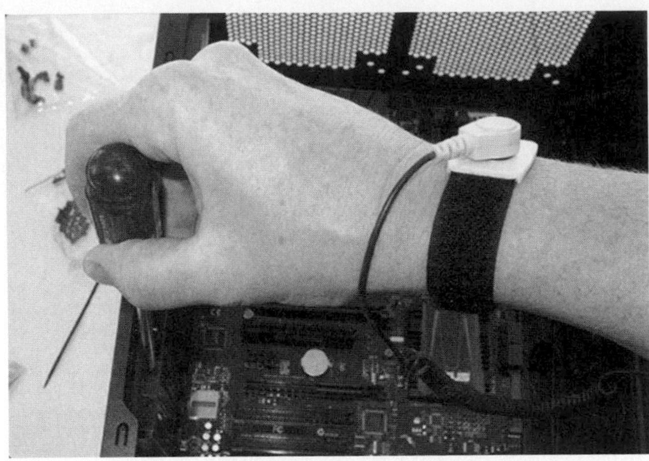

Figure 2-4 Antistatic Wrist Strap

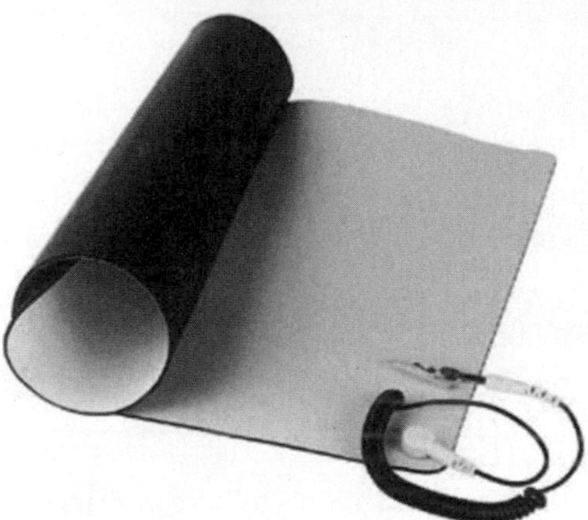

Figure 2-5 Antistatic Mat

Hand Tools (2.2.1.3)

Most tools used in the computer assembly process are small hand tools. They are available individually or as part of a computer repair toolkit. Toolkits range widely in size, quality, and price.

Cable Tools (2.2.1.4)

Tools for repairing and creating cables are also part of a computer repair toolkit. Figures 2-6 and 2-7 provide images of common cable tools.

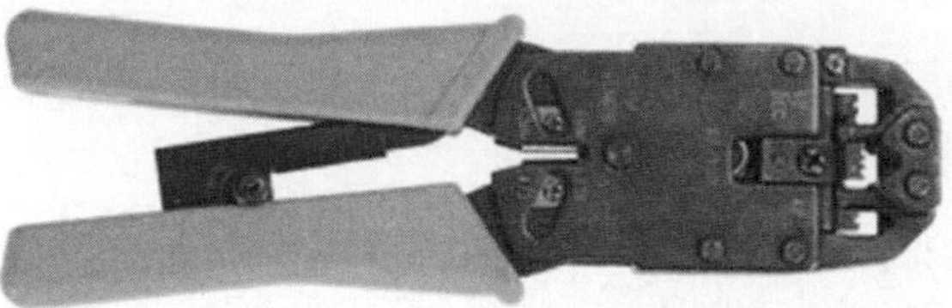

Figure 2-6 Crimper

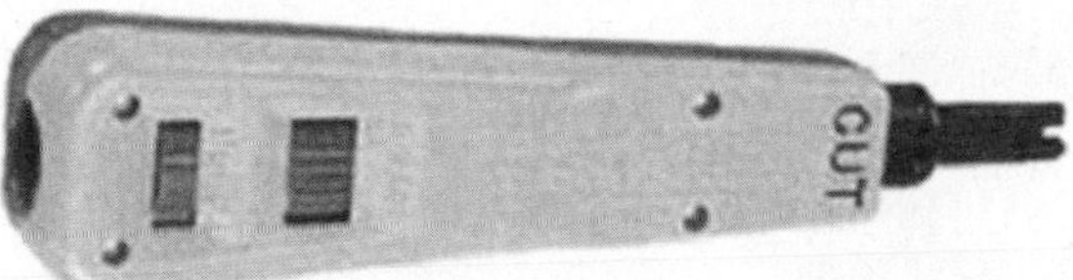

Figure 2-7 Punch Down Tool

Cleaning Tools (2.2.1.5)

Having the appropriate cleaning tools is essential when maintaining and repairing computers. Using the appropriate cleaning tools such as lint-free cloth, compressed air, cable ties, a parts organizer for small parts helps ensure that computer components are not damaged during cleaning.

Diagnostic Tools (2.2.1.6)

Diagnostic tools are used to test and diagnose equipment.

Digital Multimeter

A *digital multimeter*, as shown in Figure 2-8, is a device that can take many types of measurements. It tests the integrity of circuits and the quality of electricity in computer components. A digital multimeter displays the information on an LCD or LED screen.

Figure 2-8 Digital Multimeter

Loopback Adapter

A *loopback adapter*, also called a *loopback plug*, tests the basic functionality of computer ports. The adapter is specific to the port that you want to test.

Tone Generator and Probe

The *tone generator and probe*, as shown in Figure 2-9, is a two-part tool. The tone part is connected to a cable at one end using specific adapters. The tone generates a tone that travels the length of the cable. The probe traces the cable. When the probe is in near proximity to the cable to which the tone is attached, the tone can be heard through a speaker in the probe.

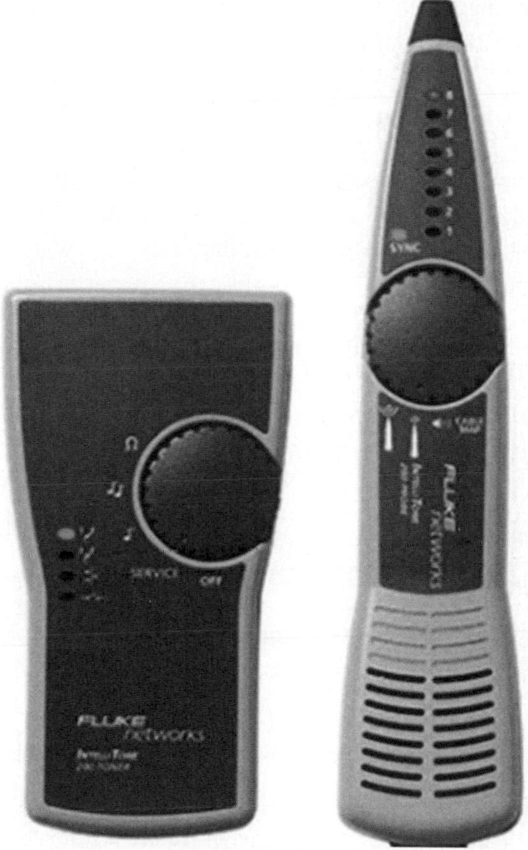

Figure 2-9 Tone Generator and Probe

WiFi Analyzer

WiFi analyzers are mobile tools for auditing and troubleshooting wireless networks. Many WiFi analyzers are robust tools designed for enterprise network planning, security, compliance, and maintenance. But WiFi analyzers can also be used for smaller, wireless LANs. Technicians can see all available wireless networks in a given area, determine signal strengths, and position access points to adjust wireless coverage.

Some WiFi analyzers can help troubleshoot a wireless network by detecting misconfigurations, access point failures, and RFI problems.

External Hard Drive Enclosure

Although an external hard drive enclosure is not a diagnostic tool, it is often used when diagnosing and repairing computers. The customer hard drive is placed into the external enclosure for inspection, diagnosis, and repair using a known-working computer. Backups can also be recorded to a drive in an external enclosure to prevent data corruption during a computer repair.

Software Tools (2.2.2)

Software tools help diagnose computer and network problems and determine which computer device is not functioning correctly. A technician must be able to use a range of software tools to diagnose problems, maintain hardware, and protect the data stored on a computer.

Disk Management Tools (2.2.2.1)

You must be able to identify which software to use in different situations. Disk management tools help detect and correct disk errors, prepare a disk for data storage, and remove unwanted files:

- *Disk Management*—Initializes disks, creates partitions, and formats partitions.
- *Format*—Prepares a hard drive to store information.
- *Scandisk* or *CHKDSK*—Checks the integrity of files and folders on a hard drive by scanning the file system. These tools might also check the disk surface for physical errors.
- **Optimize Drives**—Previously known as Defrag, optimizes space on a hard drive to allow faster access to programs and data.
- **Disk Cleanup**—Clears space on a hard drive by searching for files that can be safely deleted.
- *System File Checker (SFC)*—Scans the operating system's critical files and replaces files that are corrupt. Use the Windows 8 boot disk for troubleshooting and repairing corrupted files. The Windows 8 boot disk repairs Windows system files, restores damaged or lost files, and reinstalls the operating system. Third-party software tools are also available to assist in troubleshooting problems.

Protection Software Tools (2.2.2.2)

Each year, viruses, spyware, and other types of malicious attacks infect millions of computers. These attacks can damage operating systems, applications, and data. Computers that have been infected may even have problems with hardware performance or component failure.

To protect data and the integrity of the operating system and hardware, use software designed to guard against attacks and to remove malicious programs.

Various types of software protect hardware and data:

- *Windows Action Center*—Checks the status of essential security settings. The Action Center continuously checks to make sure that the software firewall and antivirus programs are running. It also ensures that updates download and install automatically.
- *Windows Defender*—Protects against viruses and spyware.
- *Window Firewall*—Runs continuously to protect against unauthorized communications to and from your computer.

Lab—Diagnostic Software (2.2.2.3)

In this Lab, you gather information about a hard drive diagnostic program. Refer to the Lab in *IT Essentials v6 Lab Manual.*

Organizational Tools (2.2.3)

Keeping accurate records and journals during a busy workday can be challenging. Many organizational tools, such as work-order systems, can help the technician document their work.

Reference Tools (2.2.3.1)

Good customer service includes providing the customer with a detailed description of the problem and the solution. It is important that a technician document all services and repairs and that this documentation is available to all other technicians. The documentation can then be used as reference material for similar problems.

Personal Reference Tools

Personal reference tools include troubleshooting guides, manufacturer manuals, quick reference guides, and repair journals. In addition to an invoice, a technician keeps a journal of upgrades and repairs:

- **Notes**—Make notes as you go through the troubleshooting and repair process. Refer to these notes to avoid repeating steps and to determine what needs to be done next.

- **Journal**—Include descriptions of the problem, possible solutions that have been tried to correct the problem, and the steps taken to repair the problem. Note any configuration changes made to the equipment and any replacement parts used in the repair. Your journal, along with your notes, can be valuable when you encounter similar situations in the future.
- *History of repairs*—Make a detailed list of problems and repairs, including the date, replacement parts, and customer information. The history allows a technician to determine what work has been performed on a specific computer in the past.

Internet Reference Tools

The Internet is an excellent source of information about specific hardware problems and possible solutions:

- Internet search engines
- News groups
- Manufacturer FAQs
- Online computer manuals
- Online forums and chat
- Technical websites

Miscellaneous Tools (2.2.3.2)

With experience, you will discover many additional items to add to the toolkit; for example, masking tape can be used to label parts that have been removed from a computer when a parts organizer is not available.

A working computer is also a valuable resource to take with you on computer repairs in the field. A working computer can be used to research information, download tools or drivers, and communicate with other technicians.

Figure 2-10 shows the types of computer replacement parts to include in a toolkit. Make sure that the parts are in good working order before you use them. Using known good components to replace possible bad ones in computers helps you quickly determine which component is not working properly.

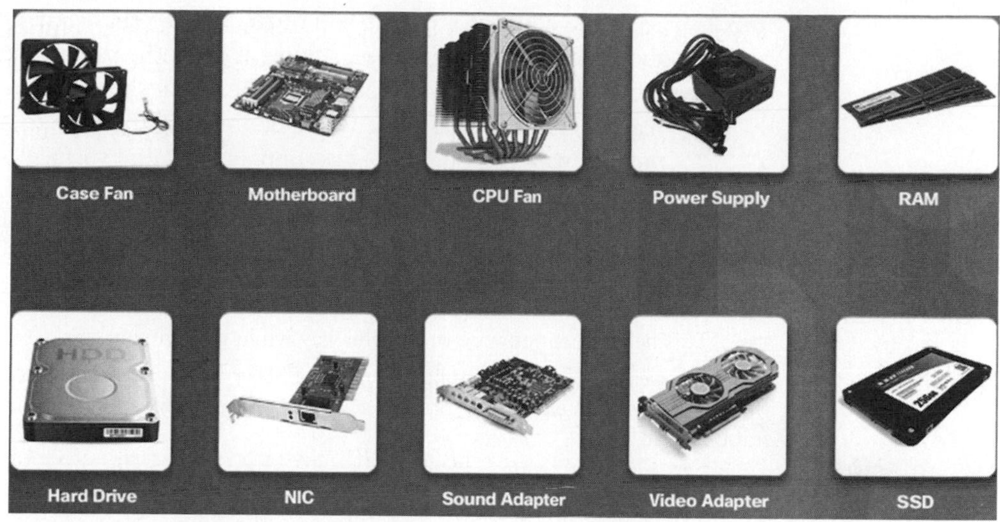

Figure 2-10 Miscellaneous Tools

Demonstrate Proper Tool Use (2.2.4)

This section describes the proper use of common tools used to protect, repair and clean computers and peripherals.

Antistatic Wrist Strap (2.2.4.1)

The *antistatic wrist strap* is a conductor that connects your body to the equipment that you are working on. When static electricity builds up in your body, the connection made by the wrist strap to the equipment, or ground, channels the electricity through the wire that connects the strap, keeping the charge between you and the equipment equal.

An example of static electricity is the small shock that you receive when you walk across a carpeted room and touch a doorknob. Although the small shock is harmless to you, the same electrical charge passing from you to a computer can damage its components. Wearing an antistatic wrist strap can prevent static electricity damage to computer components.

The wrist strap (seen previously in Figure 2-4) has two parts and is easy to wear:

How To

Step 1. Wrap the strap around your wrist and secure it using the snap or Velcro. The metal on the back of the wrist strap must remain in contact with your skin at all times.

Step 2. Snap the connector on the end of the wire to the wrist strap, and connect the other end either to the equipment or to the same grounding point that the antistatic mat is connected to. The metal skeleton of the case is a good place to connect the wire. When connecting the wire to equipment that you are working on, choose an unpainted metal surface. A painted surface does not conduct electricity as well as unpainted metal.

Note

Attach the wire on the same side of the equipment as the arm wearing the antistatic wrist strap. This helps keep the wire out of the way while you are working.

Although wearing a wrist strap helps prevent ESD, you can further reduce the risks by not wearing clothing made of silk, polyester, or wool. These fabrics are more likely to generate a static charge.

Note

Technicians should roll up their sleeves, remove scarves or ties, and tuck in shirts to prevent interference from clothing. Ensure that earrings, necklaces, rings and other loose jewelry are properly secured.

Caution

Never wear an antistatic wrist strap if you are repairing a power supply unit. Do not work on the internal components of a power supply unit unless you have specific electronics training.

Antistatic Mat (2.2.4.2)

An *antistatic mat* is slightly conductive. It works by drawing static electricity away from a component and transferring it safely from equipment to a grounding point:

How To

Step 1. Lay the mat on the workspace next to or under the computer case.

Step 2. Clip the mat to the case to provide a grounded surface on which you can place parts as you remove them from the system.

When you are working at a workbench, ground the workbench and the antistatic floor mat. By standing on the mat and wearing the wrist strap, your body has the same charge as the equipment and reduces the probability of ESD.

Reducing the potential for ESD reduces the likelihood of damage to delicate circuits or components.

Note

Always handle components by the edges.

Hand Tools (2.2.4.3)

A technician needs to be able to properly use each tool in the toolkit. This page covers many of the various hand tools used when repairing computers.

Screws

Match each screw with the proper screwdriver. Place the tip of the screwdriver on the head of the screw. Turn the screwdriver clockwise to tighten the screw and counter clockwise to loosen the screw.

Screws can become stripped if you do not use the correct size and type of screwdriver. A stripped screw may not tighten firmly or it may not be easily removed. Discard stripped screws.

Flat Head Screwdriver

Use a flat head screwdriver when you are working with a slotted screw. Do not use a flat head screwdriver to remove a Phillips head screw. Never use a screwdriver as a pry bar. If you cannot remove a component, check to see if there is a clip or latch that is securing the component in place.

Caution

If excessive force is needed to remove or add a component, something is probably wrong. Take a second look to make sure that you have not missed a screw or a locking clip that is holding the component in place. Refer to the device manual or diagram for additional information.

Phillips Head Screwdriver

Use a Phillips head screwdriver with crosshead screws. Do not use this type of screwdriver to puncture anything. This will damage the head of the screwdriver.

Hex Driver

Use a hex driver to loosen and tighten bolts that have a hexagonal (six-sided) head. Hex bolts should not be over-tightened because the threads of the bolts can be damaged. Do not use a hex driver that is too large for the bolt that you are using.

Caution

Some tools are magnetized. When working around electronic devices, be sure that the tools you are using have not been magnetized. Magnetic fields can be harmful to data stored on magnetic media. Magnetic tools can also induce current, which can damage internal computer components. Test your tool by touching the tool with a screw. If the screw is attracted to the tool, do not use the tool.

Component Retrieving Tools

A parts retriever is used to place and retrieve parts that may be hard to reach with your fingers. Do not scratch or hit any components when using these tools.

Caution

Pencils should not be used inside the computer to change the setting of switches. The pencil lead can act as a conductor and may damage the computer components.

Various specialty tools, such as Torx bits, antistatic bags and gloves, and integrated circuit pullers, can be used to repair and maintain computers. Always avoid magnetized tools, such as screwdrivers with magnetic heads, or tools that use extension magnets to retrieve small metal objects that are out of reach. Additionally, there are specialized testing devices used to diagnose computer and cable problems:

- *Multimeter*—A device that measures AC/DC voltage, electric current, and other electrical characteristics.
- *Power supply tester*—A device that checks whether the computer power supply is working properly. A simple power supply tester might just have indicator lights, whereas more advanced versions show the amount of voltage and amperage.
- *Cable tester*—A device that checks for wiring shorts, faults, or wires connected to the wrong pins.
- *Loopback plug*—A device that connects to a computer, switch, or router port to perform a diagnostic procedure called a loopback test. In a loopback test, a signal is transmitted through a circuit and then returned to the sending device to test the integrity of the data transmission.

Lab—Using a Multimeter and a Power Supply Tester (2.2.4.4)

In this lab, you learn how to use and handle a multimeter and a power supply tester. Refer to the lab in *IT Essentials v6 Lab Manual*.

Cleaning Materials (2.2.4.5)

Keeping computers clean inside and out is a vital part of a maintenance program. Dirt can cause problems with the physical operation of fans, buttons, and other mechanical components. On electrical components, an excessive buildup of dust acts like an insulator and traps the heat. This insulation impairs the ability of heat sinks and cooling fans to keep components cool, causing chips and circuits to overheat and fail.

Note

When using compressed air to clean inside the computer, blow the air around the components with a minimum distance of 4 inches (10 cm) from the nozzle. Clean the power supply and the fan blowing from inside the computer toward the fan at the back of the case so as not to blow dust back into the system.

Caution

Before cleaning any device, turn it off and unplug the device from the power source.

Computer Cases and Monitors

Clean computer cases and the outside of monitors with a mild cleaning solution on a damp, lint-free cloth. Mix one drop of dishwashing liquid with 4 oz. (118 ml) of water to create the cleaning solution. If water drips inside the case, allow enough time for the liquid to dry before powering on the computer.

When computers are in areas where there is excessive dirt and dust, use an enclosure to prevent much of the dirt from harming the computer. The enclosure should have filters to prevent dirt from entering the enclosure. These filters need to be cleaned or replaced on a regular basis.

LCD Screens

Do not use ammoniated glass cleaners or any other solution on an LCD screen, unless the cleaner is specifically designed for the purpose. Harsh chemicals damage the coating on the screen. Often, there is no glass protecting these screens, so be gentle when cleaning them and do not press firmly on the screen.

Clean dusty components with a can of compressed air. Compressed air does not cause electrostatic buildup on components. Make sure that you are in a well ventilated area before blowing the dust out of the computer. A best practice is to wear an air filter mask to make sure that you do not breathe in the dust particles.

Blow out the dust using short bursts from the can. Never tip the can or use the can upside down because doing so will cause the can to freeze. Do not allow the fan blades to spin from the force of the compressed air. Hold the fan in place. Fan motors can be ruined from spinning when the motor is not turned on.

Component Contacts

Use a lint-free cloth that is slightly moistened with isopropyl alcohol to clean the contacts on components. Do not use rubbing alcohol. Rubbing alcohol contains impurities that can damage contacts. Before reinstallation, use compressed air to blow lint off the contacts.

Keyboards

Clean a desktop keyboard with compressed air and then use a handheld vacuum cleaner with a brush attachment to remove the loose dust.

Caution

Never use a standard vacuum cleaner inside a computer case. The plastic parts of the vacuum cleaner can build up static electricity and discharge to the components. Use only vacuums that are approved for electronic components.

Mice

Use glass cleaner and a soft cloth to clean the outside of the mouse. Do not spray glass cleaner directly on the mouse. If cleaning a ball mouse, you can remove the ball and clean it with glass cleaner and a soft cloth. Wipe the rollers clean inside the mouse with the same cloth. Do not spray any liquids inside the mouse.

Table 2-1 shows the computer items that you should clean and the cleaning materials to use.

Table 2-1 Memory Modules Computer Cleaning Materials

Computer case and outside of monitor	Mild cleaning solution and lint-free cloth
LCD screen	LCD cleaning solution or distilled water and lint-free cloth
CRT screen	Distilled water and lint-free cloth
Heat sink	Compressed Air
RAM	Isopropyl alcohol and lint-free swab
Keyboard	Handheld vacuum cleaner with a brush attachment
Mouse	Mild cleaning solution and lint-free cloth

Video—Computer Disassembly (2.2.4.6)

Video

In this video demonstration, a desktop computer will be disassembled using proper lab procedures and tool use. The CPU and cooling unit are left on the motherboard and the motherboard is left in the case, but all other components are removed from the case. Its shows the steps to dissipate the static electricity by touching bare metal case and wearing an antistatic wrist strip while working in the system. It explains that you need to unplug the computer before disassembly so there is no power to it. The video demonstrates removing the process of removing the power and data cable connections, the power supply, adapter cards, and RAM.

Go to the online course to view this video.

Lab—Computer Disassembly (2.2.4.7)

In this lab, you disassemble a computer using safe lab procedures and the proper tools. Refer to the lab in *IT Essentials v6 Lab Manual*.

Summary (2.3)

This chapter emphasizes the behavior and processes that a worker should use to help in keeping the workplace a safe and productive environment.

Summary (2.3.1)

You have familiarized yourself in the lab with many of the tools used to build, service, and clean computer and electronic components. You have also learned the importance of organizational tools and how these tools help you work more efficiently. Some of the important concepts to remember from this chapter:

- Work in a safe manner to protect users and equipment.
- Follow all safety guidelines to prevent injuries to yourself and others.
- Know how to protect equipment from ESD damage.
- Know about and be able to prevent power issues that can cause equipment damage or data loss.
- Know which products and supplies require special disposal procedures.
- Familiarize yourself with the SDS for safety issues and disposal restrictions to help protect the environment.
- Be able to use the correct tools for the task.
- Know how to clean components safely.
- Use organizational tools during computer repairs.

Summary of Exercises

This is a summary of the labs and activities associated with this chapter.

Lab

The following labs cover material from this chapter. Refer to the labs in the ITE 6.0 student lab manual.

Lab—Diagnostic Software (2.2.2.3)

Lab—Using a Multimeter and a Power Supply Tester (2.2.4.4)

Check Your Understanding

You can find the answers to these questions in the appendix, "Answers to 'Check Your Understanding' Questions."

1. What is an accepted method for cleaning computer components?

   A. Using ammonia to clean the LCD screen

   B. Using glass cleaner on a soft cloth to clean the outside of the mouse

   C. Using a lint-free cloth to remove dust inside the computer case

   D. Using rubbing alcohol to clean component contacts

2. A technician accidentally spills a cleaning solution on the floor of the workshop. Where would the technician find instructions on how to properly clean up and dispose of the product?

   A. The safety data sheet

   B. The insurance policy of the company

   C. The local hazardous materials team

   D. The regulations provided by the local occupational health and safety administration

3. Which tool can be used to take resistance and voltage measurements?

   A. Loopback plug

   B. Cable tester

   C. Power supply tester

   D. Multimeter

4. Which tool would be used to create a partition on a hard drive?

   A. Format

   B. SFC

   C. Disk Management

   D. Defrag

   E. Chkdsk

5. Which statement describes the term ESD?

   A. It is a type of interference caused by electrical motors.

   B. It is a device that supplies a constant level of electrical power to a computer.

   C. It is a measurement of the current flowing though electrical devices.

   D. It is the sudden discharge of static electricity that can adversely affect a component.

6. Which tool can protect computer components from the effects of ESD?

   A. SPS
   B. Surge suppressor
   C. Antistatic wrist strap
   D. UPS

7. Which type of fastener is loosened and tightened with a hex driver?

   A. Six-sided bolt
   B. Torx bolt
   C. Slotted screw
   D. Cross head screw

8. What safety hazard might occur if a partially filled aerosol can is exposed to excessive heat?

   A. Lead poisoning
   B. Explosion
   C. Lethal voltage potential
   D. Breathing hazard

9. Which tool would be used to scan Windows critical system files and replace any corrupted files?

   A. Chkdsk
   B. Fdisk
   C. SFC
   D. Defrag

10. What tool would be used to determine which network port attaches to a specific office jack?

    A. Loopback adapter
    B. Punch down tool
    C. Tone probe
    D. Crimper

11. Which device can protect computer equipment from brownouts by providing a consistent quality of electrical power?

    A. SPS
    B. Surge suppressor
    C. UPS
    D. AC adapter

12. A technician should keep a personal ____________ where all steps taken to repair a computer problem are noted including any configuration changes made.

    A. Journal
    B. Toolkit
    C. Floppy disk
    D. Software list

13. What would make it easier for a technician to troubleshoot a problem that has been previously solved by another technician?

    A. Online computer manual
    B. Centralized closed trouble tickets
    C. Personal troubleshooting journal
    D. Online forum of manufacturer

14. Which two devices commonly affect wireless networks? (Choose two.)

    A. Microwaves
    B. External hard drives
    C. Cordless phones
    D. Incandescent light bulbs
    E. Blu-ray players
    F. Home theaters

15. What are two safety hazards when dealing with laser printers? (Choose two.)

    A. High voltage
    B. Proprietary power bricks
    C. Unwieldy card cages
    D. Heavy metals
    E. Hot components

16. What three guidelines should be followed to provide safe conditions when computer equipment is being repaired? (Choose three.)

    A. Do not open the power supply.
    B. Turn off the power to the printer and computer before beginning.
    C. If a screwdriver is unavailable, use a knife with a sharp point to loosen screws.
    D. Do not wear loose jewelry unless it is gold, because gold does not conduct electricity.

E. Ensure that your ID badge is around your neck and visible.

F. Have all of your extra parts, screws, meters, and tools beside the chassis ready for use.

G. Bend your knees when lifting heavy objects.

17. What is a proper directive for using a can of compressed air to clean a PC?

A. Spray the CPU cooling fan with the compressed air to verify that the fan blade is spinning freely.

B. Use a long, steady stream of air from the can.

C. Do not use compressed air to clean a CPU fan.

D. Do not spray the compressed air with the can upside down.

CHAPTER 3

Computer Assembly

Objectives

Upon completion of this chapter, you will be able to answer the following questions:

- How do I open the computer case?
- What is the process to install a power supply?
- How do I attach the components to the motherboard?
- How do I install a motherboard into a computer case?
- How do I handle and install a CPU with a fan and heat sink assembly?
- How do I install internal drives into a computer case?
- How do I install external devices?
- What is the process to connect external cables?
- How do I install adapter cards?
- What is the process to connect all internal cables?
- How do I reassemble the computer case?
- What should I expect the first time I boot the computer?
- What is the BIOS setup program?
- How do I use beep codes?

Key Terms

This chapter uses the following key terms. You can find the definitions in the Glossary.

Computer case *Page 105*

complementary metal oxide semiconductor (CMOS) *Page 134*

Unified Extensible Firmware Interface (UEFI) *Page 137*

basic input/output system (BIOS) *Page 132*

power-on self-test (POST) *Page 132*

LoJack *Page 140*

Secure Boot *Page 140*

Trusted Platform Module (TPM) *Page 140*

Boot Order *Page 138*

Clock Speed *Page 138*

beep codes *Page 132*

Thermal compound *Page 110*

standoffs *Page 114*

overclocking *Page 138*

SATA data cable *Page 125*

Introduction (3.0)

Assembling computers is a large part of a technician's job. As a technician, you must work in a logical, methodical manner when working with computer components. At times, you might have to determine whether a component for a customer's computer needs to be upgraded or replaced. It is important that you develop skills in installation procedures, troubleshooting techniques, and diagnostic methods.

Welcome (3.0.1)

In this section, you explore in detail the steps used to assemble a computer and to boot the system for the first time. You learn about cases and other component form factors, the main internal computer components like the CPU and RAM, as well as various peripheral components and how they work together to build a functioning PC.

Computer Assembly (3.0.1.1)

This chapter discusses building a computer and the importance of component compatibility. It also covers the need for adequate system resources to efficiently run the customer's hardware and software.

Assemble the Computer (3.1)

Choosing the right computer components when assembling a computer is important, but so is properly preparing the work area for the build.

Open the Case and Connect the Power Supply (3.1.1)

Whether you are building a computer with all new components or doing an upgrade, having the tools needed ready and understanding how to work with the case is critical. This section discusses gaining access to the inside of the computer case and installing a power supply.

Open the Case (3.1.1.1)

When building or repairing a computer, it is important that you prepare the workspace before opening the computer case. You want adequate lighting, good ventilation, and a comfortable room temperature. The workbench or table should be accessible from all sides. Avoid cluttering the surface of the work area with tools and computer components. Place an antistatic mat on the table to help prevent ESD damage to electronics. It is helpful to use small containers to hold screws and other parts as you remove them.

Computer cases are produced in a variety of form factors. Recall that form factors refer to the size and shape of the case. There are also different methods for opening cases. To learn how to open a particular computer case, consult the user manual or manufacturer's website.

Most computer cases are opened in one of the following ways:

- The computer case cover is removed as one piece.
- The top and side panels of the case are removed.
- The top of the case is removed before the side panels can be removed.
- A latch is pulled to release the side panel, which can swing open.

Figure 3-1 displays a new, empty ATX computer case. The case, or chassis, is an empty shell with a preinstalled fan(s) and cables to connect the fan(s) and front panel buttons, LED indicators, and USB, audio, or other connections.

Figure 3-1 New Empty Computer Case

Install the Power Supply (3.1.1.2)

A technician might be required to replace or install a power supply, such as the one shown in Figure 3-2. Most power supplies can only fit one way in the computer case. Always follow the power supply installation directions in the case and power supply manuals.

How To

These are the basic steps to install a power supply:

Step 1. Insert the power supply into the case.

Step 2. Align the holes in the power supply with the holes in the case.

Step 3. Secure the power supply to the case using the proper screws.

Installation Tip

Do not tighten all the screws until they have all been slightly hand-tightened. This makes it easier to tighten the last two screws.

Figure 3-2 Power Supply

Power supplies have fans that can vibrate and loosen screws that are not properly tightened. When installing a power supply, make sure that all the screws are in place and tightened correctly.

Place all unused cables into the case where they will not interfere with any other components or fans. Use cable ties, rubber bands, or hook-and-loop straps to bundle power cables and keep them out of the way. To help eliminate cable clutter inside the case, some power supplies are modular. This means that only the required cables are attached to the power supply. When components are installed in the future, additional power cables are installed as they are needed.

Installation Tip

Use a cable tie to secure all of the cables out of the way until it is time to connect them.

Lab—Install the Power Supply (3.1.1.3)

In this lab, you install a power supply in a computer case. Refer to the lab in *IT Essentials v6 Lab Manual*.

Install the Motherboard (3.1.2)

This section examines the installation of many of the components that are directly installed on a motherboard and the installation of the motherboard itself into a computer case. You also learn throughout this chapter that all components in your computer system are in some way attached to your motherboard.

Install the CPU and the Heat Sink and Fan Assembly (3.1.2.1)

The CPU and the heat sink and fan assembly should be installed on the motherboard before the motherboard is placed in the computer case. This allows for extra room to see and to maneuver components during installation.

Before installing a CPU on a motherboard, verify that it is compatible with the CPU socket, as shown in Figure 3-3.

Figure 3-3 Verify Socket Compatibility

Motherboards are designed to work with specific types of CPUs, and not all CPUs use the same motherboard socket. Table 3-1 describes the common socket types and installation notes.

Table 3-1 CPU Socket Architectures

CPU Architectures	Installation Notes
Single-edge connector (SEC)	Align the notches on the CPU to the keys in the SEC socket.
Low-insertion force (LIF) Zero-insertion force (ZIF) Pin grid array (PGA)	Align the CPU so that the connection 1 indicator is lined up with pin 1 on the CPU socket.
Land grid array (LGA)	Align the CPU so that the two notches on the CPU fit into the two socket extensions.

Note

SEC and LIF are legacy socket connections.

The CPU and motherboard are highly sensitive to electrostatic discharge (ESD). ESD can easily damage these components if they are mishandled. Therefore, always place components on an antistatic mat and wear a wrist strap (or antistatic gloves) when installing and removing CPUs.

Caution

When handling a CPU, do not touch the CPU contacts at any time. Place a CPU on the antistatic mat until you are ready to use it. Store CPUs in antistatic packaging.

To install a CPU and heat sink and fan assembly on a motherboard, follow these steps:

Step 1. Align the CPU pin 1 with the socket pin 1, as shown in Figure 3-4. Look for a dot on the CPU and a triangle on the socket to indicate pin 1. Check the CPU and motherboard documentation to ensure alignment. Place the CPU gently into the socket. Never force the CPU into its socket, as excessive force can easily damage the CPU and the socket. Stop if you encounter any resistance and make sure that you have aligned the CPU properly.

Figure 3-4 CPU Installation

Step 2. The CPU is secured to the socket on the motherboard with a latch plate. Close the CPU latch plate, as shown in Figure 3-5.

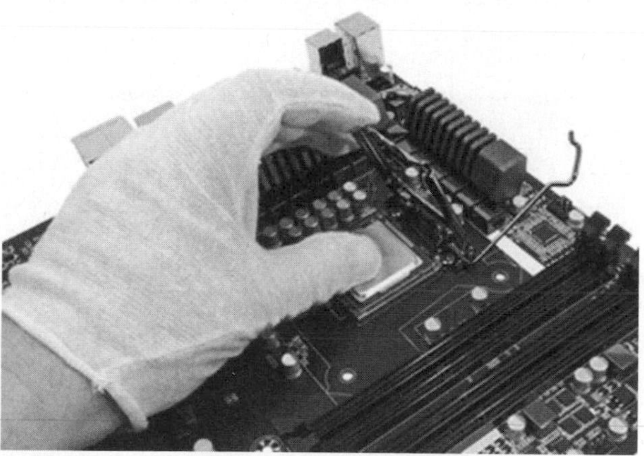

Figure 3-5 Close the Latch Plate

Step 3. Secure the latch plate in place by closing the load lever, as shown in Figure 3-6.

Figure 3-6 Close the Load Lever

Step 4. Secure the load lever under the load lever retention tab, as shown in Figure 3-7.

Figure 3-7 Secure the Load Lever

Step 5. Apply thermal compound to the CPU to the top of the CPU. *Thermal compound* helps to conduct heat away from the CPU. In most cases, only a very small amount of thermal compound is required. The compound spreads out evenly under the weight and pressure of the heat sink and fan assembly. Follow the application instructions provided by the manufacturer of the thermal compound.

Step 6. Align the heat sink and fan assembly retainers with the holes on the motherboard and place the assembly onto the CPU socket, as shown in Figure 3-8. Avoid pinching the CPU fan wires.

Figure 3-8 Install Heat Sink and Fan Assembly

Step 7. Tighten the assembly retainers to secure the assembly in place. Follow the instructions from the heat sink and fan assembly manufacturer carefully.

If you are installing a used CPU, clean the top of the CPU and the base of the heat sink with isopropyl alcohol and a lint-free cloth. This removes the old thermal compound and contaminants. Any contaminants left between the CPU and the heat sink decreases the ability of the thermal compound to absorb heat from the CPU. Follow the manufacturer recommendations about applying the thermal compound.

Installation Tip

A paper coffee filter works well as a lint-free cloth.

Note

Always follow the instructions provided with the motherboard during CPU installation. To view a sample manual, go to the online course to access this URL.

Packet Tracer
☐ Activity

Activity—Installing the CPU (3.1.2.2)

Please refer to the Activity in the Cisco Networking Academy IT Essentials 6.0 online course.

Install RAM (3.1.2.3)

RAM provides fast, temporary data storage for the CPU while the computer is operating. RAM is volatile memory, which means that its contents are lost every time the computer is powered off.

RAM may be installed on the motherboard before the motherboard is installed in the computer case. Before installation, consult the motherboard documentation or the website of the motherboard manufacturer to ensure that the RAM is compatible with the motherboard.

Like the CPU, RAM is also highly sensitive to ESD. Therefore, always work on an antistatic mat and wear a wrist strap or antistatic gloves when installing and removing RAM.

How To

To install RAM on the motherboard, follow these steps:

Step 1. Open the locking tabs on the DIMM slot, as shown in Figure 3-9.

Figure 3-9 Open Locking Tabs

Step 2. As shown in Figure 3-10, align the notches on the RAM module to the keys in the slot and firmly press straight down.

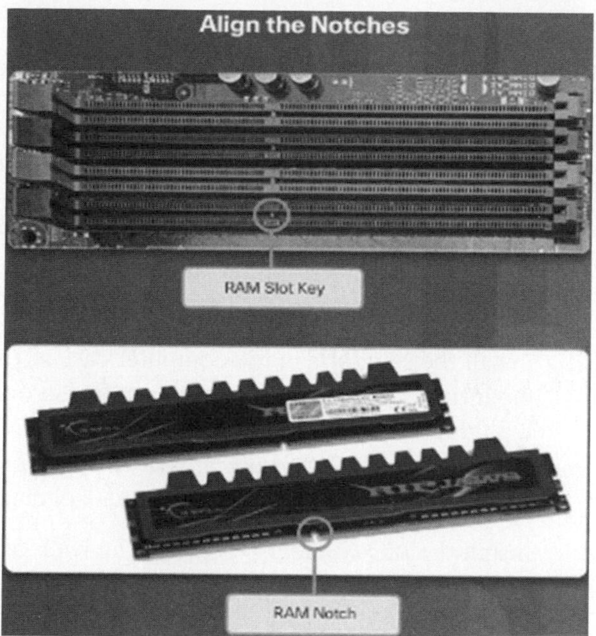

Figure 3-10 Align the Notches

Step 3. Ensure that the locking tabs click into place.

Caution

RAM can be damaged and also may cause serious damage to the motherboard if it is incorrectly aligned when the computer is powered on.

Step 4. Make sure each memory module is completely inserted into the socket and that the locking tabs have secured the RAM module.

Step 5. Visually check for exposed contacts.

Installation Tip

When a RAM module is pressed into the slot correctly, you will hear and feel a click as the locking tab moves into place.

Install Motherboard (3.1.2.4)

The motherboard is now ready to be installed in the computer case.

How To

To install the motherboard, follow these steps:

Step 1. Choose the proper motherboard *standoffs*, which are special mounting screws that connect the motherboard to the case while insulating it from contact, for the case. A motherboard printed circuit board (PCB) cannot touch any metal portion of the computer case. Therefore, it must be mounted to the case using special plastic or metal standoffs.

Step 2. Install the standoffs in the computer case at the same locations of the mounting holes in the motherboard. Install only the standoffs that align with the holes in the motherboard for an ATX motherboard. Installing additional standoffs might prevent the motherboard from being seated properly in the computer case or cause damage to the motherboard.

Step 3. Install the *I/O connector plate* in the back of the computer case, as shown in Figure 3-11. The I/O plate has cutouts that match the connector layout of the motherboard.

Figure 3-11 I/O Plate

Step 4. Align the I/O connectors on the back of the motherboard with the openings in the I/O plate.

Step 5. Align the screw holes of the motherboard with the standoffs.

Step 6. Insert all the motherboard screws and hand-tighten all of them before tightening them with a screwdriver. Do not overtighten the screws.

Installation Tips

Push the motherboard against the I/O connector plate to align the mounting holes with the standoffs and start the first screw. Also, it is helpful to use a part retriever to place screws into the mounting holes and hand-tighten them.

Activity—Installing the Motherboard (3.1.2.5)

Please refer to the Activity in the Cisco Networking Academy IT Essentials 6.0 online course.

Lab—Install the Motherboard (3.1.2.6)

In this lab, you install a CPU, a heat sink/fan assembly, and RAM module(s) on the motherboard. You then install the motherboard in the computer case. Refer to the lab in *IT Essentials v6 Lab Manual*.

Install Drives (3.1.3)

In this section, you learn the steps to install a variety of drives in both internal bays and with external connections.

Install the Hard Drive (3.1.3.1)

A computer case holds drives in drive bays. Table 3-2 describes the three most common types of drive bays.

Table 3-2 Types of Drive Bays

Drive Bay Width	Description
5.25 in. (13.34 cm)	■ Commonly used for optical drives ■ Most full-size tower cases have two or more bays.
3.5 in. (8.9 cm)	■ Commonly used for 3.5 in. HDDs. ■ Provide additional USB ports or smart card readers. ■ Most full-size tower cases have two or more internal bays.
2.5 in. (6.35 cm)	■ Intended for smaller 2.5 in. HDDS and SSDs. ■ Smallest bay width. ■ Becoming increasing popular in newer cases.

To install a hard disk drive (HDD), find an empty hard drive bay in the case that will accommodate the width of the drive. Smaller drives can often be installed in wider drive bays using special trays or adapters.

How To

To install a 3.5 in. (8.9 cm) HDD into a 3.5 in. drive bay, follow these steps:

Step 1. Position the HDD so that it aligns with the drive bay opening.

Step 2. Insert the HDD into the drive bay so that the screw holes in the drive line up with the screw holes in the case.

Step 3. Secure the HDD to the case using the proper screws.

When installing multiple drives in a case, it is recommended to maintain some space between the drives to help airflow and enhance cooling. Also, mount the drive with the metal side face up. This metal face helps to dissipate heat from the hard drive.

Installation Tip

Slightly hand-tighten all the screws before tightening any of them with a screwdriver. This makes it easier to tighten the last two screws.

Install the Optical Drive (3.1.3.2)

Optical drives are installed in 5.25 in. (13.34 cm) drive bays that are accessed from the front of the case. The bays allow access to the media without opening the case.

How To

To install an optical drive, follow these steps:

Step 1. Position the optical drive so that it aligns with the 5.25 in. (13.34 cm) drive bay opening at the front of the case.

Step 2. Insert the optical drive into the drive bay so that the optical drive screw holes align with the screw holes in the case.

Step 3. Secure the optical drive to the case using the proper screws.

Installation Tip

Slightly hand-tighten all the screws before tightening any of them with a screw driver. This makes it easier to tighten the last two screws.

Lab—Install the Drives (3.1.3.3)

In this lab, you install the hard disk and optical drives. Refer to the lab in *IT Essentials v6 Lab Manual*.

Install the Adapter Cards (3.1.4)

In this section, you go through the steps of installing different types of adapter cards into their compatible expansion slots on the motherboard.

Types of Adapter Cards (3.1.4.1)

Adapter cards add functionality to a computer. There are many different types of adapter cards, including video, Ethernet and wireless network, sound, TV tuner, video capture, external port such as USB, FireWire, Thunderbolt, and more.

Adapter cards are inserted into the following expansion slots on a motherboard:

- **PCI**—Peripheral Component Interconnect (PCI) is commonly available to support older expansion cards. Figure 3-12 shows an example of a PCI slot.

Figure 3-12 PCI Expansion Slot

- **PCIe**—PCI Express has four types of slots: x1, x4, x8, and x16, as shown in Figure 3-13. Notice how these PCIe slots vary in length from shortest (x1) to longest (x16), respectively.

Figure 3-13 PCIe x1 and x16 Expansion Slot

Adapter cards must be compatible with the expansion slots on the motherboard.

Install a Wireless NIC (3.1.4.2)

A wireless NIC enables a computer to connect to a wireless (WiFi) network. Wireless NICs use PCI or PCIe expansion slots on the motherboard. Many external wireless NICs are connected using a USB connector.

How To

To install a wireless NIC, follow these steps:

Step 1. Find an empty PCI slot on the case and remove the small metal cover, as shown in Figure 3-14.

Figure 3-14 Remove Metal Cover

Step 2. Align the card to the appropriate expansion slot on the motherboard.

Step 3. Press down gently on the card until the card is fully seated, as shown in Figure 3-15.

Figure 3-15 Insert Wireless NIC into the PCI Slot

Step 4. Figure 3-16 shows the card's mounting bracket being secured to the case with the appropriate screw.

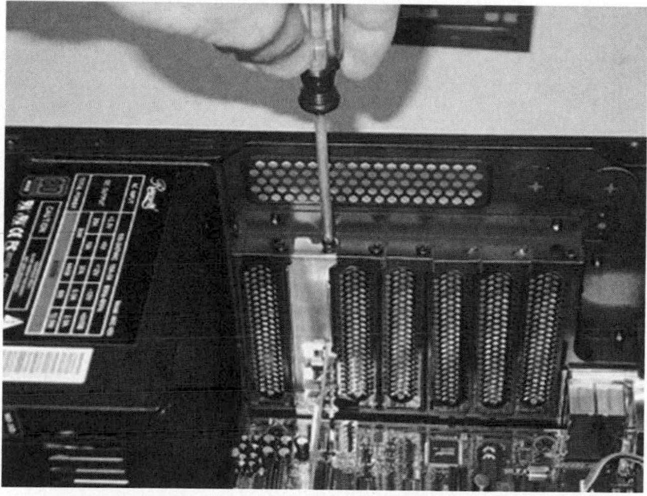

Figure 3-16 Secure the Wireless NIC

Installation Tip

Some cases have small slots at the bottom of the hole where the cover was removed. Slide the bottom of the mounting bracket into this slot before seating the card.

Install a Video Adapter Card (3.1.4.3)

Video adapter cards use PCI, AGP, or PCIe expansion slots on the motherboard.

How To

To install a video adapter card, follow these steps:

Step 1. Find an empty PCIe x16 slot on the case and remove the small metal cover.

Step 2. Align the video adapter card to the appropriate expansion slot on the motherboard.

Step 3. Press down gently on the video adapter card until the card is fully seated.

Step 4. Secure the video adapter card mounting bracket to the case with the appropriate screw.

Many video adapter cards require separate power from the power supply using a 6-pin or 8-pin power connector. Some cards may need two of these connectors. If possible, provide some space between the video adapter and other expansion cards. Video adapters create excessive heat, which is often moved away from the card with a fan.

Installation Tip

Research the length of the video card (and other adapter cards) before purchase. Longer cards may not be compatible with certain motherboards. Chips and other electronics may stand in the way of the adapter card when trying to seat them in the expansion slot. Some cases might also limit the size of adapter cards that can be installed. Some adapter cards may come with mounting brackets of different heights to accommodate these cases.

Lab—Install Adapter Cards (3.1.4.4)

In this lab, you install a NIC, a wireless NIC, and a video adapter card. Refer to the lab in *IT Essentials v6 Lab Manual*.

Install Cables (3.1.5)

Computers use cables for different purposes. There are two main types of computer cables, data and power. Data cables provide a means for communication between two devices. SATA data cable connects a storage device like a hard drive to the motherboard to carry data to and from it and other computer components. A power cable is the cable that provides power to a device. An AC power cable is an example of a power cable used for a computer. The power supply uses this AC power and converts it into DC power to give the motherboard the power it needs to operate. In this section, you learn about the many cables and connections that you need to attach to your motherboard to provide data and power to the components.

Connect Power to the Motherboard (3.1.5.1)

Motherboards require power to operate. They also transfer some of this power to various components connected to it. The number and type of power supply connectors required depends on the combination of motherboard and processor. Table 3-3 highlights the various types of connectors that can be found on a motherboard. Notice how the motherboard typically requires two power connectors.

Table 3-3 Type of Motherboard Connectors

ATX Standard	Motherboard Connection Descriptions
ATX	■ 20-pin main motherboard connector ■ 6-pin auxiliary connector
ATX12V v2.x	■ 24-pin main motherboard connector ■ 4-pin auxiliary connector
AMD GES	■ 24-pin main motherboard connector ■ 8-pin auxiliary connector
EPS12V	■ 24-pin main motherboard connector ■ 8-pin auxiliary connector often provided as 2 combined 4-pin connectors

Caution

Be careful when connecting the power supply cables to other components. Cables, connectors, and components are designed to fit together snugly. If it is difficult to plug in a cable or other part, something is wrong. Never force a connector or component. Forcing it can damage the plug and the connector. If you have a difficult time inserting a connector, check to make sure the connector is oriented properly and there are no bent pins.

How To

The steps to install motherboard power connectors include:

Step 1. Align the 24-pin (or 20-pin) ATX power connector to the socket on the motherboard. Figure 3-17 shows the ATX power connector being aligned and readied to be clicked into place.

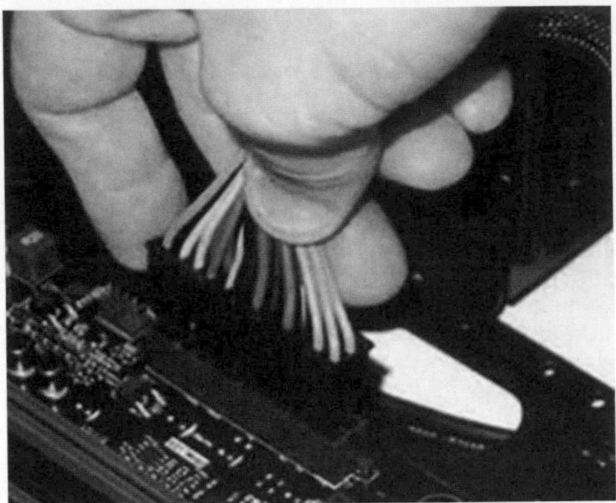

Figure 3-17 Connecting the Main Motherboard Connector

Step 2. Gently press down on the connector until the clip clicks into place.

Step 3. Align the 4-pin (or 8-pin) auxiliary power connector to the socket on the motherboard. Figure 3-18 shows the auxiliary power connector being aligned and readied to be clicked into place.

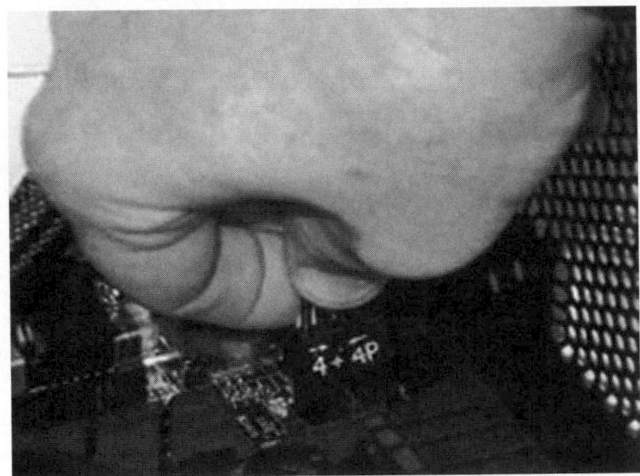

Figure 3-18 Connecting the Auxiliary Power Connector

Step 4. Gently press down on the connector until the clip clicks into place.

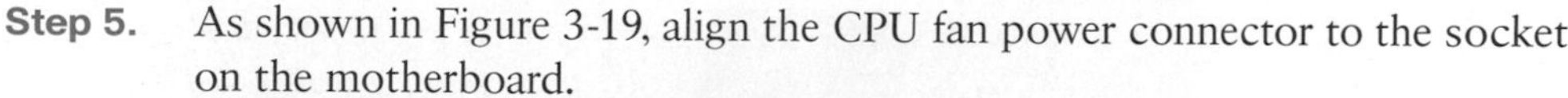

Step 5. As shown in Figure 3-19, align the CPU fan power connector to the socket on the motherboard.

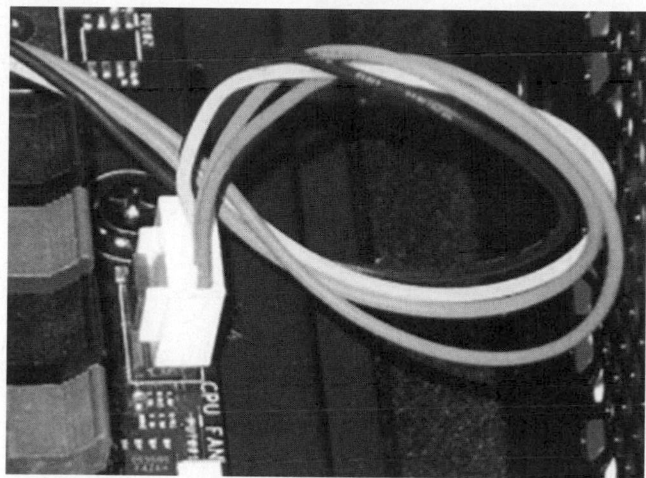

Figure 3-19 Connecting the 4-pin CPU Fan

Step 6. Gently press down on the connector until it is fully seated.

Installation Tip

Power connectors are keyed to fit into power sockets in one orientation. Some parts of the connector are square, whereas others are slightly rounded. If a connector does not look like it will fit the socket due to these shapes, remember that the slightly rounded parts will fit into square holes, but square parts will not fit into the slightly rounded holes. This is by design.

Connect Power to the Internal Drive and Case Fans (3.1.5.2)

Traditionally, HDDs and optical drives were powered by a 4-pin Molex power connector. These drives now typically use a 15-pin SATA connector, as shown in Figure 3 20.

Figure 3-20 SATA Power Connector

For flexibility, some drives have both a 15-pin SATA connector and a 4-pin Molex connector. On these drives, use only one of the power connectors, never both. Many older power supplies may not have SATA connectors. A Molex-to-SATA adapter, as shown in Figure 3-21, can be used to connect drives.

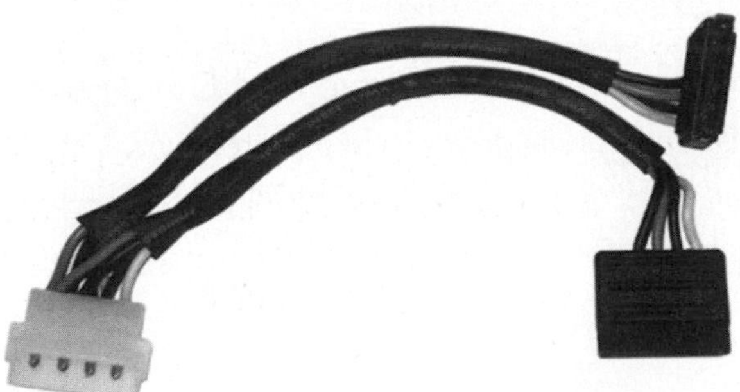

Figure 3-21 Molex-to-SATA Power Adapter

How To

The steps to connect the SATA cable to a drive are:

Step 1. Align the 15-pin SATA power connector to the port on the drive.

Step 2. Gently push in the connector until the connector is fully seated.

Installation Tip

Be very careful when connecting SATA cables. If they are pressed at an angle, they can snap the connector off of the drive.

Other peripheral devices, such as the case fans, also need to be powered. Most motherboards provide 3-pin or 4-pin connectors to connect fans.

How To

The basic steps to power case fans include:

Step 1. Align the 3-pin or 4-pin fan power connector to the port on the motherboard.

Step 2. Gently press down on the connector until the connector is fully seated.

Plug any remaining cables from the case into the appropriate connectors according to the motherboard and case manual.

Installation Tip

3-pin fan power connectors can be attached to 4-pin ports. The connector and the socket are keyed so that they will fit together even though one pin is left unconnected.

Activity—Identify the Power Connectors (3.1.5.3)

Please refer to the Activity in the Cisco Networking Academy IT Essentials 6.0 online course.

Connect the Internal Data Cables (3.1.5.4)

Internal drives and optical drives typically connect to the motherboard using SATA data cables.

The *SATA data cable* has a 7-pin connector, as shown in Figure 3-22. SATA cables are keyed to connect only one way. Many SATA cables have locking connectors that prevent the cables from coming unplugged. To remove a locked cable, depress the raised metal tab on the plug and then pull the connector out.

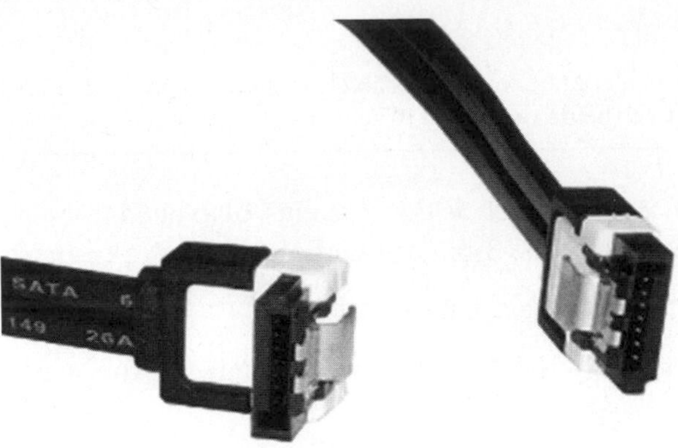

Figure 3-22 7-pin SATA Data Cable

The steps to connect a drive to the motherboard using a SATA data cable include:

Step 1. Plug one end of the SATA cable into the motherboard socket. Many motherboards have more than one SATA connector.

Step 2. Plug the other end of the SATA cable into the smaller SATA port on the drive.

Installation Tip

Use the same care when installing SATA data cables as SATA power cables. Also, avoid sharp bends or folds in the cable. These may limit transmission rates.

Lab—Install Internal Cables (3.1.5.5)

In this lab, install the internal power and data cables in the computer. Refer to the lab in *IT Essentials v6 Lab Manual.*

Install the Front Panel Cables (3.1.5.6)

A computer case has buttons to control power to the motherboard and lights to indicate activities. Connect these buttons and lights to the motherboard with the cables from the front of the case. Figure 3-23 shows some of the front panel cables commonly found in a computer case. Figure 3-24 shows a common system panel connector on a motherboard where the cables are connected. Writing on the motherboard near the system panel connector shows where each cable is connected.

Figure 3-23 Front Panel Connectors

Figure 3-24 System Panel Connector

System panel connectors are not keyed. The following guidelines for connecting cables to the system panel connectors are generic, because no standards for labeling the case cables or the system panel connectors are defined. However, each front panel cable usually has a small arrow indicating pin 1.

System panel connectors include:

- **Power button**—The power button turns the computer on or off. If the power button fails to turn off the computer, hold down the power button for five seconds.

- **Reset button**—The reset button (if available) restarts the computer without turning it off.
- **Power LED**—The power LED remains lit when the computer is on, and it often blinks when the computer is in sleep mode. Each pair of LED pins on the motherboard system panel connector has pin 1 marked with a plus sign (+).
- **Drive activity LEDs**—The drive activity LED remains lit or blinks when the system is reading or writing to hard drives.
- **System speaker**—The motherboard uses a case speaker (if available) to indicate the computer's status. For instance, one beep indicates that the computer started without problems. If there is a hardware problem, a series of diagnostic beeps is issued to indicate the type of problem. It is important to note that the system speaker is not the same as the speakers the computer uses to play music and other audio. The system speaker cable typically uses four pins on the system panel connector.
- **Audio**—Some cases have audio ports and jacks on the outside to connect microphones, external audio equipment such as signal processors, mixing boards, and instruments. Special audio panels can also be purchased and connected directly to the motherboard. These panels can install into one or more external drive bays, or be standalone panels.
- **USB**—USB ports are located on the outside of many computer cases. USB motherboard connectors often consist of 9 or 10 pins arranged in two rows. This arrangement allows for two USB connections, so USB connectors are often in pairs. Sometimes the two connectors are together in one piece and can be connected to the entire USB motherboard connector. USB connectors can also have four or five pins or individual groups of four or five pins. Most USB devices only require the connection of four pins. The fifth pin is used to ground the shielding of some USB cables.

Note

The markings on your front panel cables and system panel connectors may be different on different manufactures motherboards. Always consult the motherboard manual for diagrams and additional information about connecting front panel cables.

Caution

Make sure that the motherboard connector is marked USB. FireWire connectors are very similar. Connecting a USB cable to a FireWire connector will cause damage.

Table 3-4 provides connecting notes on various front panel indicators.

Table 3-4 Front Panel Cable Connection Specifics

Front Panel	Connection Specifics
Power button	■ Align pin 1 of the two-pin front panel power button cable with the power button pins on the motherboard.
Rest button	■ Align pin 1 of the two-pin front panel reset button cable with the reset button pins on the motherboard.
Power LED	■ Align pin 1 of the front panel power LED cable with the power LED pins on the motherboard.
Drive activity LED	■ Align pin 1 of the front panel drive activity cable with the drive activity pins on the motherboard.
System speaker	■ Align pin 1 of the front panel system speaker cable with the system speaker pins on the motherboard.
Audio cables	■ Due to the specialized function and variety of the hardware, consult the motherboard, case, and audio panel.
USB	■ Align pin 1 of the USB cable with the USB pins on the motherboard.

New cases and motherboards have USB 3.0 or maybe even USB 3.1 capabilities. The USB 3.0 and 3.1 motherboard connector is similar in design to a USB connector, but has additional pins.

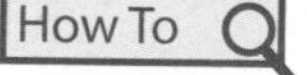

The basic steps to connect front panel cables include:

Step 1. Plug the power cable into the system panel connector in the location marked PWR_SW.

Step 2. Plug the reset cable into the system panel connector in the location marked RESET.

Step 3. Plug the power LED cable into the system panel connector in the location marked PWR_LED.

Step 4. Plug the drive activity LED cable into the system panel connector in the location marked HDD_LED.

Step 5. Plug the speaker cable into the system panel connector in the location marked SPEAKER.

Step 6. Plug the USB cable into the USB connector.

Step 7. Plug the audio cable into the audio connector.

Generally, if a button or LED does not function, the connector is incorrectly oriented. To correct this, shut down the computer and unplug it, open the case, and turn the connector around for the button or LED that does not function. To avoid wiring incorrectly, some manufacturers include a keyed pin extender that combines multiple front-panel cables (power and reset LEDs) connectors into one connector.

Installation Tip

The panel connector and case cable ends are very small. Take pictures of them to locate pin 1. Because space in the case can be limited at the end of assembly, a part retriever can be used to plug the cables into the connectors.

Activity—Identify the Front Panel Connectors (3.1.5.7)

Please refer to the Activity in the Cisco Networking Academy IT Essentials 6.0 online course.

Lab—Install Front Panel Cables (3.1.5.8)

In this lab, you install the front panel cables in the computer. Refer to the lab in *IT Essentials v6 Lab Manual*.

Reassemble the Case Assembly (3.1.5.9)

Before reattaching the side panels to the computer case, make sure that all items are correctly aligned and seated properly. This list includes the CPU, RAM, adapter cards, data cables, front panel cables, and power cables.

When the cover is in place, make sure that it is secured at all screw locations. Some computer cases use screws that are inserted with a screwdriver. Other cases have knob-type screws that you can tighten by hand.

If you are unsure about how to remove or replace the computer case, refer to the manufacturer's documentation or website.

Caution

Handle case parts with care. Some computer case covers have sharp or jagged edges.

Installation Tip

Inspect the areas where the panels meet the frame of the case. Move any cables away from these areas to avoid pinching or nicking them.

Install the External Cables (3.1.5.10)

After the case panels are reattached, connect the cables to the back of the computer.

Note

Plug in the power cable after you have connected all other cables.

When attaching cables, ensure that they are connected to the correct locations on the computer. For example, older systems use the same type of PS/2 connector for the mouse and keyboard cables, but are color-coded to avoid being connected incorrectly. Often, an icon of the connected device, such as a keyboard, mouse, monitor, or USB symbol, is shown on the connector.

Caution

When attaching cables, never force a connection.

How To

To install the various external cables, follow these steps:

Step 1. Attach the monitor cable to the video port. Secure the cable by tightening the screws on the connector. If the computer you assembled has a video adapter installed, be sure to connect the cable to the adapter and not the motherboard video port.

Step 2. Plug the keyboard cable into the PS/2 keyboard port.

Step 3. Plug the mouse cable into the PS/2 mouse port.

Step 4. Plug the USB cable into a USB port.

Step 5. Plug the power cable into the power supply.

Note

Some motherboards have only one PS/2 port. Some motherboards may not have any PS/2 ports for connecting the keyboard and mouse. Connect a USB keyboard, a USB mouse, or both to this type of motherboard.

Installation Tip

PS/2 to USB adapters can be used to connect older peripherals to motherboards that do not have PS/2 connectors.

Packet Tracer
☐ **Activity**

Activity—Identify the External Connectors (3.1.5.11)

Please refer to the Activity in the Cisco Networking Academy IT Essentials 6.0 online course.

Lab Complete the Computer Assembly (3.1.5.12)

In this lab, you install the side panels and the external cables on the computer. Refer to the lab in *IT Essentials v6 Lab Manual.*

Boot the Computer (3.2)

Booting the computer refers to turning it on and beginning the startup sequence, verifying hardware, and loading operating system software. ROM BIOS is an integral part of the boot process.

POST, BIOS, UEFI (3.2.1)

When a computer is booted (started), the *basic input/output system (BIOS)* performs a hardware check on the main components of the computer. This check is called a *power-on self-test (POST)*. This section looks at the BIOS and Unified Extensible Firmware Interface UEFI setup and POST.

BIOS Beep Codes and Setup (3.2.1.1)

The POST, shown in Figure 3-25, checks whether the computer hardware is operating correctly. If a device is malfunctioning, an error or a *beep code* alerts the technician of the problem. Typically, a single beep means that the computer is functioning properly. If there is a hardware problem, a blank screen might appear at bootup, and the computer will emit a series of beeps. Each BIOS manufacturer uses different codes to indicate hardware problems.

```
American
Megatrends
www.ami.com

1 AMD North Bridge, Rev G2
NUMM ROM Version :4.082.19
Initializing USB Controllers .. Done.
4096MB OK
USB Device(s): 1 Keyboard, 1 Mouse
Auto-Detecting SATA Port1...IDE Hard Disk
Auto-Detecting SATA Port3...ATAPI CDROM
Auto-Detecting SATA Port2...IDE Hard Disk
Auto-Detecting SATA Port4...IDE Hard Disk
SATA Port1 : ST31000340AS  SD15
             Ultra DMA Mode-6, S.M.A.R.T. Capable but Disabled
SATA Port3 : ATAPI iHAS220 6  8L07
             Ultra DMA Mode-5
SATA Port2 : ST31500341AS  CC1H
             Ultra DMA Mode-6, S.M.A.R.T. Capable but Disabled
SATA Port4 : ST31500341AS  CC1H
             Ultra DMA Mode-6, S.M.A.R.T. Capable but Disabled
Auto-detecting USB Mass Storage Devices ..
00 USB mass storage devices found and configured.
```

Figure 3-25 POST

Table 3-5 shows a sample of common beep codes. Always consult the motherboard documentation to get the beep codes for your computer.

Table 3-5 Common Beep Codes

Beep Code	Meaning	Cause
1 beep (no video)	Memory refresh failure	Bad memory
2 beeps	Memory parity error	Bad memory
3 beeps	Base 64 mem failure	Bad memory
4 beeps	Timer not operational	Bad motherboard
5 beeps	Processor error	Bad processor
6 beeps	8042 Gate A20 failure	Bad CPU or motherboard
7 beeps	Processor exception	Bad processor
8 beeps	Video memory error	Bad video card or memory
9 beeps	ROM checksum error	Bad BIOS
10 beeps	CMOS checksum error	Bad motherboard
11 beeps	Cache memory bad	Bad CPU or motherboard

A POST problem can arise before the video is activated. When troubleshooting a computer problem without video, a POST card can be used. A POST card, sometimes called a debug card, is installed in a port on the motherboard, such as PCI, PCIe, or USB port.

When the computer is started, the computer displays a series of two- or four-digit hex codes that are displayed on the POST card. If an error occurs, the post code can help diagnose the cause of the problem through the motherboard, BIOS, or POST card manufacturer.

Installation Tip

To determine if POST is working properly, remove all of the RAM modules from the computer and power it on. The computer should emit the beep code for a computer with no RAM installed. This will not harm the computer.

BIOS and CMOS (3.2.1.2)

All motherboards need BIOS to operate. *BIOS* is a ROM chip on the motherboard that contains a small program. This program controls the communication between the operating system and the hardware.

Along with the POST, BIOS also identifies:

- Which drives are available
- Which drives are bootable
- How the memory is configured and when it can be used
- How PCIe and PCI expansion slots are configured
- How SATA and USB ports are configured
- Motherboard power management features
- The motherboard manufacturer saves the motherboard BIOS settings in a *complementary metal oxide semiconductor (CMOS)* memory chip such as the one shown in Figure 3-26.

Figure 3-26 CMOS Chip

When a computer boots, the BIOS software reads the configured settings stored in CMOS to determine how to configure the hardware.

The BIOS settings are retained by CMOS using a battery such as the one shown in Figure 3-27. If the battery fails, important settings can be lost. Therefore, BIOS settings should always be documented.

Figure 3-27 CMOS Battery

Note

An easy way to document these settings is to take pictures of the various BIOS settings.

Installation Tip

If the computer's time and date is incorrect, it could indicate that the CMOS battery is bad or is getting very low.

BIOS Setup Program (3.2.1.3)

Default BIOS settings may need to be altered whenever hardware such as memory modules, storage devices, and adapter cards are added or changed. The BIOS setup program must be used to change settings.

To enter the BIOS setup program, press the proper key or key sequence during the POST. This key sequence varies between manufacturers, but they commonly use the Delete key or a function key to enter the BIOS setup program. For example, with an ASUS motherboard, use the Delete key or F2 function key during the POST to enter the BIOS program.

Note

Consult the motherboard documentation for the correct key or combination of keys for your computer.

Many motherboards display a graphic called a *splash screen* while the computer goes through the POST process. The splash screen sometimes includes the manufacturer's key combination to enter BIOS.

Although BIOS setup programs differ between manufacturers, they all provide access to similar menu items such as the following (see Figure 3-28).

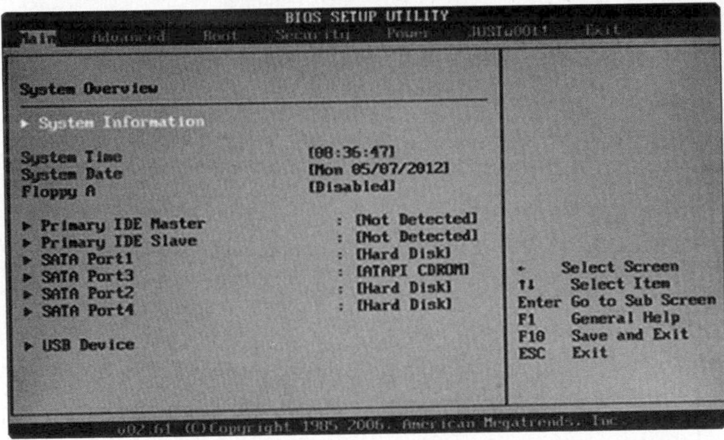

Figure 3-28 BIOS Setup Utility Program

- **Main**—Basic system configuration
- **Advanced**—Advanced system settings
- **Boot**—Boot device options and boot order
- **Security**—Security settings

- **Power**—Advanced power management configurations
- **JUSTw00t!**—Advanced voltage and clock settings
- **Exit**—BIOS exit options and loading default settings

UEFI Setup Program (3.2.1.4)

Some computers run *Unified Extensible Firmware Interface (UEFI)*. UEFI configures the same settings as traditional BIOS, but it also provides additional options. For example, UEFI provides a mouse-enabled software interface instead of the traditional BIOS screens.

BIOS and UEFI Configuration (3.2.2)

BIOS and UEFI are two firmware interfaces for computers that work as interpreters between the operating system and the computer firmware. Both of these interfaces are used at the startup of the computer to initialize the hardware components and load the operating system. In this section, you explore using the BIOS and UEFI to learn about system hardware and various configuration options in both programs. These configuration options vary depending on the BIOS manufacturer.

BIOS Component Information (3.2.2.1)

A technician can use the BIOS information to learn which components are installed in the computer and some of their attributes. This information can be useful when troubleshooting hardware that is not working properly, and to determine upgrade options. These are some of the common component information items that are displayed in the BIOS:

- **CPU**—Displays the CPU manufacturer and speed. The number of installed processors is also displayed.
- **RAM**—Displays the RAM manufacturer and speed. The number of slots and which slots the RAM modules occupy might also be displayed.
- **Hard Drive**—Displays the manufacturer, size, and type of hard drives. The type and number of hard disk controllers might also be displayed.
- **Optical Drive**—Displays the manufacturer and type of optical drives.

BIOS Configurations (3.2.2.2)

Another function of the BIOS setup program is to customize specific aspects of the computer hardware to fit individual needs. The features that can be customized are determined by the BIOS manufacturer and version. Before making changes to the

BIOS, it is important to have a clear understanding of how the changes can affect the computer. Incorrect settings can have an adverse effect.

Main BIOS configuration settings to configure include:

- **Time and Date**—The main page of the BIOS has a System Time field and a System Date field to set the system clock.
- **Disable Devices**—You can configure advanced BIOS settings to disable devices that are not needed or not used by the computer.
- *Boot Order*—Shortly after completing POST, the computer attempts to load the operating system. The BIOS checks the first device in the boot order list for a bootable partition. The boot order list, or boot sequence, is an ordered list of devices from which the computer is allowed to boot. If the device has no bootable partition, the computer checks the next device in the list. When a device with a bootable partition is found, the BIOS checks for an installed operating system. This list is typically located in the BIOS under the Boot tab. You can designate hard drives, optical drives, network boot, USB, and flash media in the boot order.
- *Clock Speed*—Some BIOS setup programs allow you to change the CPU clock speed. Reducing the CPU clock speed makes the computer run slower and cooler and is referred to as underclocking. This might result in less noise from fans and can be useful if a quieter computer is desired, such as in a home theater or bedroom. CPU *overclocking* is increasing the CPU clock speed to make the computer run faster but also hotter, possibly causing the computer to be louder due to increased fan speeds.
- **Virtualization**—Virtualization technology allows a computer to run multiple operating systems in separate files or partitions. To accomplish this, a computer virtualization program emulates the characteristics of an entire computer, including the hardware, BIOS, operating system, and programs. Enable the virtualization setting in the BIOS for a computer that will be using virtualization technology.

Table 3-6 provides BIOS setting suggestions.

Table 3-6 BIOS settings

BIOS Setting	Setting Specifics
Time and Date	■ Always set these fields to the correct time and date because they are referenced by the operating system and other programs. ■ Incorrect date and time may cause unexpected problems.

BIOS Setting	Setting Specifics
Disabling Devices	■ Disable the motherboard built-in features if installing a dedicated video card, sound card, or network card. ■ If a device is not working, check the advanced BIOS settings to see if the device is disabled by default or has been accidently disabled.
Boot Order	■ Create the boot order based on user needs. ■ Disable or remove unused devices from the boot order list.
Clock Speed	■ Overclocking a CPU voids the warranty of the CPU, can result in a shorter CPU life span, or cause damage to the CPU. ■ Always install a cooling system capable of dissipating the extra heat created by overclocking to avoid CPU damage.
Virtualization	■ Disable this setting if virtualization does not perform correctly or will not be used.

BIOS Security Configurations (3.2.2.3)

The BIOS often supports many security features to protect BIOS settings, data on the hard drive, and recovery options should the computer be stolen.

These are some common security features found in the BIOS:

- **BIOS passwords**—Passwords allow for different levels of access to the BIOS settings. There are two password settings that can be altered. The supervisor password can access all user-access passwords and all BIOS screens and settings. The supervisor password must be set before the user password can be configured. The user password gives access to the BIOS based on a defined level. Table 3-7 displays common levels of user access to BIOS.

Table 3-7 User Access Levels

Access Level	Level Description
Full Access	All screens and settings are available, except the supervisor password setting.
Limited Access	Changes can be made only to certain settings, such as, for example, the time and date.
View Only Access	All screens are available, but no settings can be changed.
No Access	No access is provided to the BIOS setup utility.

- **Drive encryption**—A hard drive can be encrypted to prevent data theft. Encryption changes the data on the drive into code. Without the correct password, the computer cannot boot and data read from the hard drive cannot be understood. Even if the hard drive is placed in another computer, the data remains encrypted.
- *LoJack*—This is a security feature that consists of two programs: the Persistence Module, which is embedded in the BIOS, and the Application Agent, installed by the user. When installed, the Persistence Module in the BIOS is activated and cannot be turned off. The Application Agent routinely contacts a monitoring center over the Internet to report device information and location. The owner can perform the functions described in Table 3-8.

Table 3-8 LoJack Functions

LoJack Functions	Description
Locate	Locate the device using Wi-Fi or IP geolocation to see the last location
Lock	■ Lock the device remotely to prevent access to your personal information ■ Display a customized message on the screen
Delete	Delete all files on the device to protect personal information and prevent identity theft

- *Trusted Platform Module (TPM)*—This is a chip designed to secure hardware by storing encryption keys, digital certificates, passwords, and data. TPM is used by Windows to support BitLocker full-disk encryption.
- *Secure Boot*—Secure Boot is a UEFI security standard that ensures that a computer only boots an OS that is trusted by the motherboard manufacturer. Secure Boot prevents an "unauthorized" OS from loading during startup.

BIOS Hardware Diagnostics and Monitoring (3.2.2.4)

The BIOS hardware monitoring features are useful for collecting information and monitoring the activity of the motherboard and connected hardware. The type and number of monitoring features varies by motherboard model. Use the hardware monitoring page to view temperatures, fan speeds, voltages, and other items. This page might also have information about intrusion detection devices.

These are some common BIOS hardware diagnostic and monitoring features:

- **Temperatures**—Motherboards have heat sensors to monitor heat-sensitive hardware. For example, a heat sensor under the CPU socket monitors the temperature of the CPU. If the CPU becomes too hot, BIOS could increase the speed of the CPU fan to cool the CPU, slow the speed of the CPU to reduce the CPU temperature, or even shut down the computer to prevent damage to the CPU. Other heat sensors monitor the temperature inside the case or power supply. Additionally, heat sensors might monitor the temperatures of the RAM modules or the chipset.

- **Fan speeds**—Some BIOS setups allow you to configure profiles to set the fan speeds to achieve a specific result. Common CPU fan speed profiles are standard, turbo, silent, and manual.
- **Voltages**—You can monitor the voltage of the CPU or the voltage regulators on the motherboard. If voltages are too high or too low, computer components can be damaged. If you find that voltages are not at or near the correct levels, make sure that the power supply is operating properly. If the power supply is not delivering the correct voltages, the motherboard voltage regulators might be damaged. In this case, the motherboard might need to be repaired or replaced.
- **Clock and bus speeds**—In some BIOS setups, you can monitor the speed of the CPU. Some BIOS setups may also allow you to monitor one or more of the busses. You might need to look at these items to determine if the correct CPU settings have been detected by the BIOS, or have been manually entered by a client or computer builder. Incorrect bus speeds can cause increased heat within the CPU and connected hardware, or cause adapter cards or RAM to malfunction.
- **Intrusion detection**—Some computer cases have a switch that triggers when a computer case is opened. You can set the BIOS to record when the switch is triggered so that the owner can tell if the case has been tampered with. The switch is connected to the motherboard.
- **Built-in diagnostics**—If you notice a problem with a device connected to the computer, such as a fan, or a basic function, such as temperature or voltage control, you might be able to use built-in diagnostics to determine where the problem is. Often, the program provides a description of the problem or an error code for further troubleshooting. Many built-in diagnostic programs retain a log that contains a record of problems encountered. You can use this information to investigate issues and error codes. When a device is under warranty, you can use this information to convey the problem to product support. Some common built-in diagnostics are: start test (which is used to check the functionality of main components when a computer does not boot correctly), hard drive test, memory test, and a battery test.

UEFI EZ Mode (3.2.2.5)

Newer computers have replaced the BIOS interface with UEFI. Although UEFI screens vary between vendors, they all offer similar features.

Figure 3-29 shows the ASUS UEFI BIOS Utility in EZ Mode. By default, the EZ Mode screen appears when you enter the UEFI. The EZ Mode provides an overview of basic system information, displays the CPU/motherboard temperature, CPU voltage output, fan speeds, memory information, and SATA information.

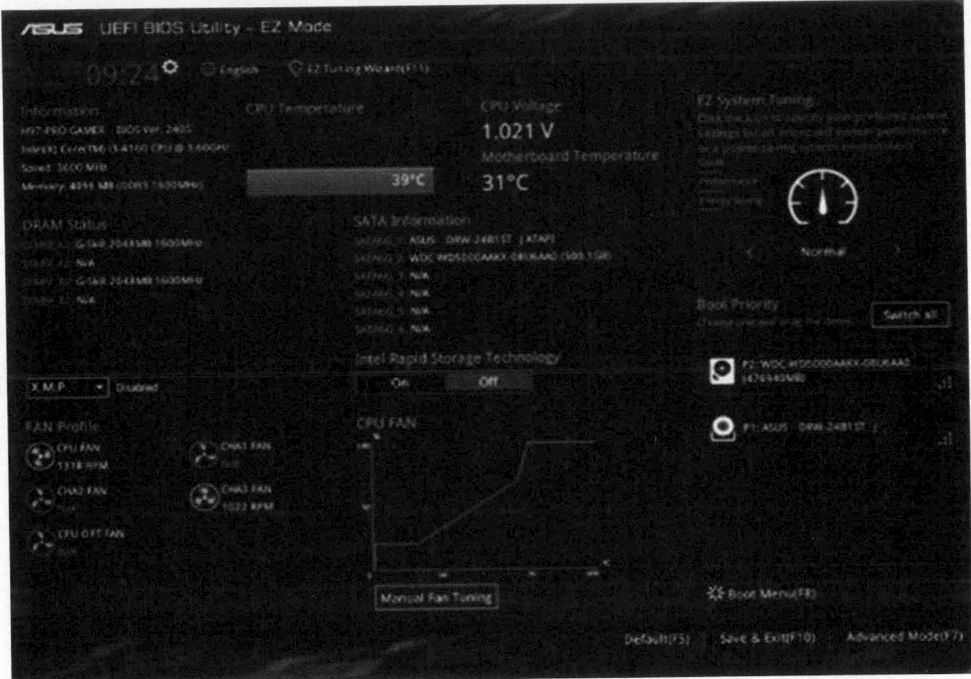

Figure 3-29 ASUS UEFI BIOS Utility EZ Mode

Specifically, from EZ Mode, you can:

- Change the time and date
- Select the language of the program
- Use the EZ Tuning Wizard to automate the creation of RAID storage and to assist with system overclocking
- Use EZ System Tuning to set the system performance mode
- Enable or disable SATA RAID
- Select the boot device priority

There is also another mode called Advanced Mode to configure and manage advanced settings.

UEFI Advanced Mode (3.2.2.6)

The ASUS Advanced Mode Main menu screen appears when you enter Advanced Mode. This mode provides options to configure advanced UEFI settings.

Note

To toggle between EZ Mode and Advanced Mode, press F7.

These are the items found on the menu at the top of the ASUS Advanced Mode Main menu screen:

- **My Favorites**—Used to provide quick access to frequently-used settings. Press **F3** or click **My Favorites (F3)** to open the Setup Tree Map Screen.
- **Main**—Used to display computer information and change the basic configuration. It allows you to set the date, time, language, and security settings.
- **Ai Tweaker**—Used for changing the CPU overclocking settings and memory operating settings. Always be cautious when changing these settings. Incorrect settings could cause the system to malfunction.
- **Advanced**—Used to change the settings for the CPU and other devices. Always be cautious when changing these settings. Incorrect settings could cause the system to malfunction.
- **Monitor**—Used for displaying temperatures, power status, and changing fan speed settings.
- **Boot**—Used for changing the boot options.
- **Tool**—Used for configuring options for special functions.
- **Exit**—Used for selecting the exit options and loading default settings.

Activity—Identify Terms (3.2.2.7)

Please refer to the Activity in the Cisco Networking Academy IT Essentials 6.0 online course.

Lab—Boot the Computer (3.2.2.8)

In this lab, you boot the computer for the first time, explore the firmware setup utility program, and change the boot order sequence. Refer to the lab in *IT Essentials v6 Lab Manual*.

Upgrade and Configure a Computer (3.3)

Computers need periodic upgrades for various reasons:

- User requirements change
- Upgraded software packages require new hardware
- New hardware offers enhanced performance

Motherboard and Related Components (3.3.1)

All components in a computer system connect to the motherboard. If you upgrade or replace a motherboard, consider that you also might have to replace other components, including the CPU, heat sink and fan assembly, and RAM. A new motherboard must also fit into the old computer case and the power supply must support it. This section examines reasons and methods for upgrading various components.

Motherboard Component Upgrades (3.3.1.1)

Changes to the computer may cause you to upgrade or replace components and peripherals. Research the effectiveness and cost for both upgrading and replacing.

When upgrading the motherboard, begin the upgrade by moving the CPU and the heat sink and fan assembly to the new motherboard if they will be reused. These items are much easier to work with when they are outside of the case. Work on an antistatic mat and wear antistatic gloves or an antistatic wrist strap to avoid damaging the CPU. If the new motherboard requires a different CPU and RAM, install them at this time. Clean the thermal compound from the CPU and heat sink. Remember to reapply thermal compound between the CPU and the heat sink.

Many older motherboards had jumpers that were moved between pins to change settings. However, newer motherboards rarely have jumpers. Advanced electronics allow these options to be configured from within the UEFI or BIOS setup program.

CMOS batteries last several years. However, if the computer does not keep the correct time and date or loses configuration settings between shutdowns, the battery is most likely dead and must be replaced. Make sure that the new battery matches the model required by the motherboard.

How To

To install a CMOS battery, follow these steps:

Step 1. Gently slide aside, or raise, the thin metal clips to remove the old battery.

Step 2. Line up the positive and negative poles to the correct orientation on the new battery.

Upgrade the Motherboard (3.3.1.2)

Before beginning an upgrade, ensure that you know where and how everything is connected. Always make notes in a journal to record how the current computer is set up. A quick way to do this is to use a cell phone and take pictures of important details, such as the way components connect to the motherboard. These pictures may prove to be surprisingly helpful when reassembling.

How To

To upgrade a motherboard from a computer case, follow these steps:

Step 1. Record how the KCP power supply, case fans, case LEDs, and case buttons attach to the old motherboard.

Step 2. Disconnect the cables from the old motherboard.

Step 3. Disconnect the expansion cards from the case. Remove each expansion card and place them in antistatic bags, or on an antistatic mat.

Step 4. Carefully record how the old motherboard is secured to the case. Some mounting screws provide support, and some may provide an important grounding connection between the motherboard and chassis. In particular, pay attention to screws and standoffs that are non-metallic, because these may be insulators. Replacing insulating screws and supports with metal hardware that conducts electricity might damage electrical components.

Step 5. Remove the old motherboard from the case.

Step 6. Examine the new motherboard and identify where all of the connectors are, such as power, SATA, fan, USB, audio, front panel connectors, and any others.

Step 7. Examine the I/O shield located at the back of the computer case. Replace the old I/O shield with the I/O shield that comes with the new motherboard.

Step 8. Insert and secure the motherboard into the case. Be sure to consult the case and motherboard manufacturer user guides. Use the proper types of screws. Do not swap threaded screws with self-tapping metal screws, because they will damage the threaded screw holes and might not be secure. Make sure that the threaded screws are the correct length and have the same number of threads per inch. If the thread is correct, they fit easily. If you force a screw to fit, you can damage the threaded hole, and it will not hold the motherboard securely. Using the wrong screw can also produce metal shavings that can cause short circuits.

Step 9. Next, connect the power supply, case fans, case LEDs, front panel, and any other required cables. If the ATX power connectors are not the same size (some have more pins than others), you might need to use an adapter. Refer to the motherboard documentation for the layout of these connections.

Step 10. After the new motherboard is in place and the cables are connected, install and secure the expansion cards.

It is now time to check your work. Make sure that there are no loose parts or unconnected cables. Connect the keyboard, mouse, monitor, and power. If a problem is detected, shut the power supply off immediately.

Upgrade the BIOS (3.3.1.3)

Motherboard manufacturers may publish updated BIOS versions to provide enhancements to system stability, compatibility, and performance. However, updating the firmware is risky. The release notes describe the upgrade to the product, compatibility improvements, and the known bugs that have been addressed. Some newer devices operate properly only with an updated BIOS installed. To check the version of the BIOS installed in a computer, consult either the BIOS Setup or UEFI BIOS utility.

Before updating motherboard firmware, record the manufacturer of the BIOS and the motherboard model. Use this information to identify the exact files to download from the motherboard manufacturer's site. Update the firmware only if there are problems with the system hardware or if you are adding functionality to the system.

Early computer BIOS information was contained in ROM chips. To upgrade the BIOS information, the ROM chip had to be replaced, which was not always possible. Modern BIOS chips are electronically erasable programmable read only memory (EEPROM), which can be upgraded by the user without opening the computer case. This process is called *flashing the BIOS*.

To download a new BIOS, consult the manufacturer's website and follow the recommended installation procedures. Installing BIOS software online may involve downloading a new BIOS file, copying or extracting files to removable media, and then booting from the removable media. An installation program prompts the user for information to complete the process.

Many motherboard manufacturers now provide software to flash the BIOS from within an operating system. For example, the ASUS EZ Update utility automatically updates a motherboard's software, drivers, and the BIOS version. It also enables a user to manually update a saved BIOS and select a boot logo when the system goes into POST. The utility is included with the motherboard, or it can be downloaded from the ASUS website.

Caution

An improperly installed or aborted BIOS update can cause the computer to become unusable.

Upgrade CPU and Heat Sink and Fan Assembly (3.3.1.4)

One way to increase the power of a computer is to increase the processing speed. You can do this by upgrading the CPU. However, the CPU must meet the requirements listed below:

- The new CPU must fit into the existing CPU socket.
- The new CPU must be compatible with the motherboard chipset.
- The new CPU must operate with the existing motherboard and power supply.

The new CPU might require a different heat sink and fan assembly. The assembly must physically fit the CPU and be compatible with the CPU socket. It must also be adequate to remove the heat of the faster CPU.

Caution

You must apply thermal compound between the new CPU and the heat sink and fan assembly.

View thermal settings in the BIOS to determine if there are any problems with the CPU and the heat sink and fan assembly. Third-party software applications can also report CPU temperature information in an easy-to-read format. Refer to the motherboard or CPU user documentation to determine if the chip is operating in the correct temperature range.

How To

To install additional fans in the case to help cool the computer, follow these steps:

Step 1. Align the fan so that it faces the correct direction to either draw air in or blow air out.

Step 2. Mount the fan using the predrilled holes in the case. It is common to mount fans near the top of the case to blow hot air out, and near the bottom of the case to bring air in. Avoid mounting two fans close together that are moving air in opposite directions.

Step 3. Connect the fan to the power supply or the motherboard, depending on the case fan plug type.

Upgrade the Ram (3.3.1.5)

Increasing the amount of RAM almost always improves computer performance. Prior to upgrading or replacing the RAM, be sure to have the answers to the following questions:

- What type of RAM does the motherboard currently use?
- Are there available RAM slots?

- Can the RAM be installed one module at a time or must it be grouped into matching banks?
- Does the new RAM match the speed, latency, and voltage of the existing RAM?

Note

Memory must often be installed in a specific order on a motherboard. Be sure to consult the motherboard user guide for more information.

To upgrade the RAM on a motherboard, follow these steps:

Step 1. Remove the existing module by freeing the retaining clips that secure it.

Step 2. Pull the module straight out from the socket.

Step 3. Insert the new module straight down into the socket.

Step 4. Lock the retaining clips.

The system discovers the newly installed RAM if it is compatible and installed correctly. If the BIOS does not indicate the presence of the correct amount of RAM, make sure that the RAM is compatible with the motherboard and that it is correctly installed.

Lab—BIOS File Search (3.3.1.6)

In this lab, you identify the current BIOS version, and then search for BIOS update files. Refer to the lab in *IT Essentials v6 Lab Manual.*

Storage Devices (3.3.2)

Storage devices are used for many purposes in a computer system. One critical use is the storage of user data. As users collect more data, they may need to increase their storage capacity. This section discusses why and how to add more storage by upgrading your hard drive.

Upgrade Hard Drives (3.3.2.1)

Instead of purchasing a new computer to get faster speed and more storage space, you might consider adding another hard drive. There are several reasons for installing an additional drive as listed:

- Increase storage space
- Increase hard drive speed
- Install a second operating system

- Store the system swap file
- Provide fault tolerance
- Back up the original hard drive

Many of the reasons suggested will be discussed in detail throughout the textbook.

How To

After selecting the appropriate hard drive for the computer, follow these general guidelines during installation:

Step 1. Place the hard drive in an empty drive bay and tighten the screws to secure the hard drive.

Step 2. Connect the drive to the motherboard using the correct cable.

Step 3. Attach the power cable to the drive.

Peripheral Devices (3.3.3)

Peripheral devices add to a computer's functionality and purpose. It is often necessary to add or upgrade peripheral devices to have a computer function to meet the need of the user. In this section, you learn why and how to upgrade peripheral devices.

Upgrade Input and Output Devices (3.3.3.1)

Peripheral devices periodically need to be upgraded. For example, if the device stops operating or if you wish to improve performance and productivity, an upgrade might be necessary.

These are a few reasons for upgrading a keyboard and/or a mouse:

- To change the keyboard and mouse to an ergonomic design. Ergonomic devices are made to be more comfortable to use and to help prevent repetitive motion injuries.
- To reconfigure the keyboard to accommodate a special task, such as typing in a second language with additional characters.
- To accommodate users with disabilities.

Monitors can be upgraded in different ways:

- Add a privacy filter to prevent people to the side of a monitor from reading information on the screen. Only the user and people directly behind the user are able to read the screen.

- Add an antiglare filter to prevent the glare of the sun and bright lights from reflecting off the screen. An antiglare filter makes it much easier to read the screen in the daylight or when a light is behind the user.
- Add multiple monitors to increase productivity by allowing the user to display more information and move data between open programs more easily and quickly. This usually requires an advanced video adapter card to support the additional connections, or a second video adapter card must be installed.

Sometimes it is not possible to perform an upgrade using the existing expansion slots or sockets. In this case, you may be able to accomplish the upgrade using a USB connection. If the computer does not have an extra USB connection, you must install a USB adapter card or purchase a USB hub, as shown in Figure 3-30.

Figure 3-30 USB Hub

After obtaining new hardware, you may have to install new drivers. You can usually do this by using the installation media. If you do not have the installation media, you can obtain updated drivers from the manufacturer's website.

Note

A *signed driver* is a driver that has passed the Windows hardware quality lab test and has been given a driver signature by Microsoft. Installing an unsigned driver can cause system instability, error messages, and boot problems. During hardware installation, if an unsigned driver is detected, you are asked whether you want to stop or continue the installation. Install unsigned drivers only if you trust the source of the drivers. Some Windows operating systems do not allow the installation of drivers that are not signed.

Lab—Upgrade Hardware (3.3.3.2)

In this lab, you gather information about hardware components in order to upgrade your customer's hardware so they can play advanced video games. Refer to the Lab in *IT Essentials v6 Lab Manual*.

Summary (3.4)

Computer assembly is an important skill for a computer technician.

Summary (3.4.1)

Assembling a computer requires a lot of planning and decision making. Component selection takes a lot of consideration and preparing the work area and tools are an important part of the process. This chapter outlined the precautions necessary to prevent component damage, the tools to use, and the questions to consider when choosing components.

This chapter also detailed the steps used to assemble a computer and to boot the system for the first time. These are some important points to remember:

- Computer cases come in a variety of sizes and configurations. Many of the computer components must match the form factor of the case.
- The CPU is installed on the motherboard with thermal compound and a heat sink and fan assembly.
- RAM is installed in RAM slots on the motherboard.
- Adapter cards are installed in PCI and PCIe expansion slots on the motherboard.
- Hard disk drives are installed in 3.5 in. (8.9 cm) drive bays located inside the case.
- Optical drives are installed in 5.25 in. (13.34 cm) drive bays that can be accessed from outside the case.
- Power supply cables are connected to all drives and the motherboard.
- Internal data cables transfer data between the motherboard and the drives.
- External cables connect peripheral devices to the computer.
- Beep codes signify hardware malfunctions.
- The BIOS setup program displays information about the computer components and allows the user to change system settings.
- Computer components require periodic upgrades and replacement parts.
- Additional hard drives can provide fault tolerance and the ability to install additional operating systems.

Summary of Exercises

This is a summary of the labs and activities associated with this chapter.

Labs

The following labs cover material from this chapter. Refer to the labs in the *IT Essentials v6 Lab Manual*.

Lab—Install the Power Supply (3.1.1.3)

Lab—Install the Motherboard (3.1.2.6)

Lab—Install the Drives (3.1.3.3)

Lab—Install Adapter Cards (3.1.4.4)

Lab—Install Internal Cables (3.1.5.5)

Lab—Install Front Panel Cables (3.1.5.8)

Lab—Complete the Computer Assembly (3.1.5.12)

Lab—Boot the Computer (3.2.2.8)

Lab—BIOS File Search (3.3.1.6)

Lab—Upgrade Hardware (3.3.3.2)

Check Your Understanding

You can find the answers to these questions in the appendix, "Answers to 'Check Your Understanding' Questions."

1. When mounting a motherboard in a computer case, what is used to prevent the motherboard from touching the bottom of the case?

   A. Standoffs

   B. Ground-fault isolators

   C. Silicon spray

   D. Grounding straps

2. What should be used to clean the base of the CPU heat sink prior to reinstallation?

   A. Rubbing alcohol

   B. Water

   C. Isopropyl alcohol

   D. Thermal compound

3. What should be done prior to the installation of RAM onto the motherboard?

   A. Consult the motherboard documentation or the website of the manufacturer to ensure that the RAM is compatible with the motherboard.

   B. Change the voltage selector to meet with the voltage specification of the RAM.

   C. Ensure the memory expansion slot tabs are in the locked position before inserting the RAM module.

   D. Populate the center memory slots first before inserting the new RAM.

4. A motherboard has a 24-pin socket for the main power connector. Which ATX power supply connector will work?

   A. 12-pin connector

   B. 16-pin connector

   C. 18-pin connector

   D. 20-pin connector

5. Which website should a technician consult to find instructions for updating the BIOS on a computer?

   A. CPU manufacturer

   B. Case manufacturer

   C. Motherboard manufacturer

   D. Operating system developer

6. Select the best answer to describe the installation step applicable for a technician installing a CPU.

   A. Align the standoffs with the case.

   B. Secure the latch plate by closing the load lever.

   C. Insert it into the appropriate bay.

   D. Align the notches with the module to the keys in the slot and firmly press straight down.

7. Select the best answer to describe the installation step applicable for a technician installing a motherboard.

   A. Align the board with the standoffs in the case.

   B. Attach the device to the case and secure screws so the internal fan does not vibrate.

   C. Align the notches with the module to the keys in the slot and firmly press straight down.

   D. Secure the latch plate by closing the load lever.

8. Given the description *ATX with up to three 3.5" drive bays*, which PC component would be being referenced?

   A. CPU

   B. Case

   C. Hard drive

   D. Motherboard

9. What part should be attached to the case and securely screwed so the internal fan does not vibrate.

   A. CPU and heatsink

   B. Hard drive

   C. Power supply

   D. RAM

10. After building the computer, the technician powers on the computer. The system beeps several times. Which component caused the beeps and where is this component located? (Choose two.)

    A. Timer

    B. Event Viewer

    C. Motherboard

    D. CMOS

    E. BIOS

    F. Hard drive

11. Where is the saved BIOS configuration data stored?

    A. RAM

    B. Cache

    C. CMOS

    D. Hard drive

12. What are two examples of settings that can be changed in the BIOS setup program? (Choose two.)

    A. Boot order

    B. Swap file size

    C. Drive partition size

    D. Device drivers

    E. Enabling and disabling devices

13. Which definition describes the term *overclocking*?

    A. Changing the bus speed of the motherboard to increase the speed of attached adaptors

    B. Modifying the motherboard clocking crystal to increase the timing signals

    C. Increasing the speed of the CPU beyond the recommendations of the manufacturer

    D. Replacing slower SDRAM with faster memory

14. What is an advantage of using signed drivers?

    A. They are guaranteed to work with all operating systems.

    B. They are guaranteed by the manufacturer to work with any hardware.

    C. They are verified to be compatible with the operating system.

    D. They never need upgrading.

15. Which procedure is performed last when installing a new motherboard?

    A. Connect the peripheral devices

    B. Secure the expansion cards

    C. Install the I/O shield

    D. Tighten the motherboard screws

16. What indicates that the charge on the CMOS battery could be getting low?

    A. Performance while accessing files on the hard drive is slow.

    B. The computer fails to boot.

    C. The computer time and date are incorrect.

    D. A beep error code occurs during POST.

CHAPTER 4

Overview of Preventive Maintenance

Objectives

Upon completion of this chapter, you will be able to answer the following questions:

- What are the benefits of preventive maintenance?
- What are the most common preventive maintenance tasks?
- What are the elements of the troubleshooting process?
- What are common problems and solutions when troubleshooting a PC?

Key Terms

This chapter uses the following key terms. You can find the definitions in the Glossary.

Preventive maintenance Page 158

Troubleshooting Page 158

data backup Page 164

Open-ended questions Page 165

Closed-ended Page 165

Device Manager Page 167

Task Manager Page 167

Introduction (4.0)

Preventive maintenance can be the key to keeping computer systems from experiencing serious problems, such as data loss and hardware failures, and it helps systems have a longer life span.

Welcome (4.0.1)

In this section, you study the need for preventive maintenance of a computer system. Following a good preventive maintenance plan can keep computer problems for being too troublesome. The type of preventive maintenance routines covered here range from tending to components and power as well as managing data. Not all problems can be avoided, so this section also covers a systematic troubleshooting process to facilitate problem solving.

Overview of Preventive Maintenance (4.0.1.1)

Preventive maintenance is the regular and systematic inspection, cleaning, and replacement of worn parts, materials, and systems. Effective preventive maintenance reduces part, material, and system faults, and keeps hardware and software in good working condition.

Troubleshooting is the systematic process used to locate the cause of a fault in a computer system and correct the relevant hardware and software issues.

In this chapter, you learn general guidelines for troubleshooting procedures and creating preventive maintenance programs. These guidelines are a starting point to help you develop your preventive maintenance and troubleshooting skills.

Preventive Maintenance (4.1)

Being "proactive, not reactive" is a good approach to problem prevention with computer systems.

PC Preventive Maintenance Overview (4.1.1)

Understanding the importance of establishing preventive maintenance routines by creating a plan and scheduling the maintenance is of major importance for PC technicians. Another critical piece to the success of preventive maintenance is tracking and ensuring the plan is implemented.

Benefits of Preventive Maintenance (4.1.1.1)

There are several considerations for preventive maintenance plans. Preventive maintenance plans are developed based on at least two factors:

- **Computer location or environment**—Computers that are exposed to dusty environments, such as those used on construction sites, require more attention than computers located in an office environment.
- **Computer use**—High-traffic networks, such as a school network, might require additional scanning and removal of malicious software and unwanted files.

Document the routine maintenance tasks that must be performed on the computer components and the frequency of each task. You can then use this list of tasks to create a preventive maintenance plan.

Be proactive in computer maintenance and data protection. By performing regular maintenance routines, you can reduce potential hardware and software problems. Regular maintenance routines reduce computer downtime and repair costs. Preventive maintenance also offers these benefits:

- Improves data protection
- Extends the life of the components
- Improves equipment stability
- Reduces the number of equipment failures

Preventive Maintenance Tasks (4.1.1.2)

Hardware

Check the condition of the cables, components, and peripherals. Clean components to reduce the likelihood of overheating. Repair or replace any component that shows signs of damage or excess wear.

Use these tasks as a guide to creating a hardware maintenance plan:

- Remove dust from fans.
- Remove dust from the power supply.
- Remove dust from the components inside the computer and peripheral equipment, such as printers.
- Clean the mouse, keyboard, and display.
- Check for and secure any loose cables.

Software

Verify that installed software is current. Follow the policies of the organization when installing security updates, operating system updates, and program updates. Many organizations do not allow updates until extensive testing has been completed. This testing is done to confirm that the update will not cause problems with the operating system and software.

Use these tasks as a guide to creating a software maintenance schedule that fits your needs:

- Review and install the appropriate security updates.
- Review and install the appropriate software updates.
- Review and install the appropriate driver updates.
- Update the virus definition files.
- Scan for viruses and spyware.
- Remove unwanted or unused programs.
- Scan hard drives for errors.
- Optimize (defragment) hard drives.

Clean the Case and Internal Components (4.1.1.3)

It is important to keep the computer case and internal components clean. The amount of dust and other airborne particles in the environment and the habits of the user determine how often to clean the computer components. Regularly cleaned (or replaced) air filters in the building in which the computer is used will significantly reduce the amount of dust in the air.

Dust or dirt on the outside of a computer can travel through cooling fans to the inside. When dust accumulates inside the computer, it prevents the flow of air and reduces the cooling of components. Hot computer components are more likely to break down than properly cooled components. Most cleaning is to prevent this accumulation of dust.

To remove dust from the inside of a computer, use a combination of compressed air, a low-air–flow ESD vacuum cleaner, and a small lint-free cloth. The air pressure from some cleaning devices can generate static and damage or loosen components and jumpers. It is important to keep these components clean:

- Heat sink and fan assembly
- RAM
- Adapter cards
- Motherboard

- Fans
- Power supply
- Internal drives

You can use a low-airflow ESD vacuum cleaner to remove collected dust and materials from inside the case. You can also use the vacuum cleaner to pull in any dust that has been blown around from the compressed air. If you use compressed air from a can, keep the can upright to prevent the fluid from leaking onto computer components. Always follow the instructions and warnings on the can to keep the compressed air a safe distance from sensitive devices and components. Use the lint-free cloth to remove any dust left behind on the component.

Caution

When you clean a fan with compressed air, hold the fan blades in place. This prevents overspinning the rotor or moving the fan in the wrong direction.

Regular cleaning also gives you a chance to do a general maintenance exam of the system factors, such as:

- Inspect components for loose screws inside the case.
- Inspect slot covers for missing expansion slot covers that let dust, dirt, or living pests into the computer and can disrupt the airflow pattern designed to remove heat from the case.
- Look for loose or missing screws that secure adapter cards.
- Look for loose connections on the motherboard or adapter cards.
- Look for loose or tangled cables that can pull free from the case and components.

Use a cloth or a duster to clean the outside of the computer case. If you use a cleaning product, do not spray it directly on the case. Instead, put a small amount onto a cleaning cloth and wipe the outside of the case.

Inspect Internal Components (4.1.1.4)

The best method of keeping a computer in good condition is to examine the computer on a regular schedule. This is a basic checklist of components to inspect:

- **CPU heat sink and fan assembly**—Examine the CPU heat sink and fan assembly for dust buildup. Make sure that the fan can spin freely. Check that the fan power cable is secure. Check the fan while the power is on to see the fan turn.
- **RAM modules**—The RAM modules should be seated securely in the RAM slots. Sometimes the retaining clips can loosen. Reseat them, if necessary. Use compressed air to remove dust.

- **Storage devices**—Inspect all storage devices. All cables should be firmly connected. Check for loose, missing, or incorrectly set jumpers. A drive should not produce rattling, knocking, or grinding sounds.
- **Adapter cards**—Adapter cards should be seated properly in their expansion slots. Loose cards can cause short circuits. Secure adapter cards with the retaining screws or clips to avoid having the cards come loose in their expansion slots. Use compressed air to remove dirt and dust on the adapter cards and the expansion slots.
- **Screws**—Loose screws can cause problems if they are not immediately affixed or removed. A loose screw in the case can cause a short circuit or roll into a position where the screw is hard to remove.
- **Cables**—Examine all cable connections. Look for broken and bent pins. Ensure that all connector retaining screws are finger-tight. Make sure cables are not crimped, pinched, or severely bent.
- **Power devices**—Inspect power strips, surge suppressors (surge protectors), and UPS devices. Make sure that there is proper and clear ventilation. Replace the power device if it does not work properly.
- **Keyboard and mouse**—Use compressed air to clean the keyboard, mouse, and mouse sensor.

Environmental Concerns (4.1.1.5)

An optimal operating environment for a computer is clean, free of potential contaminants, and within the temperature and humidity range specified by the manufacturer. With most desktop computers, the operating environment can be controlled. However, due to the portable nature of laptops, it is not always possible to control the temperature, humidity, and working conditions. Computers are built to resist adverse environments, but technicians should always take precautions to protect the computer from damage and loss of data.

Follow these guidelines to help ensure optimal computer operating performance:

- Do not obstruct vents or airflow to the internal components.
- Keep the room temperature between 45 to 90 degrees Fahrenheit (7 to 32 degrees Celsius).
- Keep the humidity level between 10 and 80 percent.

Temperature and humidity recommendations vary by computer manufacturer. You should research these recommended values if you plan to use the computer in extreme conditions.

Troubleshooting Process (4.2)

Approaching problem-solving with a logical methodical approach is essential to successful resolution. Although experience is very useful to problem-solving, following a troubleshooting model will enhance effectiveness and speed.

Troubleshooting Process Steps (4.2.1)

In this section, you learn that to troubleshoot a problem quickly and effectively you need to have of theory of how to approach the issue. Troubleshooting is a way of discovering what is causing a problem and fixing it.

Introduction to Troubleshooting (4.2.1.1)

Troubleshooting requires an organized and logical approach to problems with computers and other components. Sometimes issues arise during preventive maintenance. At other times, a customer may contact you with a problem. A logical approach to troubleshooting allows you to eliminate variables and identify causes of problems in a systematic order. Asking the right questions, testing the right hardware, and examining the right data helps you understand the problem and form a proposed solution.

Troubleshooting is a skill that you refine over time. Each time you solve a problem, you increase your troubleshooting skills by gaining more experience. You learn how and when to combine steps, or skip steps, to reach a solution quickly. The troubleshooting process is a guideline that is modified to fit your needs.

This section presents an approach to problem-solving that you can apply to both hardware and software.

Note

The term *customer*, as used in this course, refers to any user who requires technical computer assistance.

Before you begin troubleshooting problems, always follow the necessary precautions to protect data on a computer. Some repairs, such as replacing a hard drive or reinstalling an operating system, might put the data on the computer at risk. Make sure you do everything possible to prevent data loss while attempting repairs.

Caution

Always perform a backup before beginning any troubleshooting procedures. You must protect data before beginning any work on a customer's computer. If your work results in data loss for the customer, you or your company could be held liable.

Data Backup

A *data backup* is a copy of the data on a computer's hard drive that is saved to another storage device or to cloud storage. *Cloud storage* is online storage that is accessed via the Internet. In an organization, backups may be performed on a daily, weekly, or monthly basis.

If you are unsure whether a backup has been done, do not attempt any troubleshooting activities until you check with the customer. Here is a list of items to verify with the customer that a backup has been performed:

- Date of the last backup
- Contents of the backup
- Data integrity of the backup
- Availability of all backup media for a data restore

If the customer does not have a current backup and you are not able to create one, ask the customer to sign a liability release form. A liability release form contains at least the following information:

- Permission to work on the computer without a current backup available
- Release from liability if data is lost or corrupted
- Description of the work to be performed

Identify the Problem (4.2.1.2)

The first step in the troubleshooting process is to identify the problem. During this step, gather as much information as possible from the customer and from the computer.

Conversation Etiquette

When you are talking to the customer, follow these guidelines:

- Ask direct questions to gather information.
- Do not use industry jargon.
- Do not talk down to the customer.
- Do not insult the customer.
- Do not accuse the customer of causing the problem.

Table 4-1 lists some of the information to gather from the customer.

Table 4-1 Step 1: Identify the Problem

Customer information	■ Company name ■ Contact name ■ Address ■ Phone number
Computer configuration	■ Manufacturer and model ■ Operating system ■ Network environment ■ Connection type
Problem description	■ Open-ended questions ■ Closed-ended questions
Error messages	
Beep sequences	
LEDs	
POST	

Open-Ended and Closed-Ended Questions

Open-ended questions allow customers to explain the details of the problem in their own words. Use open-ended questions to obtain general information.

Based on the information from the customer, you can proceed with closed-ended questions. *Closed-ended* questions generally require a yes or no answer.

Documenting Responses

Document the information from the customer in the work order, in the repair log, and in your repair journal. Write down anything that you think might be important for you or another technician. The small details often lead to the solution of a difficult or complicated problem.

Beep Codes

Each BIOS manufacturer has a unique beep sequence, a combination of long and short beeps, for hardware failures. When troubleshooting, power on the computer and listen. As the system proceeds through the POST, most computers emit one beep to indicate that the system is booting properly. If there is an error, you might hear multiple beeps. Document the beep code sequence, and research the code to determine the specific problem.

BIOS Information

If the computer boots and stops after the POST, investigate the BIOS settings. A device might not be detected or configured properly. Refer to the motherboard documentation to ensure that the BIOS settings are correct.

Event Viewer

When system, user, or software errors occur on a computer, the Event Viewer is updated with information about the errors. The Event Viewer application, shown in Figure 4-1, records the following information about the problem:

- What problem occurred
- Date and time of the problem
- Severity of the problem
- Source of the problem
- Event ID number
- Which user was logged in when the problem occurred

Although the Event Viewer lists details about the error, you might need to further research the problem to determine a solution.

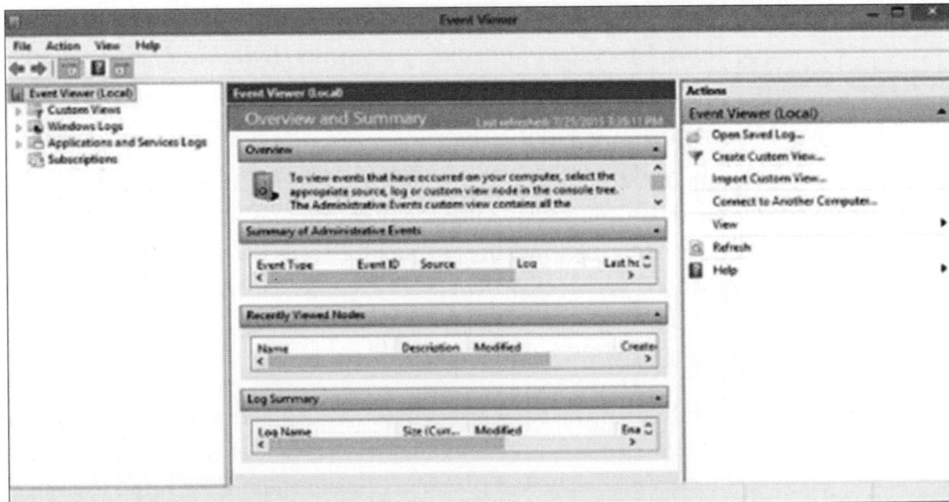

Figure 4-1 Event Viewer

Device Manager

The *Device Manager*, shown in Figure 4-2, displays all the devices that are configured on a computer. The operating system flags the devices that are not operating correctly with an error icon. A yellow circle with an exclamation point (!) indicates that the device is in a problem state. A red circle with an X means that the device is disabled. A yellow question mark (?) indicates that the system does not know which driver to install for the hardware.

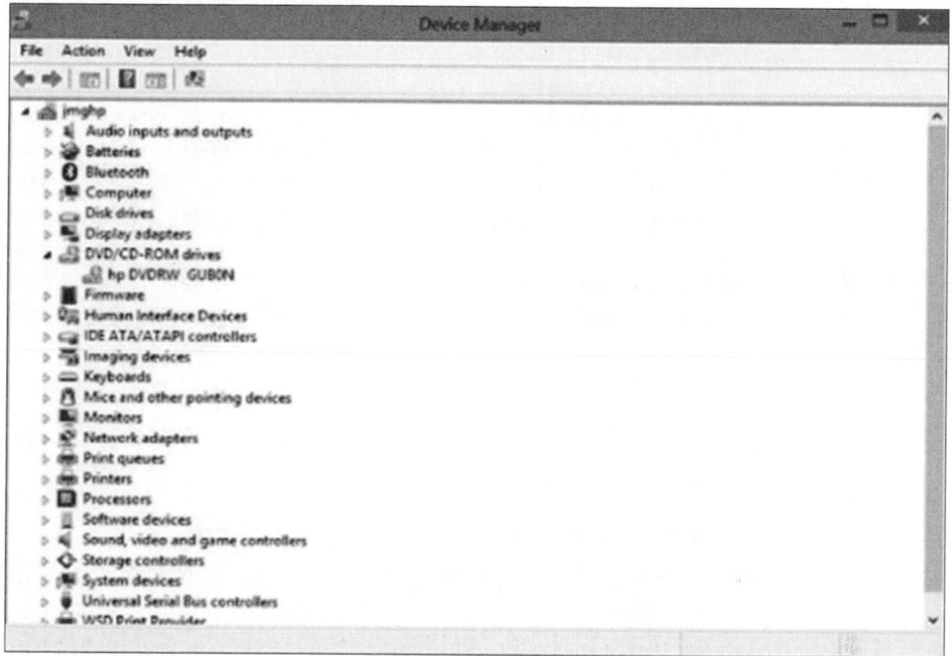

Figure 4-2 Device Manager

Task Manager

The *Task Manager*, shown in Figure 4-3, displays the applications and background processes that are currently running. With the Task Manager, you can close applications that have stopped responding. You can also monitor the performance of the CPU and virtual memory; view all processes that are currently running, and view information about the network connections.

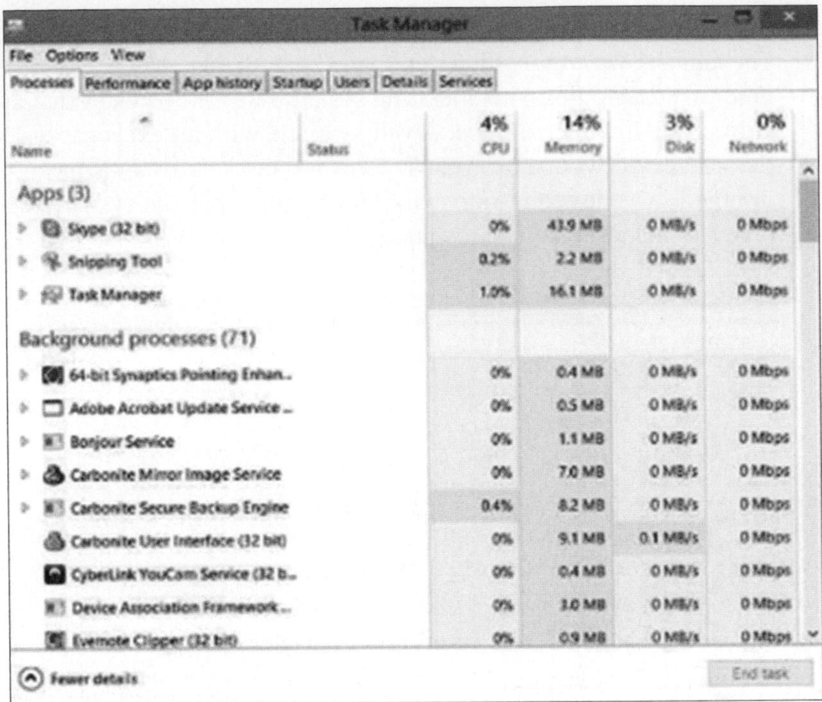

Figure 4-3 Task Manager

Diagnostic Tools

Conduct research to determine which software is available to help diagnose and solve problems. There are many programs to help you troubleshoot hardware. Manufacturers of system hardware usually provide diagnostic tools of their own. For instance, a hard drive manufacturer might provide a tool to boot the computer and diagnose why the hard drive does not start the operating system.

Activity—Identify the Problem (4.2.1.3)

Go to the online course to perform this practice activity.

Establish a Theory of Probable Cause (4.2.1.4)

The second step in the troubleshooting process is to establish a theory of probable cause. First, create a list of the most common reasons for the error. Even though the customer may think that there is a major problem, start with the obvious issues before moving to more complex diagnoses. List the easiest or most obvious causes at the top. List the more complex causes at the bottom. If necessary, conduct internal (logs, journals) or external (Internet) research, based on the symptoms. Table 4-2 is an example of a probable cause list.

Table 4-2 Step 2: Establish a Theory of Probable Cause

- Device is powered off
- Power switch for an outlet is turned off
- Surge protector is turned off
- Loose external cable connections
- Non-bootable disk in designated boot drive
- Incorrect boot order in BIOS setup

The next steps of the troubleshooting process involve testing each possible cause.

Test the Theory to Determine Cause (4.2.1.5)

You can determine an exact cause by testing your theories of probable causes one at a time, starting with the quickest and easiest. Table 4-3 identifies some common steps to determine the cause of the problem. After identifying an exact cause of the problem, you then determine the steps to resolve the problem. As you become more experienced at troubleshooting computers, you will work through the steps in the process faster. For now, practice each step to better understand the troubleshooting process.

Table 4-3 Step 3: Test the Theory to Determine Cause

- Ensure the device is powered on
- Ensure the power switch for an outlet is turned on
- Ensure the surge protector is turned on
- Ensure the external cable connections are secure
- Ensure the designated boot drive is bootable
- Verify the boot order in BIOS setup

If you cannot determine the exact cause of the problem after testing all your theories, establish a new theory of probable cause and test it. If necessary, escalate the problem to a technician with more experience. Before you escalate, document each test that you tried, as shown in Figure 4-4.

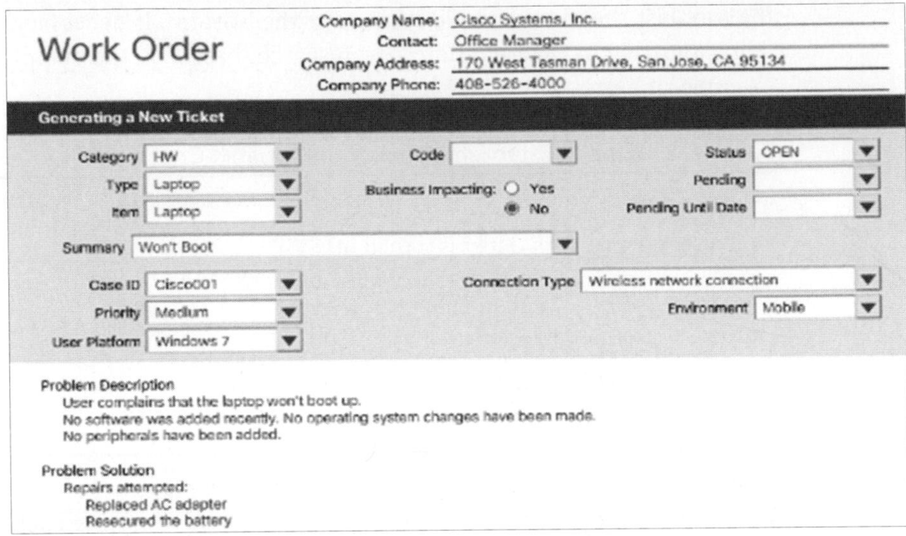

Work Order

Company Name: Cisco Systems, Inc.
Contact: Office Manager
Company Address: 170 West Tasman Drive, San Jose, CA 95134
Company Phone: 408-526-4000

Generating a New Ticket

Category: HW
Type: Laptop
Item: Laptop
Code:
Business Impacting: Yes / No (selected)
Status: OPEN
Pending:
Pending Until Date:
Summary: Won't Boot
Case ID: Cisco001
Priority: Medium
User Platform: Windows 7
Connection Type: Wireless network connection
Environment: Mobile

Problem Description
User complains that the laptop won't boot up.
No software was added recently. No operating system changes have been made.
No peripherals have been added.

Problem Solution
Repairs attempted:
Replaced AC adapter
Resecured the battery

Figure 4-4 Work Order

Establish a Plan of Action to Resolve the Problem and Implement the Solution (4.2.1.6)

After you have determined the exact cause of the problem, establish a plan of action to resolve the problem and implement the solution. Sometimes quick procedures can correct the problem. If a quick procedure does correct the problem, verify full system functionality and, if applicable, implement preventive measures. If a quick procedure does not correct the problem, research the problem further and then return to Step 3 to establish a new theory of the probable cause.

After you have established a plan of action, you should research possible solutions. Table 4-4 lists possible research locations. Divide larger problems into smaller problems that can be analyzed and solved individually. Prioritize solutions starting with the easiest and fastest to implement. Create a list of possible solutions and implement them one at a time. If you implement a possible solution and it does not correct the problem, reverse the action you just took and then try another solution. Continue this process until you have found the appropriate solution.

Table 4-4 Step 4: Establish a Plan of Action to Resolve the Problem and Implement the Solution

If no solution is achieved in the previous step, further research is needed to implement the solution.	■ Helpdesk repair logs ■ Other technicians ■ Manufacturer FAQ websites ■ Technical websites ■ News groups ■ Computer manuals ■ Device manuals ■ Online forums ■ Internet search

Verify Full System Functionality and, If Applicable, Implement Preventive Measures (4.2.1.7)

After the repairs to the computer have been completed, continue the troubleshooting process by verifying full system functionality and implementing the preventive measures needed. Table 4-5 lists the steps needed to verify functionality. Verifying full system functionality confirms that you have solved the original problem and ensures that you have not created another problem while repairing the computer. Whenever possible, have the customer verify the solution and system functionality.

Table 4-5 Step 5: Verify Full System Functionality and if Applicable Implement Preventive Measures

■ Reboot the computer
■ Ensure multiple applications work properly
■ Verify network and Internet connections
■ Print a document from at least one application
■ Ensure all attached devices work properly
■ Ensure no error messages are received

Document Findings, Actions, and Outcomes (4.2.1.8)

After the repairs to the computer have been completed, finish the troubleshooting process with the customer. Explain the problem and the solution to the customer verbally and in writing. Table 4-6 shows the steps to be taken when you have finished a repair.

Table 4-6 Step 6: Document Findings, Actions, and Outcomes

- Discuss the solution implemented with the customer
- Have the customer verify that the problem has been solved
- Provide the customer with all paperwork
- Document the steps taken to solve the problem in the work order and in the technician's journal
- Document all components used in the repair
- Document the amount of time spent to resolve the problem

Verify the solution with the customer. If the customer is available, demonstrate how the solution has corrected the computer problem. Have the customer test the solution and try to reproduce the problem. When the customer can verify that the problem has been resolved, you can complete the documentation for the repair in the work order and in your journal. Include the following information in the documentation:

- Description of the problem
- Steps to resolve the problem
- Components used in the repair

Common Problems and Solutions (4.2.2)

Computer problems can be attributed to hardware, software, networks, or some combination of the three. You will resolve some types of problems more often than others.

PC Common Problems and Solutions (4.2.2.1)

These are some common hardware problems:

Storage Devices

Storage device problems are often related to loose or incorrect cable connections, incorrect drive or media formats, and incorrect jumper or BIOS settings, as shown in Table 4-7.

Table 4-7 Common Problems and Solutions for Storage Devices

Identify the Problem	Probable Causes	Possible Solutions
The computer does not recognize a storage device.	■ The power cable is loose. ■ The data cable is loose. ■ The jumpers are set incorrectly. ■ The storage device has failed. ■ The storage device settings in the BIOS are incorrect.	■ Secure the power cable ■ Secure the data cable ■ Reset the jumpers ■ Replace the storage device ■ Reset the storage device settings in the BIOS
The computer fails to recognize an optical disc.	■ The disc is inserted upside down. ■ There more than one disc inserted into the drive. ■ The disc is damaged. ■ The disc is the wrong format. ■ The optical drive is faulty.	■ Insert the disc correctly ■ Ensure there is only one disc inserted in the drive ■ Replace the damaged disc ■ Use the correct type of disc ■ Replace the faulty optical drive
The computer will not eject the optical disc.	■ The optical drive is jammed. ■ The optical drive has been locked by software. ■ The optical drive is faulty.	■ Insert a pin in the small hole next to the eject button on the drive to manually open the tray ■ Reboot the computer ■ Replace the faulty optical drive
The computer does not recognize the removable external drive.	■ The removable external drive is not seated properly. ■ The external ports are disabled in the BIOS settings. ■ The external drive is faulty.	■ Remove and reinsert the drive ■ Enable the ports in the BIOS settings ■ Replace the removable external drive
A media reader cannot read a memory card that works properly in a camera.	■ The media reader does not support the memory card type. ■ The media reader is not connected properly. ■ The media reader is not configured correctly in the BIOS settings. ■ The media reader is faulty.	■ Use a different memory card type ■ Ensure the media reader is connected properly ■ Configure the media reader correctly in the BIOS settings ■ Install a known good media reader
Retrieving or saving data from the USB flash drive is slow.	■ The motherboard does not support USB 3.0. ■ The port is not set to the correct speed in the BIOS.	■ Update the motherboard or USB flash drive to support USB 3.0 ■ Set the port speed in the BIOS setting to a higher speed

Motherboard and Internal Components

These problems are often caused by incorrect or loose cables, failed components, incorrect drivers, and corrupted updates, as shown in Table 4-8.

Table 4-8 Common Problems and Solutions for Motherboards and Internal Components

Identify the Problem	Probable Causes	Possible Solutions
The clock on the computer is no longer keeping the correct time or the BIOS settings are changing when the computer is rebooted.	■ The CMOS battery may be loose. ■ The CMOS battery may be failing.	■ Secure the battery ■ Replace the battery
After updating the BIOS firmware, the computer will not start.	The BIOS firmware update did not install correctly.	Contact the motherboard manufacturer to obtain a new BIOS chip. If the motherboard has two BIOS chips, the second one can be used.
The computer displays the incorrect CPU information when it boots.	■ The CPU settings are not correct in the advanced BIOS settings. ■ BIOS does not properly recognize the CPU.	■ Set the advanced BIOS settings correctly for the CPU ■ Update the BIOS
The hard drive LED on the front of the computer does not light.	■ The hard drive LED cable is not connected or is loose. ■ The hard drive LED cable is incorrectly oriented to the front case panel connections.	■ Reconnect the hard drive LED cable to the motherboard ■ Correctly orient the hard drive LED cable to the front case panel connection and reconnect
The onboard NIC has stopped working.	The NIC hardware has failed.	Add a new NIC in an open expansion slot
The computer does not display any video after installing a new PCIe video card.	■ BIOS settings are set to use the onboard video. ■ The cable is still connected to the onboard video adapter port. ■ The new video card is faulty.	■ Disable the onboard video in the BIOS settings ■ Connect the cable to the new video card ■ The new video card needs to have auxiliary power connected ■ Install a known good video card

Identify the Problem	Probable Causes	Possible Solutions
The new sound card does not work.	■ The speakers are not connected to the correct jack. ■ The audio is muted. ■ The sound card is faulty. ■ BIOS settings are set to use the onboard sound device.	■ Connect the speakers to the correct jack ■ Unmute the audio ■ Install a known good sound card ■ Disable the onboard audio device in the BIOS settings

Power Supply

Power problems are often caused by a faulty power supply, loose connections, and inadequate wattage, as shown in Table 4-9.

Table 4-9 Common Problems and Solutions for Power Supplies

Identify the Problem	Probable Causes	Possible Solutions
The computer will not turn on.	■ The computer is not plugged in to the AC outlet ■ The AC outlet is faulty. ■ The power cord is faulty. ■ The power switch is not on. ■ The power switch is set to the incorrect voltage. ■ The power button is not connected correctly to the front panel connector. ■ The power supply has failed.	■ Plug the computer into a known good outlet ■ Plug the computer into a known good outlet ■ Use a known good power cord ■ Turn on the power supply switch ■ Set the power supply switch to the correct voltage ■ Correctly orient the power button to the front panel connector and connect ■ Install a known good power supply
The computer reboots, turns off unexpectedly, or there is smoke or the smell of burning electronics.	The power supply is starting to fail.	Replace the power supply

CPU and Memory

Processor and memory problems are often caused by faulty installations, incorrect BIOS settings, inadequate cooling and ventilation, and compatibility issues, as shown in Table 4-10.

Table 4-10 Common Problems and Solutions for CPUs and Memory

Identify the Problem	Probable Causes	Possible Solutions
The computer will not boot or it locks up.	■ The CPU has overheated ■ The CPU fan is failing ■ The CPU has failed	■ Reinstall the CPU ■ Replace the CPU fan ■ Add fan(s) to the case ■ Replace the CPU
The CPU fan is making an unusual noise.	The CPU fan is failing.	Replace the CPU fan
The computer reboots without warning, locks up, or displays error messages.	■ The front-side bus is set too high. ■ The CPU multiplier is set too high. ■ The CPU voltage is set too high.	■ Lower the front-side bus is settings ■ Lower the CPU multiplier settings ■ Lower the CPU voltage settings ■ Reset to the factory default settings for the motherboard to revert all previously changed settings to motherboard specifications
After upgrading from a single core CPU to a dual core CPU, the computer runs more slowly and only shows one CPU graph in the Task Manager.	The BIOS does not recognize the dual core CPU.	■ Update the BIOS firmware to support the dual core CPU ■ May need new motherboard and chip set
A CPU will not install onto the motherboard.	CPU is the incorrect type.	Replace the CPU with a CPU that matches the motherboard socket type

Identify the Problem	Probable Causes	Possible Solutions
The computer does not recognize the RAM that was added.	■ The new RAM is faulty. ■ The incorrect type of RAM was installed. ■ The RAM that has been added is not the same type of RAM already installed. ■ The New RAM is loose in the memory slot.	■ Replace the RAM ■ Install the correct type of RAM ■ Match the new RAM with the existing RAM type ■ Secure the RAM in the memory slot
After upgrading Windows, the computer runs very slowly.	■ The computer does not have enough RAM. ■ The video card does not have enough memory.	■ Install additional RAM ■ Install a video card that has more memory

Displays

Display problems are often caused by incorrect settings, loose connections, and incorrect or corrupted drivers, as shown in Table 4-11.

Table 4-11 Common Problems and Solutions for Displays

Identify the Problem	Probable Causes	Possible Solutions
Display has power but no image on the screen.	■ Video cable is loose or damaged. ■ The computer is not sending a video signal to the external display.	■ Reconnect or replace video cable ■ Use the Fn key along with the multipurpose key to toggle to the external display
The display is flickering.	■ Images on the screen are not refreshing fast enough. ■ The display inverter is damaged or malfunctioning.	■ Adjust the screen refresh rate ■ Disassemble the display unit and replace the inverter

(Continued)

Table 4-11 *Continued*

Identify the Problem	Probable Causes	Possible Solutions
The image on the display looks dim.	The LCD backlight is not properly adjusted.	Check the repair manual for instructions about calibrating the LCD backlight
Pixels on the screen are dead or not generating color.	Power to the pixels has been cut off.	Contact the manufacturer
The image on the screen appears to flash lines or patterns of different color and size (artifacts).	■ The display is not properly connected. ■ The GPU is overheating. ■ The GPU is faulty or malfunctioning.	■ Check connections to the display ■ Disassemble and clean the computer, check for dust and debris ■ Replace the GPU
Color patterns on the screen are incorrect.	■ The display is not properly connected. ■ The GPU is overheating. ■ The GPU is faulty or malfunctioning.	■ Check connections to the display ■ Disassemble and clean the computer, check for dust and debris ■ Replace the GPU
Images on the display screen are distorted.	■ Display settings have been changed. ■ The display is not properly connected. ■ The GPU is overheating. ■ The GPU is faulty or malfunctioning.	■ Restore display settings to the original factory settings ■ Check connections to the display ■ Disassemble and clean the computer, check for dust and debris ■ Replace the GPU
The display has a "ghost" image.	The display is experiencing burn-in.	■ Power off the display and unplug it from the power source for a few hours ■ Use the degauss feature if available ■ Replace the display

Identify the Problem	Probable Causes	Possible Solutions
The images on the display have distorted geometry.	■ The driver has become corrupted. ■ The display settings are incorrect.	■ Update or reinstall the driver in safe mode ■ Use the display's settings to correct the geometry
The monitor has oversized images and icons.	■ The driver has become corrupted. ■ The display settings are incorrect.	■ Update or reinstall the driver in safe mode ■ Use the display's settings to correct the geometry
The projector overheats and shuts down.	■ The fan has failed. ■ The vents are clogged. ■ The projector is in an enclosure.	■ Replace fans ■ Clean the vents ■ Remove the projector is in an enclosure or ensure proper ventilation
In a multiple monitor setup, the displays are or aligned or are incorrectly oriented.	■ The settings for multiple monitors are not correct. ■ The driver has become corrupted.	■ Use the display control panel to identify each display and set the alignment and orientation ■ Update or reinstall the driver in safe mode
The display is in VGA mode.	■ The computer is in Safe Mode. ■ The driver has become corrupted.	■ Reboot the computer ■ Update or reinstall the driver in safe mode

Summary (4.3)

This chapter discussed the concepts of preventive maintenance and the troubleshooting process.

Summary (4.3.1)

In this chapter, the need for preventive maintenance and troubleshooting problems of a computer system were detailed. It discussed why following a good preventive maintenance plan is necessary and the types of preventive maintenance routines. Because not all problems can be avoided by my preventive maintenance, this chapter also included a systematic troubleshooting process to facilitate problem-solving.

The following list summarizes important topics that are expanded upon throughout the chapter:

- Regular preventive maintenance reduces hardware and software problems.
- Before beginning any repair, back up the data on a computer.
- The troubleshooting process is a guideline to help you solve computer problems in an efficient manner.
- Document everything that you try, even if it fails. The documentation that you create is a useful resource for you and other technicians.

Summary of Exercises

This is a summary of the labs and lab activities associated with this chapter.

There are no labs associated with this chapter.

Check your Understanding

You can find the answers to these questions in the appendix, "Answers to 'Check Your Understanding' Questions."

1. A user has noticed that the hard drive LED on the front of the computer has stopped working. However, the computer seems to be functioning normally. What is the most likely cause of the problem?

   A. The motherboard BIOS needs to be updated.

   B. The power supply is not providing enough voltage to the motherboard.

   C. The hard drive LED cable has come loose from the motherboard.

   D. The hard drive data cable is malfunctioning.

2. After a problem is identified, what is the next step for the troubleshooter?
   A. Document the findings.
   B. Establish a theory of probable causes.
   C. Implement a solution.
   D. Verify the solution.
   E. Determine the exact cause.

3. What is the best way to determine if a CPU fan is spinning properly?
   A. Visually inspect the fan when the power is on to ensure it is spinning.
   B. Spin the blades of the fan quickly with a finger.
   C. Spray compressed air on the fan to make the blades spin.
   D. Listen for the sound of the fan spinning when the power is on.

4. An employee reports that the output of a workstation display is distorted. The technician checks the manufacturer website and downloads the latest version of the video driver. After the video driver is installed, what should the technician do next?
   A. Log the previous and current version numbers of the video driver.
   B. Schedule the next system checkup with the employee.
   C. Open a video-editing application to verify the video performance.
   D. Move the display card to another slot to see if the video performs better.

5. What is a symptom of a failing power supply?
   A. The power cord will not attach properly to either the power supply, wall outlet, or both.
   B. The computer sometimes does not turn on.
   C. The computer displays a POST error code.
   D. The display has only a blinking cursor.

6. An employee mentions that opening a large document file is taking longer than usual. The desktop support technician suspects that there might be a fault in the hard disk. What should the technician do next?
   A. Perform the disk cleanup procedure.
   B. Contact a data recovery company for service.
   C. Replace the hard disk with a new one to pinpoint the exact problem.
   D. Back up the user data from the workstation.

7. Which cleaning tool should be used to remove dust from components inside a computer case?

   A. Duster
   B. Cotton swabs
   C. Damp cloth
   D. Compressed air

8. What component is most suspect if a burning electronics smell is evident?

   A. Power supply
   B. Hard drive
   C. CPU
   D. RAM module

9. In which step of the troubleshooting process would a technician have to do more research on the Internet or within the computer manual in order to solve a problem?

   A. Document findings, actions, and outcomes.
   B. Identify the problem.
   C. Establish a plan of action to resolve the problem and implement the solution.
   D. Verify full system functionality and, if applicable, implement preventive measures.
   E. Test the theory to determine the cause.

10. Which task should be performed on a hard drive as part of a preventive maintenance plan?

    A. Ensure cables are firmly connected.
    B. Clean the read and write heads with a cotton swab.
    C. Blow out the inside of the drive with compressed air to remove dust.
    D. Ensure the disk spins freely.

11. What is a primary benefit of preventive maintenance on a PC?

    A. It enhances the troubleshooting processes.
    B. It extends the life of the components.
    C. It simplifies PC use for the end user.
    D. It assists the user in software development.

12. A user has just upgraded the CPU in a PC. After powering on, the computer boots but does not display the correct information about the new CPU while booting. What is the most likely cause of the problem?

    A. The CPU needs to be overclocked for it to show up correctly.
    B. The motherboard has incorrect BIOS settings.
    C. More RAM needs to be added to support the faster CPU.
    D. The operating system needs to be upgraded.

13. What method should be used by a technician to determine the exact cause of a problem?

    A. Start with most complex and most difficult probable causes to eliminate.
    B. Start with the quickest and easiest probable causes to eliminate
    C. Test theories of probable cause all at the same time.
    D. Start with what the customer thinks is the problem.

14. Which procedure is recommended when cleaning inside a computer?

    A. Invert the can of compressed air while spraying.
    B. Hold the CPU fan to prevent it from spinning and blow it with compressed air.
    C. Clean the hard drive heads with a cotton swab.
    D. Remove the CPU before cleaning.

15. A technician helps a customer to add a new 2 GB RAM module to a workstation that currently has one 2 GB RAM module installed. Three empty RAM slots are available. However, only 2 GB of RAM is reported by the BIOS after the new RAM module is added. What are two procedures that the technician should perform to pinpoint or solve the problem? (Choose two.)

    A. Make sure the new RAM module is seated properly.
    B. Replace with two 1 GB RAM modules.
    C. Check the manufacturer website for a BIOS patch.
    D. Test the new RAM module on another workstation.
    E. Upgrade the operating system to Windows 7 to support more RAM.

16. During what step in the troubleshooting process does the technician demonstrate to the customer how the solution corrected the problem?

    A. Document the findings, actions, and outcomes.
    B. Establish a theory of probable cause.
    C. Verify full system functionality.
    D. Establish a plan of action to resolve the problem.

CHAPTER 5

Windows Installation

Objectives

Upon completion of this chapter, you will be able to answer the following questions:

- What is the purpose of an operating system?
- What are the key terms to understanding the capabilities of an operating system?
- How do you determine the appropriate operating system based on customer needs?
- How do you install a Windows operating system?
- How is an operating system upgrade done?
- What is the difference between a desktop and a network operating system?
- What are different storage types and configurations for installing an operating system?
- What is the boot process of the current Windows operating system?

Key Terms

This chapter uses the following key terms. You can find the definitions in the Glossary.

operating system (OS) Page 188

Multiuser Page 189

Multitasking Page 189

Multiprocessing Page 189

Multithreading Page 189

device driver Page 190

plug-and-play (PnP) Page 190

registry Page 190

Command-line interface (CLI) Page 190

Graphical user interface (GUI) Page 190

application programming interface (API) Page 191

Open Graphics Library (OpenGL) Page 192

DirectX Page 192

Windows API Page 192

Java APIs Page 192

register Page 192

desktop operating system Page 193

Microsoft Windows Page 193

Windows 8.1 Page 193

Windows 8 Page 193

Windows 7 Page 193

Windows Vista Page 193

network operating system (NOS) Page 194

Upgrade Assistant in Windows 8.1 and 8, and Upgrade Advisor Page 196

Windows User State Migration Tool (USMT) Page 198

data migration Page 198

Windows Easy Transfer Page 198

flash memory Page 202

Solid state drives (SSD) Page 202

Solid state hybrid disks (SSHDs) Page 202

Embedded MultiMediaCard (eMMC) Page 203

partitions Page 203

master boot record (MBR) Page 204

globally unique identifier (GUID) partition table (GPT) Page 204

Primary partition Page 205

Active partition Page 205

Extended partition Page 205

Logical drive Page 205

Basic disk Page 205

Dynamic disk Page 206

Formatting Page 206

file system Page 206

File Allocation Table, 32-bit (FAT32) Page 206

New Technology File System (NTFS) Page 206

exFAT (FAT 206) Page 206

Compact Disc File System (CDFS) Page 207

NFS (Network File System) Page 207

quick format Page 207

full format Page 207

Workgroup Page 210

Homegroup Page 210

Domain Page 210

Authentication Page 210

single-sign on (SSO) authentication Page 210

Microsoft Windows Update Page 212

disk cloning Page 214

image-based Page 215

Microsoft's System Preparation (Sysprep) Page 215

remote network installation Page 217

preboot execution environment (PXE) Page 217

Unattended installation Page 218

Remote Installation Services (RIS) Page 217

Windows Recovery Environment (WinRE) Page 220

System Restore Page 220

System Image Recovery Page 220

Windows Registry Page 224

Automatic Repair Page 221

Command Prompt Page 221

cold boot Page 222

Windows Boot Manager (BOOTMGR) Page 223

WinLoad (WINLOAD.EXE) Page 223

NTOSKRNL.EXE Page 223

Safe Mode Page 224

Safe Mode with Networking Page 224

Safe Mode with Command Prompt Page 224

Last Known Good Configuration Page 224

Windows Registry keys Page 224

Dynamic Link Library (DLL) files Page 225

multiboot Page 226

Disk Management Utility Page 227

drive mapping Page 231

redundant array of independent disks (RAID) Page 231

New Spanned Volume Page 232

New Striped Volume Page 232

New Mirrored Volume Page 232

New RAID-5 Volume Page 232

mounted drive Page 235

UEFI Firmware Settings Page 221

Windows Startup Settings Page 221

Startup Repair Page 221

System Image Recovery Page 220

Windows Memory Diagnostic registry (Windows) Page 221

Cluster Page 202

Track Page 202

Sector Page 202

Cylinder Page 202

recovery partition Page 220

Introduction (5.0)

The operating system is software that most types of computers need to function. It has many roles, such as of controlling system resources, device management, memory management, and the user interface.

Welcome (5.0.1)

PCs and laptops are two types of computers that require operating systems to be useful. There are many different operating systems available, including Linux, Unix, Macintosh, and Windows. In this chapter, you learn about some of the Microsoft Windows operating systems.

Windows Installation (5.0.1.1)

The *operating system (OS)* controls almost all functions on a computer. In this chapter, you learn about the components, functions, and terminology related to the Windows 8.x, Windows 7, and Windows Vista operating systems.

Modern Operating Systems (5.1)

An operating system provides an interface for the user and manages how the hardware and applications are allocated resources. The OS boots the computer and manages the file system. Operating systems can support more than one user, task, or CPU.

Operating System Terms and Characteristics (5.1.1)

To understand the capabilities of an operating system, it is important to first understand some basic terms.

Terms (5.1.1.1)

An operating system (OS) has a number of functions. One of its main tasks is to act as an interface between the user and the hardware connected to the computer. Figure 5-1 shows the OS interaction with other components of the system.

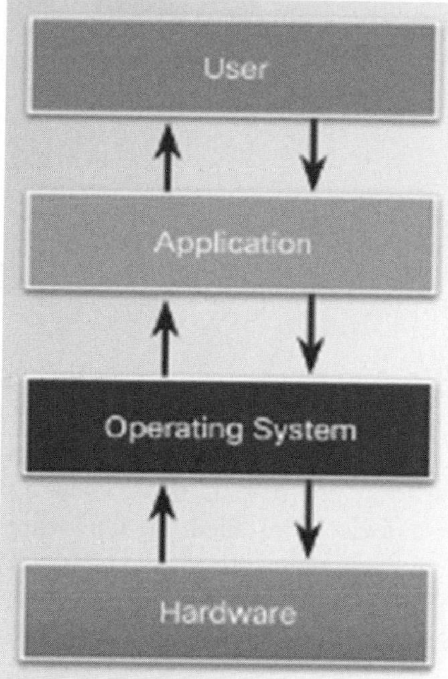

Figure 5-1 Operating System Diagram

The operating system also controls other functions:

- Software resources
- Memory allocation and all peripheral devices
- Common services to computer application software

From digital watches to computers, almost all computers require an operating system before they can be operated, hence the name.

The following terms are often used when describing operating systems:

- *Multiuser*—Two or more users can have individual accounts that allow them to work with programs and peripheral devices at the same time.
- *Multitasking*—The computer is capable of operating multiple applications at the same time.
- *Multiprocessing*—The operating system can support two or more CPUs.
- *Multithreading*—A program can be broken into smaller parts that are loaded as needed by the operating system. Multithreading allows different parts of a program to be run at the same time.

Basic Functions of an Operating System (5.1.1.2)

Regardless of the size and complexity of the computer and the operating system, all operating systems perform the same four basic functions:

- Control hardware access
- Manage files and folders
- Provide a user interface
- Manage applications

Hardware Access

The OS manages the interactions between applications and the hardware. To access and communicate with each hardware component, the OS uses a program called a *device driver*. When a hardware device is installed, the OS locates and installs the device driver for that component. Assigning system resources and installing drivers are performed with a *plug-and-play (PnP)* process. The OS then configures the device and updates the *registry*, which is a database that contains all the information about the computer.

If the OS cannot locate a device driver, a technician must install the driver manually either by using the media that came with the device or by downloading it from the manufacturer's website.

File and Folder Management

The OS creates a file structure on the hard disk drive to store data. A *file* is a block of related data that is given a single name and treated as a single unit. Program and data files are grouped together in a *directory*. The files and directories are organized for easy retrieval and use. Directories can be kept inside other directories. These nested directories are referred to as *subdirectories*. Directories are called *folders* in Windows operating systems, and subdirectories are called *subfolders*.

User Interface

The OS enables the user to interact with the software and hardware. Operating systems include two types of user interfaces:

- *Command-line interface (CLI)*—The user types commands at a prompt, as shown in Figure 5-2.
- *Graphical user interface (GUI)*—The user interacts with menus and icons, as shown in Figure 5-3.

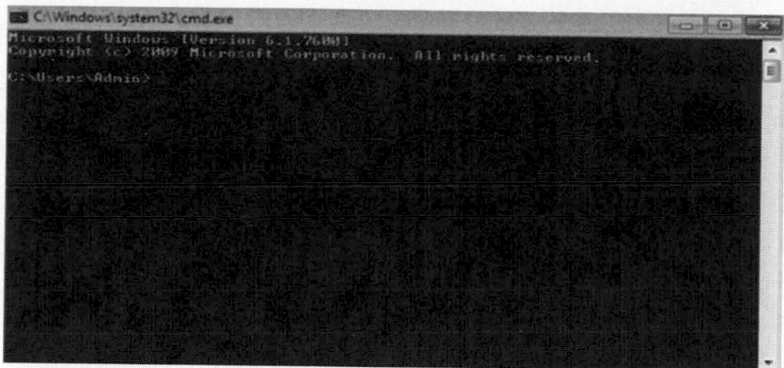

Figure 5-2 Command-line Interface

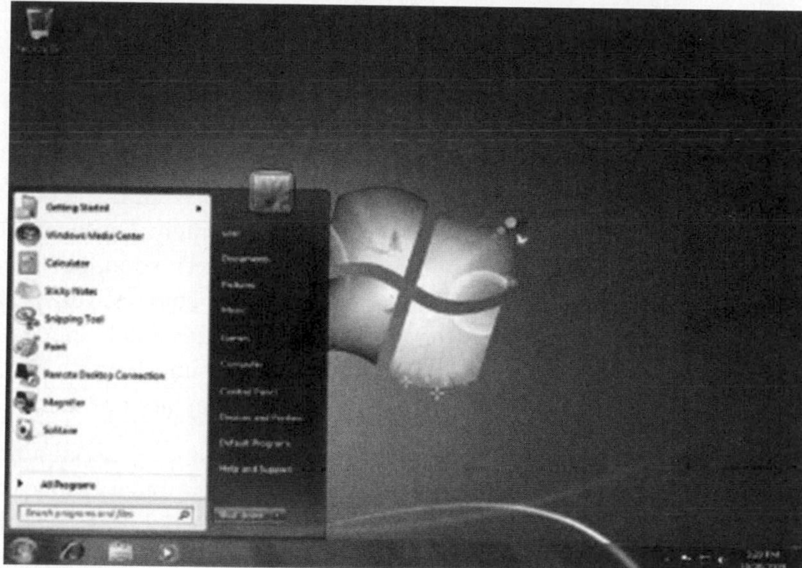

Figure 5-3 Graphical User Interface

Application Management

The OS locates an application and loads it into the RAM of the computer. Applications are software programs, such as word processors, databases, spreadsheets, and games. The OS allocates available system resources to running applications.

To ensure that a new application is compatible with an OS, programmers follow a set of guidelines known as an *application programming interface (API)*. An API allows programs to access the resources managed by the operating system in a consistent and reliable manner. Here are some examples of APIs:

- *Open Graphics Library (OpenGL)*—This is a cross-platform standard specification for multimedia graphics.
- *DirectX*—This is a collection of APIs related to multimedia tasks for Microsoft Windows.
- *Windows API*—This allows applications from older versions of Windows to operate on newer versions.
- *Java APIs*—This is a collection of APIs related to the development of Java programming.

Processor Architecture (5.1.1.3)

The processor architecture of the central processing unit (CPU) affects the performance of the computer. A CPU contains a *register*, which is a storage location where logical functions are performed on the data. A larger register can point to more addresses than a smaller register.

To better understand CPU architecture, use the analogy of a cook. He has a tool and some food in his hands. Think of his hands as a register. If the cook has very large hands, he can hold more items to be used immediately. On the counter (cache), he has other tools and ingredients that he will be using very soon, but is not using at this moment. In the kitchen (main memory) are ingredients and tools that are needed for the dish, but not as soon as the items on the counter will be needed. Other tools and ingredients related to cooking are in the stores around town (hard drive). These items can be ordered and shipped into his kitchen, if they are needed.

The terms *32-bit* and *64-bit* refer to the amount of data a computer's CPU can manage. A 32-bit register can store 2^{32} different binary values. Therefore, a 32-bit processor can directly address 4,294,967,295 bytes. A 64-bit register can store 2^{64} different binary values. Therefore, a 64-bit can directly address 9,223,372,036,854,775,807 bytes.

Table 5-1 shows the main differences between the 32-bit and 64-bit architectures.

Table 5-1 Processor Architecture

Architecture	Description
32-bit (x86-32)	■ Processes multiple instructions using a 32-bit address space ■ Supports 32-bit operating system ■ Supports maximum of 4 GB of RAM memory
64-bit (x86-64)	■ Adds additional registers specifically for instructions that use of 64-bit address space ■ Is backward compatible with the 32-bit processor ■ Supports 32-bit and 64-bit operating systems

Types of Operating Systems (5.1.2)

Desktop and network operating systems are two primary types of operating systems. *Desktop*, or *workstation*, operating systems are optimized to run applications, and although they can run services it is not their designed purpose. An *network (NOS)*, or *server*, operating system is designed to provide services to the desktop systems. Each can perform many of the same tasks, but their primary purposes are different, as described in this section.

Desktop Operating Systems (5.1.2.1)

A technician might be asked to choose and install an OS for a customer. There are two distinct types of operating systems: desktop and network. A *desktop operating system* is intended for use in a small office/home office (SOHO) environment with a limited number of users. A network operating system (NOS) is designed for a corporate environment, serving multiple users with a wide range of needs.

A desktop OS has the following characteristics:

- It supports a single user.
- It runs single-user applications.
- It shares files and folders on a small network with limited security.

In the current software market, the most commonly used desktop operating systems fall into three groups: *Microsoft Windows*, Apple Mac OS, and Linux. This chapter focuses on Microsoft operating systems:

- *Windows 8.1*—Window 8.1 is an update for Windows 8. The update includes improvements to make Windows more familiar for the users with devices that use touch or mouse and keyboard interfaces.
- *Windows 8*—Windows 8 introduced the Metro user interface that unifies the Windows look and feel on desktops, laptops, mobile phones, and tablets. Users can interact with the OS using a touchscreen or a keyboard and mouse. Another version, Windows 8 Pro, is aimed at business and technical professionals with additional features.
- *Windows 7*—Windows 7 is an upgrade from Windows XP or Vista. It is designed to run on personal computers. This version provided improved graphical user interface and better performance from the previous versions.
- *Windows Vista*—Windows Vista is a personal computer operating system. As the successor to Windows XP, it offers improvement on security and introduced the Windows Aero user interface.

Network Operating Systems (5.1.2.2)

A *network operating system (NOS)* contains features that increase functionality and manageability in a networked environment. A NOS has these specific characteristics:

- It supports multiple users.
- It runs multiuser applications.
- It provides network services to remote clients.
- It provides increased security compared to desktop operating systems.

A NOS provides certain network resources to computers:

- Server applications, such as shared databases
- Centralized data storage
- Centralized repository of user accounts and resources on the network
- Network print queue
- Redundant storage systems, such as RAID and backups

Windows Server is an example of a NOS.

Lab—Search NOC Certifications and Jobs (5.1.2.3)

In this lab, you use the Internet, a newspaper, or magazines to gather information about network operating system certifications and jobs that require these certifications. Refer to the lab in *IT Essentials v6 Lab Manual.*

Customer Requirements for an Operating System (5.1.3)

Understanding how a computer will be used is important when recommending an OS to a customer. The OS must be compatible with the existing hardware and the required applications; if not, a new computer purchase or an upgrade may be recommended.

OS Compatible Applications and Environments (5.1.3.1)

To make an OS recommendation, a technician must review budget constraints, learn how the computer will be used, and determine which types of applications will be installed and whether a new computer may be purchased. These are some guidelines to help determine the best OS for a customer:

- **Does the customer use off-the-shelf applications for this computer?** Off-the-shelf applications specify a list of compatible operating systems on the application package.
- **Does the customer use customized applications that were programmed specifically for the customer?** If the customer is using a customized application, the programmer of that application specifies which OS to use.

Minimum Hardware Requirements and Compatibility with OS Platform (5.1.3.2)

Operating systems have minimum hardware requirements that must be met for the OS to install and function correctly.

Identify the equipment that your customer has in place. If hardware upgrades are necessary to meet the minimum requirements for an OS, conduct a cost analysis to determine the best course of action. In some cases, it might be less expensive for the customer to purchase a new computer than to upgrade the current system. In other cases, it might be cost effective to upgrade one or more of the following components:

- RAM
- Hard disk drive
- CPU
- Video adapter card
- Motherboard

Figure 5-4 shows images of the components listed above.

Figure 5-4 Upgradable Computer Components

Note

If the application requirements exceed the hardware requirements of the OS, you must meet the additional requirements for the application to function properly.

After you have determined the minimum hardware requirements, ensure that all hardware in the computer is compatible with the OS that you have selected for the customer.

Operating Systems Upgrade (5.1.4)

Whether to upgrade an operating system is a decision that requires lots of thought and preparation. You may want to upgrade because you want a system that is updated or a system that can use hardware more efficiently or one that has more advanced software features; still, it is important to remember that an OS upgrade may also mean upgrading hardware, applications, and drivers for compatibility. This section addresses these topics.

Checking OS Compatibility (5.1.4.1)

An OS must be upgraded periodically to remain compatible with the latest hardware and software. It is also necessary to upgrade an OS when a manufacturer stops supporting it. Upgrading an OS can increase performance. New hardware products often require that the latest OS version be installed to operate correctly. Although upgrading an OS may be expensive, it may provide you enhanced functionality through new features and support for newer hardware.

Note

When newer versions of an OS are released, support for older versions is eventually withdrawn.

Before upgrading the operating system, check the minimum hardware requirements of the new OS to ensure that it can be installed successfully on the computer.

Upgrade Assistant and Upgrade Advisor

Microsoft provides free utilities called the *Upgrade Assistant in Windows 8.1 and 8, and Upgrade Advisor* in Windows 7 and Vista. Performing the same function, these utilities scan the system for hardware and software incompatibility issues before upgrading to newer editions of the Windows OS. Upgrade Assistant and Upgrade Advisor create a report of any problems and then guide you through the steps to resolve them. You can download the Upgrade Assistant and Upgrade Advisor from the Microsoft Windows website.

To use the Windows 7 Upgrade Advisor, follow these steps:

How To

Step 1. Download and run the correct utility depending on the version of Windows that needs to be checked.

Step 2. Click **Start check**. The program scans your computer hardware, devices, and installed software. A compatibility report is presented.

Step 3. Click **Save Report** if you want to keep it or print it later.

Step 4. Examine the report. Record any recommended fixes for the issues found.

Step 5. Click **Close**.

After making the changes to hardware, devices, or software, Microsoft recommends running the utility again before installing the new OS.

Windows OS Upgrades (5.1.4.2)

The process of upgrading the OS can be quicker than performing a new installation. The upgrade process varies depending on the version. For example, the Windows 8.1 setup utility replaces existing Windows files with Windows 8.1 files. However, the existing applications and settings are saved.

The version of an OS determines available upgrade options. For example, a 32-bit OS cannot be upgraded to a 64-bit OS. Another example is that Windows XP cannot be upgraded to Windows 8.1. Before attempting an upgrade, check the OS developer's website for a list of possible upgrade paths.

Note

Prior to performing an upgrade, back up all data in case a problem with the installation occurs.

Windows upgrade utilities differ very little across versions of the OS. The steps below are an example of upgrading to Windows 8.1 but would be valid for any Windows version:

How To

Step 1. Insert the Windows 8.1 disc into the optical drive. The Set Up window appears.

Step 2. Select the **Install now** option.

Step 3. You are prompted to download any important updates for installation.

Step 4. Agree to the End User License Agreement (EULA), and click **Next**.

Step 5. Click **Upgrade**. The system begins copying the installation files.

Step 6. Follow the prompts to complete the upgrade. When the install is complete, the computer restarts.

Data Migration (5.1.4.3)

When a new installation is required, user data must be migrated from the old OS to the new one. There are three tools available to transfer data and settings. The tool you select depends on your level of experience and your requirements.

User State Migration Tool

The *Windows User State Migration Tool (USMT)* migrates all user files and settings to the new OS, as shown in Figure 5-5. Download and install USMT from Microsoft. It is part of the Windows Assessment and Deployment Kit (Windows (ADK)). You then use the software to create a store of user files and settings that are saved in a different location from the OS. After the new OS is installed, download and install USMT again to load the user files and settings on the new OS.

Note

USMT version 5 supports *data migration* from Windows 8, 7, and Vista to Windows 8, 7, and Vista, all 32-bit and 64-bits editions.

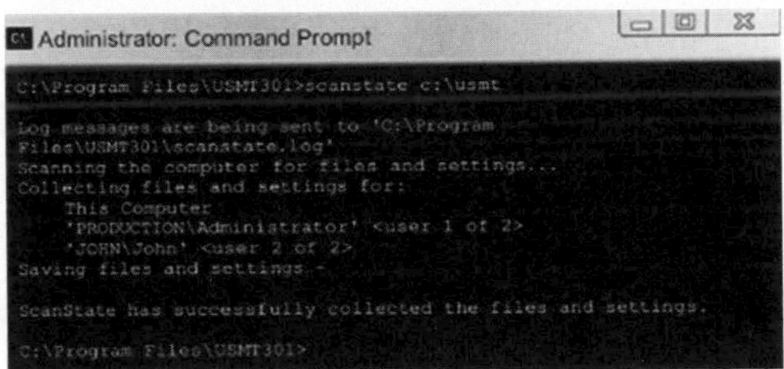

Figure 5-5 Windows User State Migration Tool

Windows Easy Transfer

If a user is switching from an old computer to a new one, use *Windows Easy Transfer* to migrate personal files and settings. You can perform the file transfer using a USB cable, CD, or DVD, a USB flash drive, an external drive, or a network connection.

Use Windows Easy Transfer to transfer information to a computer running Windows 8.1 from computers with one of the following operating systems:

- Windows 8
- Windows 7
- Windows Vista

Windows Easy Transfer cannot back up files on a Windows 8.1 computer for transfer to another computer. To back up and transfer files from a Windows 8.1 computer, manually transfer files using external storage devices.

After running Windows Easy Transfer, you can view a log of the files transferred.

Access to Windows Easy Transfer in Windows 8.1 or Windows 8 is shown below:

At the **Start Screen**, type **"windows easy transfer"** and then select **Windows Easy Transfer** from the search results.

Access to Windows Easy Transfer in Windows 7 or Windows Vista is shown below.

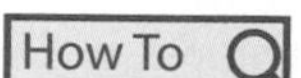

Start > All Programs > Accessories > System Tools > Windows Easy Transfer

---

Lab—Data Migration in Windows (5.1.4.4)

In this lab, you use Windows tools to select files and folders and perform a simulated migration to another Windows installation. Refer to the lab in *IT Essentials v6 Lab Manual*.

Operating System Installation (5.2)

Operating systems have varying system requirements, so be sure your system meets the ones needed for your OS installation choice. A decision needs to be made about the method of installation, such as installation media or over-the-network, and about the type of installation: Will it be a clean install, an upgrade, or even a dual boot? You also must determine where the OS will be stored upon installation. In this section, you learn about the many choices and decisions necessary for a proper OS installation.

Storage Device Setup Procedures (5.2.1)

You can choose to install the operating system to a storage media device that you have selected and prepared on your system. Several types of storage devices are available and can be used to receive the new operating system. The two most common types of data storage devices used today are hard disk drives and flash memory-based drives.

Storage Device Types (5.2.1.1)

As a technician, you might have to perform a clean installation of an OS. Performing a clean install is appropriate in the following situations:

- When a computer is passed from one employee to another
- When the OS is corrupt
- When the primary hard drive is replaced in a computer

The installation and initial booting of the OS is called the *operating system setup*. Although it is possible to install an OS over a network from a server or from a local hard drive, the most common installation method for a home or small business is through external media such as CDs, DVDs, or USB drives. To install an OS from external media, configure the BIOS setup to boot the system from the media. Most modern BIOS should support booting from CD, DVD, or USB.

Note

If the hardware is not supported by the OS, you may need to install third party drivers when performing a clean installation.

Before the operating system can be installed, a storage media device must be chosen and prepared.

Hard Disk Drives

Although hard disk drives (HDDs) are considered old technology, these drives are still common in modern computers and can be used for storing and retrieving data. HDDs contain a number of magnetic, spinning, rigid steel disks and magnetic heads mounted to a mobile arm. The magnetic head is responsible for reading and writing data off the spinning disks.

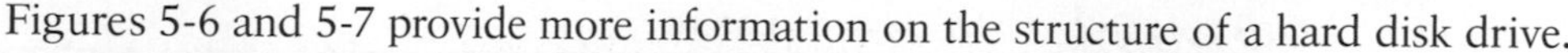

Figures 5-6 and 5-7 provide more information on the structure of a hard disk drive.

Figure 5-6 Structure of a Hard Drive

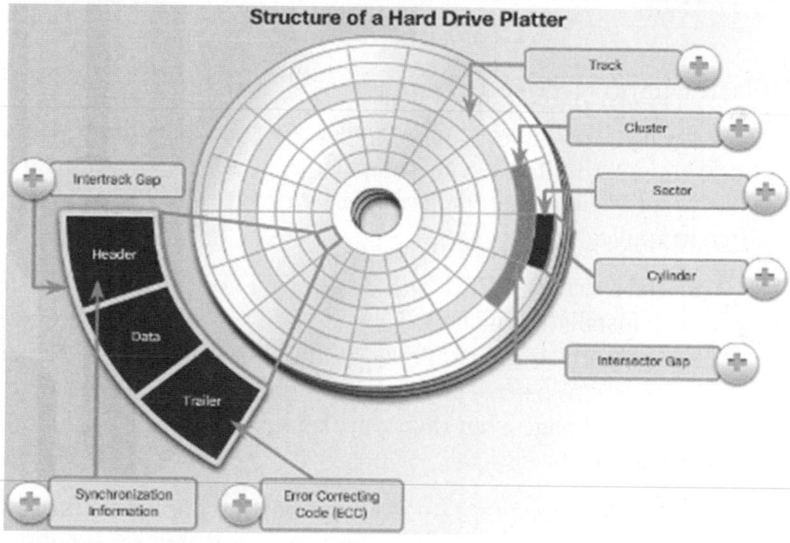

Figure 5-7 Structure of a Hard Drive Platter

Table 5-2 gives more information on structural components of the hard drive.

Table 5-2 Hard Drive Structure

Component	Description
Track	■ One complete circle on one side of the platter where data is written and read. ■ A track is broken into multiple sectors.
Cluster	■ A group of sectors allocated for data storage. ■ The file system allocates clusters for storage because most files are larger than one sector.
Sector	■ A portion of a track that contains synchronization information, data, and error-correcting code (ECC)
Cylinder	■ A track forms a concentric circle around the hard drive platter all corresponding tracks taken together, aligned above and below each other on the platter form cylinders down the platter.

Flash Memory-Based Drives

Flash memory is a type of nonvolatile data storage medium that can be electrically erased and rewritten. It became popular over the last decade as the flash technology evolved and became more reliable. Different types of flash memory are used in different applications:

- **USB flash drives**—USB flash drives are a good solution for storing operating system installation images. They are fast, reliable, resilient and inexpensive. USB flash drives are comprised of flash memory and a small control board to govern data transfer. They are most commonly used to store operating system installation images, but they can also be used to store a full installation of an OS, if space allows.
- *Solid state drives (SSD)*—Another popular application for flash memory is the SSD. An alternative to hard disks, SSDs are disks that employ high-performance flash memory technology to achieve fast data storage without the moving parts of HDDs. SSDs are faster and less prone to physical problems. Due the high-performance type of flash memory used, SSDs tend to be more efficient than USB flash drives and are a great choice for OS hosting.
- *Solid state hybrid disks (SSHDs)*—A popular and less expensive option than SSDs, SSHD devices combine the speed of SSDs with the lower price of HDDs by packing both technologies in the same enclosure. In SSHDs, data is stored in an HDD, but a small flash memory is used to cache frequently used data. This allows for frequently used data to be accessed by the operating system at SSD speeds, whereas other data is transferred at HDD speeds. SSHDs are a good option for storing operating systems.

- *Embedded MultiMediaCard (eMMC)*—Although slower and less expensive than SSD, eMMC is very popular in cell phones, PDAs and digital cameras.

Regardless of the application, flash-memory–based storage devices can be used to store entire installations of operating systems. With different levels of performance, flash-memory–based drives allow for flexibility when designing modern computer hardware.

A few different standards govern the connection between computers. Hot-swapping is a technique used in servers that allows devices such as hard drives to be connected or disconnected without powering down the computer. Although the entire computer hardware and OS must be designed to support this feature, it is very useful in servers because it allows for part replacement without interrupting service.

When the storage device type has been chosen, it must be prepared to receive the new operating system. Modern operating systems ship with an *installer* program. Installers usually prepare the disk to receive the operating system, but it is crucial for a technician to understand the terms and methods involved in this preparation.

Hard Drive Partitioning (5.2.1.2)

A hard drive is divided into areas called *partitions*. Each partition is a logical storage unit that can be formatted to store information, such as data files or applications. If you imagine a hard drive as a wooden cabinet, the partitions would be the shelves. During the installation process, most operating systems automatically partition and format available hard drive space.

Partitioning a drive is a simple a process, but to ensure a successful boot, the firmware must know what disk and partition on that disk has an operating system installed.

BIOS (basic input/output system) and UEFI (Unified Extensible Firmware Interface) are two types of firmware used in personal computers; BIOS is a legacy technology whereas UEFI is the modern replacement. UEFI addresses many of the shortcomings of BIOS. UEFI firmware performs the same functions as BIOS and more. As of 2015, modern personal computer motherboards ship with UEFI only.

When a computer is powered on, it executes the firmware program. The firmware first runs a number of tests to ensure that important computer components, such as video card and RAM memory, are present and functional. After the tests are completed and all crucial components are present and working properly, the firmware proceeds to locate and load the operating system from the disk into the RAM for execution.

Note

Differences between BIOS and UEFI during the self-test phase is beyond the scope of this course.

To find an operating system in a BIOS-based firmware, the BIOS checks the very beginning of the first installed disk. This area is called the boot sector and is specifically designed to allow the BIOS to find information about the partitions and the location of an operating system. What BIOS is looking for in the boot sector is a small program called the *boot loader*. The boot loader is the program that knows where on the disk the operating system is and how to start it. Notice that BIOS-based firmware has no information about partitions or the operating system itself; BIOS simply tries to find a valid boot loader at the beginning of the first disk and run it.

UEFI firmware is much smarter than BIOS. UEFI knows about all of the installed disks and installed operating systems. Designed as a standard by Intel and maintained by a number of companies, including Intel, Microsoft, Apple and AMD, UEFI is able to understand simple partitions and to execute boot loader code from them. This may seem like an insignificant feature, at first, but it makes the boot process much more reliable than in BIOS. Another key UEFI improvement over BIOS is the fact that the UEFI knows what operating systems are installed and their location on the disk. With UEFI, operating systems can add themselves to UEFI's boot list.

As mentioned before, an operating system is stored in a disk partition and a disk with multiple partitions can store multiple operating systems. The partition scheme has direct influence in the location of the operating systems on a disk. Finding and launching the operating system is one of the responsibilities of a computer firmware. The partition scheme is very important to the firmware. Two of the most popular partition scheme standards are MBR and GPT.

Master Boot Record

Publicly introduced in 1983, the *master boot record (MBR)* contains information on how the hard drive partitions are organized. The MBR is 512 bytes long and contains the boot loader, an executable program that allows a user to choose from multiple operating systems. MBR has become the *de facto* standard, but it has limitations that have to be addressed. MBR is commonly used in computers with BIOS-based firmware.

GUID Partition Table

Also designed as a partition table scheme standard for hard drives, the *globally unique identifier (GUID) partition table (GPT)* makes use of a number of modern techniques to expand on the older MBR partitioning scheme. GPT is commonly used in computers with UEFI firmware. Most modern operating systems now support GPT.

Table 5-3 shows a comparison between MBR and GPT.

Table 5-3 MBR and GPT Comparison

MBR	GPT
Maximum of 4 primary partitions	Maximum of 128 partitions in Windows
Maximum partition size of 2TB	Maximum partition size of 9.4ZB (9.4×10^{21} bytes)
Partition and boot data stored in one place	Partition and boot data stored in multiple locations across the disk
Any computer can boot from MBR	Computer must be UEFI-based and run a 64-bit OS

A technician should understand the process and terms relating to hard drive setup:

- *Primary partition*—The primary partition contains the operating system files and is usually the first partition. A primary partition cannot be subdivided into smaller sections. On a GPT partitioned disk, all partitions are primary partitions. On an MBR partitioned disk, there can be a maximum of four partitions.
- *Active partition*—In MBR disks, the active partition is the partition used to store and boot an operating system. Notice that only primary partitions can be marked active in MBR disks. Another limitation is that only one primary partition per disk can be marked active at one time. In most cases, the C: drive is the active partition and contains the boot and system files. Some users create additional partitions to organize files or to be able to dual-boot the computer. Active partitions are only found on drives with MBR partition tables.
- *Extended partition*—If more than 4 partitions are required on an MBR partitioned disk, one of the primary partitions can be designated an extended partition. After the extended partition is created, up to 23 logical drives (or logical partitions) can be created within this extended partition. A common setup is to create a primary partition for the OS (drive C:) and to allow an extended partition to occupy the remaining free space on a hard drive, right after a primary partition. Any extra partitions can be created within the extended partition (drives D:, E:, and so on). Although the logical drives can't be used to boot an OS, they are perfect for storing user data. Notice that there can be only one extended partition per MBR hard drive and that extended partitions are only found on drives with MBR partition tables.
- *Logical drive*—A logical drive is a section of an extended partition. It can be used to separate information for administrative purposes. Because GPT partitioned drives cannot have an extended partition, they do not have logical drives.
- *Basic disk*—A basic disk (the default) contains partitions such as primary and extended as well as logical drives, which are formatted for data storage. More space can be added to a partition by extending it into adjacent, unallocated

space, as long as it is contiguous. Either MBR or GPT can be used as the underlying partition scheme of basic disks.

- *Dynamic disk*—Dynamic disks provide features not supported by basic disks. A dynamic disk has the ability to create volumes that span across more than one disk. The size of the partitions can be changed after they have been set, even if the unallocated space is noncontiguous. Free space can be added from the same disk or a different disk, allowing a user to efficiently store large files. After a partition has been extended, it cannot be shrunk without deleting the entire partition. Either MBR or GPT can be used as the partition scheme of dynamic disks.
- *Formatting*—This process creates a file system in a partition for files to be stored.

Activity 5.2.1.3: Identify Disk Terminology

Go to the online course to perform this practice activity.

File Systems (5.2.1.4)

A new installation of an OS proceeds as if the disk were brand new. No information that is currently on the target partition is preserved. The first phase of the installation process partitions and formats the hard drive. This process prepares the disk to accept the new file system. The *file system* provides the directory structure that organizes the user's operating system, application, configuration, and data files. There are many different kinds of file systems, and each one has different structure and logic. Different file systems also differ in properties of speed, flexibility, security, size, and more. Here are five common file systems:

- *File Allocation Table, 32 bit (FAT32)*—Supports partition sizes up to 2TB or 2048GB. The FAT32 file system is used by Windows XP and earlier OS versions.
- *New Technology File System (NTFS)*—Supports partition sizes up to 16 exabytes, in theory. NTFS incorporates file system security features and extended attributes. Windows 8.1, Windows 7, and Windows Vista automatically create a partition using the entire hard drive. If a user does not create custom partitions by selecting a drive letter with "Unallocated Space" and clicking the "**New**" option, the system formats the entire available space as the partition and begins installing Windows. If users choose to create more than one partition, they will be able to determine the size of the partition.
- *exFAT (FAT 64)*—Created to address some of the limitations of FAT, FAT32, and NTFS when formatting USB flash drives, such as file size and directory size. One of the primary advantages of exFAT is that it can support files larger than 4GB.

- *Compact Disc File System (CDFS)*—Created specifically for optical disk media.
- *NFS (Network File System)*—NFS is a network-based file system that allows file access over the network. From the user's standpoint, there is no difference between accessing a file stored locally or on another computer on the network. NFS is an open standard which allows anyone to implement it.

Quick Format versus Full Format

The *quick format* removes files from the partition, but does not scan the disk for bad sectors. Scanning a disk for bad sectors can prevent data loss in the future. For this reason, do not use the quick format for disks that have been previously formatted. Although it is possible to quick format a partition or a disk after the OS is installed, the quick format option is not available when installing Windows 8.1, Windows 7, or Windows Vista.

The *full format* removes files from the partition while scanning the disk for bad sectors. It is required for all new hard drives. The full format option takes more time to complete.

Video

Video—Disk Management (5.2.1.5)

This video explores basic and dynamic disks. A drive used for OS installation in a Windows installation must be designated as a basic disk, limited to four partitions, and the partition must be primary and marked active. Windows must be installed on a basic disk, which can later be converted to a dynamic disk. A dynamic disk has the ability to create volumes instead of partitions that can span across more than one disk.

It also covers the different types of partitions and partition tables. The OS is installed on an active, primary partition and is ordinarily marked as the C: drive, which contains the boot and system files. These files are either the MBR or GPT files discussed earlier in the chapter. Extended partitions are the other type of partition that can be created. There can only be one extended partition per hard drive, which can be subdivided into smaller sections called logical drives.

Different file systems are also discussed. A file system is what a computer uses to organize data on storage devices. There are many different file systems, which each have different ways of organizing the data. Each OS has its own file system it supports, and each partition is formatted with a file system. NTFS, the most commonly used file system for current Windows operating systems, is more advanced than its predecessor, FAT32, with greater security features, more stability, and larger volume size. Two other file systems, exFAT or FAT64, which is used with USB flash drives, and CDFS, which is used for optical disks, are also introduced in the video.

Please view the video in the Cisco Networking Academy IT Essentials 6.0 online course.

OS Installation with Default Settings (5.2.1.6)

The installation process for Windows OS is similar across Windows 8.x, 7, and Vista. The process is described in detail below using Windows 8.1 as an example.

Windows 8.1

When a computer boots with the Windows 8.1 installation disc (or USB flash drive), the installation wizard presents two options:

- **Install Now**—Allows the users to install Windows 8.1.
- **Repair your computer**—Opens the Recovery Environment to repair an installation. Select the Windows 8.1 installation that needs repair and click Next. Select from a number of recovery tools, such as Startup Repair. Startup Repair locates and repairs problems with the OS files. If Startup Repair does not solve the problem, additional options, such as System Restore or System Image Recovery, are available.

Note

Before performing a repair installation, back up important files to a different physical location, such as a second hard drive, optical disc, or USB storage device.

If you select the **Install now** option, two other options are available:

- **Upgrade**—Install Windows and keep files, settings, and applications; upgrades Windows but keeps your current files, settings, and programs. Use this option to repair an installation.
- **Custom**—Install Windows only (advanced)—Installs a new copy of Windows in your choice of location and allows you to change disks and partitions.

If existing Windows installations are not found, the Upgrade option is disabled.

Note

When only upgrading the Windows OS, the previous Windows folder is retained, along with the Documents and Settings and Program Files folders. During the Windows 8.1 installation, these folders are moved to a folder named Windows.old. You can copy files from the previous installation to the new installation.

The installer copies the files and reboots a few times before presenting the Personalization screen. To simplify the process, Windows 8.1 automatically partitions and formats the drive if no partitions are found. The installation also erases any data previously stored in the drive. If partitions exist in the drive, the installer displays them and allows for partition scheme customization.

In the Personalization screen, the installer asks for a name for the computer and allows the user to select a color to be used as the basis for a theme.

The installer now attempts to connect to the network. If a network card (NIC) is present and a cable is connected, the installer will request a network address. If a wireless card is installed, the installer will list the wireless networks in range and prompt the user to pick one and to provide the password for it, if needed. If no network is available at this point, the network configuration is skipped, but this can be done later after the system is installed.

The installer presents a list of the express settings. These are the values recommended by the installer after a computer scan. Click **Use express settings** to accept and use the default settings. Alternatively, it is possible to change the default settings by clicking **Customize.**

The installer prompts for an email address for signing into a Microsoft account. Although optional, this grants access to the Windows Online Store. Enter an email address and click **Next.** To skip the account linkage and create a local user account, click **Sign In without a Microsoft account.**

The installer displays the screen to allow the creation of a local account, if no Microsoft account was created. The installer allows the user to create a Microsoft account or to use a local account. If a local user account is created, the next screen shows the request for information of a local user account.

Windows finishes the process and displays the Start Screen, as shown in Figure 5-8. When the Windows 8.1 Start Screen is presented, the installation is complete, and the computer is ready for use.

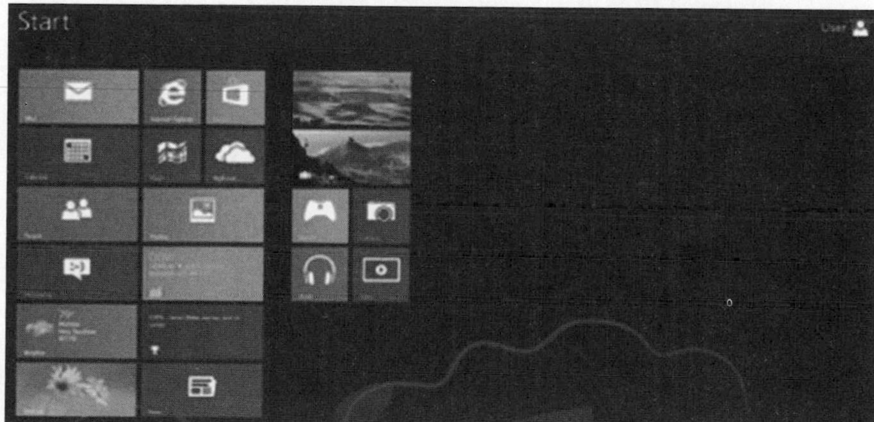

Figure 5-8 Windows 8.1 Start Screen

Depending on the current location of the computer and version of the OS, you are prompted to select a method for organizing computers and sharing resources on a network. As described in the list below, Workgroup, Homegroup, and Domain are the different ways for organizing the computers in a network.

- *Workgroup*—All the computers in the same workgroup are allowed to share files and resources over a local area network. The sharing settings are used to share specific resources on the network.
- *Homegroup*—Homegroup is a new feature that started in Windows 7 that allows computers on the same network to automatically share files and printers.
- *Domain*—A computer on a domain is governed by a central administrator and must follow the rules and procedures set by the administrator. A domain provides users with the ability to share files and devices.

Lab—Install Windows (5.2.1.7)

In this lab, you install the Windows operating system. Refer to the lab in *IT Essentials v6 Lab Manual.*

Account Creation (5.2.1.8)

When users attempt to log in to a device or to access system resources, Windows uses the process of authentication to verify the identity of the users. *Authentication* occurs when users enter a username and password to access a user account. Windows OSs use *single-sign on (SSO) authentication*, which allows users to log in once to access all system features versus requiring them to log in each time they need to access an individual resource.

User accounts allow multiple users to share a single computer using their own files and settings. Windows 8.1, Windows 7, and Windows Vista have three types of user accounts: Administrator, Standard, and Guest. Each account type provides a user with a different level of control over system resources.

In Windows 8.1, the account created during the installation process has administrator privileges. A user with administrator privileges can make changes that impact all users of the computer, such as altering security settings or installing software for all users. Accounts with administrator privileges should be used only to manage a computer and not for regular use, because drastic changes that affect everyone can be made when using the administrator account. Attackers also seek out an administrator account because it is so powerful. For this reason, it is recommended that a standard user account is created for regular use.

Standard user accounts can be created at any time by the administrator. A standard user account can use most of the capability of a computer; however, the user cannot make changes that affect other users or the security of the computer. For example, a standard user cannot install a printer.

Individuals without a user account on the computer can use a guest account. A guest account has limited permissions and must be turned on by an administrator. The Manage Accounts control panel app is used to manage user accounts. The Control Panel is a Windows location that contains many tools for manipulating windows configurations and settings. There are many ways to access the Control Panel in each version of Windows.

To access the Control Panel in Windows 7 and Vista, click the **Start** button located on the left side of the taskbar at the bottom of the desktop. This displays the Start menu. Click **Control Panel** in the Start menu. You can also click the **Start** button and type **control** in the **Search programs and files** box and press **Enter**.

The Windows 8 interface is very different from Windows 7 and Vista. To access the Control Panel from the desktop in Windows 8, place the cursor in the upper-right corner of the desktop and wait for the charms to appear. Click the **Search** charm and type control in the Search box and press **Enter**. On a touchscreen, you can also swipe your finger in from the right side of the screen to display the charms.

Windows 8 does not come with a Start menu by default. Windows 8 uses a Start screen instead. To access the Start screen, first access the charms and click the **Start** icon. To access the Control Panel from the Start screen, type **control** and press **Enter**. You can also access the Start screen in Windows 8.1 by clicking the **Start** button located on the left side of the taskbar at the bottom of the desktop.

The Control Panel can be viewed in different ways, depending on the version of Windows you are using. Throughout this course, paths to the Control Panel tools will assume that the view is set to large or small icons. This can be set by choosing **Large icons** or **Small icons** in the **View by:** drop-down menu in the Control Panel. In Windows Vista, icons can be viewed by clicking **Classic View** in the Control Panel.

Throughout this course, paths to Control Panel tools begin with **Control Panel.**

To manage a user account in Windows 8.1 and Windows 8, use the following path:

Control Panel > User Accounts > Manage Accounts

To create or remove a user account in Windows 7 and Windows Vista, use the following path:

Start > Control Panel > User Accounts > Add or remove user accounts

The Figure 5-9 shows the Windows 8.1 account management window.

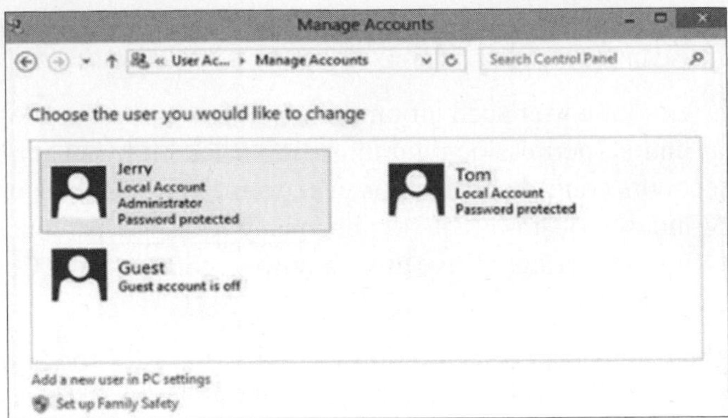

Figure 5-9 Windows 8.1 Managing Local Accounts

Finalize the Installation (5.2.1.9)

After the Windows operating system installation is complete it is important be sure the software is up to date and that all the hardware is operational.

Windows Update

To update the OS after the initial installation, *Microsoft Windows Update* is used to scan for new software and install service packs and patches.

To install patches and service packs in Windows 8 or Windows 8.1, use the following path:

Control Panel > Windows Update

To install patches and service packs in Windows 7 or Windows Vista, use the following path:

Start > All Programs > Windows Update

Figure 5-10 shows Windows Update for Windows 8.1 and Windows 8.

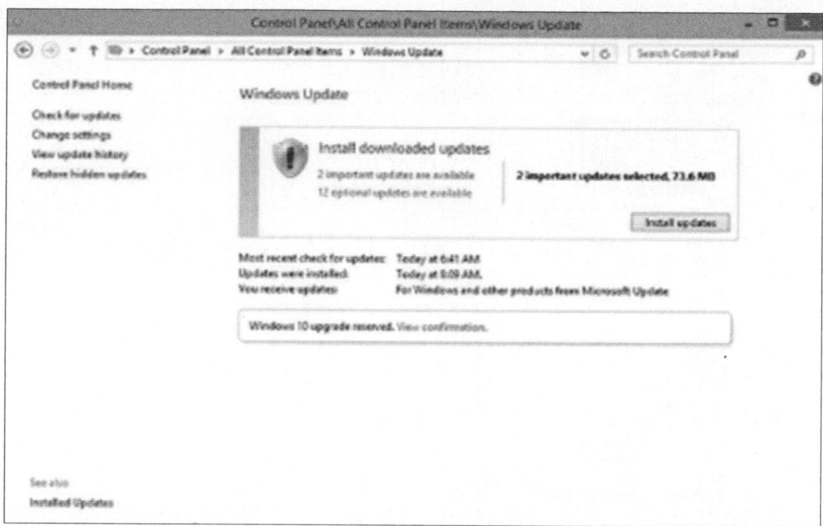

Figure 5-10 Windows 8.1 Windows Update

Device Manager

After installation, verify that all hardware is installed correctly. The Device Manager is used to locate device problems and install the correct or updated drivers in Windows Vista, Windows 7, and Windows 8.x.

In Windows 8 or Windows 8.1, use the following path:

Control Panel > Device Manager

Figure 5-11 shows Device Manager for Windows 8.1 and Windows 8.

In Windows 7 and Windows Vista, use the following path:

Start > Control Panel > Device Manager

A yellow triangle with an exclamation point indicates a problem with a device. To view a description of the problem, right-click the device and select **Properties**. A gray circle with a downward-pointing arrow indicates that a device is disabled. To enable the device, right-click the device and select **Enable**. To expand a device category, click the right-pointing triangle next to the category.

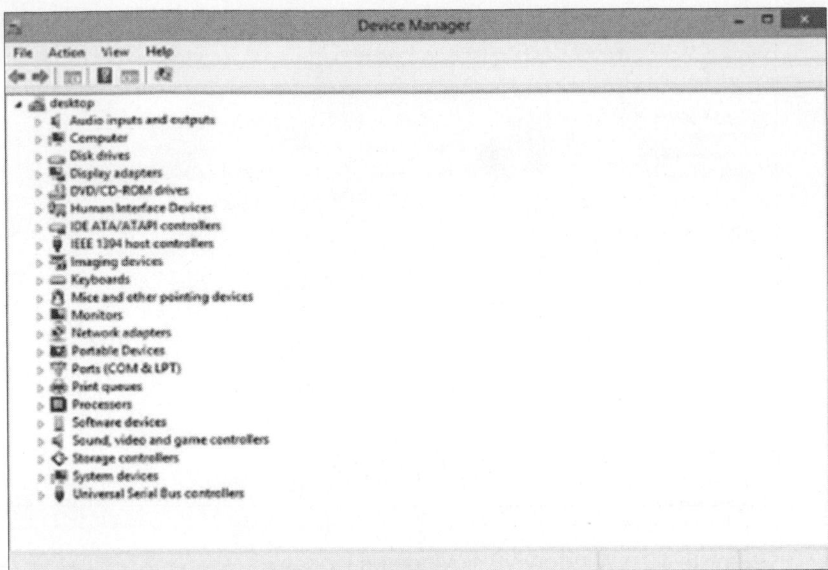

Figure 5-11 Windows 8.x Device Manager

Lab—Check for Updates in Windows (5.2.1.10)

In this lab, you configure the operating system so you can select which updates are installed and then change the settings so updates are downloaded and installed automatically. Refer to the lab in *IT Essentials v6 Lab Manual*.

Custom Installation Options (5.2.2)

A custom install can save time and money when having to deploy multiple systems with new operating system installations. Using a system image for installation can also be useful if you need to recover a system that has stopped working properly. As discussed in this section, one custom installation option is ***disk cloning***, which is copying the contents of an entire hard drive to another hard drive, thereby decreasing the time it takes to install drivers, applications, updates, and so forth on the second drive.

Disk Cloning (5.2.2.1)

Installing an OS on a single computer takes time. Imagine the time it would take to install operating systems on multiple computers, one at a time. To simplify this activity, administrators usually elect a computer to act as base system and go through the regular operating system installation process. After the operating is installed in the base computer, a specific program is used to copy all the information in its disk, sector by sector, to another disk. This new disk, usually an external device, now contains a fully deployed operating system and can be used to quickly deploy a fresh installed copy of the base operating system. Because the target disk now contains a sector-to-sector mapping of the original disk, the contents of the target disk is an image of the original disk. This is an *image-based* installation.

If an undesirable setting is accidentally included during the base installation, an administrator can use *Microsoft's System Preparation (Sysprep)* tool to remove it before creating the final image. Sysprep can be used to install and configure the same OS on multiple computers. Sysprep prepares the OS with different hardware configurations. With Sysprep, technicians can quickly install the OS, complete the last configuration steps, and install applications.

Figure 5-12 shows Sysprep in Windows 8.1 and Windows 8.

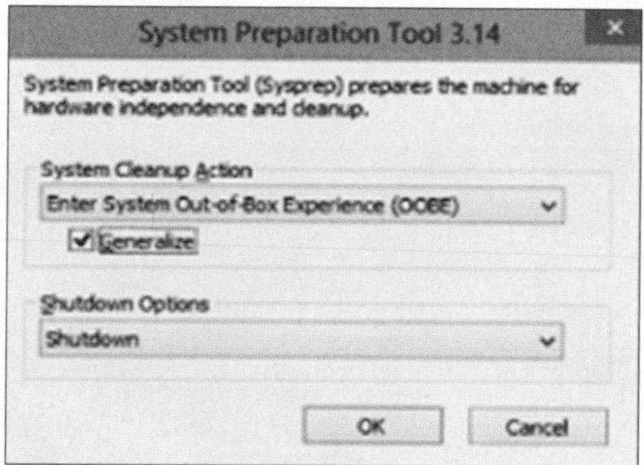

Figure 5-12 Disk Cloning

Other Installation Methods (5.2.2.2)

A standard installation of Windows is sufficient for most computers used in a home or small office environment, but there are cases when a custom installation process is required.

Take, for example, an IT support department; technicians in these environments must install hundreds of Windows systems. Performing this many installations in the standard way is not feasible.

A standard installation is done via the installation media (DVD or USB drive) provided by Microsoft and is an interactive process; the installer prompts the user for settings such as time zone and system language.

A custom installation of Windows can save time and provide a consistent configuration across computers within a large organization. A popular technique to install Windows across many computers is to perform an installation on one computer and use it as a reference installation. When the installation is completed, an image is created. An *image* is a file that contains all the data from a partition.

When the image is ready, technicians can perform a much shorter installation by simply replicating and deploying the image to all computers in the organization. If the new installation requires any adjustments, those can be done quickly after the image is deployed.

An image of a system is created based on the following steps:

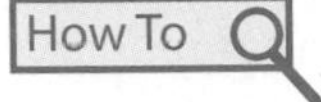

Step 1. Perform a full Windows installation on a computer. This computer must be as similar as possible to the computers that will later receive the installation to avoid driver incompatibility issues.

Step 2. Using a software tool such as imageX, create an image of the installation. The Figure 5-13 shows the **imageX** command line tool.

Step 3. The result should be one large image file containing a copy of the entire OS installation currently present on the reference system.

```
Administrator: C:\Windows\system32\cmd.exe
C:\Users>
C:\Users>
C:\Users>
C:\Users>imageX

ImageX Tool for Windows
Copyright (C) Microsoft Corp. All rights reserved.

IMAGEX [Flags] /Operation [Parameter List]

  Operation [ APPEND  | APPLY    | CAPTURE | DELETE |
              DIR     | EXPORT   | INFO    | SPLIT  |
              MOUNT   | MOUNTRW  | UNMOUNT ]

For help on a specific operation type:
  IMAGEX /Operation /?

Examples:
  IMAGEX /APPEND /?
  IMAGEX /APPLY /?
  IMAGEX /CAPTURE /?
  IMAGEX /DELETE /?
  IMAGEX /DIR /?
  IMAGEX /EXPORT /?
  IMAGEX /INFO /?
  IMAGEX /SPLIT /?
  IMAGEX /MOUNT /?
  IMAGEX /MOUNTRW /?
  IMAGEX /UNMOUNT /?

C:\Users>
```

Figure 5-13 ImageX Command-line Tool

In Windows Vista and prior, the standard installation was done based on individual files contained in the installation DVD. Today, when installing Windows 7 or 8.x, the installation process is based on an image file as it applies an image to the hard disk from the installation DVD—install.wim.

Windows has several different types of custom installations:

- **Network Installation**—This includes Preboot Execution Environment (PXE) Installation, Unattended Installation, and Remote Installation.
- **Image-based Internal Partition Installation**—This includes the pointer files to the compressed image, plus free space for any new files created by the end user, including registry files, page files, hibernation files, user data, and user-installed apps and updates.

- **Other Types of Custom Installations**—This includes Windows Advanced Startup Options, Refresh Your PC (Windows 8.x only), System Restore, Upgrade, Repair Installation, Remote Network Installation, Recovery Partition, and Refresh/restore.

Network Installation (5.2.2.3)

Network installations can reduce the costs incurred and time needed to install the operating system (OS) when physically visiting each client computer. This section explains how to install an OS throughout an enterprise network without having to physically attend to each client computer.

Remote Network Installation

A popular method for OS installation in environments with many computers is a *remote network installation*. With this method, the operating system installation files are stored on a server so that a client computer can access the files remotely to begin the installation. A software package such as *Remote Installation Services (RIS)* is used to communicate with the client, store the setup files, and provide the necessary instructions for the client to access the setup files, download them, and begin the operation system installation.

Because the client computer does not have an operating system installed, a special environment must be used to boot the computer, connect to the network, and communicate with the server to begin the installation process. This special environment is known as the *preboot execution environment (PXE)*. For the PXE to work, the NIC must be PXE-enabled. This functionality may come from the BIOS or the firmware on the NIC. When the computer is started, the NIC listens for special instructions on the network to start PXE. As shown in Figure 5-14, this is the first screen displayed during the PXE Windows installation boot. The installation options shown are installation files that were created on a Windows-based server as PXE images and then placed in a TFTP folder. PXE clients can locate and fetch files over TFTP.

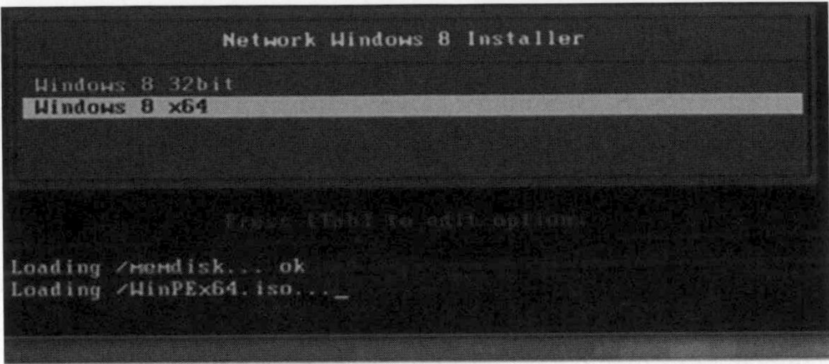

The image shows the first screen displayed during a PXE Windows installation boot. The installations displayed were created on a Windows-based server as PXE images and placed on a TFTP folder. PXE clients can locate and fetch files over TFTP.

Figure 5-14 Windows PXE Installation

Note

If the NIC is not PXE-enabled, third-party software may be used to load PXE from storage media.

Unattended Installation

Unattended installation, another network-based installation, allows a Windows system to be installed or upgraded with little user intervention. The Windows unattended installation is based on an *answer file*. This file contains simple text that instructs Windows Setup how to configure and install the OS.

To perform a Windows Unattended installation, setup.exe must be run with the user options found in the answer file. The installation process begins as usual but instead of prompting the user, Setup uses the answers listed in the answer file.

To customize a standard Windows 7 and 8.x or Windows Vista installation, the System Image Manager (SIM) is used to create the setup answer file. You can also add packages, such as applications or drivers, to answer files.

Figure 5-15 shows an example of an answer file. After all questions have been answered, the file is copied to the distribution shared folder on a server. At this point, you can do one of two things:

- Run the unattended.bat file on the client machine to prepare the hard drive and install the OS from the server over the network.
- Create a boot disk that boots the computer and connects to the distribution shared folder on the server. You then run the batch file containing a set of instructions to install the OS over the network.

Note

Windows SIM is part of the Windows Automated Installation Kit (AIK) and can be downloaded from the Microsoft website.

```
[Data]
  AutoPartition=0
  MsDosInitiated="0"
  UnattendedInstall="Yes"
  UseBIOSToBoot=1
[Unattended]
  UnattendMode=FullUnattended
  OemSkipEula=Yes
  OemPreinstall=No
  ExtendOemPartition=0
  TargetPath=*
  Repartition=No
[GuiUnattended]
  AdminPassword=*
  AutoLogon=Yes
  OEMSkipWelcome=1
  TimeZone=20
[UserData]
  ComputerName=OEMComputerName
  FullName="Windows Storage Server 2003"
  OrgName="OEM Name"
  ProductID="XXXXX-XXXXX-XXXXX-XXXXX-XXXXX"
```

Figure 5-15 Windows Unattended Installation

Restore, Refresh, and Recover (5.2.2.4)

This section explores tools that are used to recover systems to previous working states or factory default resets.

System Restore

This tool restores the computer to an earlier restore point. Because System Restore can be accessed from within Windows or at boot time, this tool can help fix a damaged system to boot up again.

Refresh Your PC (Windows 8.x Only)

This tool restores the computer's system software back to its factory state without deleting user files or removing modern apps. Computers tend to become slower as time passes. This is due to normal usage of the file systems, which can become full of fragmented files, orphan drivers, and libraries. This tool brings the system back to its factory state without much impact on user data. Refresh Your **PC (Windows 8.x Only)** will remove any installed desktop apps.

Recovery Partition

Some computers that have Windows installed contain a section of the disk that is inaccessible to the user. This partition, called a *recovery partition*, contains an image that can be used to restore the computer to its original configuration.

The recovery partition is often hidden to prevent it from being used for anything other than restoration. To restore the computer using the recovery partition, you must use a special key or key combination when the computer is starting. Sometimes, the option to restore from the factory recovery partition is located in the BIOS. Contact the computer manufacturer to find out how to access the partition and restore the original configuration of the computer.

Note

If the operating system has been damaged because of a faulty hard drive, the recovery partition may also be corrupt and unable to recover the operating system.

System Recovery Options (5.2.2.5)

When a system failure occurs, users can employ the following recovery tools:

- Windows Advanced Startup Options (Windows 8.x)
- System Recovery Options (Windows 7 and Windows Vista)
- Factory Recovery Partition

Windows 8.x Advanced Startup Options

Advanced Startup Options are a Windows 8.x set of tools that allow users to troubleshoot, recover, or restore an operating system when it cannot boot. Advanced Options are part of the *Windows Recovery Environment (WinRE)*. WinRE is a recovery platform based on the Windows Preinstallation Environment (PE).

To access Advanced Startup Options:

How To

Press F8 during boot to interrupt it. From the Choose an Option window, select **Troubleshoot**. From the Troubleshoot window, choose **Advanced Options**.

The Advanced Options window has the following tools:

- *System Restore*—This tool restores a computer to an earlier restore point. This is the same as using System Restore within Windows.
- *System Image Recovery*—This tool restores the computer using a system image file.

- *Automatic Repair*—This tool scans the system and tries to automatically repair issues that can prevent Windows from booting properly.
- *Command Prompt*—This tool opens a Recovery Environment Command Prompt, which grants access to a number of command line troubleshooting tools.
- *UEFI Firmware Settings*—This tool is shown only if the computer supports UEFI. Use this tool to change the computer's UEFI settings.
- *Windows Startup Settings*—The Startup Settings option allows you to enable Safe Mode. You can also disable automatic restart after failure and enable the error message shown on blue screen.

Windows 7 and Windows Vista

Similar to Windows 8.x Advanced Options, System Recovery Options are a set of troubleshooting tools for Windows 7 and Windows Vista. The System Recovery Options are also part of the Windows 7 Recovery Environment.

As in Windows 8.x, in Windows 7 and Windows Vista, Windows Recovery Environment can be accessed by pressing and holding the **F8** key when starting a computer. When the Advanced Boot Options screen appears, highlight **Repair your computer** and press **Enter** to access the System Recovery Options. You can then use system recovery tools to repair errors that prevent system startup. The following tools are available in the System Recovery Options menu:

- *Startup Repair*—This tool scans the hard drive for problems and automatically fixes missing or corrupt system files that prevent Windows from starting.
- *System Restore*—This tool uses restore points to restore Windows system files to an earlier point in time.
- *System Image Recovery*—This tool restores a previously created image to disk.
- *Windows Memory Diagnostic*—This tool examines computer memory to detect malfunctions and diagnose problems.
- *Command Prompt*—This tool opens a command prompt window where the bootrec.exe tool can be used to repair and troubleshoot startup issues for Windows.

When using a recovery disc, make sure that it uses the same architecture as the OS being recovered. For example, if the computer is running a 64-bit version of Windows 7, the recovery disc must use a 64-bit architecture.

Packet Tracer Activity

Activity 5.2.2.6: Identify OS Installation Terminology

Go to the online course to perform this practice activity.

Boot Sequence and Registry Files (5.2.3)

The boot process has two modes that determine the sequence of boot activities, user mode and kernel mode. In this section, you learn about the major programs that control the sequence of a normal boot process in Windows. You also learn about the Windows Registry files, which are a database containing all the information needed for a computer to run both the hardware and software installed on a Windows computer. Understanding the boot sequence and Registry is essential to a computer technician for troubleshooting and maintaining PCs.

Windows Boot Process (5.2.3.1)

Understanding the boot process in Windows can help a technician troubleshoot boot problems.

Windows Boot Process

To begin the boot process, turn on the computer. This is called a *cold boot*. When the computer is powered on, it performs a power-on self-test (POST). Because the video adapter has not yet been initialized, errors that occur at this point in the boot process are reported by a series of audible tones, called *beep codes*.

After POST, the BIOS locates and reads the configuration settings that are stored in the CMOS memory. The boot device priority, as shown in Figure 5-16, is the order in which devices are checked to locate the bootable partition. The boot device priority is set in the BIOS and can be arranged in any order. The BIOS boots the computer using the first drive that contains a valid boot sector.

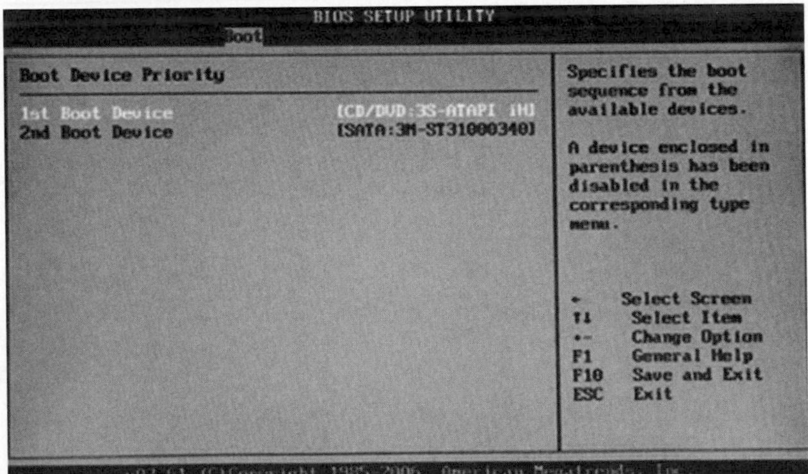

Figure 5-16 Boot Device Priority

Hard drives, network drives, USB drives, and even removable media can be used in the boot order, depending on the capabilities of the motherboard. Some BIOS also have a boot device priority menu that is accessed with a special key during computer startup. You can use this menu to select the device to boot.

Windows Boot Loader and Windows Boot Manager

At this point, the code in the boot sector is executed, and the control of the boot process is given to *Windows Boot Manager (BOOTMGR)*. BOOTMGR controls several startup steps:

1. *WinLoad (WINLOAD.EXE)* uses the path specified in BOOTMGR to find the boot partition.
2. WinLoad loads two files that make up the core of Windows: NTOSKRNL.EXE and HAL.DLL.
3. WinLoad reads the Registry files, chooses a hardware profile, and loads the device drivers.

Windows Kernel

At this point, the Windows kernel takes over the process. The name of this file is *NTOSKRNL.EXE*. It starts the login file called WINLOGON.EXE and displays the Windows Welcome screen.

Identify the BIOS Boot Process Order (5.2.3.2)

Please refer to the Activities in the Cisco Networking Academy IT Essentials 6.0 online course.

Startup Modes (5.2.3.3)

Windows can start in one of many different modes which can be selected using Advanced Boot Options menu. The Advanced Boot Options menu lets you start Windows in advanced troubleshooting modes.

Startup Modes

Some problems will prevent Windows from starting up. To troubleshoot and fix this kind of problem, use one of the many Windows Startup Modes.

Pressing the F8 key during the boot process opens the Windows Advanced Boot Options menu, as shown in Figure 5-17. This allows users to select how they wish to boot Windows. These are four commonly used startup options:

- *Safe Mode*—A diagnostic mode used to troubleshoot Windows and Windows startup issues. Functionality is limited as many device drivers are not loaded.
- *Safe Mode with Networking*—Starts Windows in Safe Mode with networking support.
- *Safe Mode with Command Prompt*—Starts Windows and loads the command prompt instead of the GUI.
- *Last Known Good Configuration*—Loads the configuration settings that were used the last time that Windows started successfully. It does this by accessing a copy of the Registry that is created for this purpose.

Note

Last Known Good Configuration is not useful unless it is applied immediately after a failure occurs. If the machine is restarted and manages to open Windows, the Registry is updated with the faulty information.

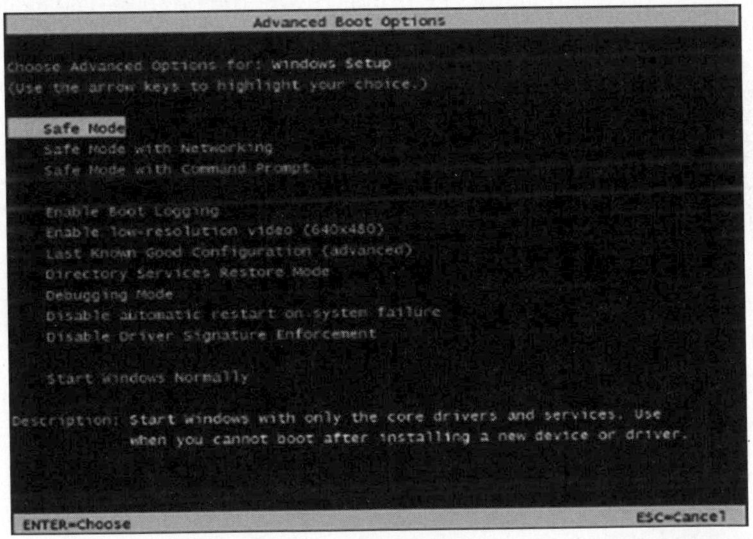

Figure 5-17 Advanced Boot Options

Windows Registry (5.2.3.4)

The *Windows Registry keys* are an important part of the Windows boot process. These keys are recognized by their distinctive names, which begin with HKEY_, as shown in Table 5-4. The words and letters that follow HKEY_ represent the portion of the OS controlled by that key. Every setting in Windows, from the background of the desktop and the color of the screen buttons to the licensing of applications, is stored in the Registry. When a user makes changes to the Control Panel settings, file associations, system policies, or installed software, the changes are stored in the Registry.

Table 5-4 Registry Keys

HKEY	Description
HKEY_CLASSES_ROOT	Information about which file extensions map to a particular application
HKEY_CURRENT_USER	Information, such as desktop settings and history, related to the current user of a PC
HKEY_USERS	Information about all users who have logged into a system
HKEY_LOCAL_MACHINE	Information relating to the hardware and software
HKEY_CURRENT_CONFIG	Information relating to all active devices on a system

Each user account has a unique section of the Registry. The Windows login process loads system settings from the Registry to reconfigure the system for each individual user account.

The Registry is also responsible for recording the location of *Dynamic Link Library (DLL) files*. A DLL file consists of program code that can be used by different programs to perform common functions. DLL files are very important to the functionality of an operating system and any applications that users may install.

To ensure that a DLL can be located by the operating system or a program, it must be registered. It is typically registered automatically during the installation process. A user may need to manually register a DLL file when a problem is encountered. Registering a DLL maps the path to the file, making it easier for programs to locate necessary files.

To register a DLL file in Windows 8.0 and 8.1 using the command-line tool, use the following path:

How To

Move the mouse to the upper right corner of the screen > The Charms Bar displays > Search and Type **Command** > click the **Command Prompt** > type **regsvr32**filename .dll

To register a DLL file in Windows 7 and Vista using the command-line tool, use the following path:

How To

Start > Type Command in the **Search Programs and Files** bar > type **regsvr32** filename.dll

Note

The filename for the dll file must contain the full path of the filename; for example, C:\Windows\System32\wuapi.dll.

Multiboot (5.2.4)

The capability for installing two or more operating systems is called *multiboot*. A separate partition is required for each operating system, and a user can choose which OS to boot from with a boot management program. In this section, multiboot procedures and disk management for installation of multiple OSs are discussed.

Multiboot Procedures (5.2.4.1)

You can have multiple operating systems on a single computer. Some software applications may require the most recent version of an OS, whereas other applications require an older version. There is a dual-boot process for multiple operating systems on a computer. During the boot process, if the Windows Boot Manager (BOOTMGR) determines that more than one OS is present, you are prompted to choose the OS that you want to load. Figure 5-18 shows the BOOTMGR for Windows 8.x. Figure 5-19 shows the BOOTMGR for Windows 7 and Vista.

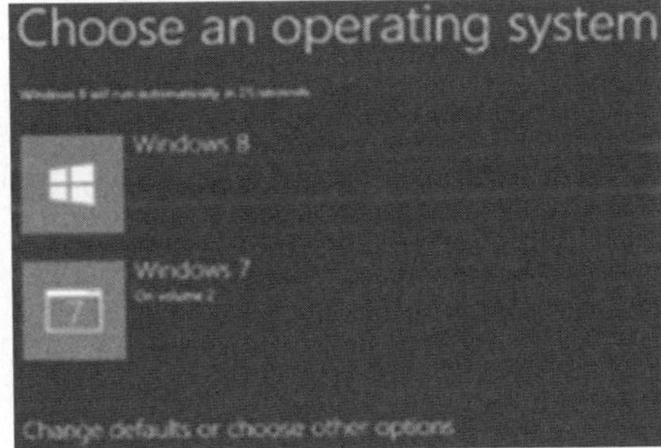

Figure 5-18 Windows 8.x Boot Manager

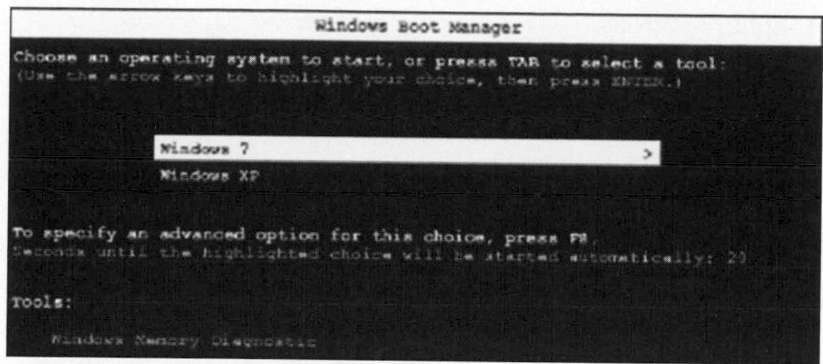

Figure 5-19 Windows 7 and Vista Boot Manager

To create a dual-boot system in Microsoft Windows, the hard drive must contain more than one partition.

The oldest OS should be installed on the primary partition or the hard drive marked as the active partition first. Install the second OS on the second partition or hard drive. The boot files are automatically installed in the active partition.

BOOTMGR File

During the installation, the BOOTMGR file is created on the active partition to allow selecting the OS to boot on startup. You can edit the BOOTMGR file to change the order of the operating systems. You can also change the length of time allowed during the boot phase to select the OS. Typically, the default time is 30 seconds. This time period delays the boot time of the computer by the specified time, unless the user intervenes to select a particular OS. If the disk has only one OS, change the time to 5 or 10 seconds to boot up the computer faster.

To change the time to display the list of operating systems, use the following path:

Select **Start** > **Control Panel** > > **System** > **Advanced System Settings** > click the **Advanced** tab > in the **Startup and Recovery** area, select **Settings**

Disk Management Utility (5.2.4.2)

A multiboot setup requires multiple hard drives or a hard drive that has multiple partitions. To create a new partition, access the *Disk Management Utility*. You can also use the Disk Management utility to complete the following tasks:

- View drive status
- Extend partitions

- Split partitions
- Assign drive letters
- Add drives
- Add arrays

To access Disk Management in Windows 8.x, access the Start Screen and start typing diskmgmt.msc. Click the Disk Manager Utility icon that will appear in the search result list.

To access the Disk Management utility in Windows 7 and Windows Vista, use the following path:

Start > right-click **Computer** > **Manage** > select **Disk Management**

Disk Management Utility is available for Windows 8.x, as shown in Figure 5-20, and for Windows 7 and Windows Vista, as shown in Figure 5-21.

Drive Status

The Disk Management utility displays the status of each disk, as shown in Figures 5-20 and 5-21.

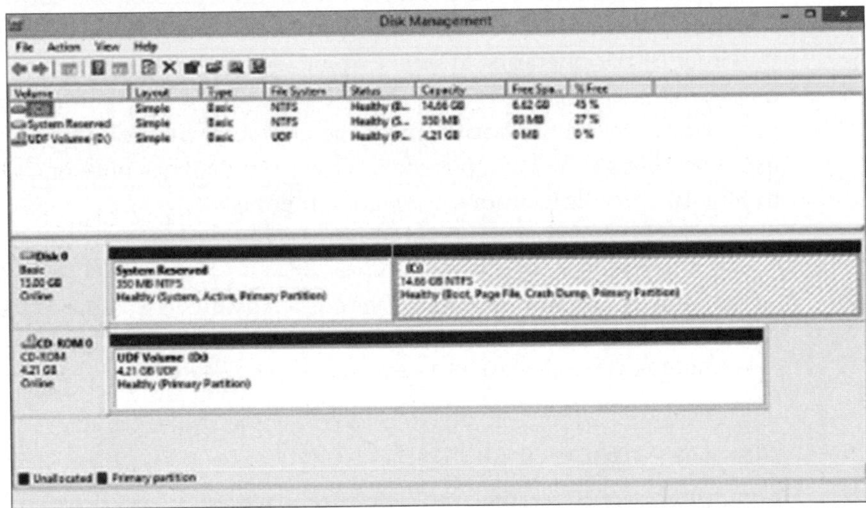

Figure 5-20 Windows 8.x Disk Management

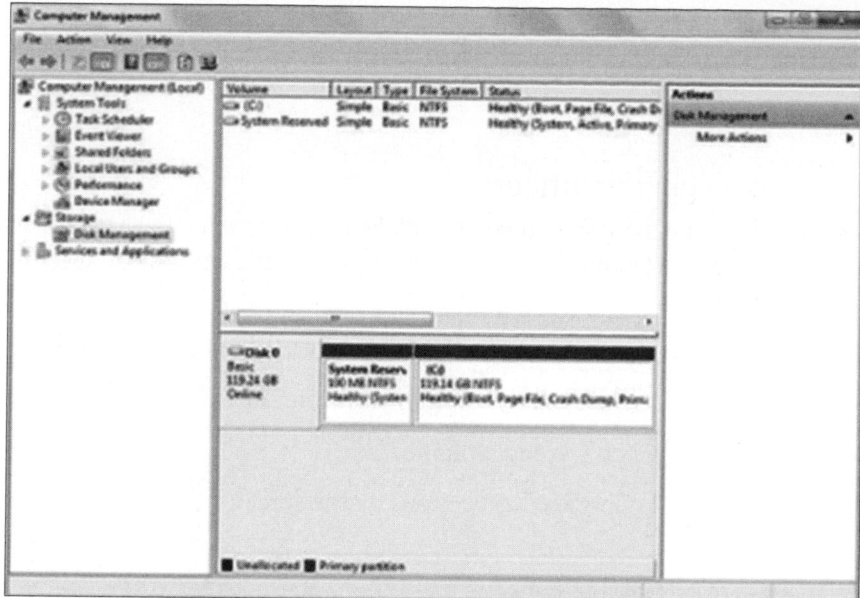

Figure 5-21 Windows 7 and Vista Disk Management

The drives in the computer display one of the following conditions:

- **Foreign**—A dynamic disk that has been moved to a computer from another computer running Windows
- **Healthy**—A volume that is functioning properly
- **Initializing**—A basic disk that is being converted into a dynamic disk
- **Missing**—A dynamic disk that is corrupted, turned off, or disconnected
- **Not Initialized**—A disk that does not contain a valid signature
- **Online**—A basic or dynamic disk that is accessible and shows no problems
- **Online (Errors)**—I/O errors detected on a dynamic disk
- **Offline**—A dynamic disk that is corrupted or unavailable
- **Unreadable**—A basic or dynamic disk that has experienced hardware failure, corruption, or I/O errors

Other drive status indicators might be displayed when using drives other than hard drives, such as an audio CD that is in the optical drive, or a removable drive that is empty.

Partitions (5.2.4.3)

In Disk Manager, you can change the size and numbers of primary partitions and logical drives.

Extending Partitions

To extend a basic volume, it must be unallocated or formatted with the NTFS file format. Extending a basic volume increases the amount of space available in a logical drive.

To extend a partition in the Disk Manager, follow these steps:

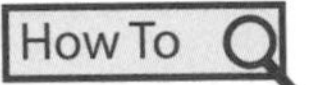

Step 1. Right-click the desired partition.

Step 2. Click **Extend Volume**.

Step 3. Follow the instructions on the screen.

Shrinking Partitions

Figure 5-22 shows that the Disk Manager can be used to shrink or split a partition that has free space. The free space, also called unallocated space, can now be used to create new partitions. To shrink a basic disk, follow these steps:

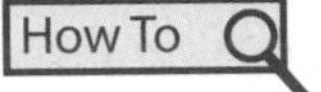

Step 1. Right-click the desired partition.

Step 2. Click **Shrink Volume**.

Step 3. Follow the instructions on the screen.

If you want to split the partition into two partitions, first use the Shrink Volume feature. After the disk has been shrunk, the partition will contain unallocated space. This space can be used to create one or more new partitions. The new partitions must be formatted and assigned drive letters.

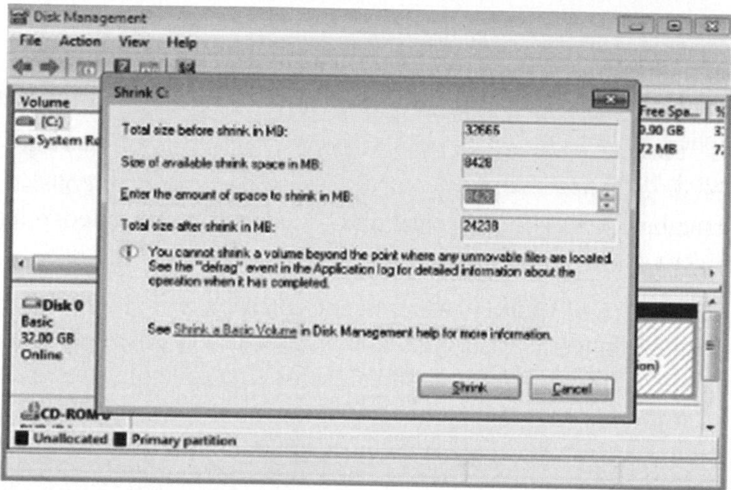

Figure 5-22 Shrink Volume

Drive Mapping or Drive Letter Assignment (5.2.4.4)

In Windows, letters are used to name physical or logical drives. This process is called *drive mapping* or *drive letter assignment*. A Windows computer can have up to 26 physical and logical drives, because there are 26 letters in the English alphabet. Drive C is reserved for the primary, active partition. In Windows Vista and Windows 7, you can assign letters A or B to drives if you do not have floppy drives. As extra storage devices are added to the system, Windows will attempt to automatically map them to the next free letter. In this way, an optical drive, extra internal disks and external storage devices are traditionally labeled as drive D, E, F, and so forth. The maximum number of additional drives is dependent on the hardware of a specific computer.

You can change, add, and remove drive letters and paths. By default, Windows assigns a letter to a partition or drive after it is created or added. You can change the drive designation to any letter as long as that letter is not already in use.

To change a drive letter in Windows from the Disk Management utility, right-click the drive and select **Change Drive Letter and Paths**.

Adding Drives

To increase the amount of storage space available on a computer, or to implement a *redundant array of independent disks (RAID)* setup, you can add drives to the computer. If the additional hard drive has been installed correctly, the BIOS should automatically recognize it. After the drive is installed, you can check if it is recognized using the Disk Management utility. If the disk is available, it probably requires formatting before it can be used. If it does not appear, troubleshoot the problem.

Adding Arrays

To set up a redundant array of independent disks (RAID), two or more drives must be installed in a computer. You can add an array with the Disk Management utility. You have the following options:

- *New Spanned Volume*—Creates a disk partition that consists of disk space from more than one physical disk. The data on a spanned volume is not fault tolerant.
- *New Striped Volume*—A dynamic partition that stores data in stripes on more than one physical disk. Also known as RAID 0, this type of volume achieves high read/write speeds. Data is spread across multiple physical disks, allowing parts of it to be accessed simultaneously. Because the data on a striped volume is not fault tolerant, this type of volume should not be used to store important data.
- *New Mirrored Volume*—Requires two physical disks. Also known as RAID 1. All data written to the volume is written to both disks simultaneously. This operation makes the data stored on a mirrored volume fault tolerant.
- *New RAID-5 Volume*—RAID 5 is a dynamic partition that stores data in stripes on more than one physical disk, while also storing recovery information for each stripe. Called parity data, this recovery information can be used to rebuild the data on a disk that has failed. The creation of parity information makes the data on a RAID-5 volume fault tolerant.

To add an array in the Disk Management utility, right-click the desired disk and select an option.

In addition to the Disk Management utility options described above, another common RAID type is RAID 10, also known as RAID 1+0. RAID 10 is a volume consisting of a mix of RAID 0 and RAID 1. RAID 10 stores data in stripes on multiple physical disks while mirroring that data on another set of disks. RAID 10 is both fast and fault tolerant.

Note

The options available for adding an array are based on system limitations. Not all options may be available.

Figure 5-23 depicts additional information about disk arrays.

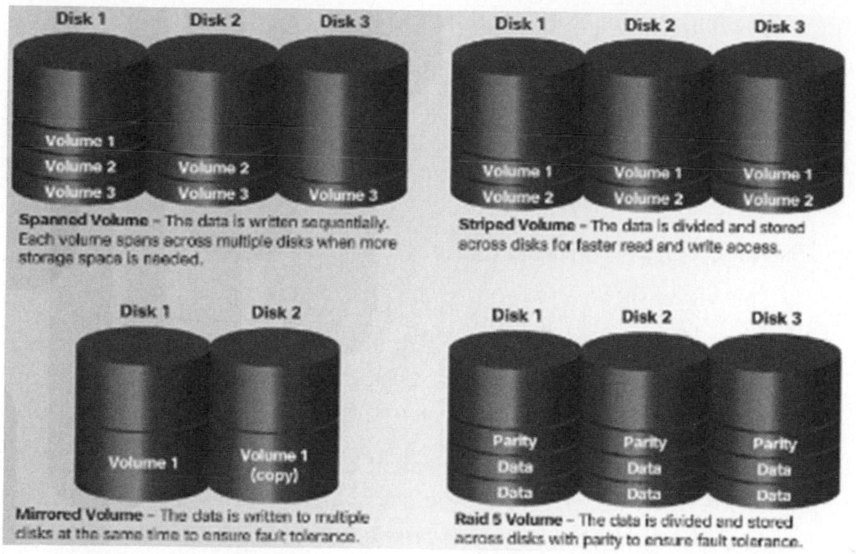

Figure 5-23 Disk Arrays

Video

Video—Disk Partitioning (5.2.4.5)

This video shows how to use the Disk Management tool to partition drives and manipulate disk volumes. The Disk Management tool allows you to create, resize, and delete partitions without having to use third-party or specialized software. The video explores using Disk Management to initialize, partition, and format with a file system two new hard drives that are added to a Windows 7 computer.

To begin you will need to access the disk management tool:

Using the path **Start Menu > Control Panel > System and Security > Administrative Tools >** select the link to **Create and format hard disk partitions** to open the Disk Management tool.

The video continues to walk through the process of initializing a disk partition and formatting it.

It goes on to show how by selecting a disk you can see the status of a disk, including characteristics such as whether it is active, whether it is primary, the amount of the storage space available, the amount of storage used, and which file system it has been formatted to use. It shows how by using Disk Management tool you can see the name, size, and type of each partition created on the disks found on your system; this includes the two newly installed hard drives.

In order to ready any hard drive to accept data, it needs to be partitioned and formatted. By selecting the newly installed hard drives, you can complete the partitioning and formatting processes. You will need to have information about the size of the partition(s) and the file system type you want to use for the drive.

The information contained here is a summary of the video content. For a more thorough explanation, viewing the video is useful.

Please view the video (5.2.4.5) in the Cisco Networking Academy IT Essentials 6.0 online course.

Video

Video—Drive Mirroring (5.2.4.6)

This video shows how to use the Disk Management tool to create a drive mirror.

This video discussed the steps to take to mirror a drive in Windows using the Disk Management tool. Mirroring a disk drive creates an exact duplicate of a drive, which is a useful way to back up drive that contains important data.

To do this in the Disk Management tool, right-click and select **Add Mirror.** This action opens a dialog box that asks whether you want to convert the disk to a dynamic disk. This is a necessary action to create a mirror, so select **Yes.** The Disk Management tool handles the rest of the operation to convert the disk and create the mirror. After the mirror is created, you will be able to view it in the Disk Management tool.

Please view the video in the Cisco Networking Academy IT Essentials 6.0 online course.

Lab—Create a Partition in Windows (5.2.4.7)

In this lab, you create a FAT32 formatted partition on a disk. You convert the partition to NTFS. You then identify the differences between the FAT32 format and the NTFS format. Refer to the lab in *IT Essentials v6 Lab Manual*.

Disk Directories (5.2.5)

In Windows, files are organized in a directory structure. A directory structure is designed to store system files, user files, and program files.

Directory Structures (5.2.5.1)

The root level of the Windows directory structure, the partition, is usually labeled drive C. Drive C contains a set of standardized directories, called folders, for the operating system, applications, configuration information, and data files. Directories may contain subdirectories. Subdirectories are commonly called subfolders.

If Windows cannot recognize the file systems already present in a new disk, the disk must be initialized and formatted before it can be used. While initializing the disk, the information about the location of the files in the disk is removed. Without the location of the disk's content, the disk appears blank to the OS. During formatting, the data on the disk is overwritten and the data is no longer accessible. Furthermore, any bad sectors of the disk are remapped and a file system structure for the OS is created during formatting.

Following the initial installation, install most applications and data in whichever directory you choose. The Windows setup program creates directories that have specific purposes, such as storing photos or music files. When files of the same type are saved to a certain location, it is easier to find them.

Note

Although initializing a disk should destroy all data in a disk, there are companies and organizations specialized in recovering data even from re-initialized disks.

Note

It is a best practice to store files in folders and subfolders rather than at the root level of a drive.

Mounting a Volume

You can map a drive to an empty folder on a volume. This is referred to as a *mounted drive*. Mounted drives are assigned drive paths instead of letters and are displayed as a drive icon in Windows Explorer. Windows Explorer is a tool that allows users to view all the drives, folders, and files on a computer in an organized manner. Use a mounted drive to configure more than 26 drives on your computer, or when you need additional storage space on a volume.

To mount a volume in Windows 8.x, follow these steps:

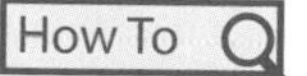

Step 1. Open **Disk Management** and right-click anywhere in the free space.

Step 2. Select New Simple Volume to start the New Simple Volume Wizard.

Step 3. Specify the size for the new partition.

Step 4. Click Next.

Step 5. Select Mount in the following empty NTFS folder: and specify the empty folder location.

Step 6. Choose whether the volume should be formatted and what file system to use.

Step 7. Finalize and Close Disk Management.

To mount a volume in Windows 7 or Vista, follow these steps:

How To

Step 1. Select **Start > Control Panel > Administrative Tools > Computer Management.**

Step 2. Click Disk Management in the left pane.

Step 3. Right-click the partition or volume to mount.

Step 4. Click Change Drive Letter and Paths.

Step 5. Click Add.

Step 6. Click Mount in the following empty NTFS folder.

Step 7. Browse to an empty folder on an NTFS volume or create one, and click OK.

Step 8. Close Computer Management.

User and System File Locations (5.2.5.2)

During installation the Windows operating system's essential folders are created. They contain operating system files and other system files necessary for the function of the OS as well as a default folder location for the user-created files.

User File Locations

By default, Windows stores most of the files created by users in the folder C:\Users\User_name\. Each user's folder contains folders for music, videos, websites, and pictures, among others. Many programs also store specific user data here. If a single computer has many users, they have their own folders containing their favorites, desktop items, and cookies. *Cookies* are files that contain information from web pages that the users have visited.

System Folder

When the Windows OS is installed, most of the files that are used to run the computer are located in the folder C:\Windows\system32.

Fonts

The folder C:\Windows\Fonts contains the fonts installed on the computer. Fonts come in several formats, including TrueType, OpenType, Composite, and PostScript. Some examples of font typefaces are Arial, Times New Roman, and Courier. You can access the Fonts folder through the Control Panel. You can install fonts by double-clicking the font file **> Install.**

Temporary Files

The Temporary Files folder contains files created by the OS and programs that are needed for a short period of time. For example, temporary files might be created while an application is being installed to make more RAM available for other applications.

Almost every program uses temporary files, which are usually automatically deleted when the application or the OS is finished using them. However, some temporary files must be deleted manually. Because temporary files take up hard drive space that could be used for other files, it is a good idea to delete them as necessary every two or three months.

In Windows, temporary files are usually located in the following folders:

- C:\Windows\Temp
- C:\Users\User_Name\AppData\Local\Temp
- %USERPROFILE%\AppData\Local\Temp

Note

%USERPROFILE% is an environment variable set by the OS with the username that is currently logged on to the computer. Environment variables are used by the operating system, applications, and software installation programs.

To see the environment variables that are configured in Windows, use the following path:

Control Panel > System > Advanced system settings > Advanced tab > Environment Variables

Program Files

The Program Files folder is used by most application installation programs to install software. In 32-bit systems, all programs are 32-bit and are installed in the folder C:\Program Files. In 64-bit systems, 64-bit programs are installed in the folder C:\Program Files, whereas 32-bit programs are usually installed in the folder C:\Program Files (x86).

File Extension and Attributes (5.2.5.3)

Files in the directory structure adhere to a Windows naming convention:

- A maximum of 255 characters is allowed.
- Characters such as a slash or a backslash (/ \) are not allowed.

- An extension of three or four letters is added to the filename to identify the file type.
- Filenames are not case sensitive.

By default, file extensions are hidden. To display the file extensions, you must disable the **Hide extensions for known file types** setting in the Folder Options control panel utility, as shown in Figure 5-24.

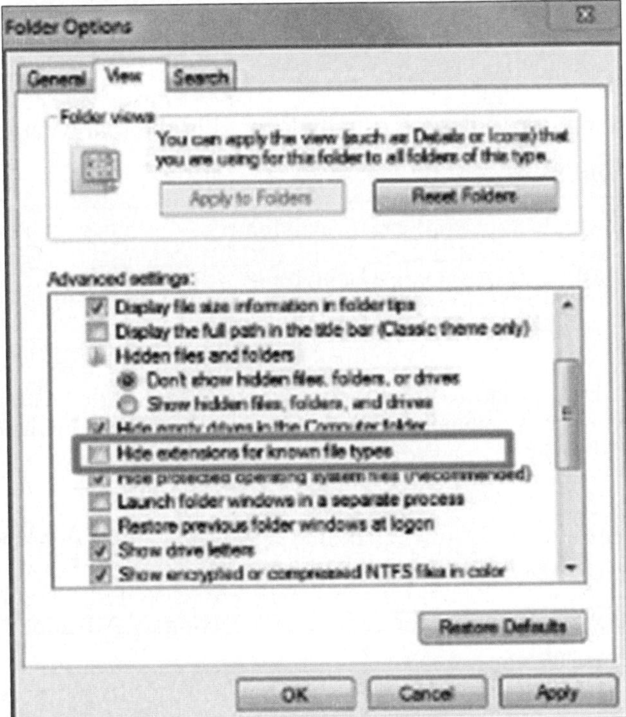

Figure 5-24 Show Known File Extensions

To display file extensions, use the following path:

Control Panel > Folder Options > View > uncheck **Hide extensions for known file types**

The following filename extensions are commonly used:

- **.docx**—Microsoft Word (2007 and later)
- **.txt**—ASCII text only

- **.jpg**—Graphics format
- **.pptx**—Microsoft PowerPoint
- **.zip**—Compression format

The directory structure maintains a set of attributes for each file that controls how the file can be viewed or altered. These are the most common file attributes:

- **R**—The file is read-only.
- **A**—The file will be archived the next time that the disk is backed up.
- **S**—The file is marked as a system file, and a warning is given if an attempt is made to delete or modify the file.
- **H**—The file is hidden in the directory display.

Application, File and Folder Properties (5.2.5.4)

To view or change the properties of an application, file, or folder, right-click the icon and select **Properties.**

Application and File Properties

The Properties view for an application or file, as shown in Figure 5-25, may contain the following tabs:

- **General**—Displays basic information, including location and the attributes.
- **Security**—Provides the option to change file access permissions for user accounts and the system.
- **Details**—Displays basic information for the file, including attributes.
- **Compatibility**—Provides options for configuring file compatibility mode and operational settings. In Windows 7, compatibility mode allows a user to run a program created for earlier versions of the Windows OS. For Windows Vista, the number of options available in compatibility mode is limited.

Figure 5-25 Application Properties

Folder Properties

The Properties view for an individual folder may contain the following tabs:

- **General**—Displays basic information, such as location and size. Provides options to change attributes, such as making a folder read-only or hidden.
- **Sharing**—Displays options for folder sharing. Users can share folders with computers on the same network. Password protection settings can also be configured.
- **Security**—Displays options for basic and advanced security settings.
- **Customize**—Displays options for customizing the appearance of the folder and optimizing it for specific file types, such as music or photo files.

Summary (5.3)

Choosing an operating system, installing the OS and understanding operating system configurations were discussed in this chapter.

Summary (5.3.1)

There are many different types of operating systems, so knowing which one is best suited for a user's needs is critical. The primary operating system presented in this chapter is Windows. It is the most widely installed and used OS, so it is important for IT technicians to understand its functions and installation processes.

This chapter introduced computer operating systems. As a technician, you should be skilled at installing Windows operating systems. The following concepts from this chapter are important to remember:

- Several different operating systems are available, and you must consider the customer's needs and environment when choosing an OS.
- The main steps in setting up a customer's computer include preparing the drive, installing the OS, creating user accounts, and configuring installation options.

Summary of Exercises

This is a summary of the Labs and activities associated with this chapter.

Labs

The following labs cover material from this chapter. Refer to the labs in the *IT Essential v6 Lab Manual*.

Lab—Search NOC Certifications and Jobs (5.1.2.3)

Lab—Data Migration in Windows (5.1.4.4)

Lab—Install Windows (5.2.1.7)

Lab—Check for Updates in Windows (5.2.1.10)

Lab—Create a Partition in Windows (5.2.4.7)

Check Your Understanding

You can find the answers to these questions in the appendix, "Answers to 'Check Your Understanding' Questions."

1. What are two ways that network operating systems (NOS) differ from desktop operating systems? (Choose two.)

   A. Network operating systems enable files and folders to be shared on a network, whereas desktop operating systems cannot share files or folders.

   B. Network operating systems have limited account user management capabilities, but desktop operating systems can manage many user accounts.

   C. Network operating systems have strong security and account management capabilities, but desktop operating systems have limited security and account management capabilities.

   D. Network operating systems support a single user, but desktop operating systems can support many users.

   E. Network operating systems can support many users at the same time, but desktop operating systems can only support a limited number of users at a time.

2. Which file system is used to access files over a network?

   A. NFS

   B. FAT

   C. CDFS

   D. NTFS

3. Technicians can use a Microsoft tool called ________________ to remove undesired settings when creating a disk image for cloning an operating system

   A. Sysprep

   B. Disk Management

   C. Disk Cleaner

   D. Partition

4. What are two types of computer user interface? (Choose two.)

   A. OpenGL

   B. CLI

   C. PnP

   D. API

   E. GUI

5. When a user makes changes to the settings of a Windows system, where are these changes stored?

   A. win.ini
   B. boot.ini
   C. Registry
   D. Control Panel

6. A technician is attempting to create multiple partitions on a hard disk that is using the boot sector standard that supports a maximum partition size of 2TB. What is the maximum number of primary partitions allowed per hard drive?

   A. 16
   B. 4
   C. 128
   D. 2
   E. 32
   F. 1

7. What term is used to describe a logical drive that can be formatted to store data?

   A. Partition
   B. Track
   C. Volume
   D. Sector
   E. Cluster

8. Which free Microsoft utility can scan Windows 7 for hardware and software incompatibility issues?

   A. Upgrade Advisor
   B. Windows Fixit Center
   C. Windows Easy Transfer
   D. Microsoft System Preparation tool

9. What type of disk volume stores data in stripes on multiple physical disks and uses parity for each stripe to provide fault tolerance?

   A. Spanned
   B. Striped
   C. RAID 5
   D. Mirrored

10. Which term best describes the process of breaking a program into smaller parts that can be loaded as needed by the operating system?

    A. Multiprocessing

    B. Multiuser

    C. Multithreading

    D. Multitasking

11. Hard drive ____________ are complete circles on one side of a hard disk platter.

    A. Partitions

    B. Tracks

    C. Volumes

    D. Sectors

    E. Clusters

12. Which key, when pressed during the boot process, allows the user to choose to start Windows in Safe Mode?

    A. F1

    B. wINDOWS

    C. F8

    D. Esc

13. What feature of an operating system allows it to support two or more CPUs?

    A. Multiprocessing

    B. Multiuser

    C. Multithreading

    D. Multitasking

14. What contains information on how hard drive partitions are organized?

    A. MBR

    B. CPU

    C. Windows Registry

    D. BOOTMGR

CHAPTER 6

Windows Configuration and Management

Objectives

Upon completion of this chapter, you will be able to answer the following questions:

- What is the purpose of the operating system?
- How do different operating systems compare with one another based on purpose, limitations, and compatibilities?
- How do you determine the appropriate operation system based on customer needs?
- How do you install an operating system?
- How do I upgrade operating systems?
- How do you navigate within an operating system GUI?
- What are some common preventive maintenance techniques for operating systems, and how are they applied?
- What can be done to troubleshoot operating systems?

Key Terms

This chapter uses the following key terms. You can find the definitions in the Glossary.

Control Panel *Page 260*

Control Panel applets *Page 247*

graphical user interface (GUI) *Page 247*

Charms *Page 248*

Aero *Page 248*

Shake *Page 249*

Peek *Page 249*

Snap *Page 249*

Sidebar *Page 249*

Personalization window *Page 250*

Task Manager *Page 253*

File Explorer *Page 256*

Windows Explorer *Page 257*

Windows libraries *Page 258*

Programs and Features utility *Page 259*

User Accounts utility *Page 262*

User Account Control (UAC) *Page 262*

Native resolution *Page 266*

Screen resolution *Page 266*

Orientation *Page 266*

Refresh rate *Page 266*

Display colors *Page 266*

Windows Action Center *Page 267*

firewall *Page 268*

Power Options utility *Page 269*

Sleep *Page 270*

Hibernate Page 270

System utility Page 270

virtual memory Page 271

paging file Page 271

Windows ReadyBoost Page 272

Roll back a driver Page 272

HomeGroup Page 276

Network and Sharing Center Page 276

Computer Management Page 277

Event Viewer Page 279

Component Services Page 279

Data Sources Page 280

service Page 281

Performance Monitor Page 282

Windows Memory Diagnostic Page 283

data object Page 283

Component Services tool Page 283

defragmentation Page 284

disk defragmenter Page 284

Disk Error-Checking Tool Page 284

CHKDSK Page 285

DXDIAG Page 289

Microsoft Management Console (MMC) Page 289

MSINFO32 Page 290

REGEDIT Page 290

virtual machine Page 290

host machine Page 290

hypervisor or Virtual Machine Manager (VMM) Page 291

Type 1 hypervisor Page 292

Type 2 hypervisor Page 292

Windows Hyper-V Page 292

Windows Virtual PC Page 293

Windows Automatic Update Page 297

Windows Task Scheduler Page 297

System Restore Page 298

Restore points Page 298

Microsoft Backup Utility Page 299

File History Page 299

Backup and Restore Page 300

shadow copies Page 301

Introduction (6.0)

Windows is an operating system that includes a graphical user interface. It is a widely used OS that has both desktop OS and network OS releases. It is intended to be a user-friendly OS using a graphical user interface for ease of navigation and for the simplification of the management of complex operations performed by the OS.

Welcome (6.0.1)

Windows has many useful and powerful tools built-in to the operating system. Some uses of these tools are modifying configurations, creating logs to record detailed information to be used to monitor performance, record settings, and track installed software while working a graphical user environment.

Windows Configuration and Management (6.0.1.1)

In this chapter, you learn how to navigate the Windows GUI. You also learn how to use the Control Panel and other tools to keep Windows operating systems running smoothly.

The Windows GUI and Control Panel (6.1)

This section examines the graphical user interface (GUI) that allows users to interact with the computer. It also explores the Control Panel. The Control Panel is the centralized configuration area in Windows where settings for the system can be modified; it is used to make modifications to and control tasks in almost every aspect of the hardware and software, including OS functions. These settings are categorized in *Control Panel* applets. Many other tools discussed are useful in fine-tuning the operation of Windows for the user.

Windows Desktop, Tools, and Applications (6.1.1)

This section examines the graphical user interface (GUI) that allows users to interact with the operating system applications and tools. It also explores the Windows Control Panel. This is where Windows centralizes many features that control the behavior and appearance of the computer.

Windows Desktop (6.1.1.1)

After the OS has been installed, you can customize the computer desktop to suit individual needs. A computer *desktop* is a graphical representation of the workspace and is commonly called a *graphical user interface, or GUI*. The desktop has icons, toolbars, and menus to manipulate files. You can add or change images, sounds, and colors on the desktop to provide a more personalized look and feel. Together, these customizable items make up a *theme*.

Windows 8 introduced a new desktop that uses tiles on the Start screen, as shown Figure 6-1. This environment is used on desktops and laptops and is optimized for mobile devices. The Start screen displays a customizable array of tiles designed to access apps and other information, such as social media updates and calendar notifications. These tiles represent notifications, applications or desktop programs. The tiles that can display dynamic content are called *live tiles*. Another new GUI element is a vertical bar known as the *Charms bar*. Charms can be accessed by swiping in with your finger from the right edge of the screen, or by placing the mouse cursor in the upper-right corner of the screen.

Figure 6-1 Windows 8 App Environment

Windows 8 has the following hardware requirements:

- 1 GHz 32-bit or 64-bit processor
- 1 GB of RAM (32-bit) or 2GB of RAM (64-bit)
- DirectX 9 supportive graphic card
- Hard disk space: 16GB (32-bit) or 20GB (64-bit)

Windows 7 and Vista have a default theme called *Aero*. Aero has translucent window borders, numerous animations, and icons that are thumbnail images of the contents of a file. Because of the advanced graphics required to support the theme, Aero is available only on computers that meet the following hardware requirements:

- 1 GHz 32-bit or 64-bit processor
- 1 GB of RAM
- 128 MB graphics card
- DirectX 9 class graphics processor that supports a Windows Display Driver Model Driver, Pixel Shader 2.0 in hardware, and 32 bits per pixel

Windows 8.1, 8.0, and 7 include the following desktop features:

- *Shake*—Minimize all windows that are not being used by clicking and holding the title bar of one window and shaking it with the mouse. Repeat the action to maximize all of the windows.
- *Peek*—View the desktop icons that are behind open windows by placing your cursor over the Show desktop button found at the right edge of the taskbar. This makes the open windows transparent. Click the button to minimize all windows.
- *Snap*—Resize a window by dragging it to one edge of the screen. Dragging the window to the left edge of the desktop fits the window to the left half of the screen. Dragging the window to the right edge of the desktop fits the window to the right half of the screen. Dragging the window to the top of the screen maximizes the window.

In Windows 7 and Vista, users can place gadgets on the desktop. *Gadgets* are small applications, such as games, sticky notes, a calendar or a clock. You can snap or position gadgets to the sides and corners of the desktop, as well as align them to other gadgets.

Note

Microsoft has retired support of the Gadgets feature.

To add gadgets to the Windows 7 or Vista desktop, follow these steps:

Step 1. Right-click anywhere on the desktop and choose Gadgets.

Step 2. Drag and drop the gadget from the menu to the desktop, or double-click the gadget to add it to the desktop, or right-click the gadget and choose Add.

Step 3. To snap a gadget, drag it to the desired desktop location. The gadget aligns itself with the screen edges and other gadgets.

In Windows Vista, you can also personalize a feature called Sidebar *Sidebar* is a graphical pane on the desktop that keeps gadgets organized.

Desktop Properties (6.1.1.2)

The Windows 8 Apps environment is highly customizable:

- To rearrange the tiles, click and drag the tiles.
- To rename a tile group, right-click on any empty area of the screen and select Name Groups.
- To add tiles to the main screen, right-click the desired Windows app, after searching for it, and select Pin to Start.
- To search for an app, click Search from the Charms bar. Alternatively, you can start typing the name of the app from the Windows Apps environment. **Search** will start automatically.

To customize the desktop, right-click anywhere on the desktop and choose **Personalize.**

Note

In Windows 8, click the **Desktop** tile to leave the Apps environment and show the desktop.

In the *Personalization window*, you can change the desktop appearance, display settings, and sound settings.

Table 6-1 shows Windows personalization desktop windows for different versions (Figures 6-2 to 6-4).

Table 6-1 Windows Personalization Desktop

Windows Personalization Desktop	Description
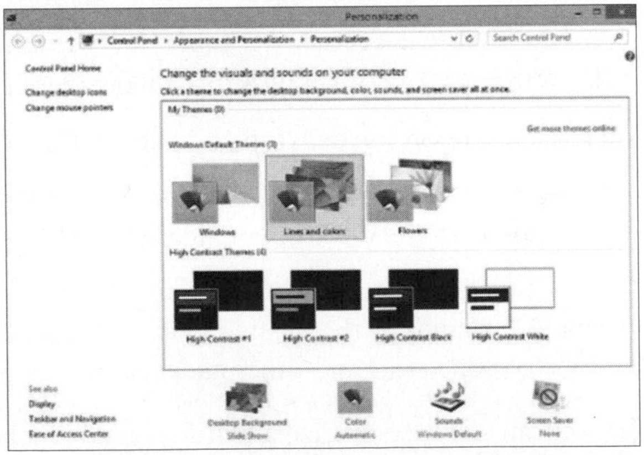 **Figure 6-2** Windows 8	In the Personalization window you can change the desktop appearance, display settings, and sound settings (Windows 8).

Windows Personalization Desktop	Description
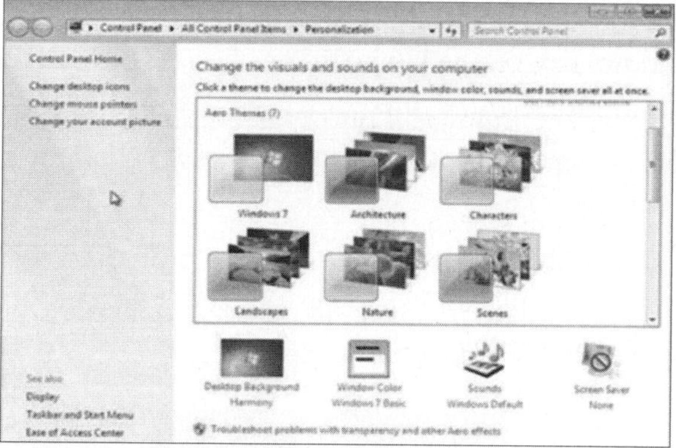 **Figure 6-3** Windows 7	Personalizing the Desktop (Windows 7).
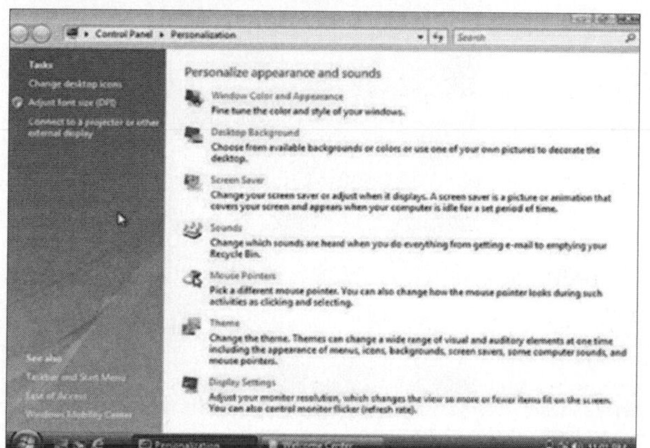 **Figure 6-4** Windows Vista	Personalizing the Desktop (Windows Vista).

Start Menu (6.1.1.3)

The Start menu is a menu like list of a computer's programs, folders, and settings. It is the central launching point for performing tasks and computer programs.

Start Menu in Windows 8.1 and 8.0

In Windows 8.0, with the introduction of Windows Apps environment, Microsoft chose to remove the Start Button and Start Menu. The Start Menu was replaced by the Start Screen, the main screen where the tiles are located.

After many requests, Microsoft brought back the Start Button in Windows 8.1 The Start Screen still plays the role of the Start Menu, but Windows 8.1 users now have a button to access the Start Screen. Other ways to access the Start Screen include pressing the Windows key on the keyboard or clicking the Start Button located on the Charms bar.

A limited Start Menu can be displayed in Windows 8.1 by right-clicking the Start Button, as shown in Figure 6-5.

The Start Menu and taskbar allow users to manage programs, search the computer, and manipulate running applications. To customize the Start Menu or the taskbar, right-click it and choose **Properties.**

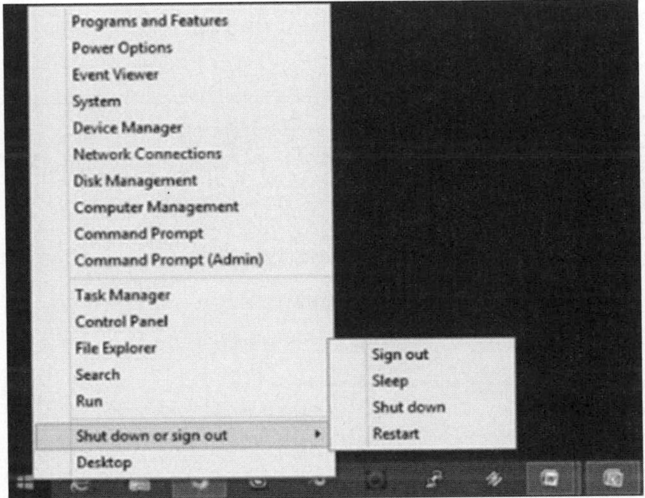

Figure 6-5 Windows 8.1 Limited Start Menu

Start Menu in Windows 7 and Vista

The Start Menu is accessed by clicking the Windows icon at the bottom-left of the desktop. The Start Menu, shown in Figure 6-6, displays all the applications installed on the computer, a list of recently opened documents, and a list of other elements, such as the search feature, help and support, and Control Panel.

To customize Start Menu settings in Windows 7 or Vista, use the following path:

Right-click an empty section of the taskbar and choose **Properties > Start Menu > Customize.**

Figure 6-6 Windows 7 and Vista Start Menu

Taskbar

In Windows 8 and 7, the following new features have been added to the taskbar to make navigating, organizing, and accessing windows and notifications easier:

- **Jump list—**To display a list of tasks that are unique to the application, right-click the application's icon in the taskbar.
- **Pinned applications—**To add an application to the taskbar for easy access, right-click the icon of an application and select Pin to taskbar.
- **Thumbnail previews—**To view a thumbnail image of a running program, hover the mouse over the program icon on the taskbar.

Task Manager (6.1.1.4)

The *Task Manager* allows you to view all running applications and to close any application.

After clicking **More details**, shown in Figure 6-7, the Windows 8 Task Manager has the following tabs:

- **Processes**—This tab shows a list of processes currently running on the computer. A *process* is a set of instructions started by the user, a program, or the OS. Running processes are categorized as apps, background processes, or Windows system processes.
- **Performance**—This tab contains system performance graphs. You can select any of the options, CPU, Memory, Disk, or Ethernet, to see a performance graph, which is shown in the right column of the tab.
- **App History**—Although the Processes tab shows live process information, this tab contains historical information, such as CPU time and network bandwidth. It is very useful when analyzing which apps consume the most resources.
- **Startup**—This tab shows what processes are automatically started during Windows 8 startup. Windows 8 also measures the impact each process has in the system's overall startup time. To keep a process from starting automatically, right-click on the process and disable automatic startup.

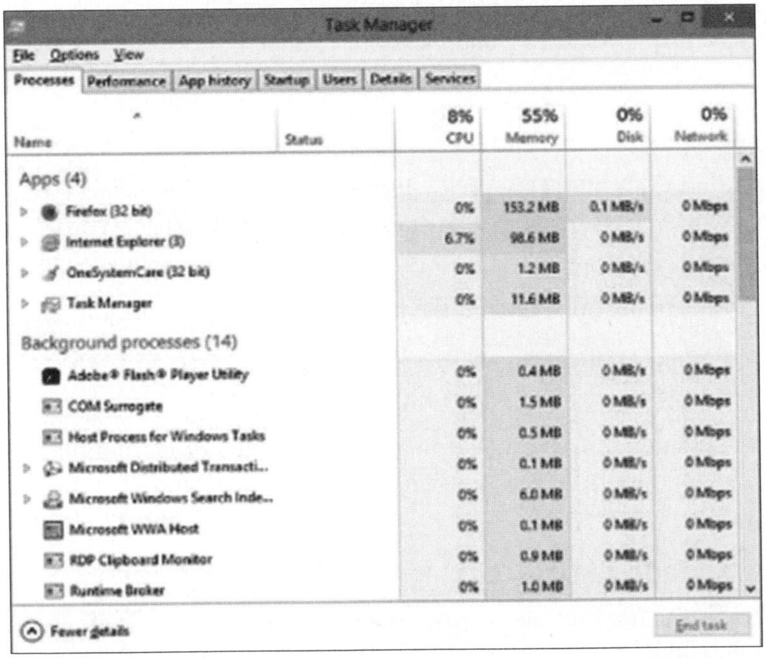

Figure 6-7 Windows 8 Task Manager

- **Users**—This tab shows how much of the system resources each user is consuming. Expand a user to display all processes owned by that user.
- **Details**—This tab allows you to tweak the level of CPU priority for a given process. It is also possible to specify which CPU a process uses to run (CPU affinity).
- **Services**—This tab displays all services currently running on the system and allows for stopping, starting, and restarting them.

The Windows 7/Vista Task Manager, shown in Figure 6-8, has the following tabs:

- **Applications**—This tab shows all running applications. From this tab you can create, switch to, or close an application that has stopped responding.
- **Processes**—This tab shows all running processes. From this tab, you can end processes or set process priorities.
- **Services**—This tab shows the available services, including their operational status.

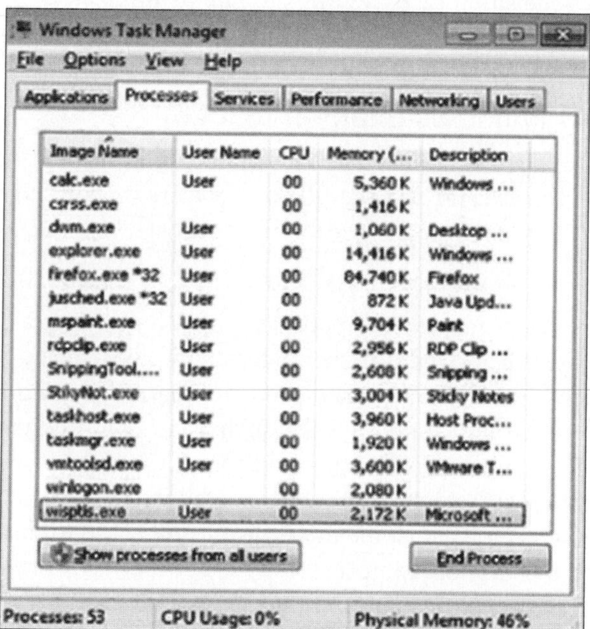

Figure 6-8 Windows 7 Task Manager

- **Performance**—This tab shows the CPU and page file usage.
- **Networking**—This tab shows the usage of all network adapters.
- **Users**—This tab shows all users that are logged on the computer. From this tab, you can disconnect remote users or log off local users.

To open the Task Manager, press **Ctrl-Alt-Delete** and select **Start Task Manager.**

Alternatively, you can open the Task Manager by right-clicking the taskbar and selecting **Task Manager** in Windows 8 or **Start Task Manager** in Windows 7 and Vista.

Be careful when ending a process or changing the priority of processes. Ending a process causes the program to end immediately without saving any information. Ending a process might prevent the system from running correctly. Also, changing the priority of a process might adversely affect the performance of the computer.

Lab—Task Manager (6.1.1.5)

In this lab, you explore Task Manager and manage processes from within Task Manager. Refer to the lab in *IT Essentials v6 Lab Manual*.

Computer and Windows Explorer (6.1.1.6)

Windows Explorer and Computer are to navigate its file system and using either program you can browse and edit the files and folders on your computer.

File Explorer and Windows Explorer

File Explorer is a file management application in Window 8. It allows you to navigate the file system and manage the folders, subfolders, and applications on your storage media. File Explorer is launched automatically when a folder or drive is opened. In File Explorer, common tasks, such as copying and moving files, and creating new folders, can be done using the Ribbon. The tabs at the top of the window change as different types of items are selected in the File Explorer. As shown in Figure 6-9, the Ribbon for the Home tab is displayed. If the Ribbon is not displaying, click the **Expand the Ribbon**, represented by a down arrow, at the upper-right corner of the window.

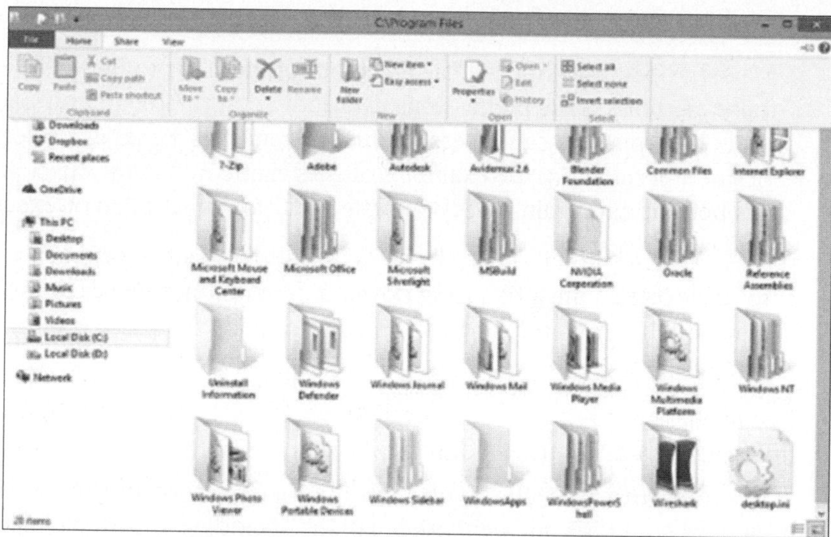

Figure 6-9 Windows 8 Explorer Ribbon Task Manager

Windows Explorer is the name of the file management application in Windows 7 and earlier. Windows Explorer performs similar functions as File Explorer without the use of the Ribbon.

This PC and Computer

In Windows 8.1, the This PC feature allows you to access the various drives installed in the computer. In Windows 7 and Vista, this same feature is called Computer.

In Windows 8.1, the This PC feature can be accessed either through File Explorer or from the Start Screen. To open This PC via File Explorer, simply open File Explorer, and it should display This PC by default. To reach This PC via the Start Screen, start typing **This PC**. Click **This PC** when it appears among the search results in the right side of the screen.

In Windows 8.0, 7, or Vista, click **Start** and select **Computer**.

Opening Files

You can open files in the same manner as applications. When opening a file, Windows determines which application is associated with the file type. For example, if you open a document, Windows will open the file with the associated program. This may be Microsoft Word, WordPad, Notepad, or another document-editing program.

Run as Administrator

Modern operating systems use a number of methods to improve security. One of these methods is file permissions. Depending on the file permission, only users with enough permission can access the file. System files, other user files, or files with elevated permissions are examples of files that could deny a user access. To override this behavior and gain access to those files, you must open or execute them as the system administrator.

To open or execute a file using elevated permission, right-click the file and choose **Run as Administrator.** You then need to provide the password for the Administrator account.

Windows Libraries (6.1.1.7)

Windows libraries allow you to easily organize content from various storage devices on your computer and network locations, including removable media, without moving the files. A library presents content from different locations in the same folder. You can search a library, and you can filter the content using criteria such as filename, file type, or date modified.

When Windows is installed, each user has four default libraries: Documents, Music, Pictures, and Videos. To access a library in Windows 7, open Windows Explorer and click **Libraries** in the left column. To add a file or folder to a library, right-click it, select **Include in library**, and choose the library to which you wish to add the item. The file or folder will be available when you open that library.

To create a new library, open a folder and select **Libraries > New library.**

To customize a library, right-click the library and click **Properties.** The Properties window allows you to add folders to the library by clicking **Include a folder.** You can also change the icon for the library and customize how items are arranged.

The Libraries feature is hidden by default. To show a link to Libraries in Windows 8.1, follow these steps:

How To

Step 1. Open File Explorer and expand the **View** tab.

Step 2. Go to **Options >** n the right side of the ribbon and click **Change folder and search options.**

Step 3. Go to the **General** tab and check the **Show Libraries** checkbox at the bottom of the window. Click **OK.**

Install and Uninstall Applications (6.1.1.8)

As a technician, you are responsible for adding and removing software from your customers' computers. Most applications use an automatic installation process when the application disc is inserted in the optical drive. The user is required to click through the installation wizard and provide information when requested.

Installing an Application

Insert the CD or DVD into the optical drive or open the downloaded program file. The program installer should start. If it does not start, run the setup or install file on the disc to begin installation, or download the program again.

After the application is installed, you can run the application from the Start Menu or the shortcut icon that the application installs on the desktop. Check the application to ensure that it is functioning properly. If there are problems, repair or uninstall the application. Some applications, such as Microsoft Office, provide a repair option within the installation program. In addition to the process described above, Windows 8 provides access to the Windows Store. Windows Store allows a user to search and install apps on a Windows 8 computer (or other Windows 8 device). To open the Windows Store app:

From the Start Screen, type **Store** and click the **Store** icon when it appears in the search results.

Uninstalling or Changing a Program

If an application is uninstalled incorrectly, you might be leaving files on the hard drive and unnecessary settings in the registry, which depletes the hard drive space and system resources. Unnecessary files might also reduce the speed at which the registry is read. Microsoft recommends that you always use the *Programs and Features utility* when removing, changing, or repairing applications. The utility guides you through the software removal process and removes every file that was installed.

In some instances, you can install or uninstall optional features of a program using the Programs and Features utility. Not all programs offer this option.

To open the Programs and Features utility, use the following path:

Control Panel > Programs and Features

To uninstall or change a program:

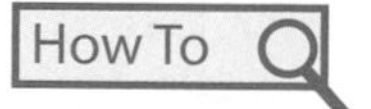

Step 1. **Click** Control Panel > Programs and Features.

Step 2. **Select a program, and then click Uninstall.** To change a program, click **Change or Repair.** Administrator permission may be required. If you are prompted for an administrator password or confirmation, type the password or provide confirmation.

Figure 6-10 shows the Windows 8 Programs and Features window.

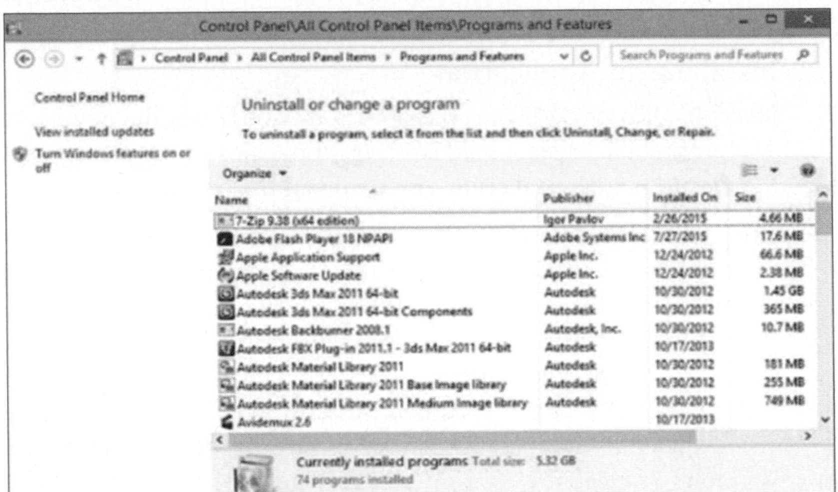

Figure 6-10 Windows 8 Programs and Features

Lab—Install Third-Party Software (6.1.1.9)

In this lab, you install and remove a third party software application. Refer to the lab in *IT Essentials v6 Lab Manual.*

Control Panel Utilities (6.1.2)

The *Control Panel* is made up of a group of individual Control Panel applets and is the central location in Windows operating systems to make changes to the configuration. When you make changes in the Control Panel you are making changes to the Windows Registry. The utilities available vary slightly depending on the version of Windows that you are running. In this section, you examine Control Panel utilities.

Introduction to Control Panel Utilities (6.1.2.1)

Windows centralizes the settings for many features that control the behavior and appearance of the computer. These settings are categorized in utilities, or small programs, found in the Control Panel, as shown in Figure 6-11.

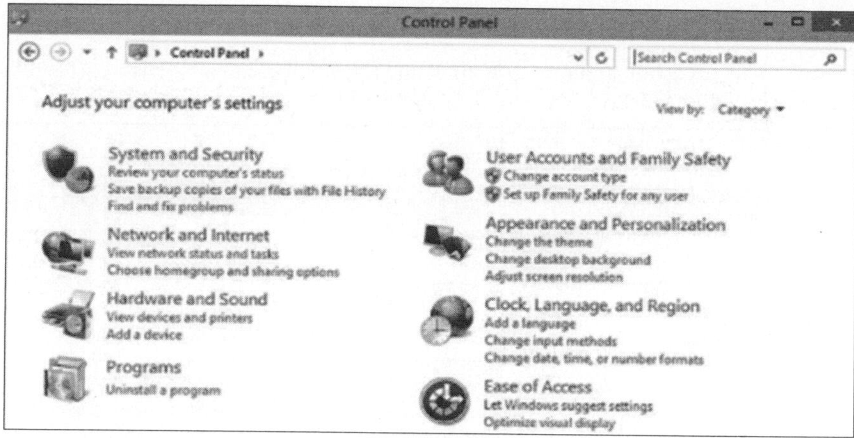

Figure 6-11 Windows 8 Control Panel in Category View

The names of various categories in the Control Panel differ slightly depending on the version of Windows installed. By default, icons are grouped into the following eight categories:

- **System and Security**—Configure system and security settings
- **Network and Internet**—Configure network connection types
- **Hardware and Sound**—Configure devices connected to the computer and settings for sound
- **Programs**—Install, uninstall, change, and repair applications
- **User Accounts and Family Safety**—Create and remove user accounts and set up parental controls
- **Appearance and Personalization**—Control the look and feel of the Windows GUI
- **Clock, Language, and Region**—Configure location and language
- **Ease of Access**—Configure Windows for vision, hearing, and mobility needs

You can change how the Control Panel is displayed. The selected view determines which utilities are immediately accessible in the Control Panel. The view options include:

- **Category**—Groups the Control Panel utilities into easy-to-navigate groups.
- **Large Icons**—Displays the utilities in alphabetical order using large icons.
- **Small Icons**—Displays the utilities in alphabetical order using small icons.

Note

This textbook assumes you are using the small icon view when paths are provided, as shown in Figure 6-12.

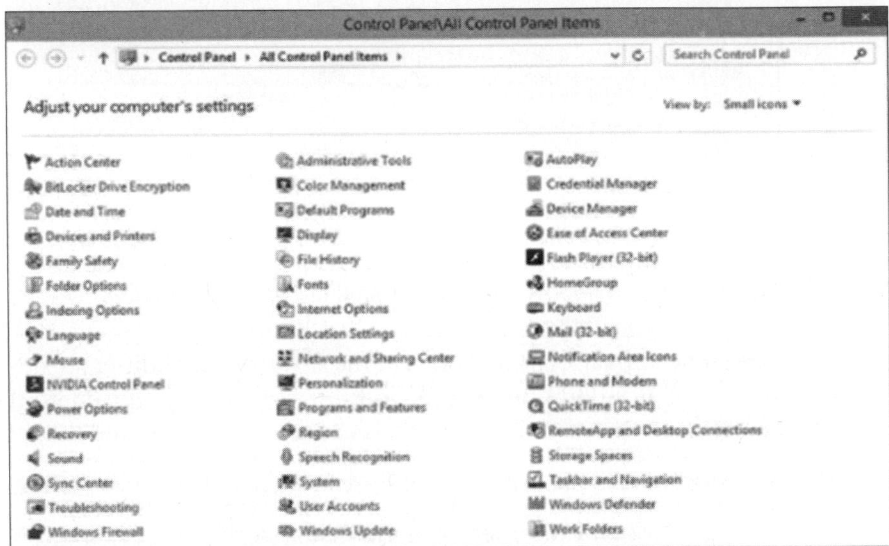

Figure 6-12 Windows 8 Control Panel Displayed with Small Icons

In Windows Vista, there are two view options:

- **Control Panel Home**—Groups the Control Panel utilities into easy-to-navigate groups.
- **Classic View**—Displays all of the Control Panel utilities individually.

User Accounts (6.1.2.2)

An administrative account is created when Windows is installed. To create a user account afterwards, open the User Accounts utility, as shown in Figure 6-13, by using the following path:

Control Panel > User Accounts.

The *User Accounts utility* provides options to help you manage passwords, change account pictures, change account names and types, and change *User Account Control (UAC)* settings.

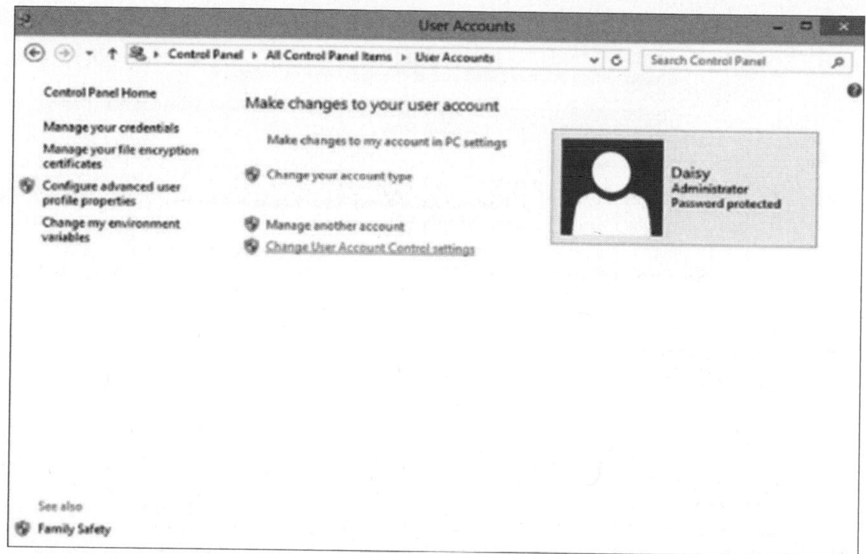

Figure 6-13 Windows 8 User Accounts

Note

Some features of the User Accounts utility require administrative privileges and might not be accessible with a standard user account.

User Account Control Settings

The *UAC* monitors programs on a computer and warns users when an action might present a threat to the computer. In Windows 8 or 7, you can adjust the level of monitoring that the UAC performs, as shown in Figure 6-14. When Windows 8 or 7 is installed, the UAC for the primary account defaults to the setting **Notify me only when programs try to make changes to my computer**, as shown in Figure 6-14. You are not notified when you make changes to these settings.

To adjust the level of UAC monitoring, use the following path:

Control Panel > User Accounts > Change User Account Control settings

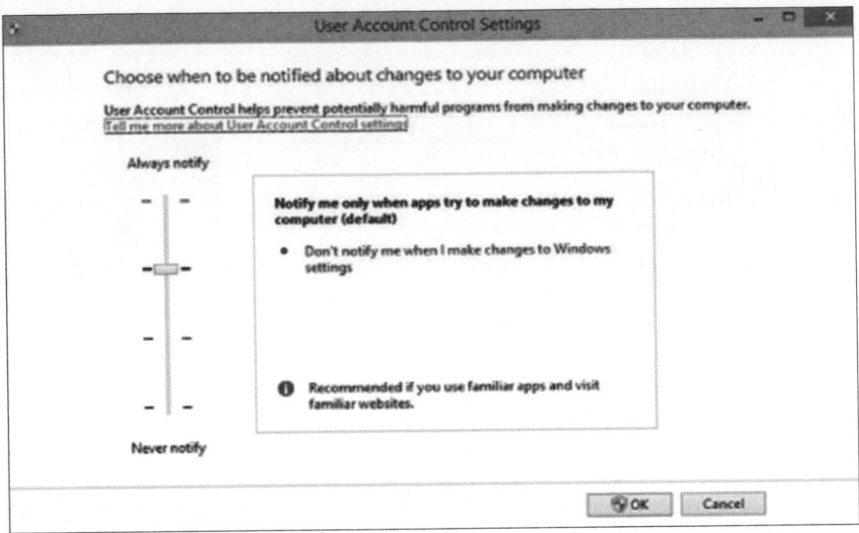

Figure 6-14 User Accounts Control Settings

Lab—Create User Accounts (6.1.2.3)

In this lab, you create user accounts in Windows. Refer to the lab in *IT Essentials v6 Lab Manual.*

Internet Options (6.1.2.4)

Internet Options has the following tabs:

- **General**—Configure basic Internet settings, such as selecting the Internet Explorer (IE) home page, viewing and deleting browsing history, adjusting search settings, and customizing the browser appearance.
- **Security**—Adjust the security settings for the Internet, local intranet, trusted sites, and restricted sites. Security levels for each zone can range from low (minimal security) to high (maximum security).
- **Privacy**—Configure privacy settings for the Internet zone, manage location services, and enable the pop-up blocker.
- **Content**—Access Parental Controls, control content viewed on the computer, adjust AutoComplete settings, and configure the feeds and web slices that can be viewed in IE. *Web slices* are specific content from websites that allow the users to subscribe and view the updated content, such as current temperature and stock quotes.
- **Connections**—Set up an Internet connection and adjust network settings.

- **Programs**—Choose the default web browser, enable browser add-ons, select the HTML editor for IE, and select programs used for Internet services. Hypertext Markup Language (HTML) is a system that tags text files to affect the appearance of web pages. An HTML editor is a computer program that can edit web pages.
- **Advanced**—Adjust advanced settings, and reset IE's settings to the default state.

To access the Internet Options utility, use the following path:

Control Panel > Internet Options

Lab—Configure Browser Settings (6.1.2.5)

In this lab, you configure browser settings in Microsoft Internet Explorer. Refer to the lab in *IT Essentials v6 Lab Manual.*

Display Settings (6.1.2.6)

You can change the appearance of the desktop by modifying the resolution and color quality with the Display Settings utility, as shown in Figure 6-15. If the screen resolution is not set properly, you might get unexpected display results from different video cards and monitors. You can also change more advanced display settings, such as the wallpaper, screensaver, power settings, and other options.

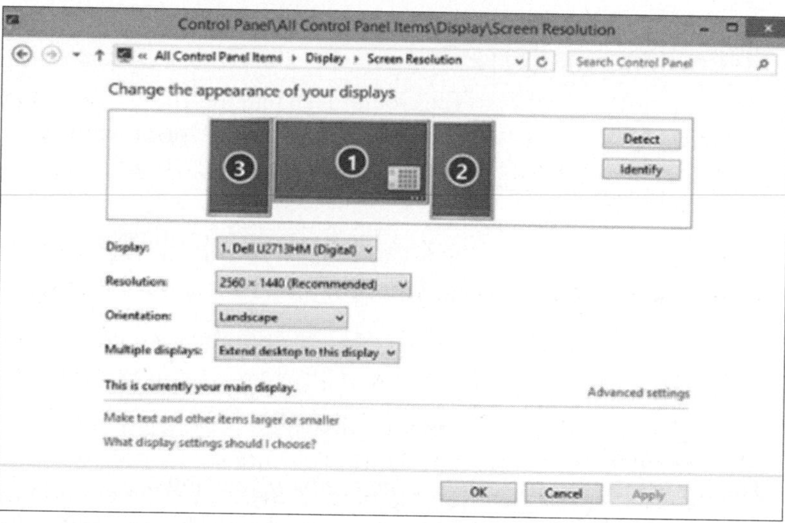

Figure 6-15 Windows 8 Display Settings

When using an LCD screen, set the resolution to native resolution. *Native resolution* sets the video output to the same number of pixels that the monitor has. If you do not use native resolution, the monitor does not produce the best picture.

To change the display settings in Windows 8 and 7, use the following path:

Control Panel > Display > Change display settings

In Windows Vista, use the following path:

Control Panel > Personalization > Display Settings

You can adjust the following features in Windows 8 and 7:

- *Screen resolution*—Specifies the number of pixels. A higher number of pixels provides better resolution.
- *Orientation*—Determines whether the display appears in landscape, portrait, flipped landscape, or flipped portrait orientations.
- *Refresh rate*—Sets how often the image in the screen is redrawn. The refresh rate is in Hertz (Hz). The higher the refresh rate, the steadier the screen image.
- *Display colors*—Specifies the number of colors visible on the screen at one time. The more bits, the greater the number of colors. The 8-bit color palette contains 256 colors. The 16-bit color (High Color) palette contains 65,536 colors. The 24-bit color (True Color) palette contains 16 million colors. The 32-bit color palette contains 24-bit color and 8 bits for other data such as transparency.

Folder Options (6.1.2.7)

Ensuring proper access to files requires managing the directory and folder settings. To configure settings for folders, use the Folder Options utility.

Folder Options has three tabs.

The General tab is used to adjust the following settings:

- **Browse folders**—Configures how a folder is displayed when it is opened.
- **Click items as follows**—Specifies the number of clicks required to open a file.
- **Navigation pane**—Determines whether all folders are displayed and whether a folder is automatically expanded when it is selected in the navigation pane.

The View tab is used to adjust the following settings:

- **Folder views**—Applies the view settings for a folder being viewed to all folders of the same type.
- **Advanced settings**—Customizes the viewing experience.

The Search tab is used to adjust the following settings:

- **What to search (Windows 7 and Vista only)**—Configures search settings based on indexed and non-indexed locations to make files and folders easier to find.
- **How to search**—Determines which options to consider during a search.
- **When searching non-indexed locations**—Determines whether system directories and compressed files are included when searching non-indexed locations.

To access the Folder Options utility, use the following path:

Control Panel > Folder Options

Action Center (6.1.2.8)

The *Windows Action Center* in Windows 8 and 7 is a centralized location to view alerts that help keep Windows running smoothly. It is divided into the Security section and the Maintenance section. Important messages are highlighted in red. These issues should be addressed quickly, such as Windows Firewall is turned off or set up incorrectly. Yellow items indicate recommended tasks that may require actions from you, such as setting up a backup. The Action Center has many utilities:

- **Change Action Center settings**—Turn messaging for security and maintenance programs on or off
- **Change User Account Control settings**—Adjust settings for the UAC
- **View archived messages**—View archived messages about past computer problems
- **View performance information**—View and rate the performance of system components

To access the Action Center in Windows 8 and 7, use the following path:

Control Panel > Action Center

Note

Windows 8.0 and Windows 7 include **View performance information** in Action Center. Microsoft removed this utility from Windows 8.1.

In Windows Vista, there is no Action Center. The Windows Vista Security Center provides only the security features of the Action Center. The Security Center displays colored-coded information about the firewall, automatic updates, malware protection, Internet security settings, and user account control.

To access the Security Center in Windows Vista, use the following path:

Control Panel > Security Center

Windows Firewall (6.1.2.9)

In addition to the security settings available in the Action Center, you can prevent malicious attacks to your computer with the Windows Firewall utility. A *firewall* implements a security policy by selectively permitting and denying data traffic to a computer. A firewall gets its name from a brick-and-mortar firewall designed to prevent fire from spreading from one part of a building to another.

You can configure firewall settings for home networks, work networks, and public networks. Further changes can be made by using the following options:

- **Allow a program or feature through Windows Firewall**—Determine which programs can communicate through the Windows Firewall in Windows 7 and Vista.
- **Allow an app or feature through Windows Firewall**—Determine which programs can communicate through the Windows Firewall in Windows 8.
- **Change notification settings**—Manage notifications from the Windows Firewall.
- **Turn Windows Firewall on or off**—Turn the Windows Firewall on or off.
- **Restore defaults**—Restore the Windows Firewall to the default settings.
- **Advanced settings**—Adjust advanced security settings.

To access the Windows Firewall, use the following path:

Start > Control Panel > Windows Firewall

Figure 6-16 displays the Windows Firewall for Window 7.

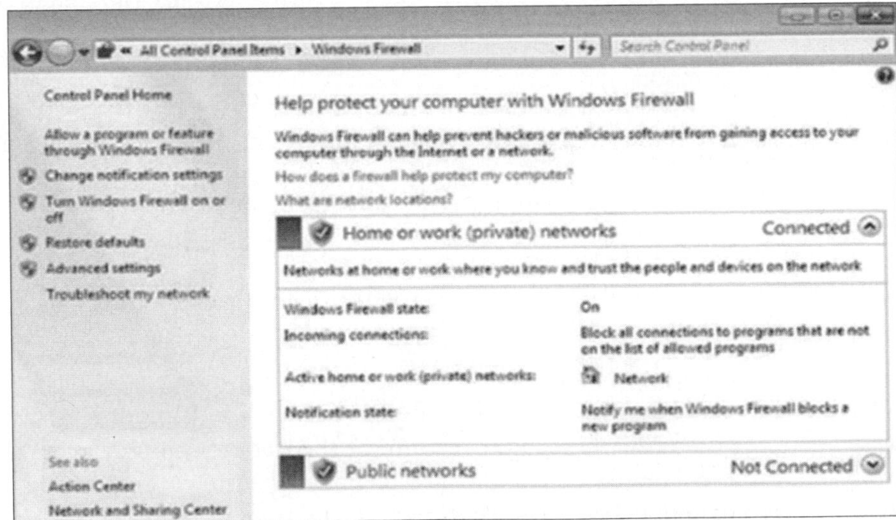

Figure 6-16 Windows Firewall on Windows 7

Power Options (6.1.2.10)

The *Power Options utility* in Windows allows you to change the power consumption of certain devices or the entire computer. Use Power Options to maximize performance or conserve energy by configuring a power plan. *Power plans* are a collection of hardware and system settings that manage the power usage of the computer.

Windows have preset power plans. These are the default settings and were created when Windows was installed. You can use the default settings or the customized plans that are based on specific work requirements.

Figure 6-17 shows Power Options in Windows 7.

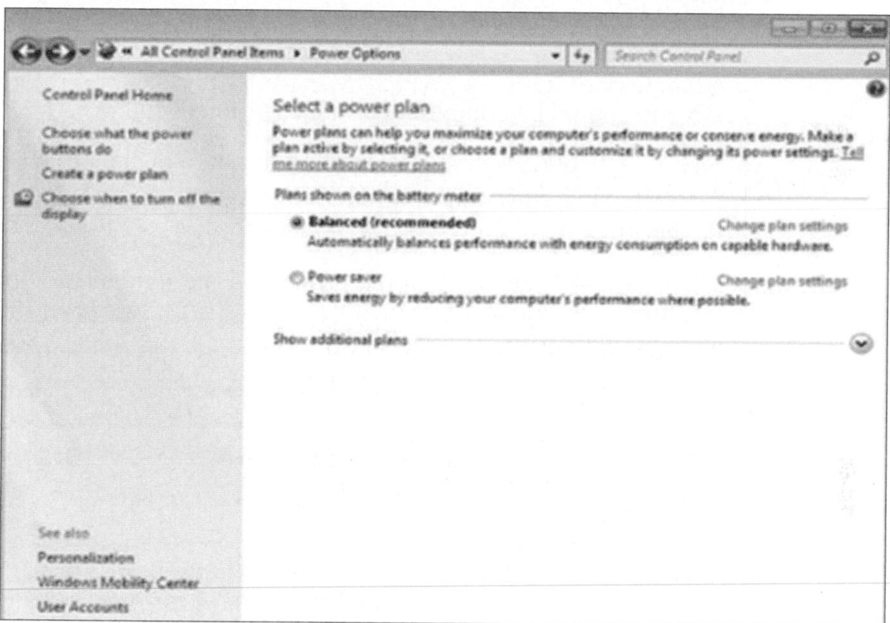

Figure 6-17 Power Options in Windows 7

> **Note**
>
> Power Options automatically detect some devices that are connected to the computer. Therefore, the Power Options windows will vary based on the hardware that is detected.

To access the Power Options, use the following path:

Control Panel > Power Options

You can choose from the following options:

- Require a password on wakeup
- Choose what the power buttons do
- Choose what closing the lid does (for laptops only)
- Create a power plan
- Choose when to turn off the display
- Change when the computer sleeps

Selecting **Choose what the power buttons do** or **Choose what closing the lid does** configures how a computer acts when power or sleep buttons are pressed or when the lid is closed. If users do not want to completely shut down a computer, the following options are available:

- **Do nothing**—The computer continues to run at full power.
- *Sleep*—Documents, applications, and the state of the operating system are saved in RAM. This allows the computer to power on quickly, but uses power to retain the information in RAM.
- *Hibernate*—Documents, applications, and the state of the operating system are saved to a temporary file on the hard drive. With this option, the computer takes a little longer to power on than the Sleep state, but does not use any power to retain the information on the hard drive.
- **Shut Down**—Shuts down the computer.

System Utility (6.1.2.11)

The *System utility* allows all users to view basic system information, access tools, and configure advanced system settings.

To access the System utility, use the following path:

Control Panel > System

The various settings can be accessed by clicking the links on the left panel.

When **Remote Settings** or **System Protection** is clicked, the System Properties utility appears with the following tabs:

- **Computer Name**—View or modify the name and workgroup settings for a computer, as well as change the domain or workgroup.
- **Hardware**—Access the Device Manager or adjust the device installation settings.
- **Advanced**—Configure settings for performance, user profiles, startup, and recovery.

- **System Protection**—Access System Restore and configure protection settings.
- **Remote**—Adjust settings for Remote Assistance and Remote Desktop.

Increasing Performance

To enhance the performance of the OS, you can change some of the settings, such as virtual memory configuration settings, as shown in Figure 6-18. The OS uses *virtual memory* and places it in the paging file on the hard drive when a computer does not have enough RAM available to run a program. A *paging file* is where data is stored until enough RAM is available to process the data. This process is much slower than accessing the RAM directly. If a computer has a small amount of RAM, consider purchasing additional RAM to reduce paging.

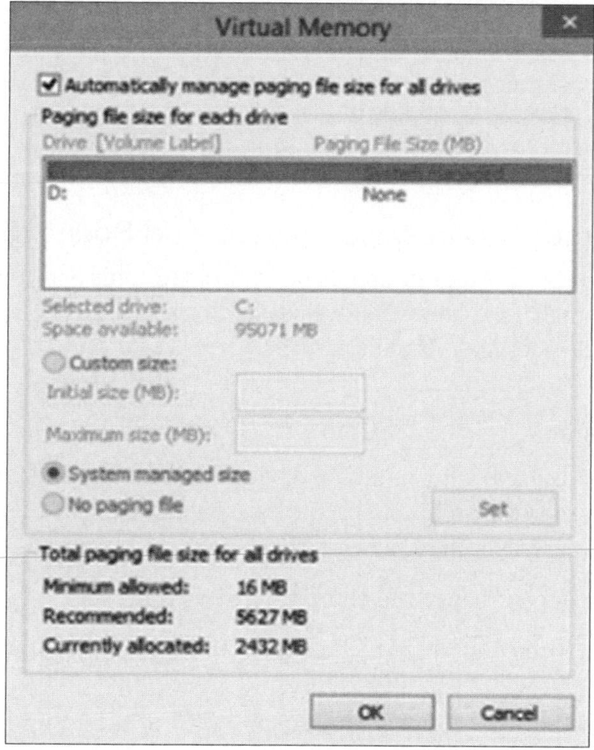

Figure 6-18 Virtual Memory Setting

To view the virtual memory setting, use the following path:

Control Panel > **System** > **Advanced system settings** > **Advanced** tab > In the **Performance** area > **Settings** button > **Advanced** tab> click **Change**

Windows ReadyBoost

If users are unable to install more RAM, they can use an external flash device and Windows ReadyBoost to enhance performance in Windows. *Windows ReadyBoost* enables Windows to treat an external flash device, such as a USB drive, as hard drive cache.

To activate Windows ReadyBoost, insert a flash device and use the following path:

Right-click the desired external flash device **>** click **Properties>** click the **ReadyBoost** tab.

After ReadyBoost has been activated for the device, determine how much space on the device will be reserved as cache. A minimum of 256 MB must be selected, with a maximum of 4GB for FAT32 file systems and 32GB for NTFS file systems.

Lab—Manage Virtual Memory (6.1.2.12)

In this lab, you customize virtual memory settings. Refer to the lab in *IT Essentials v6 Lab Manual.*

Device Manager, Devices and Printers, and Sound (6.1.2.13)

Device Manager, Devices and Printers, and Sound are tools and utilities for configuring and managing hardware devices and printers. There are several options for configuring devices and installing drivers.

Device Manager

Device Manager displays a list of all the devices installed in the computer, allowing you to diagnose and resolve device problems. You can view details about the installed hardware and drivers, as well as perform the following functions:

- **Update a driver**—Change the currently installed driver.
- *Roll back a driver*—Change the currently installed driver to the previously installed driver.
- **Uninstall a driver**—Remove a driver.
- **Disable a device**—Disable a device.

To access the Device Manager, use the following path:

Control Panel > Device Manager

You can view the properties of any device in the system by double-clicking the device name.

The Device Manager utility uses icons to indicate a problem with a device, as shown in Figure 6-19.

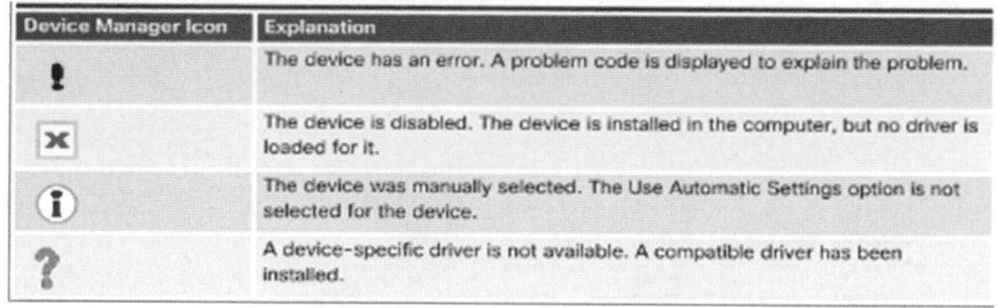

Device Manager Icon	Explanation
!	The device has an error. A problem code is displayed to explain the problem.
X	The device is disabled. The device is installed in the computer, but no driver is loaded for it.
i	The device was manually selected. The Use Automatic Settings option is not selected for the device.
?	A device-specific driver is not available. A compatible driver has been installed.

Figure 6-19 Device Manager Icon

Devices and Printers

Use Devices and Printers for a high-level look at the devices connected to the computer. Devices displayed in Devices and Printers are typically external devices you can connect to your computer through a port or network connection. Devices and Printers also allow you to quickly add a new device to the computer. Windows will automatically install any necessary drivers.

Devices listed include:

- Portable devices you carry with you and occasionally connect to your computer, such as mobile phones, portable music players, and digital cameras
- All devices you plug into a USB port on your computer, including external USB hard drives, flash drives, webcams, keyboards, and mice
- All printers connected to your computer
- Wireless devices connected to your computer, including Bluetooth devices and Wireless USB devices
- Compatible network devices connected to your computer, such as network-enabled scanners, media extenders, or network-attached storage devices (NAS devices)

To access Devices and Printers in Windows 8 and 7, use the following path:

Control Panel > Devices and Printers

To install a new device, click the **Add a device** button.

Figure 6-20 shows the Devices and Printers tool in Windows 8.

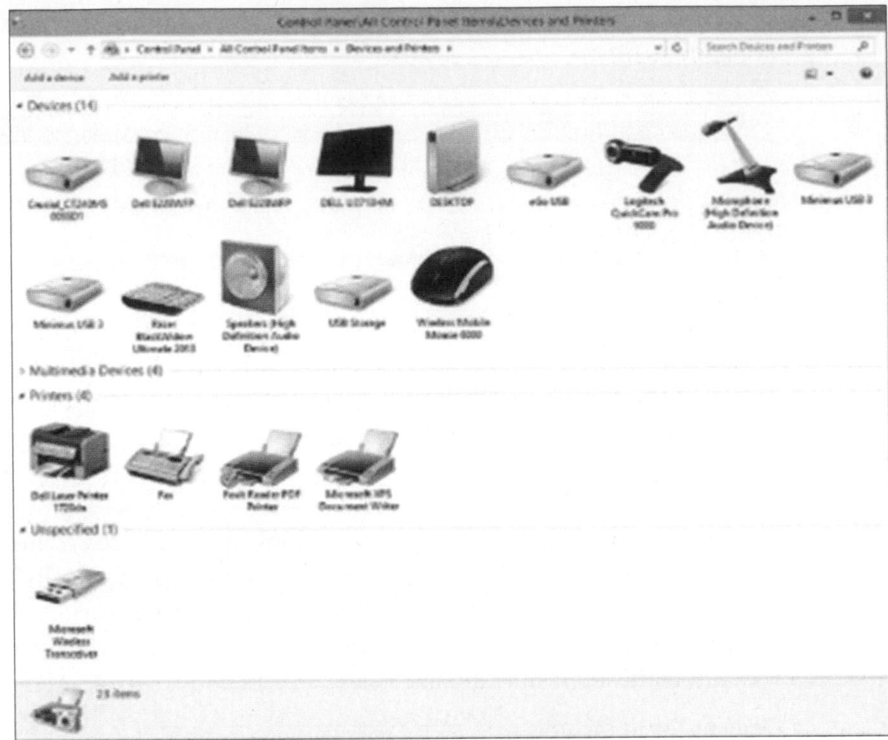

Figure 6-20 Windows 8 Devices and Printers Utility

In Windows Vista, you can use **Add Hardware** to add new devices to your computer. To access **Add Hardware**, use the following path:

Control Panel > Add Hardware

Sound

Use the Sound utility to configure audio devices or change the sound scheme of the computer. For example, you can change the email notification sound from a beep to a chime. The Sound utility also allows a user to choose which audio device is to be used for playback or recording.

To access the Sound utility, use the following path:

Control Panel > Sound

Lab—Device Manager (6.1.2.14)

In this lab, you open Device Manager to display devices listed on your computer. You also display the monitor settings. Refer to the lab in *IT Essentials v6 Lab Manual.*

Region, Programs and Features, and Troubleshooting (6.1.2.15)

Control panel is used to configure and manage many aspects of Windows, including installation and removal of programs, configure region specific information such as how date, time, currency, and numbers are formatted in Windows, as well as an applet that allows users to access troubleshooting wizards that can help fix problems that are encountered on a system.

Region

Windows 8 allows you to change the format of numbers, currencies, dates, and time by using the Region tool. You can also change the primary language or install an additional language by using Language tool.

To access the Region tool in Windows 8 use the following path:

Control Panel > Region

To access the Language tool in Windows 8 use the following path:

Control Panel > Language

Region and Language Options

In Windows 7 and Vista, the two tools are combined into one tool called Regional and Language.

To access the Region and Language tool use the following path:

Control Panel > Region and Language

Programs and Features

Use the Program and Features tool to uninstall a program from your computer if you no longer use it or if you want to free up space on your hard disk. You can use Programs and Features to uninstall programs or to change a program's configuration by adding or removing certain options.

To access Programs and Features, use the following path:

Control Panel > Programs and Features

Troubleshooting

The Troubleshooting tool has a number of built-in scripts to identify and solve problems.

To access the Troubleshooting tool in Windows 8 and 7, use the following path:

Control Panel > Troubleshooting

To display a list of all available troubleshooting scripts, click the **View All** link located in the pane on the left side of the Troubleshooting window.

Lab—Region and Language Options (6.1.2.16)

In this lab, you examine regional and language settings. Refer to the lab in *IT Essentials v6 Lab Manual.*

HomeGroup and Network and Sharing Center (6.1.2.17)

HomeGroup allows two or more computers running Windows 7 or newer on your network to share printers, media files and document libraries. *Network and Sharing Center* allows an administrator to configure and review nearly all network operations in a Windows computer.

HomeGroup (Windows 8 and 7)

A homegroup is created automatically, and the network location must be set to Home. To increase security, the homegroup is password-protected. It also allows the users to choose the files that are shared. Other users cannot change the shared files unless they are granted permission.

Join or Create a Homegroup

If a homegroup already exists on the network, you may join the homegroup. If no homegroup exists on the network, a new homegroup can be created. During the creation process, you can choose files or devices to be shared and set the permission levels, as shown in Figure 6-21. A password is generated at the end of the process to add other computers to the homegroup.

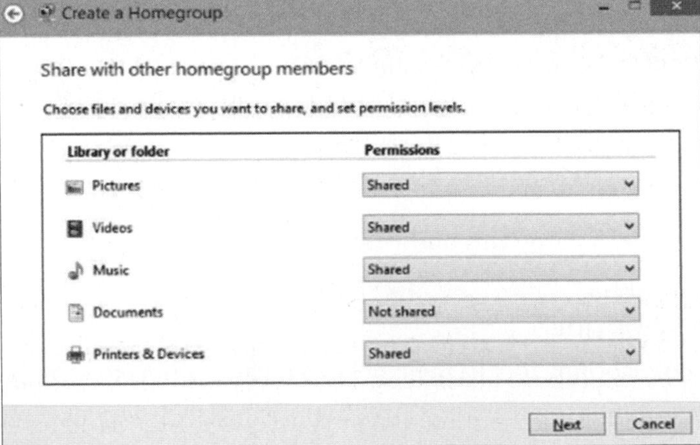

Figure 6-21 HomeGroup and Network and Sharing Center

If your computer belongs to a domain, the computer can join a homegroup to access shared resources on the network, but the computer cannot share its resources or create a new homegroup.

To join a homegroup, use the following path:

Control Panel > HomeGroup > Join Now

To create a new homegroup, use the following path:

Control Panel > HomeGroup > Create a homegroup

Create a Workgroup or Join a Workgroup or Domain

In Windows 7 and Vista, Windows automatically creates and names a workgroup in a network. You can join this workgroup or create a new one. Alternatively, you can join a domain. To join a domain, you need to know the domain name and have a user account in the domain.

In Windows Vista or later to create a workgroup, join a workgroup, or join a domain use the following path:

Start > Right-Click **Computer** > **Properties** > Under the Computer name, domain, and workgroup settings, select **Change settings**

Network and Sharing Center

Network and Sharing Center shows how your computer connects to a network. Internet connectivity, if present, is also displayed here. The bottom part of the window displays and allows the configuration of shared network resources. Some useful and common network-related tasks are displayed on the left pane of the window.

Administrative Tools (6.1.3)

Administrative Tools is a collection of very powerful tools that fundamentally change the OS. Unlike customizing the theme of the desktop, these utilities create partitions, install drivers, enable services, and perform other significant modifications.

Computer Management (6.1.3.1)

Windows contains many utilities to manage permissions and users, or to configure computer components and services. The *Computer Management* console, as shown in Figure 6-22, allows you to manage many aspects of your computer and remote computers in one tool.

The Computer Management console provides access to a number of utilities:

- Task Scheduler
- Event Viewer
- Shared Folders
- Local Users and Groups
- Performance
- Device Manager
- Disk Management

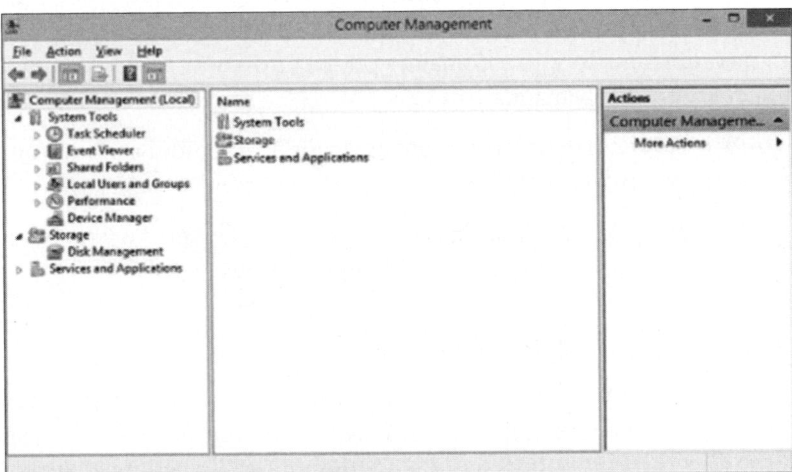

Figure 6-22 Computer Management

To open the Computer Management console, use the following path:

Control Panel > Administrative Tools > Computer Management

Alternatively, the Computer Management tool can be accessed by right-clicking **This PC** in Windows 8.1, or by right-clicking **Computer** in Windows 8.0, 7, and Vista and selecting **Manage.**

To view the Computer Management console for a remote computer, follow these steps:

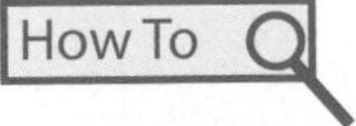

Step 1. In the console tree, click Computer Management (Local) and select Connect to another computer.

Step 2. In the Another Computer field, type the name of the computer or browse to find the computer to manage.

Event Viewer (6.1.3.2)

The *Event Viewer* logs the history of application, security, system events. These log files are a valuable troubleshooting tool because they provide information necessary to identify a problem.

To access the Event Viewer, shown in Figure 6-23, use the following path:

Control Panel > Administrative Tools > Event Viewer

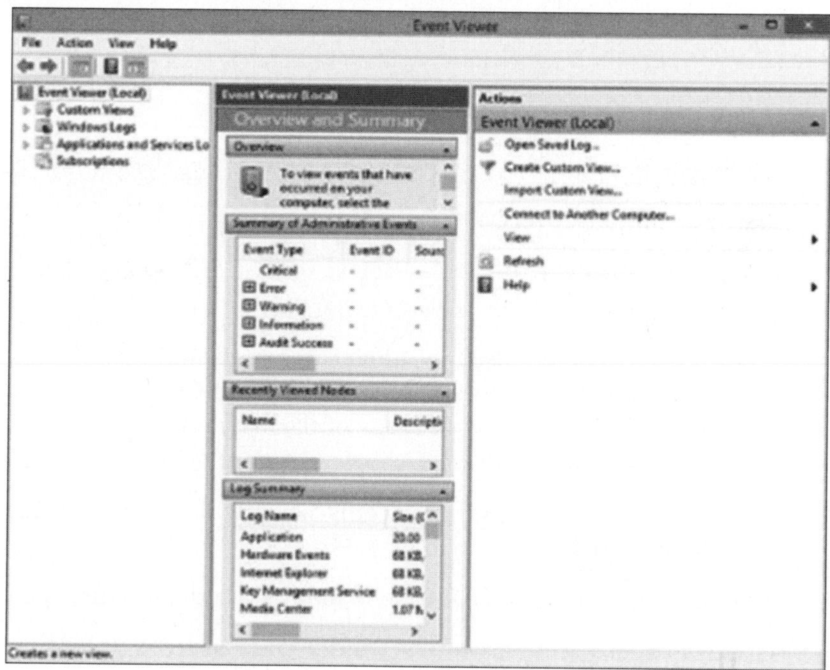

Figure 6-23 Windows Event Viewer

Component Services

Component Services is an administrative tool used by administrators and developers to deploy, configure, and administer Component Object Model (COM) components. COM is a way to allow the use of components in environments other than the environment in which they were created.

To access Component Services, shown in Figure 6-24, use the following path:

Control Panel > Administrative Tools > Component Services

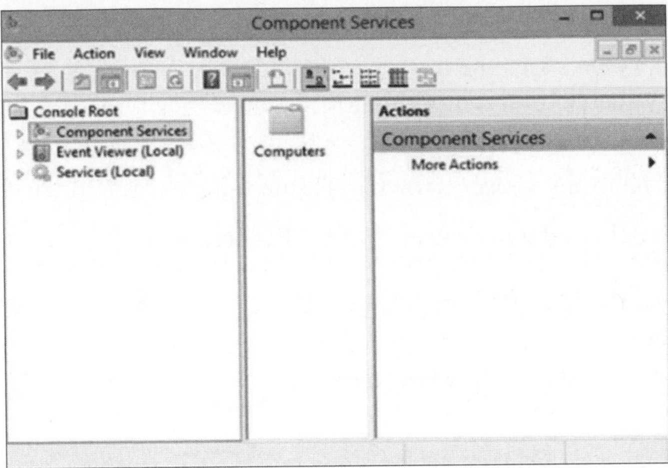

Figure 6-24 Windows Component Services

Data Sources

Data Sources is a tool used by administrators to add, remove, or manage data sources using Open Database Connectivity (ODBC). ODBC is a technology that programs use to access a wide range of databases or data sources. To access Data Sources (ODBC) in Windows 8, shown in Figure 6-25, use the following path:

Control Panel > Administrative Tools > ODBC Data Sources (32-bit) or **ODBC Data Sources (64-bit)**

To access Data Sources (ODBC) in Windows 7 and Vista, use the following path:

Control Panel > Administrative Tools > Data Sources (ODBC)

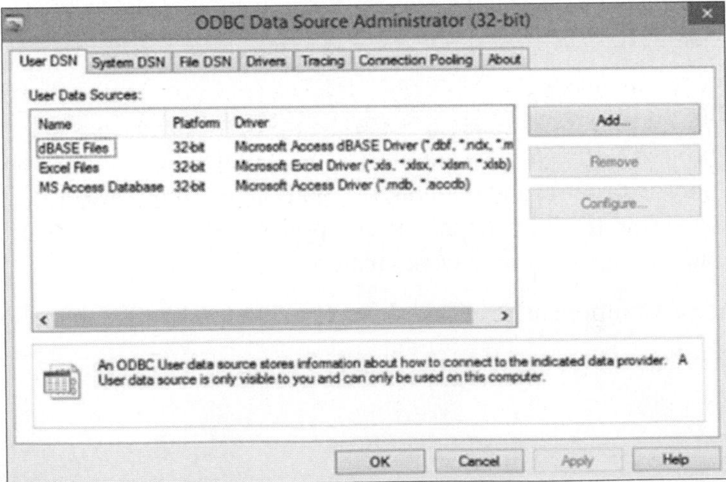

Figure 6-25 Windows 8 ODBC Data Source

Services (6.1.3.3)

The *Services console (SERVICES.MSC)* allows you to manage all the services on your computer and remote computers. A *service* is a type of application that runs in the background to achieve a specific goal, or to wait for a request. To reduce security risks, only start necessary services. You can use the following settings, or states, to control a service:

- **Automatic**—The service starts when the computer is started. This prioritizes the most important services.
- **Automatic (delayed)**—The service starts after services that are set to Automatic have started. The Automatic (delayed) setting is available only in Windows 7 and Vista.
- **Manual**—The service must be started manually by the user or by a service or program that needs it.
- **Disabled**—The service cannot be started until it is enabled.
- **Stopped**—The service is not running.

To open the Services console, use the following path:

Control Panel > Administrative Tools > Services

To view the Services console for a remote computer, follow these steps:

Step 1. In the console tree, right-click Services (Local) and select Connect to another computer.

Step 2. In the Another computer field, type the name of the computer or browse to find the computer you want to manage.

System Configuration (6.1.3.4)

System Configuration (MSCONFIG) is a tool used to identify problems that keep Windows from starting correctly. To help with isolating the issue, services, and startup programs can be turned off, and turned back on one at a time. After you have determined the cause, permanently remove or disable the program or service, or reinstall it.

Table 6-2 briefly explains the tabs and options available in System Configuration.

Table 6-2 System Configuration

Tab	Description
General	Displays a list of startup selections: ■ **Normal startup**—Starts normally. ■ **Diagnostic startup**—Starts with basic services and drivers only. ■ **Selective startup**—Starts with basic services and drivers and user-selected startup programs.
Boot	Displays a list of available Windows operating systems and shows boot options.
Services	Displays a list of the services that are started with the operation system. Allows you to disable services for troubleshooting purposes.
Startup	Displays a list of all the applications that run when the computer boots up. This list includes the applications with manufacturer name, the executable file location, and the registry location.
Tools	Displays a list of diagnostic tools that you can launch.

To open System Configuration, use the following path:

Control Panel > Administrative Tools > System Configuration

Performance Monitor and Windows Memory Diagnostics (6.1.3.5)

The *Performance Monitor*, shown Figure 6-26, displays an overview of the Performance Monitor and System Summary. You must have administrative privileges to access the Performance Monitor console. There is also a link to Resource Monitor that can be found on the homepage of the Performance Monitor tool.

The System Summary displays real-time information about the processors, disks, memory, and network usage. Use the System Summary to display detailed data about the resources that you are using when performing specific tasks or multiple tasks. The data displayed can help you understand how the computer workload affects system resources, such as the CPU, memory, and network. You can summarize usage data with histograms, graphs, and reports. The data can also help determine when an upgrade might be necessary.

To open the Performance Monitor in Windows 8, and 7, use the following path:

Control Panel > Administrative Tools > Performance Monitor

In Windows Vista, use the following path:

Control Panel > Administrative Tools > Reliability and Performance Monitor

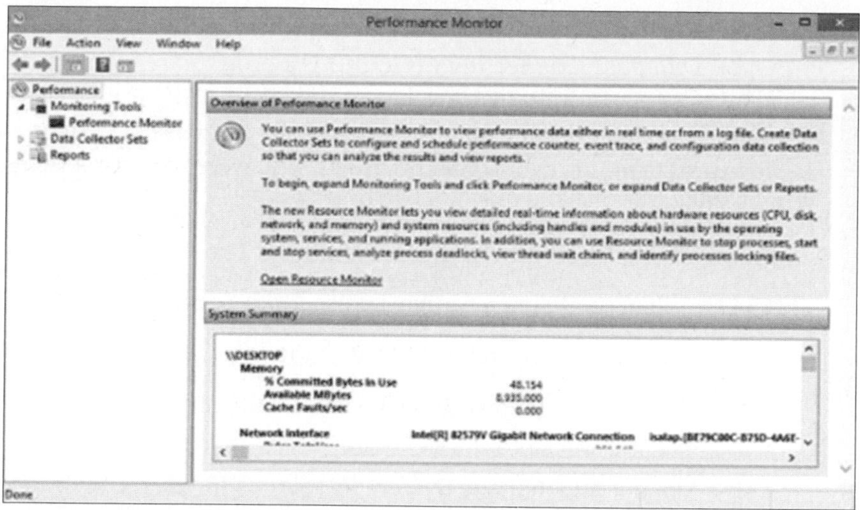

Figure 6-26 Performance Monitor

Windows Memory Diagnostic is an administrative tool that checks the physical memory that is installed on a computer for errors.

To access Windows Memory Diagnostic in Windows 8 and 7, use the following path:

Control Panel > Administrative Tools> Windows Memory Diagnostic

To access Windows Memory Diagnostic in Windows Vista, use the following path:

Control Panel > Administrative Tools> Memory Diagnostic Tools

Programming Tools (6.1.3.6)

There are also programming tools found within the Administrative tools. These tools can help someone to program some applications.

Component Services

There are many different tools developed by Microsoft that enable the sharing of data objects. Tools like COM, COM+, and DCOM are examples of these tools. A *data object* is simply a program element. allows you to make manual changes to a program so that it works better, or in a different way.

To access Component Services in Windows 8 and 7, use the following path:

Control Panel > Administrative Tools> Component Services

To access Component Services in Windows Vista, use the following path:

Search > dcomcnfg

Data Sources (ODBC)

Open Database Connectivity (ODBC) is a programming interface developed to allow access to database management systems. ODBC was created so that access to these systems was not reliant on any specific database system or operating system. This programming tool would be used if you were creating a shared database, for example.

To access Data Sources (ODBC) in Windows 7 and Vista, use the following path:

Control Panel > Administrative Tools> Data Sources (ODBC)

To access Data Sources (ODBC) in Windows 8, use the following path:

Control Panel > Administrative Tools> ODBC Data Sources

Lab—Monitor and manage System Resources (6.1.3.7)

In this lab, you use administrative tools to monitor and manage system resources. Refer to the lab in *IT Essentials v6 Lab Manual.*

Disk Defragmenter and *Disk Error-Checking Tool* (6.1.4)

Windows, as well as other OS, come with some built-in utilities that are important for PC maintenance. In this section investigates several Windows utilities.

Disk Defragmenter and Disk Error-Checking Tool (6.1.4.1)

To maintain and optimize an operating system, you can use various tools within Windows. Some of these tools include hard-drive *defragmentation*, which consolidates files for faster access, and disk error-checking, which scans the hard drive for file structure and disk surface errors.

Disk Defragmenter (or Disk Optimization)

As files increase in size, some data is written to the next available cluster on the disk. In time, data becomes fragmented and spread over nonadjacent clusters on the hard drive. As a result, it takes longer to locate and retrieve each section of the data. A *disk defragmenter* gathers the noncontiguous data into one place, making the OS run faster.

Note

It is not recommended to perform disk defragmentation on SSDs. SSDs are optimized by the controller and firmware they use. It should not be harmful to defragment Hybrid SSDs (SSHD) because they use hard disks to store data, not solid-state ram.

To access the Disk Defragmenter in Windows 8 use the following path:

Right-click the drive to check **> Properties > Tools >** click **Optimize**

To access the Disk Defragmenter in Windows 7 and Vista, use the following path:

Right-click the drive to check **> Properties > Tools >** click **Defragment Now**

Disk Error-Checking Tool

The Disk Error-Checking tool checks the integrity of files and folders by scanning the hard disk surface for physical errors. If errors are detected, the tool attempts to repair them. You can access CHKDSK through the Disk Defragmenter or by searching for *CHKDSK*. Alternatively, you can check a drive for errors using the following steps:

How To

Step 1. Right-click the drive to check and select Properties.

Step 2. Click the Tools tab.

Step 3. Under Error-checking, in Windows 8, click **Check.** In Windows 7 or Vista, click **Check Now.**

Step 4. Under the Check disk options, in Windows 8, select **Scan Drive** to attempt to recover bad sectors. In Windows 7 and Vista, select **Scan for and attempt recovery of bad sectors** and click **Start.**

The tool fixes file system errors and checks the disk for bad sectors. It also attempts to recover data from bad sectors.

Note

Use the Disk Error-Checking tool whenever a sudden loss of power causes the system to shut down.

Lab—Hard Drive Maintenance (6.1.4.2)

In this lab, you examine the results of using Disk Check and Disk Defragmenter on a hard drive. Refer to the lab in *IT Essentials v6 Lab Manual.*

System Information (6.1.4.3)

Administrators can use the System Information tool to collect and display information about local and remote computers. The System Information tool quickly finds information about software, drivers, hardware configurations, and computer components. Support personnel can use this information to diagnose and troubleshoot a computer.

To access the System Information tool in Windows 8, search for **msinfo32.exe** and press **Enter**.

To access the System Information tool in Windows 7 or Vista, use the following path:

Start > All Programs > Accessories > System Tools > System Information

You can also create a file containing all the information about the computer to send to another technician or help desk. To export a System Information file, select **File > Export**, type the filename, choose a location, and click **Save**.

Lab—Manage System Files in Windows (6.1.4.4)

In this lab, you use Windows utilities to gather information about the computer. Refer to the lab in *IT Essentials v6 Lab Manual.*

Command Line Tools (6.1.5)

Command line tools are tools that can be accessed using the command line interface (CLI) which is a text-based interface. Rather than navigate the operating system tasks through the use of icons you instruct the computer to perform those tasks by the use of text commands. Knowing the commands to use in the command line interface can be very useful when troubleshooting. In this section, you learn some of the common Windows CLI commands.

Windows CLI Commands (6.1.5.1)

Before computers had a GUI, programs and data were accessed using a command line interface (CLI). The CLI is a text-only environment where commands are issued to run programs, create and move files and folders, and perform all other functions of the computer. The CLI did not use a mouse or other input device. The CLI is still available from within Windows, although with limited capability. When troubleshooting problems with the OS, you may need to use CLI commands and options to perform tasks.

To access the CLI in Windows, search for **command.**

After the command window opens, you can enter commands to perform specific tasks. Table 6-3 describes the most common commands, how to use them, and what they do.

Table 6-3 Common Windows CLI Commands

Command	Command Function
Help [command-name]	Provides specific information for any CLI command. Alternatively, you can use [command-name]/?.
Taskkill	Stops a running application.
Bootrec	Repairs the MBR.
Shutdown	Shuts down a local or remote machine.
Tasklist	Displays currently running applications.
MD	Creates a new directory.
RD	Removes a directory.
CD	Changes to a different directory.
DEL	Deletes a file.
FORMAT	Formats a drive, mount point, or volume with a file system.
COPY	Copies files from one location to another.
XCOPY	■ Copies files, directories, or entire drives from one location to another. ■ Copies a directory and its contents from one location to another unless the directory is empty. ■ Copies only files with the archive attribute set. ■ Copies and verifies that each new file is the same as the source file. ■ Copies without prompting to overwrite existing files.
ROBOCOPY	Copies a file.
SFC	Checks and replaces all of the protected system files with known good versions if they have become corrupted or been deleted.
CHKDSK	■ Creates a report about the disk. ■ Fixes any file allocation table entries. ■ Attempts to recover data from bad sectors of the drive.
RUNAS	Allows a user to run specific tools and programs with different permissions than the user's current logon provides.
GPUPDATE	Refreshes Group Policy settings, including security settings.
GPRESULT	Refreshes Group Policy settings and Resultant Set of Policy (RSOP) for a user or a computer.
DIR	Displays a list of a directory's files and subdirectories.

(Continued)

Table 6-3 *Continued*

Command	Command Function
EXIT	Quits the command prompt.
EXPAND	Uncompresses one or more files from .CAB cabinet files.
RSTRUI	Starts the System Restore utility.
BOOTREC	Fixes boot sector problems that prevent Windows from starting. This tool is only available in the Recovery Environment. Refer to BOOTREC help for more information.
DEFRAG	Optimizes files on disks to improve system performance.
DISKPART	Creates, deletes, and resizes hard drive partitions. DISKPART can also assign or reassign drive letters. Care should be exercised when working with DISKPART.

If you are denied the use of one of these commands, you may need to access the CLI as an administrator. To access the CLI as an administrator in Windows, search for **command**. Next, right-click **Command Prompt icon>** click **Run as administrator>** click **Yes**. You will need to provide the administrator password to complete the command.

Video

Video—Common Windows CLI Commands (6.1.5.2)

This video shows how to use many CLI commands at the Windows command prompt to navigate directories and manipulate files and folders. To have the computer perform many tasks from the command prompt it is often necessary to run the command prompt from an elevated status. This means to run it with Administrative privileges. This video shows the user how to elevate the command prompt to administrator level, which varies depending on the OS version, and then steps through executing common commands such as the ones listed in Table 6-3.

Please view the video in the Cisco Networking Academy IT Essentials 6.0 online course.

Video

Video—Log User Access (6.1.5.3)

This video explores how running a batch file set by the group policy editor can be used to record the login and logoff of users on a computer. This video takes a look at executing more advanced functions in the CLI. In this video, the user is instructed on how to create files, move files, copy files, execute programs, and change the local group policy all using the command line.

Please view the video in the Cisco Networking Academy IT Essentials 6.0 online course.

Lab—Common Windows CLI Commands (6.1.5.4)

In this lab, you use CLI commands to manage files and folders in Windows. Refer to the lab in *IT Essentials v6 Lab Manual*.

System Utilities (6.1.5.5)

The Run Line utility, shown in Figure 6-27, allows you to enter commands to configure settings in Windows. Many of these commands are used for system diagnostics and modifications.

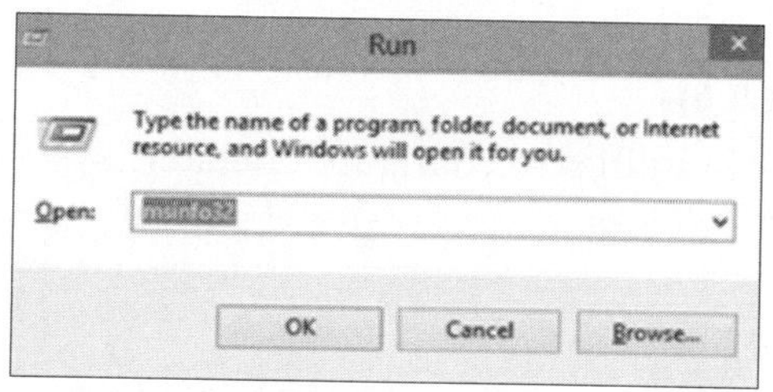

Figure 6-27 Windows Run Line Utility

Note

Because of the new GUI included in Windows 8, the Run Line utility lost much of its functionality. This is because Windows 8 allows a user to simply type commands at the Start Screen.

To access the Run Line utility in Windows, search for **Run**.

This is a list of common commands:

- COMMAND—This starts the Windows command line. It is used to execute command-line programs and utilities.
- *DXDIAG*—This displays details for all DirectX components and drivers that are installed in a computer.
- EXPLORER—This opens Windows Explorer.
- MMC—This opens the *Microsoft Management Console (MMC)* which allows you to organize management tools, called *snap-ins*, in one location for easy administration. You can also add web page links, tasks, ActiveX controls, and folders. You can create as many customized MMCs as needed, each with a different name. This is useful when multiple administrators manage different aspects of the same computer. Each administrator can have an individualized MMC for monitoring and configuring computer settings.

- *MSINFO32*—This shows the System Information window, a complete system summary of the computer, including hardware components and software information.
- MSTSC—This opens the Remote Desktop utility.
- NOTEPAD—This opens Notepad, which is a basic text editor.
- *REGEDIT*—This opens the Registry Editor, which allows a user to edit the registry. Using the Registry Editor utility incorrectly could cause hardware, application, or operating system problems, including problems that require you to reinstall the operating system.

Lab—System Utilities (6.1.5.6)

In this lab, you use Windows utilities to configure operating system settings. Refer to the lab in *IT Essentials v6 Lab Manual.*

Client-Side Virtualization (6.2)

Client-side virtualization reduces operating costs, provides a flexible environment, and centralized management. It can be deployed so that one physical device can support running multiple operating systems separately and simultaneously. This can be done through the use of a virtual machine manager.

Purpose and Requirements of Virtualization (6.2.1)

In a business environment, companies must manage technological resources in a way that allows them to stay competitive by cutting costs and allocating resources wisely. As a result, client-side virtualization has become a popular method of providing staff with critical resources, such as applications, file-sharing services, and other productivity tools. Virtualization also has advantages for small office/home office (SOHO) users, because it can provide access to programs that are not available on a specific OS.

Purpose of Virtual Machines (6.2.1.1)

Virtualization means that the system resources of a computer are used to create a virtual machine. A *virtual machine* is a computer that exists within a computer. The physical computer is called a *host*, or *host machine*. The computer within the host is the virtual machine. The virtual machine is sometimes called a *guest*.

A host machine must be a physical machine that is powered on and controlled by a user. A virtual machine uses the system resources on the host machine to boot and run an OS. The OS of the virtual machine is independent of the OS installed on the host machine. For example, a host machine running Windows 8.1 can host a virtual machine that has Windows 7 installed. This virtual machine can run software specific to Windows 7. The Windows 7 installation does not interfere with the Windows 8.1 installation on the host machine.

Host and guest operating systems do not need to be of the same family. For example, the host can be running Windows 7 while the guest runs Linux. If needed, users can further increase the functionality of their system resources by running multiple virtual machines.

Figure 6-28 shows a logical virtual machine diagram.

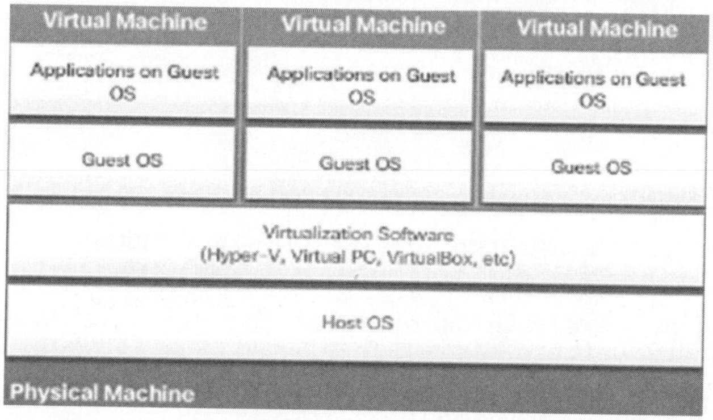

Figure 6-28 Logical Virtual Machine Diagram

Hypervisor: Virtual Machine Manager (6.2.1.2)

The software that creates and manages a virtual machine on a host machine is called the *hypervisor, or Virtual Machine Manager (VMM)*. A hypervisor can run multiple virtual machines on a single host computer. Each virtual machine runs its own operating system. The number of virtual machines that can run at the same time depends on the host machine's hardware resources. The hypervisor allocates the physical system resources, such as CPU, RAM, and hard drive, to each virtual machine as needed. This ensures that the operation of one virtual machine does not interfere with another.

Figure 6-29 shows the two types of hypervisors: Type 1 (native) and Type 2 (hosted). A *Type 1 hypervisor* runs directly on the hardware of a host and manages the allocation of system resources to virtual operating systems. A *Type 2 hypervisor* is hosted by an OS. The Windows Hyper-V and Windows Virtual PC are examples of a Type 2 hypervisor.

Figure 6-29 Hypervisor Type 1 and Type 2

Windows Hyper-V

Windows Hyper-V is a virtualization platform for Windows 8. It provides software infrastructure and basic management tools to create and manage a virtualized server computing environment. A virtualized server environment has many advantages:

- It can reduce the costs of operating and maintaining physical servers by increasing hardware utilization.
- It can increase development and test efficiency by reducing the amount of time it takes to set up hardware and software.
- It can improve server availability without using as many physical computers.

Windows Hyper-V must be enabled before it can be used. To enable Windows Hyper-V use the following path:

Control Panel > Programs and Features > click **Turn Windows features on or off > check the Hyper-V box >** click **OK.**

You may need to restart the host machine before the changes can take effect.

Figure 6-30 shows the Hyper-V manager tool in Windows 8.

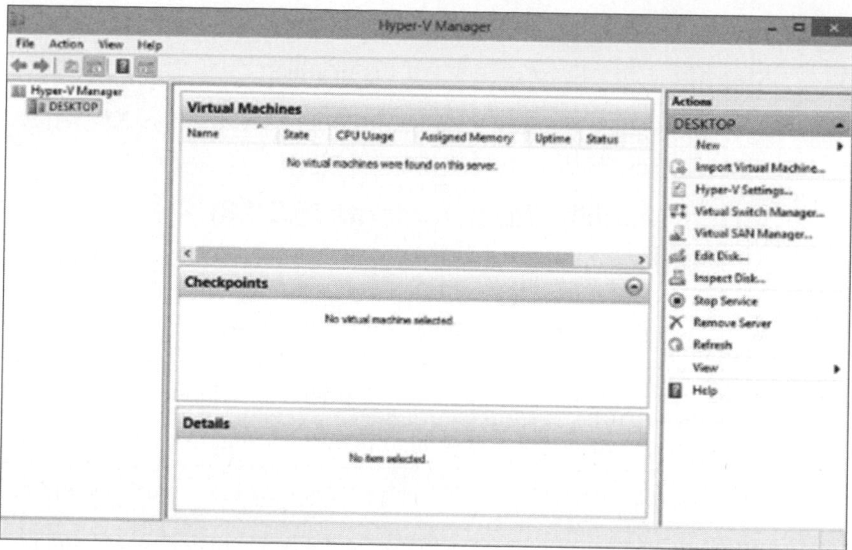

Figure 6-30 Hyper-V in Windows 8

Windows Virtual PC

Windows Virtual PC is the virtualization platform for Windows 7. Virtual PC allows you to partition system resources for a Windows OS among virtual machines running a licensed copy of Windows 7 or Vista. You can download Virtual PC from the Microsoft Windows website.

Windows XP Mode

Windows XP Mode is a program available for Windows 7. Windows XP Mode uses virtualization technology to allow users to run Windows XP programs in Windows 7. It opens a virtual machine on the Windows 7 desktop that provides a fully functional version of Windows XP, including access to all system resources. After installing a program in Windows XP Mode, you can run the program in XP Mode and access it from the Windows 7 Start Menu.

Note

Before using Windows XP Mode, download and install Windows Virtual PC.

Note

Microsoft has decommissioned Windows XP Mode, and it is not included in Windows versions later than Windows 7.

To access XP Mode in Windows 7, follow these steps:

How To

Step 1. Click **Start >** click **All Programs**.

Step 2. Click **Windows Virtual PC>** click **Windows XP Mode**.

Virtual Machine Requirements (6.2.1.3)

All virtual machines require that basic system requirements are met, such as a minimum amount of hard disk space or RAM. The minimum system requirements for Windows 8 Hyper-V are displayed in Table 6-4.

Table 6-4 Hyper-V Minimum Requirements in Windows 8

Host OS	Windows 8 Pro or Enterprise 64-bit operating system
Processor	64-bit processor with Second Level Address Translation
BIOS	BIOS-level hardware virtualization support
Memory	At least 4GB system RAM
Hard disk space	At least 15GB per virtual OS

The minimum system requirements for Windows 7 Virtual PC are displayed in Table 6-5.

Table 6-5 Virtual PC Minimum Requirements in Windows 7

Processor	1 GHz 32-bit or 64-bit processor
Memory	2GB
Hard disk space	15GB per virtual OS

Like physical computers, virtual machines are susceptible to threats and malicious attacks. Users should install security software, run a firewall, and update the operating system and programs.

To connect to the Internet, a virtual machine uses a virtual network adapter. The virtual network adapter acts like a real adapter in a physical computer, except that it connects through the physical adapter on the host to establish a connection to the Internet.

Common Preventive Maintenance Techniques for Operating Systems (6.3)

Preventive maintenance techniques should be planned and implemented to avoid preventable problems. A plan should be developed that focuses on areas that would affect productivity the most and should include detailed information about an organization's hardware and software and what needs to be done to ensure ongoing optimal operation of systems. Accurate and updated documentation is a critical component in preventive maintenance.

OS Preventive Maintenance Plan (6.3.1)

To ensure that an OS remains fully functional, you must implement a preventive maintenance plan.

Preventive Maintenance Plan Contents (6.3.1.1)

A preventive maintenance plan provides the following benefits to users and organizations:

- Decreased downtime
- Improved performance
- Improved reliability
- Decreased repair costs

Preventive maintenance plans should include detailed information about the maintenance of all computers and network equipment. The plan should prioritize equipment that would affect the organization the most if that equipment fails. Preventive maintenance for an OS includes automating tasks to perform scheduled updates. Preventive maintenance also includes installing service packs that help keep the system up to date and compatible with new software and hardware. Preventive maintenance includes the following important tasks:

- Hard drive error-checking
- Hard drive defragmentation
- Hard drive backup
- Updates to the OS and applications
- Updates to antivirus and other protective software

Perform preventive maintenance regularly, and record all actions taken and observations made. A repair log helps you determine which equipment is the most or least reliable. It also provides a history of when a computer was last fixed, how it was fixed, and what the problem was.

Preventive maintenance should take place when it causes the least amount of disruption to the users. This often means scheduling tasks at night, early in the morning, or over the weekend. There are also tools and techniques that can automate many preventive maintenance tasks.

Security

Security is an important aspect of your preventive maintenance program. Install virus and malware protection software, and perform regular scans on computers to help ensure that they remain free of malicious software. Use the Windows Malicious Software Removal Tool to check a computer for malicious software. If an infection is found, the tool removes it. Each time a new version of the tool becomes available from Microsoft, download it and scan your computer for new threats. This should be a standard item in your preventive maintenance program, along with regular updates to your antivirus and spyware removal tools.

Startup Programs

Some programs, such as antivirus scanners and spyware removal tools, do not automatically start when the computer boots. To ensure that these programs run each time the computer is booted, add the program to the Startup Folder of the Start Menu. Many programs have switches to allow the program to perform a specific action such as starting without being displayed. Check the documentation to determine if your programs allow the use of special switches.

Lab—Manage the Startup Folder (6.3.1.2)

In this lab, you customize the Startup Folder and the Run Key in the Registry to manage what applications are started automatically when Windows starts. You also use the Startup tab to manage the programs already added to the Startup Folder. Refer to the lab in *IT Essentials v6 Lab Manual.*

Updates (6.3.1.3)

Updates keep the Windows operating system, Microsoft software, and various drivers current with the latest security patches and bug fixes to keep computer systems optimized and as secure as possible.

Device Driver Updates

Manufacturers occasionally release new drivers to address issues with the current drivers. Check for updated drivers when your hardware does not work properly or to prevent future problems. It is also important to update drivers that patch or correct security problems. If a driver update does not work properly, use the Roll Back Driver feature to revert back to the previously installed driver.

Operating System Updates

Microsoft releases updates to address security issues and other functionality problems. You can install individual updates manually from the Microsoft website or automatically using the *Windows Automatic Update* utility. Downloads that contain multiple updates are called *service packs*. Installing a service pack is a good way to bring your OS up-to-date quickly. Set a restore point and back up critical data prior to installing a service pack. Add OS updates to your preventive maintenance program to ensure that your OS has the latest functionality and security fixes.

Firmware Updates

Firmware updates are less common than driver updates. Manufacturers release new firmware updates to address issues that might not be fixed with driver updates. Firmware updates can increase the speed of certain types of hardware, enable new features, or increase the stability of a product. Follow the manufacturer's instructions carefully when performing a firmware update to avoid making the hardware unusable. Research the update completely because it might not be possible to revert to the original firmware.

Scheduling Tasks (6.3.1.4)

You can schedule preventive maintenance applications to run at an assigned time. You can schedule tasks using the GUI-based *Windows Task Scheduler* or the CLI **at** command. Each of these tools allows you to run a command at a specific time, or on an ongoing basis on selected days or times. For recurring tasks, the Windows Task Scheduler is easier to learn and use than the **at** command.

Windows Task Scheduler

The Task Scheduler monitors selected, user-defined criteria and then executes the tasks when the criteria have been met. These are some common tasks that are automated using Task Scheduler:

- Disk cleanup
- Backup
- Disk defragmenter
- Restore point
- Starting other applications

To access the Windows Task Scheduler, use the following path:

Control Panel > Administrative Tools > Task Scheduler

The at Command

You can use the **at** command to schedule a command or application to run at a specific date and time. To use the **at** command, you must be logged in as an administrator.

To display more information about the **at** command, type **at /?** at the command line and press **Enter**

Lab—Task Scheduler (6.3.1.5)

In this lab, you schedule a task using the Windows Task Scheduler utility. You then make changes to your task and test your task by running it. Refer to the lab in *IT Essentials v6 Lab Manual.*

Restore Points (6.3.1.6)

Sometimes installing an application or hardware driver can cause instability or create unexpected problems. Uninstalling the application or hardware driver usually corrects the problem. If not, you can restore the computer to a time before the installation with the *System Restore* utility.

Restore points contain information about the operating system, installed programs, and registry settings. If a computer crashes or an update causes problems, the computer can be rolled back to a previous configuration using a restore point. System Restore does not back up personal data files, nor does it recover personal files that have been corrupted or deleted. Always use a dedicated backup system, such as a tape drive, optical disc, or USB storage device to back up personal files.

A technician should always create a restore point before making changes to a system in the following situations:

- When updating the OS
- When installing or upgrading hardware
- When installing an application
- When installing a driver

To open the System Restore utility in Windows 8 and create a restore point, use the following path:

Control Panel> Recovery > Configure System Restore

To open the System Restore utility in Windows 7 and Vista to create a restore point, use the following path:

Start > All Programs > Accessories > System Tools > System Restore

Lab—System Restore (6.3.1.7)

In this lab, you create a restore point and then use it to restore your computer. Refer to the lab in *IT Essentials v6 Lab Manual*.

Hard Drive Backup (6.3.1.8)

It is important to establish a backup strategy that includes data recovery of personal files. You can use the *Microsoft Backup Utility* to perform backups as required. How your computer system is used, as well as your organizational requirements, determines how often the data must be backed up and the type of backup to perform.

It can take a long time to run a backup. If the backup strategy is followed carefully, it is not necessary to back up all files every time. Only the files that have changed since the last backup need to be backed up.

In versions of earlier than Windows 8, you could use Backup and Restore to back up your files, or create and use a system image backup, or repair disc. Windows 8.1 ships with File History, which can be used to back up the files in the Documents, Music, Pictures, Videos, and Desktop folders. Over time, *File History* builds a history of your files, allowing you to go back and recover specific versions of a file. This is a helpful feature if there are damaged or lost files.

To get started with File History in Windows 8.1, shown in Figure 6-31, connect an internal or external drive, and then turn File History on by using the following path:

Control Panel > File History > click **Turn on**

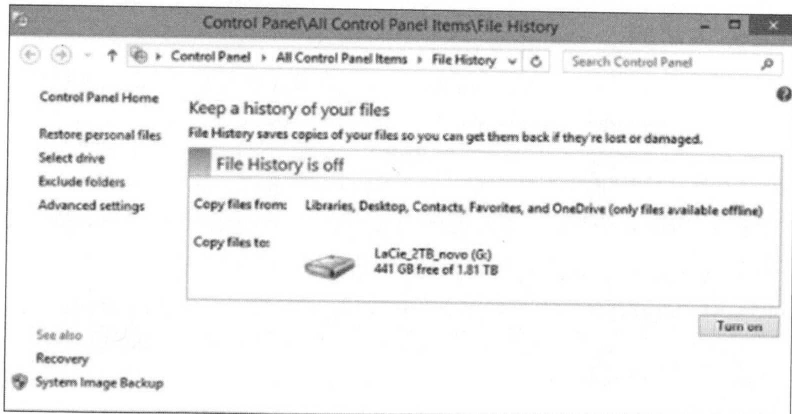

Figure 6-31 Windows 8 File History

Windows 7 and Vista ship with a different backup tool called ***Backup and Restore***. When an external drive is selected, Windows 7 will offer the chance to use the new drive a backup device. Use Backup and Restore to manage backups.

Backup and Restore is shown in Figure 6-32.

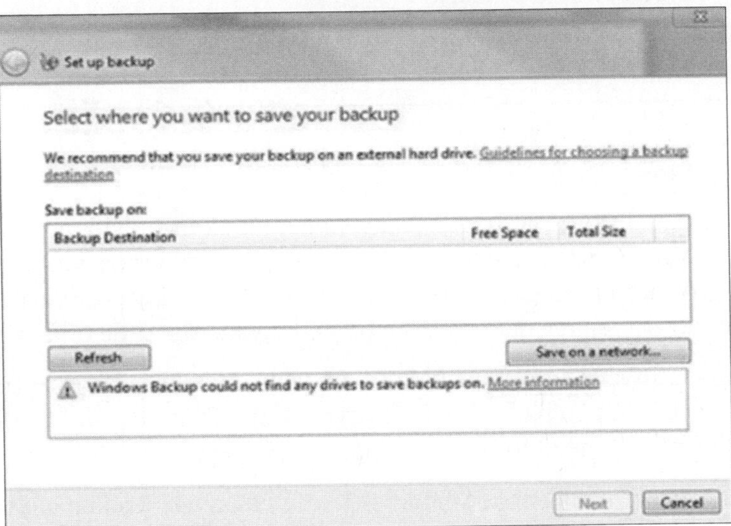

Figure 6-32 Windows 7 and Vista Backup and Restore

To access the Backup and Restore utility in Windows 7, use the following path:

Start > Control Panel > Backup and Restore

To access the Backup and Restore utility in Windows Vista, use the following path:

Start > All Programs > Accessories > System Tools > Backup Status and Configuration

Video

Video—Backup Tool (6.3.1.9)

This video explores the functions of the Backup tool, shows how to create and restore files, and also shows how to set a schedule to back up files. In this video, the use of windows 7 Backup and Restore tool is explored. You will see the various options available in the tool such as creating a system image, which is an image of the entire system. It can also create a system repair disc, use the Windows Easy Transfer Wizard, or set up manual backups and restore to those backups.

It walks you through the steps of using the Windows Backup Utility. The first thing to decide is where to save the backup, then choose between letting Windows choose what is backed up or choosing the files and folders that you want to backup manually, next you can check the Schedule and either accept the default or change the schedule to one you choose and finally you will start the backup. This can take a while, depending on what you have selected.

The video then walks through the process of checking the backed up files and doing a file restore using the Backup and Restore utility.

Please view the video in the Cisco Networking Academy IT Essentials 6.0 online course.

Video

Video—Restore Points (6.3.1.10)

This video shows how to use the backup tool to create restore points and to restore the computer using a restore point. Restore points are great for two reasons. First, you can run System Restore and restore your computer system to a previous time when your system worked. This will not delete, or change user documents, but it will restore system settings, registry settings, and system files that might have become corrupted or been altered or changed. Second, you can use it restore your user documents. In Windows 7 *PreviousVersions*, which is also known as *shadow copies*, is used to restore individual files and folders to a previous version, contained within a restore point. Windows 8.x uses File History, which replaces PreviousVersions for file restoration.

The video describes getting to System Restore by going to the **Start menu > right-click on Computer > select Properties, > click on System protection**, and this opens the **System Protection tab** within the System Properties window. From here, run the System Restore utility to restore system to a restore point.

The video continues to show operations and options available when using System Restore.

Please view the video in the Cisco Networking Academy IT Essentials 6.0 online course.

Basic Troubleshooting Process for Operating Systems (6.4)

The troubleshooting process helps resolve problems with the operations system. OS problems can result from a combination of hardware, software, and network issues. These problem range from simple, such as a driver that does not operate properly, to complex, such as a system that locks up.

Applying the Troubleshooting Process for Operating Systems (6.4.1)

Computer technicians must be able to analyze problems and determine the cause to be able to come up with solutions. This process is called *troubleshooting*. This section explores the troubleshooting steps to guide a technician in how to accurately identify, repair, and document problems.

Identify the Problem (6.4.1.1)

OS problems can result from a combination of hardware, software, and network issues. Computer technicians must be able to analyze the problem and determine the cause of the error to repair the computer. This process is called troubleshooting.

The first step in the troubleshooting process is to identify the problem. Table 6-6 is a list of open-ended and closed-ended questions to ask the customer.

Table 6-6 Step 1: Identify the Problem

Open-ended questions	■ What problems are you having? ■ What operating system is installed on the computer? ■ What updates have you performed lately? ■ What programs have you recently installed? ■ What were you doing when the problem was discovered?
Closed-ended questions	■ Can you start the operating system? ■ Can you start the operating systwem in safe mode? ■ Have you changed your password lately? ■ Have you seen any error messages on the computer? ■ Has anyone else used the computer recently? ■ Has any hardware been added recently?

Establish a Theory of Probable Cause (6.4.1.2)

After you have talked to the customer, you can establish a theory of probable causes. Table 6-7 lists some common probable causes for OS problems.

Table 6-7 Step 2: Establish a Theory of Probable Cause

Common causes of operating system problems	■ Incorrect settings in BIOS ■ Caps lock key is set to on ■ Non-bootable media during computer boot ■ Password has changed ■ Incorrect monitor setting in Control Panel ■ Operating system update failure ■ Driver update failure ■ Malware infection ■ Hard drive failure ■ Corrupt operating system files

Test the Theory to Determine Cause (6.4.1.3)

After you have developed some theories about what is wrong, test your theories to determine the cause of the problem. Table 6-8 shows a list of quick procedures that can help determine the exact cause of the problem or even correct the problem. If a quick procedure does correct the problem, you can jump to verifying the full system functionality. If a quick procedure does not correct the problem, you need to research the problem further to establish the exact cause.

Table 6-8 Step 3: Test the Theory to Determine Cause

Common steps to determine cause	■ Log in as a different user ■ Use third-party diagnostic software ■ Determine if new software or software updates have just been installed ■ Uninstall recently installed applications ■ Boot into safe mode to determine if the problem is driver related ■ Roll back newly updated drivers ■ Examine Device Manager for device conflicts ■ Examine event logs for warnings or errors ■ Check the hard drive for errors and fix file system issues ■ Use the System File Checker to recover corrupt system files ■ Use System Restore if a system update or service pack has been installed

Establish a Plan of Action to Resolve the Problem and Implement the Solution (6.4.1.4)

After you have determined the exact cause of the problem, establish a plan of action to resolve the problem and implement the solution. Table 6-9 shows some sources you can use to gather additional information to resolve an issue.

Table 6-9 Step 4: Establish a Plan of Action to Resolve the Problem and Implement the Solution

If no solution is achieved in the previous step, further research is needed to implement the solution.	■ Help desk repair logs ■ Other technicians ■ Manufacturer FAQs ■ Technical websites ■ News groups ■ Computer manuals ■ Device manuals ■ Online forums ■ Internet search

Verify Full System Functionality and Implement Preventive Measures (6.4.1.5)

After you have corrected the problem, verify full system functionality and, if applicable, implement preventive measures. Table 6-10 lists the steps to verify full system functionality.

Table 6-10 Step 5: Verify Full System Functionality and, If Applicable, Implement Preventive Measures

Verify full functionality	■ Shut down and restart computer ■ Check event logs to make sure there are no warnings or errors ■ Check Device Manager to see that there are no warnings or errors ■ Run DXDiag to make sure DirectX is running correctly ■ Make sure applications run properly ■ Make sure network shares are assessable ■ Make sure the Internet can be accessed ■ Rerun system file checker to ensure all files are correct ■ Check Task Manager to ensure that the status of all programs is Running ■ Rerun any third-party diagnostic tools

Document Findings, Actions, and Outcomes (6.4.1.6)

In the final step of the troubleshooting process, you must document your findings, actions, and outcomes. Table 6-11 lists the tasks required to document the problem and the solution.

Table 6-11 Step 6: Document Your Findings, Actions, and Outcomes

Document your findings, actions, and outcomes	■ Discuss the solution implemented with the customer ■ Have the customer verify that the problem has been solved ■ Provide the customer with all paperwork ■ Document the steps taken to solve the problem in the work order and technician's journal ■ Document any components used in the repair ■ Document the time spent to resolve the problem

Common Problems and Solutions for Operating Systems (6.4.2)

Troubleshooting computer problems is a part of every PC technician's job. No computer performs perfectly all the time so being aware of troubleshooting techniques, tools and common issues is important.

Common Problems and Solutions (6.4.2.1)

OS problems can be attributed to hardware, application, or configuration issues, or to some combination of the three. You resolve some types of OS problems more often than others. Table 6-12 shows common operating system problems and solutions.

Table 6-12 Common Problems and Solutions

Identify the Problem	Probable Causes	Possible Solutions
OS locks up.	■ Computer is overheating. ■ Some of the operating system files may be corrupted. ■ The power supply, RAM, HDD, or motherboard may be defective. ■ The BIOS settings may be incorrect. ■ An unknown event has occurred that has caused the OS to lock up. ■ An incorrect driver has been installed.	■ Clean internal components. ■ Check the fan connections to ensure fans are operating properly. ■ Run System File Checker (SFC) to replace corrupt OS files. ■ Test hardware components and replace if necessary. ■ Address any events in the event logs. ■ Examine and adjust the BIOS settings. ■ Install or roll back drivers as necessary.
The keyboard or mouse does not respond.	■ Communication between the device and computer has failed. ■ Computer has an incompatible or outdated driver. ■ Cable is damaged or disconnected. ■ Device is defective. ■ KVM switch is being used, and the active computer is not displayed.	■ Reboot the computer. ■ Install or roll back drivers. ■ Replace or reconnect the cable ■ Replace the device. ■ Change input on the KVM switch or replace the battery in a wireless device.

Identify the Problem	Probable Causes	Possible Solutions
The operating system will not start.	■ A hardware device has failed. ■ No bootable disk is available. ■ OS files corrupt. ■ MBR or boot sector is corrupt. ■ The power supply, RAM, HDD, or motherboard may be defective. ■ Hardware drivers did not install properly. ■ Windows updates have corrupted the OS.	■ Reboot the computer. ■ Remove all non-bootable media from the drives. ■ Restore Windows using the System Restore tool. ■ Recover the system disk using System Image Recovery tool. ■ Perform a repair installation on the operating system. ■ Replace the defective power supply, RAM, HDD, or motherboard with a known good component. ■ Use the Recovery Console to fix the boot sector. ■ Disconnect any newly connected devices and use the Last Known Good Configuration option to start the operating system. ■ Boot the computer into Safe Mode and address all the events in the event logs.
The computer displays an "Invalid Boot Disk Error" after the POST.	■ Media that does not have an operating system is in the drive. ■ The boot order is not set correctly in the BIOS. ■ The hard drive is not detected, or the jumpers are not set correctly. ■ Hard drive does not have an operating system installed. ■ MBR is corrupted. ■ GPT is corrupted ■ Hard drive is failing. ■ Computer has a boot sector virus.	■ Remove all media from the drives. ■ Change the boot order in the BIOs. ■ Reconnect the hard drive or reset the jumpers. ■ Install an OS. ■ Using a system repair disk, run DISKPART to repair the GPT or MBR. ■ Using a system repair disk, run BOOTREC/FixMBR to repair the MBR. ■ Replace the hard drive. ■ Run antivirus software.

(*Continued*)

Table 6-12 *Continued*

Identify the Problem	Probable Causes	Possible Solutions
The computer displays n "BOOTMGR" error after POST.	■ BOOTMGR is missing or damaged. ■ Boot configuration data is missing or damaged. ■ The boot order is not set correctly in BIOS. ■ MBR is corrupt. ■ Hard drive is failing.	■ Restore BOOTMGR from installation media. ■ Restore boot configuration data from installation media. ■ Set the correct boot order in BIOS. ■ Run **chkdsk /F/R** from Recovery Console. ■ Run **bootrec /Fixmbr** from the Recovery Environment.
A service failed to start when the computer booted.	■ The service is not enabled. ■ The service is set to Manual. ■ The failed service requires another service to be enabled.	■ Enable the service. ■ Set the service to Automatic. ■ Re-enable or reinstall the required service.
A device did not start when the computer booted.	■ The external power is not on. ■ The data cable or power cable is not connected to the device. ■ The device has been disabled in the BIOS. ■ The device has failed. ■ The device has a conflict with a newly installed device. ■ The driver is corrupted.	■ Power on external device. ■ Secure the data and power cables to the device. ■ Enable the device in the BIOS. ■ Replace the device. ■ Remove the newly installed device. ■ Reinstall or roll back the driver.
The computer continually restarts without displaying the desktop.	■ The computer is set to restart when there is a failure. ■ A startup file has become corrupted.	■ Press **F8** to open the Advanced Options menu and choose **Disable automatic restart on system failure.** ■ Run **chkdsk /F/R** from the Recovery Console. ■ Use the Recovery Environment to perform an Automatic Repair, or a System Restore

Identify the Problem	Probable Causes	Possible Solutions
The computer locks without an error messages.	■ The CPU or FSB settings are incorrect on the motherboard or in the BIOS. ■ The computer is overheating. ■ RAM is failing. ■ Hard drive is failing. ■ Power supply is failing.	■ Check and reset the CPU and FSB settings as necessary. ■ Check and replace any cooling devices as necessary. ■ Replace any failing devices with known good replacement components.
An application does not install.	■ The downloaded application installer contains a virus and was prevented from installing by the virus-protection software. ■ The installation disk of file is corrupted. ■ The installation application is not compatible with the operating system. ■ There are too many programs running and not enough system memory remaining to install the application. ■ The minimum hardware requirements of the application are not met.	■ Replace the installation disk or downloaded file with one that is virus free or not corrupt. ■ Run the installation application in compatibility mode. ■ Close other applications before attempting the installation. ■ Install hardware to meet the minimum hardware requirements of the application.
A computer with Windows 7 installed does not run Aero.	■ The computer does not meet the minimum hardware requirements for running Aero.	■ Upgrade the processor, RAM, and video card to meet the minimum Microsoft requirements for Aero.
The search feature takes a long time to find results.	■ The index service is not running. ■ The index service is not indexing the correct locations.	■ Start the index service using services.msc. ■ Change the settings of the index service in the Advanced Options panel.
The UAC no longer prompts the user for permissions.	The UAC has been turned off.	Turn on the UAC in the User Account applet in the Control Panel.

(Continued)

Table 6-12 *Continued*

Identify the Problem	Probable Causes	Possible Solutions
In Windows 7 no Gadgets appear on the desktop.	■ The gadgets have never been installed or have been uninstalled. ■ The XML necessary to render the gadget is broken, corrupt, or not installed.	■ Right-click the desktop > choose **Gadgets** > right-click a gadget > click **Add**. ■ Register the file msxml3.dll by entering **regsvr32 msxml3.dll>** at the command prompt.
The computer is running slowly and has a delayed response	A process is using most of the CPU resources.	■ Restart the process with services.msc. ■ If the process is not needed, end it with Task Manager. ■ Restart the computer.
The computer does not recognize an external drive.	The OS does not have the correct drivers for the external drive.	Download the correct drivers.
A new sound card does not work.	The volume has been muted.	Unmute the volume in the Sound Control Panel applet.
Some external devices from a 32-bit OS computer do not work in the 64-bit OS computer.	Incorrect devices drivers	Update to the 64-bit device drivers.
After an upgrade to Windows 7 or Vista, the computer runs very slowly.	Aero is causing the slowdown.	Turn off Aero.

Summary (6.5)

This chapter covered Windows installation, configuration and management.

Summary (6.5.1)

As a technician, you should be skilled at installing, configuring, and troubleshooting an operating system. The following concepts from this chapter are important to remember:

Several different operating systems are available, and you must consider the customer's needs and environment when choosing an OS.

- The main steps in setting up a customer's computer include preparing the hard drive, installing the OS, creating user accounts, and configuring installation options.
- A GUI shows icons of all files, folders, and applications on the computer. A pointing device, such as a mouse, is used to navigate in a GUI desktop.
- A CLI uses commands to complete tasks and navigate the file system.
- With a virtual machine manager, system resources on a host computer can be allocated to run virtual machines. Virtual machines run operating systems, and using them can provide users with greater system functionality.
- Preventive maintenance techniques help to ensure optimal performance of the OS. You should establish a backup strategy that allows for the recovery of data.
- Some of the tools available for troubleshooting an OS problem include administrative tools, system tools, and CLI commands.

Summary of Exercises

This is a summary of the labs activities associated with this chapter.

Labs

The following labs cover material from this chapter. Refer to the labs in the *IT Essentials v6 Lab Manual*.

Lab—Task Manager (6.1.1.5)

Lab—Install Third-Party Software (6.1.1.9)

Lab—Create User Accounts (6.1.2.3)

Lab—Configure Browser Settings (6.1.2.5)

Lab—Manage Virtual Memory (6.1.2.12)

Lab—Device Manager (6.1.2.14)

Lab—Region and Language Options (6.1.2.16)

Lab—Monitor and Manage System Resources (6.1.3.7)

Lab—Hard Drive Maintenance (6.1.4.2)

Lab—Manage System Files in Windows (6.1.4.4)

Lab—Common Windows CLI Commands (6.1.5.4)

Lab—System Utilities (6.1.5.6)

Lab—Manage the Startup Folder (6.3.1.2)

Lab—Task Scheduler (6.3.1.5)

Lab—System Restore (6.3.1.7)

Check Your Understanding

You can find the answers to these questions in the appendix, "Answers to 'Check Your Understanding' Questions."

1. What command would allow a technician to receive help with the command-line options that are used to schedule a program to run at a specific time?

   A. HELP AT

   B. AT /?

   C. ASK AT

   D. HELP

   E. CMD ?

2. What utility is used to show the system resources consumed by each user?

   A. User Accounts

   B. Event Viewer

   C. Device Manager

   D. Task Manager

3. Enabling and disabling the pop-up blocker in Internet Explorer is accomplished through which Internet Options tab?
   A. General
   B. Security
   C. Advanced
   D. Privacy

4. A workstation is configured with an advanced video capture card that was added to the system. After the OS was updated from Windows 7 to Windows 8.1, the video card stopped working. What should be done to address this problem?
   A. Update the video editing software.
   B. Update firmware on the workstation.
   C. Update Windows 8.1.
   D. Update the driver.

5. Which of these programs is an example of a Type 2 hypervisor?
   A. Windows XP Mode
   B. DirectX
   C. Virtual PC
   D. OpenGL

6. What is a characteristic of a virtual machine on a PC?
   A. A virtual machine runs its own operating system.
   B. A virtual machine only uses a physical network adapter to connect to the Internet.
   C. A virtual machine is not susceptible to threats and malicious attacks.
   D. The number of virtual machines that can be made available depends on the software resources of the host machine.

7. What is the minimum amount of system RAM that is required to run the Windows 8 Hyper-V virtualization platform?
   A. 4 GB
   B. 512 MB
   C. 1 GB
   D. 8 GB

8. A technician has installed a third-party utility that is used to manage a Windows 7 computer. However, the utility does not automatically start whenever the computer is started. What can the technician do to resolve this problem?

   A. Use the Add or Remove Programs utility to set program access and defaults.

   B. Uninstall the program and then choose Add New Programs in the Add or Remove Programs utility to install the application.

   C. Change the startup type for the utility to Automatic in Services.

   D. Set the application registry key value to one.

9. A help desk technician is talking to a user to clarify a technical problem that the user is having. What are two examples of open-ended questions that the technician might use to help determine the issue? (Choose two.)

   A. Has anyone else used the computer recently?

   B. What updates have you performed lately?

   C. What happens when you try to access your files?

   D. Can you boot up in safe mode?

   E. Can you boot the operating system?

10. Which two statements are true about restore points? (Choose two.)

    A. They are useful to restore the computer to an earlier time when the system worked properly.

    B. They back up personal data files.

    C. They contain information about the system and registry settings that are used by the Windows operating system.

    D. They recover personal files that have been corrupted or deleted.

    E. A technician should always create them after updating the operating system.

11. A technician is having difficulty resolving what appears to be a Windows 7 problem. Previously documented known solutions did not work and neither Device Manager nor Event Viewer provided useful information. Which two actions should the technician try next? (Choose two.)

    A. Ask the customer for any idea about what may be wrong.

    B. Reinstall the operating system.

    C. Check any manuals that relate to the hardware and software.

    D. Check the Internet for possible solutions.

    E. Use the recovery CD to restore the operating system.

12. A user notices that a PC is running slowly and exhibits a delayed response to keyboard commands. What is a probable cause of this symptom?

    A. A recently installed device driver is incompatible with the boot controller.

    B. One or more program files have been deleted.

    C. A process is using most of the CPU resources.

    D. The video card does not support the resolution that is being used.

13. What would be the result of having a corrupt Master Boot Record?

    A. The operating system will fail to start.

    B. A new application will fail to install.

    C. The printer will function incorrectly.

    D. The keyboard will be unresponsive to the user.

14. A user has a netbook that has the maximum amount of RAM that can be installed (1 GB), but the user performance is suffering. What Windows system utility can be used to help in this situation?

    A. Action Center

    B. HomeGroup

    C. ReadyBoost

    D. Device Manager

15. Which system tool can show hardware and software information for both local and remote computers?

    A. Chkdsk

    B. System Information

    C. Performance Monitor

    D. System Configuration

    E. Component Services

16. What GUI would allow a user to schedule a command or application to run at a specific date and time?

    A. HELP AT

    F. Task Scheduler

    B. Task Now

    C. Task Helper

CHAPTER 7

Networking Concepts

Objectives

Upon completion of this chapter, you will be able to answer the following questions:

- What are the different types of transmission media used in networking?
- What are the different types of network devices?
- What are some common communication protocols and standards?
- What is the OSI model?
- What is the TCP/IP model?
- What are common TCP and UDP protocol, ports and their purpose?
- What are the various WiFi networking standards?
- What are the different network types and their characteristics?

Key Terms

This chapter uses the following key terms. You can find the definitions in the Glossary.

Networks Page 320

host Page 321

switch Page 323

router Page 323

wireless router Page 323

access point (AP) Page 323

medium Page 323

Copper cabling Page 323

Fiber-optic cabling Page 323

Wireless connection Page 323

Bandwidth Page 325

packets Page 325

latency Page 325

Simplex Page 325

half-duplex Page 326

full-duplex Page 326

Broadband Page 326

LAN Page 326

wireless LAN (WLAN) Page 327

infrastructure mode Page 327

Ad hoc Page 328

metropolitan area network (MAN) Page 329

WAN Page 329

peer-to-peer network Page 330

client-server network Page 331

Network standards Page 332

protocol Page 334

Internet protocols Page 334

Open Systems Interconnect (OSI) reference model Page 335

DNS Page 336

BOOTP Page 336

DHCP Page 336

SMTP Page 337

IMAP Page 337

FTP Page 337

POP Page 337

TFTP Page 337

HTTP Page 337

UDP Page 337

TCP Page 337

IP Page 337

NAT Page 337

ICMP Page 338

OSPF Page 338

EIGRP Page 338

ARP Page 338

PPP Page 338

Ethernet Page 338

Interface Drivers Page 338

encapsulation process Page 338

protocol data unit (PDU) Page 338

Carrier Sense Multiple Access with Collision Detection (CSMA/CD) Page 342

backoff algorithm Page 342

full duplex transmission Page 342

IEEE 802.3 Page 342

10BASE-T Page 342

100BASE-TX Page 342

1000BASE-T Page 342

10GBASE-T Page 342

IEEE 802.11 Page 343

WiFi Page 343

Carrier Sense Multiple Access with Collision Avoidance (CSMA/CA) Page 343

Open system authentication Page 344

Shared key authentication Page 344

Wired Equivalent Privacy (WEP) Page 344

WiFi Protected Access (WPA) Page 344

IEEE 802.11i/WPA2 Page 344

modem Page 345

Hubs Page 345

Bridges Page 346

switches Page 346

Microsegmenting Page 346

switching table Page 347

Wireless access points Page 347

Routers Page 323

hardware firewall Page 349

patch panel Page 350

repeater Page 351

PoE switch Page 351

Coaxial cable Page 352

Thinnet Page 353

Optical fiber Page 358

Thicknet Page 353

Twisted-pair Page 353

UTP cable Page 353

crosstalk Page 354

electromagnetic interference (EMI) Page 354

radio frequency interference (RFI) Page 354

Shielded twisted-pair (STP) Page 354

RJ-45 connector Page 355

main distribution facility (MDF) Page 356

independent distribution facility (IDF) Page 356

plenum Page 356

Plenum-rated cables Page 356

T568A/ T568B Page 356

straight-through cable Page 357

crossover cable Page 357

Single-mode fiber (SMF) Page 359

Multimode fiber (MMF) Page 359

Subscriber Connector (SC) connectors Page 360

Straight-Tip (ST) connectors Page 359

Lucent Connectors (LC) Page 360

Duplex Multimode LC connector Page 360

MAC address Page 361

IPv4 address Page 362

IPv6 address Page 362

ipconfig Page 363

subnet mask Page 364

prefix notation Page 365

Classless Inter-Domain Router (CIDR) Page 366

supernet Page 366

static IP addressing Page 368

Default gateway Page 369

Ping Page 371

transport layer Page 373

port number Page 376

source port number Page 376

destination port number Page 376

Introduction (7.0)

Networking is the concept of sharing and communicating. When you think of networking, you think of interconnection; for example, socializing with people of similar interests or making connections. It also can describe the sharing of resources and the communication that happens when independent computers are linked together.

Welcome (7.0.1)

A *computer network* is recognized to be a system in which a group of devices connected by a transport medium exchange data and share resources while using the same rules. In this section, the specifics of those rules, protocols, and the types of media used for transporting data are discussed.

Networking Concepts (7.0.1.1)

Network concepts describe how groups or systems are interconnected and the means by which they communicate.

Principles of Networking (7.1)

Networks provide connectivity among a group of computers. The number of computers connected can be as few as two and can grow to a very large number depending on the type of network that is being used.

Computer Networks (7.1.1)

This chapter provides an overview of network principles, standards, and purposes. To meet the expectations and needs of your customers and network users, you must be familiar with networking concepts. You learn the basics of network design and how some components affect the flow of data on a network. This knowledge helps you successfully design, implement, and troubleshoot networks.

Network Definition (7.1.1.1)

Networks are systems that are formed by links. For example, roads that connect groups of people together create a physical network. Connections with your friends create your personal network. Websites that allow individuals to link to each other's pages are called *social networking sites*.

People use the following networks every day:

- Mail delivery system
- Telephone system
- Public transportation system
- Corporate computer network
- The Internet

The public transportation system is similar to a computer network. The cars, trucks, and other vehicles are like the messages that travel within the network. Each driver defines a starting point (source computer) and an ending point (destination computer). Within this system, there are rules, similar to stop signs and traffic lights, which control the flow from the source to the destination.

Host Devices (7.1.1.2)

Computer networks consist of a variety of devices. Some devices can serve either as hosts or peripherals. A host is any device that sends and receives information on the network. A printer connected to your laptop is a peripheral. If the printer is connected directly to a network, it is acting as a host.

Many different types of host devices can connect to a network. Some of the more common ones are shown in Figure 7-1.

Note

An Internet Protocol phone, which is known as an IP phone, connects to a computer network instead of the traditional telephone network.

Computer networks are used in businesses, homes, schools, and government agencies. Many networks are connected to each other through the Internet. A network can share many different types of resources, as shown in Table 7-1.

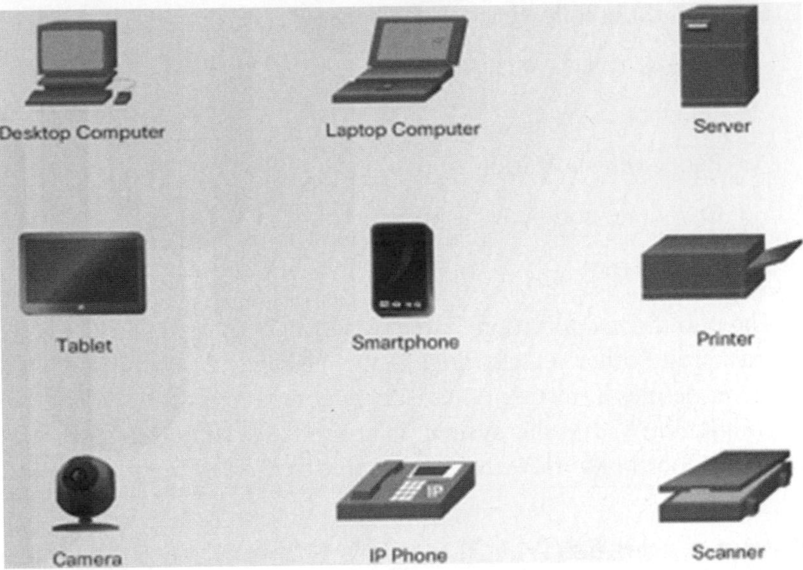

Figure 7-1 Host Device Icons

Table 7-1 Examples of Shared Resources on a Computer Network

■ Services, such as printing or scanning
■ Storage space on devices, such as hard drives or optical drives
■ Applications, such as databases
■ Information stored on other computers, such as documents and photos
■ Calendars, synchronizing between a computer and a smartphone

Intermediary Devices (7.1.1.3)

Computer networks contain many devices that exist in between the host devices. These intermediary devices ensure that data flows from one host device to another host device. The most common intermediary devices are shown in Figure 7-2.

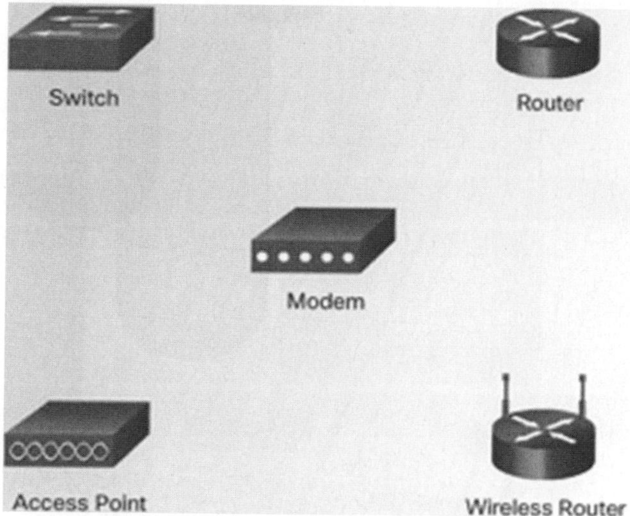

Figure 7-2 Intermediary Device Icons

A *switch* is used to connect multiple devices to the network. A *router* is used to forward traffic between networks. A *wireless router* connects multiple wireless devices to the network. In addition, a wireless router often includes a switch so that multiple wired devices can connect to the network. An *access point (AP)* provides wireless connectivity, but has fewer features than a wireless router. A modem is used to connect a home or small office to the Internet. These devices will be discussed in more detail later in the chapter.

Network Media (7.1.1.4)

Communication across a network is carried on a medium. The *medium* provides the channel over which the message travels from source to destination. The plural for medium is media.

Network devices are linked together using a variety of media. As shown in Figure 7-3, these media are:

- *Copper cabling*—Uses electrical signals to transmit data between devices
- *Fiber-optic cabling*—Uses glass or plastic fiber to carry information as light pulses
- *Wireless connection*—Uses radio signals, infrared technology, or satellite transmissions

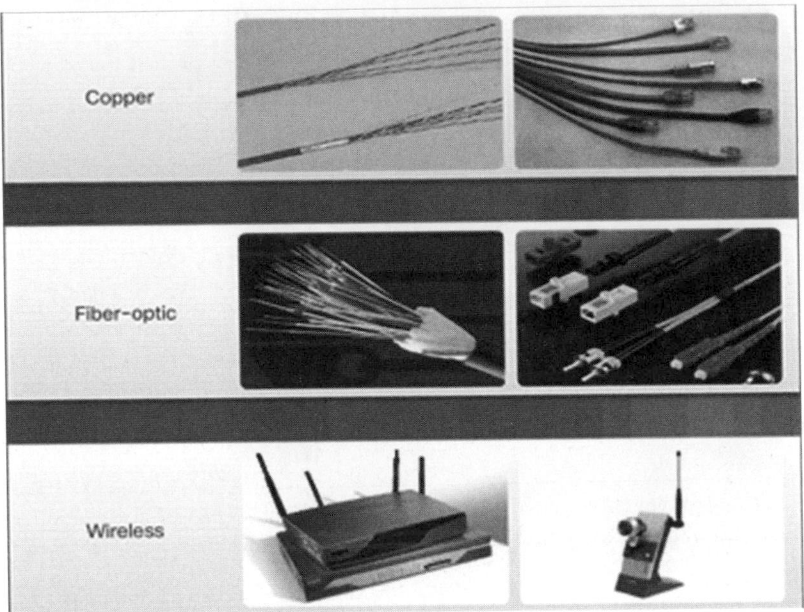

Figure 7-3 Network Media

The icons shown in Figure 7-4 are used throughout this course to represent the different types of network media. Local area networks (LANs), wide area networks (WANs), and wireless networks are discussed in the next topic. The *cloud* will be used throughout this course to represent connections to the Internet. The Internet is often the medium for communications between one network and another network.

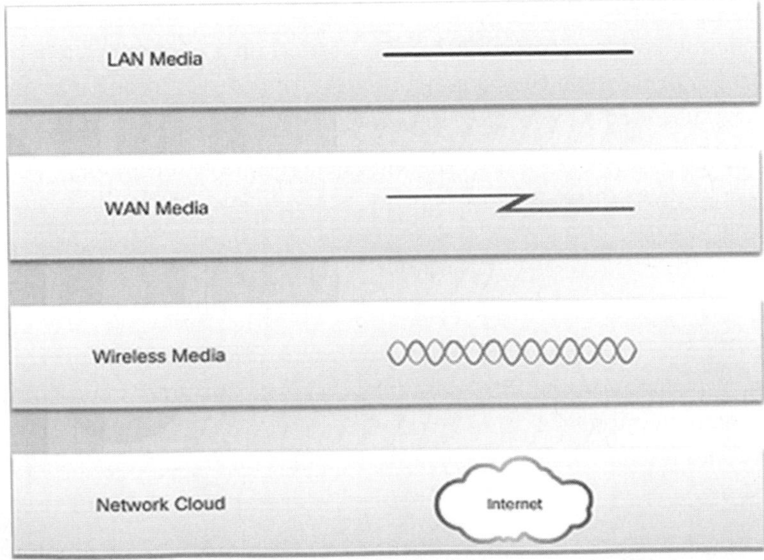

Figure 7-4 Network Media Icons

Packet Tracer
☐ Activity

Activity—Identify Network Devices and Media Representations (7.1.1.5)

To access the activities, please refer to the Cisco Networking Academy IT Essentials 6.0 online course.

Bandwidth and Latency (7.1.1.6)

Bandwidth on a network is like a highway. The number of lanes on the highway represents the amount of cars that could travel on the highway at the same time. An eight-lane highway can handle four times the number of cars that a two-lane highway can hold. In the highway example, the cars and trucks represent the data.

When data is sent over a computer network, it is broken up into small chunks called *packets*. Each packet contains source and destination address information. Packets are sent across a network one bit at a time. *Bandwidth* is measured in the number of bits that can be sent every second. The following are examples of bandwidth measurements:

- b/s—bits per second
- kb/s—kilobits per second
- Mb/s—megabits per second
- Gb/s—gigabits per second

Note

A byte is equal to eight bits, and is abbreviated with a capital letter B. The capital letter B is normally used when describing size or storage capacity, such as a file (2.5 MB) or disk drive (2 TB).

The amount of time it takes data to travel from source to destination is called *latency*. Like a car traveling across town that encounters stop lights or detours, data is delayed by network devices and cable length. Network devices add latency when processing and forwarding data. When surfing the Web or downloading a file, latency does not normally cause problems. Time-critical applications, such as Internet telephone calls, video, and gaming, can be significantly affected by latency.

Data Transmission (7.1.1.7)

The data that is transmitted over the network can flow using one of three modes: simplex, half-duplex, or full-duplex.

Simplex

Simplex is a single, one-way transmission. An example of simplex transmission is the signal that is sent from a TV station to your home TV.

Half-Duplex

When data flows in one direction at a time it is known as ***half-duplex***. With half-duplex, the channel of communications allows alternating transmission in two directions, but not in both directions simultaneously. Two-way radios, such as police or emergency communications mobile radios, work with half-duplex transmissions. When you press the button on the microphone to transmit, you cannot hear the person on the other end. If people at both ends try to talk at the same time, neither transmission gets through.

Full-Duplex

When data flows in both directions at the same time it is known as ***full-duplex***. A telephone conversation is an example of full-duplex communication. Both people can talk and be heard at the same time.

Full-duplex networking technology increases network performance because data can be sent and received at the same time. Broadband technologies, such as digital subscriber line (DSL) and cable, operate in full-duplex mode. ***Broadband*** technology allows multiple signals to travel on the same wire simultaneously. With a DSL connection, for example, users can download data to the computer and talk on the telephone at the same time.

Types of Networks (7.1.2)

Networks as you have learned are computers linked together for the purpose of sharing resources and communication. Networks are classified in many different ways such as size, geographical scope and purpose. This section examines the various network types.

LANs (7.1.2.1)

A computer network is identified by the following specific characteristics:

- Size of the area covered
- Number of users connected
- Number and types of services available
- Area of responsibility

Traditionally, a ***LAN***, as shown in Figure 7-5, is defined as a network that encompasses a small geographical area. However, the distinguishing characteristic for LANs today is that they are typically owned by an individual, such as in a home or small business, or wholly managed by an IT department, such as in a school or corporation. This individual or group enforces the security and access control policies of the network.

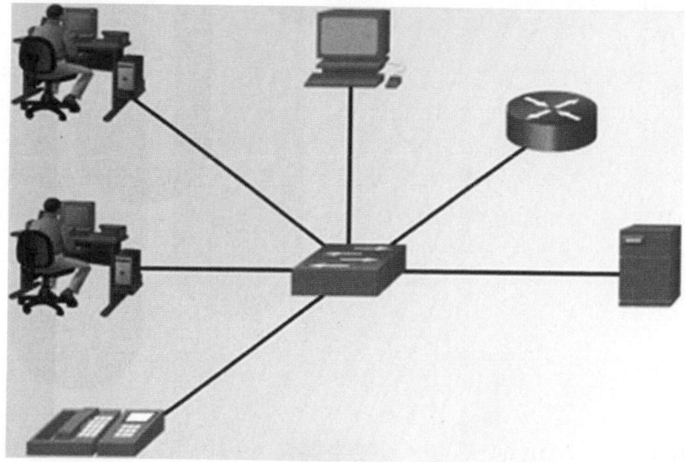

Figure 7-5 Local Area Network

WLANs (7.1.2.2)

A *wireless LAN (WLAN)* is a LAN that uses radio waves to transmit data between wireless devices. In a traditional LAN, devices are connected together using copper cabling. In some environments, installing copper cabling might not be practical, desirable, or even possible. In these situations, wireless devices are used to transmit and receive data using radio waves. As with LANs, on a WLAN, you can share resources, such as files, printers, and Internet access.

WLANs can operate in two modes. In *infrastructure mode*, as shown in Figure 7-6, wireless clients connect to a wireless router or access point (AP). The AP is connected to a switch, which provides access to the rest of the network and to the Internet. Access points are typically connected to the network using copper cabling. Instead of providing copper cabling to every network host, only the wireless access point is connected to the network with copper cabling. The range (radius of coverage) for typical WLAN systems varies from under 98.4 ft (30 m) indoors to much greater distances outdoors, depending on the technology used.

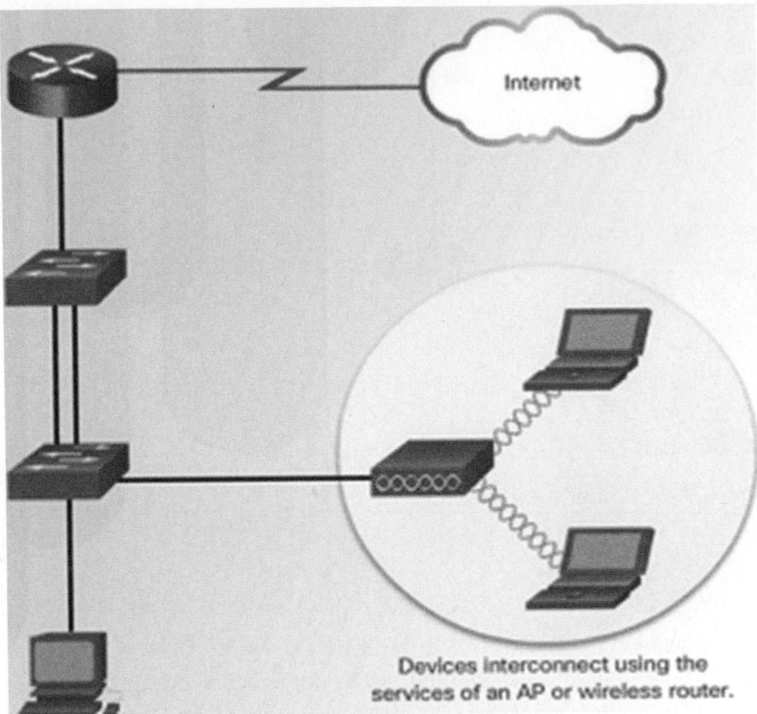
Internet
Devices interconnect using the services of an AP or wireless router.

Figure 7-6 Infrastructure Mode

Ad hoc, as shown in Figure 7-7 means the WLAN is created when it is needed. Ad hoc is usually temporary. For example, when a laptop is wirelessly connected to a smartphone, which has access to the Internet through cellular service provider.

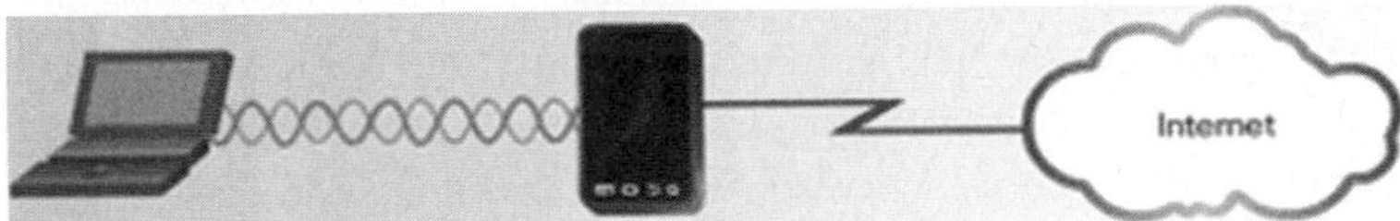
Internet

Figure 7-7 Ad hoc Mode

PANs (7.1.2.3)

A *personal area network (PAN)* is a network that connects devices, such as mice, keyboards, printers, smartphone, and tablets within the range of an individual person. All of these devices are dedicated to a single host and are most often connected with Bluetooth technology.

Bluetooth is a wireless technology that enables devices to communicate over short distances. A Bluetooth device can connect up to seven other Bluetooth devices. Described in the IEEE standard 802.15.1, Bluetooth devices are capable of handling voice and data. Bluetooth devices operate in the 2.4 to 2.485 GHz radio frequency range, which is in the Industrial, Scientific, and Medical (ISM) band. The Bluetooth standard incorporates Adaptive Frequency Hopping (AFH). AFH allows signals to "hop" around using different frequencies within the Bluetooth range, thereby reducing the chance of interference when multiple Bluetooth devices are present.

MANs (7.1.2.4)

A *metropolitan area network (MAN)*, as shown in Figure 7-8, is a network that spans across a large campus or a city. The network consists of various buildings interconnected through wireless or fiber optic backbones. The communication links and equipment are typically owned by a consortium of users, or by a network service provider who sells the service to the users. A MAN can act as a high-speed network to enable sharing of regional resources.

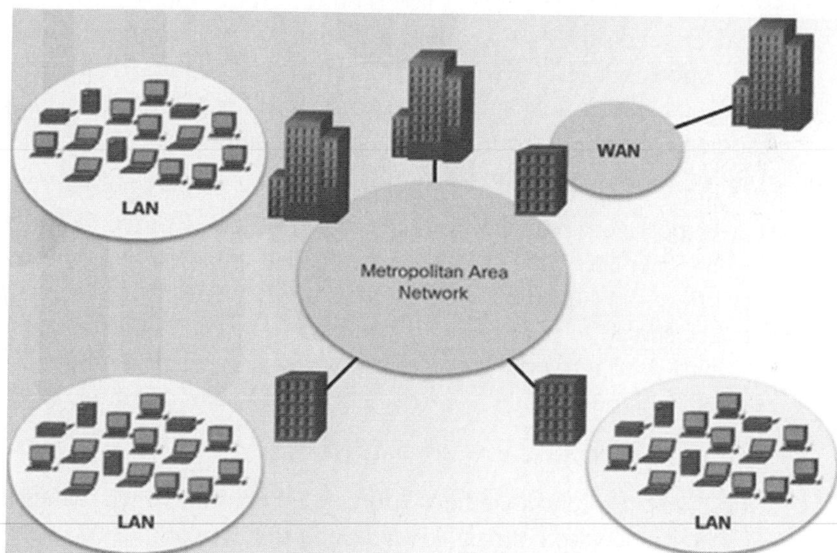

Figure 7-8 Metropolitan Area Network

WANs (7.1.2.5)

A *WAN* connects multiple networks that are in geographically separated locations. The distinguishing characteristic of a WAN is that it is owned by a service provider. Individuals and organizations contract for WAN services. The most common example of a WAN is the Internet. The Internet is a large WAN that is composed of millions of interconnected networks. In Figure 7-9, the Tokyo and Moscow networks are connected through the Internet.

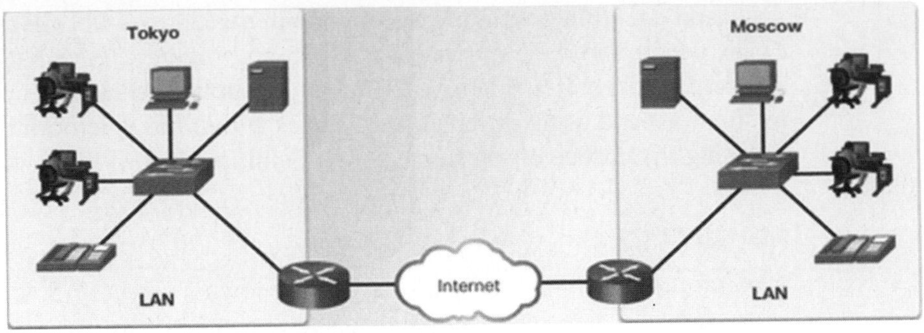

Figure 7-9 Wide Area Network

Peer-to-Peer Networks (7.1.2.6)

In a *peer-to-peer network*, there is no hierarchy among the computers, nor are there any dedicated servers. Each device, also called a client, has equivalent capabilities and responsibilities. Individual users are responsible for their own resources and can decide which data and devices to share or install. Because individual users are responsible for the resources on their own computers, the network has no central point of control or administration.

Peer-to-peer networks work best in environments with ten or fewer computers. Peer-to- peer networks can also exist inside larger networks. Even on a large client network, users can still share resources directly with other users without using a network server. In your home, if you have more than one computer, you can set up a peer-to-peer network. You can share files with other computers, send messages between computers, and print documents to a shared printer, as shown in Figure 7-10.

Peer-to-peer networks have several disadvantages:

- There is no centralized network administration, which makes it difficult to determine who controls resources on the network.
- There is no centralized security. Each computer must use separate security measures for data protection.
- The network becomes more complex and difficult to manage as the number of computers on the network increases.
- There might not be any centralized data storage. Separate data backups must be maintained. This responsibility falls on the individual users.

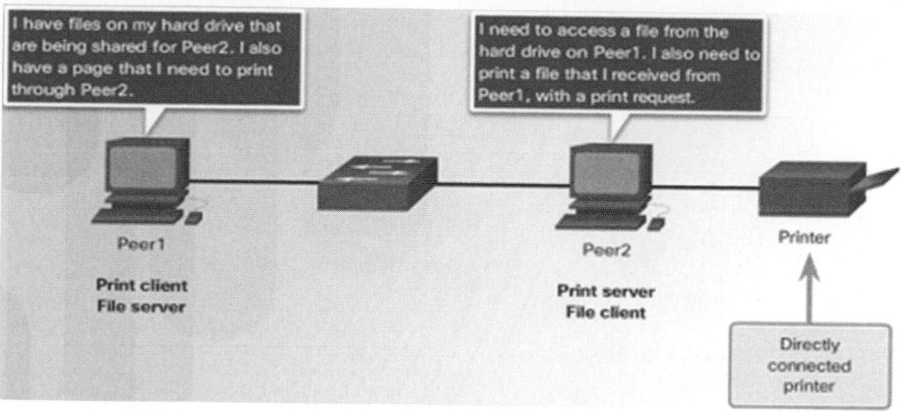

Figure 7-10 Peer-to-Peer Example

Client-Server Networks (7.1.2.7)

Servers have software installed that enables them to provide services, such as files, email, or web pages, to clients. Each service requires separate server software. For example, the server in Figures 7-11 and 7-12 requires file server software to provide clients with the ability to retrieve and store files.

In a *client-server network*, the client requests information or services from the server. The server provides the requested information or service to the client. Servers on a client-server network commonly perform some of the processing work for client machines. For example, a server can sort through a database before delivering the records requested by the client.

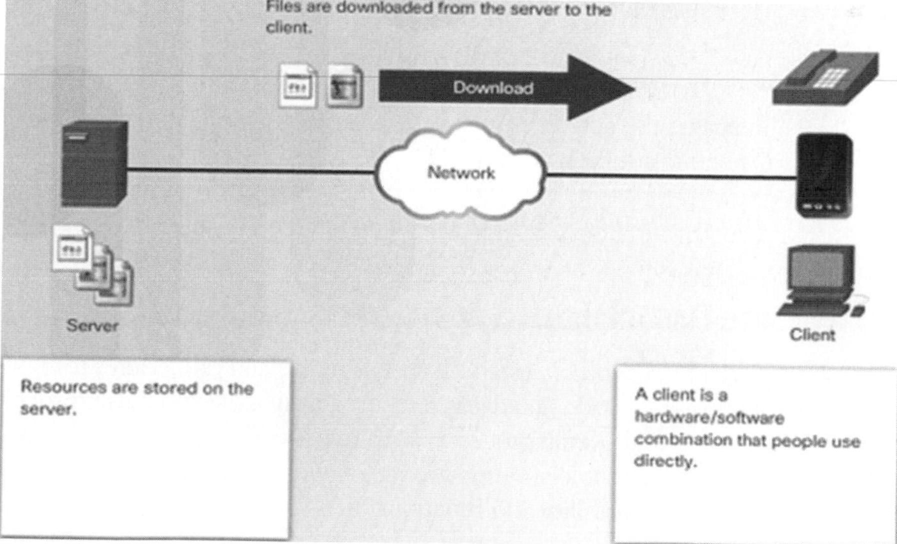

Figure 7-11 File Server and Client Download Example

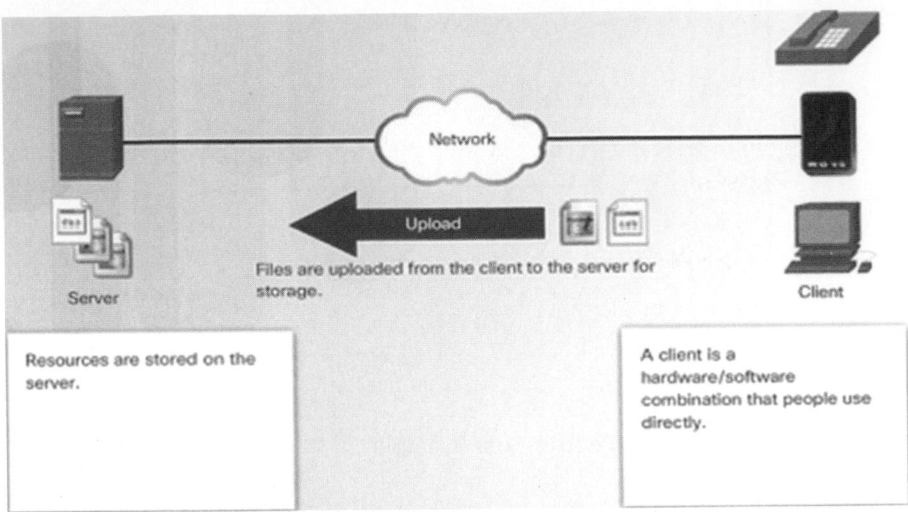

Figure 7-12 File Server and Client Upload Example

A single server can run multiple types of server software. In a home or small business, it may be necessary for one computer to act as a file server, a web server, and an email server. A client computer can also run multiple types of client software. There must be client software for every service required. With multiple client software installed, a client can connect to multiple servers at the same time. For example, a user can check email and view a web page while instant messaging and listening to Internet radio.

In a client-server network, resources are controlled by a centralized network administration. The network administrator implements data backups and security measures. The network administrator also controls user access to the server resources.

Activity—Matching Network Types (7.1.2.8)

To access the activities, please refer to the Cisco Networking Academy IT Essentials 6.0 online course.

Networking Standards (7.2)

Network standards establish specifications and procedures for how networks are supposed to work. Standards deal with many issues such as protocols, architecture, electrical and overall process related to networks. Standards are important to networking because they set a common ground on which product development can be based to ensure compatibility and functionality allowing interoperability between vendors.

Reference Models (7.2.1)

In order to provide communication among diverse devices standardization is used and communication models are utilized to define the functions and processes of a communication network. It does not describe the implementation but a way to understand how the diverse devices can communicate regardless of the network architecture.

Open Standards (7.2.1.1)

Open standards encourage interoperability, competition, and innovation. They also guarantee that no single company's product can monopolize the market, or have an unfair advantage over its competition.

A good example of this is when purchasing a wireless router for the home. There are many different choices available from a variety of vendors. All of these choices incorporate standard protocols such as Internet Protocol version 4 (IPv4), Dynamic Host Configuration Protocol (DHCP), 802.3 (Ethernet), and 802.11 (Wireless LAN). These open standards and protocols are discussed further in the chapter. They allow a client running Apple's OS X operating system to download a web page from a web server running the Linux operating system. This is because both operating systems implement the open standard protocols.

Several international standards organizations are responsible for setting networking standards some of which are listed in Table 7-2 below:

Table 7-2 International Standards Organizations

Standards Organizations	Description
International Organization for Standardization (ISO)	ISO is an independent, non-governmental international organization with a membership of 161 national standards bodies. It brings together experts to share knowledge and develop voluntary, consensus-based, market relevant International Standards that support innovation and provide solutions to global challenges. http://www.iso.org/iso/home/about.htm
ITU	ITU is the United Nations specialized agency for information and communication technologies – ICTs. http://www.itu.int/en/about/Pages/default.aspx
The Internet Engineering Task Force (IETF®)	The Internet Engineering Task Force (IETF) is a large open international community of network designers, operators, vendors, and researchers concerned with the evolution of the Internet architecture and the smooth operation of the Internet. It is open to any interested individual. http://www.ietf.org/about/

(Continued)

Table 7-2 *Continued*

Standards Organizations	Description
Internet Assigned Numbers Authority (IANA)	IANA is responsible for the global coordination of the DNS Root, IP addressing, and other Internet protocol resources. http://www.iana.org/
Internet Corporation for Assigned Names and Numbers (ICANN)	ICANN coordinates the Internet Assigned Numbers Authority (IANA) functions, which are key technical services critical to the continued operations of the Internet's underlying address book, the Domain Name System (DNS). https://www.icann.org/
Institute of Electrical and Electronics Engineers (IEEE)	IEEE is the world's largest technical professional organization dedicated to advancing technology for the benefit of humanity. http://www.ieee.org/index.html
Telecommunications Industry Association	The leading trade association representing the global information and communications technology (ICT) industry through standards development, policy initiatives, business opportunities, market intelligence and networking events. http://www.tiaonline.org/

Protocols (7.2.1.2)

A *protocol* is a system of rules. *Internet protocols* are sets of rules governing communication between computers on a network. Protocol specifications define the format of the messages that are exchanged.

Timing is crucial for the reliable delivery of packets. Protocols require messages to arrive within certain time intervals so that computers do not wait indefinitely for messages that might have been lost. Systems maintain one or more timers during the transmission of data. Protocols also initiate alternative actions if the network does not meet the timing rules. Table 7-3 lists the main functions of a protocol.

Table 7-3 Protocol Functions

Protocol Functions
■ Identifying and handling errors
■ Compressing the data
■ Determining how data is to be divided and packaged
■ Addressing data packets
■ Determining how to announce the sending and receiving of data packets

OSI Reference Model (7.2.1.3)

In the early 1980s, the International Standards Organization (ISO) developed the *Open Systems Interconnect (OSI) reference model* to standardize the way devices communicate on a network. This model was a major step toward ensuring interoperability between network devices.

The OSI model divides network communications into seven distinct layers, as shown in Table 7-4. Although other models exist, most network vendors today build their products using this framework.

Table 7-4 OSI Model

OSI Model Layer Name	Layer Number	Description
Application	7	Responsible for network services to applications
Presentation	6	Transforms data formats to provide a standard interface for the application layer
Session	5	Establishes, manages, terminates the connections between the local and remote application
Transport	4	Provides reliable transport and flow control across a network
Network	3	Responsible for logical addressing and the domain of routing
Data Link	2	Provides physical addressing and media access procedures
Physical	1	Defines all the electrical and physical specifications for devices

Note

Mnemonics can help you remember the seven layers of the OSI. Two examples are, "All People Seem To Need Data Processing" and "Please Do Not Throw Sausage Pizza Away."

TCP/IP Model (7.2.1.4)

The TCP/IP model was created by researchers in the U.S. Department of Defense (DoD). It consists of layers that perform functions necessary to prepare data for transmission over a network. Table 7-5 shows the four layers of the TCP/IP model.

Table 7-5 TCP/IP model

TCP/IP Layer	Description
Application	Where high-level protocols such as SMTP and FTP operate
Transport	Specifies which application requested or is receiving data through specific ports
Internet	Where IP addressing and routing take place
Network Access	Where MAC addressing and physical components of the network exist

TCP/IP stands for two important protocols in the suite: Transmission Control Protocol (TCP) and Internet Protocol (IP). TCP is responsible for reliable delivery. The Internet Protocol (IP) is responsible for adding source and destination addressing to the data. But the TCP/IP model includes many other protocols in addition to TCP and IP. These protocols are the dominant standard for transporting data across networks and the Internet. Table 7-6 shows a collection of some of the more popular TCP/IP protocols.

Table 7-6 Popular TCP/IP Protocols

Application Layer (7)	
Type	**Protocols**
Name System	*DNS* Translates domain names, such as cisco.com into IP addresses
Host Config	*BOOTP* ■ Enables a diskless workstation to discover its own IP address, the IP address of a BOOTP server on the network, and a file to be loaded into memory to boot the machine ■ BOOTP is being superseded by DHCP *DHCP* ■ Dynamically assigns IP addresses to client stations at startup ■ Allows the addresses to be reused when no longer needed

Type	Protocols
Email	*SMTP* ■ Enables clients to send email to a mail server ■ Enables servers to send email to other servers *POP* ■ Enables clients to retrieve email from a mail server ■ Downloads email from the mail server to the desktop *IMAP* ■ Enables clients to access email stored on a mail server Maintains email on the server
File Transfer	*FTP* ■ Sets rules that enable a user on one host to access and transfer files to and from another host over a network ■ A reliable, connection-oriented, and acknowledged file delivery protocol *TFTP* ■ A simple, connectionless file transfer protocol ■ A best-effort, unacknowledged file delivery protocol ■ Utilizes less overhead than FTP
Web	*HTTP* Set of rules for exchanging text, graphic images, sound, video, and other multimedia files on the World Wide Web

Transport Layer Protocols

UDP	*TCP*
■ Enables a process running on one host to send packets to a process running on another host ■ Does not confirm successful datagram transmission	■ Enables reliable communication between processes running on separate hosts ■ Reliable, acknowledged transmissions that confirm successful delivery

Internet Layer

Type	Protocols
Network	*IP* ■ Receives message segments from the transport layer ■ Packages messages into packets ■ Addresses packets for end-to-end delivery over an Internetwork *NAT* Translates IP addresses from a private network into globally unique public IP addresses

(*Continued*)

Table 7-6 *Continued*

Type	Protocols
IP Support	*ICMP* Provides feedback from a destination host to a source host about errors in packet delivery
Routing	*OSPF* ■ Link-state routing protocol ■ Hierarchical design based on areas ■ Open standard interior routing protocol *EIGRP* ■ Cisco proprietary routing protocol ■ Uses composite metric based on bandwidth, delay, load and reliability

Network Access Layer Protocols

ARP	*PPP*	*Ethernet*	*Interface Drivers*
Provides dynamic address mapping between an IP address and a hardware address	Provides a means of encapsulating packets for transmission over a serial link	Defines the rules for wiring and signaling standards of the network access layer	Provides instruction to a machine for the control of a specific interface on a network device

Protocol Data Units (7.2.1.5)

A message begins at the top application layer and moves down the TCP/IP layers to the bottom network access layer. As application data is passed down through the layers, protocol information is added at each level. This is known as the *encapsulation process*.

The form that a piece of data takes at any layer is called a *protocol data unit (PDU)*. During encapsulation, each succeeding layer encapsulates the PDU that it receives from the layer above in accordance with the protocol being used. At each stage of the process, a PDU has a different name to reflect its new functions. Although there is no universal naming convention for PDUs, in this course, the PDUs are named according to the protocols of the TCP/IP suite, as shown Figure 7-13.

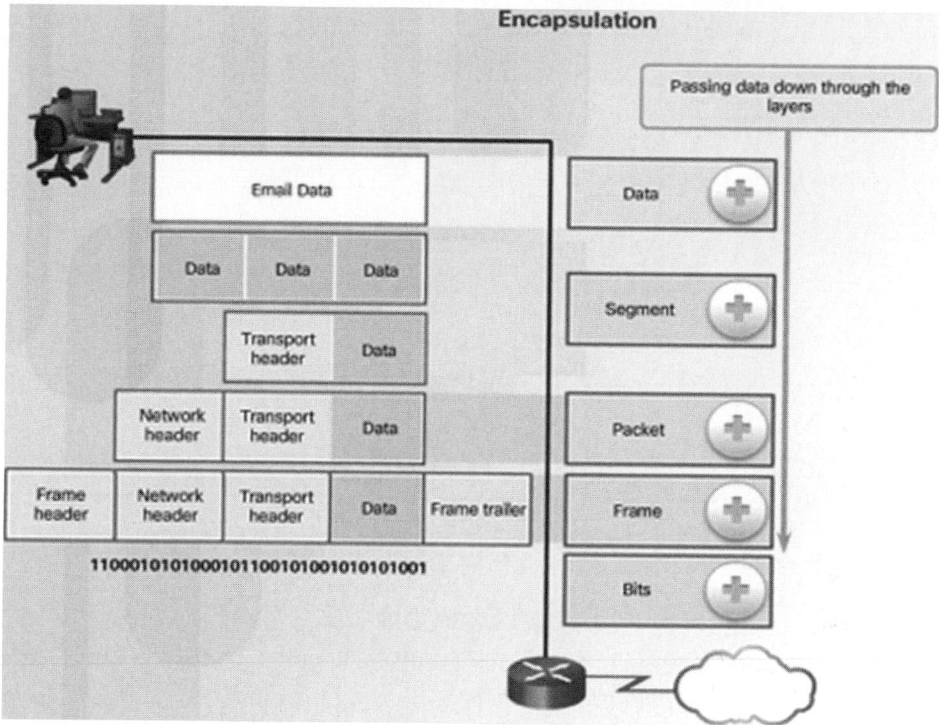

Figure 7-13 Encapsulation

Encapsulation Example (7.2.1.6)

When sending messages on a network, the encapsulation process works from top to bottom. At each layer, the upper layer information is considered data within the encapsulated protocol. For example, the TCP segment is considered data within the IP packet.

Figure 7-14 shows the encapsulation as a web server sends a web page to a web client.

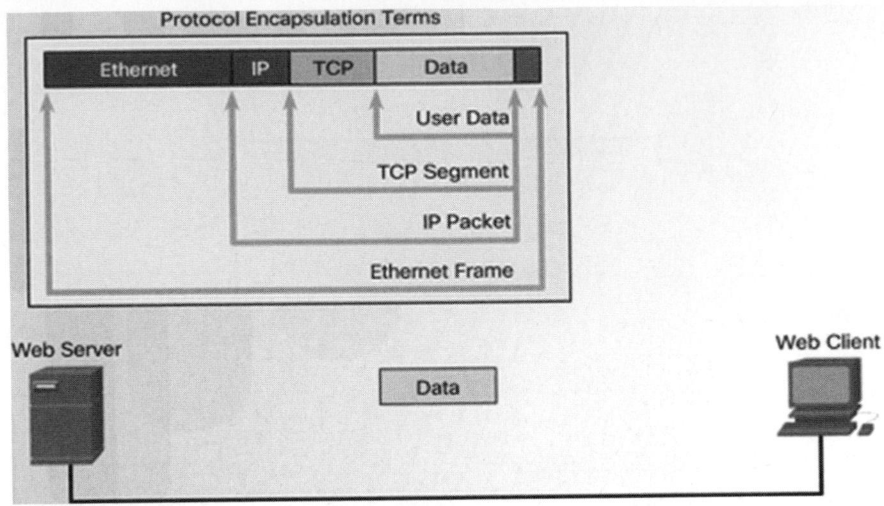

Figure 7-14 Protocol Operation of Sending a Message

De-Encapsulation Example (7.2.1.7)

This process is reversed at the receiving host, and is known as de-encapsulation. *De-encapsulation* is the process used by a receiving device to remove one or more of the protocol headers. The data is de-encapsulated as it moves up through the layers towards the end-user application.

Figure 7-15 shows the de-encapsulation process.

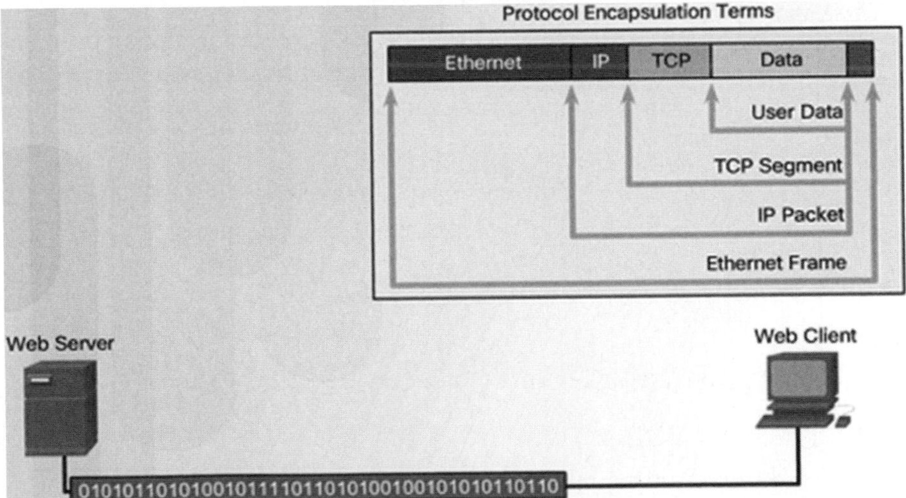

Figure 7-15 De-encapsulation Example

Comparing the OSI and TCP/IP Models (7.2.1.8)

The OSI model and the TCP/IP model are both reference models used to describe the data communication process. The TCP/IP model is used specifically for the TCP/IP suite of protocols, and the OSI model is used for the development of communication standards for equipment and applications from different vendors.

The TCP/IP model performs the same process as the OSI model, but uses four layers instead of seven. Figure 7-16 shows how the layers of the two models compare.

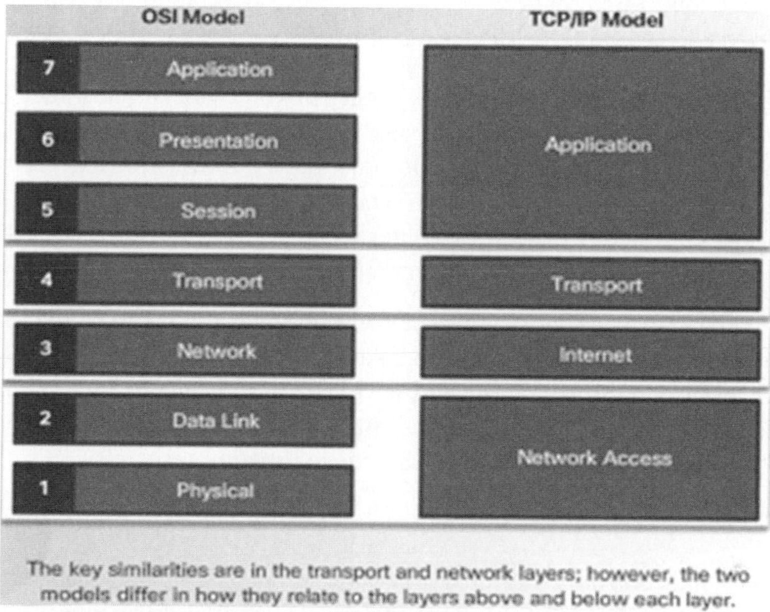

Figure 7-16 OSI and TCP/IP Model Comparison

Activity—Place the OSI and TCP/IP Model Layers (7.2.1.9)

To access the activities, please refer to the Cisco Networking Academy IT Essentials 6.0 online course.

Wired and Wireless Ethernet Standards (7.2.2)

CSMA/CD (7.2.2.1)

Ethernet protocols describe the rules that control how communication occurs on an Ethernet network. To ensure that all Ethernet devices are compatible with each other, the IEEE developed standards for manufacturers and programmers to follow when developing Ethernet devices.

The Ethernet architecture is based on the IEEE 802.3 standard. The IEEE 802.3 standard specifies that a network implement the *Carrier Sense Multiple Access with Collision Detection (CSMA/CD)* access control method:

- **Carrier**—This is the wire used to transmit data.
- **Sense**—Each device listens to the wire to determine if it is clear to send data.
- **Multiple Access**—There can be many devices accessing the network at the same time.
- **Collision Detection**—A collision causes a doubling of voltage on the wire, which is detected by the devices' NICs.

In CSMA/CD, all devices listen to the network wire for clearance to send data. This process is similar to waiting to hear a dial tone on a phone before dialing a number. When the device detects that no other device is transmitting, the device can attempt to send data. If no other device sends any data at the same time, this transmission arrives at the destination computer with no problems. If another device transmits at the same time, a collision occurs on the wire.

The first station that detects the collision sends out a jam signal that tells all stations to stop transmitting and to run a backoff algorithm. A *backoff algorithm* calculates random times in which the end station tries transmitting again. This random time is typically in 1 or 2 milliseconds (ms). This sequence occurs every time there is a collision on the network and can reduce Ethernet transmission by up to 40 percent.

Note

Most Ethernet networks today are full duplex. In *full duplex* Ethernet, there is rarely a collision because devices can transmit and receive at the same time.

Ethernet Cable Standards (7.2.2.2)

The *IEEE 802.3 standard* defines several physical implementations that support Ethernet. Table 7-7 summarizes the standards of different Ethernet cable types.

Table 7-7 Ethernet Standards

Ethernet Standards	Media	Transfer Rates
10BASE-T	Category 3	Transfer data at a rate of 10 Mb/s
100BASE-TX	Category 5	At 100 Mb/s, transfer rates of 100BASE-TX are ten time that of 10BASE-T
1000BASE-T	Category 5e, 6	1000BASE-T architecture supports data transfer rates of 1 Gb/s
10GBASE-T	Category 6a, 7	10GBASE-T architecture supports data transfer rates of 10 Gb/s

1000BASE-T is the most commonly implemented Ethernet architecture today. The name indicates the features of the standard:

- The *1000* represents a speed of 1000 Mb/s or 1 Gb/s.
- *BASE* represents baseband transmission. In baseband transmission, the entire bandwidth of a cable is used for one type of signal.
- The *T* represents twisted-pair copper cabling.

CSMA/CA (7.2.2.3)

IEEE 802.11 is the standard that specifies connectivity for wireless networks. Wireless networks use *Carrier Sense Multiple Access with Collision Avoidance (CSMA/CA)*. CMSA/CA does not detect collisions but attempts to avoid them by waiting before transmitting. Each device that transmits includes in the frame the time duration that it needs for the transmission. All other wireless devices receive this information and know how long the medium will be unavailable. This means that wireless devices operate in half-duplex mode. The transmission efficiency of an AP or wireless router is reduced as more devices are attached.

Wireless Standards (7.2.2.4)

IEEE 802.11, or WiFi, refers to a collective group of standards that specify the radio frequencies, speeds, and other capabilities for WLANs. Various implementations of the IEEE 802.11 standard have been developed over the years, as shown in Table 7-8.

The 802.11a, 802.11b, and 802.11g standards should be considered legacy. 802.11n is faster than 802.11g and the earlier 802.11b. One of its major features is a technology called multiple-input multiple-output (MIMO), a signal processing and smart antenna technique for transmitting multiple data streams through multiple antennas. New WLANs should implement 802.11ac devices. Existing WLAN implementations should upgrade to 802.11ac when purchasing new devices.

Table 7-8 Comparing 802.11 Standards

IEEE Standard	Max Speed	Max Indoor Range	Frequency	Backward Compatibility
802.11a	54 Mb/s	115 ft (35 m)	5 GHz	–
802.11b	11 Mb/s	115 ft (35 m)	2.4 GHz	–
802.11g	54 Mb/s	125 ft (38 m)	2.4 GHz	802.11b
802.11n	600 Mb/s	230 ft (70 m)	2.4 GHz and 5 GHz	802.11a/b/g
802.11ac	1.3Gb/s (1300 Mb/s)	115 ft (35 m)	5 GHz	802.11a/n

Wireless Security (7.2.2.5)

The best way to secure a wireless network is to use authentication and encryption. Two types of authentication were introduced with the original 802.11 standard, as shown in Figure 7-17:

- *Open system authentication*—Any wireless device can connect to the wireless network. This should only be used in situations where security is of no concern.
- *Shared key authentication*—Provides mechanisms to authenticate and encrypt data between a wireless client and AP or wireless router.

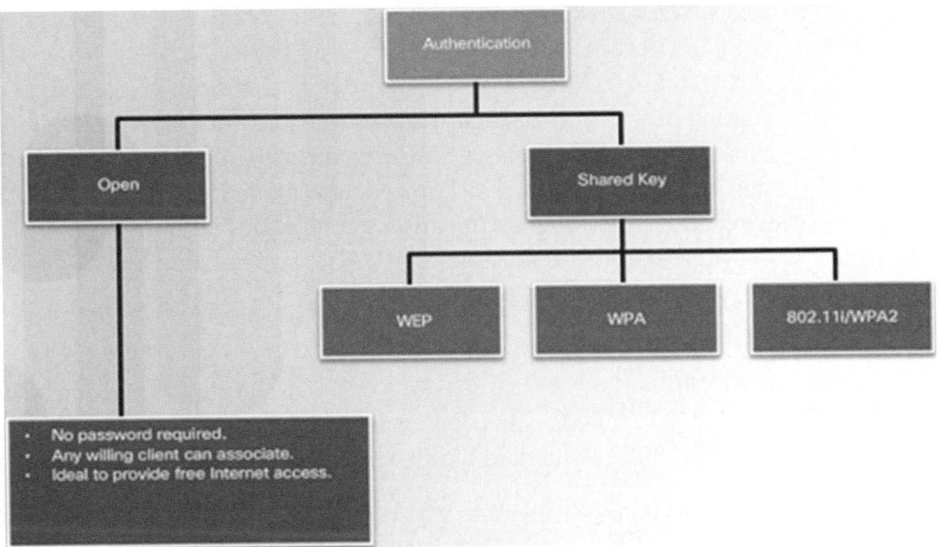

Figure 7-17 Authentication Methods

The three shared key authentication techniques for WLANs are as follows:

- *Wired Equivalent Privacy (WEP)*—This was the original 802.11 specification securing WLANs. However, the encryption key never changes when exchanging packets, making it easy to hack.
- *WiFi Protected Access (WPA)*—This standard uses WEP, but secures the data with the much stronger Temporal Key Integrity Protocol (TKIP) encryption algorithm. TKIP changes the key for each packet, making it much more difficult to hack.
- *IEEE 802.11i/WPA2*—IEEE 802.11i is now the industry standard for securing WLANs. The WiFi alliance version is called WPA2. 802.11i and WPA2 both use the Advanced Encryption Standard (AES) for encryption. AES is currently considered the strongest encryption protocol.

Since 2006, any device that bears the WiFi Certified logo is WPA2 certified. Therefore, modern WLANs should always use the 802.11i/WPA2 standard.

Physical Components of a Network (7.3)

Computer networks are made up of physical components such as cables, NICs, connections and various types of hardware that allow the interconnection of devices and end systems.

Network Devices (7.3.1)

IT technicians must understand the purpose and characteristics of common networking devices. This section discusses a variety of devices.

Modems (7.3.1.1)

A ***modem*** connects to the Internet through an Internet Service Provider (ISP). There are three basic types of modems. Modems convert a computer's digital data into a format that can be transmitted on the ISP's network. An analog modem converts digital data to analog signals for transmission over analog phone lines. A digital subscriber line (DSL) modem connects a user's network directly to the digital infrastructure of the phone company. A cable modem connects the user's network to a cable service provider, which typically uses a hybrid fiber coax (HFC) network.

Hubs, Bridges, and Switches (7.3.1.2)

The equipment used to connect devices within in a LAN has evolved from hubs to bridges to switches.

Hubs

Hubs, shown in Figure 7-18, receive data on one port and then send it out to all other ports. A hub extends the reach of a network because it regenerates the electrical signal. Hubs can also connect to another networking device, such as a switch or router, which connects to other sections of the network.

Hubs are used less often today because of the effectiveness and low cost of switches. Hubs do not segment network traffic. When one device sends traffic, the hub floods that traffic to all other devices connected to hub. The devices are sharing the bandwidth.

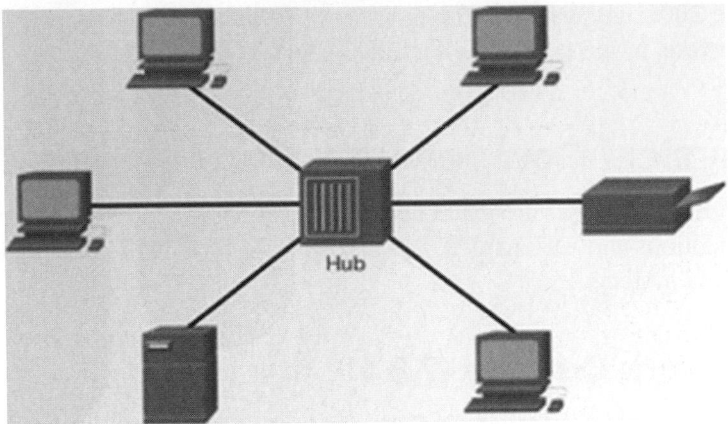

Figure 7-18 Hubs connect Device in a LAN

Bridges

Bridges were introduced to divide LANs into segments. Bridges keep a record of all the devices on each segment. A bridge can then filter network traffic between LAN segments. This helps reduce the amount of traffic between devices. For example, in Figure 7-19, if PC-A needs to send a job to the printer, the traffic will not be forward to Segment 2. However, the server will also receive this print job traffic.

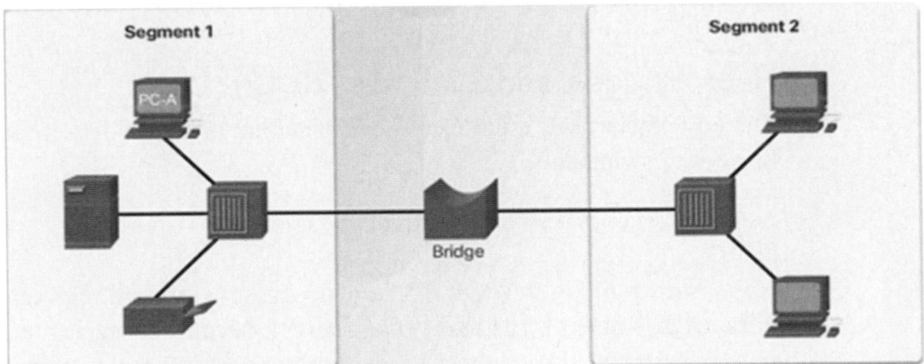

Figure 7-19 Bridges Segment a LAN

Switches

Bridges and hubs are now considered legacy devices because of the benefits and low cost of *switches*. As shown in Figure 7-20, a switch microsegments a LAN. *Microsegmenting* means that switches filter and segment network traffic by sending data only to the device to which it is sent. This provides higher dedicated bandwidth to each device on the network. If there is only one device attached to each port on a switch it operates in Full-Duplex mode. This is not the case with a hub. When PC-A sends a job to the printer, only the printer receives the traffic.

Switches maintain a switching table. The *switching table* contains a list of all MAC addresses on the network, and a list of which switch port can be used to reach a device with a given MAC address. The switching table records MAC addresses by inspecting the source MAC address of every incoming frame, as well as the port on which the frame arrives. The switch then creates a switching table that maps MAC addresses to outgoing ports. When traffic arrives that is destined for a particular MAC address, the switch uses the switching table to determine which port to use to reach the MAC address. The traffic is forwarded from the port to the destination. By sending traffic out of only one port to the destination, other ports are not affected.

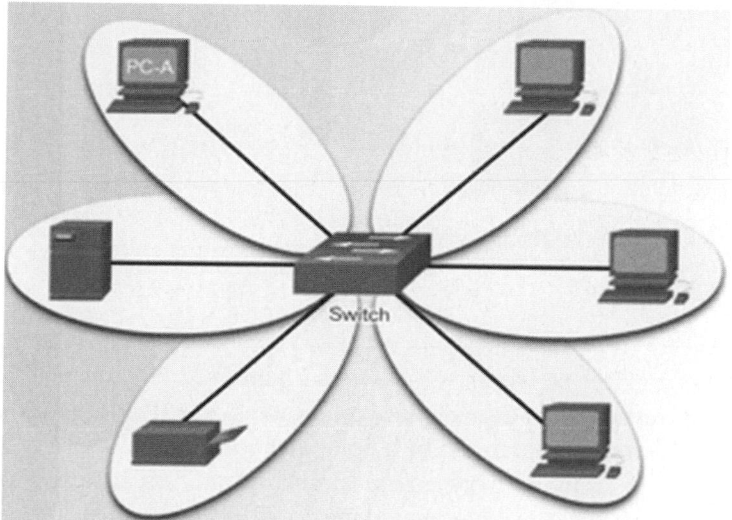

Figure 7-20 Switches Microsegment a LAN

Wireless Access Points and Routers (7.3.1.3)

Wireless Access Points

Wireless access points, shown in Figure 7-21, provide network access to wireless devices, such as laptops and tablets. The wireless access point uses radio waves to communicate with the wireless NIC in the devices and other wireless access points. An access point has a limited range of coverage. Large networks require several access points to provide adequate wireless coverage. A wireless access point provides connectivity only to the network, whereas a wireless router provides additional features.

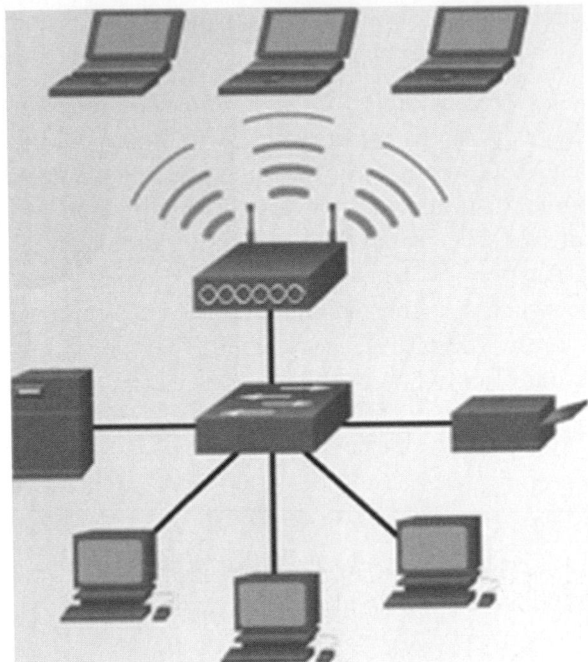

Figure 7-21 Wireless Access Points

Routers

Routers connect networks, as shown in Figure 7-22. Switches use MAC addresses to forward traffic within a single network. Routers use IP addresses to forward traffic to other networks. A router can be a computer with special network software installed, or a device built by network equipment manufacturers. In larger networks, routers connect to switches, which then connect to LANs, like the router on the right in Figure 7-22. The router serves as the gateway to outside networks.

The router on the left in Figure 7-22 is also known as a multipurpose device or integrated router. It includes a switch and a wireless access point. For some networks, it is more convenient to purchase and configure one device that serves all your needs than to purchase a separate device for each function. This is especially true for the home or small office. Multipurpose devices may also include a modem.

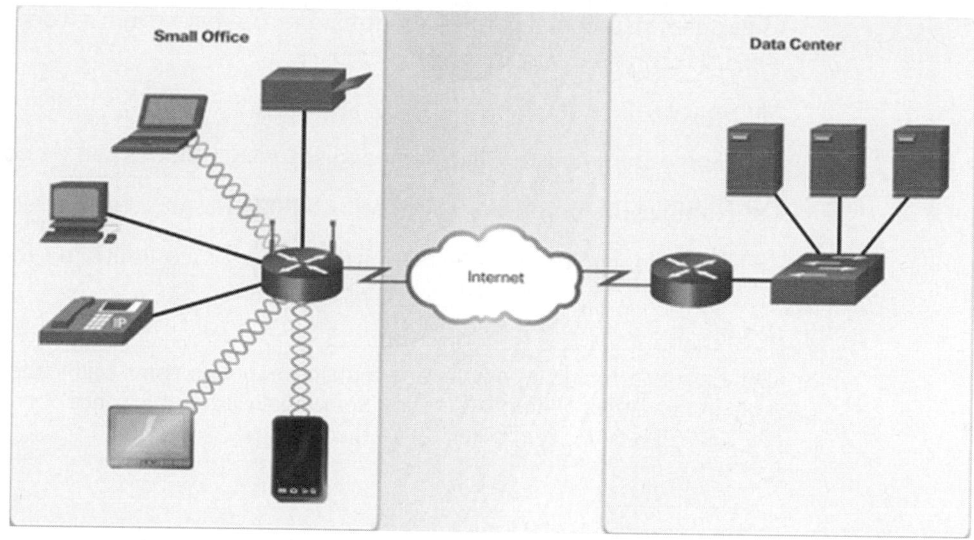

Figure 7-22 Routers

Hardware Firewalls (7.3.1.4)

An integrated router also serves as a *hardware firewall*. Hardware firewalls protect data and equipment on a network from unauthorized access. A hardware firewall resides between two or more networks, as shown in Figure 7-23. It does not use the resources of the computers it is protecting, so there is no impact on processing performance.

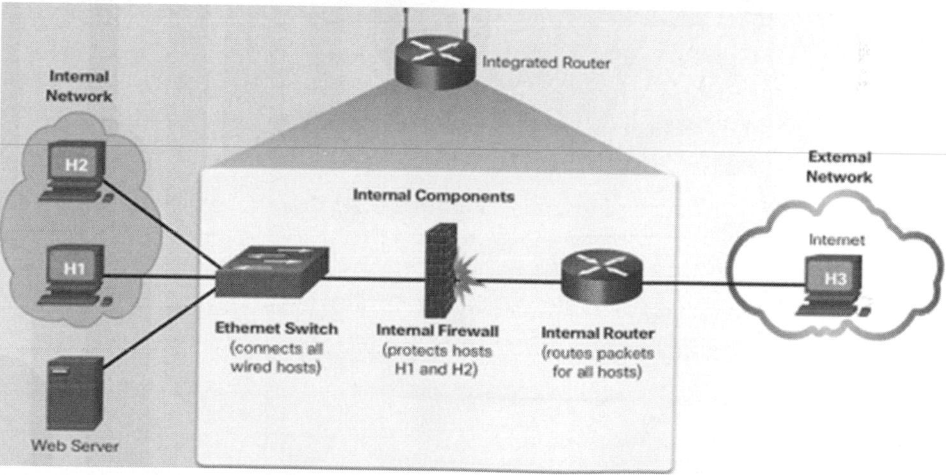

Figure 7-23 Hardware Firewalls

Firewalls use various techniques for determining what is permitted or denied access to a network segment, such as an Access Control List (ACL). This list is a file that the router uses that contains rules about data traffic between networks. Considerations when selecting a hardware firewall include

- **Space**—Free standing and uses dedicated hardware
- **Cost**—Initial cost of hardware and software updates can be costly
- **Number of computers**—Multiple computers can be protected
- **Performance requirements**—Little impact on computer performance

Note

On a secure network, if computer performance is not an issue, enable the internal operating system firewall for additional security. Some applications might not operate properly unless the firewall is configured correctly for them.

Other Devices (7.3.1.5)

Patch Panels

A *patch panel* is commonly used as a place to collect incoming cable runs from the various networking devices throughout a facility, as shown in Figure 7-24. It provides a connection point between PCs and the switches or routers. A patch panel can be unpowered or powered. A powered patch panel can regenerate weak signals before sending them on to the next device.

Figure 7-24 Patch Panel

Repeaters

Regenerating weak signals is the primary purpose of a *repeater*. Repeaters are also called extenders because they extend the distance a signal can travel. In today's networks, repeaters are most often used to regenerate signals in fiber-optic cables.

Power over Ethernet (PoE)

A *PoE switch* transfers small amounts of DC current over an Ethernet cable, along with the data, to power PoE devices. Low voltage devices that support PoE, such as WiFi access points, surveillance video devices, and IP phones, can be powered from remote locations. Devices that support PoE can receive power over an Ethernet connection at distances up to 330 ft (100 m) away. Power can also be inserted in the middle of a cable run using a PoE injector.

Activity—Identify Network Devices (7.3.1.6)

To access the activities, please refer to the Cisco Networking Academy IT Essentials 6.0 online course.

Cables and Connectors (7.3.2)

In this section you learn about cables that are used in computers and networks to carry data or power to a device. You will also learn about the connectors which are that part of the cable that plugs into a port to connect one device to another. There different types of cables and various form factors of connectors.

Coaxial Cables (7.3.2.1)

A wide variety of networking cables are available, as shown in Figure 7-25. Coaxial and twisted-pair cables use electrical signals over copper to transmit data. Fiber-optic cables use light signals to transmit data. These cables differ in bandwidth, size, and cost.

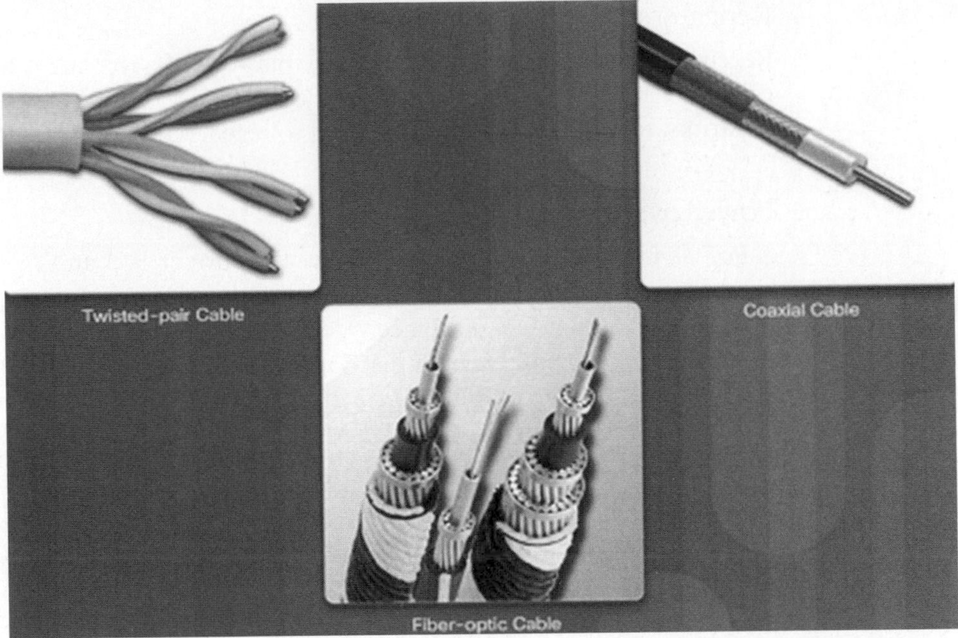

Figure 7-25 Network Cables

Coaxial cable, shown in detail in Figure 7-26, is usually constructed of either copper or aluminum. It is used by both cable television companies and satellite communication systems.

Coaxial cable (or coax) carries data in the form of electrical signals. It provides improved shielding compared to unshielded twisted-pair (UTP), so it has a higher signal-to-noise ratio and can therefore carry more data. However, twisted-pair cabling has replaced coax in LANs because, when compared to UTP, coax is physically harder to install, more expensive, and harder to troubleshoot.

Coaxial cable is enclosed in a sheath or jacket and can be terminated with a variety of connectors, as shown in Figure 7-26.

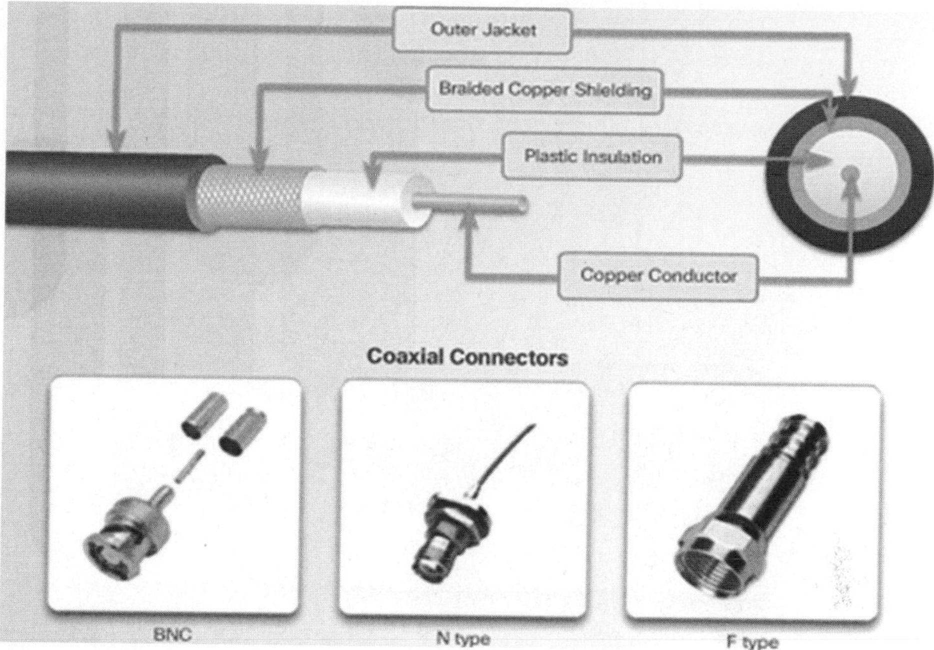

Figure 7-26 Coaxial

There are several types of coaxial cable:

- *Thicknet* **or 10BASE5**—Used in networks and operated at 10 Mb/s with a maximum length of 1640.4 ft. (500 m)
- *Thinnet* **10BASE2**—Used in networks and operated at 10 Mb/s with a maximum length of 607 ft. (185 m)
- **RG-59**—Most commonly used for cable television in the United States
- **RG-6**—Higher quality cable than RG-59, with more bandwidth and less susceptibility to interference

Coaxial cable has no specific maximum bandwidth. The type of signaling technology used determines the speed and limiting factors.

Twisted-Pair Cables (7.3.2.2)

Twisted-pair is a type of copper cabling used for telephone communications and most Ethernet networks. The pair is twisted to provide protection against crosstalk, which is the noise generated by adjacent pairs of wires in the cable. Unshielded twisted-pair (UTP) cabling is the most common variety of twisted-pair cabling.

As shown in Figure 7-27, *UTP cable* consists of four pairs of color-coded wires that have been twisted together and then encased in a flexible plastic sheath that protects from minor physical damage. The twisting of wires helps protect against *crosstalk*. However, UTP does not protect against *electromagnetic interference (EMI)* or *radio frequency interference (RFI)*. EMI and RFI can be caused by a variety of sources including electric motors and fluorescent lights.

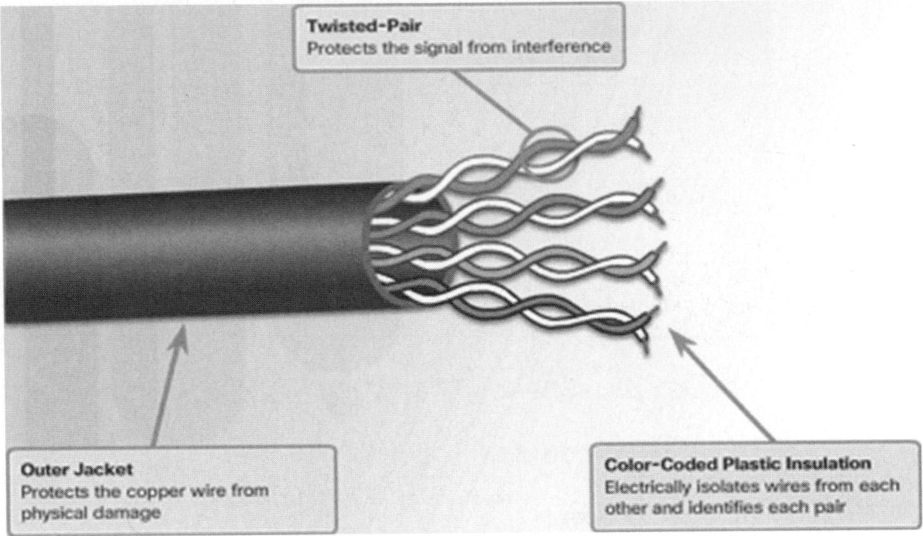

Figure 7-27 UTP Cable

There is also a thin nylon cord within the cable, which, when pulled backward along the length of the cable, will slice the jacket. This is the preferred method to access the wire pairs. It prevents nicking or cutting any of the wires in the cable.

Shielded twisted-pair (STP) was designed to provide better protection against EMI and RFI. As shown in Figure 7-28, each twisted-pair is wrapped in a foil shield. The four pairs are then wrapped together in a metallic braid or foil.

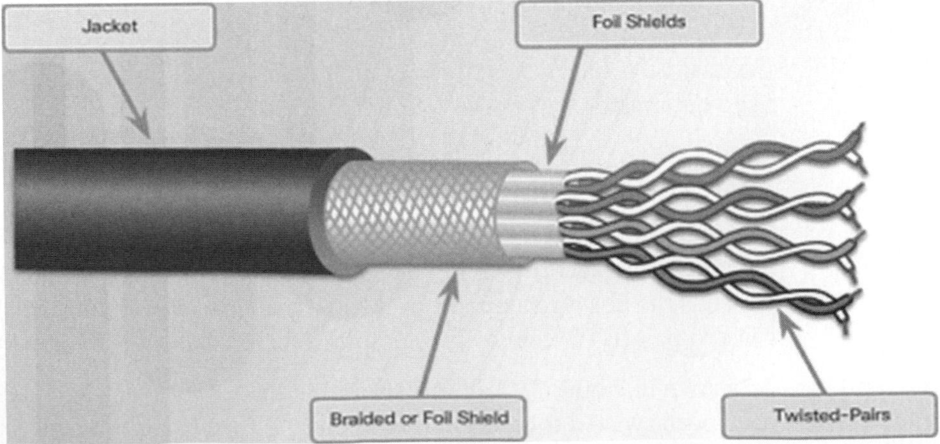

Figure 7-28 Shielded Twisted Pair

Both UTP and STP cables are terminated with an *RJ-45 connector* and plug into RJ-45 sockets, as shown in Figure 7-29. Compared to UTP cable, STP cable is significantly more expensive and difficult to install. To gain the full benefit of the shielding, STP cables are terminated with special shielded STP RJ-45 data connectors. If the cable is improperly grounded, the shield may act as an antenna and pick up unwanted signals.

Figure 7-29 RJ-45 Connector and Plug

Twisted-Pair Category Ratings (7.3.2.3)

Twisted-pair cables come in several categories (Cat). These categories are based on the number of wires in the cable and the number of twists in those wires. Most networks today are wired using twisted-pair cabling. The characteristics of twisted-pair cable are shown in Table 7-9.

Table 7-9 Twisted-Pair Cable Features

	Speed	Features
Cat 3 UTP	10 Mb/s at 16 MHz	■ Suitable for Ethernet LAN ■ Most often used for phone lines
Cat 5 UTP	100 Mb/s at 100 MHz	■ Manufactured with higher standard than Cat 3 to allow for higher data transfer rates
Cat 5e UTP	1000 Mb/s at 100 MHz	■ Manufactured with higher standard than Cat 5 to allow for higher data transfer rates ■ More twists per foot than Cat 5 to better prevent EMI and RFI from outside sources
Cat 6 UTP	1000 Mb/s at 250 MHz	■ Manufactured with higher standard than Cat 5e ■ More twists per foot than Cat 5e to better prevent EMI and RFI from outside sources

(*Continued*)

Table 7-9 *Continued*

	Speed	Features
Cat 6a UTP	1000 Mb/s at 500 MHz	■ Cat 6a has better insulation and performance than Cat 6 ■ May have a plastic divider to separate pairs of wires inside the cable to better prevent EMI and RFI ■ Good choice for customer using applications that require high bandwidth such as videoconferencing or gaming
Cat 7 ScTP	10 Gb/s at 600 MHz	ScTP (screened twisted-pair) is very expensive and not as flexible as UTP

Note

Cat 3 cables use a 6-pin RJ-11 connector, whereas all other twisted-pair cables use an 8-pin RJ-45 connector.

New or renovated office buildings often have some type of UTP cabling that connects every office to a central point called the ***main distribution facility (MDF)***. The distance limitation of UTP cabling used for data is 100 meters (330 feet). Cable runs in excess of this distance limitation need a switch, repeater, or hub to extend the connection to the MDF. These switches, repeaters, and hubs would be located in an ***IDF (independent distribution facility)***.

Cables that are installed inside plenum areas of buildings must be plenum rated. A ***plenum*** is any area that is used for ventilation, such as the area between the ceiling and a dropped ceiling. ***Plenum-rated cables*** are made from a special plastic that retards fire and produces less smoke than other cable types.

Twisted-Pair Wire Schemes (7.3.2.4)

There are two different patterns, or wiring schemes, called ***T568A and T568B***. Each wiring scheme defines the pinout, or order of wire connections, on the end of the cable. The two schemes are similar except that two of the four pairs are reversed in the termination order, as shown in Figure 7-30.

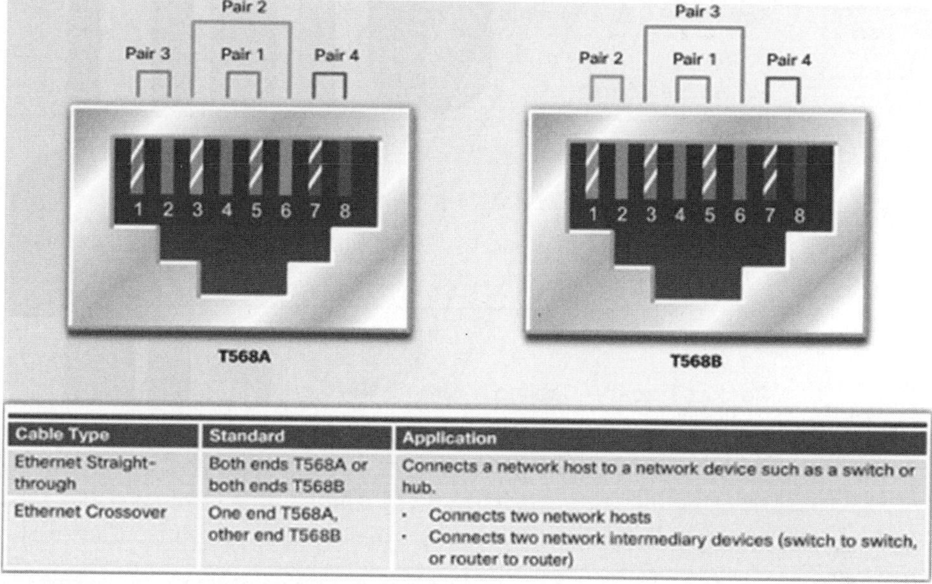

Cable Type	Standard	Application
Ethernet Straight-through	Both ends T568A or both ends T568B	Connects a network host to a network device such as a switch or hub.
Ethernet Crossover	One end T568A, other end T568B	• Connects two network hosts • Connects two network intermediary devices (switch to switch, or router to router)

Figure 7-30 Twisted-Pair Wire Schemes

On a network installation, one of the two wiring schemes (T568A or T568B) should be chosen and followed. It is important that the same wiring scheme is used for every termination in that project. If working on an existing network, use the wiring scheme that already exists.

Using the T568A and T568B wiring schemes, two types of cables can be created: a straight-through cable and a *crossover cable*. A *straight-through cable* is the most common cable type. It maps a wire to the same pins on both ends of the cable. The order of connections (the pinout) for each color is the exact same on both ends.

Two devices directly connected and using different pins for transmit and receive are known as unlike devices. They require a straight-through cable to exchange data. For example, connecting a PC to a switch requires a straight-through cable.

A crossover cable uses both wiring schemes. T568A on one end of the cable and T568B on the other end of the same cable. Devices that are directly connected and use the same pins for transmit and receive, are known as like devices. They require the use of a crossover cable to exchange data. For example, connecting a PC directly to another PC requires a crossover cable.

Note

If the incorrect cable type is used, the connection between network devices will not function. However, many newer devices can automatically sense which pins are used for transmit and receive and will adjust their internal connections accordingly.

Activity—Cable Pinouts (7.3.2.5)

To access the activities, please refer to the Cisco Networking Academy IT Essentials 6.0 online course.

Lab—Build and Test Network Cables (7.3.2.6)

In this lab, you build and test straight-through and crossover Unshielded Twisted-Pair (UTP) Ethernet network cables. Refer to the lab in *IT Essentials v6 Lab Manual*.

Packet Tracer—Cabling a Simple Network (7.3.2.7)

In this Packet Tracer activity, you develop an understanding of the basic functions of Packet Tracer, create a simple network with two hosts, and observe the importance of using the correct cable type to connect PCs. To access the activities found in this book, please refer to the instructions found in the introduction.

Fiber-Optic Cables (7.3.2.8)

Optical fiber is composed of two kinds of glass (core and cladding) and a protective outer shield (jacket). Table 7-10 explains each component in more detail.

Table 7-10 Fiber Optic Cable Components

Component	Description
Jacket	■ Typically, a PVC jacket that protects the fiber against abrasion, moisture, and other contaminants. ■ Composition varies depending on the cable usage.
Strengthening Material	■ Surrounds the buffer, prevents the fiber cable from being stretched when it is being pulled. ■ Material used is often the same material used to produce bulletproof vests.
Buffer	Used to help shield the core cladding damage.
Cladding	■ Made from slightly different chemicals then the core. ■ Tends to act like a mirror by reflecting light back into the core of the fiber keeping the light in the core as it travels down.
Core	■ Light transmission element at the center of the optical fiber. ■ Typically, silica or glass. ■ Light pulses travel through the fiber core.

Because it uses light to transmit signals, fiber-optic cable is not affected by EMI or RFI. All signals are converted to light pulses as they enter the cable, and converted back into electrical signals when they leave it. This means that fiber-optic cable can deliver signals that are clearer, can go farther, and have greater bandwidth than cable made of copper or other metals. Although the optical fiber is very thin and susceptible to sharp bends, the properties of the core and cladding make it very strong. Optical fiber is durable and is deployed in harsh environmental conditions in networks all around the world.

Types of Fiber Media (7.3.2.9)

Fiber-optic cables are broadly classified into two types:

- *Single-mode fiber (SMF)*—Consists of a very small core and uses laser technology to send a single ray of light. Popular in long-distance situations spanning hundreds of kilometers, such as those required in long haul telephony and cable TV applications.
- *Multimode fiber (MMF)*—Consists of a larger core and uses LED emitters to send light pulses. Specifically, light from an LED enters the multimode fiber at different angles. Popular in LANs because they can be powered by low-cost LEDs. It provides bandwidth up to 10 Gb/s over link lengths of up to 550 meters.

Fiber-Optic Connectors (7.3.2.10)

An optical fiber connector terminates the end of an optical fiber. A variety of optical fiber connectors are available. The main differences among the types of connectors are dimensions and methods of coupling. Businesses decide on the types of connectors that will be used, based on their equipment.

From Figures 7-31 to 7-34 of Table 7-11, you learn about the most popular types of fiber-optic connectors.

Table 7-11 Fiber Optic Connectors

	Connector Type	Description
Figure 7-31 ST Connector	*Straight-Tip (ST) connectors*	One of the first connector types used. The connector locks securely with a "twist-on/twist-off" bayonet style mechanism.

(*Continued*)

Table 7-11 *Continued*

	Connector Type	Description
 **Figure 7-32** SC Connector	*Subscriber Connector (SC) connectors*	Sometimes referred to as square connector or standard connector. It is a widely adopted LAN and WAN connector that uses a push-pull mechanism to ensure positive insertion. This connector type is used with multimode and single-mode fiber.
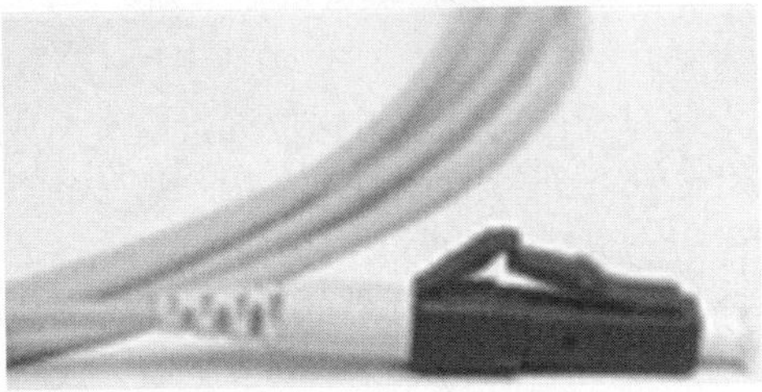 **Figure 7-33** LC Connector	*Lucent Connectors (LC)*	A smaller version of the fiber-optic SC connector. It is sometimes called a little or local connector and is quickly growing in popularity due to its smaller size.
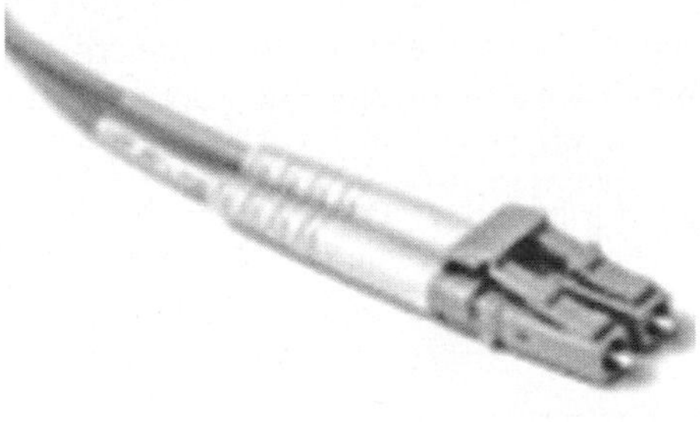 **Figure 7-34** Duplex Multimode LC Connector	*Duplex Multimode LC connector*	Similar to a LC simplex connector, but using a duplex connector.

Because light can only travel in one direction over optical fiber, two fibers are required to support the full duplex operation. Therefore, fiber-optic patch cables bundle together two optical fiber cables and terminate them with a pair of standard single fiber connectors. Some fiber connectors accept both the transmitting and receiving fibers in a single connector known as a duplex connector as shown in Figure 7-34 the Duplex Multimode LC Connector.

Basic Networking Concepts and Technologies (7.4)

Networks provide easy access to shared data and resources for an organization or home user. Understanding key elements of networking such as transmission media, communication protocols, network hardware and software, and data sharing are essential to a technician. In this section, you learn about how IP addressing is implemented, and how protocols are used by network software to perform functions and provide services over the network.

Networked Equipment Addressing (7.4.1)

Network equipment relies on two sets of address to deliver messages quickly and efficiently. Media Access Control (MAC) addressing and Internet Protocol (IP) addressing are both key components to networking but they have different purposes. MAC addresses are hardware addresses whereas IP addresses are assigned as part of connecting to a network. In this section discusses network equipment addressing.

Network Addressing (7.4.1.1)

Fingerprints and addressed letters are two ways of identifying a person. A person's fingerprints usually do not change. They provide a way to physically identify people. The mailing address of a person can change.

Devices that are attached to a network have two addresses that are similar to a person's fingerprints and a person's mailing address. These two types of addresses are the Media Access Control (MAC) address and the IP address. The *MAC address* is hard-coded onto the network interface card (NIC) by the manufacturer. The address stays with the device regardless of what network the device is connected. A MAC address is 48 bits and can be represented in one of the three hexadecimal formats shown in Table 7-12.

Table 7-12 MAC Address Format

Address Format	Description
00-50-56-BE-D7-87	Two hexadecimal digits separated by hyphens
00:50:56:BE:D7:87	Two hexadecimal digits separated by colons
0050.56BE.D787	Four hexadecimal digits separated by periods

Note

The binary and hexadecimal numbering systems are common in networking technologies. Converting between decimal, binary, and hexadecimal numbering systems is beyond the scope of this course. Search the Internet to learn more about these numbering systems.

IP Addresses (7.4.1.2)

Today, it is common for a computer to have two versions of IP addresses. In the early 1990s there was a concern about running out of IPv4 network addresses. The Internet Engineering Task Force (IETF) began to look for a replacement. This led to the development of what is now known as IP version 6 (IPv6). Currently IPv6 is operating alongside and is beginning to replace IPv4. An *IPv4 address* is 32 bits long and is represented in dotted decimal. An example of IPv4 32 bits in dotted decimal notation is: **192.168.200.8**. An *IPv6 address* is 128 bits long and is represented in hexadecimal. An example of IPv6 128 bits in hexadecimal format is: **2001:0DB8:CAFÉ:0200:0000:0000:0000:0008**.

IP addressing is assigned by network administrators based on the location within the network. When a device moves from one network to another, its IP address will most likely change. Figure 7-35 shows a topology with two LANs. This topology demonstrates that MAC addresses do not change when a device is moved. But IP addresses do change. Laptop was moved to LAN 2. Notice that laptop's MAC address did not change, but its IP addresses did change.

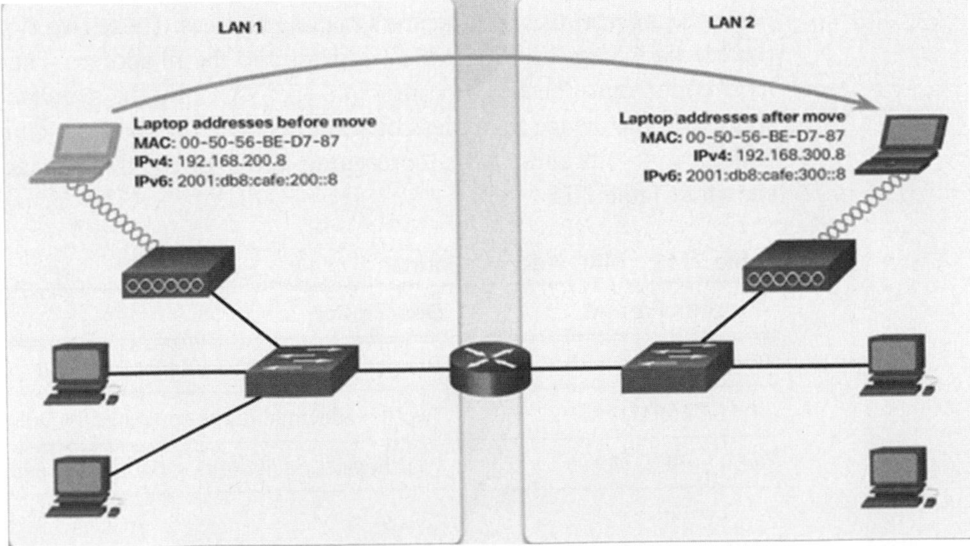

Figure 7-35 Two LAN Topology with MAC Address Change

Figure 7-36 shows output for the command *ipconfig* **/all** on the laptop. The output shows the MAC address and two IP addresses.

```
C:\> ipconfig /all

Windows IP Configuration

   Host Name . . . . . . . . . . . . : ITEuser
   Primary Dns Suffix  . . . . . . . :
   Node Type . . . . . . . . . . . . : Hybrid
   IP Routing Enabled. . . . . . . . : No
   WINS Proxy Enabled. . . . . . . . : No

Ethernet adapter Local Area Connection:

   Connection-specific DNS Suffix  . :
   Description . . . . . . . . . . . : Intel(R) PRO/1000 MT Network Connection
   Physical Address. . . . . . . . . : 00-50-56-BE-D7-87
   DHCP Enabled. . . . . . . . . . . : No
   Autoconfiguration Enabled . . . . : Yes
   IPv6 Address. . . . . . . . . . . : 2001:db8:cafe:200::8(Preferred)
   Link-local IPv6 Address . . . . . : fe80::8cbf:a682:d2e0:98a%11(Preferred)
   IPv4 Address. . . . . . . . . . . : 192.168.200.8(Preferred)
   Subnet Mask . . . . . . . . . . . : 255.255.255.0
   Default Gateway . . . . . . . . . : 2001:db8:cafe:200::1
                                       192.168.200.1
<output omitted>

C:\>
```

Figure 7-36 Laptop Addressing Information

Note

Windows OS calls the NIC an Ethernet adapter and the MAC address a physical address.

IPv4 Address Format (7.4.1.3)

When a host is configured with an IPv4 address, it is entered in dotted decimal format. Imagine if you had to enter the 32-bit binary equivalent. The address 192.168.200.8 would be entered as 11000000101010001100100000001000. If just one bit were mistyped, the address would be different. The device then might not be able to communicate on the network.

Each number separated by a period is called an octet because it represents 8 bits. Therefore, the address 192.168.200.8 has four octets. Each bit in an octet can be either a 1 (on) or a 0 (off). Also, each bit in an octet represents a value. The rightmost bit represents a 1. Each bit to its left is doubled, so that the leftmost bit represents 128. To convert the binary address, add the values of every bit that is a 1 in each octet, as shown in Figure 7-37.

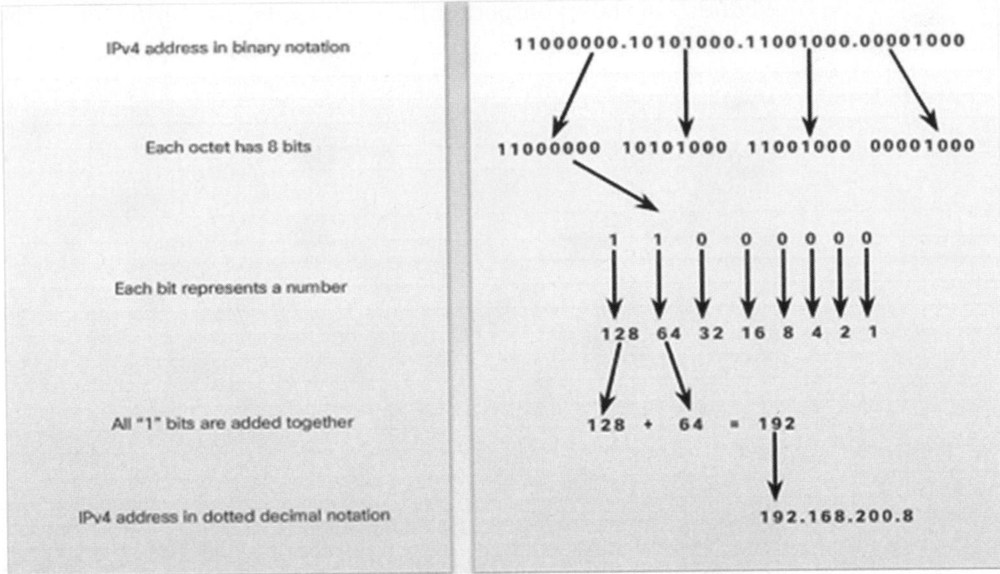

Figure 7-37 Binary to Decimal Conversion

In addition, an IPv4 address is composed of two parts. The first part identifies the network. The second part identifies a host on that network. Both parts are required.

When a computer prepares data to send out on the network, it must determine whether to send data directly to the intended receiver or to a router. It will send it directly to the receiver if the receiver is on the same network. Otherwise, it will send the data to a router. A router then uses the network portion of the IP address to route traffic between different networks.

Computers and routers use the ***subnet mask*** to calculate the network portion of the destination IPv4 address. Like an IPv4 address, the subnet mask is represented in dotted-decimal. For example, the subnet mask for the IPv4 address 192.168.200.8 might be 255.255.255.0. A computer uses both the address and the subnet mask to determine the network portion of the address. It does so at the binary level. In Figure 7-38, the 192.168.200.8 address and 255.255.255.0 subnet mask are converted to their binary equivalents. An octet with the decimal value 255 is 8 ones in binary. A one bit in the subnet mask means that bit is part of the network portion. So the first 24 bits of the 192.168.200.8 address are network bits. The last 8 bits are host bits.

	Network Portion		Host Portion
192.168.200.8	11000000.10101000.11001000	.	00001000
255.255.255.0	11111111.11111111.11111111	.	00000000
192.168.200.0	11000000.10101000.11001000	.	00000000

Figure 7-38 Role of the Subnet Mask

Classful and Classless IPv4 Addressing (7.4.1.4)

When IPv4 was first specified in 1981, addresses were divided into three classes, as shown in Table 7-13. The value of the first octet in an IPv4 address indicates which class it belongs to. Each class was assigned a default subnet mask.

Table 7-13 IP Address Classes

Class	First Octet	Subnet Mask	Network/Host N = Network, H = Host	Number of Hosts per Network
A	0-127	255.0.0.0	N.H.H.H	16,77,214
B	128-191	255.255.0.0	N.N.H.H	65,534
C	192-223	255.255.255.0	N.N.N.H	254

Subnet masks are often displayed using *prefix notation*, as shown in Table 7-14. The number after the "slash" indicates how many bits in the subnet mask are one bits. For example, the Class B network 172.16.0.0 with subnet mask of 255.255.0.0 would be written as 172.16.0.0/16. The "/16" indicates that the first 16 bits in the subnet mask are all ones.

Table 7-14 Subnet Mask in Prefix Notation

Subnet Mask	Binary	Prefix
255.0.0.0	11111111.00000000.00000000.00000000	/8
255.255.0.0	11111111.11111111.00000000.00000000	/16
255.255.255.0	11111111.11111111.11111111.00000000	/24

In the early 1990s, it was clear to network engineers that the classful IPv4 addressing system would eventually run out of space. Many businesses were too large for a Class C network address, which only had 254 host addresses. But they were too small for a Class B network address with 65,534 host addresses. Therefore, the Internet Engineering Task Force (IETF) came up with an address assignment strategy called *Classless Inter-Domain Router (CIDR, pronounced as "cider")*. CIDR was a temporary measure that allowed organizations to use addressing schemes customized to their particular situation. An organization could receive four Class C network addresses with a custom subnet mask, as shown in Table 7-15. The resulting network address is called a *supernet* because it consists of more than one classful network address.

Table 7-15 CDIR Supernet Example

192.168.20.0/24	
192.168.21.0/24	192.168.20.0/22
192.168.22.0/24	
192.168.23.0/24	

Number of IPv6 Addresses (7.4.1.5)

IPv6 addressing will eventually replace IPv4 addressing. IPv6 overcomes the limitations of IPv4 and is a powerful enhancement with features that better suit current and foreseeable network demands. The 32-bit IPv4 address space provides approximately 4,294,967,296 unique addresses. IPv6 address space provides 340, 282,366,920,938,463,463,374,607,431,768,211,456 addresses, or 340 undecillion addresses, which is roughly equivalent to every grain of sand on Earth. Table 7-16 provides a visual to compare the IPv4 and IPv6 address space.

Table 7-16 How Many Addresses Are Available with IPv6

Number Name	Scientific Notation	Number of Zeros
1 thousand	10^3	1,000
1 million	10^6	1,000,000
1 billion	10^9	1,000,000,000 *there are 4 billion IPv4 addresses
1 trillion	10^12	1,000,000,000,000
1 quadrillion	10^15	1,000,000,000,000,000
1 quintillion	10^18	1,000,000,000,000,000,000
1 sextillion	10^21	1,000,000,000,000,000,000,000
1 septillion	10^24	1,000,000,000,000,000,000,000,000

Number Name	Scientific Notation	Number of Zeros
1 octillion	10^27	1,000,000,000,000,000,000,000,000,000
1 nonillion	10^30	1,000,000,000,000,000,000,000,000,000,000
1 decillion	10^33	1,000,000,000,000,000,000,000,000,000,000,000
1 undecillion	10^36	1,000,000,000,000,000,000,000,000,000,000,000,000 *there are 340 undecillion IPv6 addresses

IPv6 Address Formats (7.4.1.6)

IPv6 addresses are 128 bits in length and written as a string of hexadecimal values. Every 4 bits is represented by a single hexadecimal digit for a total of 32 hexadecimal values. The examples shown in Table 7-17 are fully expanded IPv6 addresses.

Table 7-17 Fully Expanded IPv6 Address Examples

2001:0DB8:0000:1111:0000:0000:0000:0200:
FE80:0000:0000:0000:0123:4567:89AB:CDEF
FF02:0000:0000:0000:0000:0000:0000:0001

Two rules help reduce the number of digits needed to represent an IPv6 address.

Rule 1—Omit Leading Os

The first rule to help reduce the notation of IPv6 addresses is to omit any leading 0s (zeros) in any 16-bit section. For example:

- 01AB can be represented as 1AB
- 09F0 can be represented as 9F0
- 0A00 can be represented as A00
- 00AB can be represented as AB

Rule 2—Omit All 0 Segments

The second rule to help reduce the notation of IPv6 addresses is that a double colon (::) can replace any group of consecutive zeros. The double colon (::) can only be used once within an address, otherwise there would be more than one possible resulting address.

Table 7-18 shows examples of how to use the two rules to compress an IPv6 address.

Table 7-18 Compressing an IPv6 Address

Fully Expanded	2001:0DB8:0000:1111:0000:0000:0000:0200
No Leading 0s	2001: DB8: 0:1111: 0: 0: 0: 200
Compressed	2001: DB8:0:1111::200

Video

Video—IPv4 vs. IPv6 (7.4.1.7)

This video shows the differences between IPv4 and IPv6 addressing. IPv4 addresses are 32 bit addresses and IPv6 addresses are 128 bit addresses, but typically IPv4 addresses are represented in dotted Decimal notation and IPv6 addresses are represented by colon-separated Hexadecimal notation.

There are four octets, or four groupings of eight bits in an IPv4 address, and in an IPv6 address we have eight hextets, or eight groupings of 16 bits in each portion of an IPv6 address.

IPv4 addresses have subnet masks. With IPv4, the ones in the subnet mask define the network. In a host address of 192.168.1.100 with a 255.255.255.0 subnet mask, the 255s indicate the network portion of the address. It's the 192.168.1 network. The zeros in the subnet mask indicate the host portion of the address. In this case 100 is the host number.

IPv6 addresses have network prefixes instead of subnet masks. There are no subnet masks in IPv6. So you can see with this IPv6 address, the network prefix is slash 64. The network prefix tells us how to identify the network. In this case, the first 64 bits of the address, or the 2001:DB8:7AC:1F, defines the network, and the remaining 64 bits is the host identifier. IPv6 addresses are typically presented in a compressed format. For instance, if we look at this IPv6 address, it's been compressed.

To learn more about IPv4 and IPv6 please click the link which can be accessed in the Cisco Networking Academy IT Essentials 6.0 online course.

Static Addressing (7.4.1.8)

In a network with a small number of hosts, it is easy to manually configure each device with the proper IP address. A network administrator who understands IP addressing should assign the addresses and should know how to choose a valid address for a particular network. The IP address that is assigned is unique for each host within the same network or subnet. This is known as *static IP addressing*.

To configure a static IP address on a host, go to the TCP/IPv4 Properties window of the NIC, as shown in Figure 7-39.

You can assign the following IP address configuration information to a host:

- **IP address**—identifies the computer on the network
- **Subnet mask**—is used to identify the network on which the computer is connected
- *Default gateway*—identifies the device that the computer uses to access the Internet or another network
- **Optional values**—such as the preferred Domain Name System (DNS) server address and the alternate DNS server address

Figure 7-39 Assigning Static IPv4 Addressing

In Windows 7, use the following path:

Start > Control Panel > Network and Sharing Center > Change adapter setting > right-click **Local Area Connection > Properties > TCP/IPv4** or **TCP/IPv6 > Properties > Use the following IP address > Use the following DNS server addresses > OK > OK**

In Windows 8.0 and 8.1, use the following path:

Control Panel > Network and Sharing Center > Change adapter setting > right-click **Ethernet > Properties > TCP/IPv4** or **TCP/IPv6 > Properties > Use the following IP address > Use the following DNS server addresses > OK > OK**

Dynamic Addressing (7.4.1.9)

If more than a few computers are a part of the LAN, manually configuring IP addresses for every host on the network can be time consuming and prone to errors. A DHCP server automatically assigns IP addresses, which simplifies the addressing process. Automatically configuring some of the TCP/IP parameters also reduces the possibility of assigning duplicate or invalid IP addresses.

Before a computer on the network can take advantage of the DHCP services, the computer must be able to identify the server on the local network. A computer can be configured to accept an IP address from a DHCP server by selecting the **Obtain an IP address automatically** option in the NIC configuration window, refer to Figure 7-39. When a computer is set to obtain an IP address automatically, all other IP addressing configuration boxes are not available. The DHCP settings are configured the same for a wired or wireless NIC.

After boot up, a computer continually requests an IP address from a DHCP server until one is received. If your computer cannot communicate with the DHCP server to obtain an IP address, the Windows OS automatically assigns an Automatic Private IP Addressing (APIPA) address. This local-link address is in the range of 169.254.0.0 to 169.254.255.255. Local-link means your computer can only communicate with computers connected to the same network within this IP address range.

A DHCP server can automatically assign the following IP address configuration information to a host:

- IP address
- Subnet mask
- Default gateway
- Optional values, such as a DNS server address

In Windows 7, use the following path:

Start > Control Panel > Network and Sharing Center > Change adapter setting > right-click **Local Area Connection > Properties > TCP/IPv4** or **TCP/IPv6 > Properties >** select radio button **Obtain an IP address automatically > OK > OK**

In Windows 8.0 and 8.1, use the following path:

Control Panel > Network and Sharing Center > Change adapter setting > right-click **Ethernet > Properties > TCP/IPv4** or **TCP/IPv6 > Properties >** select radio button **Obtain an IP address automatically > OK > OK**

DNS

To access a DNS server, a computer uses the IP address configured in the DNS settings of the NIC in the computer. DNS resolves or maps host names and URLs to IP addresses.

All Windows computers contain a DNS cache that stores host names that have recently been resolved. The cache is the first place that the DNS client looks for host name resolution. Because it is a location in memory, the cache retrieves resolved IP addresses more quickly than using a DNS server and does not create network traffic.

Configuring Alternate IP Settings

Setting up an alternate IP configuration in Windows simplifies moving between a network that requires using DHCP and a network that uses static IP settings. If a computer cannot communicate with the DHCP server on the network, Windows uses the alternate IP configuration assigned to the NIC. The alternate IP configuration also replaces the APIPA address that is assigned by Windows when a DHCP server cannot be contacted.

To create the alternate IP configuration Open the NIC Properties window, double-click the Internet Protocol Version 4 (TCP/IPv4) protocol and then click the Alternate Configuration tab located in the Internet Protocol Version 4 (TCP/IPv4) Properties window. The Alternate Configuration tab only shows when **Obtain an IP address automatically** is selected.

ICMP (7.4.1.10)

Internet Control Message Protocol (ICMP) is used by devices on a network to send control and error messages to computers and servers. There are several different uses for ICMP, such as announcing network errors, announcing network congestion, and troubleshooting.

Ping is commonly used to test connections between computers. Ping is a simple but highly useful command line utility used to determine whether a specific IP address is accessible. To see a list of options that you can use with the ping command, type **ping /?** in the Command Prompt window, as shown Figure 7-40.

Ping works by sending an ICMP echo request to a destination computer or other network device. The receiving device then sends back an ICMP echo reply message to confirm connectivity. Echo requests and echo replies are test messages that determine if devices can send packets to each other. With Windows, four ICMP echo requests (pings) are sent to the destination computer, as shown in Figure 7-41. If it is reachable, the destination computer responds with four ICMP echo replies. The percentage of successful replies can help you to determine the reliability and accessibility of the destination computer. Other ICMP messages report undelivered packets and whether a device is too busy to handle the packet.

You can also use ping to find the IP address of a host when that host's name is known. If you ping the name of a website, for example, cisco.com, as shown in Figure 7-41, the IP address of the server is displayed.

```
C:\> ping /?

Usage: ping [-t] [-a] [-n count] [-l size] [-f] [-i TTL] [-v TOS]
            [-r count] [-s count] [[-j host-list] | [-k host-list]]
            [-w timeout] [-R] [-S srcaddr] [-4] [-6] target_name

Options:
    -t             Ping the specified host until stopped.
                   To see statistics and continue - type Control-Break;
                   To stop - type Control-C.
    -a             Resolve addresses to hostnames.
    -n count       Number of echo requests to send.
    -l size        Send buffer size.
    -f             Set Don't Fragment flag in packet (IPv4-only).
    -i TTL         Time To Live.
    -v TOS         Type Of Service (IPv4-only. This setting has been deprecated
                   and has no effect on the type of service field in the IP Header).
    -r count       Record route for count hops (IPv4-only).
    -s count       Timestamp for count hops (IPv4-only).
    -j host-list   Loose source route along host-list (IPv4-only).
    -k host-list   Strict source route along host-list (IPv4-only).
    -w timeout     Timeout in milliseconds to wait for each reply.
    -R             Use routing header to test reverse route also (IPv6-only).
    -S srcaddr     Source address to use.
    -4             Force using IPv4.
    -6             Force using IPv6.

C:\>
```

Figure 7-40 List of Ping Command Options

```
C:\> ping www.cisco.com

Pinging e144.dscb.akamaiedge.net [23.200.16.170] with 32 bytes of data:
Reply from 23.200.16.170: bytes=32 time=25ms TTL=54
Reply from 23.200.16.170: bytes=32 time=26ms TTL=54
Reply from 23.200.16.170: bytes=32 time=25ms TTL=54
Reply from 23.200.16.170: bytes=32 time=25ms TTL=54

Ping statistics for 23.200.16.170:
    Packets: Sent = 4, Received = 4, Lost = 0 (0% loss),
Approximate round trip times in milli-seconds:
    Minimum = 25ms, Maximum = 26ms, Average = 25ms

C:\>
```

Figure 7-41 Testing Connectivity by Hostname with Ping

Lab—Configure a NIC to Use DHCP in Windows (7.4.1.11)

In this lab, you configure an Ethernet NIC to use DHCP to obtain an IP address and test connectivity between two computers. Refer to the lab in *IT Essentials v6 Lab Manual.*

Packet Tracer—Adding Computers to an Existing Network (7.4.1.12)

In this Packet Tracer activity, you will configure the computers to use DHCP, configure static addressing, use ipconfig to retrieve host IP information, and use ping to verify connectivity. To access the activities found in this book, please refer to the instructions found in the introduction.

Transport Layer Protocols (7.4.2)

Ports and protocols are used in networking to allow communications between device, applications, and networks. Protocols define how this communication occurs and ports are used to track various communications. This section explains common transport layer protocols and ports used in data networks.

Role of the Transport Layer (7.4.2.1)

The *transport layer* is responsible for establishing a temporary communication session between two applications and delivering data between them. The transport layer is the link between the application layer and the lower layers that are responsible for network transmission.

Transport Layer Features (7.4.2.2)

Data flowing between a source application and a destination application is known as a conversation. A computer can maintain multiple conversations between multiple applications at the same time, as shown in Figure 7-42. This is possible because of the three main features of the transport layer:

- **Tracking individual conversation between applications**—a device can have multiple applications that are using the network at the same time.
- **Segmenting data and reassembling segments**—a sending device segments application data into blocks that are an appropriate size. A receiving device reassembles the segments into application data.
- **Identifying the applications**—to pass data streams to the proper applications, the transport layer must identify the target application. To accomplish this, the transport layer assigns each application an identifier called a port number.

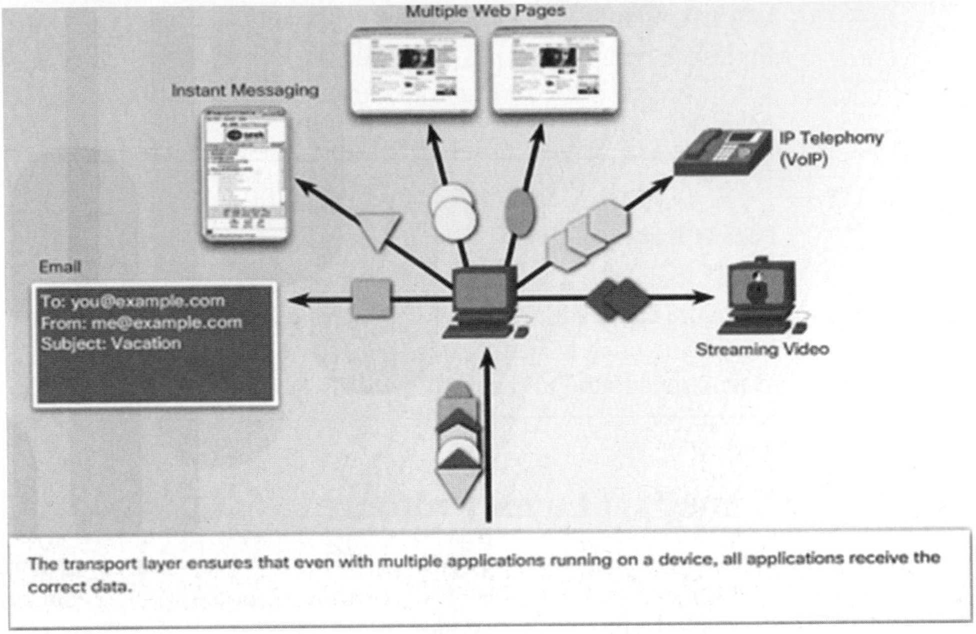

The transport layer ensures that even with multiple applications running on a device, all applications receive the correct data.

Figure 7-42 Tracking the Conversations with the Transport Layer

Transport Layer Protocol (7.4.2.3)

The two protocols that operate at the transport layer are TCP and User Datagram Protocol (UDP), as shown in Figure 7-43 TCP is considered a reliable, full-featured transport layer protocol, which ensures that all of the data arrives at the destination. In contrast, UDP is a very simple transport layer protocol that does not provide for any reliability. IP uses these transport protocols to enable hosts to communicate and transfer data. Figure 7-44 highlights the TCP and UDP properties.

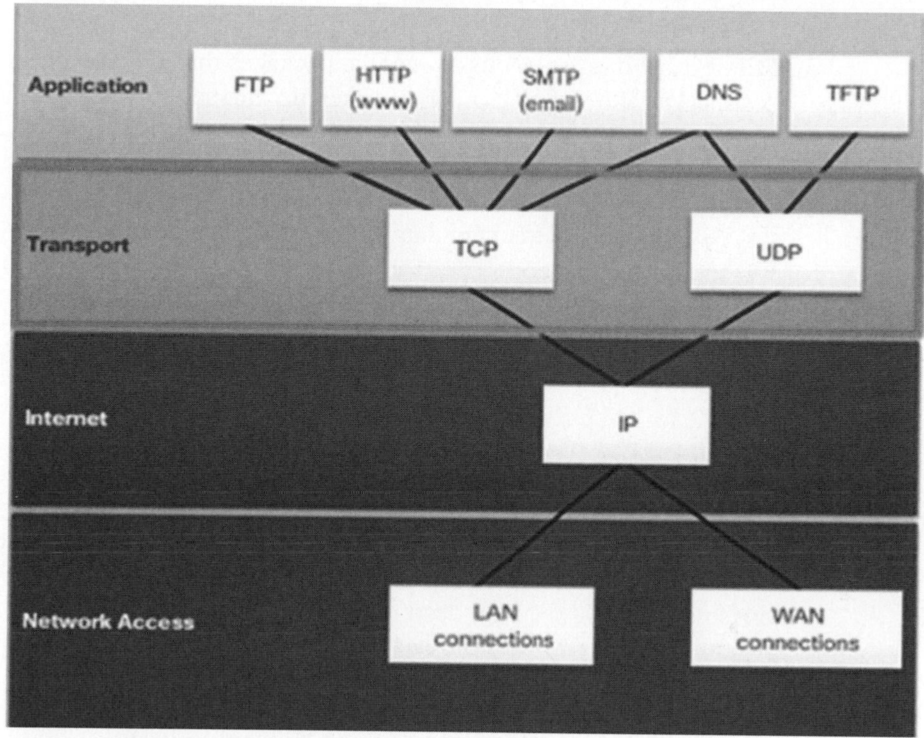

Figure 7-43 Two Transport Layer Protocols

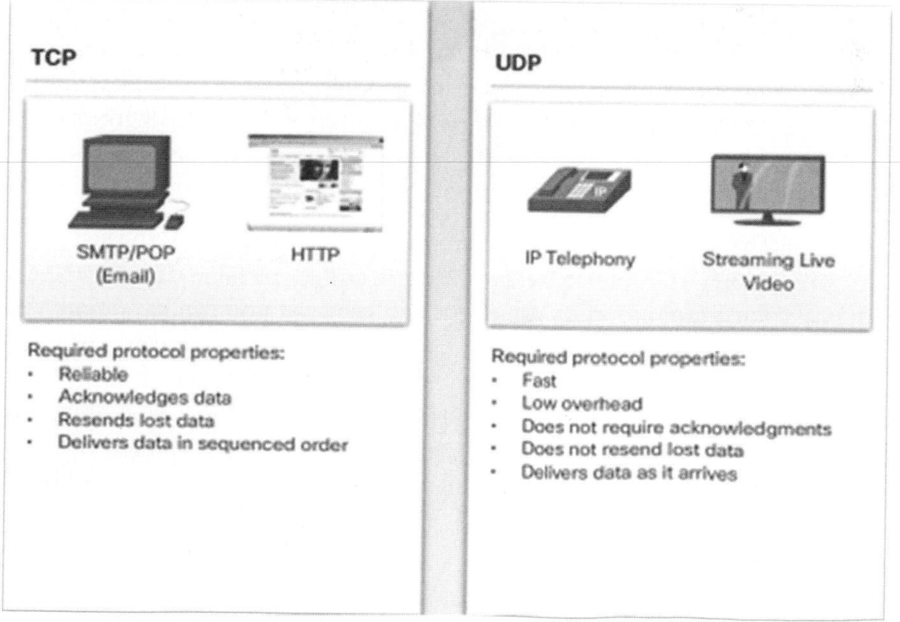

Figure 7-44 TCP and UDP Properties

TCP (7.4.2.4)

TCP transport is analogous to sending packages that are tracked from source to destination. If a shipping order is broken up into several packages, a customer can check online to see the order of the delivery.

With TCP, there are three basic operations of reliability:

- Numbering and tracking data segments transmitted to a specific device from a specific application
- Acknowledging received data
- Retransmitting any unacknowledged data after a certain period of time

UDP (7.4.2.5)

UDP is similar to placing a regular, non-registered, letter in the mail. The sender of the letter is not aware of the availability of the receiver to receive the letter. Nor is the post office responsible for tracking the letter or informing the sender if the letter does not arrive at the final destination.

UDP provides the basic functions for delivering data segments between the appropriate applications, with very little overhead and data checking. UDP is known as a best-effort delivery protocol. In the context of networking, best-effort delivery is referred to as unreliable because there is no acknowledgment that the data is received at the destination.

Port Numbers (7.4.2.6)

TCP and UDP use a source and destination *port number* to keep track of application conversations. The *source port number* is associated with the originating application on the local device. The *destination port number* is associated with the destination application on the remote device.

The source port number is dynamically generated by the sending device. This process allows multiple conversations to occur at the same time for the same application. For example, when you use a web browser, you can have more than one tab open at a time. The destination port number is 80 for regular web traffic or 443 for secure web traffic. But the source port will be different for each tab opened. This is how your computer knows which browser tab to deliver the web content. Similarly, other network applications like email and file transfer have their own assigned port numbers. The most common well-known port numbers are shown in Table 7-19.

Table 7-19 Well-Known Port Numbers

Port Number	Protocol	Application	Acronym
20	TCP	File Transfer Protocol (data)	FTP
21	TCP	File Transfer Protocol (control)	FTP
22	TCP	Secure Shell	SSH
23	TCP	Telnet	–
25	TCP	Simple Mail Transfer Protocol	SMPT
53	UDP, TCP	Domain Name Service	DNS
67	UDP	Dynamic Host Configuration Protocol (server)	DHCP
68	UDP	Dynamic Host Configuration Protocol (client)	DHCP
69	UDP	Trivial File Transfer Protocol	TFTP
80	TCP	Hypertext Transfer Protocol	HTTP
110	TCP	Post Office Protocol version 3	POP3
137-139	UDP, TCP	NetBIOS/NetBT	–
143	TCP	Internet Message Access Protocol	IMAP
161	UDP	Simple Network Management Protocol	SNMP
427	UDP, TCP	Service Location Protocol	SLP
443	TCP	Hypertext Transfer Protocol Secure	HTTPS
445	TCP	Server Message Block/Common Internet File System	SMB/CIFS
548	TCP	Apple Filing Protocol	AFP
3389	UDP, TCP	Remote Desktop Protocol	RDP

Packet Tracer Activity

Activity—TCP vs. UDP (7.4.2.7)

To access the activities, please refer to the Cisco Networking Academy IT Essentials 6.0 online course.

Activity—Protocol Definitions and Ports (7.4.2.8)

To access the activities, please refer to the Cisco Networking Academy IT Essentials 6.0 online course.

Summary (7.5)

Computer networks are part of daily life from social media connections to business operations. Networks allow users to transfer data through the use of physical and logical components or software. Physical components are comprised of things such as transmission media and networking devices. Logical components are such things as IP addressing, communication protocols, and applications like email and web browsers.

Summary (7.5.1)

This chapter introduced an overview of network principles, standards, and purposes. It described different types of hardware used in computer networks and explained various protocols and applications used to communicate. The chapter also described two models that are used to aid in the understanding of computer networks. They highlight devices that are used and the protocols that must be followed in order for networks to function properly and communicate with each other.

Many different devices can connect to today's networks including computers, laptops, tablets, smartphones, TVs, watches, and home appliances. These devices use a variety of media to connect to the network including copper, fiber, and wireless. Intermediary devices, such as switches and routers, ensure that data flows between source and destination. The type of networks these devices connect to include LANs, WLANs, PANs, MANs, and WANs.

Devices must agree on a set of rules before they can effectively communicate with each other. These rules are called standards and protocols. The OSI reference model and the TCP/IP protocol suite help network administrators and technicians understand the interaction of these various standards and protocols.

Ethernet standards come in wired and wireless varieties. The wired standard is IEEE 802.3 and the wireless standard is IEEE 802.11.

Data requires several different types of addresses and numbering to make sure it is received by the correct destination. MAC addresses are used by switches to forward traffic within a LAN. IP addresses are used by routers to determine the best path to a destination network. Port numbers are used by computers to determine which application should receive the data.

Summary of Exercises

This is a summary of the Labs Packet Tracer and videos activities associated with this chapter.

Labs

The following labs cover material from this chapter. Refer to the labs in the *IT Essentials v6 Lab Manual*.

Lab—Build and Test Network Cables (7.3.2.6)

Lab—Configure a NIC to Use DHCP in Windows (7.4.1.11)

The following Packet Tracer Activities cover material from this chapter. To access the activities found in this book, please refer to the instructions found in the introduction.

Packet Tracer Activities

Packet Tracer—Cabling a Simple Network (7.3.2.7)

Packet Tracer—Adding Computers to an Existing Network (7.4.1.12)

Please view the video link which can be accessed in the Cisco Networking Academy IT Essentials 6.0 online course.

Check Your Understanding

You can find the answers to these questions in the appendix, "Answers to 'Check Your Understanding' Questions."

1. Which standards organization publishes current Ethernet standards?

A. IEEE

B. EIA/TIA

C. ANSI

D. CCITT

2. What is the color of the wire for pin 1 in the T568B Ethernet wiring standard?

A. Blue

B. Orange

C. Brown

D. Orange/white

E. Blue/white

F. Green/white

G. Green

H. Brown/white

3. A switch is a networking device that will record ________ addresses by inspecting every incoming data frame.

   A. IP

   B. TCP/IP

   C. MAC

   D. SVI

   E. Switch Address

4. A student is helping a friend with a home computer that can no longer access the Internet. Upon investigation, the student discovers that the computer has been assigned the IP address 169.254.100.88. What could cause a computer to get such an IP address?

   A. Reduced computer power supply output

   B. Unreachable DHCP server

   C. Static IP addressing with incomplete information

   D. Interference from surrounding devices

5. Which of these programs is an example of a Type 2 hypervisor?

   A. Windows XP Mode

   B. DirectX

   C. Virtual PC

   D. OpenGL

6. What reference model divides network communications into seven distinct layers and is used to maintain equipment and application interoperability between different vendors?

   A. IEEE 802.3

   B. OSI

   C. DoD

   D. TIA

7. Which network device regenerates the data signal without segmenting the network?

   A. Switch

   B. Hub

   C. Router

   D. Modem

8. Which two protocols operate at the transport layer of the TCP/IP model? (Choose two.)

   A. IP

   B. UDP

   C. ICMP

   D. TCP

   E. FTP

9. At which layer of the TCP/IP model does routing take place?

   A. Application

   B. Internet

   C. Transport

   D. Network access

10. What is the proper CIDR prefix notation for a subnet mask of 255.0.0.0?

    A. /16

    B. /24

    C. /32

    D. /8

11. Which term is used to describe any device on a network that can send and receive information?

    A. Workstation

    B. Server

    C. Console

    D. Peripheral

    E. Host

12. How many host addresses are available on a network with a subnet mask of 255.255.0.0?

    A. 254

    B. 16,777,214

    C. 65,534

    D. 1024

13. A company is expanding its business to other countries. All branch offices must remain connected to corporate headquarters at all times. Which network technology is required to support this scenario?

    A. WLAN
    B. LAN
    C. MAN
    D. WAN

14. Which type of network will extend a short distance and connects printers, mice, and keyboards to an individual host?

    A. WLAN
    B. LAN
    C. MAN
    D. PAN

15. What is the correct compressed format of the IPv6 address 2001:0db8:eeff:000a:0000:0000:0000:0001?

    A. 2001:db8:eeff:a::0001
    B. 2001:db8:eeff:a::1
    C. 2001:db8:eeff:a:1
    D. 2001:db8:eeff:a:::1

16. Which protocol operates at the application layer of the TCP/IP model?

    A. HTTP
    B. TCP
    C. ICMP
    D. IP

17. What type of networking cable is used by television companies to carry data as electrical signals?

    A. Fiber-optic
    B. Unshielded twisted-pair
    C. Shielded twisted-pair
    D. Coaxial

CHAPTER 8

Applied Networking

Objectives

Upon completion of this chapter, you will be able to answer the following questions:

- How do I install and configure network interface cards (NICs)?
- How do I install and configure wireless routers?
- How do I connect devices to a wireless router?
- How do I configure domain memberships in Windows?
- How do I share files through network shares and drive mapping?
- What are TCP/IP services?
- What are the more common TCP/IP ports?
- How to use command line tools for troubleshooting networks?
- What are ISP broadband technologies?
- What are cloud computing technologies?
- How do I troubleshoot networks?

Key Terms

This chapter uses the following key terms. You can find the definitions in the Glossary.

Internet Service Provider (ISP) Page 385

Network components Page 386

Network design Page 386

multipurpose device Page 386

Wake on LAN Page 391

quality of service (QoS), also called 802.1q QoS Page 392

link lights Page 394

Home Network Page 395

Work Network Page 396

Public Network Page 396

cellular data network Page 421

Cellular technology Page 421

Global System for Mobile communications (GSM) Page 421

Enhanced Data Rates for GSM Evolution (EDGE) Page 422

Evolution-Data Optimized (EV-DO) Page 422

General Packet Radio Service (GPRS) Page 422

cellular WAN Page 421

cable Internet connection Page 422

satellite Page 422

Internet port Page 394

Cloud Service Models Page 426

magic packet Page 391

network location profile Page 395

network discovery Page 395

Network Address Translation (NAT) Page 399

service set identifier (SSID) Page 400

wireless channel Page 401

net commands Page 404

tracert Page 404

nslookup Page 405

domain Page 406

workgroup Page 407

homegroup Page 408

mapping network drives Page 410

nbtstat Page 404

netdom Page 404

hidden shares Page 412

virtual private network (VPN) Page 416

remote desktop Page 416

remote assistant Page 416

plain old telephone service (POTS) Page 419

dialup networking (DUN) Page 419

integrated services digital network (ISDN) Page 419

Broadband Page 419

Digital Subscriber Line (DSL) Page 420

asymetric digital subscriber line (ADSL) Page 420

Line of sight wireless Page 420

Uploading Page 420

Worldwide Interoperability for Microwave Access (WiMAX) Page 420

Multiple Input Multiple Output (MIMO) technology Page 421

Fiber broadband Page 422

Data center Page 425

Cloud computing Page 425

Software as a Service (SaaS) Page 426

Platform as a Service (PaaS) Page 426

Infrastructure as a Service (IaaS) Page 426

IT as a Service (ITaaS) Page 426

Hypertext Transfer Protocol (HTTP) Page 428

secure HTTP (HTTPS) Page 428

File Transfer Protocol (FTP) Page 428

File Transfer Protocol Secure (FTPS) Page 429

SSH File Transfer Protocol (SFTP) Page 429

Secure Copy (SCP) Page 429

Print servers Page 429

Email protocol Page 430

Proxy servers Page 430

authentication services (AAA) Page 431

Intrusion detection systems (IDSs) Page 431

intrusion prevention systems (IPSs) Page 431

Universal Threat Management (UTM) Page 431

Introduction (8.0)

Computer networks are designed with precision; devices must be compatible and must follow clearly defined rules or protocols based on the topology or type of network in order to communicate.

Welcome (8.0.1)

In this chapter, we explore how to put together a network and we put this knowledge into practice. To make a network operate, you need hardware and software so data and resources can be shared. For a small network, you need hardware like a NIC and a transmission medium to carry the signals; if you expand, you will need interconnecting devices like switches and routers. Network software includes networking services, applications, and protocols. In this section, you learn to install and configure both the necessary hardware and software. The knowledge gained throughout this section can be applied when building, maintaining, and troubleshooting a computer network.

Applied Networking (8.0.1.1)

This chapter focuses on applied networking. You learn how to install and configure network interface cards (NICs), connect devices to a wireless router, and configure a wireless router for network connectivity. You also learn how to configure domain memberships in Windows and share files through network shares and drive mapping. A large part of your networking skills includes the ability to decide which *Internet Service Provider (ISP)* to use for home or small office networks.

Networks and the Internet provide many important services. You learn about data centers and the benefits of cloud computing. You also explore some of the more important network applications, including web, email, file sharing, proxy, and security services. Finally, you learn how to apply a systemic method for troubleshooting.

Computer to Network Connection (8.1)

All it takes to connect a computer to a network is two computers, two network interface cards (NIC), and a cable. This is a peer-to-peer network, however, not the usual network installation. Rather than connecting just two computers directly, it is more common to see a central networking device such as a switch connected to the NIC in each computer so multiple computers can connect to each other.

Networking Cards (8.1.1)

Before starting, you should decide what type of network to set up and find out what kind of hardware or connections you need. A starting point for deciding about the hardware is the NIC. The NIC controls the wired or wireless connections so computers can communicate with each other and other devices on a network.

Network Installation Completion List (8.1.1.1)

Computer technicians must be able to support the networking needs of their customers. Therefore, you must be familiar with:

- *Network components*—Includes wired and wireless network interface cards (NIC) and network devices such as switches, wireless access points (APs), routers, multipurpose devices, and more.
- *Network design*—Involves knowing how networks are interconnected to support the needs of a business. For instance, the needs of a small business will differ greatly from the needs of a large business.

Consider a small business with 10 employees. The business has contracted you to connect their users. As shown in Figure 8-1, a small multipurpose device could be used for such a small number of users. A *multipurpose device* provides router, switch, firewall, and access point capabilities. A multipurpose device is typically called a wireless router.

If the business was much larger, then a wireless router would not be suitable. The organization would require dedicated switches, access points (AP), firewall appliances, and routers.

Regardless of network design, you must know how to install network cards, connect wired and wireless devices, and configure basic network equipment.

Note

This chapter focuses on connecting and configuring a home or small office wireless router. The same functionality and similar graphical user interface (GUI) elements exist in all wireless routers. You can purchase a variety of low-cost wireless routers online and from consumer electronic stores. There are a wide variety of manufacturers including Asus, Cisco, D-Link, Linksys, Netgear, and Trendnet.

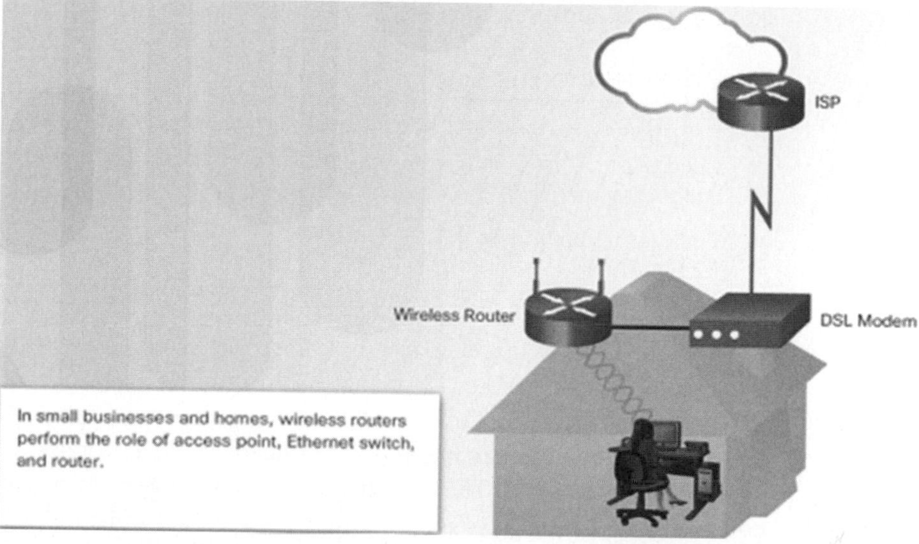
ISP
Wireless Router
DSL Modem
In small businesses and homes, wireless routers perform the role of access point, Ethernet switch, and router.

Figure 8-1 Typical Home Network

Selecting a NIC (8.1.1.2)

A NIC is required to connect to the network. As shown in Figure 8-2, there are different types of NICs. Ethernet NICs are used to connect to Ethernet networks and wireless NICs are used to connect to 802.11 wireless networks. Most NICs in desktop computers are integrated into the motherboard or connected to an expansion slot. NICs are also available in a USB form-factor.

Figure 8-2 Types of NICs

Table 8-1 lists questions to consider when purchasing a new NIC.

Table 8-1 New NIC Questions

Type of NIC:	Connection type:	Advanced NIC Features:	Cost?
■ Wired (Fast or Gigabit Ethernet)? ■ Wireless 802.11n / 802.11ac?	■ Expansion slot (PCI / PCIe)? ■ USB?	■ Wake on LAN (WoL)? ■ Quality of service (QoS)?	

You must be able to upgrade, install, and configure components when a customer asks for increased speed or new functionality to be added to a network. If your customer is adding additional computers or wireless functionality, you should be able to recommend equipment based on their needs, such as wireless access points and wireless network cards. The equipment that you suggest must work with the existing equipment and cabling, or the existing infrastructure must be upgraded. In rare cases, you might need to update the driver.

Installing and Updating a NIC (8.1.1.3)

To install a NIC in a desktop computer, you must remove the case cover. Then remove the cover of the available slot. After the NIC is securely installed, replace the case cover.

A wireless NIC has an antenna connected to the back of the card or attached with a cable so that it can be positioned for the best signal reception. You must connect and position the antenna.

Sometimes a manufacturer publishes new driver software for a NIC. A new driver might enhance the functionality of the NIC, or it might be needed for operating system compatibility. The latest drivers for all supported operating systems are available for downloading from the manufacturer's website.

When installing a new driver, disable virus protection software to ensure that the driver installs correctly. Some virus scanners detect a driver update as a possible virus attack. Install only one driver at a time; otherwise, some updating processes might conflict. A best practice is to close all applications that are running so that they are not using any files associated with the driver update.

You can also manually update a NIC driver.

In Windows 8 and 8.1, use the following path:

Control Panel > > Device Manager

In Windows 7 and Windows Vista, use the following path:

Start > Control Panel > Device Manager

In Windows 7, to view the network adapters that are installed click the arrow next to the category. To view and change the properties of the adapter, double-click the adapter. In the Adapter Properties window, select the Driver tab.

Note

Sometimes the driver installation process prompts you to reboot the computer.

If a new NIC driver does not perform as expected after it has been installed, you can uninstall the driver or roll back to the previous driver. Double-click the adapter in the **Device Manager**. In the Adapter Properties window, select the **Driver** tab and click **Roll Back Driver.** If no driver was installed before the update, this option is not available. In that case, you must find a driver for the device and install it manually if the operating system could not find a suitable driver for the NIC.

Configuring a NIC (8.1.1.4)

After the NIC driver is installed, the IP address settings must be configured. A computer can be assigned its IP configuration in one of two ways:

- **Manually**—The host is statically assigned a specific IP configuration.
- **Dynamically**—The host requests its IP address configuration from a DHCP server.

To manually configure IP settings in Windows 8 and 8.1, use the following path:

Control Panel > Network and Sharing Center > Change adapter settings > right-click **Ethernet > left click on Properties.** This opens the Ethernet Properties window.

In Windows 7 and Vista, use the following path:

Start > Control Panel > Network and Sharing Center > Change adapter setting > right-click **Local Area Connection >left-click on Properties.** This opens the Local Area Connection Properties window.

To configure IPv4 settings click **Internet Protocol Version 4 (TCP/IPv4) > Properties.** This opens the Internet Protocol Version 4 (TCP/IPv4) Properties window. The default setting is to obtain the IP settings automatically using DHCP. To configure the setting, manually click **Use the following IP address.** Next enter the appropriate IPv4 address, subnet mask, and default gateway and click **OK > OK.**

To configure IPv6 settings, click **Internet Protocol Version 6 (TCP/IPv6) > Properties.** This opens the Internet Protocol Version 6 (TCP/IPv6) Properties window. Click **Use the following IPv6 address.** Next, enter the appropriate IPv6 address, prefix length, and default gateway and click **OK > OK.**

Note

Most computers today come with an onboard NIC. If you are installing a new NIC, it is considered a best practice to disable the onboard NIC in BIOS settings.

Advanced NIC Settings (8.1.1.5)

Some NICs provide advanced features. In most network environments, the only NIC setting that you must configure is the IP address information. You can leave the advanced NIC settings at their default values. However, when a computer connects to a network that does not support some or all of the default settings, you must make the necessary changes to the advanced settings. These changes may be required so that the computer can connect to the network, enable features required by the network, or achieve a better network connection.

Note

Improperly setting the advanced features can lead to connection failure or performance degradation.

Advanced features are located in the **Advanced** tab in the NIC configuration window. The **Advanced** tab contains all the parameters that the NIC manufacturer has available.

Note

The Advanced features available and tab layout of features depend on the OS and the specific NIC adapter and driver installed.

Some advanced tab features include:

- **Speed and Duplex**—These settings must match with the device to which the NIC is connected. By default, the settings are automatically negotiated. A speed or duplex mismatch can slow down data transfer rates. If this occurs, then you may have to change either the duplex, speed, or both. Figure 8-3 shows speed and duplex settings.

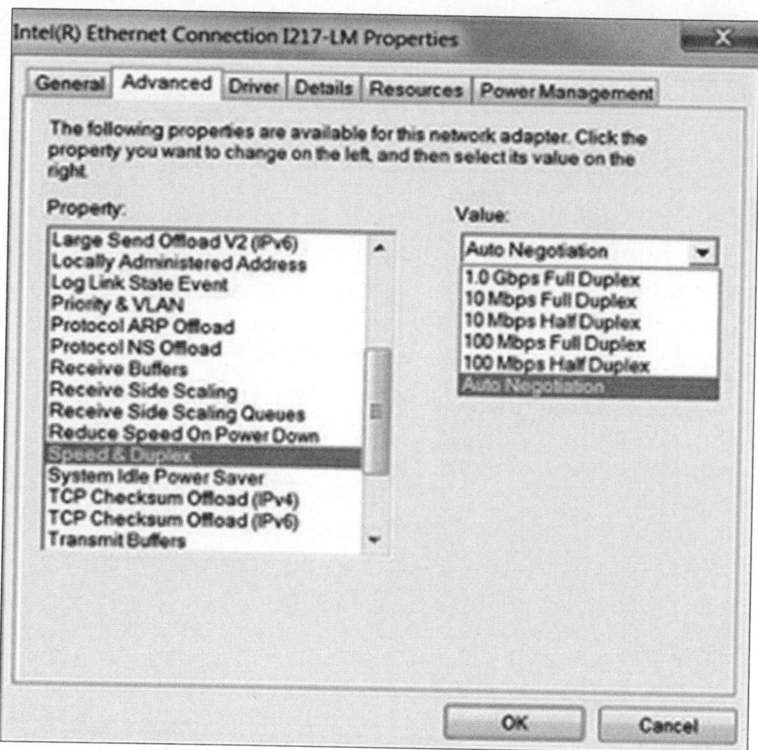

Figure 8-3 Speed and Duplex Settings

- *Wake on LAN*—WoL settings are used to wake up a networked computer from a very low power mode state. Very low power mode means that the computer is turned off but is still connected to a power source. To support WoL, the computer must have an ATX-compatible power supply and a WoL-compatible NIC. A wake-up message, called a *magic packet*, is sent to the NIC of the computer. The magic packet contains the MAC address of the NIC connected to the computer. When the NIC receives the magic packet, the computer wakes up. You configure WoL in either the motherboard BIOS or the NIC driver firmware. Figure 8-4 shows the configuration in the driver firmware.

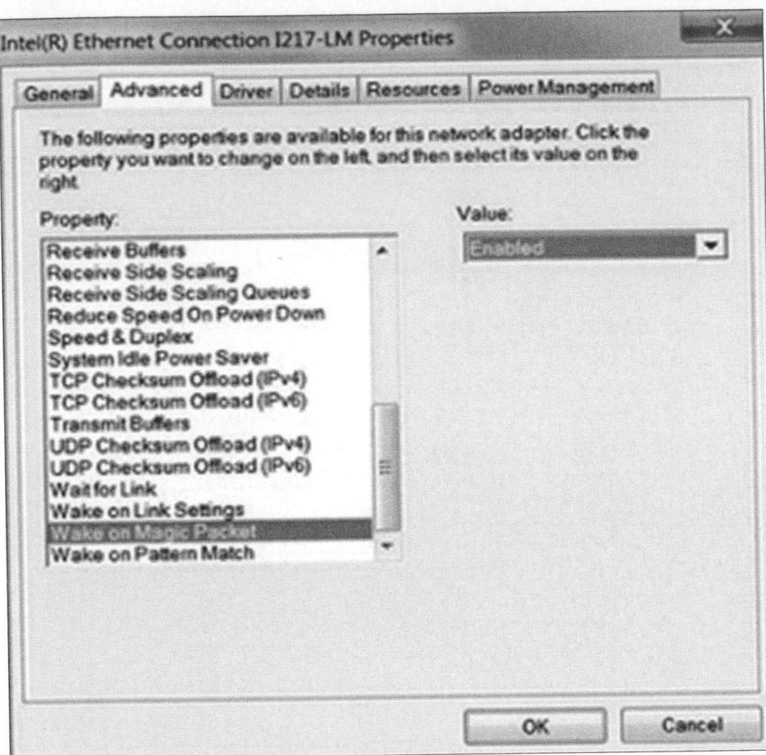

Figure 8-4 Wake on LAN Settings

- *Quality of service—QoS, also called 802.1q QoS*, is a variety of techniques that control the flow of network traffic, improve transmission speeds, and improve real-time communications traffic. Both the networked computer and the network device must have QoS enabled for the service to function. When QoS is installed and enabled on a computer, Windows can limit available bandwidth to accommodate high-priority traffic. When QoS is disabled, all traffic is treated equally. QoS is enabled by default, as shown in Figure 8-5.

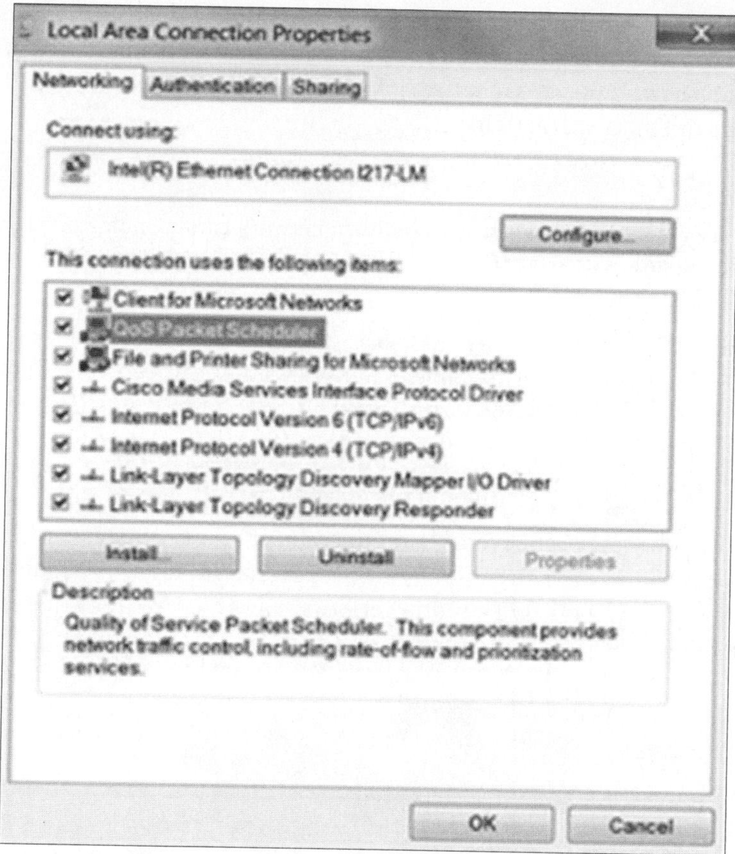

Figure 8-5 QoS Enabled by Default

Wireless and Wired Router Configurations (8.1.2)

You can use a combination of both wired and wireless connections to setup a network. That is a more common configuration in a home network environment. Home routers are actually a combination of three networking components: a router, wireless AP, and a switch. In an enterprise environment, the three pieces of hardware are kept separate, but consumer routers are almost always a combination.

Connecting the NIC (8.1.2.1)

To connect to a network, attach a straight-through Ethernet cable to the NIC port. In a home or small office network, the other end of the cable would probably be connected to an Ethernet port on a wireless router. In a business network, the computer would most likely connect to a wall jack which in turn connects to a network switch.

NICs typically have one or more green or amber LED, or *link lights*. These lights are used to indicate if there is a link connection and if there is activity. Green LEDs are often used to indicate an active link connection whereas amber LEDs are often used to indicate network activity.

Note

The meaning of LED lights varies between network card manufacturers. Refer to the motherboard or network card documentation for more information.

If the LEDs are not lit, then this indicates a problem. No activity can indicate a faulty NIC configuration, faulty cable, a faulty switch port, or even a faulty NIC. You might have to replace one or more of these devices to correct the problem.

Connecting the Router to the Internet (8.1.2.2)

A wireless router has several ports to connect wired devices. For example, the wireless router in Figure 8-6 has a USB port, an *Internet port*, and four Local Area Network (LAN) ports. The **Internet** port is an Ethernet port that is used to connect the router to a service provider device such as a broadband DSL or cable modem.

Figure 8-6 Wireless Home Router

The steps to connect a wireless router to a broadband modem port are as follows:

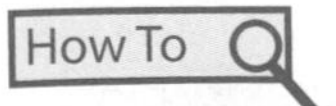

Step 1. On the router, connect a straight-through Ethernet cable to the port labeled **Internet**. This port might also be labeled **WAN**. The switching logic of the device forwards all the packets through this port when there is communication to and from the Internet and other connected computers.

Step 2. On the service provider broadband modem, connect the other end of the cable to the appropriate port. Typical labels for this port are **Ethernet**, **Internet**, or **WAN**.

Step 3. Turn on the broadband modem and plug in the power cord to the router. After the modem establishes a connection to the ISP, it will begin communicating with the router. The router Internet LEDs will light up, indicating communication. The modem enables the router to receive the network information necessary to gain access to the Internet from the ISP. This information includes public IP addresses, subnet mask, and DNS server addresses.

The topology for connecting the devices is shown in Figure 8-7.

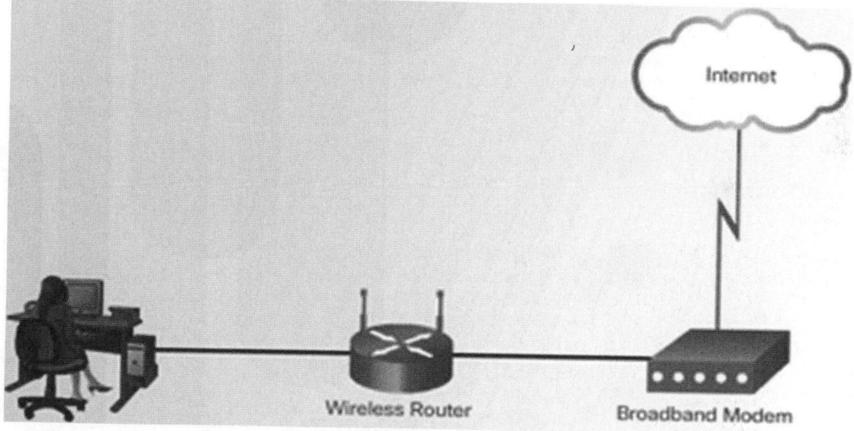

Figure 8-7 Router Connection to Internet Topology

Setting the Network Location (8.1.2.3)

The first time a computer with Windows connects to a network, a *network location profile* must be selected. Each network location profile has different default settings. Depending on the profile selected, file and printer sharing or *network discovery* can be turned off or on, and different firewall settings can be applied.

Windows has three network profiles shown in Figure 8-8:

- *Home Network*—Choose this network location for home networks or when you trust the people and devices on the network. Network discovery is turned on, which allows you to see other computers and devices on the network and other network users to see your computer.

- *Work Network*—Choose this network location for a small office or other workplace network. Network discovery is turned on. A homegroup cannot be created or joined.
- *Public Network*—Choose this network location for airports, coffee shops, and other public places. Network discovery is turned off. This network location provides the most protection. Also choose this network location if you connect directly to the Internet without using a router, or if you have a mobile broadband connection. HomeGroup is not available.

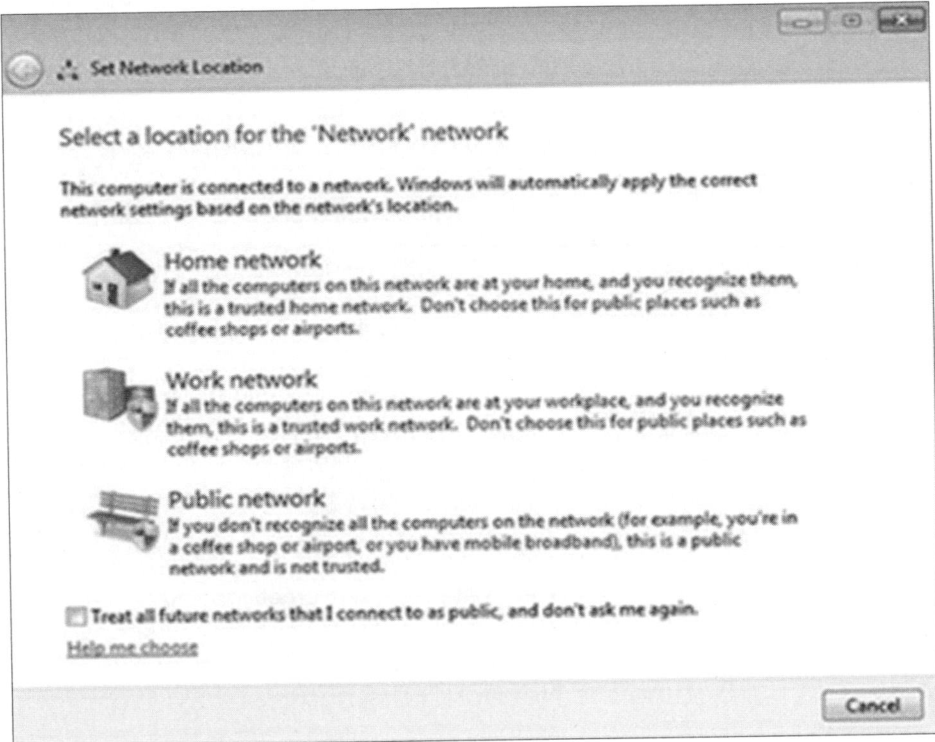

Figure 8-8 Set Network Location Window

Computers that belong to and share resources on either a Public, Work, or Home network must be members of the same workgroup. Computers on a Home network can also belong to a homegroup. A homegroup provides a simple method for file and printer sharing. Windows Vista does not support the homegroup feature.

There is a fourth network location profile called **Domain Network** and is typically used for enterprise workplaces. This profile is controlled by the network administrator and cannot be selected or changed by users connected to the enterprise.

Note

If there is only one computer on a network and file or printer sharing is not needed, the most secure choice is Public.

You can change the default settings for all network location profiles, as shown in Figure 8-9. Changes to the default profile are applied to every network that uses the same network location profile.

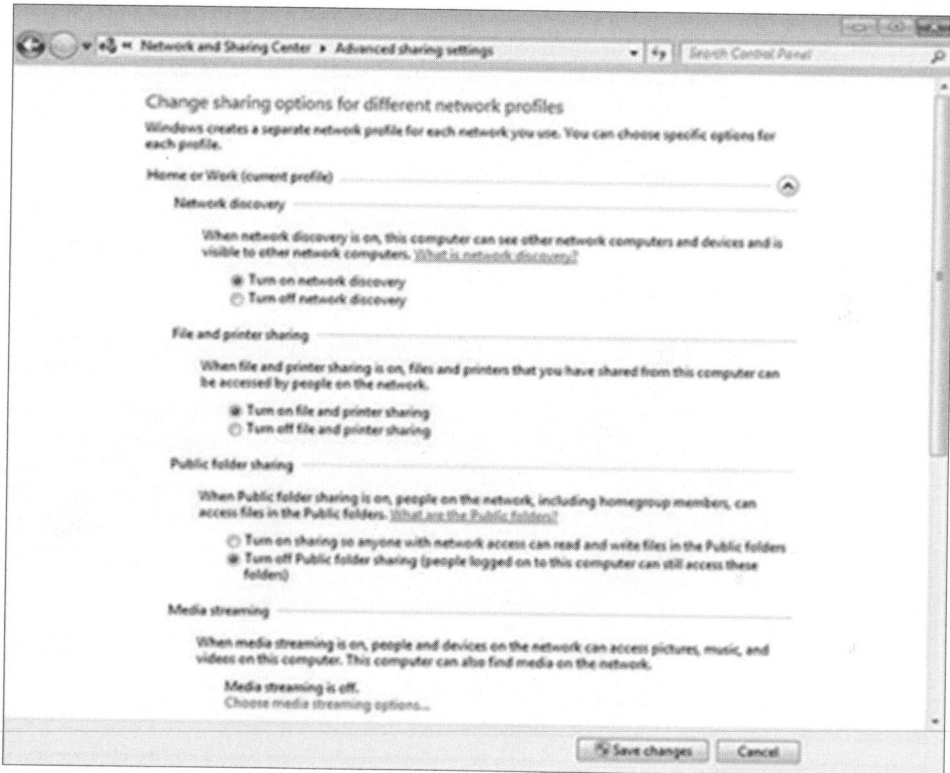

Figure 8-9 Default Sharing Options

If the Set Network Location window does not display when connecting a computer to the network for the first time, you might need to release and renew the IP address for the computer. After opening the command prompt on the computer, type **ipconfig /release** and then type **ipconfig /renew** to receive an IP address from the router.

Logging in to the Router (8.1.2.4)

Most home and small office wireless routers are ready for service out of the box. They do not require any additional configuration. However, wireless router default IP addresses, usernames, and passwords can easily be found on the Internet.

Just enter the search phrase “default wireless router ip address” or “default wireless router passwords” to see a listing of many websites that provide this information. Therefore, your first priority should be to change these defaults for security reasons.

To gain access to the wireless router’s configuration GUI, open a web browser. In the Address field, enter the default private IP address for your wireless router. The default IP address can be found in the documentation that came with the wireless router or you can search the Internet. The IP address 192.168.0.1 is a common default for some manufacturers. A security window prompts for authorization to access the router GUI. The word **admin** is commonly used as the default username and password. Again, check your wireless router’s documentation or search the Internet.

Basic Network Setup (8.1.2.5)

After logging in, a setup window opens, as shown in Figure 8-10. The setup screen will have tabs or menus to help you navigate to various router configuration tasks. It is often necessary to save the settings changed in one window before proceeding to another window.

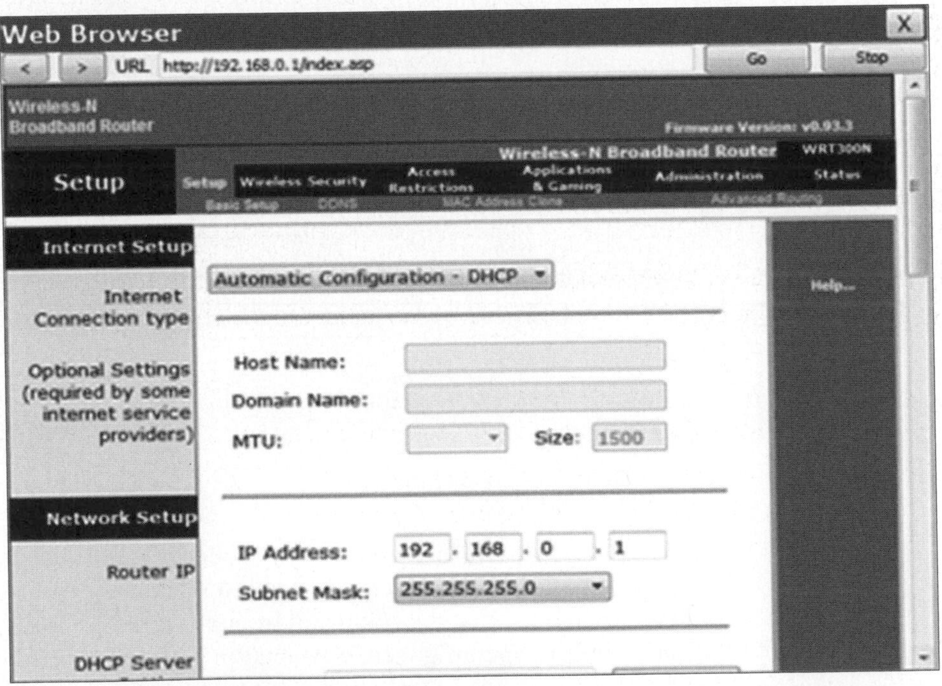

Figure 8-10 Basic Wireless Router Setup

At this point, it is a best practice to make changes to the default settings.

- **Network Device Access Permissions**—Change the default username and password. On some devices, you can only reset the password. After you change the password, the wireless router will request authorization again.
- **Router IP Address**—Change the default router IP address. It is a best practice to use private IP addressing inside your network such as the IP address 10.10.10.1. But it could be any private IP address you choose. When you click save, you will temporarily lose access to the wireless router. To regain access, renew your IP settings, using the **ipconfig /renew** command in the command prompt. Then enter the new router IP address in the web browser and authenticate with the new password.

Although some default settings should be changed, others are best left as is. Most home or small office networks share a single Internet connection provided by the ISP. Routers in this type of network receive public addresses from the ISP, which allows the router to send and receive packets to and from the Internet. The router provides private addresses to local network hosts. Because private addresses cannot be used on the Internet, a process is used for translating private addresses into unique public addresses. This allows local hosts to communicate over the Internet.

Network Address Translation (NAT) is the process used to convert private addresses to Internet-routable addresses. With NAT, a private (local) source IP address is translated to a public (global) address. The process is reversed for incoming packets. The router is able to translate many internal IP addresses into public addresses, by using NAT.

Only packets destined for other networks need to be translated. These packets must pass through the gateway, where the router replaces the private IP addresses of the source hosts with the public IP addresses of the router.

Although each host on the internal network has a unique private IP address, the hosts share Internet routable addresses that have been assigned to the router by the ISP.

Basic Wireless Settings (8.1.2.6)

After establishing the connection to a router, it is good practice to configure some basic settings to help secure the wireless network:

- **Network Mode**—Some wireless routers allow you to select which 802.11 standard to implement. Figure 8-11 shows that "Wireless-N Only" has been selected. This means that all wireless devices connecting the wireless router must have 802.11n NICs installed. Table 8-2 describes some of the network modes available in Packet Tracer, the Networking Academy network simulation tool available for download from the Cisco Networking Academy website.

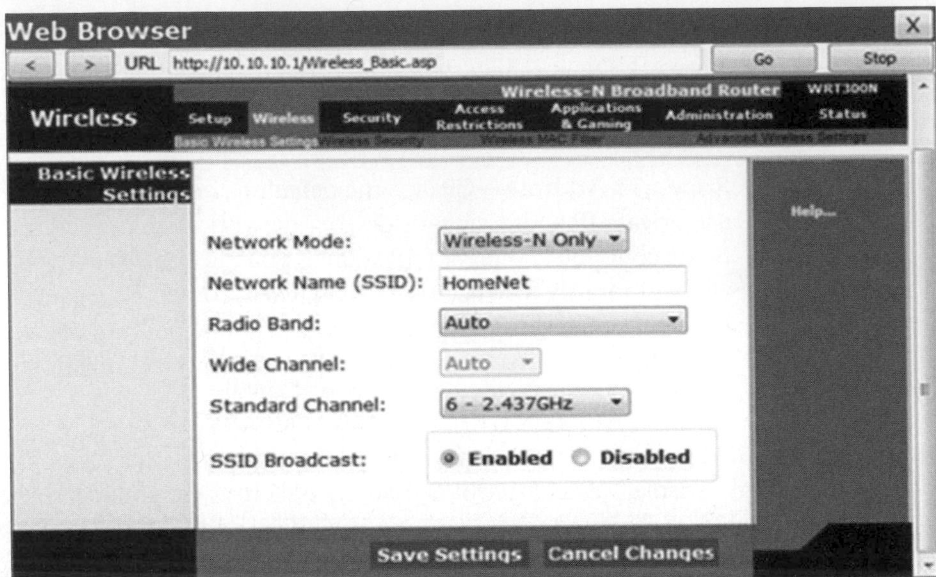

Figure 8-11 Network Mode Settings

Table 8-2 Typical Network Modes Available in Packet Tracer

Network Modes	Description
Mixed	■ Default Mode ■ Select if you have 802.11n (2.4GHz), 802.11g, 802.11b devices
Wireless—B/G Only	Select if you have 802.11g and 802.11b (2.4GHz) devices
Wireless—B Only	Select if you have only 802.11b devices
Wireless—G Only	Select if you have only 802.11g devices
Wireless—N	Select if you have only 802.11n devices
Disabled	Select to disable the wireless radio

- **Network Name (SSID)**—Assign a name or *service set identifier (SSID)* to the wireless network. The wireless router announces its presence by sending broadcasts advertising its SSID. This allows wireless hosts to automatically discover the name of the wireless network. If the SSID broadcast is disabled, you must manually enter the SSID on wireless devices.

- *Channel*—Wireless devices communicate over specific frequency ranges. Interference can be caused by other nearby wireless routers, or home electronic devices, such as cordless phones and baby monitors, using the same frequency range. These devices can slow down the wireless performance and potentially break network connections. Setting the channel number is a way to avoid wireless interference. For example, the 802.11b and 802.11g standards commonly use channels 1, 6, and 11 to avoid interference.

Wireless Security—Most wireless routers support several different security modes. Currently, the strongest security mode is WPA2 with AES encryption, as shown in Figure 8-12. Table 8-3 describes some of the security modes that are available.

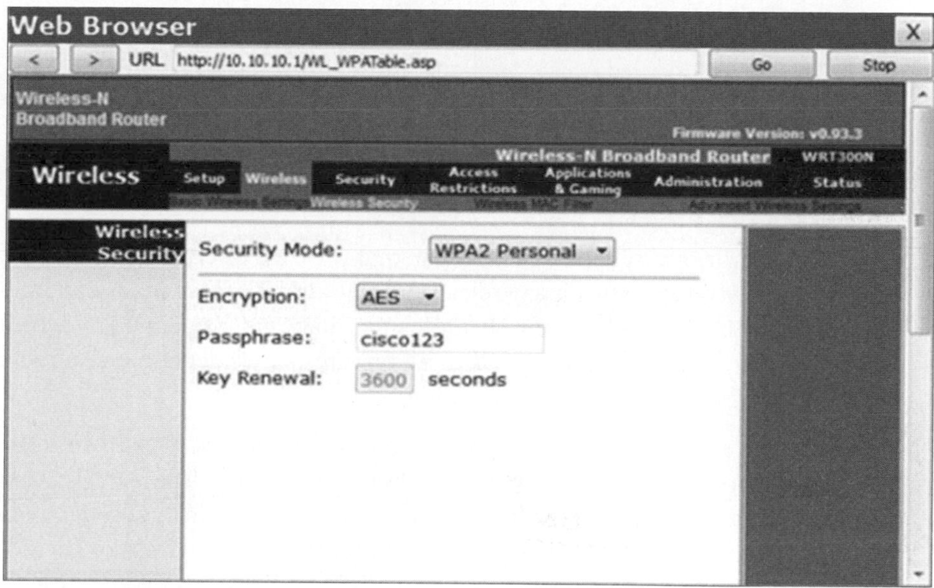

Figure 8-12 Security Mode Settings

Table 8-3 Typical Wireless Security Modes

Security Modes	Description
Wired Equivalent Privacy (WEP)	Encrypts the broadcast data between the wireless access point and the client using a 64-bit or 128-bit encryption key.
Temporal Key Integrity Protocol (TKIP)	■ This WEP patch automatically negotiates a new key every few minutes. ■ TKIP helps to prevent attackers from gaining enough data to break the encryption key.

(Continued)

Table 8-3 *Continued*

Security Modes	Description
Advanced Encryption Standard (AES)	■ A more secure encryption system than TKIP. ■ AES also requires more computing power to run the stronger encryption.
WiFi Protected Access (WPA)	■ An improved version WEP created as a temporary solution until 802.11i became ratified. ■ Now that 802.11i has been ratified, WPA2 has been released. It covers the entire 802.11i standard. ■ WPA uses much stronger encryption than WEP encryption.
WiFi Protected Access 2 (WPA2)	■ An improved version of WPA that supports robust encryption, which provides government-grade security. ■ WPA2 can be enabled with password authentication (personal) or server authentication (enterprise).

Additional security, such as parental controls or content filtering, are services that may be available in a wireless router. Internet access times can be limited to certain hours or days, specific IP addresses can be blocked, and key words can be blocked. The location and depth of these features varies depending on the manufacturer and model of the router.

Like Ethernet, wireless devices need an IP address. This IP address can be assigned through DHCP or they can be assigned statically. The wireless router can be configured to offer addresses through DHCP, or each device can be assigned a unique address. Often, you must enter the MAC address of the device to assign an IP address to a host manually.

Testing Connectivity with the Windows GUI (8.1.2.7)

When all devices are connected and all link lights are functioning, test the network for connectivity. The easiest way to test for an Internet connection is to open a web browser and see if the Internet is available. To troubleshoot a wireless connection, you can use the Windows GUI or CLI.

To verify a wireless connection in Windows Vista, use the following path:

Start > Control Panel > Network and Internet > Network and Sharing Center > Manage Network Connections.

To verify a wired or wireless connection in Windows 7, 8 or 8.1, use the following path:

Start > Control Panel > Network and Sharing Center > Change adapter settings.

In Windows 7 and Vista, wired network connections are normally called *Local Area Connection*. In Windows 8 and 8.1, wired network connections are called *Ethernet*.

Double-click the network connection icon to display the status screen. The status screen displays whether the computer is connected to the Internet, along with the duration of the connection. It also shows the number of sent and received bytes.

In all Windows versions, click the **Details** button on the Local Area Connection Status page to view IP addressing information, subnet mask, default gateway, MAC address, and other information. If the connection is not functioning correctly, close the Details page and click **Diagnose** to reset the connection information and attempt to establish a new connection. The Details and Diagnose button are shown in Figure 8-13.

Figure 8-13 Details and Diagnose Buttons on Local Area Connection Status

Testing Connectivity with the Windows CLI (8.1.2.8)

You can use several CLI commands to test network connectivity. The CLI commands can be executed from the command prompt window.

To open the Command Prompt window in Windows 8.x, bring up the Start Screen, type **command**, and select **Command Prompt**.

To open the Command Prompt window in Windows 7 and Windows Vista, select **Start** and type **command.**

As a technician, it is essential that you become familiar with the following commands:

- **ipconfig**—The command displays basic configuration information of all network adapters. Table 8-4 displays available command options. To use a command option, enter the ipconfig /option (e.g., ipconfig /all).

Table 8-4 ipconfig Command Options

ipconfig Command Options	Purpose
/all	Displays full configuration information of all networks adapters
/release	Releases the IP address of a network adapter
/renew	Renews the IP address of a network adapter
/flushdns	Empties the cache that stores DNS information
/registerdns	Refreshes the DHCP lease and re-registers the adapter with DNS
/diplaydns	Show DNS information in the cache

- **ping**—The command tests basic connectivity between devices. When troubleshooting a connectivity problem, ping your computer, the default gateway, and an Internet IP address. You can also test the Internet connection and DNS when you ping a popular website. At the command prompt, enter **ping** ***destination_name*** (e.g., **ping www.cisco.com**). To perform other specific tasks, you can add options to the ping command.
- *net*—The command is used to manage network computers, servers, and resources like drives and printers. Net commands use the NetBIOS protocol in Windows. These commands start, stop, and configure networking services.
- *netdom*—The command is used to manage computer accounts, join computers to a domain, and perform other domain-specific tasks.
- *nbtstat*—The command is used to show NetBIOS over TCP/IP statistics, current connections, and session running on local and remote computers.
- *tracert*—The command traces the route that packets take from your computer to a destination host. At the command prompt, enter tracert followed by a space

and then hostname or IP address of the destination computer. The first listing in the results is your default gateway. Each listing after that is the router that packets are traveling through to reach the destination. Tracert shows you where packets are stopping, indicating where the problem is occurring. If listings show problems after the default gateway, it may mean that the problems are with the ISP, the Internet, or the destination server.

- *nslookup*—The command tests and troubleshoots DNS servers. It queries the DNS server to discover IP addresses or host names. At the command prompt, enter nslookup followed by a space and then hostname or IP address of the destination computer. Nslookup returns the IP address for the host name entered. A reverse nslookup command, nslookup IP_address returns the corresponding host name for the IP address entered.

Note

Each of these commands have many command options. Remember to use the help option (/?) to display command options.

Video

Video—Network CLI Commands (8.1.2.9)

This video shows how to use many CLI commands at the Windows command prompt to configure and troubleshoot network connectivity. This video demonstrates using the command prompt to discover the MAC address, IP address and other IP settings by using ipconfig /all command. It also shows using the ping command to test connectivity using an IPv4 and IPv6 addresses or the hostname. It also shows using the tracert command in Windows to test connectivity. Tracert also shows the route of the packet. Both ping and tracert use the ICMP protocol.

Nslookup is demonstrated using the cisco.com domain name and resolving it to both an IPv4 and IPv6 IP address.

Please view the video in the Cisco Networking Academy IT Essentials 6.0 online course.

Lab—Connect to a Router for the First Time (8.1.2.10)

In this lab, you configure basic settings on a wireless router. Refer to the lab in *IT Essentials v6 Lab Manual*.

Packet Tracer
☐ Activity

Packet Tracer—Connect to a Wireless Router and Configure Basic Settings (8.1.2.11)

In this activity, you configure a wireless router to accept CompanyLaptop as a wireless client and route its IP packets. To access the activities found in this book, please refer to the instructions found in the introduction.

Lab—Configure Wireless Router in Windows (8.1.2.12)

In this lab, you configure and test the wireless settings on a wireless router. Refer to the lab in *IT Essentials v6 Lab Manual*.

Packet Tracer—Connect Wireless Computers to a Wireless Router (8.1.2.13)

In this activity, you configure wireless computers to connect to a network via a wireless router. You configure basic security on a wireless router by changing the SSID and password, and adding WPA2 encryption. To access the activities found in this book, please refer to the instructions found in the introduction.

Lab—Test the Wireless NIC in Windows (8.1.2.14)

In this lab, you check the status of your wireless connection, investigate the availability of wireless networks, and test connectivity. Refer to the lab in *IT Essentials v6 Lab Manual*.

Packet Tracer—Test a Wireless Connection (8.1.2.15)

In this activity, you will configure PC3 to connect to the network via a wireless router. You will also use various tools to test the functionality of the network. To access the activities found in this book, please refer to the instructions found in the introduction.

Network Sharing (8.1.3)

Domain and Workgroup (8.1.3.1)

Domain and workgroup are methods for organizing and managing computers on a network. They are defined as:

- *Domain*—A domain is a group of computers and electronic devices with a common set of rules and procedures administered as a unit. Computers in a domain can be located in different locations in the world. A specialized server called a domain controller manages all security-related aspects of users and network resources, centralizing security and administration. For example, within a domain, Lightweight Directory Access Protocol (LDAP) is a protocol used to allow computers to access data directories that are distributed throughout the network.

- *Workgroup*—A workgroup is a collection of workstations and servers on a LAN that are designed to communicate and exchange data with one another. Each individual workstation controls its user accounts, security information, and access to data and resources.

All computers on a network must be part of either a domain or a workgroup. When Windows is first installed on a computer, it is automatically assigned to a workgroup, as shown in Figure 8-14.

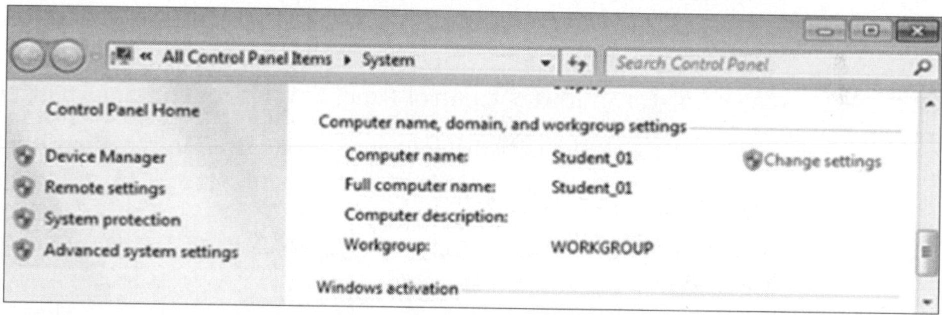

Figure 8-14 Domain or Workgroup Name

Connecting to a Workgroup or Domain (8.1.3.2)

Before computers can share resources, they must share the same domain name or workgroup name. Older operating systems have more restrictions for naming a workgroup. If a workgroup is made up of newer and older operating systems, use the workgroup name from the computer with the oldest operating system.

Note

Before changing a computer from a domain to a workgroup, you need the username and the password for an account in the local administrator group.

To change the workgroup name, use the following path for all Windows versions:

Control Panel > System > Change settings > Change

Click **Network ID** instead of **Change** to access a wizard that will guide you through the process for joining a domain or workgroup. After changing the domain name or workgroup name, you must restart the computer for the changes to take place.

Windows Homegroup (8.1.3.3)

All Windows computers that belong to the same workgroup can also belong to a *homegroup*. There can only be one homegroup per workgroup on a network. Computers can only be a member of one homegroup at a time. The homegroup option is not available in Windows Vista.

Only one user in the workgroup creates the homegroup. The other users can join the homegroup, provided they know the homegroup password. Homegroup availability depends on your network location profile:

- **Home Network**—You are allowed to create or join a homegroup.
- **Work Network**—You are not allowed to create or join a homegroup, but you can see and share resources with other computers.
- **Public Network**—No homegroup is available.

To change a computer to the Home Network profile in Windows 7, follow these steps:

Step 1. Click **Start > Control Panel > Network and Sharing Center.**

Step 2. Click the network location profile listed in the View your active networks section of the window, as shown in Figure 8-15.

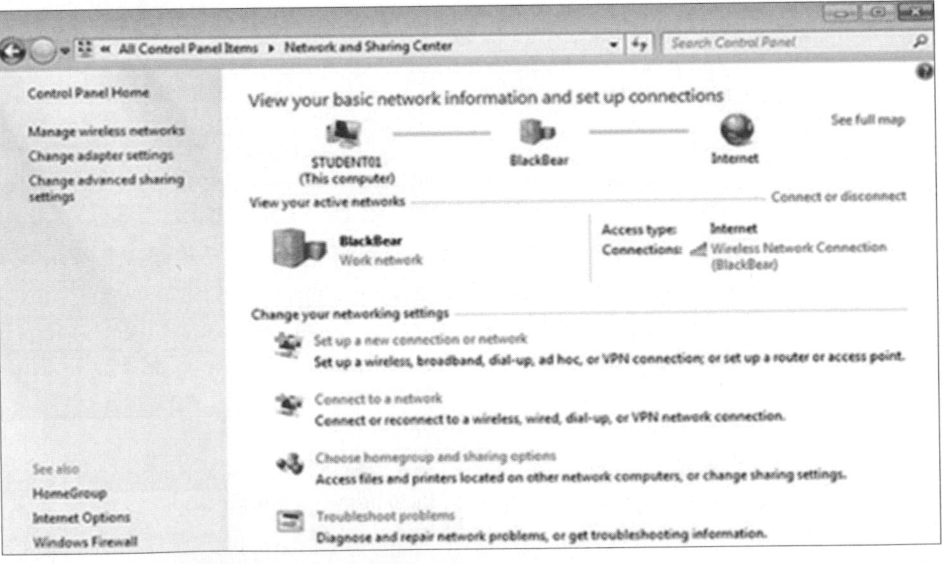

Figure 8-15 Join a Homegroup

Step 3. Click **Home network.**

Step 4. Select what you want to share (e.g., Pictures, Music, Videos, Documents, and Printers) then click **Next.**

Step 5. Join or create a homegroup.

To create a homegroup in Windows 7, follow these steps:

How To

Step 1. Click **Start > Control Panel > HomeGroup.**

Step 2. Click **Create a homegroup.**

Step 3. Select files to share then click **Next.**

Step 4. Record the homegroup password.

Step 5. Click **Finish.**

When a computer joins a homegroup, all user accounts on the computer, except the Guest account, become members of the homegroup. Being part of a homegroup makes it easy to share pictures, music, videos, documents, libraries, and printers with other people in the same homegroup. Users control access to their own resources. Users can also create or join a homegroup with a virtual machine in Windows Virtual PC.

To join a computer to a homegroup in Windows 7, follow these steps:

How To

Step 1. Click **Start > Control Panel > HomeGroup.**

Step 2. **Click Join** now.

Step 3. Select files to share then click **Next.**

Step 4. Type in the homegroup password, and then click **Next.**

Step 5. Click **Finish.**

To change the files shared on a computer, select **Start > Control Panel > HomeGroup.** After you make your changes, click **Save change.**

Note

If a computer belongs to a domain, you can join a homegroup and access files and resources on other homegroup computers. You are not allowed to create a new homegroup or share your own files and resources with a homegroup.

Sharing Resources in Windows Vista (8.1.3.4)

Windows Vista controls which resources are shared and how they are shared by turning specific sharing features on and off. Sharing and Discovery, located in the Network and Sharing Center, manages the settings for a home network. The following items can be controlled:

- Network discovery
- File sharing

- Public folder sharing
- Printer sharing
- Password protected sharing
- Media sharing

To access Sharing and Discovery, use the following path:

Start > Control Panel > Network and Internet > Network and Sharing Center

To enable sharing resources between computers connected to the same workgroup, Network Discovery and File Sharing must be turned on, as shown in Figure 8-16.

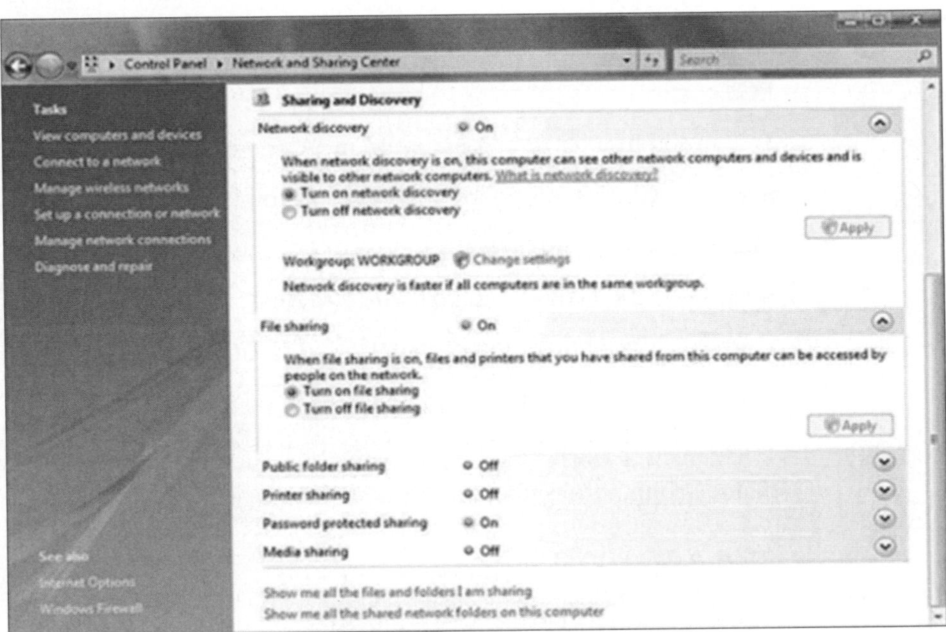

Figure 8-16 Sharing Resources in Windows Vista

Network Shares and Mapping Drives (8.1.3.5)

Network file sharing and *mapping network drives* is a secure and convenient way to provide easy access to network resources. This is especially true when different versions of Windows require access to network resources. Mapping a local drive is a useful way to access a single file, specific folders, or an entire drive between different operating systems over a network. Mapping a drive, which is done by assigning a letter (A to Z) to the resource on a remote drive, allows you to use the remote drive as if it was a local drive.

Network File Sharing

First determine which resources will be shared over the network and the type of permissions users will have to the resources. *Permissions* define the type of access a user has to a file or folder.

- **Read**—The user can view the file and subfolder names, navigate to subfolders, view data in files, and run program files.
- **Change**—In addition to Read permissions, the user can add files and subfolders, change the data in files, and delete subfolders and files.
- **Full Control**—In addition to Change and Read permissions, the user can change the permission of files and folders in an NTFS partition and take ownership of files and folders.

To share the folder, use the following path:

Right-click the folder **> Properties > Sharing > Advanced Sharing >** select **Share this folder > Permissions.** Identify who has access to the folder and which permissions. Figure 8-17 shows the permissions window of a shared folder.

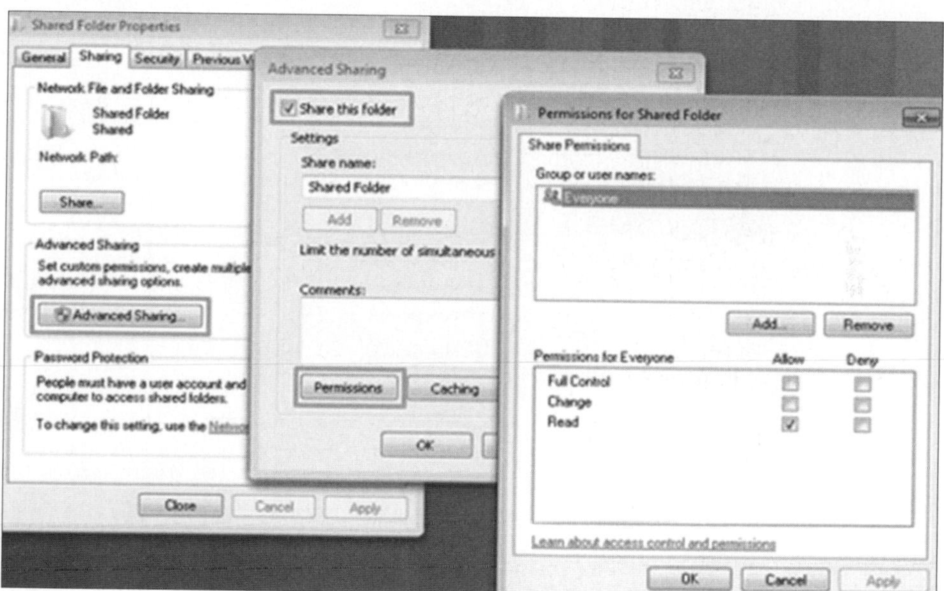

Figure 8-17 Setting Permissions for a Share Folder

Administrative Shares (8.1.3.6)

Administrative shares, also called *hidden shares*, are identified with a dollar sign ($) at the end of the share name. By default, Windows can enable the following hidden administrative shares:

- Root partitions or volumes
- The system root folder
- The FAX$ share
- The IPC$ share
- The PRINT$ share

To create your own administrative share, complete the following steps in all versions of Windows:

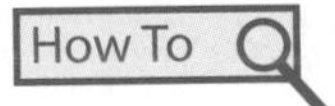

Step 1. Click Control Panel > Administrative Tools and double-click Computer Management, as shown in Figure 8-18.

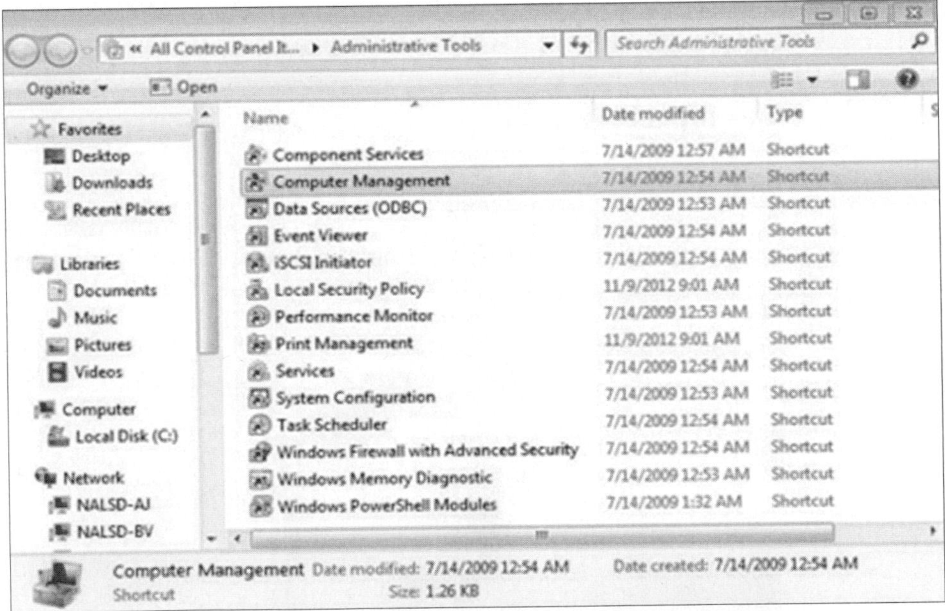

Figure 8-18 Creating Administrative Shares—Computer Management

Step 2. Expand Shared Folders, right-click Shares, and then click New Share... to open Create a Shared Folder Wizard. Click Next to get the screen shown in Figure 8-19.

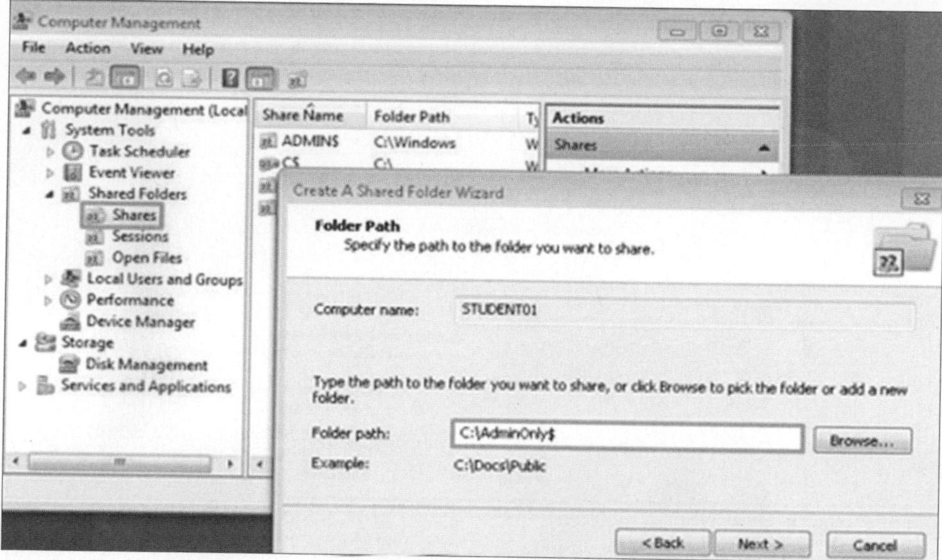

Figure 8-19 Creating Administrative Shares–Folder Path

Step 3. Type the path to the folder you want to use for the administrative share (for example, C:\AdminOnly$ in Figure 8-19). Be sure it includes a dollar sign ($) at the end of the name to identify this folder as an administrative share. Click Next. If the folder does not exist yet, Windows will ask if you want to create it.

Step 4. In the next screen, you can change the share name, add an optional description, and change the offline settings. Click Next.

Step 5. In the Share Folder Permissions window, as shown in Figure 8-20, select the Administrators have full access; other users have no access, and then click Finish.

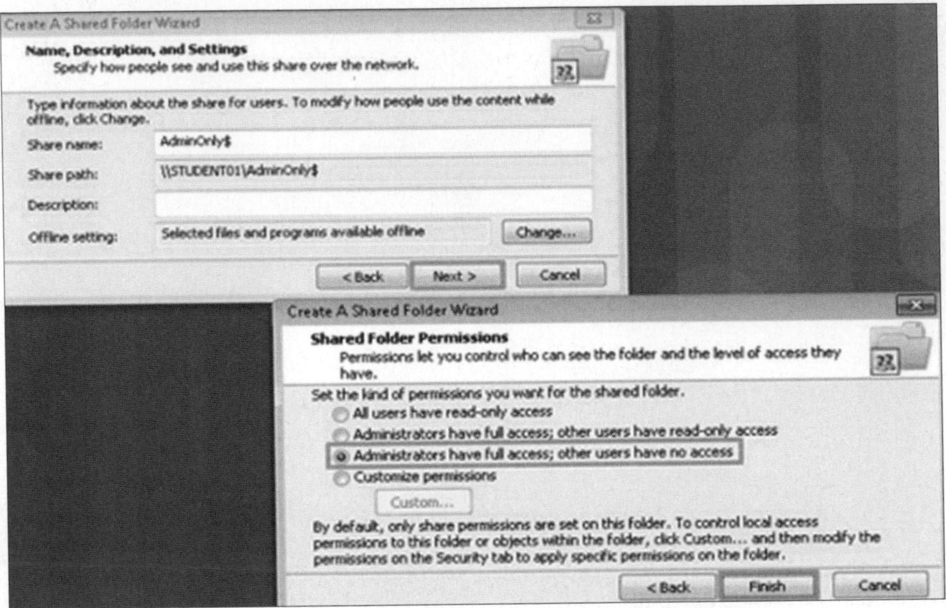

Figure 8-20 Creating Administrative Shares—Administrative Permissions

Network Drive Mapping (8.1.3.7)

To map a network drive to a shared folder in Windows 7 and Vista, use the following path:

Start > right-click **Computer > Map network drive.**

In Windows 8.0, follow these steps:

How To

Step 1. From the Start Screen type file explorer and click File Explorer to open it.

Step 2. Right-click Computer > Map network drive.

In Windows 8.1, follow these steps:

Step 1. From the Start Screen type file explorer and click File Explorer to open it.

Step 2. Right-click This PC > Map network drive.

Step 3. Locate the shared folder over the network and assign a drive letter.

Windows 7 is limited to a maximum of 20 simultaneous file-sharing connections. Windows Vista Business is limited to a maximum of 10 simultaneous file-sharing connections.

Video

Video—Share a Folder (8.1.3.8)

This video shows how to share a folder and a file over the network and allow users to connect to the share without requiring a username or password.

This video demonstrates using the Network and Sharing Center to examinc the network profile of Home and Work and how to turn on network discovery as well as file and print sharing in the profiles where you need it enabled.

It also explores the settings for shares with a password and without a password. Although it is recommended that a username and password be used for most shares, this video reviews an instance where it is useful to create a share without both.

After reviewing the advanced options in Network and Sharing Center the video walks through the steps of manually sharing a folder through the Properties window of the folder being shared. This means you will need to decide who you will share the folder with and set the necessary permissions.

Not only do you need to set the share permissions you will also learn how to set the Security permissions on the folder. These are the permissions allowed in the NTFS file and folder settings.

Please view the video in the Cisco Networking Academy IT Essentials 6.0 online course.

Lab—Share Resources in Windows (8.1.3.9)

In this lab, you create and share a folder, set permissions for the shares, create a homegroup and a workgroup to share resources, and map a network drive. Refer to the lab in *IT Essentials v6 Lab Manual*.

Remote Connections (8.1.4)

Remote access is the ability to access and control a computer from a location that is remote to your network. There are many reasons that you would want to access a computer remotely such as troubleshooting and repairing problems or sharing Internet connections or allowing teleworkers to access a corporate network from outside of the office. It can allow for more efficiency and flexibility. There are different types of remote access and implementation will depend on user and organization needs.

VPN (8.1.4.1)

When connecting to the local network and sharing files, the communication between computers is not sent beyond that network. Data remains secure because it is kept behind the router, off other networks, and off the Internet. To communicate and share resources over a network that is not secure, a *virtual private network (VPN)* is used.

A VPN is a private network that connects remote sites or users together over a public network, like the Internet. The most common type of VPN is used to access a corporate private network. The VPN uses dedicated secure connections, routed through the Internet, from the corporate private network to the remote user. When connected to the corporate private network, users become part of that network and have access to all services and resources as if they were physically connected to the corporate LAN.

Remote-access users must install the VPN client on their computers to form a secure connection with the corporate private network. The VPN client software encrypts data before sending it over the Internet to the VPN gateway at the corporate private network. VPN gateways establish, manage, and control VPN connections, also known as VPN tunnels.

To set up and configure a VPN connection, follow these steps in all Windows versions:

How To

Step 1. Select **Control Panel > Network and Sharing Center** in Windows.

Step 2. Select **Set up a new connection or network.**

Step 3. After the New Connection Wizard window opens, select **Connect to a workplace** and click **Next.**

Step 4. Select **Use my Internet connection (VPN)** and type the Internet address and the destination name.

Step 5. Select **Don't connect now; just set it up so I can connect later** and click **Next.** (Windows 7 only)

Step 6. Type the username, password, and optional domain. Then click **Create.**

Step 7. In the login window, enter the username and password and click **Connect.**

Remote Desktop and *Remote Assistance* (8.1.4.2)

Technicians can use Remote Desktop and Remote Assistance to repair and upgrade computers. Remote Desktop, as shown in Figure 8-21, allows technicians to view and control a computer from a remote location. Remote Assistance, shown in Figure 8-22, allows technicians to assist customers with problems from a remote location. Remote Assistance also allows the customer to view in real time on the screen what is being repaired or upgraded on the computer.

To access Remote Desktop in Windows 8, access the **Start Screen**, type **Remote Desktop Connection**, and click the **Remote Desktop Connection** icon.

To access Remote Desktop in Windows 7 or Vista, use the following path:

Start > All Programs > Accessories > Remote Desktop Connection

Figure 8-21 Windows Remote Desktop Client

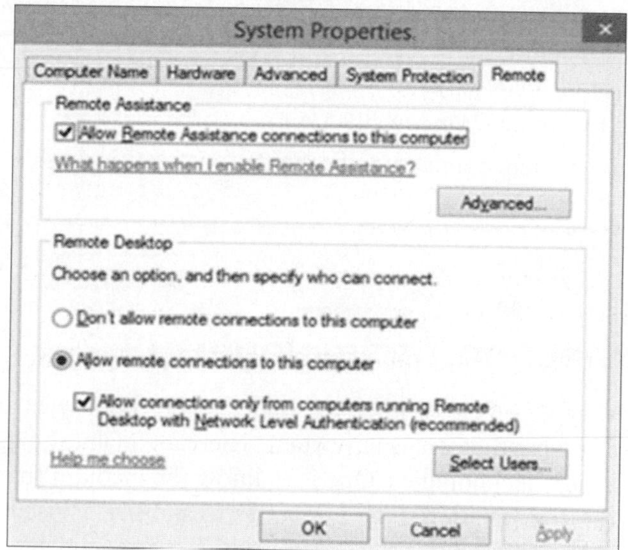

Figure 8-22 Windows Remote Assistance

Before Remote Assistance can be used in Windows, it must be enabled. To enable and access Remote Assistance follow these steps:

For Windows 8:

Step 1. Right-click **This PC** (Window 8.1) or **Computer** (Windows 8.0) and select **Properties.**

Step 2. Click **Remote Settings** in the System window and select the **Remote** tab.

Step 3. Select the **Allow Remote Assistance Connections to This Computer.**

Step 4. Click **OK.**

To access Remote Assistance in Windows 8, access the **Start Screen**, type **Invite someone to connect to your PC** and press **Enter**. Click **Invite someone you trust to help you** to allow the helper to share the control of your computer.

Note

You may need to change the Search focus to Settings.

To access Remote Assistance in Windows 7 or Vista, use the following path:

Start > All Programs > Maintenance > Windows Remote Assistance

Lab—Remote Assistance in Windows (8.1.4.3)

In this lab, you remotely connect to a computer, examine device drivers, and provide remote assistance. Refer to the lab in *IT Essentials v6 Lab Manual*.

Lab—Remote Desktop in Windows (8.1.4.4)

In this lab, you remotely connect to another Windows computer. Refer to the lab in *IT Essentials v6 Lab Manual*.

ISP Connection Technologies (8.2)

There are many types of ISP or Internet connection technologies and having an understanding of what they are is important. There are many things to consider understanding these technologies. One is to know the medium that is being used to carry a signal from one device on a network to another device on the Internet. Another aspect to understand is the signal itself. Transmission speeds are also important.

Broadband Technologies (8.2.1)

In this section you learn about various ISP connection technologies including broadband technologies which uses a single cable with multiple channels to carry large amounts of data at high speed.

Brief History of Connection Technologies (8.2.1.1)

In the 1990s, the Internet was typically used for data transfer. Transmission speeds were slow compared to the high-speed connections that are available today. The additional bandwidth allows for transmission of voice and video, as well as data. Today there are many ways to connect to the Internet. Phone, cable, satellite, and private telecommunications companies offer broadband Internet connections for businesses and home use.

Analog Telephone

Analog telephone, also called *plain old telephone service (POTS)*, transmits over standard voice telephone lines. This type of service uses an analog modem to place a telephone call to another modem at a remote site, such as an Internet service provider. The modem uses the telephone line to transmit and receive data. This method of connection is known as *dialup*.

Integrated Services Digital Network

ISDN uses multiple channels and can carry different types of services; therefore, it is considered a type of broadband. ISDN is a standard for sending voice, video, and data over normal telephone wires. ISDN technology uses the telephone wires as an analog telephone service.

Broadband

Broadband is a technology that is used to transmit and receive multiple signals using different frequencies over one cable. For example, the cable used to bring cable television to your home can carry computer network transmissions at the same time. Because the two transmission types use different frequencies, they do not interfere with each other.

Broadband uses a wide range of frequencies that can be further divided into channels. In networking, the term broadband describes communication methods that transmit two or more signals at the same time. Sending two or more signals simultaneously increases the rate of transmission. Some common broadband network connections include cable, DSL, ISDN, and satellite.

DSL and ADSL (8.2.1.2)

Digital Subscriber Line (DSL) is a broad term for a digital high-speed data connection that uses the same wiring as a regular telephone line. ADSL is the most common type of DSL connection.

Digital Subscriber Line

DSL is an always-on service, which means that there is no need to dial up each time you want to connect to the Internet. DSL uses the existing copper telephone lines to provide high-speed digital data communication between end users and telephone companies. Unlike ISDN, where the digital data communications replaces the analog voice communications, DSL shares the telephone wire with analog signals.

With DSL, the voice and data signals are carried on different frequencies on the copper telephone wires. A filter prevents DSL signals from interfering with phone signals. A DSL filter is connected between each telephone and phone jack.

The DSL modem does not require a filter. The DSL modem is not affected by the frequencies of the telephone. A DSL modem can connect directly to your computer. It can also be connected to a networking device to share the Internet connection with multiple computers.

Asymmetric Digital Subscriber Line

ADSL has different bandwidth capabilities in each direction. Downloading is the receiving of data from the server to the end user. *Uploading* is the sending of data from the end user to the server. ADSL has a fast download rate which is beneficial to users who are downloading large amounts of data. The upload rate of ADSL is slower than the download rate. ADSL does not perform well when hosting a web server or FTP server, both of which involve upload-intensive Internet activities.

Line of Sight Wireless Internet Service (8.2.1.3)

Line of sight wireless Internet is an always-on service that uses radio signals for transmitting Internet access. Radio signals are sent from a tower to the receiver that the customer connects to a computer or network device. A clear path between the transmission tower and customer is required. The tower may connect to other towers or directly to an Internet backbone connection. The distance the radio signal can travel and still be strong enough to provide a clear signal depends on the frequency of the signal. Lower frequency of 900 MHz can travel up to 40 miles (65 km), whereas a higher frequency of 5.7 GHz can only travel 2 miles (3 km). Extreme weather conditions, trees, and tall buildings can affect signal strength and performance.

WiMAX (8.2.1.4)

Worldwide Interoperability for Microwave Access (WiMAX) is an IP-based wireless 4G broadband technology that offers high-speed mobile Internet access for mobile devices. WiMAX is a standard called IEEE 802.16e. It supports a MAN-sized network and has download speeds up to 70 Mb/s and distances up to 30 miles (50 km). Security and QoS for WiMAX are equivalent to cellular networks.

WiMAX uses a low wavelength transmission, usually between 2 GHz to 11 GHz. These frequencies are not as easily disrupted by physical obstructions because they can better bend around obstacles than higher frequencies. *Multiple Input Multiple Output (MIMO) technology* is supported, which means additional antennas can be added to increase the potential throughput.

There are two methods of transmitting a WiMAX signal:

- **Fixed WiMAX**—A point-to-point or point-to-multipoint service with speeds up to 72 Mb/s and a range of 30 miles (50 km).
- **Mobile WiMAX**—A mobile service, like WiFi, but with higher speeds and a longer transmission range.

Other Broadband Technologies (8.2.1.5)

Broadband technology provides several different options for connecting people and devices for the purpose of communicating and sharing information. Each offers different features or is designed to support specific needs. It is important to have a clear understanding of the several broadband technologies and how they can best support a customer.

Cellular

Cellular technology enables the transfer of voice, video, and data. With a *cellular WAN* adapter installed, a user can access the Internet over the cellular network. There are different cellular WAN characteristics:

- **1G**—Analog voice only
- **2G**—Digital voice, conference calls, and caller ID; data speeds less than 9.6 Kb/s
- **2.5G**—Data speeds between 30 Kb/s and 90 Kb/s; supports web browsing, short audio and video clips, games, and application and ring tone downloads
- **3G**— Data speeds between 144 Kb/s and 2 Mb/s; supports full-motion video, streaming music, 3D gaming, and faster web browsing
- **3.5G**—Data speeds between 384 Kb/s and 14.4 Mb/s; supports high-quality streaming video, high-quality video conferencing, and VoIP
- **4G**—Data speeds between 5.8 Mb/s and 672 Mb/s when mobile, and up to 1 Gb/s when stationary; supports IP-based voice, gaming services, high-quality streamed multimedia, and IPv6

Cellular networks use one or more of the following technologies:

- *Global System for Mobile communications (GSM)*—Standard used by the worldwide cellular network

- *General Packet Radio Service (GPRS)*—Data service for users of GSM
- **Quad-band**—Allows a cellular phone to operate on all four GSM frequencies: 850 MHz, 900 MHz, 1800 MHz, and 1900 MHz
- **Short Message Service (SMS)**—Data service used to send and receive text messages
- **Multimedia Messaging Service (MMS)**—Data service used to send and receive text messages and can include multimedia content
- *Enhanced Data Rates for GSM Evolution (EDGE)*—Increased data rates and improved data reliability
- *Evolution-Data Optimized (EV-DO)*—Improved upload speeds and QoS
- **High Speed Downlink Packet Access (HSDPA)**—Enhanced 3G access speed

Cable

A *cable Internet connection* does not use telephone lines. Cable uses coaxial cable lines originally designed to carry cable television. A cable modem connects your computer to the cable company. You can plug your computer directly into the cable modem, or you can connect a router, switch, hub, or multipurpose network device so that multiple computers can share the connection to the Internet. Like DSL, cable offers high speeds and an always-on service, which means that even when the connection is not in use, the connection to the Internet is still available.

Satellite

Broadband *satellite* is an alternative for customers who cannot get cable or DSL connections. A satellite connection does not require a phone line or cable, but uses a satellite dish for two-way communication. The satellite dish transmits and receives signals to and from a satellite that relays these signals back to a service provider. Download speeds can reach up to 10Mb/s or more, whereas upload speed ranges about 1/10th of download speeds. It takes time for the signal from the satellite dish to relay to your ISP through the satellite orbiting the Earth. Due to this latency, it is difficult to use time-sensitive applications, such as video gaming, VoIP, and video conferencing.

Fiber Broadband

Fiber broadband provides faster connection speeds and bandwidth than cable modems, DSL, and ISDN. Fiber broadband can deliver a multitude of digital services, such as telephone, video, data, and video conferencing simultaneously.

Selecting an ISP for the Customer (8.2.1.6)

Several WAN solutions are available for connecting between sites or to the Internet. WAN connection services provide different speeds and levels of service. You should understand how users connect to the Internet and the advantages and disadvantages of different connection types. The ISP that you choose can have a noticeable effect on network service.

There are four main considerations for an Internet connection:

- Cost
- Speed
- Reliability
- Availability

Research the connection types that the ISPs offer before selecting an ISP. Check the services available in your area. Compare connection speeds, reliability, and cost before committing to a service agreement.

POTS

A *POTS* connection is extremely slow, but it is available wherever there is a landline telephone. There are two major disadvantages of using the phone line with an analog modem. The first is that the telephone line cannot be used for voice calls while the modem is in use. The second is the limited bandwidth provided by analog phone service. The maximum bandwidth using an analog modem is 56 Kb/s, but in reality, it is usually much lower than that. An analog modem is not a good solution for the demands of busy networks.

ISDN

ISDN is very reliable because it uses POTS lines. Although ISDN is not as popular as it once was, it is available in most places where the telephone company supports digital signaling to carry the data. Because it uses digital technology, ISDN offers faster connection times, faster speeds, and higher quality voice than traditional analog telephone service. It also allows multiple devices to share a single telephone line.

DSL

DSL allows multiple devices to share a single telephone line. DSL speeds are generally higher than ISDN. DSL allows the use of high-bandwidth applications or multiple users to share the same connection to the Internet. In most cases, the copper wires already in your home or business are capable of carrying the signals needed for DSL communication.

There are limitations to DSL technology:

- DSL service is not available everywhere, and it works better and faster the closer the installation is to the telephone provider's central office (CO).
- In some cases, installed telephone lines will not qualify to carry all DSL signals.
- The voice information and data carried by DSL must be separated at the customer site. A device called a filter prevents data signals from interfering with voice signals.

Cable

Most homes that have cable television have the option to install high-speed Internet service using that same cable. Many cable companies offer telephone service as well.

Satellite

People who live in rural areas often use satellite broadband because they need a faster connection than dialup, and no other broadband connection is available. The cost of installation and the monthly service fees are generally much higher than those of DSL and cable. Heavy storm conditions can degrade the quality of the connection slowing down or even disconnecting the connection.

Cellular

Many types of wireless Internet services are available. The same companies that offer cellular service may offer Internet service. PC Card/ExpressBus, USB, or PCI and PCIe cards are used to connect a computer to the Internet. Service providers may offer wireless Internet service using microwave technology in limited areas.

Packet Tracer
☐ Activity

Activity—ISP Connection Types (8.2.1.7)

Please refer to the Activity in the Cisco Networking Academy IT Essentials 6.0 online course.

Internet Technologies (8.3)

Internet technologies are important to home users, small businesses, and large enterprise because they allow wide spread sharing of resources and information across great distances and increasing speed. There are many different tools and technologies available on the internet. This section explains some of the important and evolving Internet technologies and services.

Data Centers and Cloud Computing (8.3.1)

Data centers and cloud computing are both used as data storage areas. The major difference between the two is that cloud stores are located off-premises and data centers are located on premises of an organization. Internal data are managed within the organization whereas typical cloud computing is done by third-party management. The characteristics of both are covered in more detail in the next topic areas.

Data Center (8.3.1.1)

As organizations evolve, they require increasing amounts of computing power and hard drive storage space. If left unaddressed, this will impact an organization's ability to provide vital services. The loss of vital services means lower customer satisfaction, lower revenue, and, in some situations, loss of property or life.

Large enterprises typically own a data center to manage the storage and data access needs of the organization. In these single tenant data centers, the enterprise is the only customer or tenant using the data center services. However, as the amount of data continues to expand, even large enterprises are expanding their data storage capacity by utilizing the services of third-party data centers.

Cloud Computing versus Data Center (8.3.1.2)

The terms data center and Cloud computing are often incorrectly used. These are the correct definitions of data center and Cloud computing:

- *Data center*—Typically a data storage and processing facility run by an in-house IT department or leased offsite.
- *Cloud computing*—Typically an off-premise service that offers on-demand access to a shared pool of configurable computing resources. These resources can be rapidly provisioned and released with minimal management effort.

Cloud service providers use data centers for their cloud services and Cloud-based resources. To ensure availability of data services and resources, providers often maintain space in several remote data centers. The National Institute of Standards and Technology (NIST), in their Special Publication 800-145, define a cloud model that consists of five characteristics, three service models, and four deployment models.

Characteristics of Cloud Computing (8.3.1.3)

As shown in the figure, the cloud model includes five characteristics:

- **On-demand self-service**—The network administrator can buy additional computing space in the cloud without requiring the interaction with another human.
- **Broad network access**—Access to the cloud is available using a wide variety of client devices, such as PCs, laptops, tablets, and smartphones.

- **Resource pooling**—the computing capacity of the Cloud provider is shared among all its customers and can be assigned and reassigned based on customer demand.
- **Rapid elasticity**—resource allocation to customers can quickly expand or contract with demand. To the customer, the resources and capabilities of the cloud service provider appear to be unlimited.
- **Measured service**—resource usage can be easily monitored, controlled, reported, and billed to provide full visibility to both the cloud service provide and customer.

SaaS, IaaS and PaaS (8.3.1.4)

The three main cloud services models are shown in Table 8-5. Cloud service providers have extended these models to also provide IT support for each of the cloud computing services (ITaaS), which I also included in Table 8-5.

Table 8-5 *Cloud Service Models*

Software as a Service (SaaS)	The cloud provider is responsible for access to services, such as email, communication, and virtual desktops that are delivered over the Internet.
Platform as a Service (PaaS)	The cloud provider is responsible for access to the development tools and services used to deliver the applications.
Infrastructure as a Service (IaaS)	The cloud provider is responsible for access to the network equipment, virtualized network services, and supporting network infrastructure.
IT as a Service (ITaaS)	The cloud provider is responsible for IT support for IaaS, PaaS, and SaaS service models. In the ITaaS model, an organization contracts with the cloud provider for individual or bundled services.

Cloud Types (8.3.1.5)

The four cloud deployment models are shown in Table 8-6.

Table 8-6 Cloud Types

Private	Cloud-based applications and services offered in a private cloud are intended for a specific organization or entity, such as the government. A private cloud can be set up using the organization's private network, though this can be expensive to build and maintain. A private cloud can also be managed by an outside organization with strict access security.
Public	Cloud-based applications and services offered in a public cloud are made available to the general population. Services may be free or are offered on a pay-per-use model, such as paying for online storage. The public cloud uses the Internet to provide services.

Community	These are clouds built to meet the needs of a specific industry, such as healthcare or media. Community clouds can be private or public.
Hybrid	A hybrid cloud is made up of two or more clouds (example: part Community, part public), where each part remains a distinctive object, but both are connected using a single architecture. Individuals on a hybrid cloud would be able to have degrees of access to various services based on user access rights.

Activity—Identify Cloud Terminology (8.3.1.6)

Please refer to the Activity in the Cisco Networking Academy IT Essentials 6.0 online course.

Networked Host Services (8.3.2)

Hosts on networks perform a certain role. Some of these hosts perform security tasks, whereas others provide web services. There are also many legacy or embedded systems that perform specific tasks such as file or print services.

DHCP Services (8.3.2.1)

A host needs IP address information before it can send data on the network. Two important IP address services are *Dynamic Host Configuration Protocol (DHCP)* and *Domain Name Service (DNS)*.

DHCP is the service used by ISPs, network administrators, and wireless routers to automatically assign IP addressing information to hosts.

When an IPv4, DHCP-configured device boots up or connects to the network, the client broadcasts a DHCP discover (DHCPDISCOVER) message to identify any available DHCP servers on the network. A DHCP server replies with a DHCP offer (DHCPOFFER) message, which offers a lease to the client. The offer message contains the IPv4 address and subnet mask to be assigned, the IPv4 address of the DNS server, and the IPv4 address of the default gateway. The lease offer also includes the duration of the lease.

DNS Services (8.3.2.2)

DNS is the method computers use to translate domain names into IP addresses. On the Internet, domain names, such as http://www.cisco.com, are much easier for people to remember than 198.133.219.25, which is the actual numeric IP address for this server. If Cisco decides to change the numeric IP address of www.cisco.com, it is transparent to the user because the domain name remains the same. The new address is simply linked to the existing domain name and connectivity is maintained.

Clients will make a query to a DNS server to get the IP address of a domain name it is trying to reach such as web site or when sending an email or any other location on the Internet. In response to the query a lookup is done to resolve the domain name to an IP address and that response is returned back to the client that queried the server. Now the device can communicate with the device it was trying to reach by domain name instead using the numeric IP address that it was given.

Web Services (8.3.2.3)

Web resources are provided by a web server. The host accesses the web resources using the *Hypertext Transfer Protocol (HTTP)* or the *secure HTTP (HTTPS)*. HTTP is a set of rules for exchanging text, graphic images, sound, and video on the World Wide Web. HTTPS adds encryption and authentication services using Secure Sockets Layer (SSL) protocol or the newer Transport Layer Security (TLS) protocol. HTTP operates on port 80. HTTPS operates on port 443.

To better understand how the web browser and web server interact, we can examine how a web page is opened in a browser. For this example, use the http://www.cisco.com/index.html URL.

First the browser interprets the three parts of the URL:

1. **http** (the protocol or scheme)
2. **www.cisco.com** (the server name)
3. **index.html** (the specific filename requested)

The browser then checks with a Domain Name Server (DNS) to convert www.cisco.com into a numeric address, which it uses to connect to the server. Using HTTP requirements, the browser sends a GET request to the server and asks for the index.html file.

The server sends the HTML code for this web page back to the client's browser.

Finally, the client's browser deciphers the HTML code and formats the page for the browser window.

File Services (8.3.2.4)

The *File Transfer Protocol (FTP)* was standardized in 1971 to allow for data transfers between a client and a server. An FTP client is an application that runs on a computer that is used to push and pull data from a server running FTP as a service.

As Figure 8-23 illustrates, to successfully transfer data, FTP requires two connections between the client and the server, one for commands and replies, the other for the actual file transfer.

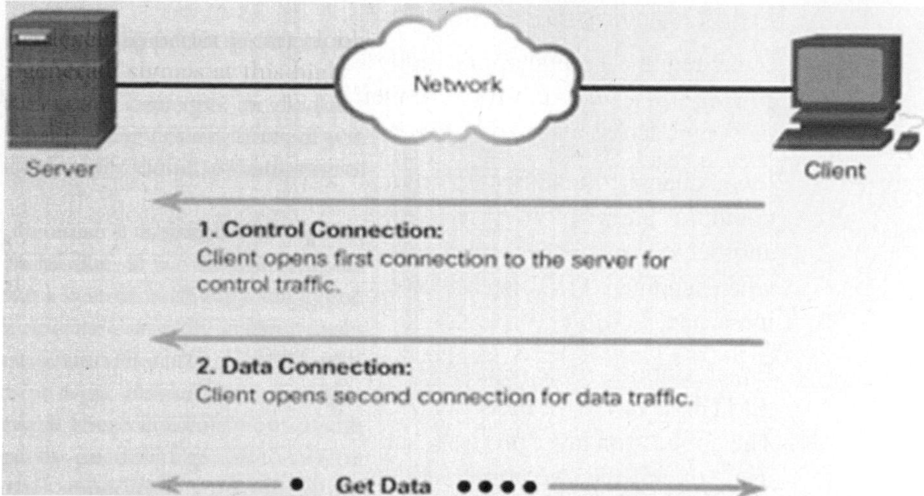

Figure 8-23 FTP Process

FTP has many security weaknesses. Therefore, a more secure file transfer services should be used, such as one of the following:

- *File Transfer Protocol Secure (FTPS)*—An FTP client can request the file transfer session be encrypted using TLS. The file server can accept or deny the request.
- *SSH File Transfer Protocol (SFTP)*—As an extension to Secure Shell (SSH) protocol, SFTP can be used to establish a secure file transfer session.
- *Secure Copy (SCP)*—SCP also uses SSH to secure file transfers.

Print Services (8.3.2.5)

Print servers enable multiple computer users to access a single printer. A print server has three functions:

- Provide client access to print resources.
- Administer print jobs by storing them in a queue until the print device is ready for them and then feeding or spooling the print information to the printer.
- Provide feedback to users.

Print servers are discussed in more detail in another chapter.

Email Services (8.3.2.6)

Email requires several applications and services, as shown in Figure 8-24. *Email protocol* is a store-and-forward method of sending, storing, and retrieving electronic messages across a network. Email messages are stored in databases on mail servers.

Email clients communicate with mail servers to send and receive email. Mail servers communicate with other mail servers to transport messages from one domain to another. An email client does not communicate directly with another email client when sending email. Instead, both clients rely on the mail server to transport messages.

Email supports three separate protocols for operation: Simple Mail Transfer Protocol (SMTP), Post Office Protocol (POP), and Internet Message Access Protocol (IMAP). The application layer process that sends mail uses SMTP. A client retrieves email using one of the two application layer protocols: POP or IMAP.

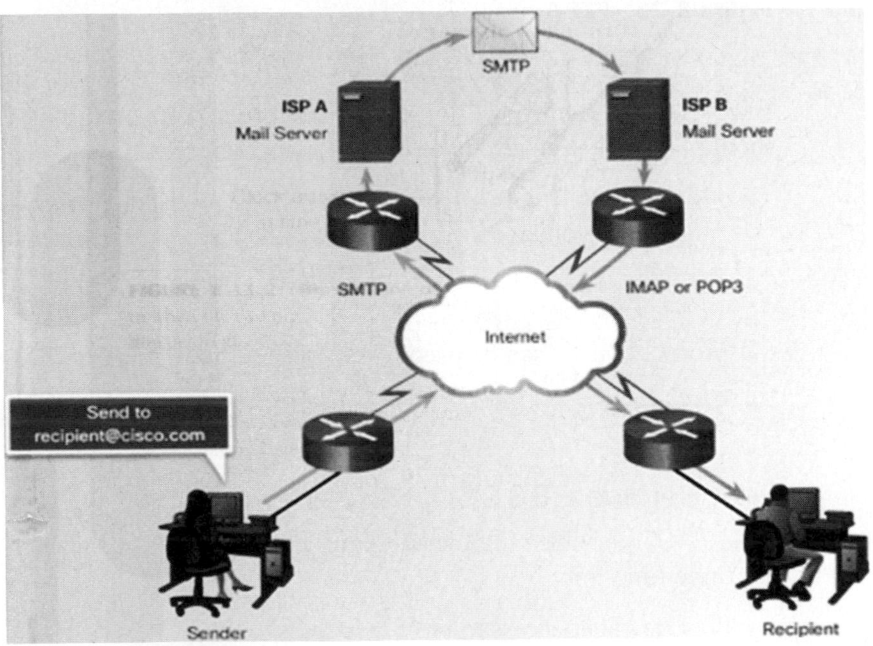

Figure 8-24 Email Process

Proxy Settings (8.3.2.7)

Proxy servers have the authority to act as another computer. A popular use for proxy servers is to act as storage or cache for web pages that are frequently accessed by devices on the internal network. For example, a proxy server could be storing the web pages for www.cisco.com. When any internal host sends an HTTP GET request to www.cisco.com, the proxy server completes the following steps:

1. It intercepts the requests.
2. It checks to see if the website content has changed.
3. If not, the proxy server responds to host with the web page.

In addition, a proxy server can effectively hide the IP addresses of internal hosts because all requests going out to the Internet are sourced from the proxy server's IP address.

Authentication Services (8.3.2.8)

Access to network devices is typically controlled through authentication, authorization, and accounting services. Referred to as *AAA* or *"triple A,"* these services provide the primary framework to set up access control on a network device. AAA is a way to control who is permitted to access a network (authenticate), what they can do while they are there (authorize), and track what actions they perform while accessing the network (accounting).

This concept is similar to using a credit card. The credit card identifies who can use it, sets how much that user can spend, and keeps account of what items or services the user purchased.

Intrusion Detection and Prevention Services (8.3.2.9)

Intrusion detection systems (IDSs) passively monitor traffic on the network. Standalone IDS systems have largely disappeared in favor of *intrusion prevention systems (IPSs)*. But the detection feature of an IDS is still part of any IPS implementation. An IDS—enabled device copies the traffic stream and analyzes the copied traffic rather than the actual forwarded packets. Working offline, it compares the captured traffic stream with known malicious signatures, similar to software that checks for viruses.

An IPS builds upon IDS technology. However, an IPS device is implemented in inline mode. This means that all ingress (inbound) and egress (outbound) traffic must flow through it for processing. An IPS does not allow packets to enter the trusted side of the network without first being analyzed. It can detect and immediately address a network problem.

Universal Threat Management (8.3.2.10)

Universal Threat Management (UTM) is a generic name for an all-in-one security appliance. UTMs include all the functionality of an IDS/IPS as well as stateful firewall services. Stateful firewalls provide stateful packet filtering by using connection information maintained in a state table. A stateful firewall tracks each connection by logging the source and destination addresses as well as source and destination port numbers.

In addition to IDS/IPS and stateful firewall services, UTMs also typically provide additional security services such as:

- Zero Day protection
- Denial of Service (DoS) and Distributed Denial of Service (DDoS) protection
- Proxy filtering of applications
- Email filtering for spam and phishing attacks
- Antispyware
- Network access control
- VPN services

These features can vary significantly, depending on the UTM vendor.

Next-generation firewalls go beyond a UTM in several important ways:

- Control the behaviors within applications
- Restricting web and web application use based on the reputation of the site
- Proactive protection against Internet threats
- Enforcement of policies based on the user, device, role, application type, and threat profile

Packet Tracer Activity

Activity—Identify the Networked Host Service (8.3.2.11)

Please refer to the Activity in the Cisco Networking Academy IT Essentials 6.0 online course.

Common Preventive Maintenance Techniques Used for Networks (8.4)

There are common preventive maintenance techniques that should continually be performed for a network to operate properly.

Network Maintenance (8.4.1)

In an organization, if one computer is malfunctioning, generally only that user is affected. But if the network is malfunctioning, many or all users are unable to work. For this reason, preventive maintenance is very important in a network environment.

Preventive Maintenance Procedures (8.4.1.1)

Preventive maintenance is just as important for the network as it is for the computers on a network. You must check the condition of cables, network devices, servers, and computers to make sure that they are kept clean and are in good working order. One of the biggest problems with network devices, especially in the server room, is heat. Network devices do not perform well when overheated. When dust gathers in and on network devices, it impedes the proper flow of cool air and sometimes even clogs the fans. It is important to keep network rooms clean and change air filters often. It is also a good idea to have replacement filters available for prompt maintenance. You should develop a plan to perform scheduled maintenance and cleaning at regular intervals. A maintenance program helps prevent network downtime and equipment failures.

As part of a regularly scheduled maintenance program, inspect all cabling. Make sure that cables are labeled correctly and labels are not coming off. Replace worn or unreadable labels. Always follow the company's cable labeling guidelines. Check that cable supports are properly installed and no attachment points are coming loose. Cabling can become damaged and worn. Keep the cabling in good repair to maintain good network performance. Refer to wiring diagrams if needed.

Check cables at workstations and printers. Cables are often moved or kicked when they are underneath desks. These conditions can result in loss of bandwidth or connectivity.

As a technician, you may notice that equipment is failing, damaged, or making unusual sounds. Inform the network administrator if you notice any of these issues to prevent unnecessary network downtime. You should also be proactive in the education of network users. Demonstrate to network users how to properly connect and disconnect cables, as well as how to move them, if necessary.

Basic Troubleshooting Process for Networks (8.5)

Network problems can be simple or complex, and can result from a combination of hardware, software, and connectivity issues.

Applying the Troubleshooting Process to Networks (8.5.1)

Computer technicians must be able to analyze the problem and determine the cause of the error to repair the network issue. This process is called *troubleshooting*.

Identify the Problem (8.5.1.1)

To assess the problem, determine how many computers on the network are experiencing the problem. If there is a problem with one computer on the network, start the troubleshooting process at that computer. If there is a problem with all computers on the network, start the troubleshooting process in the network room where all computers are connected. As a technician, you should develop a logical and consistent method for diagnosing network problems by eliminating one problem at a time.

Follow the steps outlined in this section to accurately identify, repair, and document the problem. The first step in the troubleshooting process is to identify the problem. Table 8-7 shows a list of open-ended and closed-ended questions to ask the customer.

Table 8-7 Step 1: Identify the Problem

Open-ended questions	■ What problems are you experiencing with your computer or network device? ■ What software has been installed on your computer recently? ■ What were you doing when the problem was identified? ■ What error message have you received? ■ What type of network connection is the computer using?
Closed-ended questions	■ Has anyone used your computer recently? ■ Can you see any shared files or printer? ■ Have you changed your password recently? ■ Can you access the Internet? ■ Are you currently logged into the network? ■ Is anyone else having this problem?

Establish a Theory of Probable Cause (8.5.1.2)

After you have talked to the customer, you can establish a theory of probable causes. Table 8-8 shows a list of some common probable causes for network problems.

Table 8-8 Step 2: Establish a Theory of Probable Cause

Common causes of network problems	■ Loose cable connections ■ Improperly installed NIC ■ ISP is down ■ Low wireless signal strength ■ Invalid IP address ■ DNS server issue ■ DHCP server issue ■ Network equipment issue (switch, router, etc.)

Test the Theory to Determine Cause (8.5.1.3)

After you have developed some theories about what is wrong, test your theories to determine the cause of the problem. Table 8-9 shows a list of quick procedures that can determine the exact cause of the problem or even correct the problem. If a quick procedure does correct the problem, you can then verify full system functionality. If a quick procedure does not correct the problem, you might need to research the problem further to establish the exact cause.

Table 8-9 Step 3: Test the Theory to Determine Cause

Common steps to determine cause	■ Check that all cables are connected to the proper location ■ Unseat and then reconnect cables and connectors ■ Reboot the computer or network device ■ Login as a different user ■ Repair or re-enable the network connection ■ Contact the network administrator ■ Ping your default gateway ■ Access a remote web page

Establish a Plan of Action to Resolve the Problem and Implement the Solution (8.5.1.4)

After you have determined the exact cause of the problem, establish a plan of action to resolve the problem and implement the solution. Table 8-10 shows some sources you can use to gather additional information to resolve an issue.

Table 8-10 Step 4: Establish a Plan of Action to Resolve the Problem and Implement the Solution

If no solution is achieved in the previous step, further research is needed to implement the solution	■ Helpdesk repair logs ■ Other technicians ■ Manufacturer FAQ websites ■ Technical websites ■ News groups ■ Computer manuals ■ Device manuals ■ Online forums ■ Internet search

Verify Full System Functionality and Implement Preventive Measures (8.5.1.5)

After you have corrected the problem, verify full functionality and, if applicable, implement preventive measures. Table 8-11 shows a list of the steps to verify the solution.

Table 8-11 Step 5: Verify Full System Functionality and if Applicable Implement Preventive Measures

Verify full functionality	■ Use ipconfig /all command to display IP address information for all network adapters. ■ Use Ping to check network connectivity. It will send a packet to the specified address and displays response information. ■ Use NSLookup to query an Internet domain name server. It will return a list of hosts in a domain or the information for one host. ■ Use Tracert to determine the route taken by the packets when they travel across the network. It will show where communications between your computer and another computer are having difficulty. ■ Use Net View to display a list of computers in a workgroup. It will show the available shared resources on a network.

Document Findings, Actions, and Outcomes (8.5.1.6)

In the final step of the troubleshooting process, document your findings, actions, and outcomes. Table 8-12 shows a list of the tasks required to document the problem and the solution.

Table 8-12 Step 6: Document Findings, Actions, and Outcomes

Document findings, actions, and outcomes	■ Discuss the solution implemented with the customer. ■ Ask the customer to verify the problem has been solved. ■ Provide the customer with all paperwork. ■ Document the steps taken to solve the problem in the work order and technician's journal. ■ Document any components used in the repair. ■ Document the time spent to solve the problem.

Common Problems and Solutions for Networks (8.5.2)

This section presents various network issues and approaches you can take to resolve them.

Identify Common Problems and Solutions (8.5.2.1)

Network problems can be attributed to hardware, software, or configuration issues, or to some combination of the three. You will resolve some types of network problems more often than others. Table 8-13 is a chart of common network problems and solutions.

Table 8-13 Common Problems and Solutions

Identify the Problem	Probable Causes	Possible Solutions
NIC LED lights are not lit.	■ The network cable is unplugged or damaged. ■ The NIC is damaged.	■ Reconnect or replace the network connection to the computer. ■ Replace the NIC.
User cannot SSH into a remote device.	■ The remote device is not configured for SSH access. ■ SSH is not allowed from the user or a particular network.	■ Configure the remote device for SSH access. ■ Allow SSH access from the user or the network.
Laptop cannot detect the wireless router.	■ The wireless router/access point is configured with a different 802.11 protocol. ■ The SSID is not being broadcast. ■ The wireless NIC in the laptop is disabled.	■ Configure the wireless router with a compatible protocol for the laptop. ■ Configure the wireless router to broadcast the SSID. ■ Enable the wireless NIC in the laptop.

(*Continued*)

Table 8-13 *Continued*

Identify the Problem	Probable Causes	Possible Solutions
Computer has an IP address of 169.254.x.x.	■ The network cable is unplugged. ■ The router is powered off or the connection is faulty. ■ The NIC is damaged.	■ Reconnect the network cable. ■ Ensure the router is powered on and is properly connected to the network. ■ Release and renew the IP address on the computer. ■ Replace the NIC.
Remote device does not respond to a ping request.	■ Windows firewall disables ping by default. ■ The remote device is configured to not respond to ping requests.	■ Set the firewall to enable the ping protocol. ■ Configure the remote device to respond to the ping request.
A user can access the local network but cannot access the Internet.	■ The gateway address is incorrect or not configured. ■ The ISP is down.	■ Ensure the correct gateway address is assigned to the NIC. ■ Call ISP to report outage.
The network is fully functional but the wireless device cannot connect to the network.	■ The wireless capability of the device is turned off. ■ The device is out of wireless range. ■ There is interference from other wireless devices using the same frequency range.	■ Enable wireless capability of the device. ■ Move closer to the wireless router/access point. ■ Change wireless router to a different channel.
A Windows computer, just connected to a network with only Windows computers, cannot view shared resources.	■ Workgroup name is incorrect. ■ Network location is incorrect. ■ Network Discovery and File Sharing is turned off.	■ Correct workgroup name. ■ Change to the correct network location. ■ Turn on Network Discovery and File Sharing.
A user cannot map a network drive.	■ User does not have appropriate permissions. ■ Incorrect workgroup. ■ Network Discovery and File Sharing is turned off.	■ Configure appropriate permissions for this user. ■ Change workgroup name. ■ Turn on Network Discovery and File Sharing.

Summary (8.6)

Putting a network together requires planning and an understanding of the hardware and software that work together to allow systems to connect and share resources. From installing and configuring NICs to configuring domain memberships in Windows and permissions for sharing files this chapter demonstrated applied networking content to enhance networking skills.

Summary (8.6.1)

Applied networking explains the practical application of networking principles and technologies and considers various troubleshooting examples to address real-world problems.

This chapter introduced you to the ways to connect computers to a network as well as the many services networks offer. The different aspects of troubleshooting a network were discussed with examples of how to analyze and implement simple solutions.

Summary of Exercises

This is a summary of the Labs Packet Tracer and videos activities associated with this chapter.

Labs

The following labs cover material from this chapter. Refer to the labs in the *IT Essentials v6 Lab Manual*.

Lab—Connect to a Router for the First Time (8.1.2.10)

Lab—Configure Wireless Router in Windows (8.1.2.12)

Lab—Test the Wireless NIC in Windows (8.1.2.14)

Lab—Share Resources in Windows (8.1.3.9)

Lab—Remote Assistance in Windows (8.1.4.3)

Lab—Remote Desktop in Windows (8.1.4.4)

The following Packet Tracer Activities cover material from this chapter. To access the activities found in this book, please refer to the instructions found in the introduction.

Packet Tracer Activity

Packet Tracer Activities

Packet Tracer—Connect to a Wireless Router and Configure Basic Settings (8.1.2.11)

Packet Tracer—Test a Wireless Connection (8.1.2.15)

Please view the video in the Cisco Networking Academy IT Essentials 6.0 online course.

Video

Video—Network CLI Commands (8.1.2.9)

Video—Share a Folder (8.1.3.8)

Check Your Understanding

You can find the answers to these questions in the appendix, "Answers to 'Check Your Understanding' Questions."

1. Which network service automatically assigns IP addresses to devices on the network?

   A. Telnet

   B. Traceroute

   C. DNS

   D. DHCP

2. Which technology requires customers to be within a particular range of the service provider facility in order to be provided the maximum bandwidth for Internet access?

   A. Satellite

   B. Cable

   C. ISDN

   D. DSL

3. Which operation should a network technician perform as a part of regular preventive maintenance procedures on the network?

   A. Review the access log of the server farm facility.

   B. Check the network cable connections in the wiring closet.

   C. Ensure antivirus definitions are updated to the latest version on servers.

   D. Verify the bandwidth of the WAN connection to the ISP.

4. Which special character must be included at the end of a folder name to identify a folder as an administrative share?

   A. !

   B. *

   C. #

   D. $

5. What is the difference between a data center and cloud computing?

   A. Data centers require cloud computing but cloud computing does not require data centers.

   B. Cloud computing provides access to shared computing resources, whereas a data center is a facility that stores and processes data.

   C. The data center makes use of more devices to process data.

   D. Of the two, only cloud computing is located off-site.

   E. There is no difference. These terms can be used interchangeably.

6. Which security technology is used to passively monitor network traffic with the objective of detecting a possible attack?

   A. Proxy server

   B. Firewall

   C. IDS

   D. IPS

7. Which command is used to manually query a DNS server to resolve a specific host name?

   A. net

   B. tracert

   C. nslookup

   D. ipconfig /displaydns

8. A technician wishes to update the NIC driver for a computer. What is the best location for finding new drivers for the NIC?

   A. The website for the manufacturer of the NIC

   B. The installation media that came with the NIC

   C. The website for Microsoft

   D. Windows Update

   E. The installation media for Windows

9. The process that a wireless router uses to translate a private IP address on internal traffic to a routable address for the Internet is called ________________________.

   A. NAP

   B. NAT

   C. TCP handshake

   D. Private Address Changing

10. A technician has just installed a new NIC in a laptop. When the cable is plugged in, the technician notices that the LEDs on the NIC are green and one LED is flashing. What does this usually signify?

    A. The NIC is functioning and the cable is operating at the maximum data rate.

    B. The NIC is doing a POST function to detect possible errors.

    C. The NIC is functioning and there is network activity.

    D. The NIC is attempting to establish a VPN connection but the configuration of the NIC is missing security settings.

    E. The NIC is connected to the wrong port on the wireless router.

11. Which cloud computing opportunity would provide the use of network hardware such as routers and switches for a particular company?

    A. Infrastructure as a service (IaaS)

    B. Browser as a service (BaaS)

    C. Software as a service (SaaS)

    D. Wireless as a service (WaaS)

12. _______________ technology uses different frequencies to transmit multiple signals simultaneously over the same cable.

    A. Baseband

    B. Baseboard

    C. Broadband

    D. Broadbase

13. A technician is troubleshooting a computer that has lost connectivity to the network. After data is gathered from the customer, which two tasks should the technician complete next? (Choose two.)

   A. Verify that the computer has a valid IP address.
   B. Try to log in as a different user.
   C. Verify that the computer has the most up to date version of the OS.
   D. Repair the network cable.
   E. Check that the NIC link light is lit.

14. A technician needs to check the system settings on a remote computer to make sure it will be compatible with a new software update that will be sent out. The technician will use an administrator account to log in and start a user session on the remote PC. Which Windows tool will the technician use to accomplish this?

   A. Windows VPN remote access client
   B. Windows Remote Desktop
   C. Windows file sharing services
   D. Windows Update Assistant

15. Users in a recently installed wireless network are complaining of slow data transfer and frequent loss of connectivity. The technician checks that the wireless security is correctly implemented, and there is no evidence of unauthorized users on the network. Which two problems might the technician suspect? (Choose two.)

   A. The DHCP server is faulty.
   B. The wireless signal is too weak.
   C. The antenna on the access point is too powerful.
   D. The network passwords need to be reissued to the users.
   E. There is interference from outside sources.

CHAPTER 9

Laptops and Mobile Devices

Objectives

Upon completion of this chapter, you will be able to answer the following questions:

- What are laptops and their common uses?
- What are the components of laptops and mobile devices?
- What are the best ways to select laptop components?
- What is a docking station and port replicator?
- What are different ways to configure a laptop?
- How can I repair a laptop?
- What wireless communication methods are used with laptops and mobile devices?
- What are some common preventative maintenance techniques for laptops?
- What types of displays are used with laptops and mobile devices?
- What are ways to troubleshoot laptops?

Key Terms

This chapter uses the following key terms. You can find the definitions in the Glossary.

laptop Page 448

battery Page 448

mobile device Page 448

ExpressCard slots Page 449

Thunderbolt ports Page 449

DisplayPorts Page 449

AC power adapter Page 449

Nickel-cadmium "Ni-Cad" (NiCd) Page 450

Nickel-metal hydride (NiMH) Page 450

Lithium-ion (Li-Ion) Page 451

Lithium-polymer (Li-Poly or LiPo) Page 451

Security keyhole Page 451

USB port Page 451

S-Video connector Page 451

Modem port Page 451

Ethernet port Page 451

Network LEDs Page 452

Stereo headphone jack Page 452

Microphone jack Page 452

Ventilation Page 452

PC combo expansion slot Page 452

Infrared port Page 452

Laptop latch Page 452

Hard drive access panel Page 453

Battery latch Page 453

Docking station connector Page 453

form factors Page 454

RAM access panel Page 453

CPU throttling Page 456

Function (Fn) key Page 456

built-in LCD Page 457

base station Page 457

docking station Page 457

port replicator Page 460

AC power connector Page 459

PC Card/Express slot Page 459

VGA port Page 459

Digital Visual Interface (DVI) port Page 459

Line-in connector Page 459

External diskette drive connector Page 459

Headphone connector Page 459

Mouse port Page 459

Keyboard port Page 459

Parallel port Page 459

Serial port Page 459

RJ-11 (modem port) Page 459

Ethernet port Page 451

LED monitors Page 462

Organic LED (OLED) Page 461

twisted nematic (TN) Page 461

in-plane switching (IPS) Page 461

LCD cutoff switch Page 461

inverter Page 462

backlight Page 461

Advanced Configuration and Power Interface (ACPI) Page 464

Hibernate Page 466

low battery warning Page 468

critical battery level Page 468

Bluetooth Page 468

cellular WAN capabilities Page 471

wireless adapters Page 471

Mini-PCI Page 471

Mini-PCIe Page 471

PCI Express Micro Page 471

flash drive Page 474

flash card Page 474

flash card reader Page 475

small outline dual inline memory modules (SODIMMs) Page 455

customer-replaceable units (CRUs) Page 478

field-replaceable units (FRUs) Page 478

DC jack Page 481

touchpad Page 453

Mobile hotspot Page 496

tethering Page 471

embedded MultiMediaCard (eMMC) Page 492

hot-swappable Page 473

smart card Page 475

Subscriber identity module (SIM) card Page 492

Near field communication (NFC) Page 496

Memory card Page 492

touchscreen Page 493

Lightning connector Page 495

Micro/Mini universal serial bus (USB) Page 495

Double touch Page 493

electronic readers Page 499

Expansion ports Page 472

Fitness monitors Page 498

gestures Page 493

Global positioning system Page 499

hotspot Page 471

Infrared Page 496

LED monitors Page 462

Liquid-crystal display (LCD) Page 461

Light-emitting diode (LED) Page 461

Long touch Page 493

Multi-touch Page 493

phablets Page 499

Pinch Page 494

Proprietary vendor specific ports Page 495

proximity sensor Page 494

Scroll Page 493

Slide or swipe Page 493

Smart headsets Page 498

smartphone Page 492

Smart watches Page 498

Spread Page 494

tablet Page 492

Wearable devices Page 498

Introduction (9.0)

The first laptops were used primarily by business people who needed to access and enter data when they were away from the office. The use of laptops was limited due to expense, weight, and limited capabilities compared to less expensive desktops.

Welcome (9.0.1)

The most significant feature of a *laptop* is its compact size. The design of the laptop places the keyboard, screen, and internal components into a small, portable case. As a result, laptops can be used to take notes in school, present information in a business meeting, or access the Internet in a coffee shop. A rechargeable *battery* allows the laptop to function when it is disconnected from an external power source. The compact design, convenience, and evolving technology of laptops have made them popular. A *mobile device* is any device that is hand-held and lightweight, typically with a touchscreen for input. With the increase in demand for mobility, the popularity of laptops and other mobile devices continues to grow.

Laptops and Mobile Devices (9.0.1.1)

Improvements in technology have allowed the laptop to become lightweight, powerful, and much more affordable. Because of this, laptops are found in just about every setting today.

Laptops run the same operating systems as desktop computers and most come with built-in WiFi, webcam, microphone, speakers, and ports to attach external components.

Like a desktop or laptop computer, mobile devices use an operating system to run applications (apps), games, and play movies and music. Mobile devices also have a different CPU architecture, designed to have a reduced instruction set compared to laptop and desktop processors.

This chapter focuses on many features of laptops, mobile devices, and their capabilities.

Laptop Components (9.1)

The following section looks closely at both internal and external laptop components. Components can be located in different places on different laptop models. It is important to know each component to make informed decisions on the selection of components for purchases and upgrades. Understanding laptop components is necessary for troubleshooting when they malfunction or fail.

Features of Laptop Components (9.1.1)

Laptops are becoming as versatile desktop computers and have much more powerful components that in the past. There is a large selection in features and price, size, and platforms so usability should be a strong consideration when considering the device.

External Features Unique to Laptops (9.1.1.1)

Laptop and desktop computers use many of the same hardware features so that peripherals can be interchangeable. The placement of ports, connections, and drives is unique because of the compact design of a laptop. Ports, connections, and drives are located on the exterior of the laptop, in the front, back, and side panels. USB ports allow external devices such as optical drives, Bluetooth, and WiFi to be attached to a laptop. Some laptops contain *ExpressCard slots*, *Thunderbolt ports*, and *DisplayPorts* as well.

Status indicators, ports, slots, connectors, bays, jacks, vents, and a keyhole are on the exterior of the laptop.

In this chapter, figures and lists are examples of the common components that laptops have but not all of them will have each of these components. The vendor and purpose of use will determine the exact features of the model of laptop.

Figure 9-1 shows three LEDs on the top of a laptop.

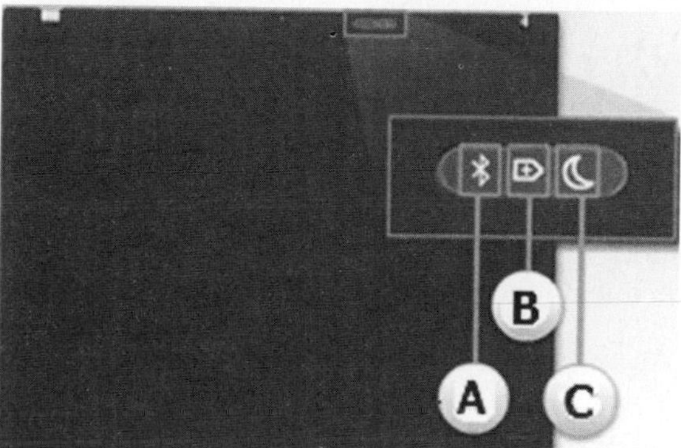

Figure 9-1 Top View of a Laptop

The LED symbols in Figure 9-1 are explained in the list:

- A—The Bluetooth status LED indicates when the Bluetooth wireless transceiver is enabled. Bluetooth is a wireless industry standard that enables portable devices to communicate over short distances is Bluetooth.
- B—The battery status LED indicates the status of the battery. A laptop computer can use a battery or an *AC power adapter* to operate. The type of battery and how the laptop is used affects how long a battery charge will last.

- C—The standby LED indicates whether the laptop is in standby or not. Standby mode reduces the amount of electricity used by the laptop by shutting off the monitor, hard drive, and CPU. A small amount of electricity is used to keep the RAM active and to make the data available. A laptop computer may enter standby mode when it has not been used for a predefined amount of time.

Note

LED displays vary among laptops. Consult the laptop manual for a list of specific status displays.

Figure 9-2 shows three components on the back of a laptop.

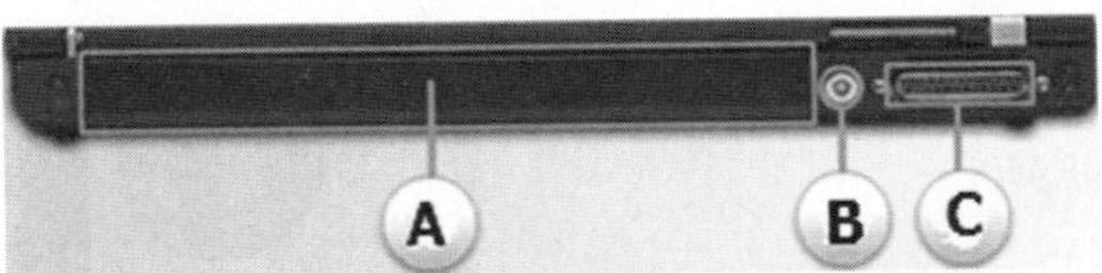

Figure 9-2 Laptop Rear View

The three components shown in Figure 9-2 are explained in the list:

- A—The battery bay is a connector that is used to attach a laptop battery.
- B—The AC power connector is a connector that is used to attach the AC power adapter to the laptop and to charge the battery.
- C—The parallel port is a socket that is used to connect a device such as a printer or scanner.

Laptops require a port for external power and can operate using either a battery or an AC power adapter. You can use this port to power the computer or to charge the battery. Laptop batteries are manufactured in various shapes and sizes. They use different types of chemicals and metals to store power.

Table 9-1 compares rechargeable batteries.

Table 9-1 Laptop Battery Comparison

Type of Battery	Characteristics	Common Use
Nickel-cadmium "Ni-Cad" (NiCd)	Heavy for the power it holds, long life (many charging cycles), may exhibit memory effect.	Toys, cordless phones, emergency lighting, power tools, camera flash
Nickel-metal hydride (NiMH)	Moderate weight for power, moderate lifespan, may experience "polarity reversal" at end of cycle, shut down, or recharge at once. May need several charge/discharge cycles to reach full capability.	Cell phones, digital cameras, GPS units, flashlights, and other consumer electronics

Type of Battery	Characteristics	Common Use
Lithium-ion (Li-Ion)	Lightweight battery for power, no memory effect, can easily overheat. Keep cool, charge often, seek freshest batteries (most recently manufactured).	Cell phones, laptops
Lithium-polymer (Li-Poly or LiPo)	Costly, small, lightweight battery for power, moderate capacity, fast recharge, moderate lifespan, do not short circuit, is not flammable.	PDAs, laptops, portable MP3 players, portable gaming devices, radio-controlled airplanes

The left side components are shown in Figure 9-3.

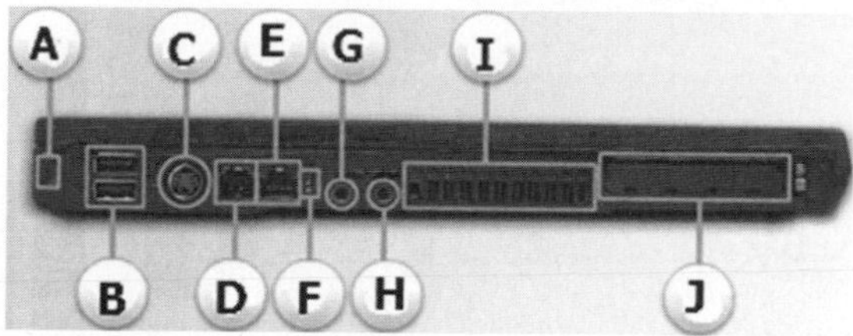

Figure 9-3 Laptop: Left-Side View

The left side of a laptop may have all or some of these 10 components explained in the list:

- A—*Security keyhole:* A small slot designed to receive a specially shaped lock to reduce the risk of physical theft. A security keyhole enables a user to connect a laptop to a stationary location, such as a desk, by using a combination or keyed lock
- B—*USB port:* A socket that is used to connect one or more peripherals.
- C—*S-Video connector:* A four-pin mini-DIN connector that is used to output video signals to a compatible device. S-video separates the brightness and color portions of a video signal. Connects the laptop to an external monitor or projector
- D—*Modem port:* The RJ-11 modem port is a device that is used to connect the laptop to a standard telephone line. The modem can be used to connect the computer to the Internet, to fax documents, and to answer incoming calls. Communicates on analog phone networks
- E—*Ethernet port:* An RJ-45 socket that is used to connect the laptop to a cabled local area network.

- F—*Network LEDs:* The two network LEDs are lights that indicate the status of the network connection. The green link light indicates network connectivity. The other LED light indicates the traffic to and from the laptop.
- G—*Stereo headphone jack:* Audio to external speakers or headphones connects the laptop to external speakers or headphones.
- H—*Microphone jack:* Connects a microphone to the laptop.
- I—*Ventilation:* A series of vents that allow hot air to be expelled from the interior of the laptop.
- J—*PC Combo Card slot:* An expansion slot that supports expansion cards like PCMCIA and PC Card/ExpressCard.

The front of the laptop is shown in Figure 9-4.

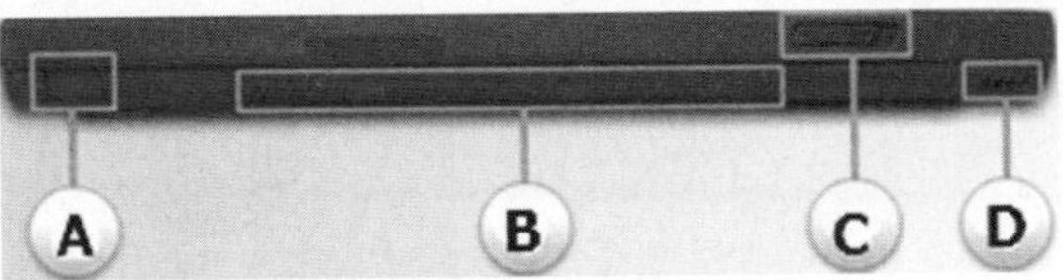

Figure 9-4 Laptop: Front View

The front of a laptop may have all or some of these components explained in the list:

- A—*Infrared port:* Allows the laptop to communicate with other infrared-enabled devices
- B—*Speakers:* Provide sound output
- C—*Laptop latch:* Keeps the lid closed
- D—*Ventilation:* Removes heat from the case

The right of a laptop may have all or some of these four components explained in the list:

The right side of the laptop is shown in Figure 9-5.

Figure 9-5 Laptop: Right-Side View

- A—*Optical drive:* Reads CDs, DVDs, and Blu-ray discs
- B—*Optical drive status indicator:* Displays activity on the optical drive

- C—*Drive bay status indicator:* Displays activity on that drive bay
- D—*Video Graphics Array (VGA) port:* Allows for external monitor or projector

The bottom of the laptop is shown in Figure 9-6.

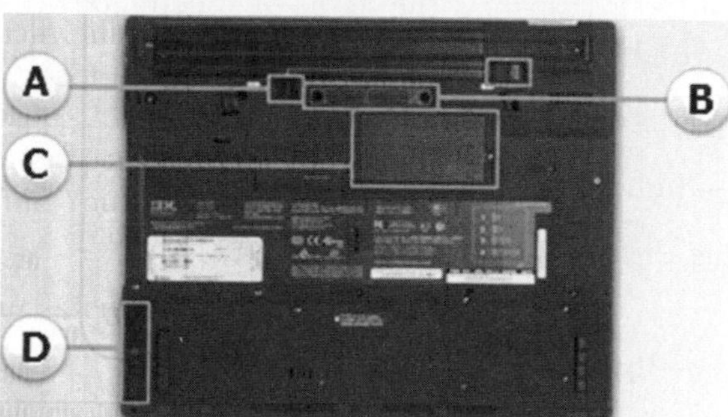

Figure 9-6 Laptop: Bottom View

The bottom of the laptop may have all or some of these components explained in the list:

- A—*Battery latches (two areas):* Release the battery from the battery bay
- B—*Docking station connector:* Connects the laptop to a docking station or port replicator
- C—*RAM access panel:* Provides access to the RAM
- D—*Hard drive access panel:* Provides access to the hard drive

Common Input Devices and LEDs in Laptops (9.1.1.2)

Laptops are designed to be compact and portable, while maintaining much of the same functionality provided by desktop computers. As a result, essential input devices are built into laptops. When a laptop lid is lifted, the following input devices may be present:

- *Touchpad*—Consists of right and left click buttons. The touchpad can be used instead of a mouse for the laptop.
- **Pointing stick**—The pointer controller, which can be used instead of a mouse for the laptop.
- **Keyboard**—A compact input device and has multi-functional keys.
- *Fingerprint readers*—Are used for security authentication.
- **Microphone**—Used for recording with your laptop.
- **Web camera**—A camera attached to your computer to transmit video.

Note

Input devices that are built into laptops can be configured in the same manner as input devices for desktops.

Laptops may feature LEDs that show the status of specific devices or components. LEDs are commonly found below the display screen or directly above the keyboard.

Types of common status LEDs found on a laptop include the following:

- **Wireless LED**—Indicates the activity of the wireless network connection.
- **Bluetooth status LED**—Indicates when the Bluetooth wireless transceiver is enabled.
- **Num Lock LED**—Indicates the on/off status of the ten-key number pad.
- **Caps Lock LED**—Indicates the on/off status of the caps lock.
- **Hard drive activity LED**—Indicates the activity of the hard drive.
- **Power on LED**—Indicates the on/off status of the laptop.
- **Battery status LED**—Indicates the status of the laptop battery.
- **Hibernate/standby LED**—Indicates whether the computer is in standby mode or if it is entering or leaving hibernate mode.

Note

LEDs vary by laptop model.

Internal Components (9.1.1.3)

The compact nature of laptops requires a number of internal components to fit in a small amount of space. The size restrictions result in a variety of form factors for a number of laptop components, such as the motherboard, RAM, CPU, and storage devices. Some laptop components, such as the CPU, may be designed to use less power to ensure that the system can operate for a longer period of time when using a battery source.

Motherboards

Desktop motherboards have standard *form-factors*. The standard size and shape allow motherboards from different manufacturers to fit into common desktop cases. In comparison, laptop motherboards vary by manufacturer and are proprietary. When you repair a laptop, you must often obtain a replacement motherboard from the laptop manufacturer. Figure 9-7 shows a comparison between a desktop motherboard and a laptop motherboard.

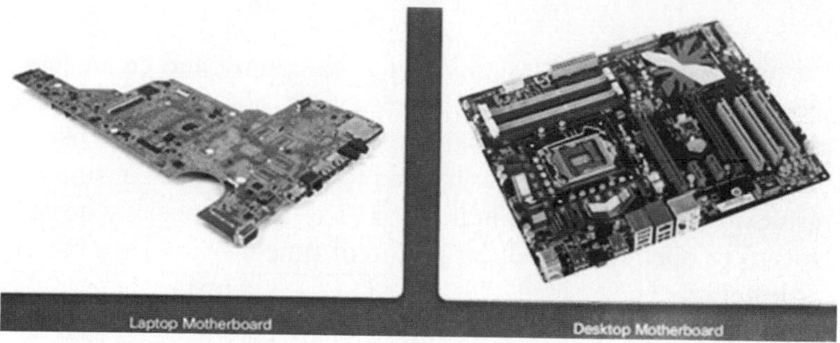

Figure 9-7 Motherboard Comparison

Laptop motherboards and desktop motherboards are designed differently. Components designed for a laptop generally cannot be used in a desktop. Laptop and desktop designs are compared in Table 9-2.

Table 9-2 Laptop and Desktop Comparison

Component	Laptop	Desktop
Motherboard form-factor	Proprietary	AT, LPX, NLX, ATX, BTX
Expansion slot	Mini-PCI	PCI, PCIe, ISA, AGP
RAM slot type	SODIMM	SIMM, DIMM, RIMM

RAM

Because of the limited amount of spacc within laptops, memory modules are much smaller than those used in desktops. Laptops use *small outline dual inline memory modules (SODIMMs)*, as shown in Figure 9-8.

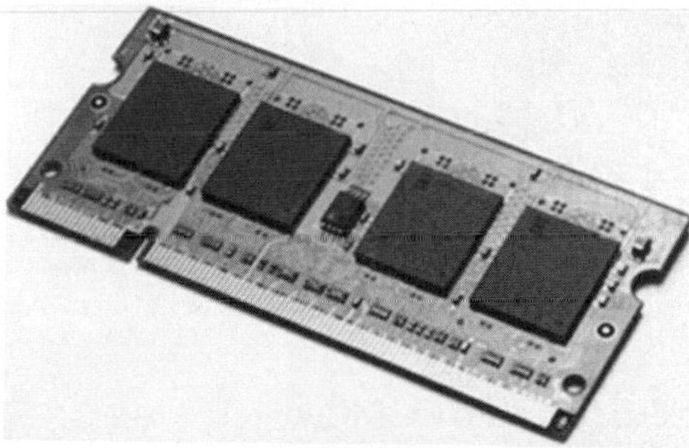

Figure 9-8 SODIMM

CPUs

Laptop processors are designed to use less power and create less heat than desktop processors. As a result, laptop processors do not require cooling devices that are as large as those found in desktops. Laptop processors also use ***CPU throttling*** to modify the clock speed as needed to reduce power consumption and heat. This results in a slight decrease in performance. These specially designed processors allow laptops to operate for a longer period of time when using a battery.

Note

Refer to the laptop manual for compatible processors and for replacement instructions.

Storage

Laptop storage devices are 1.8 in. (4.57 cm) or 2.5 in. (6.35 cm) in width, whereas desktop storage devices are typically 3.5 in. (8.9 cm). The 1.8 in. drives are mostly found in ultraportable laptops because they are smaller, lighter, and consume less power. However, their spin rate is usually slower than that of 2.5 in. drives which have spin rates of up to 10,000RPMs.

There has been an increase in the use of SSD storage in laptops. SSDs can generally transfer data faster and with less latency than hard drives, running silently and consuming less power. They have no moving parts.

Special Function Keys (9.1.1.4)

The purpose of the ***Function (Fn) key*** is to activate a second function on a dual-purpose key. The feature that is accessed by pressing the Fn key in combination with another key is printed on the key in a smaller font or different color. Several functions can be accessed:

- Display settings
- Display brightness
- Screen orientation
- Keyboard backlighting
- Volume
- Media options such as fast forward or rewind
- Sleep states

- WiFi functionality
- Bluetooth functionality
- Battery status
- Touchpad power
- Airplane mode

Note

Some laptops may have dedicated function keys that perform functions without requiring users to press the Fn key.

A laptop monitor is a ***built-in LCD*** or LED screen. You cannot adjust the laptop monitor for height and distance because it is integrated into the lid of the case. You can often connect an external monitor or projector to a laptop. Pressing the Fn key with the appropriate function key on the keyboard toggles between the built-in display and the external display.

Do not confuse the Fn key with function keys F1 through F12. These keys are typically located in a row across the top of the keyboard. Their function depends on the OS and application that is running when they are pressed. Each key can perform up to seven different operations by pressing it with one or more combinations of the Shift, Ctrl, and Alt keys.

Docking Station Versus Port Replicator (9.1.1.5)

A *base station* attaches to AC power and to desktop peripherals. When you plug the laptop into the base station, you have access to power and the attached peripherals as well as an increased number of ports.

There are two types of base stations that are used for the same purpose: docking stations and port replicators.

Docking Station

A *docking station* allows a laptop to function as a desktop computer. Peripheral devices, such as monitor, mouse, and keyboard can be permanently connected to the docking station. When a user decides to use the laptop in desktop mode, the user connects the laptop to the docking station via the docking connector as shown in Figure 9-9.

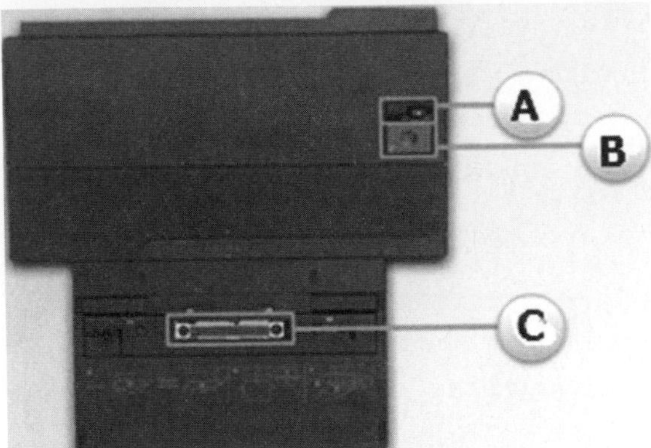

Figure 9-9 Docking Station: Top View

The following list provides more information about the components located on the TOP of the docking station:

- A—*Power button:* A control that turns the power on and turns the power off to the laptop when the laptop is connected to the docking station.
- B—*Eject button:* A lever that releases the laptop from the docking station so that the laptop can be removed.
- C—*Docking connector:* A socket that is used to attach a laptop to a docking station.

The docking connector allows the laptop to communicate with the peripheral devices. Some docking stations can provide addition ports beyond what is available on the laptop, such as additional USB ports. The docking stations may also have built-in peripheral devices, such as speakers or an optical drive, as shown in Figure 9-10.

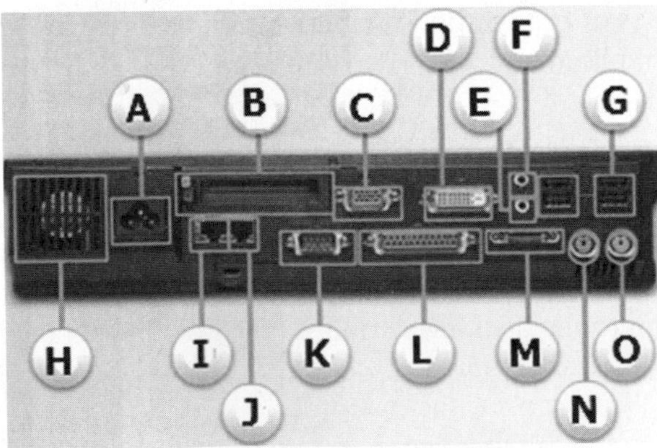

Figure 9-10 Docking Station: Rear View

The following list provides more information about the components typically located on the rear of the docking station:

- A—*AC power connector:* Provides power to charge the battery
- B—*PC Card/ExpressCard slot:* Connects laptops to expansion cards
- C—*VGA port:* Allows for external monitor or projector
- D—*Digital Visual Interface (DVI) port:* Allows for external monitor or projector
- E—*Headphone connector:* Allows audio output for headphones
- F—*Line-in connector:* Allows audio input from pre-amplified sources like iPods
- G—*USB port:* Connects the laptop to most peripheral devices
- H—*Exhaust vent:* Lets hot air out of the laptop
- I—*Ethernet port:* Communicates on Ethernet networks
- J—*RJ-11 (modem port):* Communicates on analog phone networks
- K—*Serial port:* A legacy port that connects devices like mice, keyboards and modems before widespread use of USB
- L—*Parallel port:* Connects legacy devices such as printers and scanners that do not support USB
- M—*External diskette drive connector:* Connects laptop to an external diskette drive
- N—*Keyboard port:* Connects older keyboards to the laptop
- O—*Mouse port:* Connects older mice to the laptop

When a laptop is connected to the docking station, it can be secured using a locking mechanism, as shown in Figure 9-11.

Figure 9-11 Docking Station: Right-Side View

Many docking stations are proprietary and only work with particular laptops. Before buying a docking station, check the laptop documentation or the website of the manufacturer to determine the appropriate make and model for the laptop.

Port Replicator

A *port replicator* also allows a laptop to connect multiple peripheral devices quickly. The peripheral devices are plugged into the port replicator permanently, and the laptop usually connects to the port replicator via a USB port. A port replicator can provide a more universal solution by connecting to the laptop via the USB port. An advantage to using a port replicator is that multiple laptops from different vendors can use most, if not all, of its functionality.

The available connection types depend on the docking station, port replicator, and the make and model of the laptop:

- Manufacturer-specific and model-specific
- USB, FireWire, and Thunderbolt
- PC-Card or ExpressCard

Most laptops can be docked both when in use or while shut off. Adding devices when docking can be handled by plug-and-play technology or by using a separate hardware profile for the docked and undocked state. The docking stations and port replicators allow for easy connection and disconnection of a laptop from all of the peripherals to which it is connected.

Lab—Research Docking Stations (9.1.1.6)

In this lab, you use the Internet, a newspaper, or a local store to gather information and then record the specifications for a laptop docking station. Refer to the lab in *IT Essentials v6 Lab Manual.*

Laptop Displays (9.1.2)

Laptop *display* is the output device that shows all the onscreen content and is one of the most expensive components of the laptop. There are three different display types, and they come in various sizes and resolutions. Understanding the screen display types and the internal display components of a laptop is important when purchasing or repairing a system. Laptop monitors are built-in displays. They are similar to desktop monitors, except that you can adjust the resolution, brightness, and contrast using software or button controls. You cannot adjust the laptop monitor for height and distance because it is integrated into the lid of the case. You can connect a desktop monitor to a laptop, providing the user with multiple screens and increased functionality.

This section describes the different types of displays and the internal components for each type.

LCD, LED, and OLED Displays (9.1.2.1)

There are three types of laptop displays:

- *Liquid-crystal display (LCD)*
- *Light-emitting diode (LED)*
- Organic light-emitting diode (OLED)

The two most common technologies used in the manufacturing of LCD displays are *twisted nematic (TN)* and *in-plane switching (IPS)*. TN is the most common and the oldest. TN displays offer high brightness, uses less power than IPS, and are inexpensive to manufacture. IPS displays offer better color reproduction and better viewing angles, but have low contrast and slow response time. Manufactures are now producing Super-IPS (S-IPS) panels, at reasonable prices, that have improved response times and contrast.

LED displays use less power and have a longer lifespan than LCD displays, making them the display choice for many laptop manufactures.

Organic LED (OLED) technology is commonly used for mobile devices and digital cameras, but can also be found in some laptops. With OLED displays, every pixel is individually lit.

Some laptops now come with detachable touch screens that can be used like a tablet when the display is detached. Other laptops permit the keyboard to fold back behind the display to allow the laptop to function like a tablet. To accommodate these types of laptops, Windows will rotate the display 90, 180, or 270 degrees automatically or by pressing the Ctrl + Alt keys simultaneously with the arrow key for which way you want the laptop to face.

Laptops with touchscreens have a special glass piece attached to the front of the screen, known as a digitizer. The digitizer converts the touch actions (press, swipe, and so on) into a digital signal that is processed by the laptop.

On many laptops, a small pin on the laptop cover contacts a switch when the case is closed, called a *LCD cutoff switch*. The cutoff switch helps conserve power by turning off the display. If this switch breaks or is dirty, the display remains dark while the laptop is open. Carefully clean this switch to restore normal operation.

Backlights and Inverters (9.1.2.2)

An inverter and backlight are two important display components. The inverter is essentially the power supply for the backlight and the backlight supplies the main source of light to the screen without it the image on the screen would not be visible.

LCDs do not produce any light by themselves. A *backlight* shines through the screen and illuminates the display. Two common types of backlights are cold cathode fluorescent lamp (CCFL) and LED. With CCFL, fluorescent tubes are connected to an *inverter*, used to convert direct current (DC) to alternating current (AC). The florescent backlight, as shown in Figure 9-12, is behind the LCD screen.

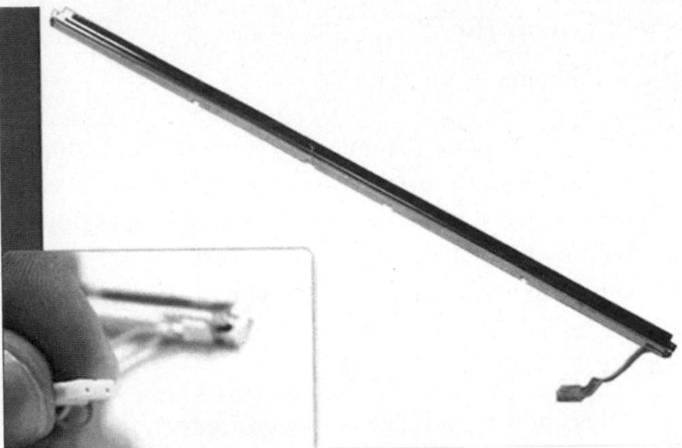

Figure 9-12 Backlight

To replace the backlight, you must completely disassemble the display. The inverter, as shown in Figure 9-13, is behind the screen panel and close to the LCD.

Figure 9-13 Inverter

LED monitors use LED-based backlights and do not have fluorescent tubes or inverters. LED technology increases the longevity of the display because it consumes less power. Also, LED technology is safer for the environment because LEDs do not contain mercury. Mercury is a key ingredient in fluorescent backlights used in LCDs.

WiFi Antenna Connectors (9.1.2.3)

WiFi antennas transmit and receive data carried over radio waves. WiFi antennas in laptops are typically located above the screen, as shown in Figure 9-14.

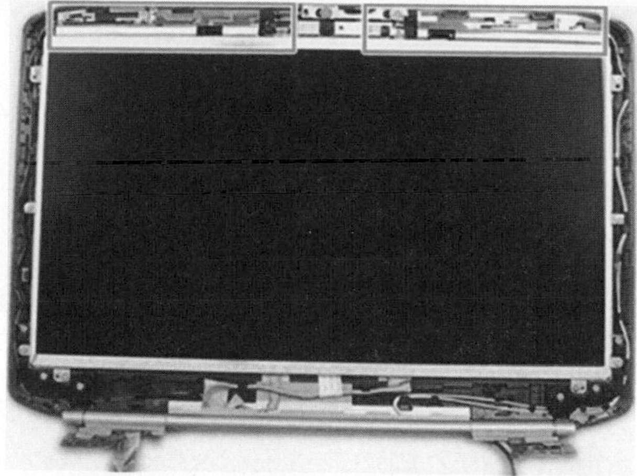

Figure 9-14 WiFi Antenna

The WiFi antenna is connected to a wireless card by an antenna wire and antenna leads, as shown in Figure 9-15.

Figure 9-15 WiFi Antenna Leads

The wires are fastened to the display unit by wire guides, which are located on the sides of the screen.

Webcam and Microphone (9.1.2.4)

Most laptops today have a webcam and microphone built in. The webcam is normally positioned at the top, center of the display. The internal microphone can often be found next to the webcam. Some manufactures may place the microphone next to the keyboard, or on the side of the laptop.

Laptop Configuration (9.2)

Power conservation and management are important aspects to consider for laptops because they are intended for portable use. Laptops use batteries as a power source when disconnected from an external power source.

Power Settings Configuration (9.2.1)

Software can be used to extend the life of the laptop battery and maximize battery usage. This section introduces methods of power management and settings for optimizing power management through software and the BIOS on a laptop.

Power Management (9.2.1.1)

Advances in power management and battery technology are increasing the amount of time that a laptop can be powered from a battery. Many batteries can power a laptop for 10 hours or more. Configuring laptop power settings to better manage power usage is important to ensure that the battery is used efficiently.

Power management controls the flow of electricity to the components of a computer. The *Advanced Configuration and Power Interface (ACPI)* creates a bridge between the hardware and the operating system and allows technicians to create power management schemes to get the best performance from a laptop. The ACPI states are applicable to most computers, but they are particularly important when managing power in laptops.

Table 9-3 shows the ACPI standards.

Table 9-3 Laptop and Desktop Comparison

Standard	Description
S0	The computer is on and the CPU is running.
S1	The CPU and RAM are still receiving power, but unused devices are powered down.
S2	The CPU is off, but RAM is refreshed. The system is in a lower mode than S1.
S3	The CPU is off, and the RAM is set to a slow refresh rate. This mode is often called "save to RAM." This state is known as sleep or suspend mode.
S4	The CPU and RAM are off. The contents of RAM have been saved to a temporary file on the hard disk. This mode is also called "save to disk." This state is known as hibernate mode.
S5	The computer is off.

Managing ACPI Settings in the BIOS (9.2.1.2)

Technicians are frequently required to configure power settings by changing the settings in the BIOS or UEFI setup. Configuring the power settings affects the following:

- System states
- Battery and AC modes
- Thermal management
- CPU PCI bus power management
- Wake on LAN (WOL)

Note

WOL might require a cable connection inside the computer from the network adapter to the motherboard.

The ACPI power management mode must be enabled in the BIOS setup to allow the OS to configure the power management states, as shown in the figure.

How To

To enable ACPI mode in the BIOS setup, follow these steps:

Step 1. Enter BIOS setup.

Step 2. Locate and enter the Power Management settings menu item.

Step 3. Use the appropriate keys to enable ACPI mode.

Step 4. Save and exit BIOS setup.

Note

These steps are common to most laptops, but be sure to check the laptop documentation for specific configuration settings. There is no standard name for each power management state. Different manufacturers might use different names for the same state.

Activity—Match ACPI Standards (9.2.1.3)

Go to the online course to perform this practice activity.

Managing Laptop Power Options (9.2.1.4)

The Power Options utility in Windows allows you to reduce the power consumption of specific devices or the entire system. To configure power settings in Windows, use the following path:

Control Panel > Power Options

Types of Laptop Power Options

If you do not want to completely shut down the laptop when you press the power button, you can change what the button does.

To access the **Define power buttons and turn on password protection** menu in Windows, click the **Choose what the power buttons do** link on the left-hand side of the Power Options utility.

The options are:

- **Do nothing**—The computer continues to run at full power.
- **Sleep**—Documents and applications are saved in RAM, allowing the computer to power on quickly.
- *Hibernate*—Documents and applications are saved to a temporary file on the hard drive. The laptop takes longer to power on than from the Sleep state.
- **Shutdown**—Closes all open programs, closes the Windows OS, and then turns off your computer and display. Shutting down doesn't save your work, so you must save your files first.

Figure 9-16 shows Hibernate enabled in the Power Options utility of Windows 7.

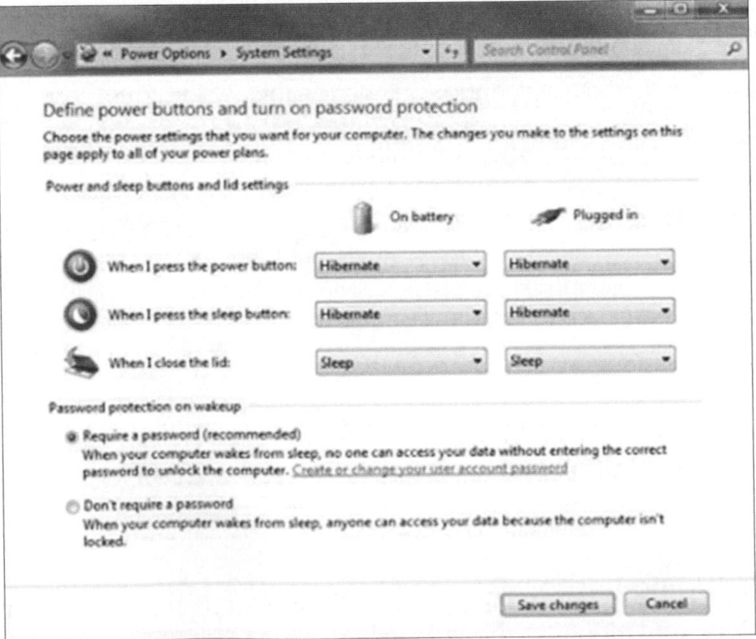

Figure 9-16 Hibernate Enabled in Windows 7 Power Options Utility

Hard Drive and Display Power Management

Two of the biggest power consumers on a laptop are the hard drive and display. As shown in Figure 9-17, you can select when to turn the hard drive or display off when the laptop is running on a battery or AC adapter.

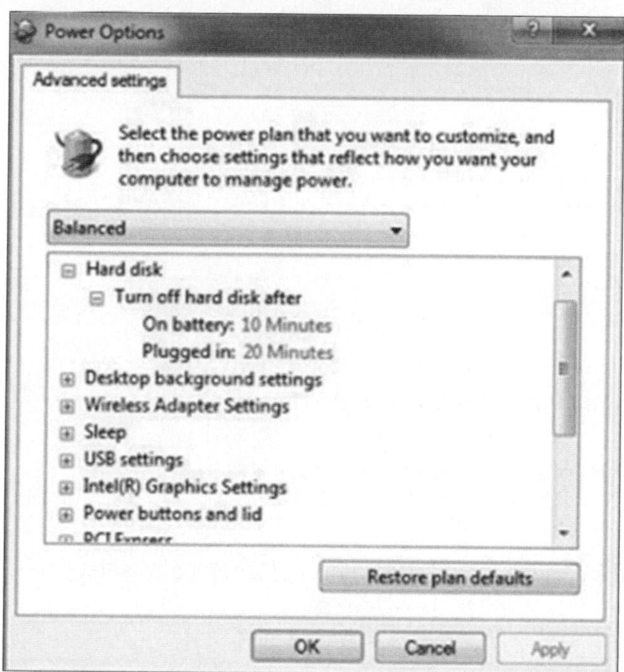

Figure 9-17 Power Options Advanced Settings

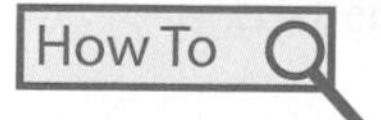

To adjust the power settings for a hard drive, display, or other computer component in Windows, follow these steps:

Step 1. Click **Control Panel > Power Options**

Step 2. Locate the power plan.

Step 3. Click **Change plan settings.**

Step 4. Click **Change advanced power settings.**

Sleep Timers

Customized sleep timer settings for Windows Power Plans are shown in Figure 9-18.

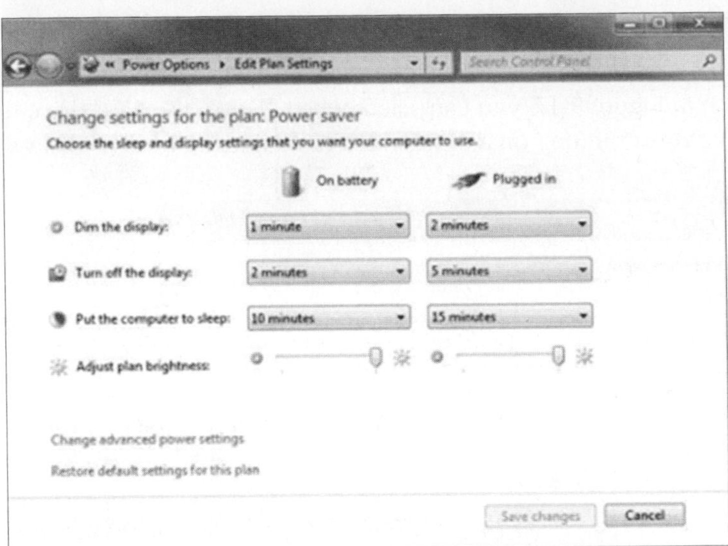

Figure 9-18 Edit Power Plans Settings Windows

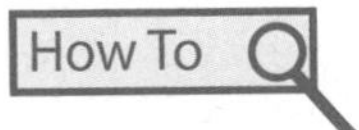

To configure sleep timers, follow these steps:

Step 1. **Click** Control Panel > Power Options.

Step 2. **Click** Change when the computer sleeps **and select the desired time.**

Battery Warnings

The default for a *low-battery warning* is 10 percent remaining capacity. The default for *critical battery level* is 5 percent. You can also set the type of notification and the action to take, such as whether to sleep, hibernate, or shut down the laptop when the battery capacity reaches a specified level.

Wireless Configuration (9.2.2)

A major advantage of a laptop is that it is portable and adding the use of wireless technologies increases the functionality of the laptop in any location. Laptop users can connect to the Internet, wireless peripheral devices, or other laptops through the use of wireless technologies. Most laptops have built-in wireless devices, adding to their flexibility and portability compared to desktop computers. This section takes a look at various wireless technologies available.

Bluetooth (9.2.2.1)

The *Bluetooth* technical specification is described by the Institute of Electrical and Electronics Engineers (IEEE) 802.15.1 standard. Bluetooth devices are capable of handling voice, music, videos, and data.

Table 9-4 shows common Bluetooth characteristics.

Table 9-4 Bluetooth Characteristics

A short-range wireless technology designed to eliminate the need for cables between portable or fixed-configuration devices.
Operates at 2.4 to 2.485 GHz in the unlicensed Industrial, Scientific, and Medical band.
Low power, low cost, and small size.
Uses adaptive frequency hopping.
Version 1.2 operates at up to 1.2 Mbps.
Version 2.0 + Enhanced Data Rate (EDR) operates at up to 3 Mbps.
Version 3.0 + High Speed (HS) operates at up to 24 Mbps.
Version 4.0 + Low Energy (LE) operates at up to 24 Mbps, also called Bluetooth Smart
Version 4.0 has added technology to support products that use very little energy, called Bluetooth low energy (BLE)
Version 4.1 is an update to improve things such as coexistence with mobile wireless service
Version 4.2 added support for technology needed by Internet of Things (IoT) devices

The distance of a Bluetooth personal area network (PAN) is limited by the amount of power used by the devices in the PAN. Bluetooth devices are broken into three classifications, as shown in Table 9-5. The most common Bluetooth network is Class 2, which has a range of approximately 33 feet (10 m).

Table 9-5 Bluetooth Characteristics

Class	Maximum Permitted Power (mW)	Approximate Distance
Class 1	100 mW	~330 feet (100 m)
Class 2	2.5 mW	~33 feet (10 m)
Class 3	1 mW	~3 feet (1 m)

Four specifications of Bluetooth technology define the standards for data transfer rates. Each subsequent version offers enhanced capabilities. For instance, Version 1 is older technology with limited capabilities, and Version 4 features more advanced capabilities.

Table 9-6 shows the four Bluetooth technology specifications that define the standards for data transfer rates.

Table 9-6 Bluetooth Specifications

Specification	Version	Data Transfer Rate
1.0	v1.2	1 Mbps
2.0	v2.0 + EDR	3 Mbps
3.0	v3.0 +HS	24 Mbps
4.0	v4.0 +LE	24 Mbps

Security measures are included in the Bluetooth standard. The first time that a Bluetooth device connects, the device is authenticated using a PIN. This is known as pairing. Bluetooth supports both 128-bit encryption and PIN authentication.

Bluetooth Installation and Configuration

Windows activates connections to Bluetooth devices by default. If the connection is not active, look for a switch on the front face or on the side of the laptop to enable the connection. If a laptop does not feature Bluetooth technology, you can purchase a Bluetooth adapter that plugs into a USB port.

Before installing and configuring a device, make sure that Bluetooth is enabled in the BIOS.

Turn on the device and make it discoverable. Check the device documentation to learn how to make the device discoverable. Use the Bluetooth Wizard to search and discover Bluetooth devices that are in discoverable mode.

How To

To discover a Bluetooth device in Windows 7 and 8, follow these steps:

Step 1. Click **Control Panel > Devices and Printers > Add a device.**

Step 2. Select the discovered device and click **Next.**

Step 3. Enter the pairing code provided by Windows into the Bluetooth device.

Step 4. When the device has been successfully added, click **Close.**

How To

In Windows Vista, follow these steps:

Step 1. Click **Control Panel > Bluetooth Devices > Add a Wireless Device.**

Step 2. Choose the device from the list and click **Next.**

Step 3. If prompted, click **Continue.** The Add Bluetooth Device Wizard starts.

Step 4. Click **My device is set up and ready to be found > Next.**

Step 5. Select the discovered device and click **Next.**

Step 6. If prompted, enter a passkey and click **Finish.**

Cellular WAN (9.2.2.2)

Laptops with integrated *cellular WAN capabilities* require no software installation and no additional antenna or accessories. When you turn on the laptop, the integrated WAN capabilities are ready to use. If the connection is not active, look for a switch on the front face or on the side of the laptop to enable the connection.

Many cell phones provide the ability to connect other devices. This connection, known as *tethering*, can be made using WiFi, Bluetooth, or by using an USB cable. After a device is connected, it is able to use the phone's cellular connection to access the Internet. When a cellular phone allows WiFi devices to connect and use the mobile data network, this is called a *hotspot*.

You can also access a cellular network by using a cellular hotspot device.

WiFi (9.2.2.3)

Laptops usually access the Internet by using *wireless adapters*. Wireless adapters can be built in to the laptop or attached to the laptop through an expansion port. Three major types of wireless adapters are used in laptops, as shown in Figure 9-19.

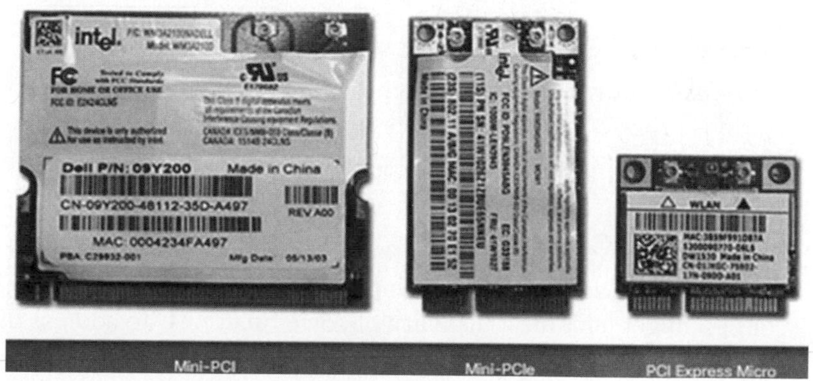

Figure 9-19 Wireless Adapter Types

- *Mini-PCI*—Mini-PCI cards have 124 pins and are capable of 802.11a, 802.11b, and 802.11g wireless LAN connection standards.
- *Mini-PCIe*—Mini-PCIe cards have 54 pins and support the same standards as Mini-PCI with the addition of 802.11n and 802.11ac wireless LAN standards.
- *PCI Express Micro*—Commonly found in newer and smaller laptops, such as Ultrabooks, because they are half the size of Mini-PCIe cards. PCI Express Micro cards have 54 pins and support the same standards ad Mini-PCIe.

How To

To configure wireless settings on a laptop running Windows, follow these steps:

Step 1. Select Control Panel > Network and Sharing Center > Set up a new connection or network.

Step 2. If a connection or network has already been established, click Connect and select the network.

Step 3. Use the Set up a new connection or network wizard to establish the new connection or configure the new network.

Laptop Hardware and Component Installation and Configuration (9.3)

Compactness and portability are two major reasons laptops are so popular. These two factors also cause the limitations in some areas of technology that users want to have available. This section discusses enhancing the functionality of a laptop through the installation and configuration of expansion devices.

Expansion Slots (9.3.1)

Expansion ports are different types of connection ports on a laptop that allow various types of peripheral devices to be connected to the system externally. There are many types, including USB ports and ExpressCard slots.

Expansion Cards (9.3.1.1)

One of the disadvantages of laptops in comparison to desktops is that their compact design might limit the availability of some functions. To address this problem, many laptops contain *ExpressCard slots* to add functionality.

Figure 9-20 shows an example of the two types of ExpressCards.

Figure 9-20 ExpressCards

Table 9-7 shows a comparison of the two ExpressCard models: ExpressCard/34 and ExpressCard/54. The models are 34 mm and 54 mm in width, respectively.

Table 9-7 ExpressCard Specifications

Express Bus	Size	Thickness	Interface	Examples
ExpressCard/34	75 mm × 34 mm	5 mm	PCI Express or USB 2.0 or USB 3.0	FireWire, TV tuner, wireless NIC
ExpressCard/54	75 mm × 54 mm	5 mm	PCI Express or USB 2.0 or USB 3.0	Smart card reader, CompactFlash reader, 1.8-in. disk drive

Here are some examples of functionality that can be added when using ExpressCards:

- Additional memory card reader
- External hard drive access
- TV turner cards
- USB and FireWire ports
- WiFi connectivity

To install a card, insert the card into the slot and push it all the way in. To remove the card, press the eject button to release it.

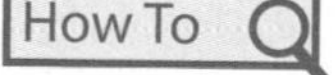

If the ExpressCard is hot-swappable, follow these steps to safely remove it:

Step 1. Click the Safely Remove Hardware icon in the Windows system tray to ensure that the device is not in use.

Step 2. Click the device that you want to remove. A message pops up to tell you that it is safe to remove the device.

Step 3. Remove the hot-swappable device from the laptop.

Caution

ExpressCards and USB devices are commonly ***hot-swappable***. However, removing a device that is not hot-swappable while the computer is powered on can cause damage to data and devices.

Flash Memory (9.3.1.2)

Flash memory uses the same type of nonvolatile memory chips as SSDs and does not require power to maintain the data. It is a popular non-volatile, rewritable storage media. Very durable it is used in many electronic devices including USB drives, cameras, external hard disk drives, and mobile devices. This section discusses various types of flash memory.

External Flash Drive

An *external flash drive* is a removable storage device that connects to an expansion port such as USB, eSATA, or FireWire. External flash drives can be an SSD drive or a smaller device. Flash drives provide fast access to data, high reliability, and reduced power usage. These drives are accessed by the operating system in the same way that other types of drives are accessed. An external flash drive is shown in Figure 9-21.

Figure 9-21 Flash Drive

Flash Cards and Flash Card Readers

A *flash card* is a data storage device that uses flash memory to store information. Flash cards are small, portable, and require no power to maintain data. They are commonly used in laptops, mobile devices, and digital cameras. A large variety of flash card models are available, and each varies in size and shape. Most modern laptops feature a flash card reader for Secure Digital (SD) and Secure Digital High Capacity (SDHC) flash cards, as shown in Figure 9-22.

Figure 9-22 Flash Cards

A *flash card reader* on a laptop is shown in Figure 9-23.

Figure 9-23 Flash Card Reader

Note

Flash memory cards are hot-swappable and should be removed by following the standard procedure for hot-swappable device removal.

Smart Card Reader (9.3.1.3)

A *smart card* is similar to a credit card, but it has an embedded microprocessor that can be loaded with data. It can be used for telephone calling, electronic cash payments, and other applications. The microprocessor on the smart card is there for security, and can hold much more information than that of a magnetic stripe found on a credit card.

Smart cards have been around for more than a decade but were found mostly in Europe. Recently, their popularity has increased in the United States.

Smart card readers are used to read and write to smart cards and can be connected to a laptop using a USB port. There are two types of smart card readers:

- **Contact**—This type of reader requires a physical connection to the card, made by inserting the card into the reader, as shown in the figure.
- **Contactless**—This type of reader works on a radio frequency that communicates when the card comes close to the reader.

Many smart card readers support contact and contactless read operations all in one device.

SODIMM Memory (9.3.1.4)

The make and model of the laptop determines the type of RAM needed. It is important to select the memory type that is physically compatible with the laptop. Most desktop computers use memory that fits into a DIMM slot. Most laptops use a smaller profile memory chip that is called ***small outline dual inline memory module (SODIMM)***. SODIMM has 72-pin and 100-pin configurations for support of 32-bit transfers and 144-pin, 200-pin, and 204-pin configurations for support of 64-bit transfers.

Note

SODIMMs can be further classified as DDR, DDR2, DDR3, and DDR4. Different laptop models require different types of SODIMMs.

Before purchasing and installing additional RAM, consult the laptop documentation or the website of the manufacturer for form-factor specifications. Use the documentation to find where to install RAM on the laptop. On most laptops, RAM is inserted into slots behind a cover on the underside of the case. On some laptops, the keyboard must be removed to access the RAM slots. As shown in Figure 9-24, SODIMM is installed into the underside of the case.

Figure 9-24 SODIMM Installed in a Laptop

Consult the manufacturer of the laptop to confirm the maximum amount of RAM each slot can support. You can view the currently installed amount of RAM in the POST screen, BIOS, or System Properties window.

Figure 9-25 shows where the amount of RAM is displayed in the System utility.

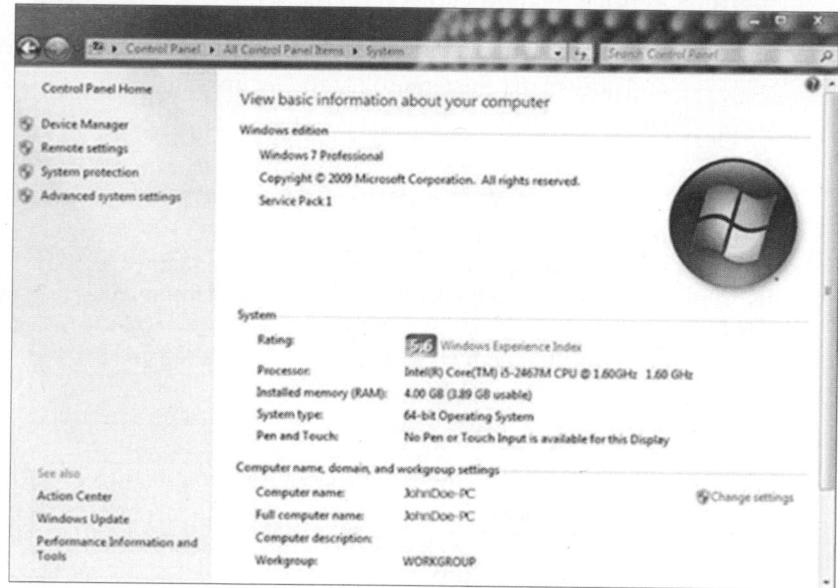

Figure 9-25 RAM Information in the System Utility

To replace or add memory, determine if the laptop has available slots and that it supports the quantity and type of memory to be added. In some instances, there are no available slots for the new SODIMM.

How To

To remove the existing SODIMM, follow these steps:

Step 1. Remove the AC adapter and battery from the laptop.

Step 2. Remove the screws on the cover above the memory socket to expose the module.

Step 3. Press outward on the clips that hold the sides of the module.

Step 4. Lift up to loosen the module from the slot and remove it.

How To

To install a SODIMM, follow these steps:

Step 1. Remove the AC adapter and battery from the laptop.

Step 2. Remove the screws on the cover above the memory socket to expose the module.

Step 3. Align the notch of the memory module at a 45-degree angle and gently press it into the socket.

Step 4. Gently press down on the memory module into the socket until the clips lock.

Step 5. Replace the cover and install the screws.

Step 6. Insert the battery and connect the AC adapter. Turn the computer on and access the System utility to ensure that the RAM has been identified successfully.

Note

Throughout this chapter, steps are provided for replacing laptop hardware with a specific make and model of laptop. There are many different models of laptops. Not all laptops have the same steps for hardware replacement. Consult the laptop repair manual before replacing any hardware.

Lab—Research Laptop RAM (9.3.1.5)

In this lab, you use the Internet, newspaper, or a local store to gather information about expansion memory for a laptop. Refer to the lab in *IT Essentials v6 Lab Manual*.

Replacing Hardware Devices (9.3.2)

Some components of a laptop might need to be replaced. Always remember to make sure that you have the correct replacement component and tools as recommended by the manufacturer.

Overview of Hardware Replacement (9.3.2.1)

Some parts of a laptop, typically called *customer-replaceable units (CRUs)*, can be replaced by the customer. CRUs include such components as the laptop battery and RAM. Parts that should not be replaced by the customer are called *field-replaceable units (FRUs)*.

FRUs include components such as the motherboard, LCD display, as shown in Figure 9-26.

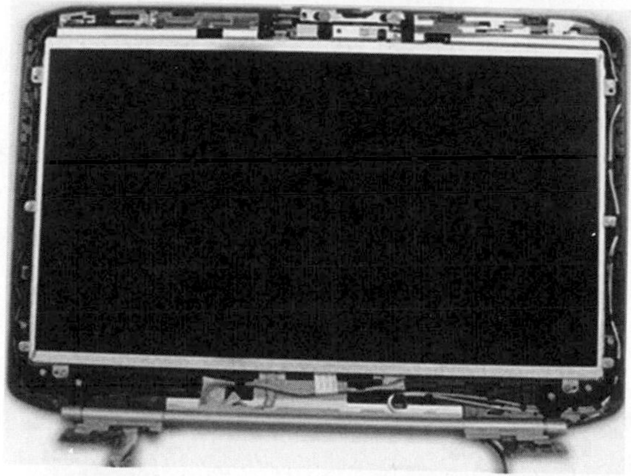

Figure 9-26 Laptop Display Screen

Another component considered a FRU is a keyboard, as shown in Figure 9-27.

Figure 9-27 Removing the Laptop Keyboard

Replacing FRUs typically requires a considerable amount of technical skill. In many cases, the device may need to be returned to the place of purchase, a certified service center, or the manufacturer.

A repair center might provide service on laptops made by different manufacturers or just specialize in a specific brand and be considered an authorized dealer for warranty work and repair. The following are common repairs performed at local repair centers:

- Hardware and software diagnostics
- Data transfer and recovery
- Keyboard and fan replacement

- Internal laptop cleaning
- Screen repair
- LCD inverter and backlight repair

Most repairs to displays must be performed in a repair center. The repairs include replacing the screen, the backlight, or the inverter.

If no local services are available, you might need to send the laptop to a regional repair center or to the manufacturer. If the laptop damage is severe or requires specialized software and tools, the manufacturer can decide to replace the laptop instead of attempting a repair.

Caution

Before attempting to repair a laptop or portable device, check the warranty to see if repairs during the warranty period must be done at an authorized service center to avoid invalidating the warranty. If you repair a laptop yourself, always back up the data and disconnect the device from the power source. Always consult the service manual before beginning a laptop repair.

Power (9.3.2.2)

These are some signs that the battery may need to be replaced:

- The battery does not hold a charge.
- The battery overheats.
- The battery is leaking.

If you experience problems that you suspect are battery-related exchange the battery with a known good battery that is compatible with the laptop. If a replacement battery cannot be located take the battery to an authorized repair center for testing.

A replacement battery must meet or exceed the specifications of the laptop manufacturer. New batteries must use the same form factor as the original battery. Voltages, power ratings, and AC adapters must also meet manufacturer specifications.

Note

Always follow the instructions provided by the manufacturer when charging a new battery. The laptop can be used during an initial charge, but do not unplug the AC adapter.

Caution

Handle batteries with care. Batteries can explode if they are shorted, mishandled, or improperly charged. Be sure that the battery charger is designed for the chemistry, size, and voltage of your battery. Batteries are considered toxic waste and must be disposed of according to local laws.

Replacing a Battery

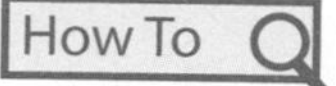

To remove and install a battery, follow these steps:

Step 1. Power off the laptop and disconnect the AC adapter.

Step 2. Remove the cover for the battery, if needed.

Step 3. Move the battery lock to the unlocked position.

Step 4. Hold the release lever in the unlock position and remove the battery.

Step 5. Ensure that the battery contacts inside of the laptop and on the battery are clear of dirt and corrosion.

Step 6. Insert the new battery.

Step 7. Make sure that both battery levers are locked.

Step 8. Reinstall the cover for the battery, if needed.

Step 9. Connect the AC adapter to the laptop and power on the computer.

Replacing a DC Jack

A *DC jack* receives power from a laptop's AC/DC power converter and supplies the power to the motherboard.

If your DC jack is replaceable, follow these steps:

Step 1. Power off the laptop and disconnect the AC adapter.

Step 2. Remove the battery.

Step 3. Unfasten the DC jack from the case.

Step 4. Unfasten the power cable that is attached to the DC jack.

Step 5. Disconnect the power cable connector from the motherboard and remove the DC jack from the case.

Step 6. Connect the power cable connector to the motherboard.

Step 7. Secure the power cables that are attached to the new DC jack to the case.

Step 8. Secure the DC jack to the case.

Step 9. Insert the battery.

Step 10. Connect the AC adapter to the laptop and power on the computer.

A laptop DC jack is shown in Figure 9-28.

Figure 9-28 DC Jack

Note

If the DC jack is soldered onto the motherboard, the jack will need to be replaced by someone who knows how to properly use a soldering iron, or the motherboard should be replaced according to the manufacturer of the laptop.

Lab—Research Laptop Batteries (9.3.2.3)

In this lab, you use the Internet, newspaper, or a local store to gather information and then record the specifications for a laptop battery. Refer to the lab in *IT Essentials v6 Lab Manual*.

Keyboard, Touchpad, and Screen (9.3.2.4)

The keyboard and *touchpad* are input devices considered to be FRUs. Replacing a keyboard or touchpad typically requires removing the plastic casing that covers the inside of a laptop, as shown in Figure 9-29. In some instances, a touchpad is attached to the plastic casing.

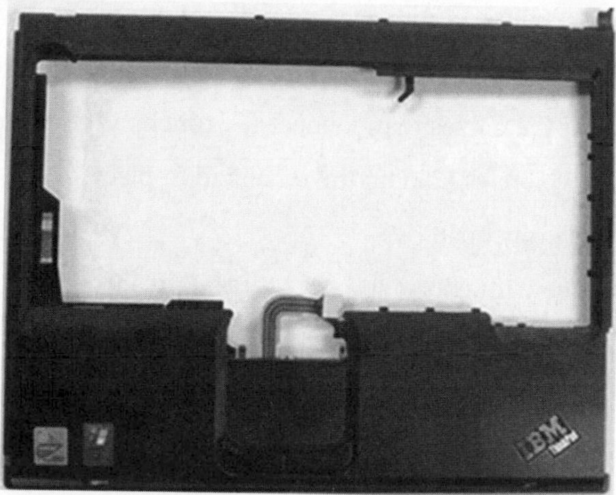

Figure 9-29 Plastic Casing Surrounding a Laptop Keyboard

Replacing a Keyboard

How To

To remove and replace a keyboard, follow these steps:

Step 1. Power off the laptop, disconnect the AC adapter, and remove the battery.

Step 2. Open the laptop.

Step 3. Remove any screws holding the keyboard in place.

Step 4. Remove any plastics holding the keyboard in place.

Step 5. Lift up the keyboard and detach the keyboard cable from the motherboard.

Step 6. Remove the keyboard.

Step 7. Plug the new keyboard cable into the motherboard.

Step 8. Insert the keyboard and attach any plastics that hold the keyboard in place.

Step 9. Replace all necessary screws to secure the keyboard.

Step 10. Close the screen and turn the laptop over.

Step 11. Connect the AC adapter to the laptop and power on the computer.

Replacing a Touchpad

How To

Be sure to power off the laptop, disconnect the AC adapter, and remove the battery before beginning to remove and replace a touchpad, as shown in Figure 9-30. Follow these steps to remove and replace a touchpad:

Step 1. If the touchpad is attached to the laptop casing, remove the casing. If it is a separate component, remove all devices that block access to the touchpad.

Step 2. Close the screen and turn the computer over.

Step 3. Remove the bottom casing of the laptop.

Step 4. Disconnect the cables that connect the touchpad to the motherboard.

Step 5. Remove the screws holding the touchpad in place.

Step 6. Remove the touchpad.

Step 7. Insert the new touchpad and fasten it to the laptop casing.

Step 8. Replace the screws to hold the touchpad in place.

Step 9. Connect the cables from the touchpad to the motherboard.

Step 10. Replace the bottom casing of the laptop.

Step 11. Turn over the laptop and open the screen.

Step 12. Turn on the laptop and ensure that the touchpad is working correctly.

Figure 9-30 shows disconnecting the cables that connect the touchpad to the motherboard.

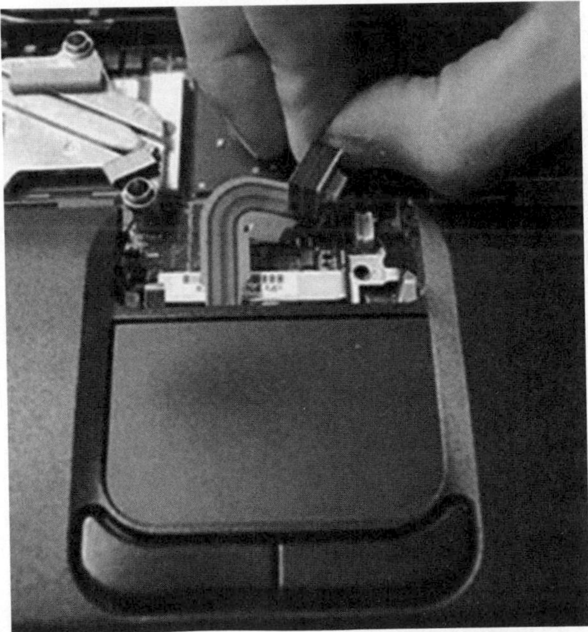

Figure 9-30 Touchpad Attached to Plastic Casing

Replacing a Screen

A laptop's display screen is often the most expensive component to replace. Unfortunately, it is also one of the most susceptible to damage.

How To

To replace a screen, follow these steps:

Step 1. Remove the AC adapter and battery from the laptop.

Step 2. Remove the top part of the laptop case and the keyboard.

Step 3. Disconnect the display cable from the motherboard.

Step 4. Remove any screws securing the display to the laptop frame.

Step 5. Detach the display assembly from the laptop frame.

Step 6. Insert the display assembly into the laptop frame.

Step 7. Secure the display assembly by replacing the screws.

Step 8. Connect the display cable to the motherboard.

Step 9. Reattach the keyboard and the top part of the laptop case.

Step 10. Insert the battery and connect the AC adapter. Turn the computer on to check that the new display is working.

Lab—Research Laptop Screens (9.3.2.5)

In this activity, you use the Internet, newspaper, or a local store to gather information and then record the specifications for a laptop display onto this worksheet. Refer to the lab in *IT Essentials v6 Lab Manual*.

Internal Storage Drive and Optical Drive (9.3.2.6)

The form factor of an internal storage device is smaller for a laptop than for a desktop computer. Laptop drives are 1.8 in. (4.57 cm) or 2.5 in. (6.35 cm) in width. Most storage devices are CRUs, unless a warranty requires technical assistance.

Before purchasing a new internal or external storage device, check the laptop documentation or the website of the manufacturer for compatibility requirements. Documentation often contains FAQs that may be helpful. It is also important to research known laptop component issues on the Internet.

On most laptops, the internal hard drive and the internal optical drive are connected behind a cover on the underside of the case. On some laptops, the keyboard must be removed to access these drives. Optical drives might not be interchangeable in the laptop. Some laptops may not include optical drives at all.

To view the currently installed storage devices, check the POST screen or BIOS. If installing a second drive or an optical drive, confirm that there are no error icons next to the device in the Device Manager.

Replacing a Hard Drive

To remove and replace a hard drive, follow these steps:

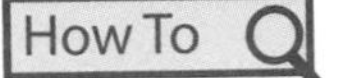

Step 1. Power off the laptop, disconnect the AC adapter, and remove the battery.

Step 2. On the bottom of the laptop, remove the screw that holds the hard drive in place.

Step 3. Slide the assembly outward.

Step 4. Remove the hard drive faceplate from the hard drive.

Step 5. Attach the hard drive faceplate to the new hard drive.

Step 6. Slide the hard drive into the hard drive bay.

Step 7. On the bottom of the laptop, install the screw that holds the hard drive in place.

Step 8. Insert the battery, connect the AC adapter to the laptop, and power on the computer.

Replacing an Optical Drive

To remove and replace an optical drive, follow these steps:

Step 1. Power off the laptop, disconnect the AC adapter, and remove the battery.

Step 2. Press the button to open the drive and remove any media in the drive. Close the tray.

Step 3. On the bottom of the laptop remove the screws that hold the optical drive in place.

Step 4. Slide the latch to release the lever that secures the drive.

Step 5. Pull on the lever to expose the drive then remove the drive.

Step 6. Insert the new drive securely.

Step 7. Push the lever inward.

Step 8. Replace the screw that holds the optical drive in place.

Step 9. Insert the battery, connect the AC adapter to the laptop and power on the computer.

Lab—Research Laptop Hard Drives (9.3.2.7)

In this lab, you use the Internet, newspaper, or a local store to gather information about hard drives for a laptop. Refer to the lab in *IT Essentials v6 Lab Manual*.

Wireless Card (9.3.2.8)

Before replacing a wireless card, determine which form factor is required by the laptop by checking the label on the wireless card or the laptop documentation.

To remove and install a wireless card, follow these steps:

How To

Step 1. Power off the laptop, disconnect the AC adapter, and remove the battery.

Step 2. Locate the wireless card compartment on the bottom of the computer.

Step 3. Remove the cover if needed.

Step 4. Disconnect all wires and remove any screws holding the wireless card in place.

Step 5. Slide the wireless card out of the compartment and remove it.

Step 6. Slide the new wireless card into its compartment.

Step 7. Connect all wires and replace any screws holding the wireless card in place.

Step 8. Replace the cover if needed, including any screws holding it into place.

Step 9. Insert the battery, connect the AC adapter to the laptop, and power on the computer.

Figure 9-31 shows removing a wireless card.

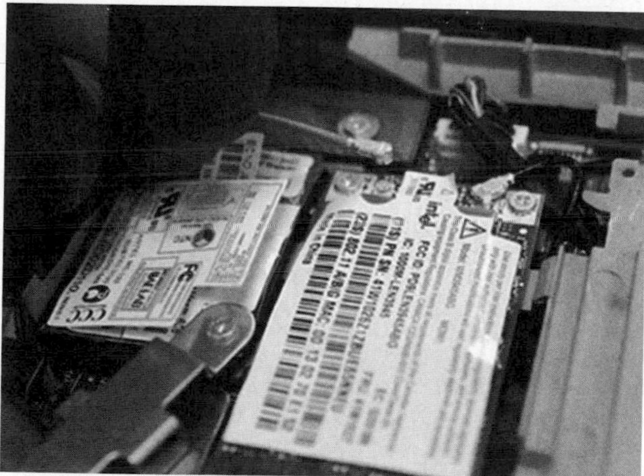

Figure 9-31 Removing a Wireless Card

Speakers (9.3.2.9)

Before replacing laptop speakers, check that the volume is not muted by increasing volume or unmuting the sound.

To remove and replace the speaker unit, follow these steps:

Step 1. Power off the computer and then disconnect the AC adapter.

Step 2. Remove the battery and any other components recommended by the manufacturer, including the keyboard or top casing.

Step 3. Disconnect any cables connecting the laptop to the motherboard.

Step 4. Remove any screws securing the speakers to the laptop frame.

Step 5. Remove the speakers.

Step 6. Insert the new speakers.

Step 7. Tighten all screws to secure the speakers to the laptop frame.

Step 8. Connect any cables connecting the laptop to the motherboard.

Step 9. Insert the battery, along with all other components that were removed.

Step 10. Connect the AC adapter and power on the computer to check for functionality.

CPU (9.3.2.10)

Before a CPU can be replaced, a technician must remove the fan or heat sink. Fans and heat sinks might be joined together as a single module or installed as separate units. If the fan and heat sink are separate, remove both components individually.

To replace a CPU with a separate fan and heat sink, follow these steps:

Step 1. Power off the computer and disconnect the AC adapter.

Step 2. Remove the battery.

Step 3. Turn the laptop over, if necessary, and remove any plastics covering the fan.

Step 4. Locate the fan and remove any screws holding the fan in place.

Step 5. Disconnect the power cable connecting the fan to the motherboard.

Step 6. Remove the fan from the laptop.

Step 7. Remove the heat sink from the CPU by removing any screws holding it in place.

Step 8. Remove the screw that locks the latch holding the CPU in the socket.

Step 9. Open the latch and remove the CPU from the socket.

Step 10. Remove any thermal paste from the CPU and store the CPU in an anti-static bag.

Step 11. Gently place the new CPU into the socket.

Step 12. Fasten the latch that holds the CPU in place and tighten the screws holding it down.

Step 13. Apply thermal paste to the CPU before replacing the heat sink.

Step 14. Insert the heat sink and replace all necessary screws.

Step 15. Insert the fan and connect the power cable to the motherboard.

Step 16. Fasten the fan to the motherboard by replacing all necessary screws.

Step 17. Replace the base cover of the laptop.

Step 18. Insert the battery and replace all necessary components.

If the fan and heat sink are joined together, use the following procedure.

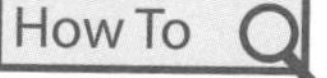

To remove and replace a CPU and heat sink assembly, follow these steps:

Step 1. Power off the computer and disconnect the AC adapter.

Step 2. Remove the battery.

Step 3. Turn the laptop over, if necessary, and remove any plastics covering the heat sink.

Step 4. Locate the heat sink or fan and heat sink assembly and remove any screws holding it in place.

Step 5. Disconnect the fan power cable from the motherboard.

Step 6. Remove the heat sink or fan and heat sink assembly.

Step 7. Remove the screw that locks the latch holding the CPU in the socket.

Step 8. Open the latch and remove the CPU from the socket.

Step 9. Remove any thermal paste from the CPU and store the CPU in an anti-static bag.

Step 10. Gently place the new CPU into the socket.

Step 11. Fasten the latch that holds the CPU in place and tighten the screws holding it down.

Step 12. Apply thermal paste to the CPU before replacing the heat sink.

Step 13. Insert the heat sink or fan and heat sink assembly and connect the power cable to the motherboard.

Step 14. Fasten the heat sink or fan and heat sink assembly to the system frame by replacing all necessary screws.

Step 15. Replace the base cover of the laptop.

Step 16. Insert the battery and replace all necessary components.

Note

A CPU is one of the most fragile components in a laptop. It should be handled with great care.

Note

It is important to note how the CPU is positioned. The replacement must be installed the same way.

Motherboard (9.3.2.11)

Replacing the motherboard in a laptop normally requires a technician to remove all other components from a laptop. Before replacing a laptop motherboard, make sure that the replacement meets the design specifications of the laptop model.

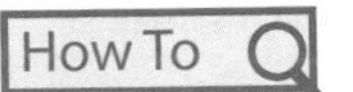

To remove and replace the motherboard, follow these steps:

Step 1. Power off the computer and disconnect the AC adapter.

Step 2. Remove the battery.

Step 3. Detach the DC jack from the laptop casing. Unclip the power cable from the case and disconnect it from the motherboard.

Step 4. Remove any remaining screws connecting the motherboard to the case.

Step 5. Remove the motherboard.

Step 6. Attach the new motherboard to the laptop casing. Tighten any necessary screws.

Step 7. Attach the DC jack to the laptop casing, clip the power cable to the case, and connect it to the motherboard.

Step 8. Replace any removed components.

Step 9. Insert the battery, connect the AC adapter, and power on the computer to ensure that the system is functioning.

Plastic Frames (9.3.2.12)

The exterior of a laptop is typically comprised of multiple plastic parts. This includes the plastic parts that are responsible for covering the memory, wireless card, and hard drive, as well as the casing that surrounds the touchpad and keyboard.

How To

To remove and replace the plastics, follow these steps:

Step 1. Disconnect the AC adapter and remove the battery.

Step 2. Adjust the positioning of the laptop so that the desired plastic component is facing upward.

Step 3. Unscrew the desired plastic component, or pry it off gently using the technique suggested by the manufacturer.

Step 4. Attach the new plastic component and replace all necessary screws, or insert and fasten the component.

Step 5. Insert the battery and connect the AC adapter.

Video

Video—Replace Laptop Components (9.3.2.13)

This video shows how to replace many of the components of a laptop. In it there is a demonstration of how to remove RAM memory modules as well as how to remove and replace your laptop hard drive from a laptop. It will remind you that first thing that you're going to want to do is go to your laptop manufacturer's website and download the maintenance manual for your particular make and model of laptop. You will also learn about the tool that should be on hand such as Phillips-head screwdrivers, a flathead screwdriver, a set of torques wrenches, an anti-static wrist strap, reading glasses with 200 percent zoom to zoom in small characters, screws, and documentation on the motherboard, as well as possibly needing a flashlight in case there's not enough light. After powering down the laptop the process of following the manufacturer's documentation to remove all the necessary components to reach the RAM and hard drive are demonstrated.

Go to the online course to view this video.

Lab—Research Building a Specialized Laptop (9.3.2.14)

In this lab, you use the Internet, a newspaper, or a local store to gather information about building a specialized laptop that supports hardware and software that allows a user to perform tasks that an off-the-shelf system cannot perform. Refer to the lab in *IT Essentials v6 Lab Manual*.

Mobile Device Hardware Overview (9.4)

With the increase in demand for mobility the popularity of mobile devices continues to grow. Like a laptop, mobile devices use an operating system to run applications (apps) and games and play movies and music. Android and iOS are examples of mobile device operating systems.

Mobile Device Hardware (9.4.1)

Although mobile devices have similar hardware to desktops and laptops, there are many important differences. Hardware in a mobile device usually is not repaired by the field technician, but some parts may be replaceable.

Mobile Device Parts (9.4.1.1)

Unlike laptops, mobile devices, such as smartphone and tablets, are typically small enough to be handheld. A *smartphone* can be carried in a pocket. A *tablet* can be carried in a purse or small backpack. Because of their small size, mobile devices usually do not have *field-serviceable parts*. Mobile devices consist of several compact components integrated into a single unit. When a mobile device malfunctions, it is usually sent to the manufacturer for repair or replacement.

There are parts and instructions available from many websites for replacing broken mobile device parts, including touchscreens, front or back glass, and batteries. Installing parts from sources other than the manufacturer voids the manufacturer's warranty and might harm the device. For example, if a replacement battery is installed that does not meet the exact electrical specification for the phone the phone could short out or overload, becoming unusable.

Some mobile devices might have one or more of the following field-replaceable parts:

- **Battery**—Some mobile device batteries can be replaced.
- *Memory card*—Many mobile devices use memory cards to add storage.
- *Subscriber identity module (SIM) card*—This small card contains information used to authenticate a device to mobile telephone and data providers. SIM cards can also hold user data such as contacts and text messages.

Non-Upgradeable Hardware (9.4.1.2)

Mobile device hardware is typically not upgradeable. The design and dimensions of the internal hardware do not allow for replacement with upgraded hardware. Many of the components in a mobile device are connected directly to circuit boards, which cannot be replaced with upgraded components. For example, an *embedded MultiMediaCard (eMMC)* is flash memory that is a component of the circuit board. The eMMC is used as main storage for most mobile devices.

Batteries and removable memory cards, however, can often be replaced with items that have larger capacities. This might not increase the speed or capability of the mobile device, but it does allow for longer run times between charges or increased storage capacity for data.

Some functionality can be added to mobile devices through the use of built-in ports and docking stations. These connections offer expandability, such as video or audio output, a connection to a docking station, or docking to a clock radio. Some smartphones can even be docked to a device with a keyboard, track pad, and monitor to create a version of a laptop. There are also tablet cases that have a keyboard on the inside.

When a mobile device no longer possesses the capabilities or operates at the speeds required by the user, it must be replaced. Often, old mobile devices can be traded in for credit when purchasing a new one. The items are refurbished and resold or donated. Basic mobile devices can be donated to be reused when they cannot be traded in. Check for local donation programs in your area to find where these devices can be taken.

Touchscreens (9.4.1.3)

Most mobile devices do not have a keyboard or a pointing device. They use *touchscreens* to allow users to physically interact with what is shown on the screen and type on a virtual keyboard. Fingers or a stylus are used in place of a mouse pointer. Icons, like those found on desktops and laptops, are clicked with a touch rather than a mouse button. Mobile device manufacturers use the word tap or touch when describing operations and steps when using a mobile device. You will see both of these terms in instruction manuals, and they mean the same thing. This course uses the term touch.

In addition to a single touch, mobile devices have the ability to recognize when two or more points of contact are made on the screen. This is called *multi-touch*. These are some common finger movements, called *gestures*, used to perform functions:

- *Slide or swipe*—Move between screens horizontally or vertically. Touch the screen, slide your finger quickly in the direction you want to move the screen and let go.
- *Double touch*—Zoom items such as photographs, maps, and text. Touch the screen twice quickly to zoom in. Touch the screen twice quickly again to zoom out.
- *Long touch*—Select items, such as text, icons, or photos. Touch and hold the screen until options become available for the item you are touching.
- *Scroll*—Scroll items that are too large for the screen, such as photos or web pages. Touch and hold the screen, moving your finger in the direction you want to move the item. Lift your finger when you reach the area of the screen you want to see.

- *Pinch*—Zoom out from objects, such as photographs, maps, and text. Touch the screen with two fingers and pinch them together to zoom out from the object.
- *Spread*—Zoom in on objects, such as photographs, maps, and text. Touch the screen with two fingers and spread them apart to zoom in on the object.

These gestures may be different between devices. Many other gestures can also be used, depending on the device and operating system version. Check the device documentation for additional information.

Some smartphones have a *proximity sensor* that turns off the touchscreen when the phone is up to your ear and turns it on when you pull the device away from your ear. This prevents functions from being activated by contact with your face or ear, and also saves power.

Solid State Drives (9.4.1.4)

Mobile devices use the same components found in solid state drives (SSDs) to store data. To reduce the size requirements, there is no case surrounding the components as shown in Figure 9-32. The circuit board, flash memory chips, such as eMMC, and memory controller in SSDs are installed directly inside the mobile device.

Figure 9-32 SSD Board

These are some of the advantages of using flash memory storage in mobile devices:

- **Power efficiency**—Flash memory requires very little power to store and retrieve data. This reduces the frequency with which mobile devices need to be recharged.
- **Reliability**—Flash memory can withstand high levels of shock and vibration without failing. Flash memory is also highly resistant to heat and cold.
- **Lightweight**—The weight of mobile devices is not significantly affected by the amount of memory installed.

- **Compact**—Because flash memory is compact, mobile devices can remain small regardless of the amount of memory installed.
- **Performance**—Flash memory does not have any moving parts, so there is no spin-up time for platters like a conventional hard drive. There is also no drive head to move, reducing the seek time to locate data.
- **Noise**—Flash memory makes no noise.

Connection Types (9.4.1.5)

Mobile devices can connect to other devices to use shared peripherals or other resources. They can be wired or wireless connections.

Wired Connections

- *Micro/Mini universal serial bus (USB)* **connectors**—These USB connectors can charge a device and transfer data between devices.
- *Lightning connector*—allows Apple mobile devices to connect to host computers and other peripherals, such as USB battery chargers, monitors, and cameras.
- *Proprietary vendor specific ports*—Proprietary vendor specific ports can be found on some mobile devices. These ports are not compatible with other vendors, but often compatibles with other products from the same vendor. These ports are used to charge the device and communicate with other devices.

Examples of wired connections are shown in Figure 9-33.

Figure 9-33 Wired connections

Wireless Connections

Besides WiFi, mobile devices also use the following wireless connections:

- *Near field communication (NFC)*—NFC enables mobile devices to establish radio communications with other devices by placing the devices close together or by touching them together.
- *Infrared (IR)*—If a mobile device is IR enabled, it can be used to control other IR controlled devices remotely, such as a TV, set top box, or audio equipment.
- **Bluetooth**—This wireless technology allows data exchange over a short distance between two Bluetooth-enabled devices or connect to other Bluetooth-enabled peripheral devices, such as speakers or headphones.

Shared Internet Connections

A smartphone's Internet connection can be shared with other devices. There are two ways to share the smartphone's Internet connection: tethering and mobile hotspot. The ability to share the connection depends on the cellular carrier and the plan with the carrier.

- *Tether*—This uses your cellular phone as a modem for another device, such as a tablet or laptop. The connection is made over a USB cable or Bluetooth.
- *Mobile hotspot*—A hotspot is where devices connect using WiFi to share a cellular data connection.

Packet Tracer
☐ Activity

Activity—Identify Connection Types (9.4.1.6)

Go to the online course to perform this practice activity.

Accessories (9.4.1.7)

Mobile device accessories are not necessary for the functions of the devices as intended by the manufacturer. However, accessories can enhance the user's experience. The accessories, except for protective covers, can be connected to the laptops and mobile devices via wired or wireless technologies.

Protective covers

Mobile devices are portable electronic devices. Cases and protective covers can protect these devices from physical damage during travel or use. Furthermore, some protective covers also provide protection from water damage.

Power sources

- **External batteries/portable chargers**—While you're on the go, the external batteries can provide the extra power for mobile devices. Portable chargers, such as wireless QI, pronounced *key*, chargers, solar chargers, and car chargers, can replenish power.
- *Docking stations*—These allow mobile devices to easily connect to other devices. Most docking stations will also act as a charger while the mobile device is connected. Some docking stations also have speakers or keyboards.

Some examples of power sources are shown in Figure 9-34.

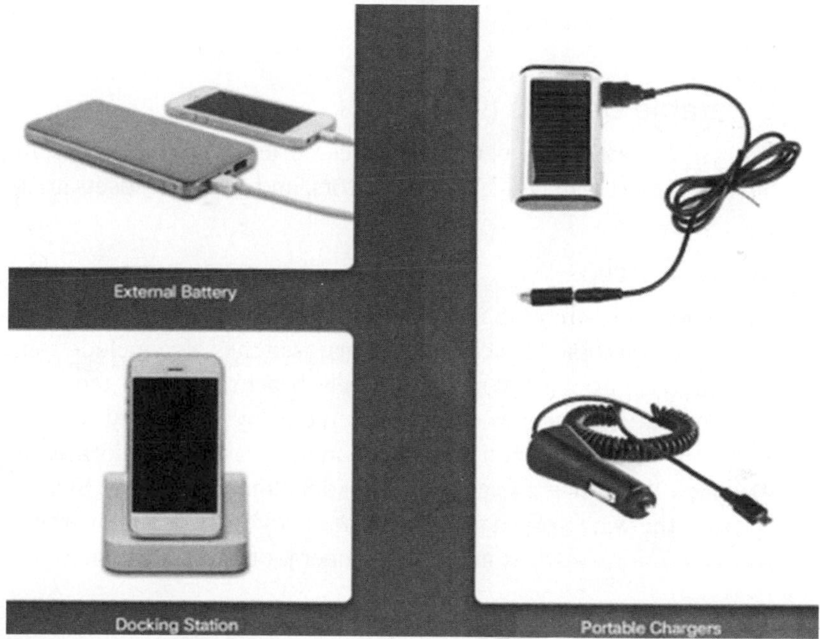

Figure 9-34 Power Sources

There are mobile device cases that contain an external battery. These cases make the device larger and heavier when the case is attached, but the battery life of the device is increased and an external battery or portable charge is no longer necessary.

Audio Accessories

- **Headsets/ear buds**—These allow a user to listen to audio output privately. If the headset or ear buds have a microphone, the user can have phone conversation while keeping their hands free. Both wireless and wired connections are available.
- **Speakers**—These speakers can come in different colors, shapes, and sizes. Speakers can also be wireless or wired.

Other

- **Credit card readers**—People can use their smartphones with credit card readers to accept credit card payments from anyone.
- **Game pad**—These are peripheral devices used for playing video games.
- **Memory/MicroSD**—Like a laptop, built-in memory card readers increase storage capacity.

Other Mobile Devices (9.4.2)

Types of mobile devices are growing and changing. Although the number of different types of devices is growing, the size of some devices are shrinking.

Wearable Devices (9.4.2.1)

Wearable devices are clothing or accessories that have miniature computing devices. Smart watches, fitness monitors, and smart headsets are some examples.

Smart Watches

Smart watches are watches that combine the functions of a watch and some functions of mobile devices. Some smartwatches also include sensors to measure body and environmental metrics such as heart rate, body temperature, elevation, or air temperature. They have touchscreen displays, and they can function on their own or paired with smartphones. These watches can display notifications of incoming messages, incoming phone calls, and social media updates. Smartwatches can run apps on the watch or via a smartphone. They may also allow the users to control some functions, such as music and camera, on a smartphone.

Fitness Monitors

Fitness monitors are designed to clip onto clothing or be worn on the wrist. They are used for tracking a person's daily activity and body metrics as they work toward their fitness goals. These devices measure and collect activity data. They can also connect with other Internet-connected devices to upload the data for later review. Some fitness monitors may also have basic smartwatch capabilities, such as displaying caller ID and text messages.

Smart Headsets

Smart headsets are designed to be worn like a pair of eyeglasses. The headset has a small screen built into the frame or projected onto glass. The headset is often connected to a smartphone for network connectivity. Functions might be controlled by a touchpad on the side or voice commands. These devices have many of the same functions as smartphones. A user can see notifications, read emails, get directions, or take calls via the headset rather than on a smartphone. The display is always visible to the wearer; all they have to do is focus on it.

Specialty Devices (9.4.2.2)

There are many other types of smart devices. These devices benefit from network connectivity and advanced functions.

Global Positioning System

Global positioning system (GPS) is a satellite-based navigation system. GPS satellites are located in space and transmit signals back to Earth. The GPS receiver locks onto the signals and constantly calculates its position relative to these satellites. After the position has been determined, the GPS receiver calculates other information, such as speed and time and distance to a programmed destination.

Smart Cameras

A *smart camera* allows images to be transferred onto a PC using built-in wireless connections. Furthermore, with WiFi enabled, the images can be shared on social media, emailed, or transferred to cloud-based storage directly from the camera.

Some smart cameras can connect to other smart devices to add functionality. When the smart camera is connected to a smartphone, the smartphone controls some features on the camera such as remote control or displaying pictures on the smartphone from the camera. The smart camera can also connect to a smart TV to display images.

Electronic Readers

An *electronic reader*, or *e-reader*, is a device optimized for reading electronic books, e-books, newspapers, and other documents. They have WiFi or cellular connectivity to download content. An e-reader has a similar form factor as a tablet, but the screen provides much better readability, especially in sunlight. E-readers are often lighter weight and have longer battery life than an average tablet. This is done by using electronic paper technology. This technology makes text and images look similar to ink on paper.

Phablets

A *phablet* is a mobile device with a size between a typical smartphone and a typical tablet. The phablet screen is about 5 to 7 in. (12.7 cm to 17.8 cm) measured diagonally. A phablet offers the portability and functionality of a smartphone with a larger screen.

Common Preventive Maintenance Techniques for Laptops and Mobile Devices (9.5)

Preventive maintenance should be scheduled at regular intervals to keep laptops and mobile devices running properly. It is important to keep them clean and to ensure that it is being used an optimal environment. The following section covers preventive maintenance techniques for the laptops and mobile devices.

Scheduled Maintenance for Laptops and Mobile Devices (9.5.1)

The preventive maintenance schedule for a laptop may include practices that are unique to a particular organization, but should also include these standard procedures: cleaning, hard drive maintenance, and software updates.

Preventative maintenance for mobile devices requires only three basic tasks: cleaning, backing up data and keeping the operating system and applications up to date.

Scheduling Maintenance (9.5.1.1)

Because laptops and mobile devices are portable, they are used in different types of environments. As a result, they are more likely than desktop computers to be exposed to these harmful materials and situations:

- Dirt and contamination
- Spills
- Drops
- Excessive heat or cold
- Excessive moisture

In a laptop, many components are placed in a very small area directly beneath the keyboard. Spilling liquid onto the keyboard can result in severe internal damage. It is important to keep a laptop clean. Proper care and maintenance can help laptop components run more efficiently and extend the life of the equipment.

Laptop Preventive Maintenance Program

A preventive maintenance program is important in addressing such issues and must include a routine schedule for maintenance. Most organizations have a preventive maintenance schedule in place. If a schedule does not exist, work with the manager to create one. The most effective preventive maintenance programs require a set of routines to be conducted monthly, but still allow for maintenance to be performed when usage demands it.

The preventive maintenance schedule for a laptop may include practices that are unique to a particular organization, but should also include these standard procedures:

- Cleaning
- Hard drive maintenance
- Software updates

To keep a laptop clean, be proactive, not reactive. Keep fluids and food away from the laptop. Close the laptop when it is not in use. When cleaning a laptop, never use harsh cleaners or solutions that contain ammonia. These are some nonabrasive materials for cleaning a laptop:

- Compressed air
- Mild cleaning solution
- Cotton swabs
- Soft, lint-free cleaning cloth

Caution

Before you clean a laptop, disconnect it from all power sources and remove the battery.

Routine maintenance includes the monthly cleaning of these laptop components:

- **Exterior case**—Wipe the case with a soft, lint-free cloth that is lightly moistened with water or mild cleaning solution.
- **Cooling vents and I/O ports**—Use compressed air or a non-electrostatic vacuum to clean out the dust from the vents and from the fan behind the vent. Use tweezers to remove any debris.
- **Display**—Wipe the display with a soft, lint-free cloth that is lightly moistened with a computer-screen cleaner.
- **Keyboard**—Wipe the keyboard with a soft, lint-free cloth that is lightly moistened with water or mild cleaning solution.
- **Touchpad**—Wipe the surface of the touchpad gently with a soft, lint-free cloth that is moistened with an approved cleaner. Never use a wet cloth.

Note

If it is obvious that the laptop needs to be cleaned, clean it. Do not wait for the next scheduled maintenance.

Mobile Device Preventive Maintenance Program

Mobile devices are often carried in pockets or purses. They can be damaged by drops, excess moisture, heat, or cold. Although mobile device screens are designed to prevent light scratching, the touchscreen should be protected using a screen protector if possible.

Preventative maintenance for mobile devices requires only three basic tasks: cleaning, backing up data and keeping the operating system and applications up to date.

- **Cleaning**—Use a soft, lint-free cloth and a cleaning solution designed for touchscreen to keep the touchscreen clean. Do not use ammonia or alcohol to the clean the touchscreen.
- **Backing up the data**—Keep a backup copy of the information on the mobile device to another source, such as a cloud drive. The information includes: contacts, music, photos, video, apps, and any customized settings.
- **Updating the system and applications**—When a new version of the operating system or applications is available, the device should be updated to ensure that the device is working at its best. An update can include new features, fixes, or improvements to performance and stability.

Basic Troubleshooting Process for Laptops and Mobile Devices (9.6)

Troubleshooting is a skill that is developed with experience. Technicians can better develop their troubleshooting skills through gaining experience and using an organized approach to problem solving.

Applying (9.6.1)

This section outlines a systematic approach that can be employed to properly troubleshoot and gives specifics on how to address issues that are particular to laptops and mobile devices.

Identify the Problem (9.6.1.1)

Laptop and mobile device problems can result from a combination of hardware, software, and network issues. Technicians must be able to analyze the problem and determine the cause of the error to repair the device. This process is called troubleshooting.

The first step in the troubleshooting process is to identify the problem.

Table 9-8 shows a list of open-ended and closed-ended questions to ask laptop and mobile device customers.

Table 9-8 Step 1: Identify the Problem

Identify the Problem for Laptop	
Open-ended questions	■ What problems are you experiencing with your laptop? ■ What software has recently been installed? ■ What were you doing when the problem was identified? ■ What error messages have you received?
Close-ended questions	■ Is the laptop under warranty? ■ Is the laptop currently using the battery? ■ Can the laptop operate using the AC adapter? ■ Can the laptop boot and show the desktop OS?
Identify the Problem Mobile Devices	
Open-ended questions	■ What problems are you experiencing? ■ What is the make and model of your mobile device? ■ What service provider do you have?
Closed-ended questions	■ Has the problem happened before? ■ Has anyone else used the mobile device? ■ Is your mobile device under warranty?

Establish a Theory of Probable Cause (9.6.1.2)

After you have talked to the customer, you can establish a theory of probable causes.

Table 9-9 shows a list of some common probable causes for laptop and mobile device problems.

Table 9-9 Step 2: Establish a Theory of Probable Cause

Common causes of laptop problems	■ Battery does not have a charge. ■ Battery will not charge. ■ Loose cable connections. ■ Keyboard does not lock. ■ Num Lock key is on. ■ Loose RAM.
Common causes of mobile device problems	■ Power button is broken ■ Battery can no longer hold a charge. ■ There is excessive dirt in the speaker, microphone, or charging port ■ The mobile device has been dropped ■ The mobile device has been submerged

Test the Theory to Determine Cause (9.6.1.3)

After you have developed some theories about what is wrong, test your theories to determine the cause of the problem. If a quick procedure does not correct the problem, research the problem further to establish the exact cause.

Table 9-10 shows a list of quick procedures that can determine the exact cause of the problem or even correct the problem.

Table 9-10 Step 3: Test the Theory to Determine Cause

Common steps to determine cause for laptop problems	■ Use an AC adapter with the laptop ■ Replace the battery ■ Reboot the laptop ■ Check BIOS settings ■ Disconnect and reconnect the cables ■ Disconnect the peripherals ■ Toggle Num Lock key ■ Remove and reinstall RAM ■ Caps Lock key is on ■ Check for non-bootable media in a boot device

Common steps to determine cause for mobile device problems	■ Restart the mobile device ■ Plug the mobile device into an AC outlet ■ Replace the mobile device battery ■ Remove any removable battery and reinstall it ■ Clean the speaker, microphone, charging port, or other connection ports

Establish a Plan of Action to Resolve the Problem and Implement the Solution (9.6.1.4)

After you have determined the exact cause of the problem, establish a plan of action to resolve the problem and implement the solution. Table 9-11 shows some sources you can use to gather additional information to resolve an issue.

Table 9-11 Step 4: Establish a Plan of Action to Resolve the Problem and Implement the Solution

If no solution is achieved in the previous step, further research is needed to implement the solution.	■ Help desk repair logs ■ Other technicians ■ Manufacturer FAQs ■ Technical websites ■ Newsgroups ■ Manuals ■ Online forums ■ Internet research

Verify Full System Functionality and Implement Preventive Measures (9.6.1.5)

After you have corrected the problem, verify full functionality and, if applicable, implement preventive measures. Table 9-12 shows a list of steps to verify the solution.

Table 9-12 Step 5: Verify Full System Functionality and Implement Preventive Measures

Verify solution and full functionality for laptops	■ Reboot the laptop ■ Attach all peripherals ■ Operate laptop using only battery ■ Print a document from an application ■ Type a sample document to test the keyboard ■ Check Event Viewer for warnings or errors

(*Continued*)

Table 9-12 *Continued*

Verify solution and full functionality for mobile devices	■ Reboot the mobile device ■ Browse the Internet using WiFi ■ Browse the Internet using 4G, 3G, or other carrier network type ■ Make a phone call ■ Send a text message ■ Open different types of apps ■ Operate the mobile device using only the battery

Document Findings, Actions, and Outcomes (9.6.1.6)

In the final step of the troubleshooting process, document your findings, actions, and outcomes. Table 9-13 shows a list of the tasks required to document the problem and the solution.

Table 9-13 Step 6: Document Findings, Actions, and Outcomes

Document your findings, actions, and outcomes	■ Discuss the solution implemented with the customer ■ Ask the customer to verify that the problem has been solved ■ Provide the customer with all paperwork ■ Document the steps taken to solve the problem in the work order and technician's journal ■ Document any components used in the repair ■ Document the time spent to resolve the problem

Common Problems and Solutions for Laptops and Mobile Devices (9.6.2)

Laptop and mobile device problems can be attributed to hardware, software, networks, or some combination of the three.

Identify Common Problems and Solutions (9.6.2.1)

You will resolve some types of laptop problems more often than others. Table 9-14 shows common laptop problems and solutions.

Table 9-14 Common Problems and Solutions for Laptops

Identify the Problem	Probable Causes	Possible Solutions
Laptop does not power on.	■ Laptop is not plugged in. ■ Battery is not charged. ■ Battery will not hold a charge.	■ Plug the laptop into AC power ■ Remove and einstall the battery. ■ Replace battery if will not charge
Laptop battery supports the system for a reduced period of time.	■ Proper battery charging and discharging practices have not been followed. ■ Extra peripherals are draining the battery. ■ Power plan isn't correct. ■ Battery is not holding a charge for very long.	■ Follow the battery charging procedures described in the manual ■ Remove unneeded peripherals and disable wireless NIC if possible ■ Modify power plan to decrease battery usage ■ Replace the battery
External display has power but no image on the screen.	■ A video cable is loose or damaged. ■ The laptop is not sending a video signal to the external display.	■ Reconnect or replace video cable ■ Use the Fn key along with the multipurpose key to toggle to the external display
Laptop is powered on, but nothing is displayed on the LCD screen when the laptop lid is reopened.	■ The LCD cutoff switch is dirty or damaged. ■ The laptop has gone into sleep mode.	■ Check the laptop repair manual for instructions about cleaning or replacing the LCD cutoff switch ■ Press a key on the keyboard to bring the computer out of sleep mode
The image on a laptop looks dull and pale	LCD backlight is not properly adjusted	Check the laptop repair manual for instructions about calibrating the LCD backlight
The image on a laptop display is pixilated.	Display properties are incorrect.	Set the display to native resolution
The laptop display is flickering.	■ Images on the screen are not refreshing fast enough. ■ The inverter is damaged or malfunctioning.	■ Adjust the screen refresh rate ■ Disassemble the display and replace the inverter

(*Continued*)

Table 9-14 *Continued*

Identify the Problem	Probable Causes	Possible Solutions
A user is experiencing a ghost cursor that moves on its own.	■ The track pad is dirty. ■ A track pad and mouse are being used at the same time. ■ A part of the hand has touched the track pad while typing.	■ Clean the track pad ■ Disconnect the mouse ■ Try not to touch the track pad while typing
Pixels on the screen are dead or not generating color.	Power to the pixels has been cut off.	Contact the manufacturer
The image on the screen appears to flash lines or patterns of different color and size (artifacts).	■ The display is not properly connected. ■ The GPU is overheating. ■ The GPU is faulty or malfunctioning.	■ Disassemble the laptop to check display connections ■ Disassemble and clean the computer, checking for dust and debris ■ Replace the GPU
Color patterns on a screen are incorrect.	■ The display is not properly connected. ■ The GPU is overheating. ■ The GPU is faulty or malfunctioning.	■ Disassemble the laptop to check display connections ■ Disassemble and clean the computer, checking for dust and debris ■ Replace the GPU
Images on a display screen are distorted.	■ Display setting have been changed. ■ The display is not properly connected. ■ The GPU is overheating. ■ The GPU is faulty or malfunctioning.	■ Restore display setting to the original factory settings ■ Disassemble the laptop to check display connections ■ Disassemble and clean the computer, checking for dust and debris ■ Replace the GPU
The network is fully functional and the wireless laptop connection is enabled, but the laptop cannot connect to the network.	■ WiFi is turned off. ■ Out of wireless range.	■ Turn laptop wireless on using the wireless NIC properties or the Fn key along with the appropriate multipurpose key. ■ Move closer to the wireless access point.

Identify the Problem	Probable Causes	Possible Solutions
Input devices connected with Bluetooth are not functioning properly.	■ Bluetooth capability is turned off. ■ Batteries in the input device are not providing enough power. ■ The input device is out of range.	■ Turn laptop Bluetooth on by using the Bluetooth setting applet or the Fn key along with the appropriate multipurpose key ■ Replace the batteries ■ Move the input device closer to the laptop's Bluetooth receiver ■ Verify that the Bluetooth device is turned on
Keyboard is inserting numbers instead of text and Num Lock indicator light is on.	Num Lock is enabled.	Turn off Num Lock using the Num Lock key or the Fn key along with the appropriate multipurpose key
The battery is swollen	■ The battery has been overcharged ■ An incompatible charger has been used ■ The battery is defective	■ Replace the battery with a new one from the manufacturer

Table 9-15 displays common problems and solution for mobile devices.

Table 9-15 Common Problems and Solutions for Mobile Devices

Identify the Problem	Probable Causes	Possible Solutions
The mobile device will not connect to the Internet	■ WiFi is not available ■ The device is in airplane mode ■ WiFi settings are incorrect ■ WiFi is turned off ■ There is no carrier data network in range	■ Move within the boundaries of a WiFi network ■ Turn WiFi on ■ Turn off airplane mode ■ Configure WiFi settings ■ Move within the boundaries of a network carrier
The mobile device will not turn on	■ The battery is drained ■ The power button is broken ■ The device has failed	■ Charge the mobile device or replace the battery with a charged battery ■ Contact customer support to determine the next course of action

(Continued)

Table 9-15 *Continued*

Identify the Problem	Probable Causes	Possible Solutions
A tablet fails to charge or charges very slowly when connected to AC power	■ The tablet is in use when being charged ■ The AC adapter does not have enough amperage	■ Turn off the tablet when charging ■ Use an AC adapter from the manufacturer or came with the tablet ■ Use an AC adapter that has have enough amperage
A smart phone cannot connect to the carrier's network	The SIM card is not installed	Install the SIM
Mobile device battery won't hold a charge	Device settings are incorrectly configured	■ Modify the power plan to decrease the battery usage ■ Replace the battery
Mobile device won't connect to Bluetooth	■ Bluetooth capability is turned off. ■ The devices are not paired ■ The input device is out of range.	■ Turn on Bluetooth ■ Pair the devices ■ Bring the devices into range
The battery is swollen	■ The battery has been overcharged ■ An incompatible charger has been used ■ The battery is defective	Replace the battery with a new one from the manufacturer
The touchscreen is not responsive	■ The touchscreen is dirty ■ The touchscreen has shorted out due to damage or water ■ The touchscreen has failed	■ Clean the touchscreen ■ Replace the touchscreen
The device exhibits very short battery life	■ The battery has been cycled so many times that it does not hold a high charge ■ The battery is defective	Replace the battery
The device is overheating	■ A power-intensive app is running while the device is charging ■ Many radios are on while the device is charging ■ The battery is defective	■ Close any unnecessary apps or remove the device from the charger ■ Turn off any unnecessary radios or remove the device from the charger ■ Replace the battery

Lab—Research Laptop Problems (9.6.2.2)

Laptops often use proprietary parts. To find information about the replacement parts, you may have to research the website of the laptop manufacturer. Refer to the lab in *IT Essentials v6 Lab Manual.*

Lab—Gather Information from the Customer (9.6.2.3)

In this lab, you act as a call center technician and create closed-ended and open-ended questions to ask a customer about a laptop problem. Refer to the lab in *IT Essentials v6 Lab Manual.*

Lab—Investigating Support Websites (9.6.2.4)

In this lab, you investigate the services provided by a local laptop repair company, or a laptop manufacturer's support website. Use the Internet or a local phone directory to locate a local laptop repair company or laptop manufacturer's support website. Refer to the lab in *IT Essentials v6 Lab Manual.*

Summary (9.7)

This chapter discussed the features and functionality of laptops and mobile devices, as well as how to remove and install internal and external components.

Summary (9.7.1)

Laptops and mobile devices have become very important in our daily lives. Internet browsing, online purchasing, media streaming, social media are used more and more with a mobile device rather than the desktop computer. This is a global occurrence. Although laptops are not usually used while moving around, they are portable devices that allow for convenience and productivity outside of the office because users can do the same tasks on a laptop as their desktop but from anywhere. The rising usage of these devices makes it critical for an IT professional to become familiar with the technology.

The following concepts from this chapter are important to remember:

- Laptops and mobile devices are lightweight and can operate on battery power.
- Laptops use the same types of ports as desktop computers so that peripheral devices can be interchangeable. Mobile devices can also use some of the same peripheral devices.
- Essential input devices, such as a keyboard and track pad, are built into laptops to provide similar functionality as desktop computers. Some laptops and mobile devices use touchscreens as input devices.
- The internal components of laptops are typically smaller than desktop components because they are designed to fit into compact spaces and conserve energy. The internal components of mobile devices are usually connected to the circuit board to keep the device compact and light weight.
- Laptops feature function keys that can be pressed in combination with the Fn key. The functions performed by these keys are specific to the laptop model.
- Docking stations and port replicators can increase the functionality of laptops by providing the same types of ports that are featured on desktop computers. Some mobile devices use docking station to charge or use peripheral devices.
- Laptops and mobile devices most commonly feature LCD or LED screens, many of which are touchscreen.

- Backlights illuminate LCD and LED laptop displays. OLED displays have no backlight.
- The power settings of laptop batteries can be configured to ensure that power is used efficiently.
- Laptops and mobile devices can feature a number of wireless technologies, including Bluetooth, Infrared, WiFi and the ability to access Cellular WANs.
- Laptops provide a number of expansion possibilities. Users can add memory to increase performance, make use of flash memory to increase storage capacity, or increase functionality by using expansion cards. Some mobile devices can add more storage capacity by upgrading or adding more flash memory, such as MicroSD cards.
- Laptop components consist of CRUs and FRUs.
- Laptop components should be cleaned regularly in order to extend the life of the laptop.

Summary of Exercises

This is a summary of the Labs and activities associated with this chapter.

Labs

The following labs cover material from this chapter. Refer to the labs in the IT Essentials v6 Lab Manual.

Lab—Research Docking Stations (9.1.1.6)

Lab—Research Laptop RAM (9.3.1.5)

Lab—Research Laptop Batteries (9.3.2.3)

Lab—Research Laptop Screens (9.3.2.5)

Lab—Research Laptop Hard Drives (9.3.2.7)

Lab—Research Building a Specialized Laptop (9.3.2.14)

Lab—Research Laptop Problems (9.6.2.2)

Lab—Gather Information from the Customer (9.6.2.3)

Lab—Investigating Support Websites (9.6.2.4)

Check Your Understanding

You can find the answers to these questions in the appendix, "Answers to 'Check Your Understanding' Questions."

1. Which statement describes a mobile device feature?

   A. When a mobile device is not operating at the speed required by the user, the user must perform a memory upgrade.

   B. Docking stations can add some functionality to mobile devices such as video output.

   C. Like laptops and desktops, most mobile device hardware is upgradeable.

   D. There are no field-replaceable parts for mobile devices, but there are some which are field-serviceable.

2. What is an example of an expansion slot on a laptop?

   A. ExpressCard

   B. EISA

   C. AGP

   D. Internal USB

   E. ISA

   F. External PCI

3. What are three problems laptop computers are more likely to face because of being portable? (Choose three.)

   A. Excessive moisture

   B. Drops

   C. Wrong BIOS configuration

   D. Poor performance

   E. Excessive wear

   F. Outdated drivers

4. What is a closed-ended question that a technician may ask when troubleshooting a possible laptop battery failure?

   A. What software has been installed recently?

   B. Can the laptop operate using the AC adapter?

   C. Have you recently upgraded your display driver?

   D. What problems are you experiencing with your laptop?

5. Which type of RAM modules are designed for the space limitations of laptops?

   A. DIMMs

   B. SIMMs

   C. SODIMMs

   D. SRAM

6. Which statement describes the S4 ACPI power state?

   A. The CPU and RAM are still receiving power, but unused devices are powered down.

   B. The laptop is on and the CPU is running.

   C. The laptop is off and nothing has been saved.

   D. The CPU and RAM are off. The contents of the RAM have been saved to a temporary file on the hard disk.

7. What is the maximum range of a Class 2 Bluetooth network?

   A. 50 meters

   B. 10 meters

   C. 5 meters

   D. 2 meters

8. A technician troubleshooting a laptop notices that some keyboard keys are not working properly. What should the technician check first?

   A. Is the WordPad program corrupted?

   B. Is the touchpad working?

   C. Is the Num Lock key on?

   D. Is the AC adapter charging correctly?

9. Which situation would indicate a failing laptop battery?

   A. Extra peripherals are draining the battery.

   B. The battery is not holding the charge for very long.

   C. The external hard drive has no power from the USB port.

   D. The screen is not showing full brightness.

10. What is a proactive way to keep a laptop clean?

   A. Use mild soap to clean the screen.

   B. Use compressed air to blow the dust off the optical drive.

   C. Clean the keyboard using cotton swabs.

   D. Keep fluids away from the laptop computer.

11. A customer brings in a mobile device for repair. After asking a few questions, the service technician determines that the device is unable to connect to any WiFi network. Which step of the troubleshooting process has just taken place?

    A. Document findings.

    B. Establish a theory of probable causes.

    C. Implement a solution.

    D. Identify the problem.

    E. Determine the exact cause.

12. Which statement is true of laptop motherboards?

    A. The form-factor varies by manufacturer.

    B. They follow standard form factors so they can be interchanged easily.

    C. They are interchangeable with most desktop motherboards.

    D. Most of them use the ATX form factor.

13. Which component is part of a solid state drive?

    A. Flash memory chip

    B. Spindle

    C. Drive head

    D. Disk platter

14. What would be considered a form of removable, non-mechanical, non-volatile memory?

    A. A CMOS chip

    B. An external hard drive

    C. An external flash drive

    D. A SODIMM memory module

CHAPTER 10

Mobile, Linux, and OS X Operating Systems

Objectives

Upon completion of this chapter, you will be able to answer the following questions:

- What are the GUIs on Android and OS X operating systems?
- What are major characteristics of Linux OS?
- What are main characteristics of Apple OS X?
- What is the command-line interface?
- What is Open Source software?
- What are command-line tools that can be used for OS optimization in Linux?
- What is a graphical user interface (GUI)?
- How can I use GUI tools in OS X operating system?
- What is data synchronization?
- What is a passcode and why use it?
- What is cloud storage?
- How is cloud storage used to backup mobile devices?
- How is device tracking done on a mobile device?
- What is a sandbox?
- How does Bluetooth work on a mobile device?

Key Terms

This chapter uses the following key terms. You can find the definitions in the Glossary.

source code Page 520

open source Page 521

closed source Page 521

Android Page 521

iOS Page 521

apps Page 521

software development kit (SDK) Page 521

Xcode Page 521

Android Studio Page 522

Quick Response (QR) code Page 523

Android Application Package (APK) Page 523

Metro-style apps Page 524

Push Page 524

Pull Page 524

sideloading Page 525

launcher Page 527

Widgets Page 528

Home button Page 531

Siri Page 531

Spotlight Page 532

alert badge *Page 534*

accelerometer *Page 539*

GPS *Page 540*

Navigation *Page 540*

Geocaching *Page 540*

Geotagging *Page 540*

Specialized search results *Page 540*

Device tracking *Page 540*

WiFi calling *Page 541*

Mobile payment *Page 542*

Premium SMS-based transactional payments *Page 542*

Direct Mobile Billing *Page 542*

Mobile Web Payments *Page 542*

Contactless NFC (Near Field Communication) *Page 542*

VPN *Page 543*

digital assistant *Page 543*

Google Now *Page 543*

Cortana *Page 543*

Wireless Emergency Alerts (WEA) *Page 544*

International Mobile Equipment Identity (IMEI) *Page 545*

passcode lock *Page 546*

Swipe *Page 546*

Pattern *Page 546*

Personal Identification Number (PIN) *Page 546*

Simple Passcode *Page 547*

Touch ID *Page 547*

Trusted Devices *Page 547*

Trusted Places *Page 547*

Trusted Face *Page 547*

Trusted Voice *Page 547*

On-body detection *Page 547*

remote backup *Page 551*

locator app *Page 551*

Cellular towers *Page 552*

Remote Lock *Page 553*

Remote wipe *Page 553*

sandbox *Page 553*

Rooting *Page 554*

Jailbreaking *Page 554*

Preferred Roaming List (PRL) *Page 557*

Primary Rate ISDN (PRI) *Page 557*

tethering *Page 559*

3G *Page 560*

4G *Page 560*

Mobile WiMAX *Page 560*

LTE *Page 560*

Short Message Service (SMS) *Page 560*

Multimedia Message Service (MMS) *Page 560*

hotspot *Page 560*

Airplane Mode *Page 561*

Bluetooth *Page 563*

Bluetooth pairing *Page 564*

Email servers *Page 566*

email clients *Page 566*

Post Office Protocol 3 (POP3) *Page 567*

Internet Message Access Protocol (IMAP) Page 567

Simple Mail Transfer Protocol (SMTP) Page 567

Multipurpose Internet Mail Extension (MIME) Page 567

Secure Sockets Layer (SSL) Page 568

Exchange Page 568

iCloud Page 570

Internet email Page 571

Messaging Application Programming Interface (MAPI) Page 568

Data synchronization Page 572

Sync process on Android Page 573

Backup on iOs Page 575

Sync on iOS Page 575

OneDrive Page 577

UNIX Page 577

Linux Page 577

OS X Page 578

Netboot Page 579

Ubuntu Linux Page 579

Mission Control Page 582

Finder Page 582

command-line interface (CLI) Page 582

shell Page 582

kernel Page 582

terminal Page 583

backup data Page 585

Time Machine Page 588

Déjà Dup Page 585

Partition management Page 589

Mount or Unmount disk partitions Page 589

Disk format Page 589

Bad sector check Page 589

cron service Page 592

Self-Monitoring, Analysis and Reporting Technology, S.M.A.R.T patches Page 589

Multiboot Page 591

boot manager Page 591

boot camp Page 591

grub Page 591

firmware Page 596

root Page 554

signature files Page 596

Gnome-keyring Page 597

Introduction (10.0)

The three most common operating systems for computers, laptops and mobile devices are Microsoft Windows, Mac OS X, and Linux. Windows has been discussed in previous chapters and in this chapter you will learn about OS X and Linux as well as mobile devices.

Welcome (10.0.1)

Understanding various operating systems and the hardware they run on is critical to the success of a technician. It is necessary to know PC and mobile device operations, applications, the operating systems that they use. OS X and Linux are two popular OSs in addition to Windows.

Mobile, Linux, and OS X Operating Systems (10.0.1.1)

The operating system (OS) controls almost all functions on a computer. In this chapter, you learn about the components, functions, and terminology related to mobile operating systems, Linux, and OS X.

Mobile Operating Systems (10.1)

Operating systems on mobile devices manage apps and services, and determine the ways users interact with the device. This section focuses on an introduction to mobile device operating systems and key features of each of the two main mobile operating systems and the difference between them.

Android versus iOS (10.1.1)

Like desktops and laptops, mobile devices use an operating system (OS) to run software. This chapter focuses on the two most commonly used mobile operating systems: Android and iOS. Android is developed by Google, and iOS is developed by Apple.

Open Source versus Closed Source (10.1.1.1)

Before users can analyze and modify software, they must be able to see the *source code*. Source code is the sequence of instructions that is written in human readable language, before it is turned into machine language (zeroes and ones). The source code is an important component of free software as it allows the users to analyze and eventually modify the code. When the developer chooses to provide the source code, the software is said to be *open source*. If the program's source code is not published, the software is said to be *closed source*.

Android is an open source OS developed by Google. *iOS* is a closed source OS developed by Apple.

Released in 2008 on the HTC Dream, the Android OS has been customized for use on a wide range of electronic devices. Because Android is open and customizable, programmers can use it to operate devices like laptops, smart TVs, and e-book readers. There have even been Android installations in devices like cameras, navigation systems, and portable media players.

Released in 2007 on the first iPhone, the Apple iOS source code was not released to the public. To copy, modify or redistribute iOS requires permission from Apple.

This chapter focuses on Android 5.0.1 (Lollipop) and iOS 8.4 as these were the latest versions available at the time of writing.

Mobile Application Development (10.1.1.2)

Mobile operating systems are not just stand alone products. Mobile operating systems are platforms on which other products can be created and marketed for use on that OS. Examples of such products are mobile applications, which are simply called *apps*. Apps are programs created to perform specific tasks on mobile devices. Calendars, maps, notes, and email are a few examples of apps commonly found in mobile devices.

In the iOS ecosystem, apps were originally designed by Apple. Similarly, Google originally designed Android apps. When it became clear these operating systems were actually software platforms, Apple and Google each released their own *software development kit (SDK)*. An SDK contains a number of software tools designed to allow external programs to be written for a specific software package.

Developers who want to create Apple iOS apps must download and install *Xcode*, Apple's official integrated development environment (IDE). XCode can be downloaded at no cost and allows developers to write and test their iOS apps in an iPhone simulator. Loading and running apps on the actual iOS device requires the payment of a yearly iOS Developer Program subscription fee. Xcode also contains a debugger, libraries, a handset simulator, documentation, sample code and tutorials.

Xcode is shown in Figure 10-1.

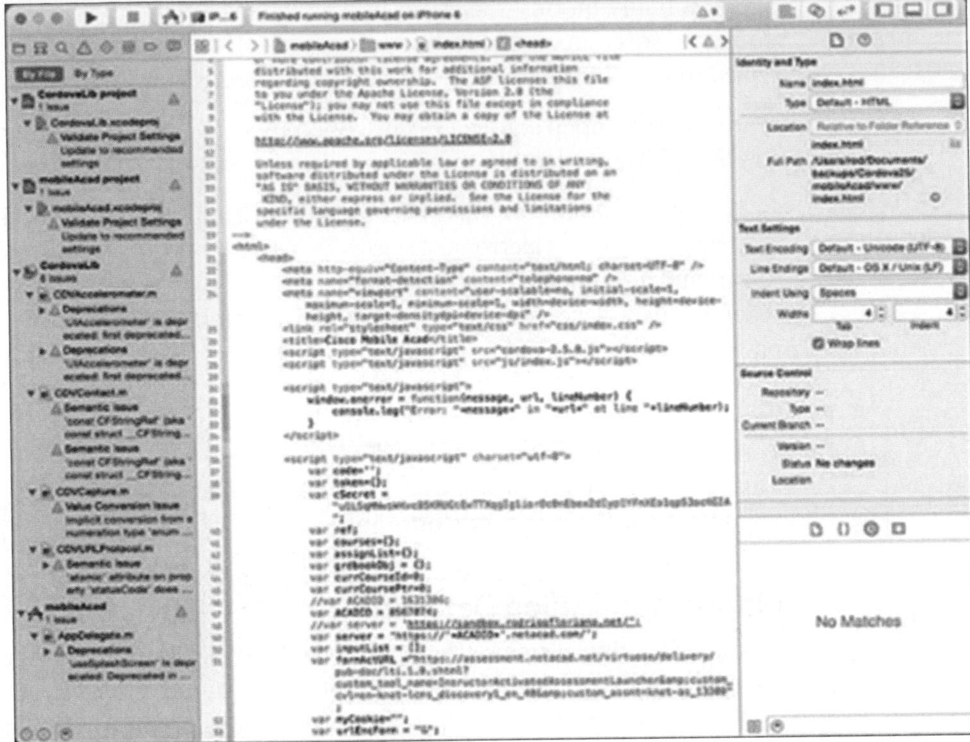

Figure 10-1 Xcode

The Google Android SDK also includes many of the items listed above for Xcode, as well as a number of tutorials. The Android SDK supports several development platforms which include computers running Linux, Mac OS X 10.5.8 or later, and Windows XP or later. *Android Studio* is a Google IDE for Android development.

Application and Content Sources (10.1.1.3)

Apps are the programs that are executed on mobile devices. Mobile devices come with a number of different apps preinstalled to provide basic functionality. There are apps to make phone calls, send and receive email, listen to music, take pictures, and play video or video games. Many other types of apps enable information retrieval, device customization, and productivity.

Apps are used on mobile devices the same way that programs are used on computers. Instead of being installed from an optical disk, apps are downloaded from a content source. Some apps can be downloaded for free, and others must be purchased. Although Apple apps are available only through Apple's store, several content sources are available for Android mobile devices:

- Google Play
- Amazon App Store
- Androidzoom
- AppsAPK
- 1Mobile

There are many other websites where Android apps can be found. It is important to install apps only from trusted sources. If a questionable site contains a desired app, check Google Play or the Amazon App Store to see if it can be downloaded from there instead. Apps downloaded from trusted sources are less likely to contain malicious code. The Google Play store only allows installation of apps on devices that are compatible with the device.

Sometimes a website contains a *Quick Response (QR) code*. QR codes are similar to a bar code, but can contain much more information. To use a QR code, a special app accesses the camera on a mobile device to scan the code. The code contains a web link that allows the direct download of an app. Be careful when using QR codes, and only allow downloads and installations from trusted sources.

QR code is shown in Figure 10-2.

Figure 10-2 QR code

On Android, applications are packaged into an archive format called *Android Application Package or APK* for short. When an Android application is compiled and ready for distribution, it is placed inside an APK file. Along with the app's compiled code, the APK contains resources, certificates, and assets required for the app's proper operation.

The Apple App Store is the only content source that iOS users are allowed to use to get apps and content. This ensures that Apple has cleared the content to be free of harmful code, meet strict performance guidelines, and does not infringe on copyrights.

Similar to Apple's App Store and Google's Google Play, Microsoft launched its own application store in 2012. Starting with Windows 8 and Windows Server 2012, the Windows Store allows Windows users to search, download and install Windows Store Apps (also known as *Metro-style apps*).

Other types of content are also available for download. Like apps, some content is free, whereas other content must be purchased. Content that you currently own can also be loaded onto mobile devices through a data cable connection or over WiFi. Some types of content that are available include:

- Music
- Television programs
- Movies
- Magazines
- Books

Push versus *Pull*

There are two main methods for installing apps and content on mobile devices: push and pull. When a user runs the Google Play app or the Apple App Store app from a mobile device, apps and content that are downloaded are pulled from a server to the device.

With Android devices, a user can browse Google Play using any desktop or laptop computer and purchase content. The content is pushed to the Android device from the server. iOS users are able to purchase content from iTunes on a desktop or laptop computer that is then pushed to an iOS device.

When an Android app is being installed, a list of all the required permissions is displayed, as shown in Figure 10-3. You must agree to grant the listed permissions to the app so that it can be installed. Always read the list of permissions carefully and do not install apps that request permission to access items and features that it should not need.

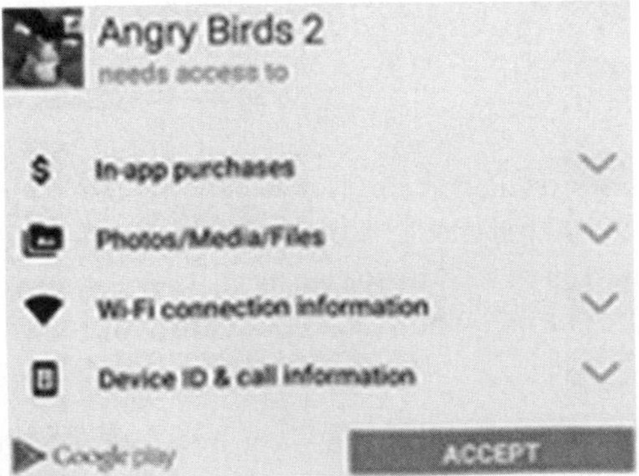

Figure 10-3 Installation Permissions

Sideloading

There is another way to install apps on Android mobile devices. Apps can be downloaded from different sources on the Internet and transferred to a mobile device through WiFi, Bluetooth, data cable, or other methods. This is called *sideloading*. Sideloading an application is not recommended, because many sources for apps cannot be trusted. Only install apps from trusted sources and developers.

Note

iOS devices do not support sideloading by default.

Android Touch Interface (10.1.2)

Android supports a selection of touch screens

Home Screen Items (10.1.2.1)

Much like a desktop or laptop computer, mobile devices organize icons and widgets on multiple screens for easy access. One screen is designated as the home screen, as shown in Figure 10-4.

Figure 10-4 Android Main Home Screen

Additional screens are accessed by sliding the home screen to the left or right. Each screen contains navigation icons, the main area where icons and widgets are accessed, and notification and system icons. The screen indicator displays which screen is currently being displayed.

Navigation Icons

The Android OS uses the system bar to navigate apps and screens. The system bar is always displayed at the bottom of every screen.

The system bar contains the following buttons:

- **Back—**Returns to the previous screen. If the on-screen keyboard is displayed, this button closes it. Continuing to press the Back button navigates to through each previous screen until the home screen is displayed.
- **Home—**Returns to the home screen.
- **Recent Apps—**Opens thumbnail images of recently used apps. To open an app, touch its thumbnail. Swipe a thumbnail to remove it from the list.
- **Menu—**If available, Menu shows additional options for the current screen.

Google Search

Android devices often come with a default Google search app preinstalled. Touch and then type text into the box to search the device and the Internet for anything. Touch the microphone icon to enter the pattern to be searched using speech.

Special Enhancements

As a result of Android's open source code, some manufacturers add functionality to the Android OS before deploying it in their devices. For example, some Samsung Android tablets have a feature called the Mini App Tray, which contains shortcuts to apps that can be used at any time. Many manufacturers have followed that trend resulting in apps or GUI elements that are only present in devices built by that specific manufacturer. This chapter focuses on an unmodified version of Android.

Notification and System Icons

Each Android device has an area that contains system icons, such as the clock, battery status, and radio signal status for WiFi and provider networks. Apps such as email, text messaging, and Facebook often display status icons to indicate communication activity.

To open the notification area on Android devices, swipe down from the top of the screen. You can do the following when notifications are open:

- Respond to a notification by touching it.
- Dismiss a notification by swiping it off the screen to either side.

- Dismiss all notifications with the icon.
- Toggle often-used settings.
- Adjust the brightness of the screen.
- Open the Settings menu with the quick settings icon.

Another element of the Android User Interface (UI) is the *launcher*. The launcher defines the format of the home screens, the look and feel of its icons, buttons, color scheme and animations. Although Android includes a stock launcher, there are also other launchers available in the Google Play store:

- **Nova Launcher—**This launcher offers many animation options, folder views and desktop screen behavior. Although the free version should suit most users, the paid version allows for gesture customization.
- **Google Now Launcher—**Created by Google, this launcher comes installed by default in Nexus devices. It turns the left most screen into Google Now, allowing quick access to Google Now cards, searches and various voice commands.
- **Action Launcher—**This launcher introduces a slide-in side bar to house the apps to allow quicker app access.

Managing Apps, Widgets, and Folders (10.1.2.2)

Apps

Each home screen is set up with a grid where apps can be placed.

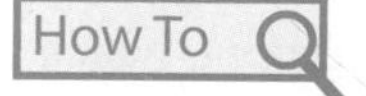

To move an app, follow these steps:

Step 1. Touch and hold the app.

Step 2. Drag it to an empty area of any home screen.

Step 3. Release the app.

To remove an app from a home screen, follow these steps:

Step 1. Touch and hold the app.

Step 2. Drag it to **X Remove** on the top of the screen.

Step 3. Release the app.

To execute an app, touch it. After the app is running, there are often options which can be configured by touching the menu button.

There are usually three different ways to close an app:

- Touch the Back button continually to reach the home screen. It is common for the program to prompt to exit the app.
- Touch the Home button.
- Touch the Exit option in the menu for the app.

Widgets

Widgets are programs (or pieces of programs) that display information right on the home screen. A weather widget, for example, can be placed on the Home screen to display weather conditions. Often, a widget can be touched to launch an associated app. In the case of a weather widget, touching the widget would open a weather app on full screen mode to display more information about the weather. Widgets are helpful because they give you quick access to often-used information or functions. These are some examples of popular widgets:

- **Clock**—Displays a large version of a customizable clock.
- **Weather**—Displays current conditions for one or more locations.
- **WiFi On/Off**—Allows the user to turn WiFi on or off quickly without navigating to the settings menu.
- **Power Control**—Displays multiple widgets, such as WiFi On/Off, Bluetooth, and Vibrate.

There are many other types of widgets that can be used to customize Android screens. Refer to the documentation of programs or Google Play to determine which apps have widgets.

How To

To add a widget to the home screen, follow these steps:

Step 1. Touch and hold an empty area of the home screen.

Step 2. Touch Widgets.

Step 3. Identify the desired Widget from the list.

Step 4. Touch and hold the desired widget and drag it to the home screen.

Folders

On some mobile devices, multiple apps can be grouped into folders to help organize them. If folders are not available, an app can be installed to provide this feature. Apps can be grouped in any way you want.

How To

To create a folder on an Android device, follow these steps:

Step 1. Touch and hold an app on a home screen.

Step 2. Drag the app onto another app that you want to put in the same folder.

Step 3. Release thc app.

Touch any folder to open it. Touch any app in the folder to open it. To rename a folder, touch the folder, touch the folder name, and type a new name for the folder. To close a folder, touch outside the folder, or touch the Back or Home button. Move folders around on home screens the same way apps are moved.

How To

To remove an app from a folder, follow these steps:

Step 1. Open the folder.

Step 2. Touch and hold the app to remove.

Step 3. Drag the app to an empty area of a home screen.

Step 4. Release the app.

On Android devices, if a folder has two apps and one is removed, the folder is removed, but the remaining app replaces the folder on the home screen.

All Apps Icon

The All Apps icon opens the All Apps screen. This displays all of the apps that are installed on the device. These are some common tasks that can be performed from the All Apps screen:

- **Launch an app**—Touch any app to launch it.
- **Place apps on a home screen**—Touch and hold an app. The home screen is displayed. Release the app on any open area of any home screen.
- **Uninstall apps**—Touch and hold an app. Drag the app to either the trashcan icon or the X icon.
- **Access the Play Store**—Touch the menu icon and touch Google Play.

Figure 10-5 shows a breakdown of Android's GUI.

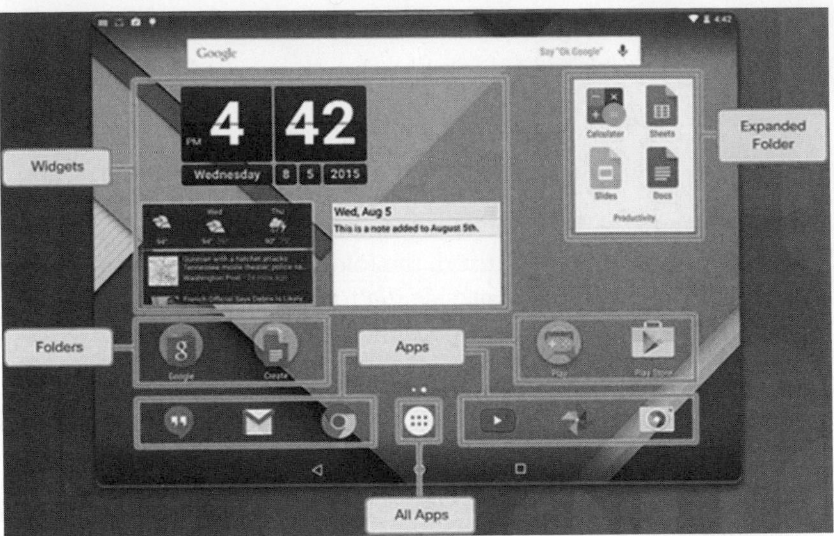

Figure 10-5 Android's GUI

Lab—Working with Android (10.1.2.3)

In this lab, you place apps and widgets on the home screen and move them between different screens. You also create folders. Finally, you install and uninstall apps from the Android device. Refer to the lab in IT *Essentials v6 Lab Manual*.

iOS Touch Interface (10.1.3)

iOs Interface is made up of elements such as sliders, switches, and buttons designed around a touch screen. Like the Android OS there is no clicking to open an app or access a program all you need to do is tap.

Home Screen Items (10.1.3.1)

The iOS interface works in much the same way as the Android interface. Screens are used to organize apps, and apps are launched with a touch. There are some very important differences:

- **No navigation icons**—A physical button must be pressed instead of touching navigation icons.
- **No widgets**—Only apps and other content can be installed on iOS device screens.
- **No app shortcuts**—Each app on a home screen is the actual app, not a shortcut.

Home Button

Unlike Android, iOS devices do not use navigation icons to perform functions. A single physical button called the *Home button* performs many of the same functions as the Android navigation buttons. The Home button is located physically at the bottom of the devicc. The Home button performs the following functions:

- **Wake the device**—When the device's screen is off, press the Home button once to turn it on.
- **Return to the home screen**—Press the Home button while using an app to return to the last home screen that was used.
- **Open the multitasking bar**—Double-click the Home button to open the multitasking bar. The multitasking bar shows the most recent apps that have been used.
- **Start Siri or voice control**—Press and hold the Home button to start Siri or voice control. *Siri* is special software that understands advanced voice controls. On devices without Siri, basic voice controls can be accessed in the same way.
- **Open audio controls**—Double-click the Home button when the screen is locked to open the audio controls.

Notification Center

iOS devices have a notification center that displays all alerts in one location. To open the notification area on iOS devices, touch the top of the screen and swipe a finger down the screen. The following actions can be taken when notifications are open:

- Respond to an alert by touching it.
- Remove an alert by touching the X icon and touching clear.

To change the options for notifications on a per-app basis, use the following path:

Settings > Notifications

Commonly Used Settings

iOS devices allow the user to quickly access common settings and switches, even if the device is locked. To access the commonly used settings menu, swipe up from the very bottom of any screen. From the commonly used settings screen a user can:

- Toggle often used settings such as airplane mode, WiFi, Bluetooth, do not disturb mode and screen rotation lock
- Adjust screen brightness

- Control the music player
- Access Airdrop
- Access Flashlight, Clock, Calendar and Camera

Spotlight (Search tool)

From any screen of an iOS device, touch the screen and drag down to reveal the *Spotlight* search field. Any part of the screen except the very top or the very bottom should work. When Spotlight search field is revealed, type what you're looking for. Spotlight shows suggestions from many sources including the Internet, iTunes, App Store, movie show times, locations nearby.

Spotlight also automatically updates the results as you type, as shown in Figure 10-6.

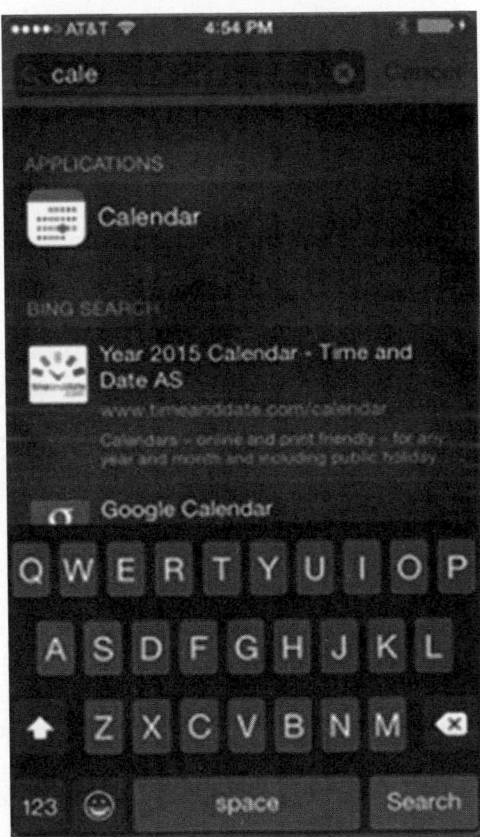

Figure 10-6 iOS Spotlight

Managing Apps and Folders (10.1.3.2)

Managing app and folders on a mobile device can be very different from managing them on desktops and PCs. Android and iOS have specifics steps for managing apps and folders on mobile devices. The following paragraphs explain how to work with apps and folders in iOS.

Apps

iOS apps and folders work similarly to the Android OS. Instead of an All Apps button, all the apps that are installed on the device are located on the home screens. Apps can be uninstalled from the device, but can be re-installed on the device using iTunes.

Each home screen has a grid in which apps can be placed. To move an app, follow these steps:

How To

Step 1. Touch and hold the app until it jiggles.

Step 2. Drag it to an empty area of any home screen.

Step 3. Release the app.

Step 4. Move any additional apps.

Step 5. Press the Home button to save the changes.

How To

To remove an app from an iOS device, follow these steps:

Step 1. Touch and hold the app until it jiggles.

Step 2. Touch the X icon on the app.

Step 3. Delete any additional apps.

Step 4. Press the Home button to save the changes.

Multitasking Bar

iOS allows multiple apps to run at the same time. While you are working in one app, others may run in the background. The multitasking bar is used to quickly switch between the apps that have been used recently, close apps that are running, and access commonly used settings. To open the multitasking bar, double-click the Home button. While the multitask bar is visible, iOS will also show favorite and recent contacts on the top of the screen. The following actions can be performed in the multitasking bar:

- Touch any app to open it.
- Swipe the multitasking bar to the right or to the left to see more apps.
- Tap on any favorite or recent contact on the top of screen to access it.
- Swipe an app up to force the app to close.

Folders

Folders can also be created on iOS devices to help organize them.

How To

To create a folder, follow these steps:

Step 1. Touch and hold an app on a home screen until it jiggles.

Step 2. Drag the app onto another app that you want to put in the same folder.

Step 3. Release the app.

Step 4. Add any additional apps to the folder.

Step 5. Touch the Home button to save changes.

Touch any folder to open it. Touch any app in the folder to open it. To rename a folder, touch the folder, touch the folder name, and type a new name for the folder. To close a folder, touch outside the folder or touch the Home button. Move folders around on home screens the same way apps are moved.

How To

To remove an app from a folder, follow these steps:

Step 1. Open the folder.

Step 2. Touch and hold the app you want to remove.

Step 3. Drag the app to an empty area of a home screen.

Step 4. Release the app.

To remove a folder, remove all apps from the folder.

Many of the apps on iOS devices are able to show an *alert badge*. An alert badge is displayed as a small icon over an app, as shown in Figure 10-7. This icon is a number that indicates the amount of alerts from the app. This number might be how many missed calls you have, how many text messages that you have, or how many updates are available. If an alert badge displays an exclamation mark, there is a problem with the app. Alert badges for apps inside a folder are displayed on the folder. Touch the app to attend to the alerts.

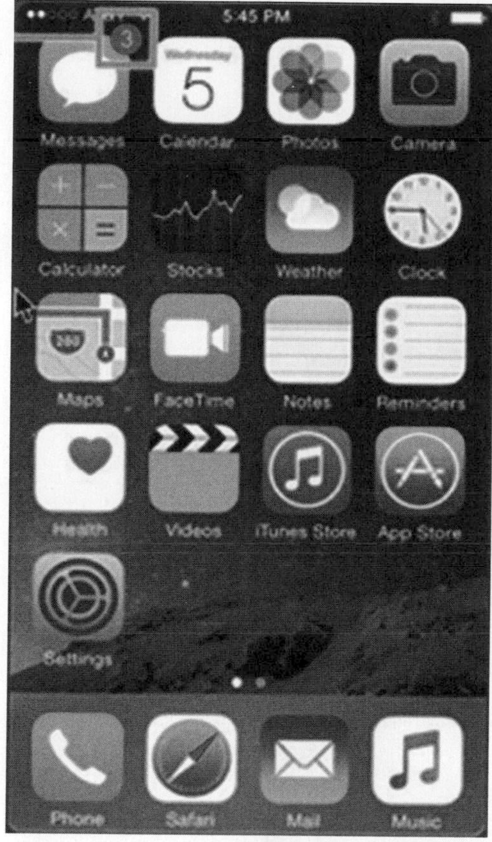

Figure 10-7 iOS Alert Badge

Lab—Working with iOS (10.1.3.3)

In this lab, you place apps on the home screen and move them between different home screens. You also create folders. Finally, you install apps on the iOS device and uninstall them. Refer to the lab in *IT Essentials v6 Lab Manual.*

Windows Phone Touch Interface (10.1.4)

Similar to Android, Windows Phone apps do not live on the Start screen; they can be pinned or unpinned without uninstalling them from the device.

Start Screen Items (10.1.4.1)

The Start screen on Windows phones is based on tiles, as shown in Figure 10-8. Instead of displaying icons as a reference to apps, tiles are apps that can display dynamic information and allow interaction right on the start screen. A tile can display live information, such as text messages, news or photos. If the user needs more information, the tile can be tapped, and the app is expanded to take up the entire screen.

Tiles are squares or rectangles. The user can choose how big a tile can be. This is helpful as it allows the user to create a visual sense of priority among tiles.

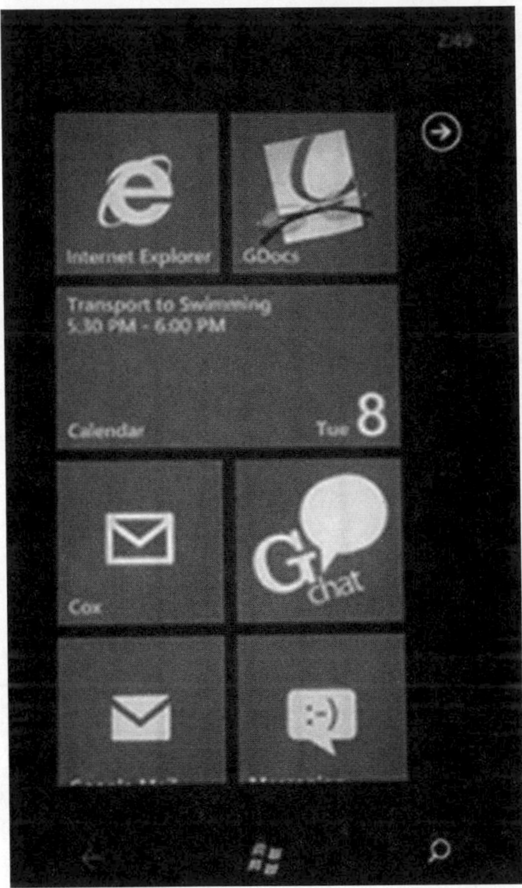

Figure 10-8 Start Screen on Windows Phone

Pinning to Start

The Windows Phone allows users to pin content to the Start screen for easy access. Users can pin practically any content available in the phone including apps, contacts, maps, videos or websites. Pinned content will appear as tiles on Start.

How To

To pin to Start, look for the pinning icon or, in the case of pinning an app to start, follow these steps:

Step 1. Tap and hold the app until the **pin to start** bar appears.

Step 2. Tap the **pin to start** bar.

To unpin from Start, tap and hold them item and then tap the unpin icon.

Navigation Icons

Windows Phones have a physical row of buttons used for navigation. The buttons are:

- **Back**—Returns to the previous screen. Continuing to press the Back button navigates to each previous screen until the Start screen is displayed. Tap and hold the back button to access App Switcher, a list of recently used apps.
- **Start**—Returns to the Start screen.
- **Search**—Tap the Search button to start a Bing search from anywhere on the phone. Tap and hold the Search button to access Cortana, Windows Phone digital assistant.

Managing Apps and Folders (10.1.4.2)

The Start screen on a Windows Phone is customizable. Tiles can be easily moved, resized and grouped.

Rearranging Tiles

How To

To move a tile, follow these steps:

Step 1. Tap and hold the tile you want to move until it pops into the foreground.

Step 2. Push the tile where you want it to go.

Step 3. When you are done moving tiles, press the Start button.

Resizing Tiles

How To

To resize a tile, follow these steps:

Step 1. Tap and hold the tile you want to change to a different size.

Step 2. Tap the resize icon until the tile changes to the size you want.

Step 3. When you are done, press the Start button.

Creating and Naming Folders

To create and name a folder, follow these steps:

Step 1. On Start button, tap and hold a tile.

Step 2. Move the tile on top of another tile until the folder pops into the foreground.

Step 3. To name the folder, tap Name folder, give it a name, and then tap Enter.

To add another tile to the folder, simply tap and hold the tile, and then push it into the folder.

To Open Apps in a Folder

To open apps in a folder, follow these steps:

Step 1. To get to any of the apps in the folder, just tap the folder to open it, and then tap the app you want.

Step 2. To close the folder, tap the tile for the folder that appears above it.

To Remove a Tile from a Folder

To remove a tile from a folder, follow these steps:

Step 1. Tap the folder to open it.

Step 2. Tap and hold the tile you want to remove from the folder.

Step 3. Push the tile to anywhere on Start.

Common Mobile Device Features (10.1.5)

Mobile devices offer set of capabilities, services, and applications to the user, and although users have a choice of different vendors and models for the devices, there are common features among them. This section describes capabilities, services and applications that are common to devices as well as explaining others that are unique to vendor's devices.

Screen Orientation and Calibration (10.1.5.1)

Screen orientation is the way in which a rectangular page is oriented for normal viewing. The two most common types of orientation are portrait and landscape. Calibration is used to set your touchscreen so that your touches get detected more accurately.

Screen Orientation

Most mobile device screens are rectangular in shape. This shape allows content to be viewed in two different ways: portrait and landscape. Some content fits better in a specific view. For example, video fills the screen in landscape mode, but may not fill half the screen in portrait mode. An e-book viewed in portrait mode seems very natural because it is similar in shape to an actual book. Typically, users can choose the viewing mode that is the most comfortable for them for each type of content.

Many mobile devices contain sensors, such as an *accelerometer*, that can determine how they are being held. Content is automatically rotated to the position of the device. This feature is useful, for example, when taking a photograph. When the device is turned to landscape mode, the camera app also turns to landscape mode. Also, when a user is creating a text, turning the device to landscape mode automatically turns the app to landscape mode, making the keyboard larger and wider.

When using an Android device, to enable automatic rotation use the following path:

Settings > Display > check Auto-rotate screen

When using an iOS device, to enable automatic rotation use the following path:

Swipe up from the very bottom of the screen **> tap** the **lock icon on the far right in the top row**

Screen Calibration

When using a mobile device, you may need to adjust the brightness of the screen. Increase the screen brightness level when using a mobile device outdoors because bright sunlight makes the screen very difficult to read. In contrast, a very low brightness is helpful when reading a book on a mobile device at night. Some mobile devices can be configured to auto-adjust the brightness depending on the amount of surrounding light. The device must have a light sensor to use auto-brightness.

The LCD screen for most mobile devices uses the most battery power. Lowering the brightness or using auto-brightness helps conserve battery power. Set the brightness to the lowest setting to get the most battery life from the device.

When using an Android device, to configure screen brightness use the following path:

Settings > Display > Brightness > slide the brightness to the desired level

Alternatively, tap the **Adaptive Brightness** toggle to allow the device to decide the optimal screen brightness based on the amount of light availed.

When using an iOS device, to configure screen brightness, use the following path:

Swipe up from the very bottom of the screen > Drag the slider below the first row of icons to adjust the brightness.

Alternatively, to configure brightness in the Settings menu, use the following path:

Settings > Display & Brightness > slide the brightness to the desired level or tap the **Auto-Brightness** toggle.

GPS (10.1.5.2)

Another common feature of mobile devices is the *global positioning system (GPS)*. GPS is a navigation system that determines the time and geographical location of the device by using messages from satellites in space and a receiver on Earth. A GPS radio receiver uses at least four satellites to calculate its position based on the messages. GPS is very accurate and can be used under most weather conditions. However, dense foliage, tunnels, and tall buildings can interrupt satellite signals.

There are GPS devices for cars, boats, and hand-held devices used by hikers and backpackers. In mobile devices, GPS receivers have many different uses:

- *Navigation*—A mapping app that provides turn-by-turn directions to a location, an address, or coordinates.
- *Geocaching*—A mapping app that shows the location of geocaches. Geocaches are containers that are hidden around the world. Users find them and often sign a log book to show that they found it.
- *Geotagging*—Embeds location information into a digital object, like a photograph or a video, to record where it was taken.
- *Specialized search results*—For example, displays results based on proximity, such as restaurants that are close by when searching for the keyword restaurants.
- *Device tracking*—Locates the device on a map if it is lost or stolen.

To enable GPS on Android devices use the following path:

Settings > Location > Tap on the toggle to turn location services on

To enable GPS on iOS devices use the following path:

Settings > Privacy > Location services > Turn location services on

Note

Some Android and iOS devices do not have GPS receivers. These devices use information from WiFi networks and cellular networks, if available, to provide location services.

Lab—Mobile Device Features (10.1.5.3)

In this lab, you set the auto rotation and brightness, and turn GPS on and off. Refer to the lab in *IT Essentials v6 Lab Manual*.

Lab—Mobile Device Information (10.1.5.4)

In this activity, you use the Internet, a technical journal, or a local store to gather information about an Android and an iOS device. You then document the specifications of each Android and iOS device onto this lab. Refer to the lab in *IT Essentials v6 Lab Manual*.

Convenience Features (10.1.5.5)

Modern mobile devices are essentially small computers. As a result, a number of convenience features are being developed for modern smartphones. Below are a few of these features:

WiFi Calling

Instead of using the cellular carrier's network, modern smartphones can use the Internet to transport voice calls by taking advantage of a local WiFi hotspot. This is called *WiFi calling*. Locations, such as coffee shops, work places, libraries, or homes, usually have WiFi networks connected to the Internet. The phone can transport voice calls through the local WiFi hotspot. If there is no WiFi hotspot within reach, the phone will use the cellular carrier's network to transport voice calls.

WiFi calling is very useful in areas with poor cellular coverage because it uses a local WiFi hotspot to fill the gaps. The WiFi hotspot must be able to guarantee a throughput of at least 1Mbps to the Internet for a good quality call. When WiFi calling is enabled and in use during a voice call, the phone will display "WiFi" next to the carrier name.

To enable WiFi calling on Android use the following path:

Settings > More (under Wireless & networks section) **> WiFi Calling >** Tap on the toggle to turn it on

To enable WiFi calling on iOS use the following path:

Settings > Phone and turn on WiFi Calling

Note

All major cell phone carriers now support WiFi calling, with support for the most recent iPhones and Android phones. The expectation is that it will become more widespread. One reason it is thought to be becoming so wide spread is to alleviate the provider network traffic and still have service provided.

Mobile Payments

A few mobile payment methods include:

- *Premium SMS-based transactional payments*—Consumers send a SMS message to a carrier's special phone number containing a payment request. The seller is informed the payment has been received and is cleared to release the goods. The charge is then added to the customer's phone bill. Slow speed, poor reliability, and poor security are a few shortcomings of this method.
- *Direct Mobile Billing*—Using a mobile billing option during check-out, a user identifies him or herself (usually through a two-factor authentication) and allows the charge to be added to the mobile service bill. This is very popular in Asia and has the following benefits: security, convenience, and no need for bank cards or credit cards.
- *Mobile Web Payments*—The consumer uses the web or dedicated apps to complete the transaction. This method relies on the Wireless Application Protocol (WAP) and usually requires the use of credit cards or a pre-registered online payment solution, such as PayPal.
- *Contactless NFC (Near Field Communication)*—This method is used mostly in physical store transactions. A consumer pays for good or services by waving the phone near the payment system. Based on an unique ID, the payment is charged directly against a prepaid account or bank account. NFC is also used in mass—transportation services, the public parking sector, and many more consumer areas.

Mobile payments refer to any payments made through a mobile phone, as shown in Figure 10-9.

Figure 10-9 NFC Payment

Virtual Private Network

A *virtual private network (VPN)* is a private network that uses a public network (usually the Internet) to connect remote sites or users together. Instead of using a dedicated leased line, a VPN uses "virtual" connections routed through the Internet from the company's private network to the remote site or employee.

Many companies create their own Virtual Private Networks (VPNs) to accommodate the needs of remote employees and distant offices. With the proliferation of mobile devices, it was a natural move to add VPN clients to smartphones and tablets.

When a VPN is established from a client to a server, the client accesses the network behind the server as if it was connected directly to that network. Because VPN protocols also allow for data encryption, the communication between client and server is secure and attractive to businesses.

To create a new VPN connection on Android, use the following path:

Settings > More (under Wireless & networks section) **> VPN >** Tap on the + sign to add a VPN connection

When the VPN information has been added to the device, that device must be started before traffic can be sent and received through it.

To start a VPN on Android use the following path:

Settings > General > VPN > Select the desired VPN connection **>** enter username and password **>** tap **CONNECT**

To create a new VPN connection on iOS use the following path:

Settings > General > VPN > Add VPN Configuration...

When the VPN information has been added to the device, that device must be started before traffic can be sent and received through it.

To start a VPN on iOS use the following path:

Settings > Toggle VPN to on

Information Features (10.1.5.6)

Virtual assistants

A *digital assistant*, sometimes called a virtual assistant, is a program that can understand natural conversational language and perform tasks for the end user. Modern mobile devices are powerful computers, making them the perfect platform for digital assistants. Popular digital assistants currently include *Google Now* for Android, *Siri* for iOS, and *Cortana* for Windows Phone 8.1.

These digital assistants rely on artificial intelligence, machine learning, and voice recognition technology to understand conversational-style voice commands. As the end user interacts with these digital assistants, sophisticated algorithms predict the user's needs and fulfill requests. By pairing simple voice requests with other inputs, such as GPS location, these assistants can perform several tasks, including playing a specific song, performing a web search, taking a note, or sending an email.

Google Now

To access Google Now on an Android device follow these steps:

Simply say "Okay google". Google Now will activate and start listening to requests.

Siri

To access Siri on an iOS device press and hold the Home button. Siri will activate and start listening to requests.

Alternatively, Siri can be configured to start listening to commands when it hears "Hey Siri. To enable "Hey Siri", use the following path:

Settings > General > Siri > Toggle Allow "Hey Siri" to on.

Cortana

To access Cortana on a Windows device, follow these steps:

Press and hold the Search button. Cortana will activate and start listening to requests.

Emergency Notification

Wireless Emergency Alerts (WEA) are emergency messages sent by authorities through mobile carriers. In the U.S.A., government partners include: local and state public safety agencies, FEMA, the FCC, the Department of Homeland Security, and the National Weather Service. Mobile carriers do not charge for WEA messages.

Timely alerts can help to save lives during an emergency. With WEA, alerts can be sent to mobile devices without the user having to download an app or subscribe to a service.

WEAs look like a regular text message and contain the type and time of the alert, any recommended action and the agency issuing the alert. WEAs are relatively short, having no more than 90 characters. To differentiate from a regular message, WEA messages will be followed by a distinct pattern vibration and audio tone.

There are three different kinds of alerts:

- **Presidential Alerts**—Alerts issued by the President or a designee.
- **Imminent Threat Alerts**—Alerts include severe manmade or natural disasters, such as hurricanes, earthquakes, and tornadoes, where an imminent threat to life or property exists.
- **AMBER Alerts**—Alerts meet the U.S. Department of Justice's criteria to help law enforcement to search for and locate an abducted child.

You may need to register a device with a carrier, or provide some kind of unique identifier. Every mobile device has a unique 15-digit number called an *International Mobile Equipment Identity (IMEI)*. This number identifies the device to a carrier's network. The numbers come from a family of devices called the Global System for Mobile Communications (GSM). The number can often be found in the configuration settings of the device, or in a battery compartment, if the battery is removable.

The user of the device is also identified using a unique number called the International Mobile Subscriber Identity (IMSI). The IMSI is often programmed on the subscriber identity module (SIM) card, or can be programmed on the phone itself, depending on the network type.

Methods for Securing Mobile Devices (10.2)

Many issues exist when it comes to securing mobile devices from the physical security to encryption of data. It is easy to forget how vulnerable mobile devices can be with such ease of use and network access from libraries to airplanes everything is connected. There are many ways to secure a mobile device and knowing them can help ensure that users are practicing good security rather than leaving themselves vulnerable due to poor security practices. Mobile device threats are increasing and can result in data loss, security breaches and regulatory compliance violations. As a technician it is important to know security methods to prevent problems.

Passcode Locks (10.2.1)

Setting a passcode is one method to use to help protect your data. It is like a gatekeeper to prevent immediate access to a device for an intruder.

Overview of Passcode Locks (10.2.1.1)

Smartphones, tablets, and other mobile devices contain sensitive data. If a mobile device is lost, anyone who finds the device has access to contacts, text messages, and web accounts. One method to help prevent theft of private information from mobile devices is to use a passcode lock. A *passcode lock* locks a device and puts it in a power-saving state. The lock can also be delayed to engage after a specified amount of time passes after the device goes into the power-saving state. One common method for placing a mobile device into a sleep state is by quickly pressing the main power button. The device can also be set to enter a sleep state after a certain amount of time.

Many different types of passcode locks are available, as shown in Figure 10-10.

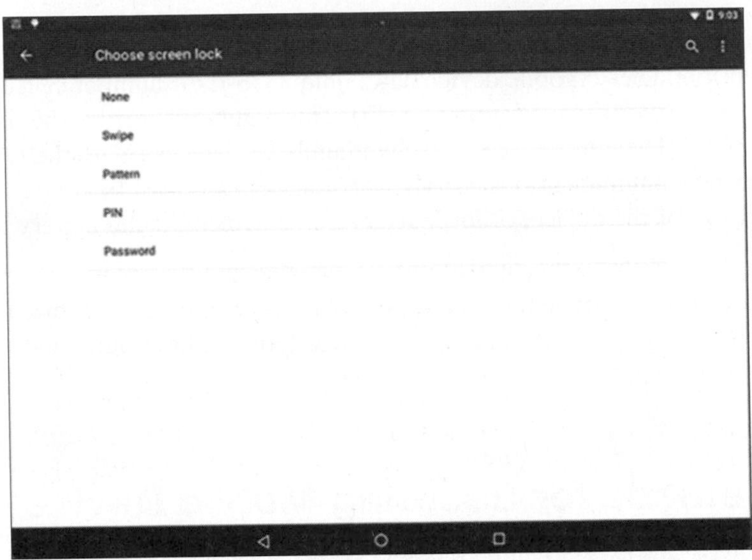

Figure 10-10 Passcode Lock Types on Android

Some types of passcode locks are more difficult to guess than others. The passcode must be entered each time the device is turned on or resumes from a power-saving state. These are some common types of passcode locks:

- **None**—Removes any type of existing passcode lock for that device.
- *Swipe*—The user slides an icon, such as a lock or arrow, to unlock the device. This option is the least secure.
- *Pattern*—Locks the device when the user slides a finger over the screen in a certain pattern. To unlock the device, the exact pattern must be repeated on the screen.
- *PIN*—Uses a private Personal Identification Number (PIN) to secure the device. A PIN is a series of numbers. When the PIN is entered correctly, the device unlocks.
- **Password**—Uses a password to secure the device. This option is the least convenient, especially if the word is complicated or long, but can be very secure.

- *Simple Passcode*—iOS devices only. When this option is set to On, the passcode must be a four-digit number. When set to Off, more complex passwords using characters, numbers, and symbols can be used.
- *Touch ID*—iOS devices only. Starting with the iPhone 5S, it is also possible to unlock an iOS device based on the user's fingerprints. The Home button in selected iPhone devices contain a fingerprint scanner that can be used to unlock the device, authorize payments and access to apps. Although Google has announced similar feature, fingerprint unlocking was not very popular among Android devices at the time this chapter was written.

To set a passcode on an Android device, use the following path:

Settings > Security > Screen Lock > Choose the type of passcode to use from the list, and set the remaining Screen Security settings.

After a passcode is set, it must be entered each time the device is turned on or resumes from a power-saving state.

Android 5.0 (Lollipop) allows an extra set of unlock options. Placed under the Smart Lock feature, the extended Android unlock options are:

- *Trusted Devices*—This feature unlocks the Android phone or tablet whenever it is paired with a specific Bluetooth device or NFC tag of the user's choice. For example, it is convenient to be able to keep the Android phone or tablet unlocked when paired to a car's Bluetooth.
- *Trusted Places*—By using the GPS chip built into the device, Android allows the user to define home and work locations. The device will no longer require unlocking when it is in either one of those locations.
- *Trusted Face*—When activated, Trusted Face allows Android to unlock itself based on a pre-registered image of the user's face.
- *Trusted Voice*—This feature relies on the user's unique voiceprint to unlock the Android device when a registered user says "Okay, Google."
- *On-body detection*—This feature will use the device's accelerometer to detect if the user has the device on his possession. By detecting some specific pattern of movement, Android assumes the device is in the user's hands, pocket or bag and will not require unlocking until it is set down by the user.

To set a Smart Lock on an Android device, use the following path:

Settings > Security > Smart Lock > Choose the type of lock to use from the list, and set the remaining details based on the chosen option.

To set a passcode on an iOS device, use the following path:

Settings > Touch ID & Passcode > Turn Passcode On. Enter a four-digit number, as shown in Figure 10-11. Enter the same number a second time for verification.

To use Touch ID, the user must register at least one fingerprint and can register up to five fingerprints. Touch ID configuration and behavior can also be set in the screen described above.

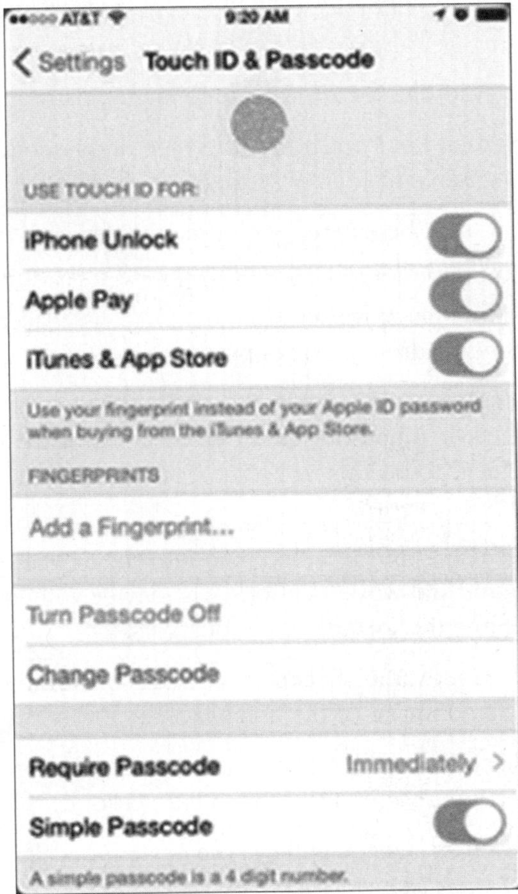

Figure 10-11 Passcode Lock on iPhone

Note

To increase security, some services will force the user to create a passcode lock before they can be enabled. VPN and Microsoft Exchange accounts are two examples of such services.

Lab—Passcode Locks (10.2.1.2)

In this lab, you set a passcode lock, change a passcode lock, and fail passcode authentication. You also remove a passcode lock. Refer to the Lab in *IT Essentials v6 Lab Manual*.

Restrictions on Failed Login Attempts (10.2.1.3)

To unlock a mobile device when a passcode has been properly implemented requires entering the correct PIN, password, pattern, or other passcode type. In theory, a passcode, such as a PIN, could be guessed given enough time and perseverance. To prevent someone from trying to guess a passcode, mobile devices can be set to perform defined actions after a certain number of incorrect attempts have been made.

For Android devices, the number of failed attempts before lockout depends on the device and version of Android OS. It is common that an Android device will lock when a passcode has failed from 4 to 12 times. After a device is locked, you can unlock it by entering the Gmail account information used to set up the device.

For iOS devices, the device is disabled after five failed attempts, as shown in Figure 10-12.

Figure 10-12 iPhone Temporarily Disabled After Incorrect Passcode Entered

On the sixth failed attempt, the device remains disabled for one minute. Each failed attempt after six results in additional waiting time.

Table 10-1 shows the results of failing to enter the correct passcode.

Table 10-1 iOs Failed Passcode Attempts

Failed Attempts	Additional Time Device is Disabled	Total Time Device is Disabled
1 to 5	0	0
6	1 minute	1 minute
7	5 minutes	6 minutes
8	15 minutes	21 minutes
9	60 minutes	81 minutes
10	60 minutes	144 minutes
11	Device Data Deleted	

Note

The incorrect passwords must be different from each other to trigger the waiting time.

If the passcode fails 10 times and the Turn on the Erase data option is enabled, the screen goes black, and all data on the device is deleted. To restore the iOS device and data, you must connect it to the computer to which it was last synchronized and use the Restore option in iTunes.

On iOS, to increase security, the passcode is used as part of the encryption key for the entire system. Because the passcode is not stored anywhere, no one can gain access to the user data on iOS devices, including Apple. The system depends on the user to provide the passcode before the system can be unlocked and decrypted for use. A forgotten passcode will render user data unreachable, forcing the user to perform a full restore through iTunes on the computer, where the device was last synchronized.

Cloud-Enabled Services for Mobile Devices (10.2.2)

Just like mobile devices provide access to the network wherever and whenever cloud-enabled services provide access to data and applications wherever and whenever you want or need them. Smartphones and tablets are increasingly used for this access. Data processing and data storage are now happening beyond the mobile device.

Remote Backup (10.2.2.1)

Mobile device data can be lost due to device failures or the loss or theft of the device. Data must be backed up periodically to ensure that it can be recovered if needed. With mobile devices, storage is often limited and not removable. To overcome these limitations, remote backups can be performed. A *remote backup* is when a device copies its data to cloud storage using a backup app. If data needs to be restored, run the backup app and access the website to retrieve the data.

For Android devices, the following items are automatically backed up remotely:

- Calendar
- Mail
- Contacts

Google also keeps track of all apps and content that you have purchased, so they can be downloaded again. Many apps are also available to remotely back up other items. Research the apps in the Google Play Store to find backup apps that meet your needs.

iOS users are given 5 GB of storage for free. Additional storage can be purchased for a yearly fee. These are the items that can use iCloud as backup location:

- Calendar
- Mail
- Contacts
- Content that you have purchased from the Apple App Store (This content does not count against the 5 GB total)
- Photos taken with the device
- Settings configured on the device
- Accumulated App data from running apps
- Screen icons and locations
- Text and media messages
- Ringtones

Locator Applications (10.2.2.2)

If a mobile device is misplaced or stolen, it is possible to find it using a locator app. A *locator app* should be installed and configured on each mobile device before it is lost. Both Android and iOS have many different apps for remotely locating a device.

Similar to Apple's Find My Phone, Android Device Manager allows a user to locate, ring, or lock a lost Android device, or to erase data from the device. To manage a lost device, the user must visit Android Device Manager Dashboard hosted at https://www.google.com/android/devicemanager and log in with the Google account used on the Android device. Android Device Manager is included and enabled by default on Android 5.x and can be found under **Settings > Security > Device Administration.**

Most iOS users use the Find My iPhone app. The first step is to install the app, start it, and follow the instructions to configure the software. The Find My iPhone app can be installed on different iOS devices to locate the lost device. If a second iOS device is not available, the device can also be found by logging in to the iCloud website and using the Find My iPhone feature. After initiating the location option from a website or second iOS device, the locator app uses location data from the following sources to locate the device:

- *Cellular towers*—The app calculates the location of the device by analyzing the signal strength from the towers to which it can connect. Because the towers are at known locations, the location of the device can be determined. This is called triangulation.
- **WiFi hotspots**—The app looks up the approximate location of WiFi hotspots that the missing device can detect. A file containing many known hotspots and their location is stored on the device.
- **GPS**—The app uses data from the GPS receiver to determine the location of the device.

Note

If the app is unable to locate the lost device, the device might be turned off or disconnected. The device must be connected to a cellular or wireless network to receive commands from the app, or to send location information to the user.

After the device is located, you might be able to perform additional functions, such as sending a message or playing a sound. These options are useful if you have misplaced your device. If the device is close by, playing a sound indicates exactly where it is. If the device is at another location, sending a message to display on the screen allows someone to contact you if it has been found.

Remote Lock and Remote Wipe (10.2.2.3)

If attempts to locate a mobile device have failed, there are other security features that can prevent data on the device from being compromised. Usually the same apps that perform remote location have security features. Two of the most common remote security features are:

- *Remote lock*—The remote lock feature for iOS devices is called lost mode. The Android Device Manager calls this feature Lock. It allows you to lock the device with a passcode so others cannot gain access to the data in the device. For example, the user can display custom messages, or keep the phone from ringing due to incoming calls or text messages.
- *Remote wipe*—The remote wipe feature for iOS devices is called erase phone. The Android Device Manager calls this feature Erase. It deletes all data from the device and returns it to a factory state. To restore data to the device, Android users must set up the device using a Gmail account, and iOS users must synchronize their device to iTunes.

Note

For these remote security measures to function, the device must be powered on and connected to a cellular or WiFi network.

Software Security (10.2.3)

Applications need to be protected from internal design flaws and external threats. Applications developers embed security measures inside applications to prevent hackers from compromising a program and technicians need to take additional measures to keep applications including operating systems from being compromised.

Antivirus (10.2.3.1)

All computers are vulnerable to malicious software. Smartphones and other mobile devices are computers, so they are also vulnerable. Antivirus apps are available for both Android and iOS. Depending on the permissions granted to antivirus apps when they are installed on an Android device, the app might not be able to scan files automatically or run scheduled scans. File scans must be initiated manually. iOS does not allow automatic or scheduled scans. This is a safety feature to prevent malicious programs from using unauthorized resources or contaminating other apps or the OS. Some antivirus apps also provide locator services, remote lock, or remote wipe.

Mobile device apps run in a sandbox. A *sandbox* is a location of the OS that keeps code isolated from other resources and other code. It is difficult for malicious programs to infect a mobile device because apps are run inside the sandbox. An Android app asks for permission to access certain resources upon installation. A malicious app has access to any resources that were allowed permission during installation. This is another reason why it is important to download apps only from trusted sources.

Due to the nature of the sandbox, malicious software does not usually damage mobile devices; it is far more likely for a mobile device to transfer a malicious program to another device, such as a laptop or desktop. For example, if a malicious program is downloaded from email, the Internet, or another device, the malicious program could be placed on a laptop the next time it is connected to the mobile device.

Rooting and Jailbreaking

Mobile operating systems are usually protected by a number of software restrictions. An unmodified copy of iOS for example, will only execute authorized code and allow very limited user access to its file system.

Rooting and *Jailbreaking* are two names for removing restrictions and protections added to mobile operating systems. Rooting is the term used for Android devices, and Jailbreaking is used for iOS devices. The manufacturer restrictions are removed from these devices, allowing them to run arbitrary user-code, granting users full access to the file system and full access to kernel modules.

Rooting or jailbreaking a mobile device usually voids the manufacturer's warranty. It is not recommended that you modify a customer's mobile device in this way. Nevertheless, a large group of users choose to remove their own devices' restrictions. These are some of the benefits of rooting or jailbreaking a mobile device:

- The GUI can be heavily customized.
- Modifications can be made to the OS to improve the speed and responsiveness of the device.
- The CPU and GPU can be overclocked to increase performance of the device.
- Features such as tethering that are disabled by a carrier can be enabled free of cost.
- Apps can be installed from secondary or unsupported sources.
- Apps that cannot be removed from within the default OS, known as bloatware, can be removed.

Jailbreaking exploits vulnerabilities in iOS. When a usable vulnerability is found, a program is written. This program is the actual jailbreak software and it is then distributed on the Internet. Apple discourages jailbreaking, and actively works towards eliminating vulnerabilities that make jailbreaking possible on iOS. In addition to the OS updates and bug fixes, new iOS releases usually include patches to eliminate known vulnerabilities that allow jailbreaking. When iOS vulnerabilities are fixed by updates, it forces hackers to start over.

Note

The jailbreak process is completely reversible. To remove the jailbreak and bring the device back to its factory state, connect it to iTunes and perform a Restore.

Android is based on Linux and therefore, open source by nature. Because of this, Google has chosen to support rooting, deliberately allowing it in every Android release. Users who wish to root an Android device can do so without the need to search for vulnerabilities.

Rooting or jailbreaking a device is risky and may void the manufacturer's warranty. A rooted or jailbroken device greatly increases the risk of infection by a virus, because it might not properly create or maintain sandboxing features. A modified OS also provides user access to the root directory. This also grants malicious programs access to this sensitive area of the file system.

Figure 10-13 shows a few commands executed on a jailbroken iPhone. A Terminal app is used to provide a CLI interface and allow for commands to be issued at an elevated user level known as root. Root user has the highest level of rights and permissions.

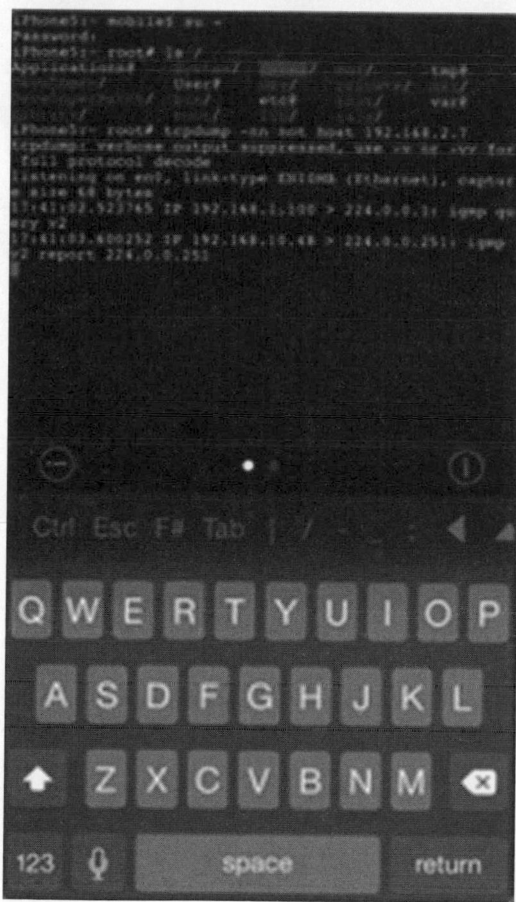

Figure 10-13 Jailbreaking on iOS Device-Terminal on iPhone

Figure 10-14 shows the root user again performing tasks with an iPhone that would not be possible without jailbreaking. The phone is now hosting an SSH session established from a desktop PC to a jailbroken iPhone. An openSSH server was installed on the jailbroken phone so that the phone can receive the connection and allow the remote shell. Among the commands issued on the phone, **uname -a**, displays the kernel version and proves this is indeed a session to an iPhone5. The **netstat** command shows the SSH service bound to port 22 and in ESTABLISHED state.

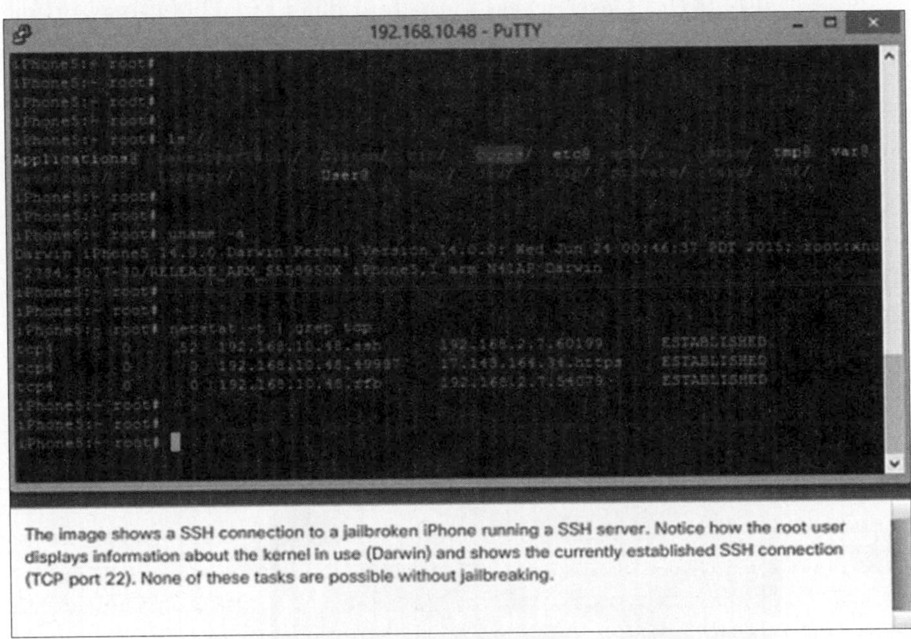
192.168.10.48 - PuTTY
The image shows a SSH connection to a jailbroken iPhone running a SSH server. Notice how the root user displays information about the kernel in use (Darwin) and shows the currently established SSH connection (TCP port 22). None of these tasks are possible without jailbreaking.

Figure 10-14 Jailbreaking on iOS Device-iPhone as SSH Server

Patching and Updating Operating Systems (10.2.3.2)

Like the OS on a desktop or laptop, you can update or patch the OS on mobile devices. Updates add functionality or increase performance. Patches can fix security problems or issues with hardware and software.

Because there are so many different Android mobile devices, updates and patches are not released as one package for all devices. Sometimes a new version of Android cannot install on older devices where the hardware does not meet the minimum specifications. These devices might receive patches to fix known issues, but not receive OS upgrades.

Android updates and patches use an automated process for delivery. When a carrier or manufacturer has an update for a device, a notification on the device indicates that an update is ready. Touch the update to begin the download and installation process.

iOS updates also use an automated process for delivery, and devices that do not meet the hardware requirements are also excluded. To check for updates to iOS, connect the device to iTunes. A notice to download opens if updates are available. To manually check for updates, click the **Check for Update** button in the iTunes Summary pane.

There are two other types of updates for mobile device radio firmware that are important. These are called baseband updates and consist of the *Preferred Roaming List (PRL)* and the *Primary Rate ISDN (PRI)*. The PRL is configuration information that a cellular phone needs to communicate on networks other than its own, so that a call can be made outside of the carrier's network. The PRI configure the data rates between the device and the cell tower. This ensures that the device is able to communicate with the tower at the correct rate.

Network Connectivity and Email (10.3)

Mobile devices give people the freedom to work, learn, play, and communicate wherever they want. People using mobile devices do not need to be tied to a physical location to send and receive voice, video, and data communications.

Wireless and Cellular Data Network (10.3.1)

A connection to the Internet through a cellular company is expensive and relies on cellular towers and satellites to create a mesh of global coverage. Typically, cellular companies charge their customers based on the amount of data they transport through the cellular network. A cellular connection can become expensive. Using a service provider for Internet connection and supplying local wireless connections in many businesses is a reasonable alternative to using cellular data in some places.

Wireless Data Network (10.3.1.1)

College campuses use wireless networks to allow students to sign up for classes, watch lectures, and submit assignments in areas where physical connections to the network are unavailable. With mobile devices becoming more powerful, many tasks that needed to be performed on large computers connected to physical networks can now be completed using mobile devices on wireless networks.

Coffee shops, libraries, work places or homes typically use a different type of connection to Internet. These connections are usually based on established cable TV or telephone lines to connect the building to the service provider. Companies providing this type of connection to the Internet usually charge a flat fee for a specific speed, regardless of the amount of data transported. The relatively low cost of this type connection makes it possible for businesses to provide a free Internet connection to their customers. The customers connect to the Internet through the local wireless network of that business.

Almost all mobile devices are capable of connecting to WiFi networks. It is advisable to connect to WiFi networks when possible because data used over WiFi does not count against the cellular data plan. Also, because WiFi radios use less power than cellular radios, connecting to WiFi networks conserves battery power. Like other WiFi-enabled devices, it is important to use security when connecting to WiFi networks. These precautions should be taken to protect WiFi communications on mobile devices:

- Use the highest WiFi security framework possible. Currently WPA2 security is the most secure.
- Enable security on home networks.
- Never send login or password information using clear, unencrypted text.
- Use a VPN connection when possible.

To turn WiFi on or off, use the following path for Android and iOS

Settings > WiFi > turn WiFi on or off

To connect an Android device when it is within the range of a WiFi network, turn on WiFi, and the device then searches for all available WiFi networks, and displays them in a list. Touch a WiFi network in the list to connect. Enter a password if needed.

When a mobile device roams out of the range of the WiFi network, it attempts to connect to another WiFi network in range. If no WiFi networks are in range, the mobile device connects to the cellular data network. When WiFi is on, it automatically connects to any WiFi network that it has connected to previously. If the network is new, the mobile device either displays a list of available networks that can be used or asks if it should connect to it.

If a mobile device does not prompt to connect to a WiFi network, the network SSID broadcast may be turned off, or the device may not be set to connect automatically. Manually configure the WiFi settings on the mobile device.

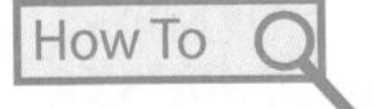

To connect to a WiFi network manually on an Android device, follow these steps:

Step 1. Select **Settings > Add network.**

Step 2. Enter the network SSID.

Step 3. Touch **Security** and select a security type.

Step 4. Touch **Password** and enter the password.

Step 5. Touch **Save**.

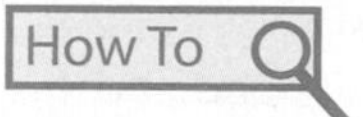

To connect to a WiFi network manually on an iOS device, follow these steps:

Step 1. Select **Settings > WiFi > Other.**

Step 2. Enter the network SSID.

Step 3. Touch **Security** and select a security type.

Step 4. Touch **Other Network.**

Step 5. Touch **Password** and enter the password.

Step 6. Touch **Join.**

Tethering

If a user wants to synchronize data, share files or an Internet connection, a connection can be made between two devices using a cable, WiFi, or Bluetooth. This connection is called *tethering*. For example, a user may need to connect a computer to the Internet but no WiFi or wired connection is available. A cell phone can be used as a bridge to the Internet, through the cellular carrier's network.

Lab—Mobile WiFi (10.3.1.2)

In this lab, you turn the WiFi radio on and off, forget a found WiFi network, and find and connect to a WiFi network. Refer to the lab in *IT Essentials v6 Lab Manual*.

Cellular Communications (10.3.1.3)

When people began to use cell phones, there were few industry-wide standards for cell phone technology. Without standards, it was difficult and expensive to make calls to people who were on another network. Today, cell phone providers use industry standards, making it less expensive to use cell phones to make calls.

Cellular standards have not been adopted uniformly around the world. Some cell phones are capable of using multiple standards, whereas others can use only one standard. As a result, some cell phones can operate in many countries, and other cell phones can only be used locally.

The first generation (1G) of cell phones began service in the 1980s. First-generation phones primarily used analog standards. With analog, interference and noise cannot easily be separated from the voice in the signal. This factor limits the usefulness of analog systems. Few 1G devices are in use today.

In the 1990s, the second generation (2G) of mobile devices was marked by a switch from analog to digital standards. Digital standards provide higher call quality.

As 3G cell phone standards were being developed, extensions to the existing 2G standards were added. These transitional standards are known as 2.5G standards.

Third-generation (3G) standards enable mobile devices to go beyond simple voice and data communications. It is now common for mobile devices to send and receive text, photos, audio, and video. 3G even provides enough bandwidth for video conferencing. 3G mobile devices are also able to access the Internet to browse, play games, listen to music, and watch video.

Fourth-generation (4G) standards provide ultra-broadband Internet access. Higher data rates allow users to download files much faster, perform video conferencing, or watch high-definition television. These are some common 4G standards:

- Mobile WiMAX
- Long Term Evolution (LTE)

The specification for 4G devices sets peak speed requirements at 100 Mb/s for highly mobile devices (devices in cars or trains) and 1 Gb/s for devices being used by people moving slowly or standing still.

Mobile WiMAX and LTE

Even though *Mobile WiMAX* and *LTE* fall short of the data rate to be compliant with 4G (128 Mb/s and 100 Mb/s, respectively), they are still considered 4G standards, because they offer so much improvement over the performance of 3G. WiMAX and LTE are also forerunners to versions that will be compliant with the full specification of 4G.

Technologies that add multimedia and networking functionality can be bundled with cellular standards. The two most common are *Short Message Service (SMS)*, used for text messaging, and *Multimedia Message Service (MMS)*, used for sending and receiving photos and videos. Most cellular providers charge extra for adding these features.

To turn on or off cellular data on an Android device, use the following path:

Settings > Touch **More** under Wireless and Networks **>** Touch **Mobile Networks >** Touch **Data** enabled

To turn on or off cellular data on an iOS device use the following path:

Settings > General > Cellular Data > turn cellular data on or off

As a mobile device moves from an area of 4G coverage to 3G coverage, the 4G radio shuts off and turns on the 3G radio. Connections are not lost during this transition.

Hotspot

A *hotspot* is a physical location where an Internet connection is shared among wireless users. As shown in Figure 10-15, a personal hotspot can be created using a mobile device with a cellular data connection. The mobile device with hotspot enabled can offer Internet connection to other devices in the wireless LAN.

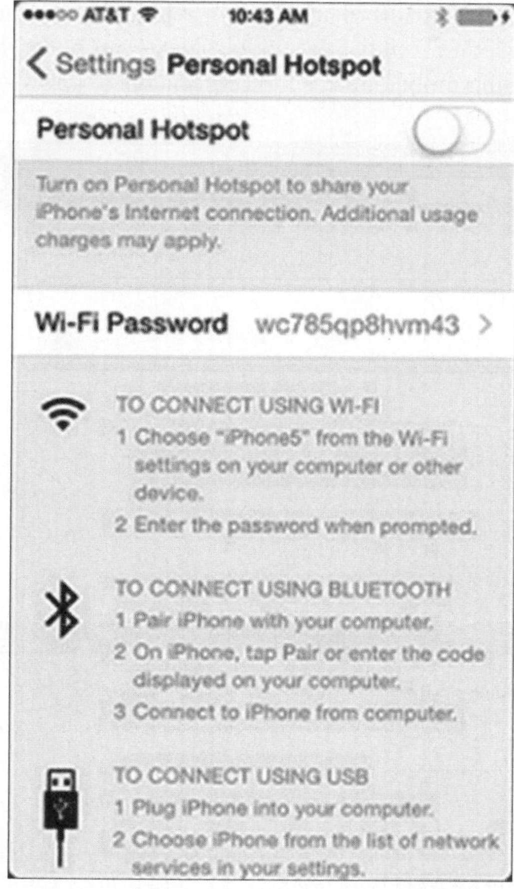

Figure 10-15 Personal Hotspot on iOS

Airplane Mode

Most mobile devices also have a setting called *Airplane Mode* that turns off all cellular, WiFi, and Bluetooth radios. Airplane Mode is useful when traveling on an airplane or when located where accessing data is prohibited or expensive. Most mobile device functions are still usable, but communication is not possible.

To turn Airplane Mode on or off on an Android device use the following path:

Settings > More (under the Wireless & Networks section) **>** Airplane mode toggle

To turn Airplane Mode on or off on an iOS device use the following path:

Settings and turn **Airplane mode** on or off Figures 10-16 and 10-17 show Airplane mode found Android and iOS, respectively.

There are apps available for mobile devices that can display available networks, signal strength of access points and towers, and even locations of networks. A WiFi analyzer can be used to display information about wireless networks, whereas a cell tower analyzer can be used on cellular networks. These can be very useful tools to start with when diagnosing mobile device radio problems.

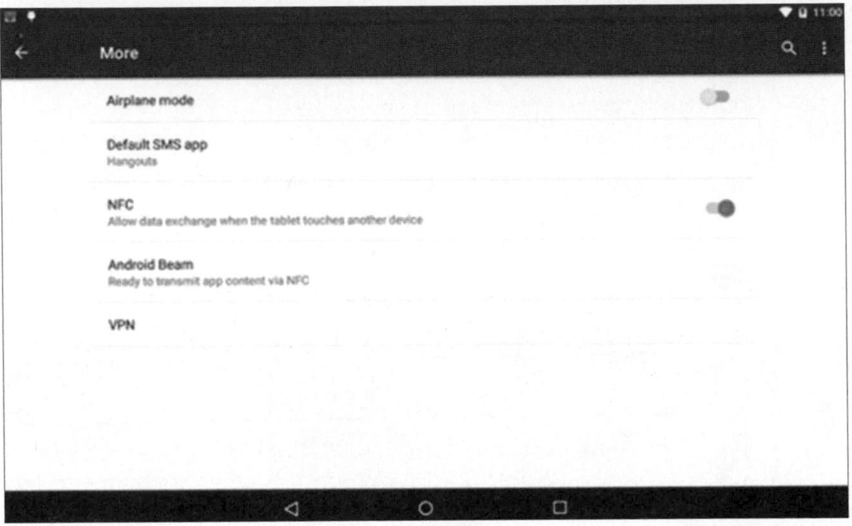

Figure 10-16 Airplane Mode Toggle Android

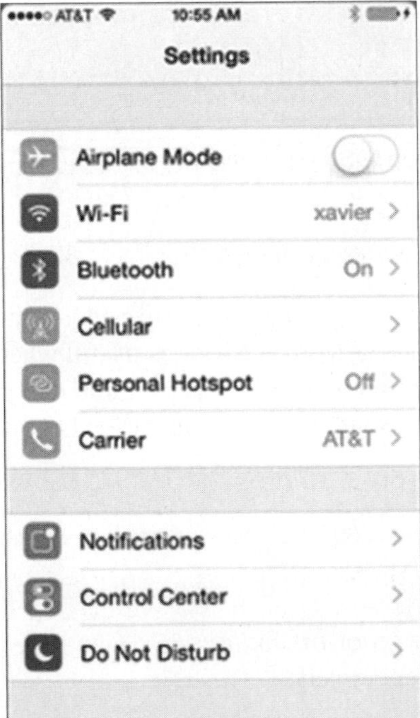

Figure 10-17 Airplane Mode Toggle iOS

Bluetooth (10.3.2)

Bluetooth was designed for communicating wirelessly over short distances with no user intervention after the initial configuration takes place. It uses low power and therefore a good choice for mobile devices running on battery. Bluetooth is a networking standard operating in the 2.45 GHz frequency, does not require line of sight, can connect multiple devices simultaneously because of the weak signal it uses, and when the Bluetooth capable devices are in range they automatically detect each other and form a personal area network. Although WiFi is used for carrying larger amounts of data, Bluetooth is used for brief and occasional communications. It is integrated into many Android and iOS devices and applications.

Bluetooth for Mobile Devices (10.3.2.1)

Mobile devices connect using many different methods. Cable connections are not always practical when connecting headsets or speakers. Bluetooth technology provides a simple way for mobile devices to connect to each other and to wireless accessories. *Bluetooth* is wireless, automatic, and uses very little power, which helps conserve battery life. Up to eight Bluetooth devices can be connected together at any one time.

These are some examples of how mobile devices use Bluetooth:

- **Hands-free headset**—A small earpiece with a microphone used for making and receiving calls.
- **Keyboard or mouse**—A keyboard or mouse can be connected to a mobile device to make input easier.
- **Stereo control**—A mobile device can connect to a home or car stereo to play music.
- **Car speakerphone**—A device that contains a speaker and a microphone used for making and receiving calls.
- **Tethering**—To synchronize data, share files, or share an Internet connection, a mobile device can be connected to another device over a physical cable such as a USB cable, or using a wireless connection such as WiFi or Bluetooth.
- **Mobile speaker**—Portable speakers can connect to mobile devices to provide high-quality audio without a stereo system.

Bluetooth is a networking standard that has two levels, physical and protocol. At the physical level, Bluetooth is a radio frequency standard. At the protocol level, devices agree on when bits are sent, how they are sent, and that what is received is the same as what was sent.

Bluetooth Pairing (10.3.2.2)

Bluetooth pairing is when two Bluetooth devices establish a connection to share resources. In order for the devices to pair, the Bluetooth radios must be turned on, and one device begins searching for other devices. Other devices must be set to discoverable mode, also called visible, so that they can be detected. When a Bluetooth device is in discoverable mode, it transmits the following information when another Bluetooth device requests it:

- Name
- Bluetooth class
- Services that the device can use
- Technical information, such as the features or the Bluetooth specification that it supports

During the pairing process, a PIN may be requested to authenticate the pairing process. The PIN is often a number, but can also be a numeric code or passkey. The PIN is stored using pairing services, so it does not have to be entered the next time the device tries to connect. This is convenient when using a headset with a smartphone, because they are paired automatically when the headset is turned on and within range.

How To

To pair a Bluetooth device with an Android device, follow these steps:

Step 1. Follow the instructions for your device to place it in discoverable mode.

Step 2. Check the instructions for your device to find the connection PIN.

Step 3. Select **Settings > Bluetooth** (under Wireless & Networks section).

Step 4. Touch the **Bluetooth** toggle to turn it on.

Step 5. Wait until Android scans and locates the Bluetooth device previously placed in discoverable mode.

Step 6. Touch the discovered device to select it.

Step 7. Enter the PIN.

How To

To pair a Bluetooth device with an iOS device, follow these steps:

Step 1. Follow the instructions for your device to place it in discoverable mode.

Step 2. Check the instructions for your device to find the connection PIN.

Step 3. Select **Settings > Bluetooth**.

Step 4. Touch **Bluetooth** to turn it on.

Step 5. Touch the discovered device to select it.

Step 6. Type the PIN.

Figures 10-18 and 10-19 show Bluetooth devices being found Android and iOS, respectively.

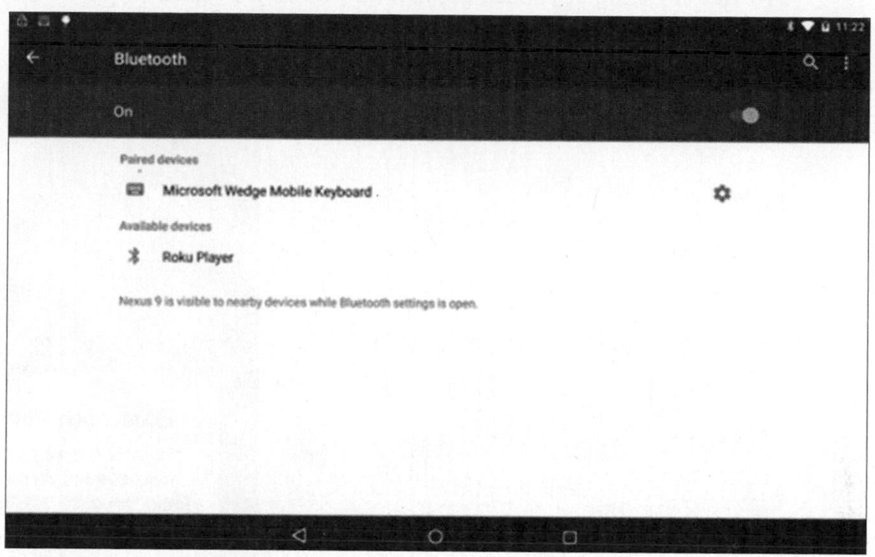

Figure 10-18 Bluetooth Toggle Android

Figure 10-19 Bluetooth Toggle iOS

For some devices, this process may vary slightly. Figures 10-20 and 10-21 show a Microsoft Bluetooth Keyboard being paired with Android and iOS, respectively. Notice how the keyboard provides a PIN to be typed on the keyboard before the pairing process can be completed.

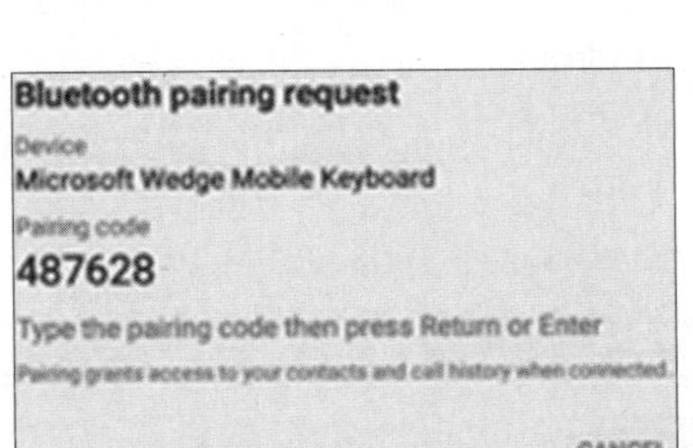

Figure 10-20 Bluetooth Pairing Android

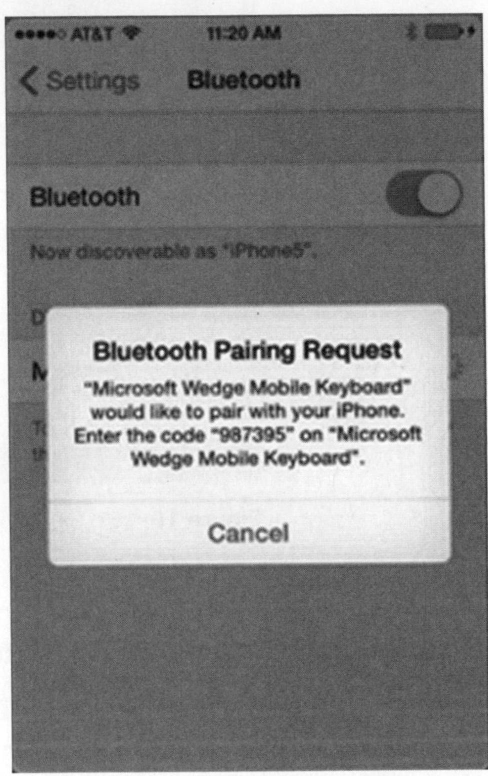

Figure 10-21 Bluetooth Pairing iOS

Configuring Email (10.3.3)

The email structure relies on servers and clients. *Email servers* are responsible for forwarding email messages sent by their users. Users utilize *email clients* to compose, read, and manage their messages. Email clients can be web-based or standalone applications. Standalone email clients are platform dependent. This section focuses on email clients for mobile devices.

Introduction to Email (10.3.3.1)

The following information is required when setting up an email account:

- **Display name**—This can be your real name, nickname, or any name that you want people to see.

- **Email address**—This is the address people need to send email to you. An email address is a username followed by the @ symbol and the domain of the email server (user@example.net).
- **Email protocols used by the incoming mail server**—Different protocols provide different email services.
- **Incoming and outgoing mail server names**—These names are provided by the network administrator or ISP.
- **Username**—This is used to log in to the mail servers.
- **Account password**—The password should be strong, because mail accounts are often available from websites.

The protocols used in email include the following:

- *Post Office Protocol version 3 (POP3)*—This retrieves emails from a remote server over TCP/IP. POP3 does not leave a copy of the email on the server; however, some implementations allow users to specify that mail be saved for some period of time. POP3 supports end users that have intermittent connections, such as dialup. A POP3 user can connect, download email from the server, and then disconnect. POP3 usually uses port 110.
- *Internet Message Access Protocol (IMAP)*—This allows local email clients to retrieve email from a server. Like POP3, IMAP allows you to download email from an email server using an email client. The difference is that IMAP allows the user to organize email on the network email server, and to download copies of email. The original email remains on the network email server. Unlike POP3, IMAP typically leaves the original email on the server until you move the email to a personal folder in your email application. IMAP synchronizes email folders between the server and client. IMAP is faster than POP3, but IMAP requires more disk space on the server and more CPU resources. The most recent version of IMAP is IMAP4. IMAP4 is often used in large networks, such as a university campus. IMAP usually uses port 143.
- *Simple Mail Transfer Protocol (SMTP)*—This is a text-based protocol that transmits emails across a TCP/IP network. It is an email format for text that uses only ASCII encoding. SMTP must be implemented to send email. SMTP sends email from an email client to an email server or from one email server to another. A message is sent after recipients are identified and verified. SMTP usually uses port 25.
- *Multipurpose Internet Mail Extensions (MIME)*—This extends the email format to include text in ASCII standard as well as other formats, such as pictures and word processor documents. MIME is normally used in conjunction with SMTP.

- *Secure Socket Layer (SSL)*—This was developed to transmit files securely. All data exchanged between the email client and the email server is encrypted. When configuring an email client to use SSL, make sure to use the correct port number for the email server.

Exchange

Exchange is an email server, contact manager, and calendaring software created by Microsoft. Exchange uses a proprietary messaging architecture called *Messaging Application Programming Interface (MAPI)*. MAPI is used by Microsoft Office Outlook to connect to Exchange servers, to provide email, calendar, and contact management.

You need to know how to configure a device to accept the correct incoming mail format. You can configure the email client software using a wizard.

Activity—Matching Email Protocols (10.3.3.2)

Please refer to the Activity in the Cisco Networking Academy IT Essentials 6.0 online course.

Android Email Configuration (10.3.3.3)

Android devices are capable of using advanced communication applications and data services. Many of these applications and features require the use of web services provided by Google. When you configure an Android mobile device for the first time, you are prompted to sign in to your Google account with your Gmail email address and password.

By signing in to your Gmail account, the Google Play store, data and settings backup, and other Google services become accessible. The device synchronizes contacts, email messages, apps, downloaded content, and other information from Google services. If you do not have a Gmail account, you can use the Google account sign-in page to create one.

Note

If you want to restore Android settings to a tablet that you have previously backed up, you must sign in to the account when setting up the tablet for the first time. You cannot restore your Android settings if you sign in after the initial setup.

After initial setup, access your mailbox by touching the Gmail app icon. Android devices also have an email app for connecting to other email accounts., If there are no other accounts created it simply redirects the user to the Gmail app in later versions of Android.

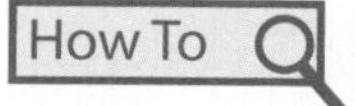

To add an email account, perform the following steps:

Step 1. Touch the **Email** or the **Gmail** app icon.

Step 2. Choose the type of account and tap **NEXT**.

Step 3. Enter the device's passcode if needed.

Step 4. Enter the email address you want to use and password.

Step 5. Tap **Create New Account**.

Step 6. Enter your first name, last name, email address and password.

Step 7. Provide a phone number for account recovery purposes (optional).

Step 8. Review the account information and tap Next.

Figures 10-22 and 10-23 show the Android email account setup screens.

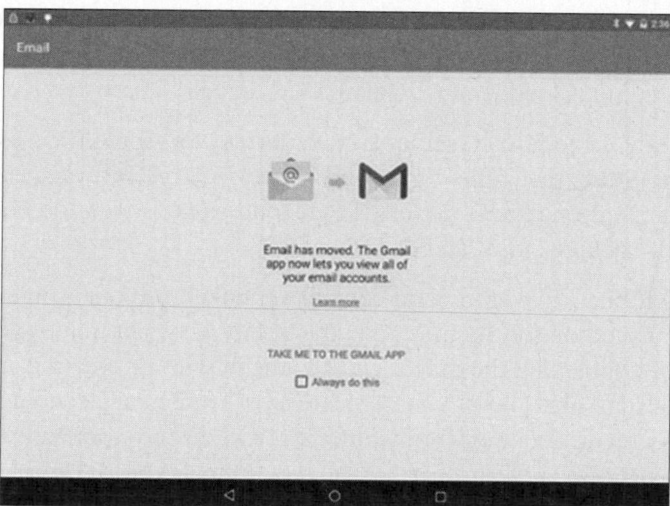

Figure 10-22 Android Email Configuration

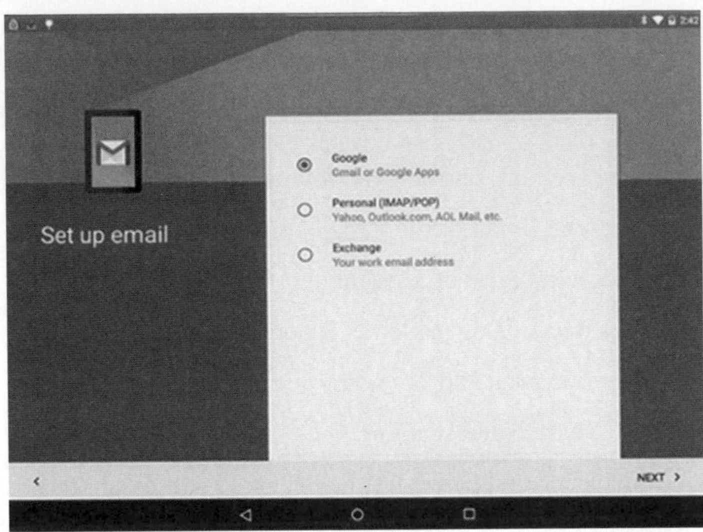

Figure 10-23 Android Email Configuration—Email Account Type

iOS Email Configuration (10.3.3.4)

iOS devices ship with a stock Mail app which can handle multiple email accounts simultaneously. The Mail app also supports a number of different email account types including iCloud, Yahoo, Gmail, Outlook and Microsoft Exchange.

An Apple ID is required to set up an iOS device. An Apple ID is used to access the Apple App Store, the iTunes Store, and iCloud. *iCloud* provides email and the ability to store content on remote servers. The iCloud email is free and comes with remote storage for backups, mail, and documents.

All of the iOS devices, apps, and content are linked to your Apple ID. When an iOS device is turned on for the first time, the Setup Assistant guides you through the process of connecting the device and signing in with or creating an Apple ID. The Setup Assistant also allows you to create an iCloud email account. You can restore settings, content, and apps from a different iOS device from an iCloud backup during the setup process.

To setup the iCloud, use the following path:

Settings > iCloud.

To set up additional email accounts follow these steps:

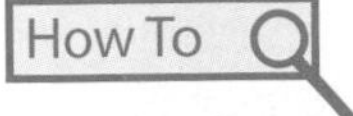

Step 1. Select **Settings > Mail, Contacts, Calendars > Add Account.**

Step 2. Tap the account type.

Step 3. If the account type is not listed, touch Other.

Step 4. Enter the account information.

Step 5. Touch **Save**.

Figures 10-24 and 10-25 show email configuration tools found on Android and iOS.

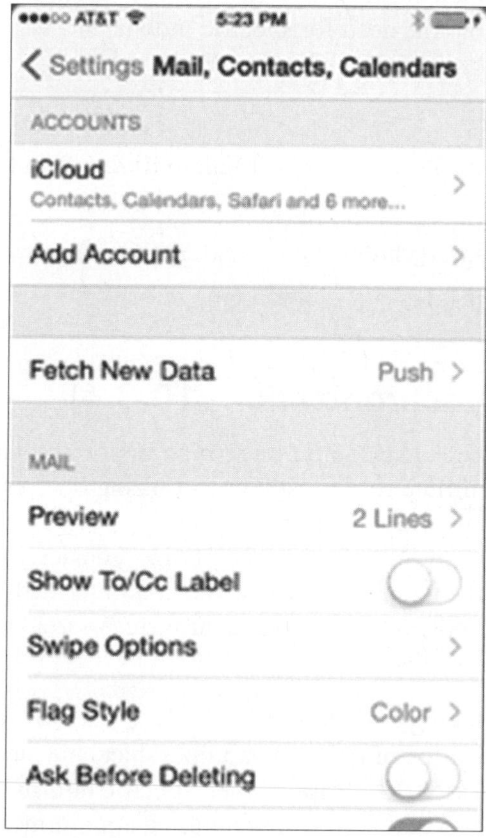

Figure 10-24 Email Configuration iOS

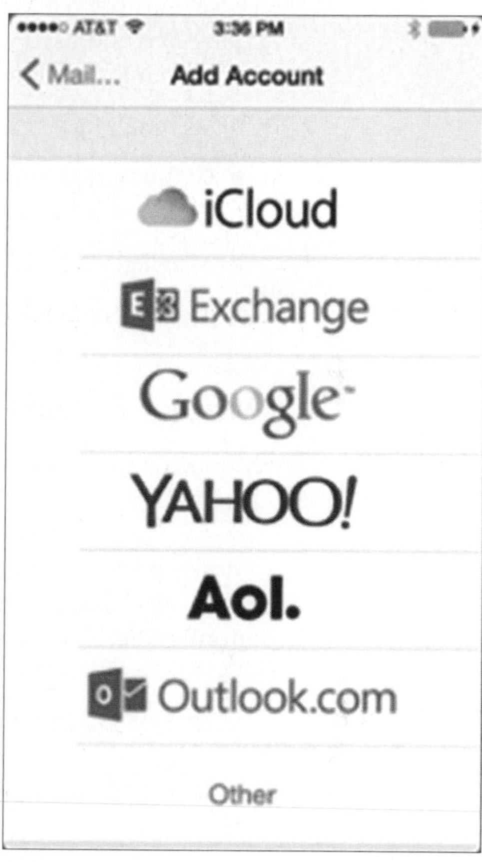

Figure 10-25 Email Configuration iOS Account Type

Internet Email (10.3.3.5)

Unlike local email where the server is controlled by an in-house administrator, *Internet email* refers to an email service that is hosted somewhere on the Internet and controlled by a third party team of administrators.

As more people began to use email, there became a need for an email service for people with little to no technical knowledge. Companies deploy, host and manage the service, leaving the users the task of managing their personal messages. Internet Email services usually provide a web-based interface to allow users to access their mailboxes through any web browser. In addition to the web interface, companies often also provide an email client app that can be downloaded and installed on mobile devices. Email client apps provide a better user experience when compared to the web interface.

Mobile device manufacturers typically add email apps to their operating systems. These apps often allow for a number of different Internet email services to be configured and used without the need for specific mobile email client apps. These are some common options for accessing an Internet Email account:

- Web interface
- GUI-based Desktop email client, such as Mail, Outlook, Windows Live Mail and Thunderbird
- Mobile email client apps, including Gmail and Yahoo
- Stock OS mobile email apps such as iOS Mail

Mobile Device Synchronization (10.3.4)

Mobile devices are used much like computers storing important data that would be hard to replace and cause difficulties if lost. Synchronizing devices is one way to help prevent that loss. Synchronization occurs when a mobile device communicates with a desktop computer or a server. When you synchronize a device with your computer, it typically updates both the mobile device and the computer with the most recent information. This section addresses ways to synchronize Android and iOS devices.

Types of Data to Synchronize (10.3.4.1)

Many people use a combination of desktop, laptop, tablet, and smartphone devices to access and store information. It is helpful when specific information is the same across multiple devices. For example, when scheduling appointments using a calendar program, each new appointment would need to be entered in each device to ensure that each device is up to date. Data synchronization eliminates the need to make changes to every device.

Data synchronization is the exchange of data between two or more devices, while maintaining consistent data on those devices. These are some of the types of data that can be synchronized:

- Contacts
- Email

- Calendar entries
- Pictures
- Music
- Apps
- Video
- Browser links and settings
- Location Data

Although the term Sync means data synchronization in the sense covered above, it has slight differences on Android and iOS.

Android

Sync essentially synchronizes your contacts and other data with Google and other services.

The *Sync process on Android* synchronizes user data to services, including Facebook, Google, and Twitter. As a result, all devices associated to that Google account have access to the same data, making it easier to replace a damaged device without data loss. The synchronizing process on Android is also simple; just add the account and turn on Auto Sync.

You may see all accounts on your device by visiting **Settings > Accounts,** as shown in Figure 10-26.

Auto-sync will synchronize your device with the service's servers automatically, without user intervention. To turn on Auto-Sync, from the same Accounts panel shown in Figure 10-27, select the triple dot icon on the upper right corner and tap **Auto-sync data.**

Android Sync also allows the user to choose what types of data gets synchronized. To turn on or off data sync per-data type on Android, use the following path:

Settings > Accounts > tap on the account you want to configure **>** toggle the data types on or off accordingly, as shown in Figure 10-27.

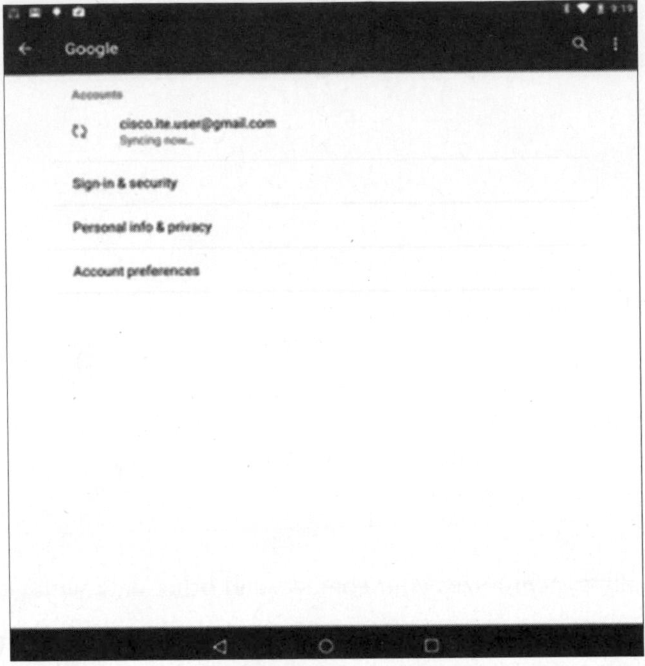

Figure 10-26 Syncing Data on Android

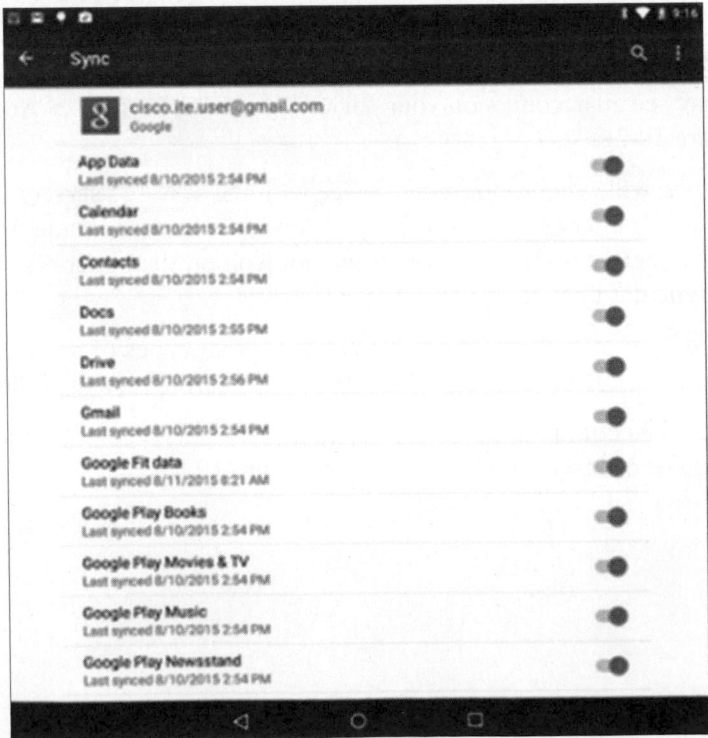

Figure 10-27 Specifying Type of Data to Backup on Android

iOS

Two different processes exist on iOS to synchronize device data. They are Backup and Sync.

Backup copies your personal data from your phone to your computer. That includes application settings, text messages, voicemails, and other data types.

Sync copies new apps, music, video, or books from iTunes to your phone and from your phone to iTunes, resulting on full synchronization on both devices.

Backup saves a copy of the all data created by the user and by apps. Sync copies only media downloaded via the iTunes Store mobile app, respecting what was specified through iTunes' Sync definitions. For example, a user can keep movies from syncing to the phone if the user does not watch movies on the phone.

As a general rule, when connecting an iOS device to iTunes, always perform a Backup first, and then Sync. This order can be changed in iTunes' Preferences.

A few more useful options are available when performing Sync or Backup on iOS:

- **Backup storage location—**iTunes allows backups to be stored on the local computer hard drive or on the iCloud online service.
- **Backup straight from iOS device—**In addition to backing up data from an iOS device to the local hard drive or iCloud through iTunes, users can configure the iOS device to upload a copy of its data directly to iCloud. This is useful as Backups can be performed automatically, eliminating the need to connect to iTunes. Similar to Android, the user can also specify what type of data is sent to the iCloud backup, as shown in Figure 10-28.

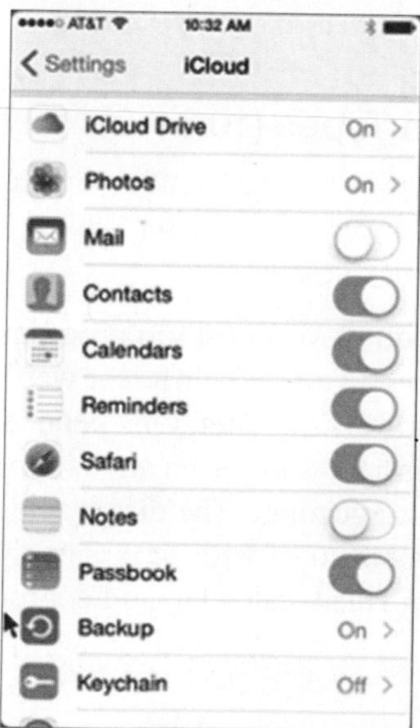

Figure 10-28 Specifying Type of Data to Backup on iOS

- **Sync over WiFi**—iTunes can scan and connect to iOS on the same WiFi network. When connected, the Backup process can be initiated automatically between iOS devices and iTunes. This is useful as Backups can be performed automatically every time iTunes and the iOS device are on the same WiFi, eliminating the need for a wired USB connection.

When a new iPhone is connected to the computer, iTunes will offer to restore it using the most recent backup of data from other iOS devices, if available. Figure 10-29 shows the iTunes window on a computer.

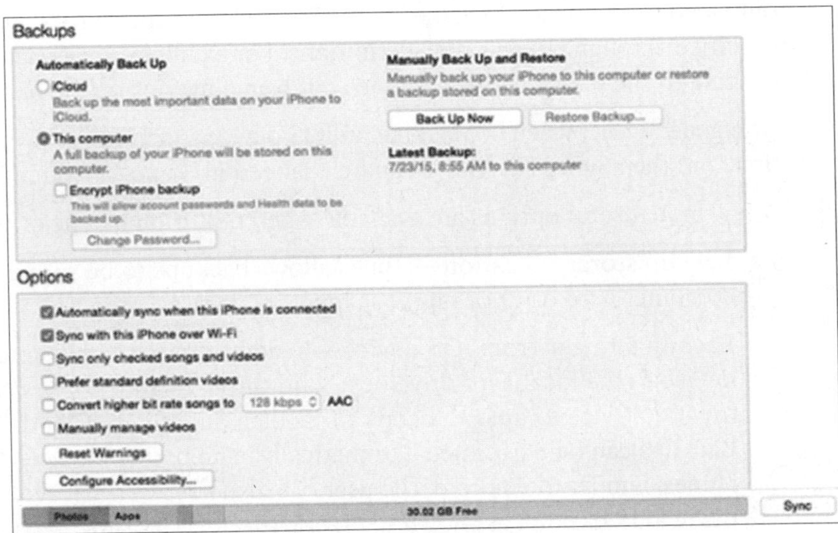

Figure 10-29 Syncing Data on iOs

Synchronization Connection Types (10.3.4.2)

To synchronize data between devices, the devices must use a common communication medium. USB and WiFi connections are the most common connection types used to synchronize data between devices.

Because most Android devices do not have a desktop program for performing data synchronization, most users sync with Google's different web services, even when synchronizing with a desktop or laptop computer. One benefit of synchronizing data using this method is that the data is accessible from any computer or mobile device at any time by signing in to a Google account. The disadvantage to this arrangement is that it can be difficult to synchronize data with programs that are installed locally on a computer, such as Outlook for email, calendar, and contacts.

Before iOS 5, synchronization was limited to using a USB connection cable to connect the device to a computer. You can now use WiFi Sync to synchronize with iTunes. To use WiFi Sync, you must first synchronize the iOS device with iTunes using a USB cable. You must also turn on Sync over WiFi Connection in the Summary pane of iTunes. After that, you can use WiFi Sync or a USB cable. When the iOS device is on the same wireless network as the computer running iTunes and it is plugged into a power source, it automatically synchronizes with iTunes.

Microsoft also offers cloud storage for synchronizing data between devices through the use of OneDrive. *OneDrive* is also able to synchronize data between mobile devices and PCs.

Linux and OS X Operating Systems (10.4)

Linux and OS X are the operating systems that are most familiar to users besides Microsoft Windows.

Linux and OS X Tools and Features (10.4.1)

This section explores the operating system in iOS devices, OS X, and the OS for Android which is a modified Linux. Both of these OSs contribute open source code for development.

Introduction to Linux and OS X Operating Systems (10.4.1.1)

UNIX is a non-proprietary operating system based on the C programming language and user command interface. Some popular desktop operating systems are based on UNIX, such as Linux, OS X, Android and iOS.

Linux

Linux operating systems are used in practically every platform, including embedded-systems, wearable devices, smartwatches, cellphones, netbooks, PCs, servers and super computers. Although Linux is getting a larger user base, Android, a modified version of Linux, may be responsible for the operating system's spread throughout the consumer market.

Figure 10-30 shows the desktop of Ubuntu Linux.

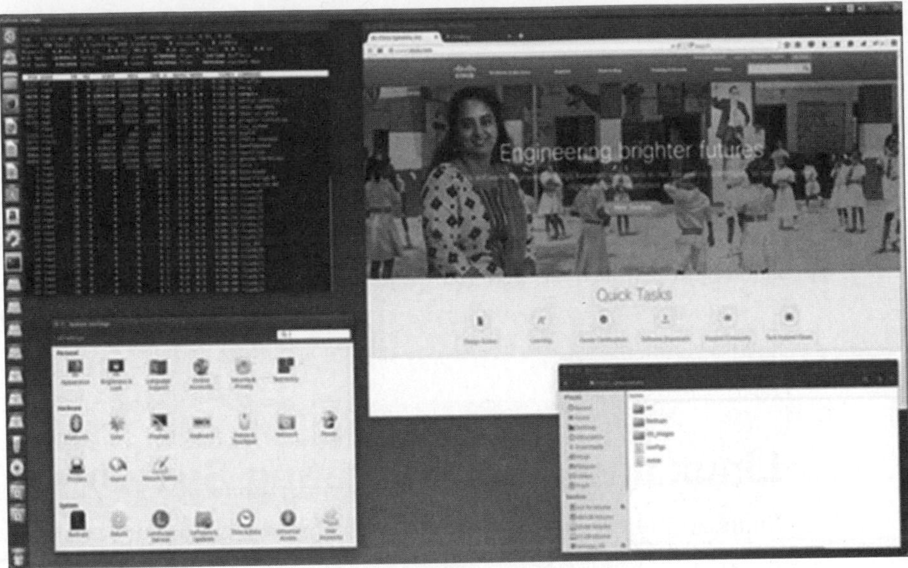

Figure 10-30 Ubuntu Desktop—Unity

OS X (Formerly known as Mac OS X)

The operating system for Macintosh computers is *OS X*. It is formerly known as Mac OS X. OS X is streamlined for Macintosh computer hardware, and it can work seamlessly with other Apple devices, such as iPhones.

Figure 10-31 shows the desktop of OS X 10.10 Yosemite.

Figure 10-31 OS X Yosemite Desktop

Note

This chapter focuses on Ubuntu Linux 14.04 LTS (Trusty Tahr) and Apple OS X 10.10 (Yosemite).

A special tool built in to OS X allows some unique installation configurations. The tool is called *Netboot*, and it can boot multiple OS X machines remotely. After the machines are rebooted, any content from the session is gone. This can be used in a setting such as a classroom to reset the computers at the end of a class or day. The tool can also place an OS installation or a program on multiple computers at the same time. This would be useful in a corporate enterprise to image or upgrade all computers.

Overview of Linux and OS X GUI (10.4.1.2)

Most operating systems include one or more GUI component to facilitate the user-computer interaction.

Linux GUI

Different Linux distributions ship with different software packages, but users decide what stays in their system by installing or removing packages. The graphical interface in Linux is comprised of a number of subsystems that can also be removed or replaced by the user. Although the details about these subsystems and their interactions are beyond the scope of this course, it is important to know the Linux GUI as whole can be easily replaced by the user. As a result of the extremely large number of Linux distributions, this chapter focuses on Ubuntu when covering Linux.

Ubuntu Linux uses Unity as its default GUI. Another feature in the Linux GUI is the ability to have multiple desktops or workspaces. This allows the users to arrange the windows on a particular workspace.

Canonical has a website that simulates Unity's UI and also provides a tour through the Unity's main features. To experience Unity via Canonical's website visit this URL: http://tour.ubuntu.com/en/. You can go to the online course to access the link.

Figure 10-32 shows a breakdown of the main components of Ubuntu Unity Desktop.

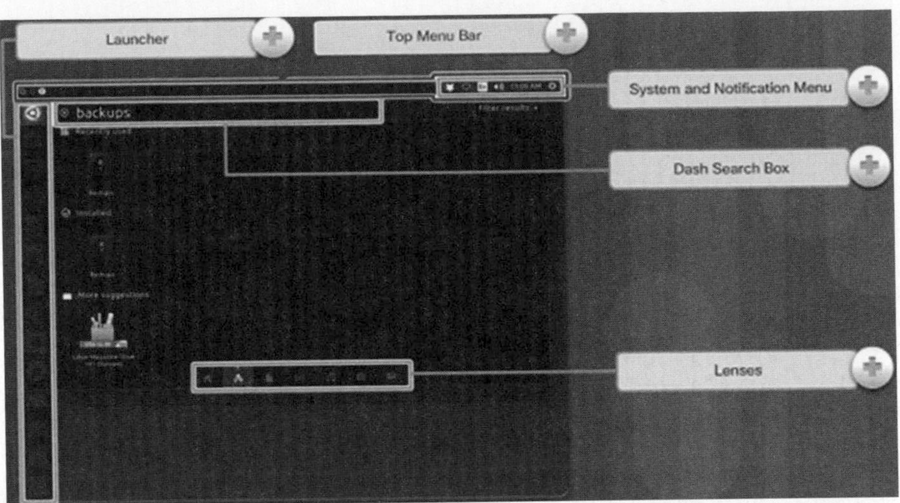

Figure 10-32 Ubuntu Unity GUI

Table 10-2 describes the main components of Ubuntu Unity Desktop GUI.

Table 10-2 Main Components of Ubuntu Unity GUI

Component	Description
Launcher	A dock placed on the left side of the screen that serves as application launcher and switcher. Right-click any application hosted on the Launcher to access a short list of tasks the application can perform.
Top Menu bar	A multipurpose menu bar containing the currently running application, buttons to control the active window, and system controls and notifications.
System and Notification menu	Many important functions are located in the indicator menus at the top right corner of your screen. Use the indicator menu to switch users, shut down your computer, control the volume level, or change network settings.
Dash search box	Holds the Search tool and a list of recently used applications. Dash includes lenses at the bottom of the Dash area, which allow the user to fine tune Dash search results. To access Dash, simply click the Ubuntu button on the top of the Launcher.
Lenses	Allows the user to fine tune the results

OS X GUI

Among the major differences between older versions of Mac OS and OS X is the addition of the Aqua GUI. Aqua was designed around the theme of water, with components resembling droplets and a deliberate use of reflection and translucency. The latest release of OS X 10.10 Yosemite introduces a flatter Aqua theme.

Figure 10-33 shows a breakdown of the OS X Aqua desktop.

Figure 10-33 Ubuntu Unity GUI

Table 10-3 describes the main components of OS X Aqua desktop GUI.

Table 10-3 Main Components of OS X Aqua Desktop GUI

Component	Description
Apple menu	Access system preferences, software updates, power controls, and more.
Application menu	Displays the name of the active application in bold and the menu of the active application.
Menu bar	Contains the Apple menu, currently active application menus, status menus and indicators, Spotlight, and Notification Center.
Notification Center icon	Allows the user to see all notifications
Spotlight icon	Used for searching for apps, documents, images and other file
Status menu	Displays date and time and status of your computer and some features, such as Bluetooth and wireless.
Dock	Displays thumbnails of frequently used applications and the running applications that are minimized. One of the important functions included in the Dock is Force Quit. By right-clicking a running application in the Dock, the user can choose to close an unresponsive application.

With OS X, *Mission Control* is a quick way to see everything that is currently open on your Mac. Mission Control can be accessed by using a three or four finger swipe up gesture, depending on your touch pad or mouse settings. Mission Control allows you to organize your apps on multiple desktops. To navigate the file system, OS X includes Finder. *Finder* is very similar to the Windows File Explorer.

OS X also allows screen sharing. Screen sharing is a feature that lets other people using MACs to be able to view your screen. They can even be allowed to take control of your computer. This is very useful when you may need help or wish to help someone else.

Overview of Linux and OS X CLI (10.4.1.3)

In both Linux and OS X, the user can communicate with the operating system by using the *command-line interface (CLI)*. Command-line interface (CLI) is a text-based interface in which at a prompt users type commands in a specified format or syntax to which the system responds. To add flexibility, commands (or tools) that support parameters, options and switches, are usually preceded by the dash ("—") character. The options and switches supported by a command are also entered by the user along with the command.

A program called a *shell* interprets the commands from the keyboard and passes them to the operating system. When a user logs in the system, the login program checks the username and password; if the credentials are correct, the login program starts the shell. From this point on, an authorized user can begin interacting with the OS through text-based commands.

The shell acts as an interface layer between the user and kernel. The *kernel* is responsible for allocating CPU time and memory to processes. It also manages the file system and communications in response to system calls.

As shown in Figure 10-34, users interact with the kernel through a shell.

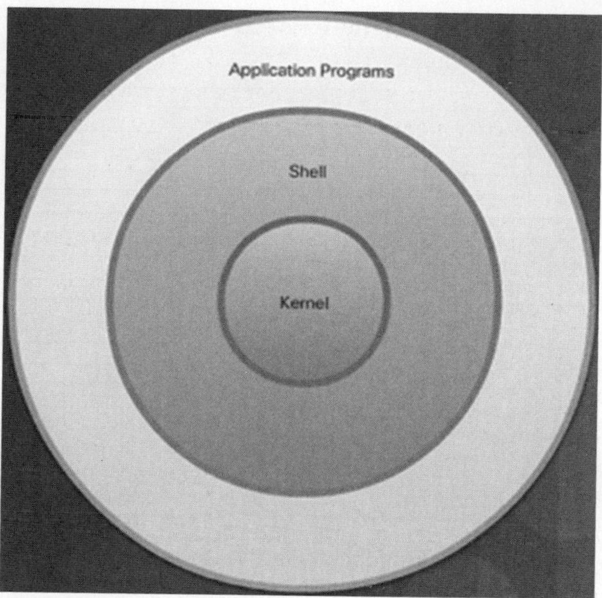

Figure 10-34 UNIX High Level Diagram

Most operating systems include a graphical interface. Although a command-line interface is still present, the OS often boots into the GUI by default, hiding the command-line interface from the user. One way to access the command-line interface in a GUI-based operating system is through a terminal emulator application. These applications provide user access to the command-line interface and are often named as some variation of the word *terminal*. On Linux, popular terminal emulators are Terminator, eterm, xterm, konsole, and gnome-terminal. OS X includes a terminal emulator called Terminal but a number of third-party emulators are available.

Figure 10-35 shows gnome-terminal, a popular Linux terminal emulator.

Figure 10-36 shows Terminal, a popular OS X terminal emulator.

```
rod@desktop: ~
rod@desktop:~$ uname -a
Linux desktop 3.13.0-32-generic #57-Ubuntu SMP Tue Jul 15 03:51:08 UTC 2014 x86_
64 x86_64 x86_64 GNU/Linux
rod@desktop:~$
rod@desktop:~$
rod@desktop:~$ ls -l Documents/
total 12
drwxrwxr-x 3 rod rod 4096 Dec  8  2013 air
drwxrwxr-x 3 rod rod 4096 Aug 13 13:24 backups
-rw-rw-r-- 1 rod rod    0 Aug 13 13:27 configs
-rw-rw-r-- 1 rod rod    0 Aug 13 13:27 notes
drwxrwxr-x 2 rod rod 4096 Aug 13 13:26 OS_images
rod@desktop:~$
rod@desktop:~$
rod@desktop:~$ ls -l Documents/ | grep OS
drwxrwxr-x 2 rod rod 4096 Aug 13 13:26 OS_images
rod@desktop:~$
rod@desktop:~$
rod@desktop:~$
```

Figure 10-35 Linux Terminal Emulator—Gnome-Terminal

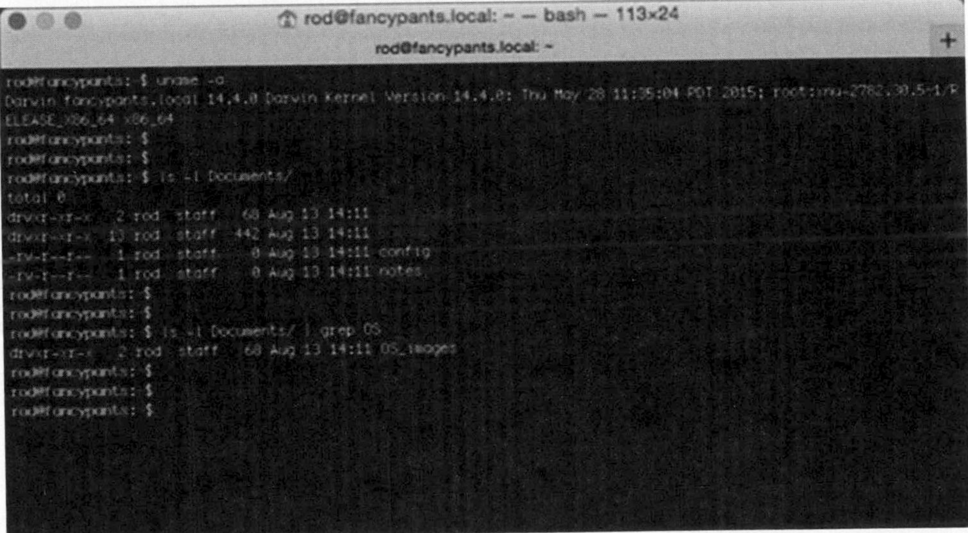

Figure 10-36 OS X Terminal Emulator

Note

The same commands were issued in both terminals to illustrate how similar the command-line interfaces are in UNIX-like systems.

Note

To experience a Linux command-line interface in your web browser, go to the online class and visit the NDG Linux CompTIA A+ supplemental module.

Linux and OS X File Systems

Linux and OS X have unique file systems.

The commonly used file systems in Linux are ext3 and ext4 (third and fourth extended file system). They are journaled file systems that keep journals, or logs, of all the changes about to be made to the file system. These journals minimize the risk of file system corruption in the event of a sudden power loss because the journals can be used to apply the changes after power is restored. Both filesystems can support large file sizes up to 32 TiB (tebibytes) for ext4.

HFS+ (Hierarchical File System Plus) is the principle file system used by OS X. Like ext3 and ext4, HFS+ also supports journaled volumes. HFS+ volumes can support large file sizes up to almost 8 EiB (exbibyte) in OS X 10.4 and later.

Lab—Install Linux in a Virtual Machine and Explore the GUI (10.4.1.4)

In this lab, you install a Linux OS in a virtual machine using a desktop virtualization application, such as VirtualBox. After completing the installation, you explore the GUI interface. Refer to the lab in *IT Essentials v6 Lab Manual.*

Overview of Backup and Recovery (10.4.1.5)

The process of *backing up data* refers to creating a copy (or multiple copies) of data for safekeeping. When the backing up process is complete, the copy is called a backup. The primary goal is the ability to restore or recover the data in case of failure. Gaining access to an earlier version of the data is often seen as a secondary goal of the backing up process.

Although backups can be achieved with a simple copy command, many tools and techniques exist to make the process automatic and transparent to the user.

Linux

Several backup tools and solutions are available for Linux. *Déjà Dup* is an easy and efficient tool for backing up data.

Figure 10-37 shows the Deja Dup program on Ubuntu Linux.

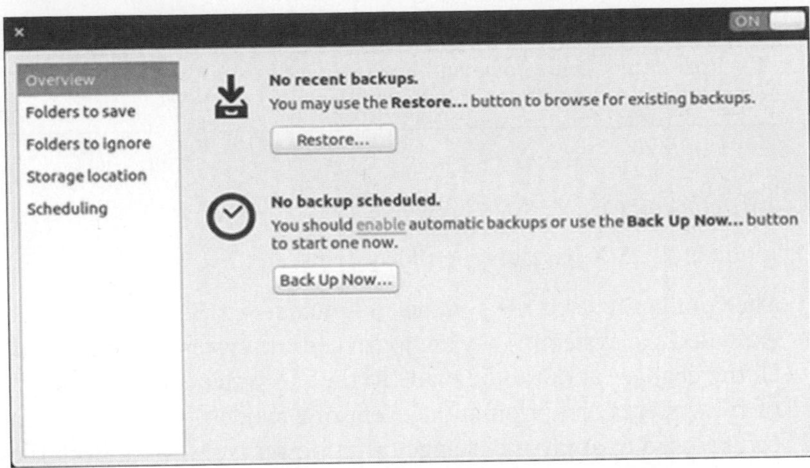

Figure 10-37 Déjà Dup

Déjà Dup supports a number of features including local, remote, or cloud backup locations. Figure 10-38 shows the Deja Dup program backup location feature.

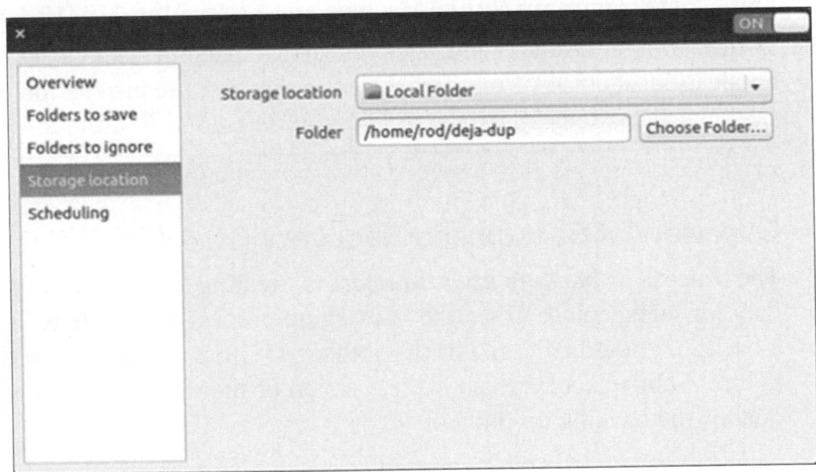

Figure 10-38 Déjà Dup Backup Location

Other features such as data encryption compression, incremental backs up, periodic scheduled backups, and GNOME desktop integration are also choices. Figure 10-39 shows the Deja Dup program backup scheduling.

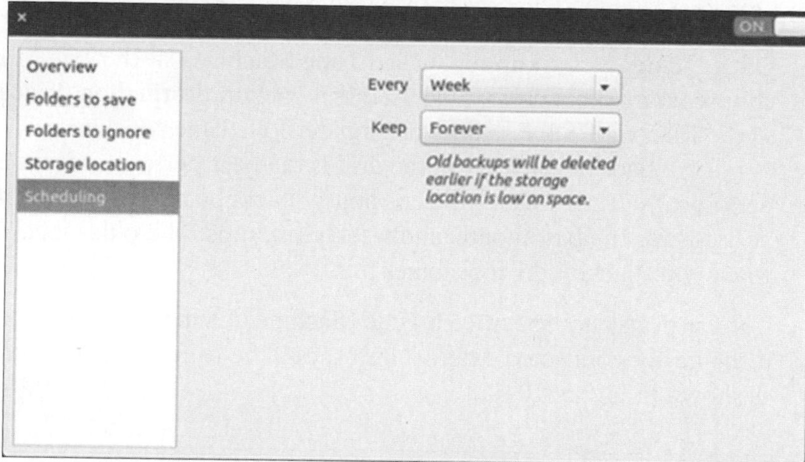

Figure 10-39 Déjà Dup—Backup Scheduling

It also restores from any particular backup. Figure 10-40 shows the option to choose where to restore the data from using the Deja Dup program on Ubuntu Linux.

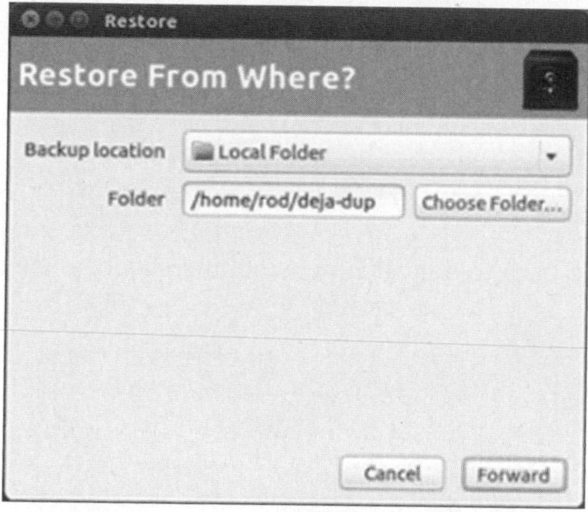

Figure 10-40 Déjà Dup Restoring a Backup

To enable automatic backups on Ubuntu Linux, use the following path:

Click the Ubuntu button at the top of **Launcher >** type **deja dup > click** the **Déjà Dup** icon **> Click** the toggle switch located on the upper right corner of Déjà Dup's window to turn backups **On.**

OS X

OS X includes a backup tool called Time Machine. With *Time Machine*, users choose an external drive to be used as a backup destination device and connect it to the Mac via USB, FireWire or Thunderbolt. Time Machine will prepare the disk to receive backups and, when the disk is ready, it performs incremental backups periodically. Time Machine keeps hourly backups for the past 24 hours, daily backups for the past month, and weekly backups. The oldest backups are deleted when your backup drive becomes full.

If the user has not specified a Time Machine destination disk, Time Machine will ask if the newly connected external disk should be used as the destination backup disk, as shown in Figure 10-41.

Figure 10-41 Time Machine—Destination Backup Disk

To adjust Time Machine settings, use the following path:

Settings > Time Machine

Figure 10-42 shows the path to adjust Time Machine settings use the following path.

Figure 10-42 Time Machine—Settings

If Time Machine is configured and the destination disk is connected, Time Machine will perform automatic backups based on its time schedule. Alternatively, a user can start a backup at any time by clicking **Back up Now** on the Time Machine menu bar menu.

To restore data from Time Machine, make sure the destination backup disk is connected to the Mac and click **Enter Time Machine** in the Time Machine menu. Time Machine allows the user to restore the data to any previous version currently available in the destination backup disk.

Overview of Disk Utilities (10.4.1.6)

Most operating systems are quite reliable, but problems could still occur and damage the system. A disk that is damaged or has corrupted sectors could lose data, or the OS could malfunction. Most disk problems are the same regardless of the operating system used. To help diagnose and solve disk-related problems, most modern operating systems include disk utility tools. Below are a few common maintenance tasks that can be performed using disk utility software:

- *Partition management*—When working with computer disks, partitions may need to be created, deleted, or resized. If the OS is running off a partition that needs attention, the computer should be booted from an external disk before any work is done in the system partition.
- *Mount or Unmount disk partitions*—On UNIX-like systems, mounting a partition relates to the process of binding a partition of a disk or a disk image file (usually an .iso) to a folder location. This is a common task in UNIX-like systems.
- *Disk format*—Before a partition can be used by the user or the system, it must be formatted.
- *Bad sector check*—Modern disks are able to detect and flag bad sectors. When a disk sector is flagged as bad, it becomes harmless to the OS because it will no longer be used to store data. Although it is common to have a few bad sectors in any disk, a large number of bad sectors could be an indicator of a failing disk. Disk utilities can be used not only to search, detect and flag bad sectors, but also to attempt salvaging data stored in bad sectors by moving it to healthy disk sectors.
- **Query S.M.A.R.T. attributes**—An abbreviation for *Self-Monitoring, Analysis and Reporting Technology, S.M.A.R.T.* is a great feature added to modern disks. Included in the disk's controller itself, S.M.A.R.T. can detect and report a number of attributes about the disk's health. The goal of S.M.A.R.T. is to anticipate disk failure, allowing the user to move the data to a healthy disk before the failing disk becomes inaccessible. Modern disk utilities are able to query S.M.A.R.T. attributes, alert the user and recommend repairing actions.

Ubuntu Linux includes Disks, as shown in Figure 10-43.

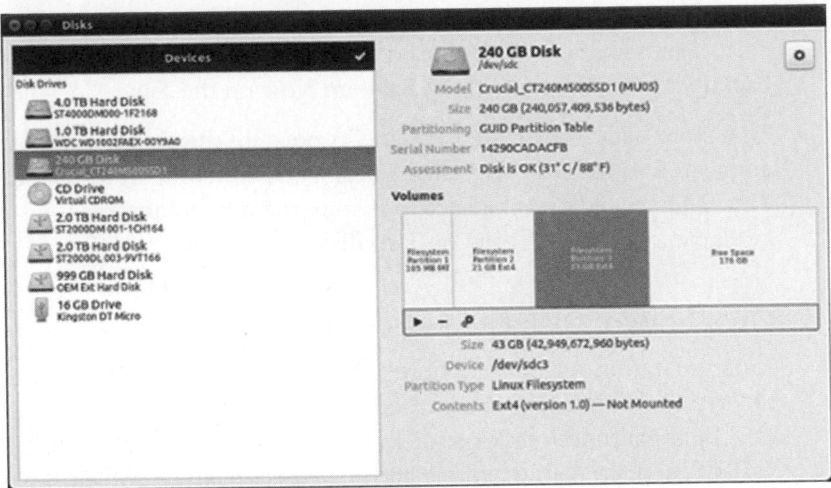

Figure 10-43 Ubuntu Utility—Disks

With Disks, users can perform the most common disk-related tasks including partition management, mount or unmount, format disks, and query S.M.A.R.T.

To access Disks, use the following path:

Click the Ubuntu button at the top of Launcher **>** type **Disks >** click the Disks' icon

OS X includes Disk Utility, as shown in Figure 10-44.

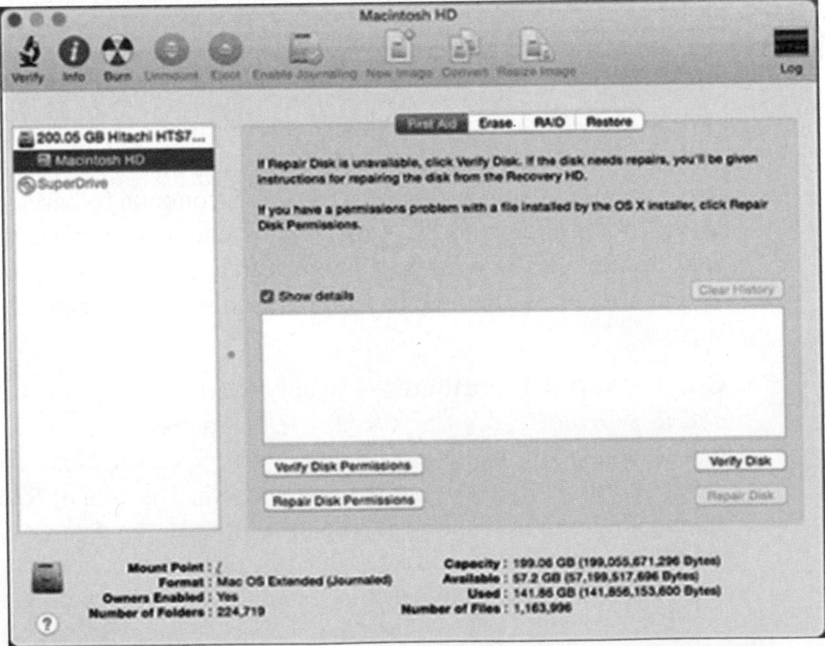

Figure 10-44 Disk Utility—OS X program

In addition to supporting the main disk maintenance tasks, Disk Utility also supports Verify Disk Permissions and Repair Disk Permissions. Repair Disk Permission is a common troubleshoot step in OS X.

To start Disk Utility on OS X, use the following path:

Applications > Utilities > Disk Utility

Disk Utility can also be used to backup disks to image files and perform an image recovery to disk from image files. These files contain the entire contents of a disk.

Multiboot

Sometimes it is necessary to have more than one operating system installed in the computer. In those situations, the user must perform the installation of one OS, install a boot manager and then install the second OS. A *boot manager* is a program that is located in the boot sector and allows the user to choose which OS to use at boot time. By tracking the partition where a specific OS was installed, a boot manager can direct the BIOS to the correct partition, allowing it to load the desired operating system.

A popular boot manager for Linux is *grub*. For OS X, a common boot manager is *boot camp*.

The maximum number of operating systems allowed depends on the size of the disk, and although the boot manager technology allows a computer to have multiple OSs installed, only one OS can be used at a time. To switch from one OS to another, a reboot is necessary.

Note

Before working on disks containing important data, a full disk backup is advised and considered best practice.

Video

Video—Multiboot (10.4.1.7)

This video shows how to set up multiboot on a computer with Windows 7 and Windows 8. This video walks through the steps of readying a newly installed second hard drive to receive data and install an OS on to the second hard drive. It also shows how to use Startup and Recovery options to boot to a multiboot computer and adjust settings. Another thing that is demonstrated is using the msconfig utility to view the boot options on the system.

Please view the video in the Cisco Networking Academy IT Essentials 6.0 online course.

Linux and OS X Best Practices (10.4.2)

Computer systems need periodic preventive maintenance to ensure best performance. Maintenance tasks should be scheduled and performed frequently to prevent problems or to detect problems early. To avoid missing maintenance tasks due to human error, computer systems can be programmed to perform tasks automatically.

Scheduled Tasks (10.4.2.1)

Two tasks that should be scheduled and performed automatically are Backups and Disk checks.

Scheduling backups are important to ensure that important data is not lost due to a hardware failure. The more frequent the backups, the smaller the risk of data loss.

Magnetic-based media's ability to hold the electromagnetic charges for storing data wears out with time. By periodically checking the disk for bad sectors, an administrator can become aware of the potential for a failure, allowing for planning and data migration.

Backups and disk checks are usually time-consuming tasks. An additional benefit of scheduled maintenance tasks is that it allows the computer to perform these tasks when no users are using the system. The CLI utility, cron, can schedule these tasks during off-peak hours.

How to Schedule a Task—The Cron Service

In Linux and OS X, the *cron service* is responsible for scheduled tasks. As a service, **cron** runs in the background and executes tasks at specific dates and times. **cron** uses a schedule table called a *cron table* that can be edited with the **crontab** command.

The cron table is a plaintext file that has 6 columns, formatted as shown in Figure 10-45.

Figure 10-45 cron Table

A task is usually represented by a command, a program or a script. To schedule a task, the user adds a row to the cron table. The new row specifies the minute, hour, day of the month, and the day of the week the task should be executed by the **cron** service. When the specified date and time arrives, the task is executed.

Table 10-4 has an explanation of the cron table fields. The center column shows the data type acceptable for the fields.

Table 10-4 Cron Table Fields

Minute	0–59	The minute the command executes.
Hour	0–23	The hour the command executes.
Day	1–31	Day of the month the command executes.
Month	1–12	The month the command executes.
Weekday	0–6	Day of the week the command executes. 0 = Sunday, 1 = Monday, and so forth
Command	varies	The command or set of commands. This must be compatible with the shell and use.

The crontab shown in Figure 10-46 has two entries.

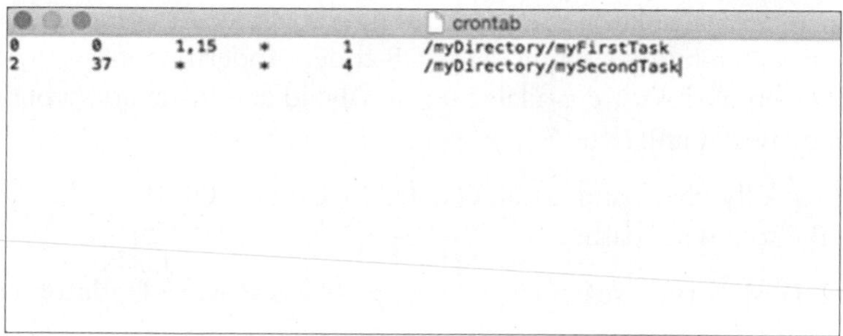

Figure 10-46 crontab Example

The first entry tells the **cron** service to execute **myFirstTask** script, located at **/myDirectory/**, on the first and fifteenth day of each month and also on Mondays, always at midnight (0h 0m). The second entry shows that the **cron** service will execute **mySecondTask** script, also located at **/myDirectory/**, every Wednesday at 2h 37m in the morning.

As stated above, **cron** uses a schedule table called a cron table that can be edited with the **crontab** command. Open a terminal window to use with the following:

To create or edit the cron table, use the **crontab -e** command from a terminal.

To list the current cron table, use the **crontab -l** command.

To remove the current cron table, use **crontab -r** command.

Security (10.4.2.2)

Despite continued efforts to create a perfectly secure operating system, vulnerabilities continue to be found. Malicious users probe operating systems searching for vulnerabilities in the code. When a vulnerability is found, it can be used as basis for the creation of a virus or other malicious software.

A number of measures can be taken to help prevent malicious software from infecting a computer system. The most common of these measures include operating system updates, firmware updates, antivirus, and antimalware.

Operating System Updates

Also known as *patches*, OS updates are released periodically by OS companies to address any known vulnerability in their operating systems. Although companies have update schedules, the release of unscheduled OS updates is common when a major vulnerability is found in the OS code. Modern operating systems will alert the user when updates are available for download and installation, but the user can check for updates at any time.

To manually check and install updates on Ubuntu Linux, as shown in Figure 10-47, use the following path:

Click **Dash >** type **software updater >** click **Software Updater** icon

Figure 10-47 Check and Install Updates on Ubuntu Linux

To manually check and install updates on OS X, as shown in Figure 10-48, use the following path:

Click the Apple logo on the upper left corner of the screen **>** Select **About This Mac >** On the Overview tab, select Software Update **Software Update... >** Select the **Update** Tab

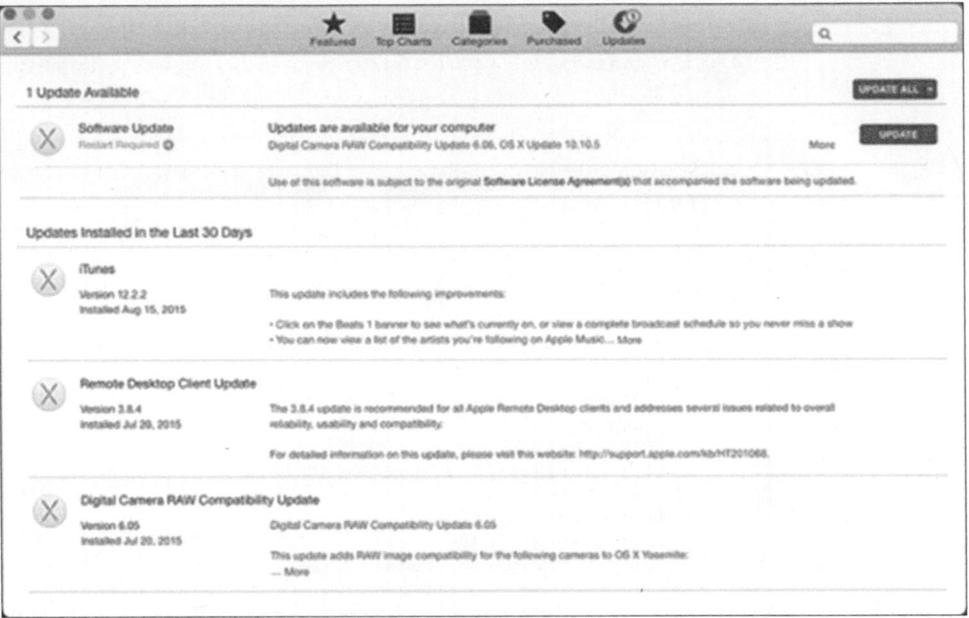

Figure 10-48 Check and Install Updates on OS X

Firmware Updates

Usually held in nonvolatile memory, such as ROM or Flash, *firmware* is a type of software designed to provide low-level functionality for a device. Firmware is commonly found in embedded devices, such as digital watches, traffic lights, and home appliances. It is also common in computers and computer peripherals, digital cameras, and cell phones. Firmware is susceptible to vulnerabilities and software exploits; however, the process for updating firmware can be more complicated than with operating systems. Check for firmware updates with the manufacturer and update the system if new versions are available.

Antivirus and Antimalware

In general, antivirus and antimalware rely on code signatures to operate. *Signatures* or *signature files* are files containing a sample of the code used by viruses and malware. Based on these signature files, antivirus and antimalware scan the contents of a computer disk comparing the contents of the files stored on the disk with the samples stored in the signature file. If a match is found, the antivirus or antimalware alerts the user of the possible presence of malware.

New malware is created and released every day; therefore, the signature files of antivirus and antimalware programs must be updated just as frequently.

Security Credentials Manager

Usernames, passwords, digital certificates, encryption keys are just a few of the security credentials associated to a user. Due to the increasing number of necessary security credentials, modern operating systems include a service to manage them. Applications and other services can then request and utilize the credentials stored by the security credentials manager service.

Gnome-keyring is a security credentials manager for Ubuntu Linux. To access Gnome-Keyring on Ubuntu Linux use the following path:

Click **Dash** > Search for **Key** > Click **Passwords and Keys**

Keychain is a security credentials manager for OS X. To access Keychain on OS X use the following path:

Applications > **Utilities** > **Keychain Access**

Basic CLI (10.4.3)

The command-line interface (CLI) is a user interface used to execute commands by typing text at a prompt instead of using a mouse to point and click icons in a GUI shell.

File and Folder Commands (10.4.3.1)

A number of command-line tools are included in UNIX-like systems by default. To adjust the command-line tool operation, users can enter parameters and switches along with the command.

Table 10-5 lists a few basic CLI commands.

Table 10-5 Basic CLI commands

Command	Description
man	Displays the documentation for a specific command
ls	Displays the files inside a directory
cd	Changes the current directory
mkdir	Creates a directory under the current directory
cp	Copies files from source to destination
mv	Moves files to a different directory
rm	Removes files
grep	Searches for specific strings of characters within a file or other commands' output
cat	List the contents of a file and expects the file name as the parameter

It is easy to create and edit text files in the CLI. The command **vi** opens a text editor. The command **q** is used to exit the editor when you are finished.

Administrative Commands (10.4.3.2)

In order to organize the system and reinforce boundaries within the system, UNIX utilizes file permissions. File permissions are built into the file system structure and provide a mechanism to define permissions to every file. Every file on UNIX systems carries its file permissions which define the actions that the owner, the group and others can do with the file. The possible permissions rights are Read, Write, and Execute.

Using the **ls** command and the **-l** parameter to list additional information about the file, consider the output of the **ls -l** command below:

rod@machine: $ ls -l my_awesome_file

-rwxrw-r-- 1 rod staff 1108485 Aug 14 7:34

My_Awesome_File

rod@machine: $

The output above provides lots of information about: **My_Awesome_File.**

The first portion of the output above displays the permissions associated to **My_Awesome_File.** File permissions are always displayed in the User, Group, and Other order which leads to the conclusion that **My_Awesome_File** can be:

- The user who owns the file can Read, Write, and eXecute the file. This is represented by rwx.
- The group that owns the file can Read and Write to the file. This is represented by rw-.
- Any other user or group in the system can only Read the file. This is represented by r--.

The next portion is the number of hard links to the file, in this instance it is a numeral 1. This portion is not in the scope of this course.

The third portion displays the username of the owner of the file. The fourth portion displays the name of the group that owns the file. In this case, the user **rod** and the group **staff** both have some level of ownership over the file.

The fifth portion displays the file size in bytes.

My_Awesome_File has 1108485 bytes or about 1.1MB.

The sixth portion displays the date and time of the last modification.

The seventh portion displays the file name.

Figure 10-49 shows a breakdown of file permissions in UNIX.

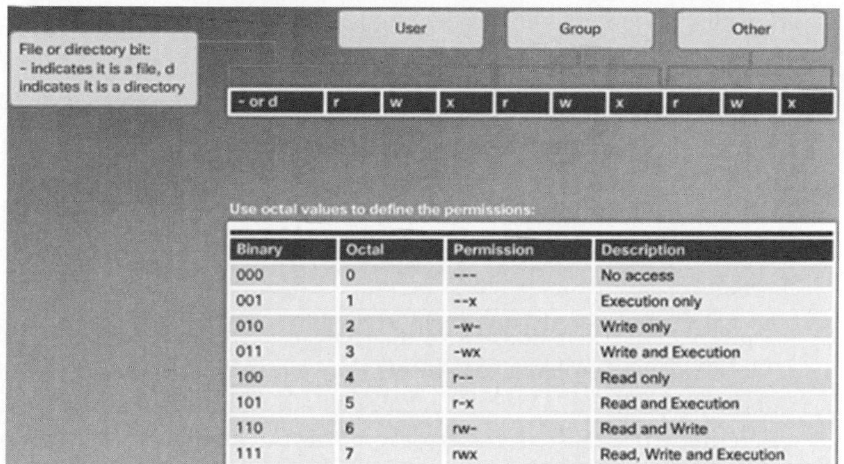

Binary	Octal	Permission	Description
000	0	---	No access
001	1	--x	Execution only
010	2	-w-	Write only
011	3	-wx	Write and Execution
100	4	r--	Read only
101	5	r-x	Read and Execution
110	6	rw-	Read and Write
111	7	rwx	Read, Write and Execution

Figure 10-49 UNIX File Permissions

The only user who can override file permissions in UNIX is the *root* user. Having the power to override file permissions, the root user can write to any file. Because everything is treated as a file, the root user has full control over the UNIX operating system. Root access is often required before performing maintenance and administrative tasks.

Note

Because Linux and OS X are based on UNIX, both operating systems are in full compliance with UNIX file permissions.

Lab—Working with the Linux Command Line (10.4.3.3)

In this lab, you use the Linux command line to manage files and folders and perform some basic administrative tasks. Refer to the lab in *IT Essentials v6 Lab Manual*.

Basic Troubleshooting Process for Mobile, Linux, and OS X Operating Systems (10.5)

When troubleshooting problems with mobile devices, find out if the device is under warranty. If it is, it can often be returned to the place of purchase for an exchange. If the device in no longer under warranty, determine if a repair is cost-effective. To determine the best course of action, compare the cost of the repair with the replacement cost of the mobile device. Because many mobile devices change rapidly in design and functionality, they are often more expensive to repair than to replace. For this reason, mobile devices are usually replaced.

Applying the Troubleshooting Process to Mobile, Linux, and OS X Operating Systems (10.5.1)

Follow the steps outlined in this section to accurately identify, repair, and document the problem.

Identify the Problem (10.5.1.1)

Mobile device problems can result from a combination of hardware, software, and network issues. Mobile technicians must be able to analyze the problem and determine the cause of the error to repair the mobile device. This process is called *troubleshooting*.

The first step in the troubleshooting process is to identify the problem. The figures show a list of open-ended and closed-ended questions to ask the customer.

Table 10-6 focuses on mobile device operating systems.

Table 10-6 Step 1: Identify the Problem for Mobile Device Operating Systems

Open-ended questions	■ What is the problem you are experiencing? ■ What is the version of mobile OS you are using? ■ What service provider do you have? ■ What apps have you installed recently?
Closed-ended questions	■ Has this problem happened before? ■ Has anyone else used the mobile device? ■ Is your mobile device under warranty? ■ Have you modified the operating system on the mobile device? ■ Have installed any apps from an unapproved source? ■ Does the mobile device connect to the Internet?

Table 10-7 focuses on Linux and OS X operating system problems.

Table 10-7 Step 1: Identify the Problem for Linux and OS X

Open-ended questions	■ What is the problem you are experiencing? ■ What is the make and model of your computer? ■ What is the version of Linux or OS X you are using? ■ What programs of drivers have you installed recently? ■ What OS updates have you installed recently? ■ What system configuration have you changed recently?
Closed-ended questions	■ Has this problem happened before? ■ Has anyone else used the mobile device? ■ Is your –mobile device under warranty? ■ Have you modified the operating system on the mobile device? ■ Does the mobile device connect to the Internet?

Establish a Theory of Probably Cause (10.5.1.2)

After you have talked to the customer, you can establish a theory of probable causes.

Table 10-8 shows a list of some common probable causes for mobile device operating systems, Linux, and OS X problems.

Table 10-8 Step 2: Establish a Theory of Probable Cause

Common causes of mobile device operation system problems	■ Mobile device cannot send or receive email. ■ An app has stopped working. ■ A malicious app has been sideloaded. ■ Mobile device software or apps are not up to date. ■ A user has forgotten their passcode.
Common causes of Linux or OS X problems	■ Computer cannot send or receive email. ■ An application has stopped working. ■ A malicious app has been installed. ■ The computer has stopped responding. ■ A user has forgotten their login credentials. ■ The OS is not up to date.

Test the Theory to Determine Cause (10.5.1.3)

After you have developed some theories about what is wrong, test your theories to determine the cause of the problem. If a quick procedure does correct the problem, you can then verify full system functionality. If a quick procedure does not correct the problem, you might need to research the problem further to establish the exact cause.

Table 10-9 shows a list of quick procedures that can determine the exact cause of the problem or even correct the problem.

Table 10-9 Step 3: Test the Theory to Determine Cause

Common steps to determine cause of mobile device operation system problems	■ Force a running app to close ■ Reconfigure email account settings ■ Restart the mobile device ■ Restore the mobile device from backup ■ Connect an iOS device to iTunes ■ Update the operating system ■ Reset the mobile device to factory defaults
Common steps to determine cause of Linux or OS X problems	■ Force a running program to close ■ Reconfigure email account settings ■ Restart the computer ■ Restore the computer from backup ■ Perform a full OS installation to restore the computer to factory defaults ■ Update the operating system

Establish a Plan of Action to Resolve the Problem and Implement the Solution (10.5.1.4)

After you have determined the exact cause of the problem, establish a plan of action to resolve the problem and implement the solution.

Table 10-10 shows some sources you can use to gather additional information to resolve an issue.

Table 10-10 Step 4: Establish a Plan of Action to Resolve the Problem and Implement the Solution

If no solution is achieved in the previous step, further research is needed to implement the solution.	■ Help desk repair logs ■ Other technicians ■ Manufacturer FAQs ■ Technical websites ■ Newsgroups ■ Manuals ■ Online forums ■ Internet research

Verify Full System Functionality and Implement Preventive Measures (10.5.1.5)

After you have corrected the problem, verify full functionality and, if applicable, implement preventive measures.

Table 10-11 shows a list of the steps to verify the solution.

Table 10-11 Step 5: Verify Full System Functionality and Implement Preventive Measures

Verify solution and full functionality for mobile device operation systems.	■ Reboot the mobile device ■ Browse the Internet using WiFi ■ Browse the Internet using 4G, 3G, or another carrier network type ■ Make a phone call ■ Send a text message ■ Open different types of apps ■ Operate the mobile device using only the battery
Verify solution and full functionality for Linux or OS X.	■ Reboot the computer ■ Browse the Internet using WiFi ■ Browse the Internet using a wired connection ■ Make a phone call ■ Send a test email ■ Open different programs

Document Findings, Actions, and Outcomes (10.5.1.6)

In the final step of the troubleshooting process, you must document your findings, actions, and outcomes.

Table 10-12 lists the tasks required to document the problem and the solution.

Table 10-12 Step 6: Document Findings, Actions, and Outcomes

Document your findings, actions, and outcomes	■ Discuss the solution implemented with the customer ■ Have the customer verify that the problem has been solved ■ Provide the customer with all paperwork ■ Document the steps taken to solve the problem in the work order and technician's journal ■ Document any components used in the repair ■ Document the time spent to resolve the problem

Common Problems and Solutions for Mobile, Linux, and OS X Operating Systems (10.5.2)

Mobile device problems can be attributed to hardware, software, networks, or combination of the three. You will resolve some types of problems more than others.

Identify Common Problems and Solutions (10.5.2.1)

Table 10-13 is a chart of common mobile device problems and solutions.

Table 10-13 Common Problems and Solutions for Mobile Devices

Identify the Problem	Probable Causes	Possible Solutions
The mobile device will not connect to the Internet	■ WiFi is not available ■ Airplane mode is turned on. ■ WiFi settings are incorrect ■ WiFi is turned off	■ Turn WiFi on ■ Turn off airplane mode ■ Reconfigure WiFi settings
The mobile device cannot install additional apps or save photos.	The mobile device is out of storage space.	■ Insert a memory card or replace the memory card with a larger one if possible ■ Remove unnecessary files ■ Uninstall unnecessary apps

Identify the Problem	Probable Causes	Possible Solutions
Mobile device won't connect to Bluetooth	■ Bluetooth capability is turned off. ■ The Bluetooth device is not turned on ■ The input device is out of range.	■ Enable Bluetooth ■ Turn on Bluetooth ■ Bring the devices into range
Mobile device cannot pair with a Bluetooth device.	■ Bluetooth capability is turned off. ■ The Bluetooth device is not turned on ■ The PIN code is incorrect	■ Enable Bluetooth ■ Turn on Bluetooth ■ Correct the PIN code
Mobile device display looks dim.	■ Brightness is set too low in the display settings ■ Auto brightness does not work well in well-lit areas. ■ Auto brightness is not calibrated correctly.	■ Increase the brightness in the display settings ■ Turn off auto brightness ■ Recalibrate the light sensor
The mobile device cannot broadcast to an external monitor.	■ No wireless display-capable device is available. ■ Miracast, WiDi, AirPlay, or other wireless display technology is not enabled.	■ Install a wireless display-capable device of turn on the one that is available ■ Enable the wireless display-capabilities
The device exhibiting slow performance.	■ A GPS application is running ■ One or more power-intensive apps is running	■ Turn off the GPS or close the app ■ Close all unnecessary apps ■ restart the device
The mobile device is unable to decrypt email.	■ Your email client is not set up to decrypt email. ■ You do not have the correct decryption key.	■ Configure the email to decrypt email ■ Attain the correct decryption key from the sender of the encrypted email
The mobile device OS has frozen	■ An app is not compatible with the device. ■ Network connectivity is poor. ■ The device has failing hardware.	■ Uninstall the incompatible app ■ Move to an area with better network coverage ■ Replace any failing hardware

(*Continued*)

Table 10-13 *Continued*

Identify the Problem	Probable Causes	Possible Solutions
The mobile device has no sound coming from the speakers.	■ The volume is set too low in the audio setting or in an app. ■ The volume is muted. ■ The speaker has failed	■ Turn up the volume in the audio setting or in an app ■ Unmute the volume ■ Replace the speaker
The mobile device OS has frozen	■ An app is not compatible with the device. ■ Network connectivity is poor. ■ The device has failing hardware.	■ Uninstall the incompatible app ■ Move to an area with better network coverage ■ Replace any failing hardware

Table 10-14 is a chart of common mobile device OS security problems.

Table 10-14 Common Problems and Solutions for Mobile OS Security

Identify the Problem	Probable Causes	Possible Solutions
The mobile device has a weak signal or the signal has been dropped	■ There are not enough cell towers in the area. ■ The area is between coverage areas of the carrier.	■ Move to a more populated area the will have more cell towers ■ Move to an area within the range of the carrier
The power of a mobile device is draining more quickly than normal.	■ The device is roaming between cell towers or coverage areas. ■ The display is set too bright ■ An app is using too many resources. ■ Too many radios are in use.	■ Move to an area within the range of the carrier ■ Set the display to a lower brightness ■ Close any unnecessary apps ■ Reboot the device
Mobile device has slow data speeds.	■ The connected cell is too far away for high speed data. ■ The mobile is roaming. ■ Data transmission has gone the usage for a device ■ The device is experiencing high resource utilization.	■ Move closer to a cell tower ■ Move to an area within the range of the carrier ■ Raise the data limit of the device ■ Turn off data usage for the device ■ Close any unnecessary apps. ■ Reboot the device

Identify the Problem	Probable Causes	Possible Solutions
A mobile device connects to a WiFi network unintentionally.	The device is set to automatically connect to unknown WiFi networks.	Set the device so it will only connect to known WiFi networks.
A mobile device pairs to a Bluetooth device unintentionally.	The device is set to automatically pair with unknown devices.	Set the device to turn off Bluetooth pairing by default.
A mobile device has leaked personal files and data.	■ The device has been lost or stolen. ■ The device has been compromised by malware.	■ Remote lock or wipe the device ■ Scan for and remove malware from the device
A mobile device account has been accessed by unauthorized personnel.	■ Credentials are being stored by default. ■ No VPN is being used. ■ No passcode is set on the device. ■ The passcode had been discovered. ■ The device has been compromised by malware.	■ Set the device so it does not store credentials by default ■ Used VPN connection ■ Set a passcode on the device ■ Change passcode to a stronger one ■ Scan for and remove malware from the device
An app has achieved unauthorized access to root.	The device has been compromised by malware.	Scan for and remove malware from the device
The mobile device is being tracked without permission.	■ The GPS is on but not in use by any apps. ■ An app allows connection to the GPS ■ The device has been compromised by malware.	■ Turn off GPS when not in use ■ Shut down or remove any unwanted apps allows connection to the GPS ■ Scan for and remove malware from the device
The mobile device camera or microphone is being accessed without permission.	■ An app allows connection to the camera or microphone ■ The device has been compromised by malware.	■ Shut down or remove any unwanted apps allows connection to the camera or microphone ■ Scan for and remove malware from the device

Computer problems can be attributed to hardware, software, networks, or some combination of the three. You will resolve some types of computer problems more often than others.

Table 10-15 is chart of common Linux and OS X problems and solutions.

Table 10-15 Common Problems and Solutions for Linux and OS X Operating Systems

Identify the Problem	Probable Causes	Possible Solutions
The automatic backup operation does not start.	■ Time Machine is turned off in OS X. ■ Deja Dup is turned off in Linux.	■ Turn on Time Machine in OS X ■ Turn on Deja Dup in Linux
The directory appears empty.	■ The directory is the mount point for another disk or partition ■ The files were accidently deleted	■ Remount the disk using the correct directory with Disk Utility for OS X ■ Remount the disk using the correct directory with Disks for Linux ■ Restore the deleted files from a backup using Time Machine or Déjà Dup
An application stops responding in OS X.	■ The application has stopped working. ■ The application was using resources that became unavailable.	Force-quit the application
WiFi is not accessible using Ubuntu.	The wireless NIC driver did not install correctly.	■ Install the Linux driver from the manufacturer's website if available ■ Install the Linux driver from the Ubuntu repositories if available
OS X cannot read the remote optical disc using Remote Disc	■ The MAC already has an optical drive installed. ■ The option to request permission to use the optical drive has been enabled.	■ Place the media in the local optical drive ■ Accept the request for permission to use the optical drive
Linus fails to boot and you receive a "Missing GRUB" or "Missing LILO" message.	■ GRUB or LILO has been corrupted. ■ GRUB or LILO has been deleted.	■ Run Linux from installation media, open a terminal and install the boot manager with the command: sudo grub-install or sudo lilo-install
Linus or OS X freezes on startup and exhibits kernel panic where there is a stop screen.	■ A driver has become corrupted. ■ Hardware is failing.	■ Update all device drivers from the manufacturer's website ■ Replace any failing hardware

Many computer problems can be solved by simply turning off the device and turning it back on. When a mobile device does not respond to a reboot, a reset may need to be performed.

These are some of the ways that Android devices can be reset, check the documentation for your mobile device to determine how to reset your device:

- Hold down the power button until the mobile device turns off. Turn the device on again.
- Hold down the power button and the volume down button until the mobile device turns off. Turn the device on again.

This is how iOS devices can be reset: Press and hold both the Sleep/Wake button and the Home button for 10 seconds, until the Apple logo appears.

In some cases, when a standard reset does not correct the problem, a factory reset may need to be performed. To perform a factory reset on an Android device, use the following path:

Settings > Backup and reset > Factory data reset > Reset device

To perform a factory reset on an iOS device, use the following path:

Settings > General > Reset > Erase All Content and Settings

Caution

A factory reset restores the device to the state when it left the factory. All settings and user data is deleted from the device when a factory reset is performed. Be sure to back up any data and record any settings before performing a factory reset because all data and settings will be lost after performing a factory reset.

When a reboot does not fix a PC, more investigation should be done. You may find that some configuration should be changed, software updates are required or a misbehaving program is the culprit and must be reinstalled.

Lab—Troubleshooting Mobile Devices (10.5.2.2)

In this lab, you analyze scenarios involving common problems for mobile devices and identify the solutions. Refer to the lab in *IT Essentials v6 Lab Manual.*

Summary (10.6)

Operating systems are software programs that allow computers, laptops, smartphones, tablet PCs, and other devices to run applications and programs. Among the most popular computer operating systems are Microsoft's Windows and Apple's OS X and various distributions of Linux. In previous chapters you have learned about Windows and in this chapter you have learned about Apple's OS X and Ubuntu Linux as well as mobile devices.

Mobile devices are closer to handheld computers than ever before. They are a permanent part of the computing and network landscape and understanding them and the operating systems that run them is important for a technician.

Summary (10.6.1)

This chapter introduced you to mobile devices, the operating systems used on mobile devices, how to secure mobile devices, the uses of cloud-enabled services for mobile devices, and the way that mobile devices connect to networks, devices, and peripherals.

This chapter also covered Ubuntu Linux and Apple OS X operating systems and some of its main characteristics including, command-line interface, command-line-based tools, graphical user interfaces used and some GUI-based tools. This chapter also covered the main maintenance tasks and its related tools.

The basics of troubleshooting mobile operating systems, Linux and OS X were discussed with examples of simple solutions for common problems. The following concepts from this chapter are important to remember.

- Open source software can be modified by anyone with little or no cost.
- Use only trusted content sources to avoid malware and unreliable content.
- Both Android and iOS have similar GUIs for using apps and other content.
- Email accounts are closely tied to mobile devices and provide many different data synchronization services.
- Android devices use apps to synchronize data not automatically synchronized by Google.
- iOS devices use iTunes to synchronize data and other content.
- Passcode locks can secure mobile devices.
- Remote backups can be performed to backup mobile device data to the cloud.
- Remote lock or remote wipe are features to secure a mobile device that has been lost or stolen.
- Antivirus software is often used on mobile devices to prevent the transfer of malicious programs to other devices or computers.

Summary of Exercises

This is a summary of the Labs and activities associated with this chapter.

Labs

The following labs cover material from this chapter. Refer to the labs in the *IT Essentials v6 Lab Manual*.

Lab—Working with Android (10.1.2.3)

Lab—Working with iOS (10.1.3.3)

Lab—Mobile Device Features (10.1.5.3)

Lab—Mobile Device Information (10.1.5.4)

Lab—Passcode Locks (10.2.1.2)

Lab—Mobile WiFi (10.3.1.2)

Lab—Install Linux in a Virtual Machine and Explore the GUI (10.4.1.4)

Lab—Working with the Linux Command Line (10.4.3.3)

Lab—Troubleshooting Mobile Devices (10.5.2.2)

Check Your Understanding

You can find the answers to these questions in the appendix, "Answers to 'Check Your Understanding' Questions."

1. What three tasks can be done with the iOS device Home button? (Choose three.)

   A. Place apps into folders

   B. Respond to an alert

   C. Return to the home screen

   D. Wake the device

   E. Display the navigation icons

   F. Open audio controls

2. Which two terms describe unlocking Android and iOS mobile devices to allow users full access to the file system and full access to the kernel module? (Choose two.)

   A. Patching
   B. Remote wipe
   C. Jailbreaking
   D. Rooting
   E. Sandboxing

3. What two sources of information are used to enable geocaching, geotagging and device tracking on Android and iOS devices? (Choose two.)

   A. GPS signals
   B. The relative position to other mobile devices
   C. Cellular or WiFi network
   D. Images of the environment from the integrated camera
   E. The user profile

4. How is the representation of apps in the Windows Phone operating system interface different from the representations used in Android and iOS?

   A. Windows Phone uses badges that indicate the system resources used by each app.
   B. Windows Phone uses widgets that, when deleted from the Start screen, also delete the associated app.
   C. Windows Phone uses buttons that must be tapped before an app can be seen.
   D. Windows Phone uses rectangles that can display active content and that can also be resized.

5. True or False?

   Android and OS X are based on the UNIX operating system.

      False

      True

6. What two preventive maintenance tasks should be scheduled to occur automatically? (choose two)

   A. Resetting devices by applying the factory reset feature
   B. Checking the disks for bad sectors
   C. Executing a backup
   D. Scanning the signature files
   E. Updating the operating system software

7. A person with an Android mobile device holds down the power button and the volume down button until the device turns off. The person then turns the device back on. What was this person doing to the device?

   A. A standard reset of the device
   B. A full backup to the iCloud
   C. A normal power off
   D. A factory reset
   E. An operating system update

8. What are two types of cloud-enabled services for mobile devices? (Choose two.)

   A. Screen app locking
   B. Screen calibration
   C. Remote backup
   D. Passcode configuration
   E. Locator apps

9. Which term is used to describe the process of establishing a connection between any two Bluetooth devices?

   A. Matching
   B. Joining
   C. Syncing
   D. Pairing

10. Which feature of an Android or iOS mobile device helps prevent malicious programs from infecting the device?

    A. The phone carrier prevents the mobile device app from accessing some smartphone features and programs.
    B. Mobile device apps are run in a sandbox that isolates them from other resources.
    C. The passcode restricts the mobile device app from access to other programs.
    D. The remote lock feature prevents malicious programs from infecting the device.

11. Which statement describes the Airplane Mode feature found on most mobile devices?

    A. It automatically lowers the volume of the audio output from the device.
    B. It allows the device to roam from one cellular network to another.
    C. It locks the device so that it cannot be used by someone else if it is lost or stolen.
    D. It turns off cellular, WiFi, and Bluetooth radios on the device.

12. Which email protocol used by mobile devices allows pictures and documents to be included in email messages?

    A. MIME
    B. SMTP
    C. POP3
    D. IMAP

13. What are two features of the Android operating system? (Choose two.)

    A. Android has been implemented on devices such as cameras, smart TVs, and e-book readers.
    B. All available Android applications have been tested and approved by Google to run on the open source operating system.
    C. Android is open source and allows anyone to contribute to its development and evolution.
    D. Each implementation of Android requires a royalty to be paid to Google.
    E. Android applications can only be downloaded from Google Play.

14. What Linux CLI command removes files?

    A. rm
    B. man
    C. ls
    D. cd
    E. mkdir

15. What Linux CLI command displays the documentation for a specific command?

    A. rm
    B. man
    C. ls
    D. cd
    E. mkdir

16. What Linux CLI command displays the files inside a directory

    A. rm
    B. man
    C. ls
    D. cd
    E. mkdir

17. What Linux CLI command changes the current directory

A. rm

B. man

C. ls

D. cd

E. mkdir

18. What Linux CLI command creates a directory under the current directory

A. rm

B. man

C. ls

D. cd

E. mkdir

CHAPTER 11

Printers

Objectives

Upon completion of this chapter, you will be able to answer the following questions:

- What types of printers are currently available?
- What is the process of installation and configuration for local printers?
- How do I install and configure a local printer and scanner?
- How do I share a printer on a network?
- What does it take to upgrade printers?
- How can I identify and apply common preventive maintenance techniques to printers?
- How can I troubleshoot printers?

Key Terms

This chapter uses the following key terms. You can find the definitions in the Glossary.

pages per minute (ppm) Page 620

dots per inch (dpi) Page 621

Mean time between failures (MTBF) Page 621

total cost of ownership (TCO) Page 621

Serial data transfer Page 622

Parallel data transfer Page 622

IEEE 1284 Page 623

FireWire (i.LINK or IEEE 1394) Page 623

Ethernet connection Page 623

all-in-one device Page 635

Inkjet printer Page 623

Thermal Page 624

Piezoelectric Page 624

laser printer Page 625

Processing Page 626

Charging Page 626

Exposing Page 626

Developing Page 626

Transferring Page 626

Fusing Page 627

Cleaning Page 627

conditioning Page 626

thermal printer Page 628

Impact printer Page 629

daisy wheel printer Page 629

dot matrix printer Page 629

Print to file Page 630

Virtual printers Page 630

Cloud printing Page 631

Page Description Language (PDL) Page 632

What You See Is What You Get (WYSIWYG) Page 632

Printer Command Language (PCL) Page 633

PostScript (PS) Page 633

printer drivers Page 633

primary corona Page 626

print server Page 644

HEPA filtration Page 651

Introduction (11.0)

Printers are an important peripheral device in many organizations. Most people still print their office documents, so hard copy has not gone away. At the same time, they don't give much thought to how their printer works until it doesn't. All they care is that their printer works when they want it to work. When it doesn't the support professional's knowledge of printers and their operation becomes relevant and necessary. Training in this content brings a high level of professionalism and customer support to the organization and IT support person.

Welcome (11.0.1)

Printers produce paper copies of electronic files. Many situations, such as government regulations, require physical records; therefore, hard copies of computer documents are often as important today as they were when the paperless revolution began several years ago.

Printers (11.0.1.1)

This chapter provides essential information about printers. You will learn how printers operate, what to consider when purchasing a printer, and how to connect printers to an individual computer or to a network.

You must understand the operation of various types of printers to be able to install and maintain them, as well as troubleshoot any problems that arise.

Common Printer Features (11.1)

Printers come in various models and types, chosen to meet the different needs and necessities of an organization. Choosing the right model saves time, is cost effective and an efficient use of company resources.

Characteristics and Capabilities (11.1.1)

The many types of printer have common features but also different capabilities to decide on based on the different needs and necessities. Features including printing speeds, monochrome or color, cost and availability of cartridges, driver compatibility, power consumption, network type, and the total cost of ownership are some of the many factors that need to be considered when purchasing, repairing, and maintaining printers.

Characteristics and Capabilities of Printers (11.1.1.1)

As a computer technician, you might be required to purchase, repair, or maintain a printer. The customer might request that you perform the following tasks:

- Select a printer
- Install and configure a printer
- Troubleshoot a printer

The printers available today are usually either laser printers using imaging drums or inkjet printers using electrostatic spray technology. Dot matrix printers using impact technology are used in applications that require carbon copies. Figure 11-1 shows three types of printers.

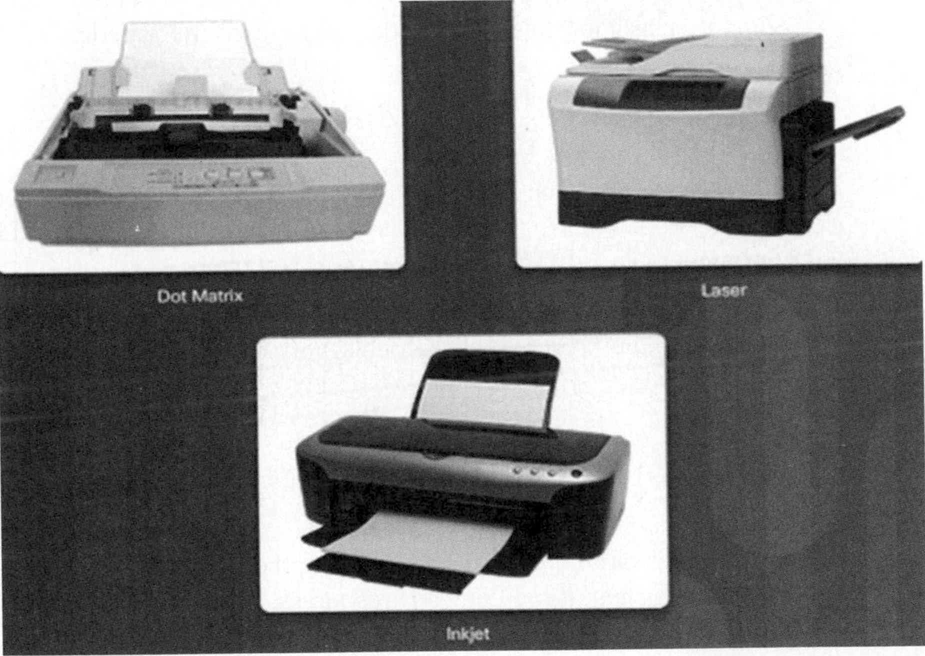

Figure 11-1 Three Types of Printers

Capabilities and Speed

Printer capabilities and speed are factors to consider when selecting a printer. The speed of a printer is measured in *pages per minute (ppm)*. Printer speed varies between makes and models. Speed is also affected by the complexity of the image and the quality desired by the user. For example, a draft quality page of text prints faster than a high-quality page of text. A draft quality image of a color digital photograph prints faster than a photo quality print. Inkjet printers are usually slower, but they are often sufficient for a home or small office.

Color or Black and White

The color printing process uses the primary colors cyan, magenta, and yellow (CMY). For inkjet printing, the color black servers as the base or key color. Thus, the acronym CMYK refers to the inkjet color printing process.

The choice between a black-and-white printer and a color printer depends on the needs of the customer. If the customer is primarily printing letters and does not need color capability, a black-and-white printer is sufficient and can be less expensive. An elementary school teacher might need a color printer to add excitement to lessons.

Quality

The quality of printing is measured in *dots per inch (dpi)*. The larger the dpi number, the better the image resolution. When the resolution is higher, text and images are clearer. To produce the best high-resolution images, use high-quality ink or toner and high-quality paper.

Reliability

A printer should be reliable. Because so many types of printers are on the market, research the specifications of several printers before selecting one. Here are some manufacturer options to consider:

- **Warranty**—Identify what is covered within the warranty.
- **Scheduled servicing**—Servicing is based on expected usage. Usage information is in the documentation or on the manufacturer's website.
- *Mean time between failures (MTBF)*—The printer should work without failing for an average length of time. This information is in the documentation or on the manufacturer's website.

Total Cost of Ownership

When buying a printer, there is more than just the initial cost of the printer to consider. The *total cost of ownership (TCO)* includes a number of factors:

- Initial purchase price
- Cost of supplies, such as paper and ink
- Pages per month
- Price per page
- Maintenance costs
- Warranty costs

When calculating the TCO, consider the amount of printing required and the expected lifetime of the printer.

Printer Connection Types (11.1.1.2)

A printer must have a compatible interface with the computer to print. Typically, printers connect to home computers using a parallel, USB, or wireless interface. Figure 11-2 shows examples of the various connection types. However, printers may also connect directly to a network using a network cable or a wireless interface.

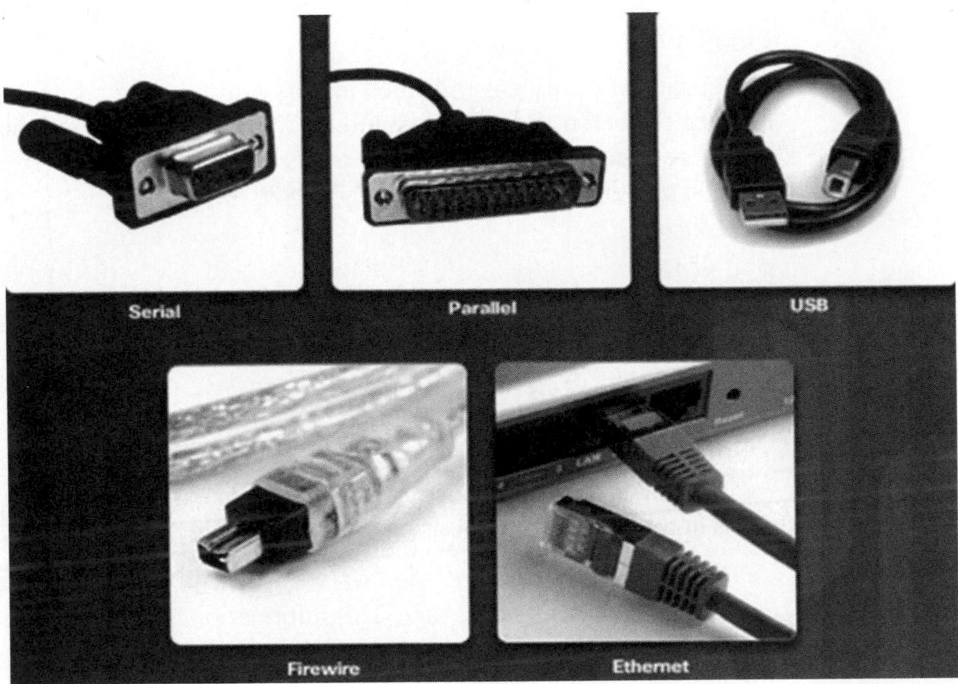

Figure 11-2 Printer Connection Types

Serial

Serial data transfer is the movement of single bits of information in a single cycle. A serial connection can be used for dot matrix printers because the printers do not require high-speed data transfer. A serial connection for a printer is often referred to as COM.

Parallel

Parallel data transfer is faster than serial data transfer. Parallel data transfer moves multiple bits of information in a single cycle. The data transfer path is wider than the serial data transfer path, allowing data to move more quickly to or from the printer.

IEEE 1284 is the standard for parallel printer ports. Enhanced Parallel Port (EPP) and Enhanced Capabilities Port (ECP) are two modes of operation within the IEEE 1284 standard that allow bidirectional communication. A parallel connection for a printer is often referred to as Line Print Terminal (LPT).

USB

USB is a common interface for printers and other devices. When a USB device is added to a computer system that supports plug-and-play, the device is automatically detected and starts the driver installation process.

FireWire

FireWire, also known as i.LINK or IEEE 1394, is a high-speed communication bus that is platform independent. FireWire connects digital devices such as digital printers, scanners, digital cameras, and hard drives.

Ethernet

Connecting a printer to the network requires cabling that is compatible with both the network and the network port installed in the printer. Most network printers use an RJ-45 interface and an *Ethernet connection* to connect to a network.

Wireless

Many home printers include a wireless antenna and wireless software to connect wirelessly to your home or small office network.

Printer Types (11.1.2)

This section describes the characteristics of many types of printers. Knowing the features and characteristics of different printer types is necessary to make the best choice for the printer use. The intended use of the printer is also important in the purchasing decision. Will this be a business printer or home use, networked or local, is it a special use printer, these are some of the questions to ask to help in the decision.

Inkjet Printers (11.1.2.1)

Inkjet printers produce high-quality prints. Inkjet printers are easy to use and somewhat less expensive when compared with laser printers. The print quality of an inkjet printer is measured in dpi. Higher dpi numbers provide better image details. Figure 11-3 shows inkjet printer components.

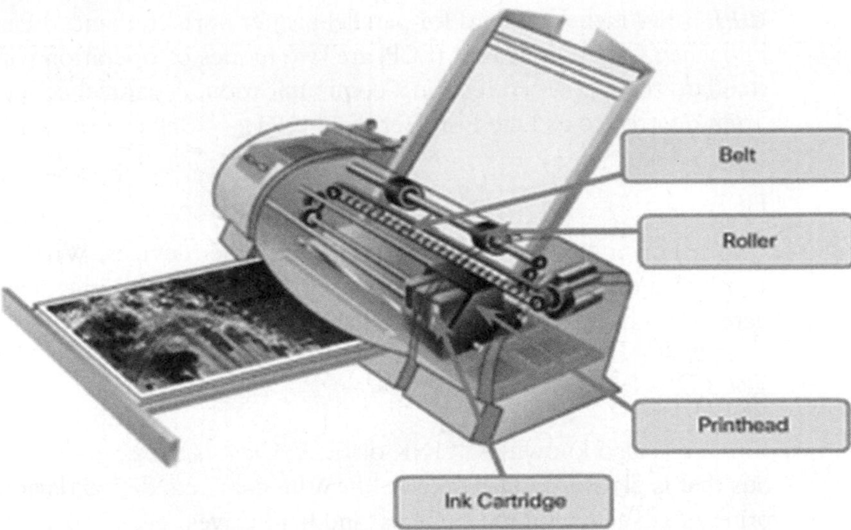

Figure 11-3 Inkjet Printer Components

Inkjet printers use ink cartridges that spray ink onto a page through tiny holes. The tiny holes are called nozzles and are located in the print head. The print head and ink cartridges are located on the carriage, which is attached to a belt and motor. As rollers pull paper in from the feeder, the belt moves the carriage back and forth along the paper as the ink is sprayed in a pattern on the page.

There are two types of inkjet nozzles:

- *Thermal*—A pulse of electrical current is applied to heating chambers around the nozzles. The heat creates a bubble of steam in the chamber. The steam forces ink out through the nozzle and onto the paper.
- *Piezoelectric*—Piezoelectric crystals are located in the ink reservoir at the back of each nozzle. A charge is applied to the crystal, causing it to vibrate. This vibration of the crystal controls the flow of ink onto the paper.

Inkjet printers use plain paper to make economical prints. Special-purpose paper can be used to create high-quality prints of photographs. An inkjet printer with a duplex assembly can print on both sides of a sheet of paper. When the paper leaves the printer, the ink is often wet. You should avoid touching printouts for 10 to 15 seconds to prevent smearing. If inkjet printer quality degrades, check the printer calibration by using the printer software.

Table 11-1 lists some advantages and disadvantages of an inkjet printer:

Table 11-1 Inkjet Printer Pros and Cons

Advantages	Disadvantages
Initial low cost	Nozzles are prone to clogging.
High resolution	Ink cartridges are expensive.
Quick to warm up	Ink is wet after printing.

Laser Printers (11.1.2.2)

A *laser printer* is a high-quality, fast printer that uses a laser beam to create an image. Figure 11-4 shows an example of a laser printer.

Figure 11-4 Laser Printers

The central part of the laser printer is its imaging drum. The drum is a metal cylinder that is coated with a light-sensitive insulating material. When a beam of laser light strikes the drum, it becomes a conductor at the point where the light hits it.

As the drum rotates, the laser beam draws an electrostatic image upon the drum. This undeveloped image is passed by a supply of dry ink or toner. The electrostatic charge attracts toner to the image. The drum turns and brings the exposed image in contact with the paper, which attracts the ink from the drum. The paper is then passed through a fuser assembly that is made up of hot rollers, which melts the toner into the paper.

These are some advantages of a laser printer:

- Low cost per page
- High ppm
- High capacity
- Prints are dry

These are some disadvantages of a laser printer:

- High cost of start up
- Toner cartridges are expensive
- Require a high level of maintenance

Laser Printing Process (11.1.2.3)

The laser printer process involves seven steps to print information onto a single sheet of paper.

The details of this process are explained below and shown in Figure 11-5.

1. *Processing*—The data from the source must be converted into a printable form. The printer converts data from common languages, such as Adobe PostScript (PS) or HP Printer Command Language (PCL), to a bitmap image stored in the printer's memory. Some laser printers have built in Graphical Device Interface (GDI) support. GDI is used by Windows applications to display printed images on a monitor so there is no need to convert the output to another format such as PostScript or PCL.
2. *Charging*—The previous latent image on the drum is removed and the drum is conditioned for the new latent image. A wire, grid, or roller receives a charge of approximately –600 volts DC uniformly across the surface of the drum. The charged wire or grid is called the *primary corona*. The roller is called a *conditioning* roller.
3. *Exposing*—To write the image, the photosensitive drum is exposed with the laser beam. Every portion of the drum that is scanned with the light has the surface charge reduced to about –100 volts DC. This electrical charge has a lower negative charge than the remainder of the drum. As the drum turns, an invisible latent image is created on the drum.
4. *Developing*—The toner is applied to the latent image on the drum. The toner is a negatively charged combination of plastic and metal particles. A control blade holds the toner at a microscopic distance from the drum. The toner then moves from the control blade to the more positively charged latent image on the drum.
5. *Transferring*—The toner attached to the latent image is transferred to the paper. A corona wire places a positive charge on the paper. Because the drum was charged negatively, the toner on the drum is attracted to the paper. The image is now on the paper and is held in place by the positive charge. Because color printers have three cartridges of ink, a colored image must go through multiple transfers to be complete. To ensure precise images, some color printers write multiple times onto a transfer belt that transfers the complete image to paper.

6. *Fusing*—The toner is permanently fused to the paper. The printing paper is rolled between a heated roller and a pressure roller. As the paper moves through the rollers, the loose toner is melted and fused with the fibers in the paper. The paper is then moved to the output tray as a printed page. Laser printers with duplex assemblies can print on both sides of a sheet of paper.

7. *Cleaning*—When an image has been deposited on the paper and the drum has separated from the paper, the remaining toner must be removed from the drum. A printer might have a blade that scrapes the excess toner. Some printers use an AC voltage on a wire that removes the charge from the drum surface and allows the excess toner to fall away from the drum. The excess toner is stored in a used toner container that is either emptied or discarded.

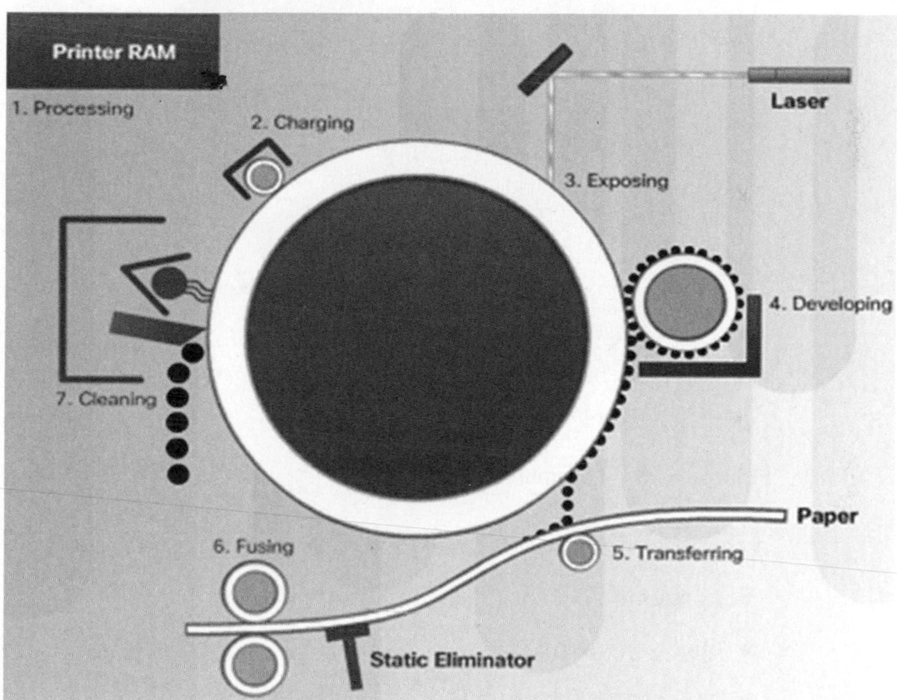

Figure 11-5 Laser Printer Process

Activity—Laser Printing Process (11.1.2.4)

Please refer to the Activity in the Cisco Networking Academy IT Essentials 6.0 online course.

Thermal Printers (11.1.2.5)

Some retail cash registers or older fax machines might contain *thermal printers*. Thermal paper is chemically treated and has a waxy quality. Thermal paper becomes black when heated. After a roll of thermal paper is loaded, the feed assembly moves the paper through the printer. Electrical current is sent to the heating element in the print head to generate heat. The heated areas of the print head make the pattern on the paper.

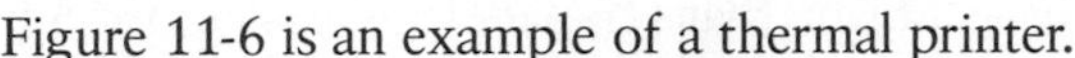

Figure 11-6 is an example of a thermal printer.

Figure 11-6 Thermal Printer

A thermal printer has the following advantages:

- Longer life because there are few moving parts
- Quiet operation
- No cost for ink or toner

A thermal printer has the following disadvantages:

- Paper is expensive.
- Paper has a short shelf life.
- Images are poor quality.
- Paper must be stored at room temperature.
- Color printing is not available.

Impact Printers (11.1.2.6)

Impact printers have print heads that strike an inked ribbon, causing characters to be imprinted on the paper. Dot matrix and daisy wheel are examples of impact printers.

Figure 11-7 is an example of an impact printer.

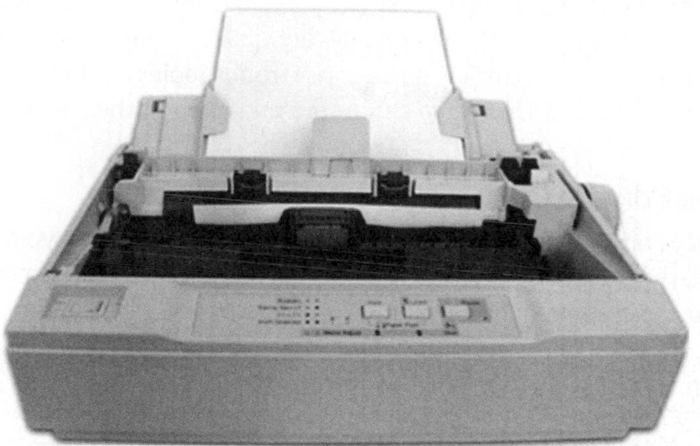

Figure 11-7 Impact Printer

The following are some advantages of an impact printer:

- Uses less expensive ink than inkjet or laser printers
- Uses continuous feed paper
- Has carbon-copy printing ability

The following are some disadvantages of an impact printer:

- Noisy
- Low-resolution graphics
- Limited color capability

Types of Impact Printers

A *daisy wheel printer* uses a wheel that contains letters, numbers, and special characters. The wheel rotates until the required character is in place, and then an electromechanical hammer pushes the character into the ink ribbon. The character then strikes the paper, imprinting the character on the paper.

A *dot matrix printer* is similar to a daisy wheel printer, except that it has a print head containing pins that are surrounded by electromagnets instead of a wheel.

When energized, the pins push forward onto the ink ribbon, creating a character on the paper. The number of pins on a print head, 9 or 24, indicates the quality of the print. The highest quality of print that is produced by the dot matrix printer is referred to as near letter quality (NLQ).

Most dot matrix printers use continuous-feed paper, also known as *tractor feed*. The paper has perforations between each sheet, and perforated strips on the side are used to feed the paper and to prevent skewing or shifting. Sheet feeders that print one page at a time are available for some higher quality printers. A large roller, called the platen, applies pressure to keep the paper from slipping. If a multiple-copy paper is used, you can adjust the platen gap to the thickness of the paper.

Virtual Printers (11.1.2.7)

Virtual printing does not send a print job to a printer within your local network. Instead, the print software either sends the job to a file or transmits the information to a remote destination in the cloud for printing.

Typical methods for sending a print job to a file include the following:

- *Print to file*—Originally, print to file saved your data in a file with the .prn extension. The .prn file then could be quickly printed at any time without opening the original document. Print to file can now save in other formats, as shown in Figure 11-8.

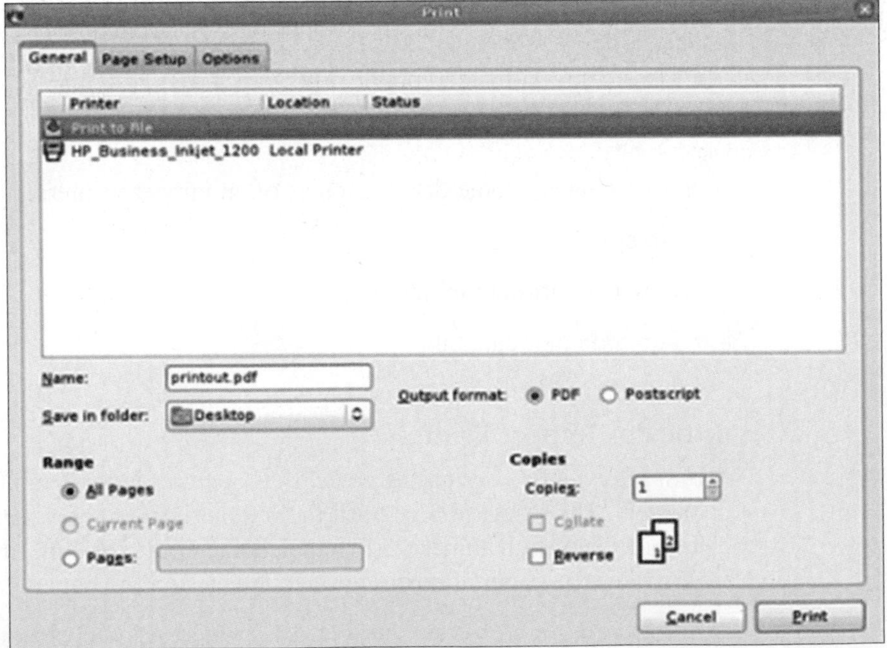

Figure 11-8 Print to File

- **Print to PDF**—Adobe's Portable Document Format (PDF) was released as an open standard in 2008.
- **Print to XPS**—Introduced by Microsoft in Windows Vista, the XML Paper Specification (XPS) format was meant to be an alternative to PDF.
- **Print to image**—To prevent others from easily copying the content in a document, you can choose to print to an image file format, such as JPG or TIFF.

Cloud printing is sending a print job to a remote printer, as shown in Figure 11-9. The printer could be at any location within your organization's network. Some printing companies provide software that you can install and then send print jobs to their closest location for processing.

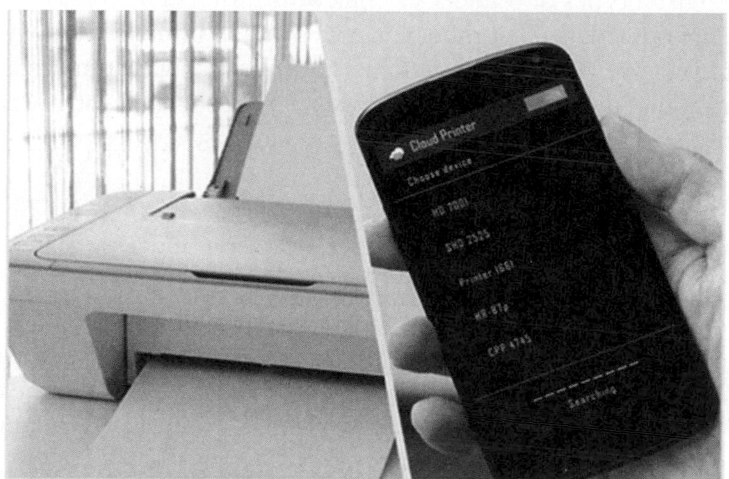

Figure 11-9 Cloud Printing

Another cloud printing example is Google Cloud Print, which allows you to connect your printer to the web. After you're connected, you can send print jobs to your printer from anywhere.

Installing and Configuring Printers (11.2)

A printer is a commonly added peripheral device for home users and businesses. After you've chosen the type of printer you need and purchased it, then the next step is installing and configuring the device. This section provides information about both the installation and configuration of a printer. When installing a printer, you need the printer hardware itself, as well as the appropriate drivers for the operating system so that it can communicate properly with that printer. The printer drivers must be compatible with the operating system being used.

Installing and Updating a Printer (11.2.1)

A computer printer does not work until you install the included drivers and software. In the planning of installing and/or updating a printer, it is necessary to have all of the right components to make both the hardware and software work properly.

Installing a Printer (11.2.1.1)

When you purchase a printer, the installation and configuration information is usually supplied by the manufacturer. An installation CD that includes the drivers, manuals, and diagnostic software is included with the printer. If there is no CD, you can download the tools from the manufacturer's website.

Although all types of printers are somewhat different to connect and configure, there are procedures that should be applied to all printers. Before you install a printer, remove all packing material. Remove anything that prevents moving parts from shifting during shipping. Keep the original packing material in case you need to return the printer to the manufacturer for warranty service.

Note

Before connecting the printer to the PC, read the installation instructions. In some cases, the printer driver needs to be installed first before the printer is connected to the PC.

If the printer has a USB, FireWire, or parallel port, connect the corresponding cable to the printer port. Connect the other end of the data cable to the corresponding port on the back of the computer. If you are installing a network printer, connect the network cable to the network port.

After the data cable has been properly connected, attach the power cable to the printer. Connect the other end of the power cable to an available electrical outlet. When you turn on the power to the device, the computer tries to determine the correct device driver to install.

Types of Print Drivers (11.2.1.2)

Printer *drivers* are software programs that make it possible for computers and printers to communicate with each other. Configuration software provides an interface that enables users to set and change printer options. Every printer model has its own type of driver and configuration software.

Page Description Language (PDL) is a type of code that describes the appearance of a document in a language that a printer can understand. The PDL for a page includes the text, graphics, and formatting information. A software application uses a PDL to send *What You See Is What You Get (WYSIWYG)* images to the printer. The printer translates the PDL file so that whatever is on the computer screen is what is printed. PDLs speed up the printing process by sending large amounts of data at one time. They also manage the computer fonts.

Adobe Systems developed *PostScript* to allow fonts and text types to share the same characteristics on the screen as on paper. Hewlett-Packard developed *Printer Command Language (PCL)* for communication with early inkjet printers. PCL is now an industry standard for nearly all printer types.

Table 11-2 is a PostScript and PCL comparison.

Table 11-2 PostScript and PCL Comparison

PostScript	PCL
Page is rendered by the printer.	Page is rendered on local workstation.
Better quality output.	Faster print job.
Handles more complex print jobs.	Requires less printer memory.
Output is identical on different printers.	Output varies slightly on different printers.

Updating and Installing Printer Drivers (11.2.1.3)

After you have connected the power and data cables to the printer, the operating system discovers the printer and installs the driver.

A *printer driver* is a software program that enables the computer and the printer to communicate with each other. The driver also provides an interface for the user to configure printer options. Each printer model has a unique driver. Printer manufacturers frequently update drivers to increase the performance of the printer, to add options, or to fix problems. You can download updated printer drivers from the manufacturer's website.

To install a printer driver, follow these steps:

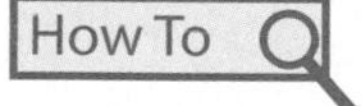

Step 1. Determine if a newer driver is available. Most manufacturers' websites have a link to a page that offers drivers and support. Make sure that the driver is compatible with the computer and operating system that you are updating.

Step 2. Download the printer driver files to your computer. Most driver files are compressed or zipped. Download the file to a folder and uncompress the contents. Save instructions or documentation to a separate folder on your computer.

Step 3. Install the downloaded driver automatically or manually. Most printer drivers have a setup file that automatically searches the system for older drivers and replaces them with the new one. If no setup file is available, follow the directions supplied by the manufacturer.

Step 4. Test the new printer driver. Run multiple tests to make sure that the printer works properly. Use a variety of applications to print different types of documents. Change and test each printer option.

The printed test page should contain text that is readable. If the text is unreadable, the problem could be a bad driver program or the wrong PDL is being used.

Printer Test Page (11.2.1.4)

After installing a printer, print a test page to verify that the printer is operating properly. The test page confirms that the driver software is installed and working correctly, and that the printer and computer are communicating.

To manually print a test page in Windows Vista, use the following path:

Step 1. **Control Panel > Printers** to display the **Printers** window.

Step 2. Right-click the desired printer and follow this path **Properties > General Tab > Print Test Page**

A dialog box asks if the page printed correctly. If the page did not print, built-in help files assist you in troubleshooting the problem.

To manually print a test page in Windows 7, use the following path:

Step 1. Choose **Devices and Printers** to display the **Devices and Printers** control panel.

Step 2. Right-click the desired printer and follow this path:

Printer Properties > General Tab > Print Test Page

To manually print a test page in Windows 8.0 or 8.1, use the following path:

Step 1. **Control Panel > Devices and Printers** to display the **Devices and Printers** control panel

Step 2. Right-click the desired printer and follow this path:

Printer Properties > General Tab > Print Test Page

You can test the printer by printing a test page from an application, such as Notepad or WordPad. To access Notepad in Windows 7 and Vista, use the following path:

Step 1. **Start > All Programs > Accessories > Notepad**

Step 2. To open Notepad in Windows 8.0 and 8.1, from the **Start Screen**, type Notepad and click Notepad to open it.

Step 3. In the blank document that opens, type some text. Print the document using the following path:

File > Print

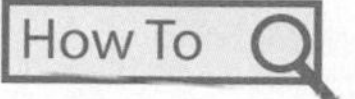

Test the Printer from the Printer Panel

Most printers have a front panel with controls to allow you to generate test pages. This method of printing enables you to verify the printer operation separately from the network or computer. Consult the printer manufacturer's website or documentation to learn how to print a test page from the front panel of the printer.

Test Printer Functions (11.2.1.5)

The installation of any device is not complete until you have successfully tested all its functions. Printer functions might include:

- Print double-sided documents.
- Use different paper trays for different paper sizes.
- Change the settings of a color printer so that it prints in black and white or grayscale.
- Print in draft mode.
- Use an optical character recognition (OCR) application.
- Print a collated document.

Note

Collated printing is ideal when you need to print several copies of a multiple page document. The **Collate** setting will print each set, in turn, as shown in Figure 11-10. Some copiers will even staple each printed set.

Functions for an *all-in-one* printer include the following:

- Fax to another known working fax
- Create a copy of a document
- Scan a document
- Print a document

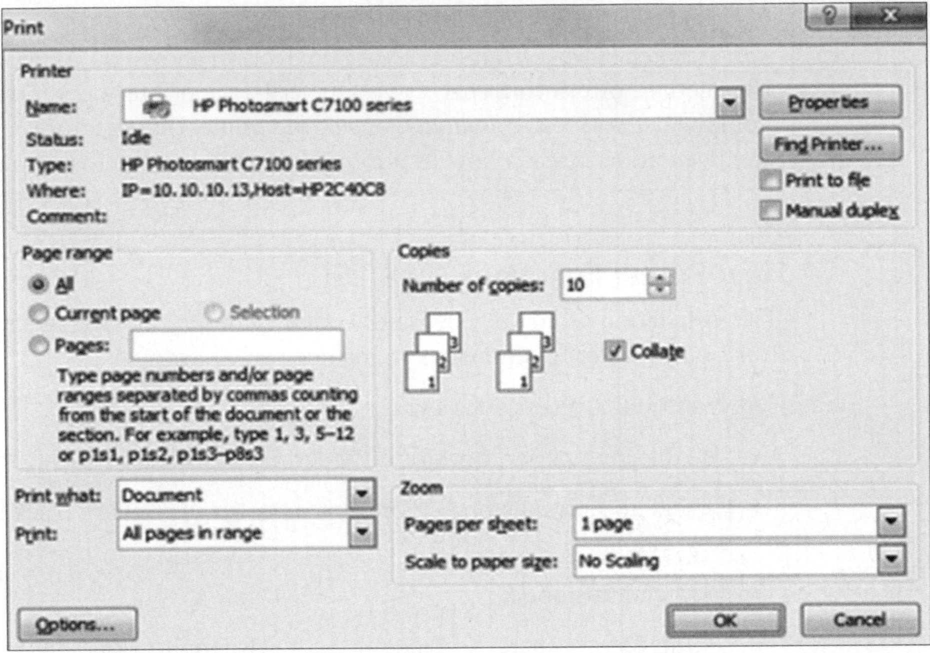

Figure 11-10 Collated Printing

Note

For information on clearing paper jams, installing ink cartridges, and loading the paper trays, check the manufacturer's documentation or website.

Lab—Install a Printer (11.2.1.6)

In this lab, you install a printer. You find, download, and update the driver and the software for the printer. Refer to the lab in *IT Essentials v6 Lab Manual*.

Configuring Options and Default Settings (11.2.2)

Because of a printer's hardware characteristics, some of the configuration options will be device-specific properties such as resolution and memory. Other configurations such as document printing options are common across printer models. There are settings that will be defaults and describe how that hardware can be used to perform a printing task. Unless you override them, a program uses the default document properties that are set for a printer. This section discusses the various configuration and setting options.

Common Configuration Settings (11.2.2.1)

Each printer may have different configurations and default options. Check the printer documentation for specific information about its configuration and default settings. Figure 11-11 shows an example of printer configuration settings.

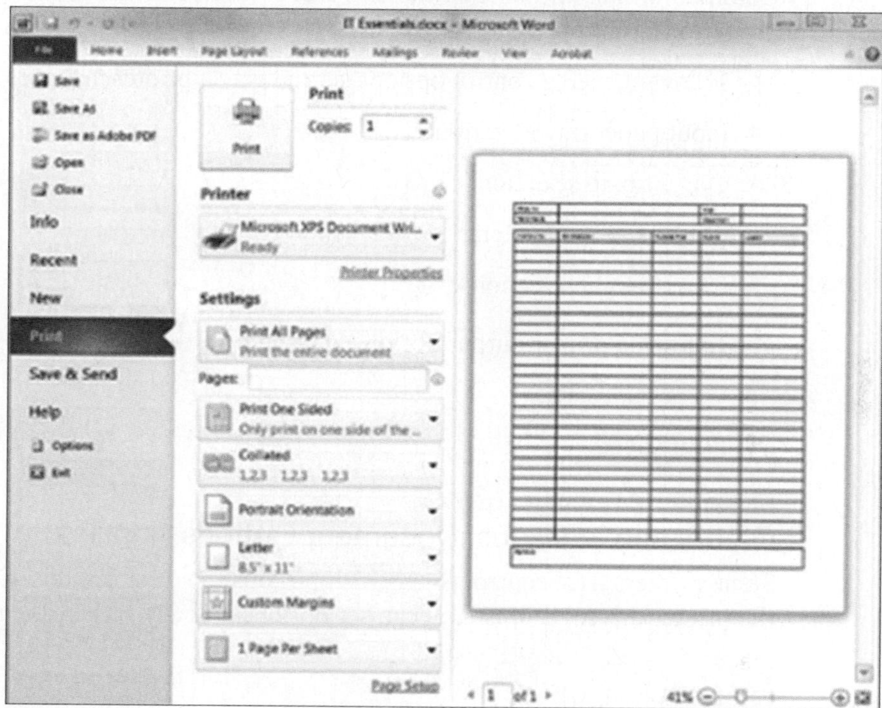

Figure 11-11 Printer Configuration Settings

Here are some common configuration options available for printers:

- **Paper type**—Standard, draft, gloss, or photo
- **Print quality**—Draft, normal, or photo
- **Color printing**—Multiple colors is used
- **Black-and-white printing**—Only black ink is used
- **Grayscale printing**—Images printed using only black ink in different shades
- **Paper size**—Standard paper sizes or envelopes and business cards
- **Paper orientation**—Landscape or portrait

- **Print layout**—Normal, banner, booklet, or poster
- **Duplex**—Two-sided printing
- **Collate**—Print sets of a document with multiple pages

Common printer options that the user can configure include media control and printer output.

The following media control options set the way a printer manages media:

- Input paper tray selection
- Output path selection
- Media size and orientation
- Paper weight selection

The following printer output options manage how the ink or toner goes on the media:

- Color management
- Print speed

Global and Individual Document Options (11.2.2.2)

Some printers have control panels with buttons to select options. Other printers use the printer driver options. You can set options globally or per document.

Global Method

The *global method* refers to printer options that are set to affect all documents. Each time a document is printed, the global options are used, unless they are overridden by per-document selections.

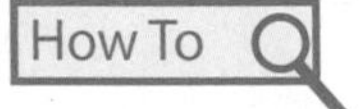

To change the global configuration of a printer in Windows 8 or 7, use the following path:

Step 1. **Control Panel > Devices and Printers >** right-click the printer

Step 2. To designate a default printer, right-click the printer and select **Set as default** printer as shown in Figure 11-12.

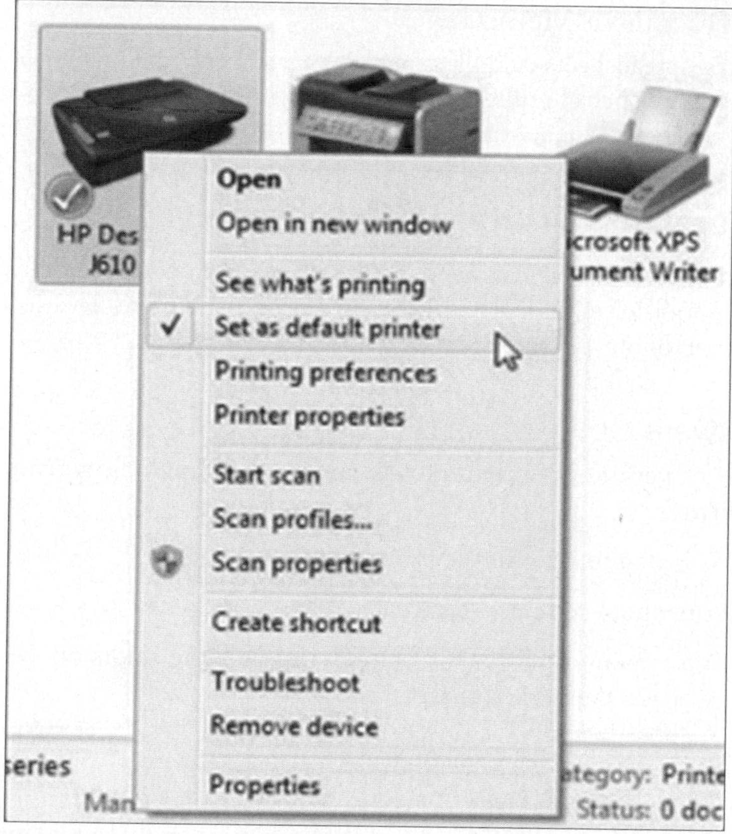

Figure 11-12 Set as Default Printer

To change the global configuration of a printer in Windows Vista, use the following path:

How To

Step 1. **Control Panel > Printers and Faxes >** right-click the printer

Step 2. To designate a default printer, right-click the printer and select **Set as default printer.**

Note

Depending on the driver installed, the **Set as default printer** option might not be available. In this case, double-click the printer to open the Document Status window, and then choose **Printer > Set as default printer.**

Per-Document Method

Letters, spreadsheets, and digital images are some of the document types that may require special printer settings. You can change the settings for an individual document by changing the document print settings.

Optimizing Printer Performance (11.2.3)

Printing performance can be improved with modifications to the printer tray settings, print spool settings, device calibration settings, and more. This section explains common optimization settings.

Software Optimization (11.2.3.1)

With printers, most optimization is completed through the software supplied with the drivers.

The following tools optimize performance:

- **Print spool settings**—Cancel or pause current print jobs in the printer queue
- **Color calibration**—Adjust settings to match the colors on the screen to the colors on the printed sheet
- **Paper orientation**—Select landscape or portrait image layout

Printers are calibrated using the print driver software. *Calibration* makes sure that the print heads are aligned and that they can print on different kinds of media, such as cardstock, photographic paper, and optical discs. Some inkjet print heads are fitted to the ink cartridge, so you might have to recalibrate the printer each time you change a cartridge.

Hardware Optimization (11.2.3.2)

Some printers can be upgraded to print faster and to accommodate more print jobs by adding hardware. The hardware may include additional paper trays, sheet feeders, network cards, and expansion memory.

Firmware

Firmware is a set of instructions stored on the printer. The firmware controls how the printer operates. The procedure to upgrade firmware is similar to installing printer drivers. Because firmware updates do not take place automatically, visit the home page of the printer manufacturer to check the availability of new firmware.

Printer Memory

All printers have RAM. Printers usually arrive from the factory with enough memory to handle jobs that involve text. However, print jobs involving graphics, and especially photographs, run more efficiently if the printer memory is adequate to store the entire job before it starts. Upgrading the printer memory increases the printing speed and enhances complex print job performance.

Print job buffering is when a print job is captured in the internal printer memory. Buffering allows the computer to continue with other work instead of waiting for the printer to finish. Buffering is a common feature in laser printers and plotters, as well as in advanced inkjet and dot matrix printers.

If you receive low memory errors, this can indicate that the printer is out of memory or has a memory overload. In this instance, you may need more memory.

Sharing Printers (11.3)

Printer sharing is an effective way to give users access to the printer while saving on hardware purchases. This section outlines the processes to share a printer in Windows operating systems.

Operating System Settings for Sharing Printers (11.3.1)

Connecting a printer to a network print server is not all that needs to be completed to make the printer available to network users. The printer is a resource on the server it must be shared to the network before it can be accessed. In a server-based network, access to the printer can be controlled in the same way as access to any other resource on the server.

Configuring Printer Sharing (11.3.1.1)

Windows allows computer users to share their printers with other users on the network.

In Windows 7, to configure the computer with the printer attached to accept print jobs from other network users, follow these steps:

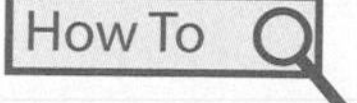

Step 1. Select **Control Panel > Network and Sharing Center > Change advanced sharing settings.**

Step 2. **Expand the network listing to view the network profile.**

Step 3. **If printer sharing is off, under** File and printer sharing, **select** Turn on file and printer sharing, **and then click** Save changes.

In Windows Vista, to configure the computer with the printer attached to accept print jobs from other network users, follow these steps:

Step 1. Select Control Panel > Printers.

Step 2. Right-click the printer to share and choose Sharing. The Printer Properties dialog box opens.

Step 3. Select Share this printer and enter the desired shared printer name. This name is displayed to other users.

Step 4. Verify that sharing has been successful. In the Printers window, check whether the printer has a share icon under it, indicating that it is a shared resource.

In Windows 8.0 and 8.1, to configure the computer with the printer attached to accept print jobs from other network users, follow these steps:

Step 1. Select Control Panel > Network and Sharing Center > Change advanced sharing settings.

Step 2. Expand the network listing to view the network profile.

Step 3. If printer sharing is off, under File and printer sharing, select Turn on file and printer sharing, and then click Save changes.

Users who can now connect to the shared printer might not have the required drivers installed. They might also be using different operating systems than the computer that is hosting the shared printer. Windows can automatically download the correct drivers to these users. On the Printer Properties sheet, click open the Sharing tab and then click the Additional Drivers button to select operating systems that the other users are using. When you close that dialog box by clicking OK, Windows will ask to obtain those additional drivers. If the other users are also using the same Windows OS, you do not need to click the Additional Drivers button.

Connecting to a Shared Printer (11.3.1.2)

To connect to the printer from another computer on the network in Windows 7, follow these steps

Step 1. Choose Devices and Printers > Add a Printer.

Step 2. The Add Printer wizard appears.

Step 3. Select Add a network, wireless or Bluetooth printer.

Step 4. A list of shared printers will appear. If the printer is not listed, select The printer that I wanted is not listed.

Step 5. After selecting the printer, click Next.

Step 6. A virtual printer port is created and displayed in the Add a Printer window. The required print drivers are downloaded from the print server and installed on the computer. The wizard then finishes the installation.

To connect to the printer from another computer on the network in Windows Vista, follow these steps:

Step 1. Choose Control Panel > Printers > Add a Printer.

Step 2. The Add Printer wizard appears.

Step 3. Select Add a network, wireless or Bluetooth printer.

Step 4. A list of shared printers will appear. If the printer is not listed, select The printer that I wanted is not listed.

Step 5. After selecting the printer, click Next.

Step 6. A virtual printer port is created and displayed in the Add a Printer window. The required print drivers are downloaded from the print server and installed on the computer. The wizard then finishes the installation.

To connect to the printer from another computer on the network in Windows 8.0 or 8.1, follow these steps:

Step 1. Choose Devices and Printers > Add a Printer.

Step 2. The Add Printer wizard appears.

Step 3. A list of shared printers will appear. If the printer is not listed, select The printer that I wanted is not listed.

Step 4. After selecting the printer, click Next.

Step 5. A virtual printer port is created and displayed in the Add a Printer window. The required print drivers are downloaded from the print server and installed on the computer. The wizard then finishes the installation.

Printer Is Not Listed

In all versions of Windows, if you click **The printer I wanted is not listed**, you will have one of the following options to map a path to the network printer as shown in Figure 11-13:

- Browse for a printer on the network
- Enter the exact path to a printer on the network
- Enter the IP address or hostname of a printer on the network

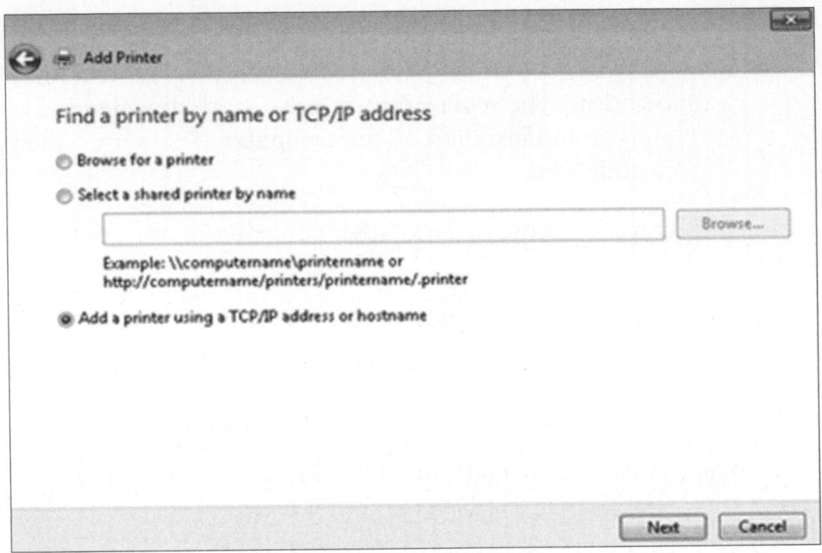

Figure 11-13 Finding a Printer on the Network

Wireless Printer Connections (11.3.1.3)

Wireless printers allow hosts to connect and print wirelessly using Bluetooth or a wireless LAN (WLAN) connection. For wireless printers to use Bluetooth, both the printer and the host device must have Bluetooth capabilities and be paired. If necessary, you can add a Bluetooth adapter to the computer, usually in a USB port. Wireless Bluetooth printers allow for easy printing from mobile devices.

Wireless printers designed for 802.11 standards are equipped with installed wireless NICs and connect directly to a wireless router or access point. Setup is completed by connecting the printer to the computer with the supplied software or using the printer display panel to connect to the wireless router.

Print Servers (11.3.2)

Print servers can be wireless, internal, external or embedded devices. The *print server* is the device that interfaces between a computer and a printer. This section discusses the purpose and function of print servers.

Purposes of Print Servers (11.3.2.1)

Some printers require a separate print server to allow network connectivity because these printers do not have built-in network interfaces. Print servers enable multiple computer users, regardless of device or operating system, to access a single printer. A print server has three functions:

- To provide client access to print resources
- To administrate print jobs by storing them in a queue until the print device is ready for them and then feeding or spooling the print information to the printer
- To provide feedback to users

Software Print Servers (11.3.2.2)

In a previous topic, you learned how a Windows computer can share an attached printer with other Windows computers on the network. But what if the computer sharing the printer is running a different operating system, such as Mac OS X? In such a situation, you can use print server software.

One example is Apple's free Bonjour Printer Server, which is a built-in service in Mac OS X. It is automatically installed on a Windows computer if you install the Apple Safari Browser. You can also download the Bonjour Printer Server for Windows for free from the Apple website.

After it's downloaded and installed, the Bonjour Printer Server operates in the background, automatically detecting any compatible printers connected to the network. Open the Bonjour Printer Wizard to configure the Windows computer to use a printer.

Sharing a printer from a computer also has disadvantages. The computer sharing the printer uses its own resources to manage the print jobs coming to the printer. If the computer user on the desktop is working at the same time as a user on the network is printing, the desktop computer user might notice a performance slowdown. In addition, the printer is not available to others if the user reboots or powers off the computer with a shared printer.

Hardware Print Servers (11.3.2.3)

A *hardware print server* is a simple device with a network card and memory. It connects to the network and communicates with the printer to enable print sharing. The print server can be connected to the printer through a USB cable. A hardware print server may be integrated with another device, such as a wireless router. In this case, the printer would connect directly to the wireless router, most likely through a USB cable.

Apple's AirPort Extreme is an example of a hardware print server. Through the AirPrint service, the AirPort Extreme can share a printer with any device on the network.

Hardware print servers allow many users on a network to access a single printer. A hardware print server can manage network printing through either wired or wireless connections. An advantage of using a hardware print server is that the server accepts incoming print jobs from computers, thereby freeing the computers for other tasks. A hardware print server is always available to users, unlike a printer shared from a user's computer.

Dedicated Printer Servers (11.3.2.4)

For larger networking environments with multiple LANs and many users, a dedicated print server is needed to manage printing services. A dedicated print server is more powerful than a hardware print server. It handles client print jobs in the most efficient manner and can manage more than one printer at a time. A dedicated print server must have the following resources to meet the requests of print clients:

- **Powerful processor**—Because the dedicated print server uses its processor to manage and route printing information, it must be fast enough to handle all incoming requests.
- **Adequate hard disk space**—A dedicated print server captures print jobs from clients, places them in a print queue, and sends them to the printer in a timely manner. This process requires the computer to have enough storage space to hold these jobs until completed.
- **Adequate memory**—The processor and RAM handle sending print jobs to a printer. If memory is not large enough to handle an entire print job, the hard drive must send the job, which is much slower.

Lab—Share a Printer (11.3.2.5)

In this lab, you share a printer, configure the printer on a networked computer, and print a test page from the remote computer. Refer to the lab in *IT Essentials v6 Lab Manual*.

Maintaining and Troubleshooting Printers (11.4)

Preventive maintenance is a proactive way to decrease printer problems and increase the life span of the hardware. Using manufacturer's guidelines, a preventive maintenance plan should be established and implemented. This section examines preventive maintenance guidelines and best practices.

Printer Preventive Maintenance (11.4.1)

Like any computer or network component, printers require attention and maintenance to head off major malfunctions, avoid costly repairs that results from neglect and can reduce downtime for troubleshooting and emergency repairs.

Vendor Guidelines (11.4.1.1)

Preventive maintenance decreases downtime and increases the service life of the components. It is important to maintain printers to keep them working properly. A good maintenance program guarantees good quality prints and uninterrupted operation. The printer documentation contains information on how to maintain and clean the equipment.

Read the information manuals that come with every new piece of equipment. Follow the recommended maintenance instructions. Use the supplies listed by the manufacturer. Less expensive supplies can save money, but may produce poor results, damage the equipment, or void the warranty.

Caution

Be sure to unplug the printer from the electrical source before beginning any type of maintenance.

When maintenance is completed, reset the counters to allow the next maintenance to be completed at the correct time. On many types of printers, the page count is viewed through the LCD display or a counter located inside the main cover.

Most manufacturers sell maintenance kits for their printers. For laser printers, the kit might contain replacement parts that often break or wear out:

- Fuser assembly
- Transfer rollers
- Separation pads
- Pickup rollers

Figure 11-14 shows a maintenance kit that includes replacements for parts that often break or wear out.

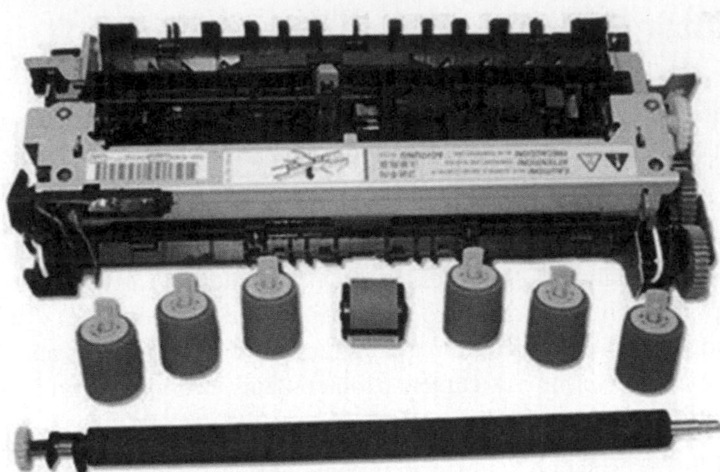

Figure 11-14 Maintenance Kit

When you install new parts or replace toners and cartridges, visually inspect all internal components and perform the following tasks:

- Remove bits of paper and dust
- Clean spilled ink or toner
- Look for worn gears, cracked plastic, or broken parts

If you do not know how to maintain printing equipment, call a manufacturer-certified technician.

Replacing Consumables (11.4.1.2)

The type and quality of paper and ink used can affect the life of the printer. Many types of printer paper are available, including inkjet and laser. The printer manufacturer might recommend which type of paper to use for best results. Some papers, especially photo paper, transparencies, and multilayered carbon paper, have a right and wrong side. Load the paper according to the manufacturer's instructions.

The manufacturer recommends the brand and type of ink to use. If the wrong type of ink is installed, the printer might not work or the print quality might deteriorate. Avoid refilling ink cartridges because the ink can leak.

When an inkjet printer produces blank pages, the ink cartridges might be empty. Some inkjet printers may refuse to print any pages if one of the ink cartridges is empty. Laser printers do not produce blank pages. Instead, they begin to print poor quality prints. Most inkjet printers have a utility that shows ink levels in each cartridge, as shown in Figure 11-15. Some printers have LCD message screens or LED lights that warn users when ink supplies are low.

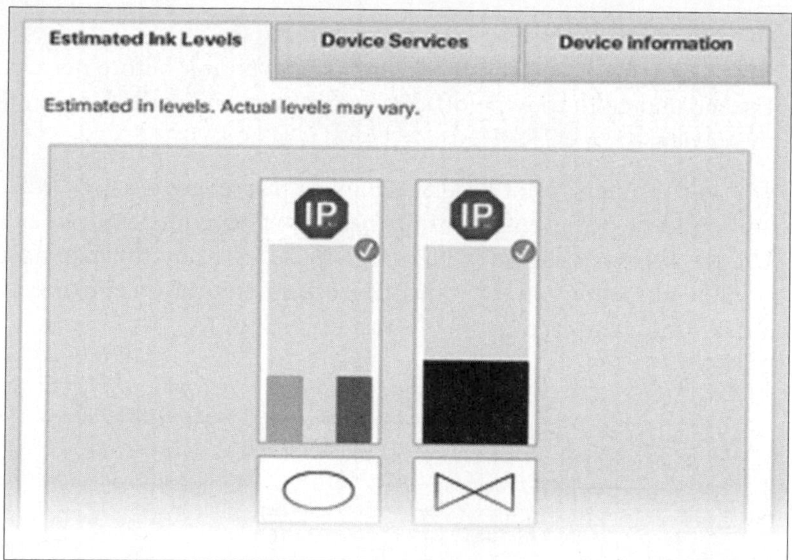

Figure 11-15 Estimated Ink Levels

A method for checking ink levels is to look at the page counter inside the printer or the printer software to determine how many pages have been printed. Then look at the cartridge label information. The label should show how many pages the cartridge can print. You can then easily estimate how many more pages you can print. To help keep track of usage, each time you replace the cartridge, reset the counter. In addition, some printouts use more ink than others do. For example, a letter uses less ink than a photograph.

You can set the printer software to toner save or draft quality to reduce the amount of ink or toner that the printer uses. These settings also reduce the print quality of laser and inkjet products, as well as the time it takes to print a document on an inkjet printer.

An impact printer is similar to a typewriter because the print head strikes an inked ribbon to transfer ink to the printout. When the impact printer produces faded or light characters, the ribbon is worn out and needs to be replaced. If a consistent flaw is produced in all characters, the print head is stuck or broken and needs to be replaced.

Cleaning Methods (11.4.1.3)

Always follow the manufacturer's guidelines when cleaning printers. Information on the manufacturer's website or documentation explains the proper cleaning methods.

Caution

Unplug printers before cleaning to prevent danger from high voltage.

Printer Maintenance

Make sure that you turn off and unplug any printer before performing maintenance. Use a damp cloth to wipe off dirt, paper dust, and spilled ink on the exterior of the device.

On some printers, print heads in an inkjet printer are replaced when the cartridges are replaced. However, sometimes print heads become clogged and require cleaning. Use the utility, as shown in Figure 11-16, supplied by the manufacturer to clean the print heads. After you clean them, test them. Repeat this process until the test shows a clean and uniform print.

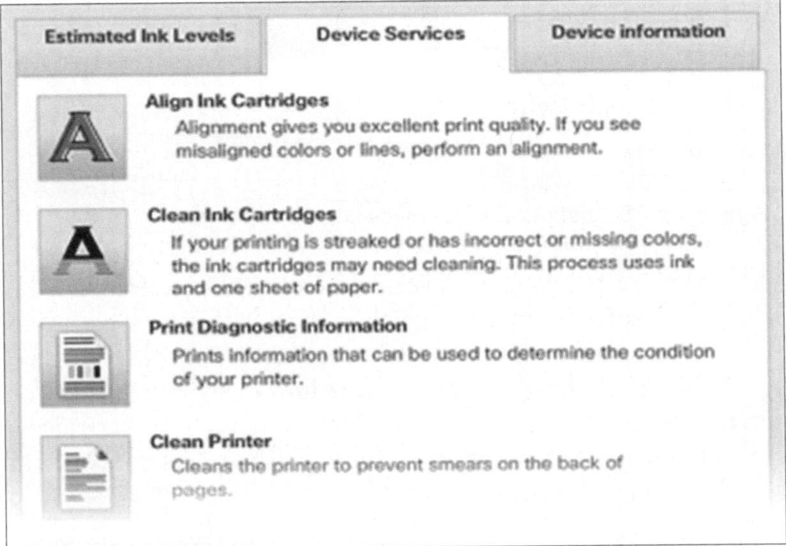

Figure 11-16 Printer Utility

Printers have many moving parts. Over time, the parts collect dust, dirt, and other debris. If not cleaned regularly, the printer may not work well or could stop working completely. When working with dot-matrix printers, clean the roller surfaces with a damp cloth. On inkjet printers, clean the paper-handling machinery with a damp cloth. Some printer parts must be lubricated with special grease. Check the documentation to determine if your printer needs this grease and the locations to use it.

Caution

Do not touch the drum of a laser printer while cleaning because you can damage the drum surface.

Laser printers do not usually require much maintenance unless they are in a dusty area or are very old. When cleaning a laser printer, use a specially designed vacuum cleaner to pick up toner particles. A standard vacuum cleaner cannot hold the tiny particles of toner and may scatter them about. Use only a vacuum cleaner with ***high efficiency particulate air (HEPA) filtration***. HEPA filtration catches microscopic particles within the filters.

Thermal printers use heat to create an image on special paper. To extend the life of the printer, clean the heating element of the thermal printer regularly with isopropyl alcohol.

Choosing the correct paper type for a printer helps the printer last longer and print more efficiently. Several types of paper are available. Each type of paper is labeled with the type of printer for which it is intended. The manufacturer of the printer may also recommend the best type of paper.

Operational Environment (11.4.1.4)

Printers, like all other electrical devices, are affected by temperature, humidity, and electrical interference. Laser printers produce heat and should be operated in well-ventilated areas to prevent overheating.

Keep paper and toner cartridges in their original wrappers. These supplies should also be stored in a cool, dry, dust-free environment. High humidity causes paper to absorb moisture from the air. This can cause the paper to wave, which causes pieces of paper to stick together or jam during the printing process. High humidity can also make it difficult for the toner to attach to the paper correctly. If the paper and printer are dusty, you can use compressed air to blow away the dust. Table 11-3 lists common operating environment guidelines.

Table 11-3 Operating Environment Guidelines

- Keep paper dry
- Keep printer in a cool, dust free environment
- Store toner in a clean, dry environment
- Clean glass on scanners

Troubleshooting Printer Issues (11.4.2)

Troubleshooting is a valuable skill. Using an organized approach to problem solving will help technicians develop their troubleshooting skills. This section outlines a systematic troubleshooting approach and offers specifics on how to address issues that are particular to printers.

Identify the Problem (11.4.2.1)

Printer problems can result from a combination of hardware, software, and connectivity issues. A technician must be able to determine if the problem exists with the device, a cable connection, or the computer to which the printer is connected. Computer technicians must be able to analyze the problem and determine the cause of the error to repair the printer issues.

The first step in the troubleshooting process is to identify the problem. The following list shows examples of open-ended and closed-ended questions to ask the customer:

Identify the Problem

Open-ended questions:

- What problems are you experiencing with your printer or scanner?
- What software or hardware has been changed recently on your computer?
- What were you doing when the problem was discovered?
- What error messages have you received?

Closed-ended questions:

- Is the printer under warranty?
- Can you print a test page?
- Is this a new printer?
- Is the printer powered on?

Establish a Theory of Probable Cause (11.4.2.2)

After you have talked to the customer, you can establish a theory of probable cause. The following shows a list of some common probable causes for printer problems. If necessary, conduct internal and external research based on the symptoms of the problem. The following list shows of some common probable causes for printer problems:

Establish a Theory of Probable Cause

Common causes for printer problems:

- Loose cable connections
- Paper jams
- Equipment power
- Low ink warning

- Out of paper
- Error on equipment display
- Errors on computer screen

Test the Theory to Determine Cause (11.4.2.3)

After you have developed some theories about what is wrong, test them to determine the cause of the problem. The following shows a list of quick procedures that can determine the exact cause of the problem or even correct the problem. If a quick procedure does correct the problem, you can verify full system functionality. If a quick procedure does not correct the problem, you may need to research the problem further to establish the exact cause:

Test the Theory to Determine Cause

Common steps to determine cause:

- Restart the printer
- Disconnect and reconnect the cables
- Restart computer
- Check for paper jams
- Reseat paper in tray
- Open and close printer tray
- Ensure printer doors are closed
- Install a new ink or toner cartridge

Establish a Plan of Action to Resolve the Problem and Implement the Solution (11.4.2.4)

After you have determined the exact cause of the problem, establish a plan of action to resolve the problem and implement the solution. The following list shows some sources you can use to gather additional information to resolve an issue:

Establish a Plan of Action to Resolve the Problem and Implement the Solution

If no solution is achieved in the previous step, further research is needed to implement the solution:

- Help desk repair logs
- Other technicians

- Manufacturer FAQs
- Technical websites
- Newsgroups
- Manuals
- Online forums
- Internet research

Verify Full System Functionality and Implement Preventive Measures (11.4.2.5)

After you have corrected the problem, verify full functionality and, if applicable, implement preventive measures. The following shows a list of the steps to verify the solution:

Verify Full System Functionality and, If Applicable, Implement Preventive Measures

Verify full functionality:

- Reboot the computer
- Reboot the printer
- Print a test page from the printer control panel
- Print a document from an application
- Reprint the customer's problem print job

Document Findings, Actions, and Outcomes (11.4.2.6)

In the final step of the troubleshooting process, document your findings, actions, and outcomes. The following shows a list of the tasks required to document the problem and the solution.

Document Your Findings, Actions, and Outcomes

Document your findings, actions, and outcomes:

- Discuss the solution implemented with the customer
- Ask the customer to verify that the problem has been solved
- Provide the customer with all paperwork

- Document the steps taken to solve the problem in the work order and technician's journal
- Document any components used in the repair
- Document the time spent to resolve the problem

Common Problems and Solutions for Printers (11.4.3)

Printer problems can stem from many sources; the printer hardware, printer drivers, the print server, or, in the case of a network printer, the network. Recognizing the source of a problem and identifying a solution are the topics of this section.

Identify Common Problems and Solutions (11.4.3.1)

Printer problems can be attributed to hardware, software, networks, or some combination of the three. You will resolve some types of problems more often than others. Table 11-4 shows a chart of common problems and solutions.

Table 11-4 Common Problems and Solutions

Identify the Problem	Probable Causes	Possible Solutions
An application document does not print.	There is a document error in the print queue.	Manage the print jobs by deleting the document from the print queue and print again
Printer cannot be added or there is a print spooler error.	The printer service is stopped or not working properly.	Start the print spooler and if necessary reboot both the computer and printer
Printer jobs are sent to the print queue but are not printed.	The printer has been installed on the wrong port.	Use printer properties and settings to configure the printer port
Print queue is functioning properly but the printer does not print.	■ There is a bad cable connection. ■ The printer is in standby. ■ The printer has an error such as out paper, out of toner, or paper jam.	■ Check for bent pins on the printer cable connections to the printer and computer ■ Manually resume printer from standby, or power cycle the printer ■ Check the printer status and correct any errors

(Continued)

Table 11-4 *Continued*

Identify the Problem	Probable Causes	Possible Solutions
Printer is printing unknown characters or does not print anything.	■ Printer may be plugged into a UPS. ■ Incorrect print driver installed. ■ Printer cables are loose. ■ No paper in printer.	■ Plug the printer directly into the wall outlet or surge protector ■ Uninstall incorrect print driver and install correct driver ■ Secure printer cables ■ Add paper to the printer
Printer is printing unknown characters or does not print a test page.	Wrong or outdated printer driver is installed.	Uninstall incorrect print driver and install correct driver
Paper jams when printing.	■ Printer is dirty. ■ The wrong paper type is being used. ■ Humidity causes the paper to stick together.	■ Clean the printer ■ Replace paper with the manufacturer's recommended paper type ■ Insert new paper in the paper tray
Print jobs are faded.	■ The toner cartridge is low. ■ The toner cartridge is defective. ■ The paper is incompatible with the printer.	■ Replace the toner cartridge ■ Replace the paper
The toner is not fusing to the paper.	■ The toner cartridge is empty. ■ The toner cartridge is defective. ■ The paper is incompatible with the printer.	■ Replace the toner cartridge ■ Replace the paper
The paper is creasing after printing.	■ The paper is defective. ■ The paper is loaded incorrectly.	■ Remove the paper from the printer, check for defects, and replace ■ Remove, align, and replace the paper
The paper is not being fed into the printer.	■ The paper is wrinkled. ■ Printer set to print to a different paper size than currently loaded.	■ Remove the wrinkled paper from the tray ■ Change paper size in print settings

Identify the Problem	Probable Causes	Possible Solutions
User receives a "Document failed to print" message.	■ A cable is loose or disconnected. ■ A printer is no longer shared.	■ Check and reconnect cables ■ Configure printer sharing
User receives an "Access Denied" message when trying to install a printer.	User does not have administrative or power user privileges.	Log out and log back in as an administrative or power user
Printer is printing incorrect colors.	■ Print cartridge is empty. ■ Print cartridge defective. ■ Incorrect cartridge type installed. ■ Print heads need to be cleaned and calibrated.	■ Replace cartridge with correct cartridge ■ Clean and calibrate print heads
Printer is printing blank pages.	■ The printer is out of ink or toner ■ The print head is clogged. ■ The corona wire has failed ■ The high voltage power supply has failed.	■ Replace the printer ink or toner ■ Replace the ink cartridge ■ Replace the corona wire ■ Replace the high voltage power supply
The printer display has no image.	■ The printer is not turned on. ■ The contrast of the screen is set too low. ■ The display is broken.	■ Turned on printer ■ Turn up the screen contrast ■ Replace the display

Summary (11.5)

In this chapter, various types of printers were discussed.

Summary (11.5.1)

You learned that there are many different types and sizes of printers, each with different capabilities, speeds, and uses. You also learned that printers can be connected directly to computers or shared across a network.

The chapter introduced the different types of cables and interfaces available to connect a printer.

The following concepts from this chapter are important to remember:

- Some printers have low output and are adequate for home use, whereas other printers have high output and are designed for commercial use.
- Printers can have different speeds and quality of print.
- Older printers use parallel cables and ports. Newer printers typically use USB or FireWire cables and connectors.
- With newer printers, the computer automatically installs the necessary drivers.
- If the device drivers are not automatically installed by the computer, download them from the manufacturer's website or use the supplied CD.
- Most optimization is done through software drivers and utilities.
- After you have set up the printer, you can share the device with other users on the network. This arrangement is cost-efficient because every user does not need to have a printer.
- A good preventive maintenance program extends the life of the printer and keeps it performing well.
- Always follow safety procedures when working with printers. Many parts inside printers contain high voltage or become very hot with use.
- Use a sequence of steps to fix a problem. Start with simple tasks before you decide on a course of action. Call a certified printer technician when a problem is too difficult for you to fix.

Summary of Exercises

This is a summary of the Labs, Packet Tracer, videos, and activities associated with this chapter.

Labs

The following labs cover material from this chapter. Refer to the labs in the *IT Essentials v6 Lab Manual*.

Lab—Install a Printer (11.2.1.6)

Lab—Share a Printer (11.3.2.5)

Check Your Understanding

You can find the answers to these questions in the appendix, "Answers to 'Check Your Understanding' Questions."

1. What term is used to describe dual-sided printing?

   A. IR printing

   B. Spooling

   C. Duplex printing

   D. Buffering

2. Which statement describes the print buffering process?

   A. A document is being prepared by the application to be printed.

   B. A document is being printed on the printer.

   C. A PC is encoding a photograph into a language that the printer understands.

   D. Large documents are stored temporarily in internal printer memory while waiting for the availability of the printer.

3. What are two potential disadvantages of replacing printer consumables with parts or components that are not recommended by the manufacturer? (Choose two.)

   A. Non-recommended parts may be less expensive.

   B. The printer may need cleaning more often.

   C. Print quality may be poor.

   D. Non-recommended parts may be more readily available.

   E. The manufacturer warranty may be voided.

4. How could a user share a locally connected printer with other users on the same network?

   A. Enable print sharing

   B. Install shared PCL drivers

   C. Install a USB hub

   D. Remove the PS drivers

5. A technician wants to share a printer on the network but according to the company policy, no PC should have a directly connected printer. Which device would the technician need?

   A. A hardware print server

   B. A USB hub

   C. A LAN switch

   D. A docking station

6. Which is common printer paper type configuration option?

   A. Typical

   B. Gloss

   C. Thick

   D. Shiny

   E. Color printing

7. What is the first action that should be taken when performing preventive maintenance on a printer?

   A. Remove the paper from the printer paper tray

   B. Disconnect the printer from the power source

   C. Clean the print heads using the printer software utility

   D. Disconnect the printer from the network

8. While troubleshooting a printer problem, a technician discovers that the printer has been connected to the wrong computer port. Which printer problem would this mistake have caused?

   A. Blank pages are printed by the printer.

   B. The print spooler displays an error.

   C. When a document is printed, there are unknown characters on the page.

   D. The print queue is functioning, but print jobs are not printed.

9. Which method is recommended for cleaning the print heads in an inkjet printer?

   A. Use the printer software utility
   B. Use compressed air
   C. Wipe the print heads with a damp cloth
   D. Wipe the print heads with isopropyl alcohol

10. What are two closed-ended questions that a technician could ask a user while trying to identify the problem with a printer? (Choose two.)

    A. What recent software or hardware changes have been made to your computer?
    B. Can you print a test page on the printer?
    C. What were you doing when the problem occurred?
    D. Is the printer powered on?
    E. What error messages were displayed when the problem occurred?

11. Which type of document typically takes the longest time to print?

    A. A digital color photograph
    B. A high quality page of text
    C. A draft text
    D. A draft photo quality printout

12. A small business has connected several printers to the web using Google Cloud Print. Mobile workers can then print job orders while they are on the road. This is an example of using what type of printer?

    A. Inkjet
    B. Thermal
    C. Laser
    D. Virtual

13. What software enables users to set and change printer options?

    A. Firmware
    B. Word processing applications
    C. Configuration software
    D. Drivers

14. What are two disadvantages of sharing a directly connected printer from a computer? (Choose two.)

    A. Only one computer at a time can use the printer.
    B. Other computers do not need to be cabled directly to the printer.
    C. All the computers using the printer need to use the same operating system.
    D. The computer sharing the printer uses its own resources to manage all the print jobs coming to the printer.
    E. The computer directly connected to the printer always needs to be powered on, even if not in use.

15. Dots per inch is used as a measure for which characteristic of a printer?

    A. Cost of ownership
    B. Speed
    C. Reliability
    D. Quality of printing

CHAPTER 12

Security

Objectives

Upon completion of this chapter, you will be able to answer the following questions:

- What are some types of security threats that involve malicious software?
- What are some types of security threats that involve Internet Security software?
- What are some types of security threats that involve access to data and equipment?
- What are some types of security procedures?
- What are the elements of a strong security policy?
- How can physical security be implemented?
- What are some disaster and recovery techniques?
- How can TCP/IP attacks be identified?
- How do configure wireless security?
- What are some of the preventive maintenance techniques for security?
- What can be done to troubleshoot security?
- What is the process to troubleshoot security?

Key Terms

This chapter uses the following key terms. You can find the definitions in the Glossary.

Malware Page 667

virus Page 667

Trojan horse Page 667

antivirus program Page 669

antispyware program Page 669

anti-adware programs Page 669

Phishing Page 669

spear phishing Page 669

Spam Page 670

Denial of service (DoS) Page 670

Distributed denial of service (DDoS) Page 670

SYN flood attack Page 671

Spoofing Page 671

man-in-the-middle attack Page 671

replay attack Page 672

DNS poisoning Page 672

Grayware Page 719

virus protection software Page 722

web tools Page 680

pop-up Page 681

Worm Page 668

Adware Page 668

Spyware Page 668

Ransomware Page 668

Rootkit Page 669

zero day attack Page 672

zero hour Page 672

Social engineering Page 673

Pretexting Page 673

Tailgating Page 673

Something for Something (Quid pro quo) Page 673

Baiting Page 673

security policy Page 675

Windows Local Security Policy Page 675

Active X controls Page 681

Active X filtering Page 681

SmartScreen filter Page 682

InPrivate Browsing Page 682

software firewall Page 683

Biometric Security Page 685

profile Page 685

fingerprint reader Page 685

Smart card Page 686

Security key fob Page 686

data backup Page 687

Permissions Page 687

DNS poisoning Page 672

Data wiping Page 691

Degaussing Page 692

high-level formatting Page 694

Low-level formatting Page 694

principle of least privilege Page 688

Encryption Page 689

Encrypting File System (EFS) Page 689

BitLocker Page 689

Trusted Platform Module (TPM) Page 689

Data wiping software Page 691

Degaussing wand Page 692

Standard Format or high-level formatting Page 694

Low-level Format Page 694

rogue antivirus Page 695

signatures Page 697

mirrors Page 697

Hash encoding Page 698

message digest Page 698

Secure Hash Algorithm (SHA) Page 698

Message Digest 5 (MD5) Page 698

Symmetric encryption Page 699

Triple Date Encryption Standard (3DES) Page 699

Asymmetric encryption Page 700

Public key encryption Page 700

private key Page 700

digital signatures Page 700

RSA Page 700

service set identifier (SSID) Page 701

Wired Equivalent Privacy (WEP) Page 702

WiFi Protected Access (WPA) Page 702

WiFi Protected Access 2 (WPA2) Page 702

Advanced Encryption Standard (AES) Page 699

WiFi Protected Setup (WPS) Page 702

hardware firewall Page 703

Packet filtering Page 704

Stateful packet inspection (SPI) Page 704

Proxy Page 704

demilitarized zone (DMZ) Page 704

Port forwarding Page 705

Port triggering Page 705

AutoRun Page 707

AutoPlay Page 707

Multifactor authentication Page 707

two-factor authentication Page 686

bring your own device (BYOD) Page 708

security profile Page 708

Card key Page 708

Conduit Page 708

Biometric devices Page 709

privacy screen Page 709

Patches Page 710

service pack Page 710

Introduction (12.0)

In IT, security protecting an organization's assets is the goal. One of the major assets is information in any form. It involves protecting the confidentiality, integrity, and availability of information. This section explores identifying the threats and vulnerabilities and the methodologies used for protection.

Welcome (12.0.1)

In this chapter, you learn about processes, tools, and policies that are important in discovering, preventing, and documenting threats and vulnerabilities to information and assets of an organization with the goal permitting authorized users to carry out legitimate and useful tasks within a secure computing environment.

Security (12.0.1.1)

This chapter reviews the types of attacks that threaten the security of computers and the data contained on them. A technician is responsible for the security of data and computer equipment in an organization. You will learn how to work with customers to ensure that the best possible protection is in place.

To successfully protect computers and the network, a technician must understand both types of threats to computer security:

- **Physical**—Events or attacks that steal, damage, or destroy equipment, such as servers, switches, and wiring
- **Data**—Events or attacks that remove, corrupt, deny access to authorized users, allow access to unauthorized users, or steal information

Security Threats (12.1)

Security threats are always there, can be difficult to control, and have the potential to impact valuable resources negatively but threats can be mitigated by understanding which assets are at risk and vulnerable then treating the vulnerabilities. Although it is not possible to prevent an earthquake, measures can be taken to build using specifications that guard against collapse if an event does occur. That is the approach that is taken in IT security. This section examines various threats in information systems.

Types of Security Threats (12.1.1)

The focus of this section is to learn the types of threats and tools involved mitigating computer and network attacks. Information systems security threats are relentless, ingenious and constantly evolving. It is important that technicians prepare themselves with information and resources to defend against complicated and growing computer security threats.

Malware (12.1.1.1)

Computers and the data contained on them must be secured against malware:

- *Malware* is any software created to perform malicious acts. The word malware is an abbreviation of malicious software.
- It is usually installed on a computer without the knowledge of the user. These programs open extra windows on the computer or change the computer configuration.
- Malware is capable of modifying web browsers to open specific web pages that are not the desired web page. This is known as browser redirection.
- It is also capable of collecting information stored on the computer without the user's consent.

The first and most common type of malware is a computer *virus*. A virus is transferred to another computer through email, USB drives, file transfers, and even instant messaging. The virus hides by attaching itself to computer code, software, or documents on the computer. When the file is accessed, the virus executes and infects the computer.

Examples of what a virus can do are listed in Table 12-1.

Table 12-1 Viruses Can ...

■ Alter, corrupt, delete files or even erase an entire hard drive on a computer
■ Prevent the computer from booting, cause applications to not load or operate correctly
■ Use the users email account to spread the virus to other computers
■ Lay dormant until summoned by the attacker
■ Record keystrokes to capture sensitive information, such as passwords and credit card numbers and send that data to the attacker

Another type of malware is a *Trojan horse*. A Trojan horse usually looks like a useful program but it carries malicious code. For example, Trojan horses are often provided with free online games. These games are downloaded to the user computer but also contain a Trojan horse. While playing the game, the Trojan horse is installed on the user's system and continues operating even after the game has been closed.

There are several types of Trojan horses as described in Table 12-2.

Table 12-2 Types of Trojan Horses

Types of Trojan Horses	Description
Remote access	Trojan enables unauthorized remote access.
Data-sending	Trojan provides the attacker with sensitive data, such as passwords.
Destructive	Trojan corrupts or deletes files.
Proxy	Trojan will use the victim's computer as the source device to launch attacks and perform other illegal activities.
FTP	Trojan enables unauthorized file transfer services on end devices.
Security software disabler	Trojan stops antivirus programs or firewalls from functioning.
Denial of service (DOS)	Trojan slows or halts network activity.

Over the years, malware has continued to evolve.

Table 12-3 describes other types of malware.

Table 12-3 Varieties of Malware

Security Modes	Description
Worms	■ A worm is a self-replicating program that is harmful to networks with the intent to slow or disrupt network operations. ■ Worms typically spread automatically by exploiting known vulnerabilities in legitimate software.
Adware	■ Usually distributed by downloading online software. ■ It displays advertising on your computer most often as in a pop-up window. ■ Adware pop-up windows are sometimes difficult to control and open new windows faster than users can close them.
Spyware	■ Similar to adware but used to gather information about a user and send the information to another entity, without the user's consent ■ Spyware can be low threat, gathering browsing data, or it can be high threat where personal or financial information is gathered.
Ransomware	■ Similar to adware but denies access to the infected computer system ■ The *ransomware* then demands a paid ransom for the restriction to be removed

Security Modes	Description
Rootkits	■ Program used by hackers to gain Administrator account level access to a computer ■ Very difficult to detect because it can control security programs to conceal itself ■ Special rootkit removal software can be used but sometimes a reinstallation of the OS is necessary to ensure that the rootkit is completely removed.

To detect, disable, and remove malware before it infects a computer, always use *antivirus software*, *antispyware*, and *adware removal tools*.

It is important to know that these software programs become outdated quickly. Therefore, it is the responsibility of the technician to apply the most recent updates, patches, and virus definitions as part of a regular maintenance schedule. Many organizations establish a written security policy stating that employees are not permitted to install any software that is not provided by the company.

Activity—Identify Malware Types (12.1.1.2)

Go to the online course to perform this practice activity.

Phishing (12.1.1.3)

Phishing is when a malicious party sends an email, calls on the phone, or places a text with the intent to trick the recipient into providing personal or financial information. Phishing attacks are also used to persuade users to unknowingly install malware on their devices.

For example, a user has received an email which looks like it originated from a legitimate outside organization, such as a bank. The attacker might ask for verification of information, such as a username, password, or PIN number, to possibly prevent some terrible consequence from occurring. If the user provides the requested information, the phishing attack is successful.

A form of phishing attack is called *spear phishing*. This is when a phishing attack is targeted at a specific individual or organization.

Organizations must educate their users regarding phishing attacks. There is rarely a need to provide sensitive personal or financial information online. Legitimate businesses will not ask for sensitive information through email. Be suspicious. When in doubt, make contact by mail or phone to ensure the validity of the request.

Spam (12.1.1.4)

Spam, also known as *junk mail*, is unsolicited email. In most cases, spam is used as a method of advertising. However, spam can be used to send harmful links, malware, or deceptive content. The goal is to obtain sensitive information such as a social security number or bank account information. Most spam is sent out by multiple computers on networks that have been infected by a virus or worm. These compromised computers send out as much bulk email as possible.

Spam cannot be stopped, but its effects can be diminished. For example, most ISPs filter spam before it reaches the user's inbox. Many antivirus and email software programs automatically perform email filtering. This means that they detect and remove spam from an email inbox.

Even with these security features implemented, some spam still might get through. Watch for some of the more common indicators of spam:

- An email has no subject line.
- An email is requesting an update to an account.
- The email is filled with misspelled words or strange punctuation.
- Links within the email are long and/or cryptic.
- An email is disguised as correspondence from a legitimate business.
- The email requests that you open an attachment.

Organizations must also make employees aware of the dangers of opening email attachments that may contain a virus or a worm. Do not assume that email attachments are safe, even when they are sent from a trusted contact. The sender's computer may be infected by a virus that is trying to spread itself. Always scan email attachments before opening them.

TCP/IP Attacks (12.1.1.5)

To control communication on the Internet, your computer uses the TCP/IP protocol suite. Unfortunately, some features of TCP/IP can be manipulated, resulting in network vulnerabilities.

TCP/IP is vulnerable to the following types of attacks:

- *Denial of service (DoS)*—DoS is a type of attack that creates an abnormally large amount of requests to network servers, such as email or web servers. The goal of the attack is to completely overwhelm the server with false requests creating a denial of service for legitimate users.
- *Distributed DoS (DDoS)*—A DDoS attack is like a DoS attack but is created using many more computers, sometimes in the thousands, to launch the attack.

The computers are first infected with DDoS malware and then become zombies, an army of zombies, or botnets. After the computers become infected, they sit dormant until they are required to create a DDoS attack. Zombie computers located at different geographical locations make it difficult to trace the origin of the attack.

- *SYN flood*—A SYN request is the initial communication sent to establish a TCP connection. A SYN flood attack randomly opens TCP ports at the source of the attack and ties up the network equipment or computer with a large amount of false SYN requests. This causes sessions to be denied to others. A SYN flood attack is a type of DoS attack.

Figure 12-1 shows the process of a TCP SYN flood attack.

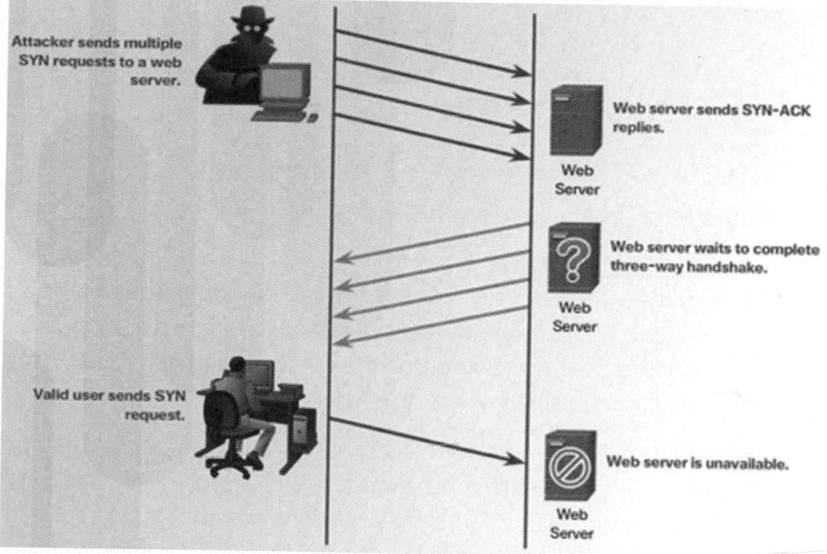

Figure 12-1 TCP SYN Flood Attack

- *Spoofing*—In a spoofing attack, a computer pretends to be a trusted computer to gain access to resources. The computer uses a forged IP or MAC address to impersonate a computer that is trusted on the network.
- *Man-in-the-middle*—An attacker performs a man-in-the-middle (MitM) attack by intercepting communications between computers to steal information transiting through the network. A MitM attack could also be used to manipulate messages and relay false information between hosts, because the hosts are unaware that the messages have been modified.

Figure 12-2 shows the process of a man-in-the-middle attack.

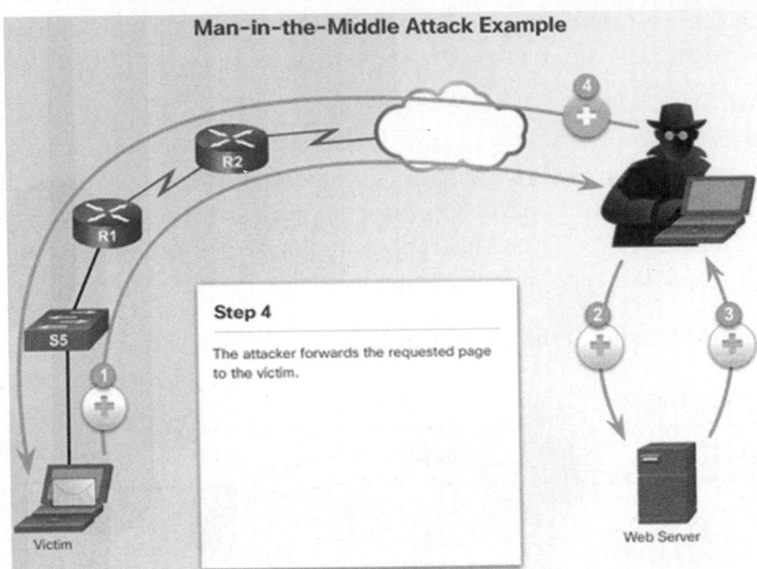

Figure 12-2 Man-in-the-Middle Attack

- **Replay**—To perform a *replay attack*, data transmissions are intercepted and recorded by an attacker. These transmissions are then replayed to the destination computer. The destination computer handles these replayed transmissions as authentic and sent by the original source.
- *DNS poisoning*—DNS records on a system are changed to point to imposter servers. The user attempts to access a legitimate site, but traffic is diverted to an imposter site. The imposter site is used to capture confidential information, such as usernames and passwords. An attacker can then retrieve the data from that location.

Activity—Identify the TCP/IP Attacks (12.1.1.6)

Go to the online course to perform this practice activity.

Zero-Day Attacks (12.1.1.7)

A *zero-day attack*, sometimes referred to as a *zero-day threat*, is a computer attack that tries to exploit software vulnerabilities that are unknown or undisclosed by the software vendor. The term *zero-hour* describes the moment when the exploit is discovered. During the time it takes the software vendor to develop and release a patch, the network is vulnerable to these exploits. Defending against these fast-moving attacks requires network security professionals to adopt a more sophisticated view of the network architecture. It is no longer possible to contain intrusions at a few points in the network.

Social Engineering (12.1.1.8)

Social engineering occurs when an attacker tries to gain access to equipment or a network by tricking people into providing the necessary access information. For example, a social engineer gains the confidence of an employee by pretending to be a help desk worker at their company and convinces the employee to divulge their username and password information.

Table 12-4 describes some social engineering techniques used to gain information.

Table 12-4 Social Engineering Techniques

Techniques	Description
Pretexting	An attacker pretends to need personal or financial data in order to confirm the identity of the recipient.
Phishing	An attacker sends a fraudulent email disguised as being from a legitimate, trusted source. The intention of this message is to trick the recipient into installing malware on their device, or to share personal or financial information.
Spear Phishing	An attacker creates a targeted phishing attack tailored for a specific individual or organization.
Spam	Attacker uses spam email to trick a user to click an infected link or download an infected file.
Tailgating	An attacker quickly follows an authorized person into a secure location. The hacker then has access to a secure area.
Something for Something (Quid pro quo)	This is when a hacker requests personal information from a party in exchange for something like a free gift.
Baiting	This is when an attacker leaves something like a thumb drive or external drive for an employee to find.

Here are some basic precautions to help protect against social engineering:

- Never give out your login credentials (e.g., username, password, PIN)
- Never post credential information in your work area
- Lock your computer when you leave your desk

To secure a physical location, the business should:

- Implement an access or entry control roster listing who is permitted in
- Do not let anyone follow you through a door that requires an access card
- Always ask for the ID of unknown persons
- Restrict access to visitors
- Escort all visitors

Security Procedures (12.2)

Businesses need to implement rules and regulations around the protection of information and the systems that store and process this information. Security policies are designed to be living documents that outline the rules that must be followed in various areas of asset protection. There are usually different policies to address the various areas. Security procedures are the instructions and steps to implement the policies and ensure compliance with them.

Windows Local Security Policy (12.2.1)

Security policies need to be implemented as part of a business's operation for all resources in an organization. Windows Local Security Policy setting allows administrators to enforce rules on a computer or multiple computers running a Windows OS.

What Is a Security Policy? (12.2.1.1)

A *security policy* is a set of security objectives that ensure the security of a network, the data, and the computer systems in an organization. The security policy is a constantly evolving document based on changes in technology, business, and employee requirements.

The security policy is usually created and managed by the organization management and the IT staff. Together they create a document that should answer the questions listed:

- Which assets require protection?
- What are the possible threats?
- What to do in the event of a security breach?
- What training will be in place to educate the end users?

A *security policy* typically includes the items described in Table 12-5. This list is not exhaustive and could include other items related specifically to the operation of an organization.

Table 12-5 Security Policy

Policy Item	Description
Identification and Authentication Policies	Specifies authorized persons that can have access to network resources and outlines verification procedures.
Password Policies	Ensures passwords meet minimum requirements and are changed regularly.
Acceptable Use Policies	Identifies network resources and usages that are acceptable to the organization. It may also identify ramifications if this policy is violated.
Remote Access Policies	Identifies how remote users can access a network and what is accessible via remote connectivity.
Network Maintenance Policies	Specifies network device operating systems and end user application update procedures.
Incident Handling Policies	Describes how security incidents are handled.

In this course, we focus on configuring the Local Security Policy in Windows.

Accessing Windows Local Security Policy (12.2.1.2)

In most networks that use Windows computers, Active Directory is configured with Domains on a Windows Server. Windows computers are members of a domain, computers and devices on a network that are administered as a group with common rules and procedures. The administrator configures a Domain Security Policy that applies to all computers that join. Account policies are automatically set when a user logs in to Windows.

Windows Local Security Policy can be used for standalone computers that are not part of an Active Directory domain. To access Local Security Policy in Windows 7 and Vista, use the following path:

Start > Control Panel > Administrative Tools > Local Security Policy

In Windows 8 and 8.1, use the following path:

Search > secpol.msc and then click **secpol**.

The Local Security Policy Tool opens, as shown in Figure 12-3.

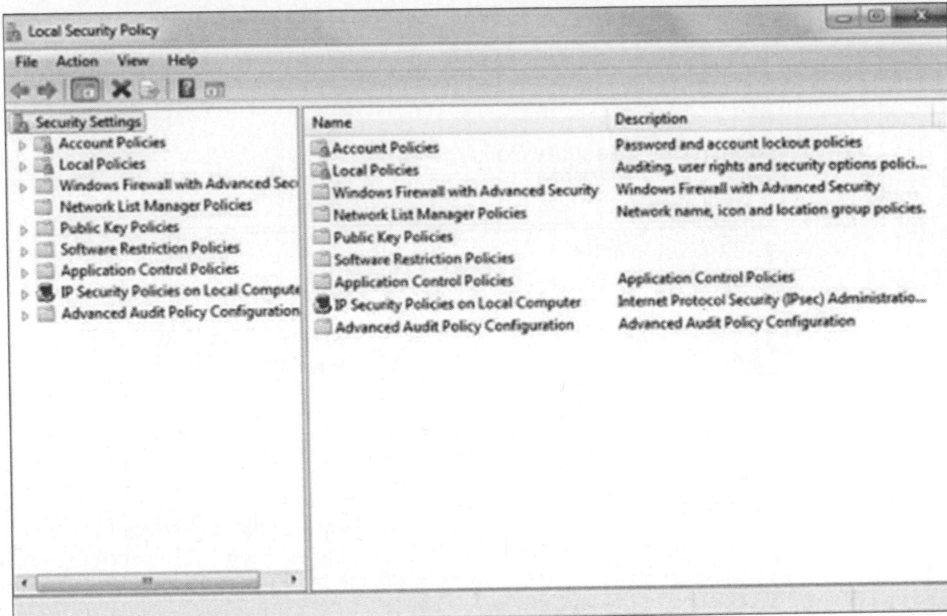

Figure 12-3 Windows Local Security Policy Tool

Note

In all versions of Windows, you can use the **Run** command **secpol.msc** to open the Local Security Policy tool.

Usernames and Passwords (12.2.1.3)

The system administrator usually defines a naming convention for usernames when creating network logins. A common example of a username is the first letter of the person's first name and then the entire last name. Keep the naming convention simple so that people do not have a hard time remembering it. Usernames, like passwords, are an important piece of information and should not be revealed.

Password guidelines are an important component of a security policy. Any user that must log on to a computer or connect to a network resource should be required to have a password. Passwords help prevent theft of data and malicious acts. Passwords also help to confirm that the logging of events is valid by ensuring that the user is the correct person.

Three levels of password protection are recommended:

- **BIOS**—Prevents the operating system from booting and the BIOS settings from being changed without the appropriate password.

- **Login**—Prevents unauthorized access to the local computer.
- **Network**—Prevents access to network resources by unauthorized personnel.

Security Settings for Account Policies (12.2.1.4)

When assigning passwords, the level of password control should match the level of protection required. Assign strong passwords whenever possible.

Table 12-6 shows guidelines for creating strong passwords.

Table 12-6 Guidelines for Strong Passwords

Password Characteristic	Guideline
Minimum Length	Use at least eight characters.
Complexity	Include letters, numbers, symbols, and punctuation. Use a variety of keys on the keyboard, not just common letters and characters.
Variety	Use a different password for each site or computer that you use.
Expiration	Passwords should be made to expire within an acceptable time period. The shorter the time period, the more secure the computer will be. Also, set a reminder to change the passwords you have for email, banking, and credit card websites on the average of every three to four months.

Use the **Password Policy** in **Account Policies** to enforce password requirements. The configurations in Figure 12-4 meet the following requirements:

- **Enforce password history**—The user may reuse a password after 24 unique passwords have been saved.
- **Maximum password age**—The user must change the password after 90 days.
- **Minimum password age**—The user must wait one day before changing a password again. This prevents users from entering a different password 24 times in order to use a previous password again.
- **Minimum password length**—The password must be at least eight characters.
- **Password must meet complexity requirements**—The password must not contain the user's account name or parts of the user's full name that exceed two consecutive characters. The password must contain three of the following four categories: uppercase letters, lowercase letters, numbers, and symbols.

- **Store passwords using reversible encryption**—Storing passwords using reversible encryption is essentially the same as storing plaintext versions of the passwords. For this reason, this policy should never be enabled unless application requirements outweigh the need to protect password information.

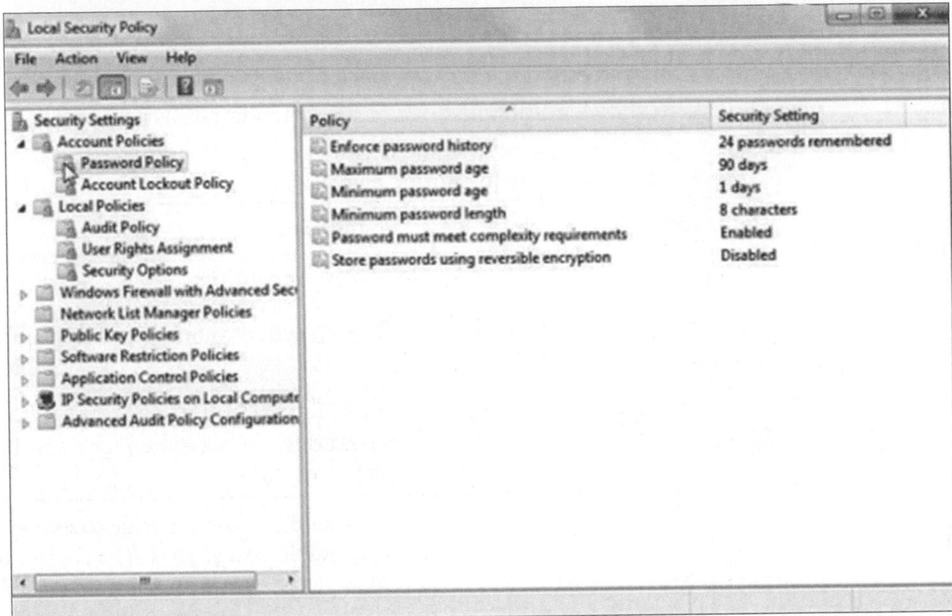

Figure 12-4 Configuring the Password Requirements

Use the **Account Lockout Policy** in **Account Policies** to prevent brute-force login attempts. For example, an option is to allow the user to enter the wrong username and/or password five times. After five attempts, the account is locked out for 30 minutes. After 30 minutes, the number of attempts is reset to zero and the user can attempt to login again. This policy would also protect against a dictionary attack, where every word in the dictionary is entered to try to gain access.

Local Password Management (12.2.1.5)

Password management for standalone Windows computers is done locally through the **User Accounts** tool. To create, remove, or modify a password in Windows, use the following path.

Control Panel > User Accounts

To prevent unauthorized users from accessing local computers and network resources, lock your workstation, laptop, or server when you are not present.

It is important to make sure that computers are secure when users are away. A security policy should contain a rule about requiring a computer to lock when the screensaver starts. This ensures that after a short time away from the computer, the screen saver will start and then the computer cannot be used until the user logs in.

In all versions of Windows, use the following path:

Control Panel > Personalization > Screen Saver. Choose a screen saver and a wait time, and then select the **On resume, display logon screen option.**

Security Settings for Local Policies (12.2.1.6)

Most of the settings in the **Local Policies** branch of the **Local Security Policy** are beyond the scope of this course. However, you should enable auditing for each **Audit Policy**. For example, auditing for all logon events can be enabled.

Some settings in **User Rights Assignment** and **Security Options** will be modified in lab 12.2.1.8.

Exporting the Local Security Policy (12.2.1.7)

If the *local security policy* on every standalone computer is the same, then use the Export Policy feature. Save the policy with a name, such as *workstation.inf*. Then copy the policy file to an external media or network drive to use on other standalone computers. This is particularly helpful if the administrator needs to configure extensive local policies for user rights and security options.

Lab—Configure Windows Local Security Policy (12.2.1.8)

In this lab, you configure Windows Local Security Policy. You modify password requirements, enable auditing, configure some user rights, and set some security options. You then use Event Manager to view logged information. Refer to the lab in *IT Essentials v6 Lab Manual*.

Securing Web Access (12.2.2)

Web browsers such as Microsoft Internet Explorer, Mozilla Firefox, and Google Chrome are installed on almost all computers and are a frequently used application that can be vulnerable and exploited. This section focuses on understanding technologies available when using a web browser and can increase the functionality of the program while also exposing it to exploitation. You will learn about the features, the vulnerabilities and how to secure systems against them.

Web Security (12.2.2.1)

There are various web tools (e.g., ActiveX, Flash) that can be used by attackers to install a program on a computer.

To prevent this, browsers have features that can be used to increase web security:

- ActiveX Filtering
- Pop-up Blocker
- SmartScreen Filter
- InPrivate Browsing

Figure 12-5 displays the path to Tools in Internet Explorer 11, which is where you can access features that can be used to increase web security.

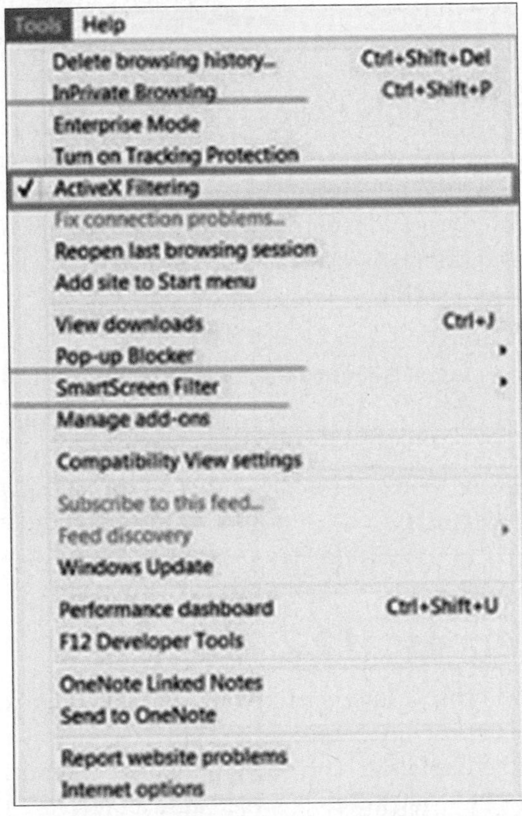

Figure 12-5 Features That Can Be Used to Increase Web Security

ActiveX Filtering (12.2.2.2)

When browsing the web, some pages may not work properly unless you install an ActiveX control. Some *ActiveX* controls are written by third parties and may be malicious. ActiveX filtering allows for web browsing without running ActiveX controls.

After an ActiveX control has been installed for a website, the control runs on other websites as well. This may degrade performance or introduce security risks. When *ActiveX filtering* is enabled, you can choose which websites are allowed to run ActiveX controls. Sites that are not approved cannot run these controls, and the browser does not show notifications for you to install or enable them.

To enable ActiveX filtering in Internet Explorer 11, use the following path:

Tools > ActiveX Filtering

Clicking the **ActiveX Filtering** again would disable ActiveX.

To view a website that contains ActiveX content when ActiveX filtering is enabled, click the blue **ActiveX Filtering** icon in the address bar, and click **Turn off ActiveX Filtering.**

After viewing the content, you can turn ActiveX filtering for the website back on by following the same steps.

Pop-up Blocker (12.2.2.3)

A *pop-up* is a web browser window that opens on top of another web browser window. Some pop-ups are initiated while browsing, such as a link on a page that opens a pop-up to deliver additional information or a close-up of a picture. Other pop-ups are initiated by a website or advertiser and are often unwanted or annoying, especially when multiple pop-ups are opened at the same time on a web page.

Most web browsers offer the ability to block pop-up windows. This enables a user to limit or block most of the pop-ups that occur while browsing the web.

To enable the Internet Explorer 11 Pop-up Blocker feature, use the following path:

Tools > Pop-up Blocker > Turn on Pop-up Blocker

When the Pop-up Blocker is enabled, the Pop-up Blocker settings can be customized. To change the settings of the Pop-up Blocker in Internet Explorer:

Tools > Pop-up Blocker > Pop-up Blocker settings

The following Pop-up Blocker settings can be configured:

- Add a website to allow pop-ups.
- Change notifications when blocking pop-ups.
- Change the level of blocking. **High** blocks all pop-ups, **Medium** blocks most automatic pop-ups, and **Low** allows pop-ups from secure sites.

SmartScreen Filter (12.2.2.4)

Web browsers may also offer additional web filtering capabilities. For instance, Internet Explorer 11 provides the *SmartScreen Filter* feature. This feature detects phishing websites, analyzes websites for suspicious items, and checks downloads against a list that contains sites and files known to be malicious.

To enable the Internet Explorer 11 SmartScreen Filter feature, use the following path:

Safety > SmartScreen Filter > Turn on SmartScreen Filter

This opens the Microsoft SmartScreen Filter window. From this window, the user can enable or disable the feature.

To enable the feature, click **Turn on SmartScreen Filter (recommended)** and click **OK**.

The content of a webpage can also be verified. To analyze the current web page, use the following path:

Tools > SmartScreen Filter > Check this website

To report a suspicious web page, use the following path:

Tools > SmartScreen Filter > Report unsafe website

InPrivate Browsing (12.2.2.5)

Web browsers retain information about the web pages that you visit, the searches that you perform, and other identifiable information including usernames, passwords, and more. This is a convenient feature when using a computer at home that is secured with a password. However, this is a concern when using a public computer such as a computer in a library, hotel business center, or an Internet café.

The information retained by web browsers can be recovered and exploited by others. They could use the information to steal your identity, steal your money, or change your passwords on important accounts.

To improve security when using a public computer, web browsers provide the ability to browse the web anonymously without retaining information. For instance, the *InPrivate Browsing* feature in Internet Explorer 11. While you're browsing, the InPrivate Browser temporarily stores files and cookies and then deletes them when the InPrivate session is ended. This prevents the storing of the information usually stored during a browsing session.

Displayed in Table 12-7 is the kind of information usually stored by the browser:

Table 12-7 Information InPrivate Browsing Prevents from Being Stored by the Browser

■ Usernames
■ Passwords
■ Cookies
■ Browsing history
■ Temporary Internet files
■ Form data

An InPrivate Browsing window can be opened from the Windows desktop or from within the browser.

To start InPrivate Browsing in Windows 7, right-click the **Internet Explorer** icon then click **Start InPrivate Browsing.**

This opens a new InPrivate Browser window. The window explains the InPrivate feature and confirms that the feature is enabled. The address bar now identifies this as an InPrivate window by adding an InPrivate indicator at the address bar. Closing the browser window ends the InPrivate Browsing session. It is important to note that only this browser window and any new tabs opened within this window provide privacy. Other opened browser windows are not protected by InPrivate Browsing.

To open an InPrivate Browsing window from within Internet Explorer 11, use the following path:

Tools > InPrivate Browsing

As an alternative, you could press **Ctrl+Shift+P** to open an InPrivate window.

Protecting Data (12.2.3)

One of the most important goals of information security is to protect data. It is critical that the data being stored, processed, and transported is being safeguarded. While operating systems and applications can be reinstalled user data is unique and if damaged it not easily replaced if it can be replaced at all.

Software Firewalls (12.2.3.1)

A *software firewall* is a program that runs on a computer to allow or deny traffic between the computer and other computers to which it is connected. The software firewall applies a set of rules to data transmissions through inspection and filtering of data packets. Windows Firewall, shown in Figure 12-6, is an example of a software firewall. It is installed by default when the OS is installed.

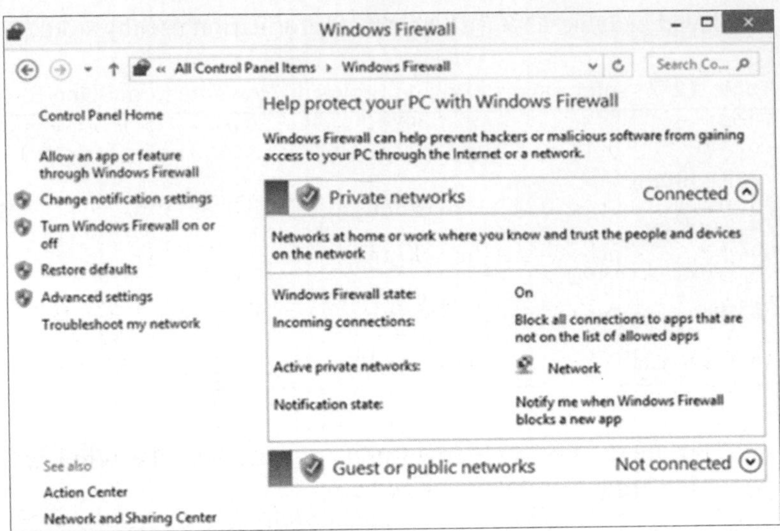

Figure 12-6 Software Firewall

You can control the type of data sent to and from the computer by selecting which ports will be open and which will be blocked. Firewalls block incoming and outgoing network connections, unless exceptions are defined to open and close the ports required by a program.

To enable or disable a port on the Windows Firewall in Windows 7, 8.0, or 8.1, follow these steps:

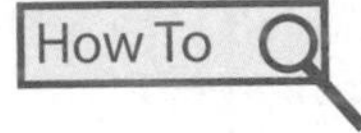

Step 1. Control Panel > Windows Firewall > Advanced settings.

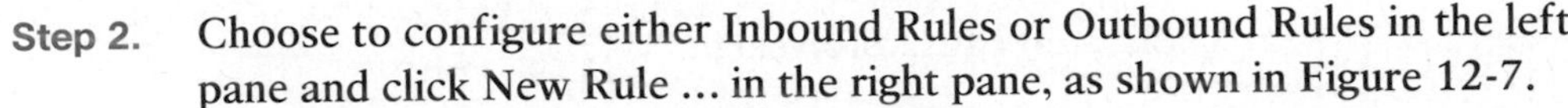

Step 2. Choose to configure either Inbound Rules or Outbound Rules in the left pane and click New Rule ... in the right pane, as shown in Figure 12-7.

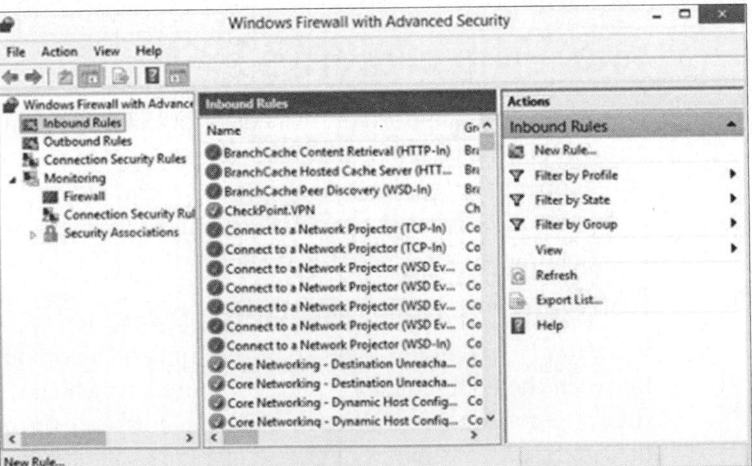

Figure 12-7 Configuring Firewall Rules

Step 3. Select the **Port** radio button and click **Next.**

Step 4. Choose **TCP** or **UDP.**

Step 5. **Choose All local ports or Specific local ports to define individual ports or a port range and click Next.**

Step 6. Choose **Block the connection** and click **Next.**

Step 7. Choose when the rule applies and click **Next.**

Step 8. **Provide a name and optional description for the rule and click Finish.**

To enable or disable a port on the Windows Firewall in Windows Vista, follow these steps:

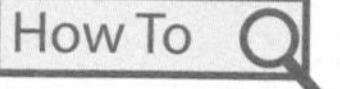

Step 1. **Control Panel > Windows Firewall**, and then click **Allow a program through Windows Firewall.**

Step 2. Click **Add port ...** and configure the name, port number, and protocol (TCP or UDP).

Step 3. Click **OK.**

Biometrics and Smart Cards (12.2.3.2)

Additional methods of securing access to devices include:

- *Biometric security*—Biometric security compares physical characteristics against stored profiles to authenticate people. A *profile* is a data file containing known characteristics of an individual. The user is granted access if their characteristics match saved settings. A *fingerprint reader* is a common biometric device as shown in Figure 12-8.

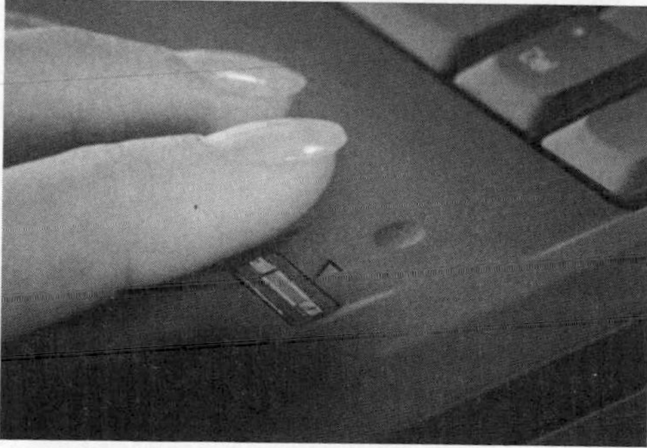

Figure 12-8 Laptop Fingerprint Reader

- *Smart card security*—A smart card is a small plastic card, about the size of a credit card, with a small chip embedded in it. The chip is an intelligent data carrier, capable of processing, storing, and safeguarding data. Smart cards store private information, such as bank account numbers, personal identification, medical records, and digital signatures. Smart cards provide authentication and encryption to keep data safe.
- *Security key fob*—A security key fob is a device that is small enough to attach to a key ring. It uses a process called two-factor authentication, which is more secure than a username and password combination. First, the user enters a personal identification number (PIN). If correctly entered, the security key fob will display a number. This is the second factor which the user must enter to login to the device or network. Figure 12-9 depicts a type of key fob.

Figure 12-9 Key Fob

Data Backups (12.2.3.3)

Data can be lost or damaged in circumstances such as theft, equipment failure, or a disaster. For this reason, it is important to regularly perform a data backup.

A *data backup* stores a copy of the information on a computer to removable backup media that can be kept in a safe place. Backing up data is one of the most effective ways of protecting against data loss. If the computer hardware fails, the data can be restored from the backup to functional hardware.

Data backups should be performed on a regular basis and included in the security policy. Data backups are usually stored offsite to protect the backup media if anything happens to the main facility. Backup media is often reused to save on media costs. Always follow the organization's media rotation guidelines.

These are some considerations for data backups:

- **Frequency**—Backups can take a long time. Sometimes it is easier to make a full backup monthly or weekly, and then do frequent partial backups of any data that has changed since the last full backup. However, having many partial backups increases the amount of time needed to restore the data.
- **Storage**—For extra security, backups should be transported to an approved offsite storage location on a daily, weekly, or monthly rotation, as required by the security policy.
- **Security**—Backups can be protected with passwords. The password is entered before the data on the backup media can be restored.
- **Validation**—Always validate backups to ensure the integrity of the data.

To perform a data backup in Windows 7 or Vista, use the following path:

Control Panel > Backup and Restore

From here, you can backup up a hard drive to a removable disk, create a system image, or create a system repair disc.

In Windows 8.0 and 8.1, the Control Panel item **Backup and Restore** was removed. Instead, you use **File History** to back up the files. **File History** is found in the Control Panel. First, you will need to set up a File History drive and turn File History on. You can choose an attached external drive or internal drive by clicking **Select drive** from the left side panel. Or you can **Select a network location.**

File and Folder Permissions (12.2.3.4)

Permissions are rules you configure to limit folder or file access for an individual or for a group of users. To configure file- or folder-level permissions in all versions of Windows, use the following path:

Right-click the file or folder and select **Properties > Security > Edit ...**

Table 12-8 lists the permissions that are available for files and folders.

Table 12-8 Guidelines for Strong Passwords

Permission Level	Description
Full Control	Users can see the contents of a file or folder, change and delete existing files and folders, create new files and folders, and run programs in a folder.
Modify	Users can change and delete existing files and folders, but cannot create new ones.
Read and Execute	Users can see the contents of existing files and folders and can run programs in a folder.
Read	Users can see the contents of a folder and open files and folders.
Write	Users can create new files and folders and make changes to existing files and folders.

Principle of Least Privilege

Users should be limited to only the resources they need in a computer system or on a network. For example, they should not be able to access all files on a server if they only need access to a single folder. It may be easier to provide users access to the entire drive, but it is more secure to limit access to only the folder that is needed to perform their job. This is known as the *principle of least privilege*. Limiting access to resources also prevents malicious programs from accessing those resources if the user's computer becomes infected.

Restricting User Permissions

File and network share permissions can be granted to individuals or through membership within a group. These share permissions are much different than file and folder level NTFS permissions. If an individual or a group is denied permissions to a network share, this denial overrides any other permissions given. For example, if you deny someone permission to a network share, the user cannot access that share, even if the user is the administrator or part of the administrator group. The local security policy must outline which resources and the type of access allowed for each user and group.

When the permissions of a folder are changed, you are given the option to apply the same permissions to all sub-folders. This is known as permission propagation. Permission propagation is an easy way to apply permissions to many files and folders quickly. After parent folder permissions have been set, folders and files that are created inside the parent folder inherit the permissions of the parent folder.

Also, the location of the data and the action performed on the data determine how the permissions are propagated:

- **Data is moved to the same volume**—It will keep the original permissions
- **Data is copied to the same volume**—It will inherit new permissions

- **Data is moved to a different volume**—It will inherit new permissions
- **Data is copied to a different volume**—It will inherit new permissions

File and Folder Encryption (12.2.3.5)

Encryption is often used to protect data. *Encryption* is where data is transformed using a complicated algorithm to make it unreadable. A special key must be used to return the unreadable information back into readable data. Software programs are used to encrypt files, folders, and even entire drives.

Encrypting File System (EFS) is a Windows feature that can encrypt data. EFS is directly linked to a specific user account. Only the user that encrypted the data will be able to access it after it has been encrypted using EFS.

To encrypt data using EFS in all Windows versions, follow these steps:

Step 1. Select one or more files or folders.

Step 2. Right-click the selected data **>Properties**.

Step 3. Click **Advanced ...**

Step 4. Select the **Encrypt contents to secure data** check box.

Step 5. Files and folders that have been encrypted with EFS are displayed in green.

Windows BitLocker (12.2.3.6)

You can also choose to encrypt an entire hard drive using a feature called *BitLocker*. To use BitLocker, at least two volumes must be present on a hard disk. A system volume is left unencrypted and must be at least 100 MB. This volume holds the files required by Windows to boot.

Before using BitLocker, the *Trusted Platform Module (TPM)* must be enabled in BIOS. The TPM is a specialized chip installed on the motherboard. The TPM stores information specific to the host system, such as encryption keys, digital certificates, and passwords. Applications like BitLocker that use encryption can make use of the TPM chip.

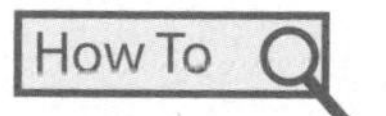

To enable TPM, follow these steps:

Step 1. Start the computer, and enter the BIOS configuration.

Step 2. Look for the **TPM** option within the BIOS configuration screens. Consult the manual for your motherboard to locate the correct screen.

Step 3. Choose **Enable** or **Activate** the security chip.

Step 4. Save the changes to the BIOS configuration.

Step 5. Reboot the computer.

To turn on BitLocker in all versions of Windows, follow these steps:

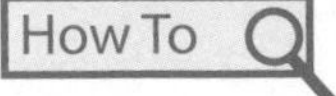

Step 1. Click **Control Panel > BitLocker Drive Encryption.**

Step 2. On the **BitLocker Drive Encryption** page, click **Turn On BitLocker** on the operating system volume.

Step 3. If TPM is not initialized, the **Initialize TPM Security Hardware** wizard appears. Follow the instructions provided by the wizard to initialize the TPM. Restart your computer.

Step 4. The **Save the recovery password** page has the following options:

- **Save the password on a USB drive**—This option saves the password to a USB drive.
- **Save the password in a folder**—This option saves the password to a network drive or other location.
- **Print the password**—This option will print the password.

Step 5. After saving the recovery password, click **Next.**

Step 6. On the **Encrypt the selected disk volume** page, select the **Run BitLocker System Check** check box.

Step 7. Click **Continue.**

Step 8. Click **Restart Now.**

Step 9. The **Encryption in Progress** status bar is displayed. After the computer reboots, you can verify BitLocker is active as shown in Figure 12-10. You can click **TPM Administration** to view the TPM details, as shown in Figure 12-11.

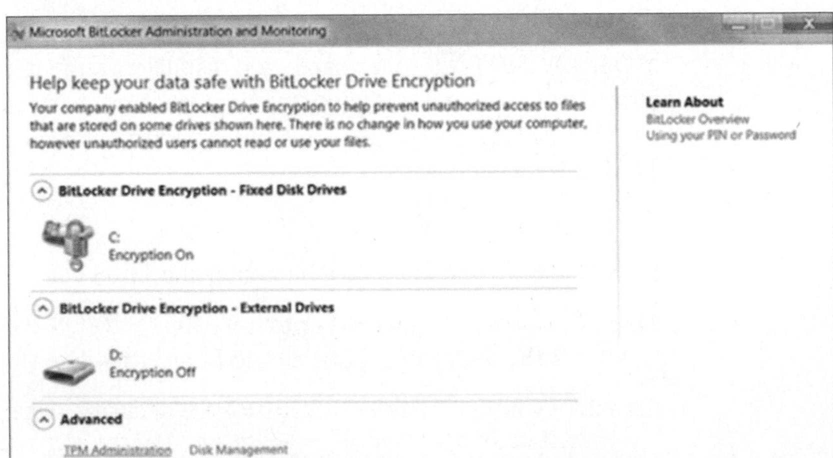

Figure 12-10 Verify BitLocker is Active

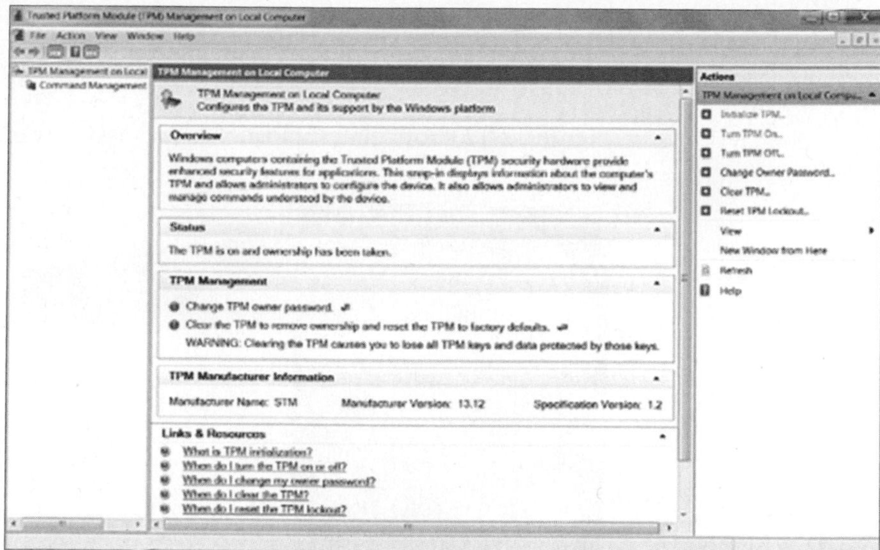

Figure 12-11 View TPM Details

Note

BitLocker encryption can also be used with removable drives by using BitLocker To Go. BitLocker To Go does not use a TPM chip, but still provides encryption for the data and requires a password.

Data Wiping (12.2.3.7)

Protecting data also includes removing files from storage devices when they are no longer needed. Simply deleting files or reformatting the drive may not be enough to ensure your privacy. For instance, deleting files from a hard disk drive does not remove them completely. The operating system only removes the reference to the file in the file allocation table. However, the data still remains on the drive. This data is not completely removed until the hard drive stores other data in the same location, overwriting the previous data.

For this reason, software tools can be used to recover folders, files, and even entire partitions. This could be a blessing if the erasure was accidental. But it could also be disastrous if the data is recovered by a malicious user.

For this reason, storage media should be fully erased using one or more of the following methods:

- *Data wiping software*—Also known as *secure erase*, consists of a software tool specifically designed to overwrite existing data multiple times, rendering the data unreadable.

- *Degaussing wand*—Consists of a wand with very powerful magnets which is held over exposed hard drive platters to disrupt or eliminate the magnetic field on a hard drive.
- Figure 12-12 shows an example of a degaussing wand.

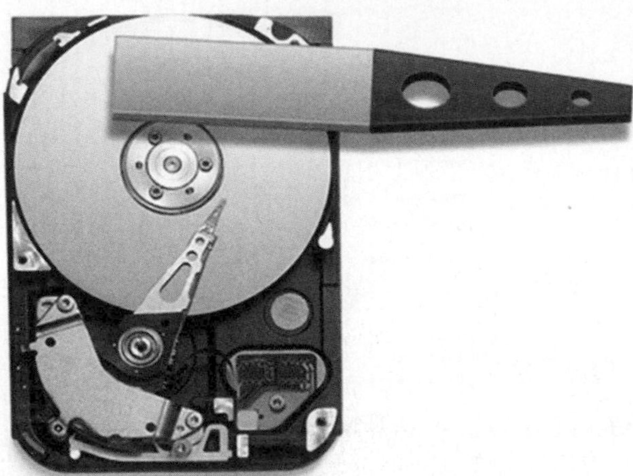

Figure 12-12 Degaussing Wand

- **Electromagnetic degaussing device**—Consists of a magnet with an electrical current applied to it to create a very strong magnetic field. The device can very quickly disrupt or eliminate the magnetic field on a hard drive.

These methods are described in more detail in Table 12-9.

Table 12-9 Guidelines for Strong Passwords

Data Wiping Method	Description
Data wiping	■ Useful when needing to occasionally wipe a drive. ■ Software tool takes a long time to erase a disk. ■ Tool may offer multiple data overwriting choices including using special patterns of 1s and 0s, mathematical algorithms, and random bits. ■ Data wiping tools are available for free.
Degaussing wand	■ Useful when needing to occasionally wipe a drive. ■ Hard drive platters must be exposed to the wand for approximately two minutes. ■ Costs much less than an electromagnetic degaussing device.

Data Wiping Method	Description
Electromagnetic degaussing device	■ Useful to bulk erase multiple drives. ■ Degaussing devices take very little time (e.g., 10 seconds) to wipe out a hard drive. ■ A degaussing tool can be very expensive (e.g., US$20,000).

Note

It is important to remember that data wiping and degaussing techniques are irreversible, and the data can never be recovered.

SSDs are comprised of flash memory instead of magnetic platters. Common techniques used for erasing data such as degaussing are not effective. To fully ensure that data cannot be recovered from an SSD, perform a secure erase. This also applies to hybrid SSD.

Other storage media and documents (e.g., optical disks, eMMC, USB sticks) must also be destroyed. Use a shredding machine or incinerator that is designed to destroy documents and each type of media. For sensitive documents that must be kept, such as those with classified information or passwords, always keep them locked in a secure location.

When thinking about what devices must be wiped or destroyed, remember that devices besides computers and mobile devices store data. Printers and multifunction devices may also contain a hard drive that caches printed or scanned documents. This caching feature can be turned off in some instances, or the device needs to be wiped on a regular basis to ensure data privacy. It is a good security practice to set up user authentication on the device, if possible, to prevent an unauthorized person from changing any settings that concern privacy.

Hard Drive Recycling and Destruction (12.2.3.8)

Companies with sensitive data should always establish clear policies for storage media disposal. There are two choices available when a storage media is no longer needed.

The media can either be:

- **Recycled**—Hard drives that have been wiped can be reused in other computers. The drive can be reformatted and a new operating system installed
- **Destroyed**—Destroying the hard drive fully ensures that data cannot be recovered from a hard drive. Specifically designed devices such as hard drive crushers, hard drive shredders, incinerators, and more can be used for large volumes of drives. Otherwise physically damaging the drive with hammer is effective.

Two types of formatting can be performed as described in Table 12-10.

Table 12-10 Destroying a Hard Disk Drive

Data Wiping Method	Description
Standard format	■ Also called *high-level formatting*. ■ A boot sector is created and a file system is set up on the disk. A standard format can only be performed after a low-level format has been completed.
Low-level format	■ The surface of the disk is marked with sector markers to indicate where data will be stored physically on the disk, and tracks are created. ■ *Low-level formatting* is most often performed at the factory after the hard drive is built.

A company may choose an outside contractor to destroy their storage media. These contractors are typically bonded and follow strict governmental regulations. They may also offer a certificate of destruction. This certificate provides evidence that the media has been completely destroyed.

Activity—Identify Data Protection Terminology (12.2.3.9)

Go to the online course to perform this practice activity.

Protection Against Malicious Software (12.2.4)

Malware is malicious software that can infect computers and network devices in several ways. Malware comes in a number of varieties, including viruses, worms, Trojans, and spyware. It is important individuals and organizations are practicing due diligence in preventing attacks from malware breaches. It can be devastating and can pose major legal and financial problems if personal and business data is stolen or destroyed. This section discusses how to defend your system against various forms of malicious software with planning and protective tools.

Malicious Software Protection Programs (12.2.4.1)

Malware includes viruses, worms, Trojan horses, keyloggers (which capture keystrokes), spyware, and adware. These are designed to invade privacy, steal information, damage the system, or delete corrupt data.

It is important that you protect computers and mobile devices using reputable antimalware software. The following types of antimalware programs are available:

- **Antivirus protection**—Program continuously monitors for viruses. When a virus is detected, the user is warned, and the program attempts to quarantine or delete the virus.
- **Adware protection**—Program continuously looks for programs that display advertising on your computer.
- **Phishing protection**—Program blocks the IP addresses of known phishing websites and warns the user about suspicious sites.
- **Spyware protection**—Program scans for keyloggers and other spyware.
- **Trusted/untrusted sources**—Program warns you about unsafe programs about to be installed or unsafe websites before they are visited.

It may take several different programs and multiple scans to completely remove all malicious software. Run only one malware protection program at a time.

Several reputable security organizations such as McAfee, Symantec, and Kaspersky, offer all-inclusive malware protection for computers and mobile devices.

Be cautious of malicious *rogue antivirus* products that may appear while browsing the Internet. Most of these rogue antivirus products display an ad or pop-up that looks like an actual Windows warning window. They usually state that the computer is infected and must be cleaned. Clicking anywhere inside the window may begin the download and installation of the malware.

When faced with a warning window that is suspect, never click inside the warning window. Close the tab or the browser to see if the warning window goes away. If the tab or browser does not close, press ALT+F4 to close the window or use the task manager to end the program. If the warning window does not go away scan the computer using a known good antivirus or adware protection program to ensure that the computer is not infected.

To find a link to a blog about rogue antivirus malware go to 12.2.4.1 in the online course.

Unapproved, or non-compliant, software is not just software that is unintentionally installed on a computer. It can also come from users that meant to install it. It may not be malicious, but it still may violate security policy. This type of non-compliant system can interfere with company software or network services. Unapproved software must be removed immediately.

Remediating Infected Systems (12.2.4.2)

When a malware protection program detects that a computer is infected, it removes or quarantines the threat. But the computer is most likely still at risk. The first step to remediating an infected computer is to remove the computer from the network to prevent other computers from becoming infected. Physically unplug all network cables from the computer and disable all wireless connections.

The next step is to follow any incident response policies that are in place. This may include notifying IT personnel, saving log files to removable media, or turning off the computer. For a home user, update the malicious software protection programs that are installed and perform full scans of all media installed in the computer. Many antivirus programs can be set to run on system start before loading Windows. This allows the program to access all areas of the disk without being affected by the operating system or any malware.

Viruses and worms can be difficult to remove from a computer. Software tools are required to remove viruses and repair the computer code that the virus has modified. These software tools are provided by operating system manufacturers and security software companies. Make sure that you download these tools from a legitimate site.

Boot the computer in Safe Mode to prevent most drivers from loading. Install additional malware protection programs and perform full scans to remove or quarantine additional malware. It may be necessary to contact a specialist to ensure that the computer has been completely cleaned. In some cases, the computer must be reformatted and restored from a backup, or the operating system may need to be reinstalled.

The system restore service may include infected files in a restore point. After the computer has been cleaned of any malware, the system restore files should be deleted, as shown in Figure 12-13.

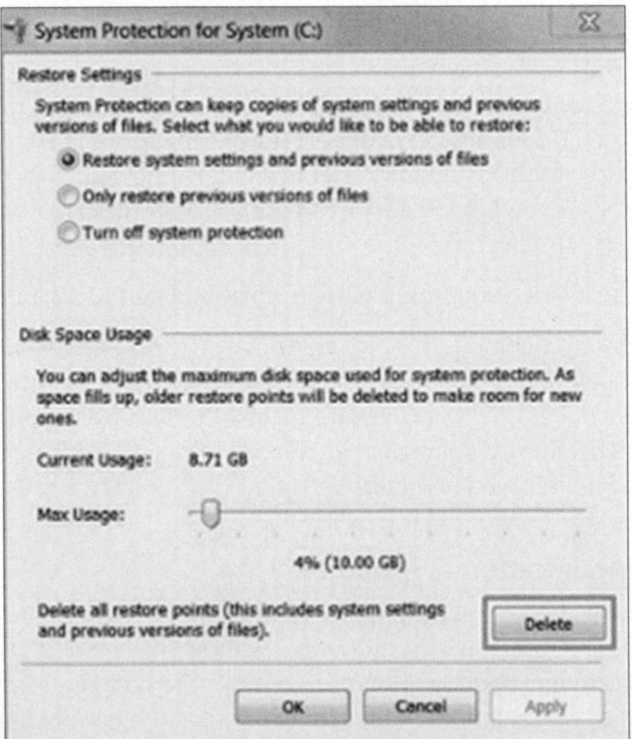

Figure 12-13 Deleting Restore Points

Signature File Updates (12.2.4.3)

Software manufacturers must regularly create and dispense new patches to fix flaws and vulnerabilities in products. Because new viruses are always being developed, security software must be continually updated. This process can be performed automatically, but a technician should know how to manually update any type of protection software and all customer application programs.

Malware detection programs look for patterns in the programming code of the software in a computer. These patterns are determined by analyzing viruses that are intercepted on the Internet and on LANs. These code patterns are called *signatures*. The publishers of protection software compile the signatures into virus definition tables. To update signature files for antivirus software, first check to see if the signature files are the most recent files. You can check the file status by navigating to the **About** option of the protection software or by launching the update tool for the protection software.

To update signature file, follow these steps:

How To

Step 1. Create a Windows Restore Point. If the file you load is corrupt, setting a restore point allows you to go back to the way things were.

Step 2. Open the antivirus program. If the program is set to execute or obtain updates automatically, you may need to turn the automatic feature off to perform these steps manually.

Step 3. Click the **Update** button.

Step 4. After the program is updated, use it to scan the computer.

Step 5. When the scan is complete, check the report for viruses or other problems that could not be treated and delete them yourself.

Step 6. Set the antivirus program to automatically update and run on a scheduled basis.

Always retrieve the signature files from the manufacturer's website to make sure the update is authentic and not corrupted by viruses. This can put great demand on the manufacturer's website, especially when new viruses are released. To avoid creating too much traffic at a single website, some manufacturers distribute their signature files for download to multiple download sites. These download sites are called *mirrors*.

Caution

When downloading signature files from a mirror, ensure that the mirror site is a legitimate site. Always link to the mirror site from the manufacturer's website.

Security Techniques (12.2.5)

Security is a difficult task and takes a lot of effort to maintain that secure environment by applying strategies that can significantly reduce the risk level. There are many layers of security that need to be managed to keep the risks low and mitigate threats. Multiple layers of protection can isolate and protect computers and networks should one of the layers be compromised. Security needs to include a plan to secure both physically as well as logically. In this section, you learn about layering both physical and logical security techniques as well as monitoring logs and how to take action as needed.

Common Communication Encryption Types (12.2.5.1)

Communication between two computers may require a secure communication. To do so, the following protocols are required:

- Hash encoding
- Symmetric encryption
- Asymmetric encryption

Hash encoding, or *hashing*, ensures the integrity of the message. This means it ensures that the message is not corrupt or been tampered with during transmission. Hashing uses a mathematical function to create a numeric value, called a *message digest* that is unique to the data. If even one character is changed, the function output will not be the same. The function can only be used one way. Therefore, knowing the message digest does not allow an attacker to recreate the message, making it difficult for someone to intercept and change messages. The most popular hashing algorithm is now *Secure Hash Algorithm (SHA)*, which is replacing the older *Message Digest 5 (MD5)* algorithm.

Hash encoding is illustrated in Figure 12-14.

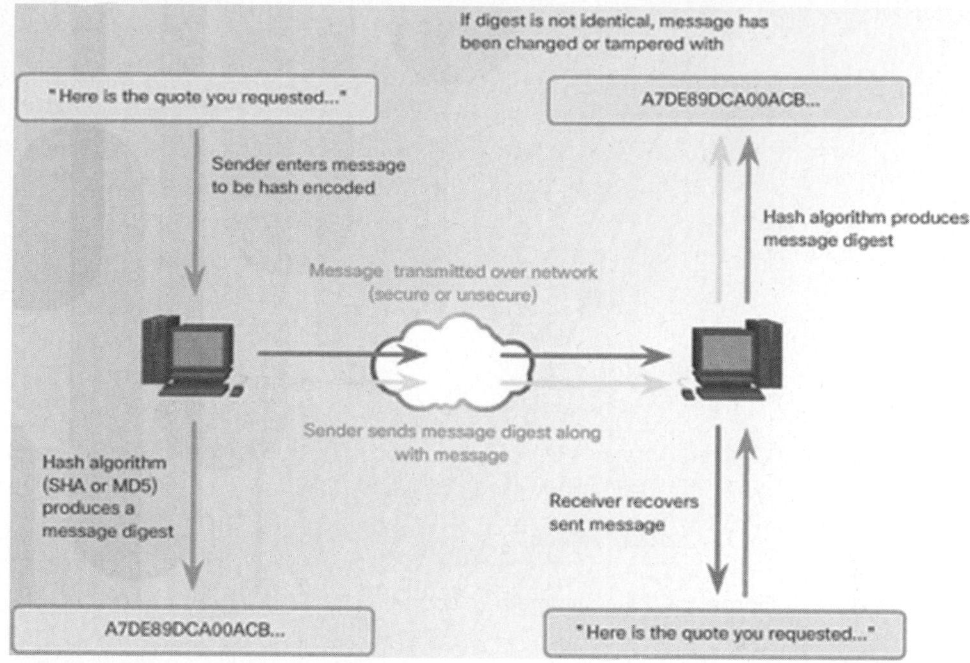

Figure 12-14 Hash Encoding

Symmetric encryption ensures the confidentiality of the message. If an encrypted message is intercepted, it cannot be understood. It can only be decrypted (i.e., read) using the password (i.e., key) that it was encrypted with. Symmetric encryption requires both sides of an encrypted conversation to use an encryption key to encode and decode the data. The sender and receiver must use identical keys. *Advanced Encryption Standard (AES)* and the older *Triple Data Encryption Algorithm (3DES)* are examples of symmetric encryption.

Symmetric encryption is shown in Figure 12-15.

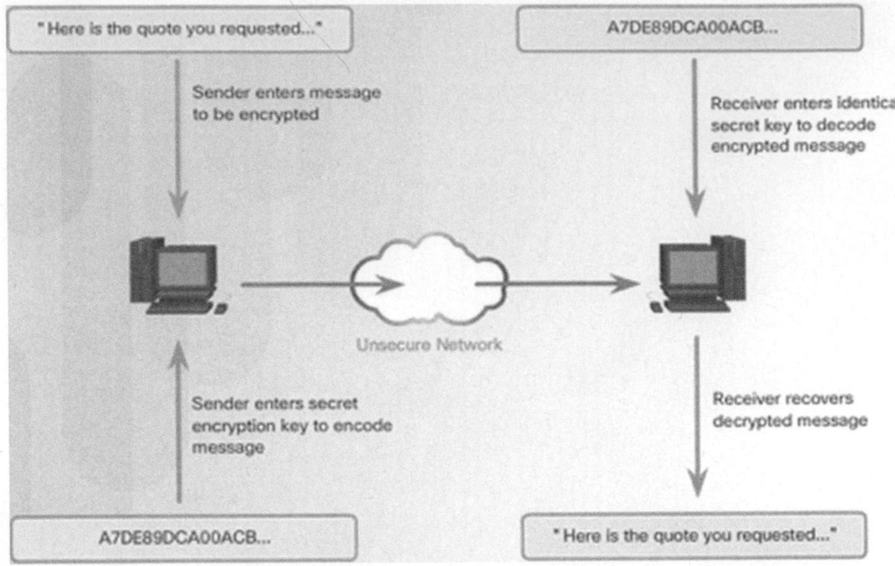

Figure 12-15 Symmetric Encryption

Asymmetric encryption also ensures confidentiality of the message. It requires two keys, a private key and a public key. The *public key* can be widely distributed, including emailing in plaintext or posting on the web. The *private key* is kept by an individual and must not be disclosed to any other party. These keys can be used in two ways:

- *Public key encryption* is used when a single organization needs to receive encrypted text from a number of sources. The public key can be widely distributed and used to encrypt the messages. The intended recipient is the only party to have the private key, which is used to decrypt the messages.
- In the case of *digital signatures*, a private key is required for encrypting a message, and a public key is needed to decode the message. This approach allows the receiver to be confident about the source of the message because only a message encrypted using the originator's private key could be decrypted by the public key. *RSA* is the most popular example of asymmetric encryption.

Asymmetric encryption using a public key is shown in Figure 12-16.

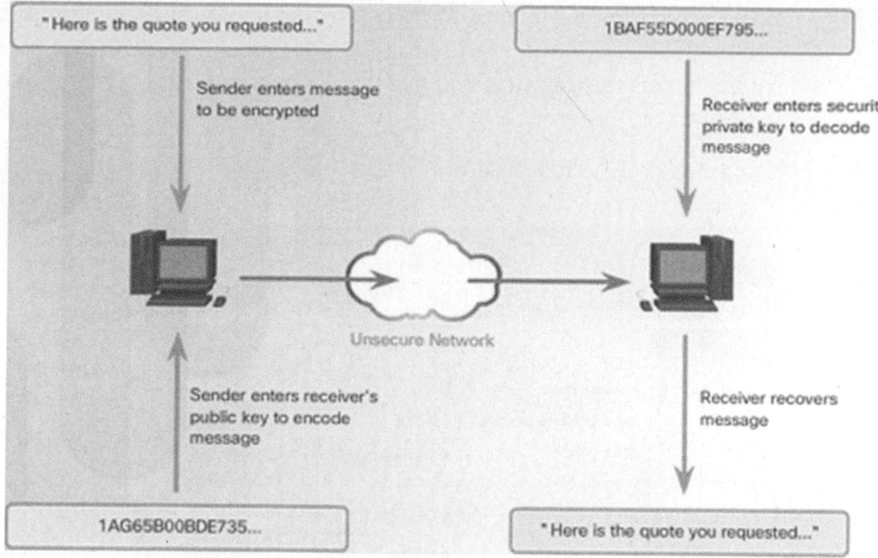

Figure 12-16 Asymmetric Encryption

Note

Symmetric encryption requires that the two systems be preconfigured with a secret key. Asymmetric encryption requires that only one system has the private key.

Service Set Identifiers (12.2.5.2)

Because radio waves are used to transmit data in wireless networks, it is easy for attackers to monitor and collect data without physically connecting to a network. Attackers gain access to a network by being within range of an unprotected wireless network. A technician needs to configure access points and wireless NICs to an appropriate level of security.

When installing wireless services, apply wireless security techniques immediately to prevent unwanted access to the network. Wireless access points should be configured with basic security settings that are compatible with the existing network security.

The *service set identifier (SSID)* is the name of the wireless network. A wireless router or access point broadcasts the SSID by default so that wireless devices can detect the wireless network. When the SSID broadcast has been disabled on the wireless router or access point manually enter the SSID on wireless devices to connect to the wireless network.

Disabling the SSID broadcast provides very little security. If the SSID broadcast is disabled, a user who wants to connect to the wireless network and who knows the

SSID of that network can simply enter it manually. When a computer is searching for a wireless network, it will broadcast the SSID. An advanced hacker can easily intercept this information and use it to impersonate your router and capture your credentials.

In Figure 12-17 SSID broadcast is disabled.

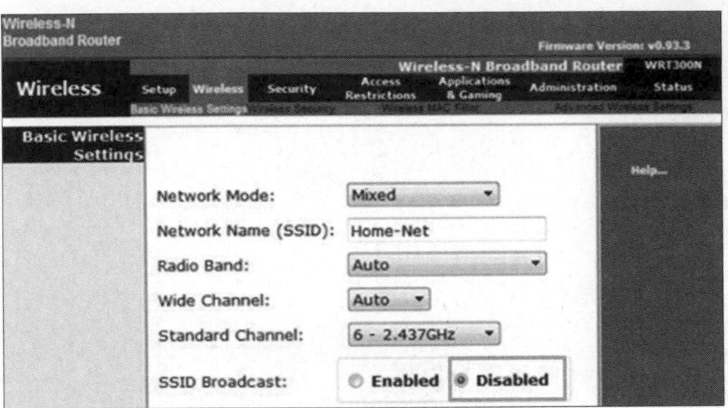

Figure 12-17 Disabled SSID Broadcast

Wireless Security Modes (12.2.5.3)

Use a wireless encryption system to encode the information being sent to prevent unwanted capture and use of data.

Most wireless access points support several different security modes the most common ones are:

- *Wired Equivalent Privacy (WEP)*—The first generation security standard for wireless. Attackers quickly discovered that QEP encryption was easy to break.
- *WiFi Protected Access (WPA)*—An improved version of WEP. WPA uses much stronger encryption than WEP.
- *WiFi Protected Access 2 (WPA2)*—An improved version of WPA. This protocol introduces higher levels of security than WPS. WPA2 supports robust encryption, providing government-grade security.

It is important to always implement the strongest security mode (WPA2) possible if available.

Many routers offer *WiFi Protected Setup (WPS)*. WPS allows very easy WiFi security setup. With WPS, both the router and the wireless device will have a button that, when both are pressed, automatically configures WiFi security between the devices. A software solution using a PIN is also common. It is important to know that WPS is not secure. It is vulnerable to brute-force attack, a method of password cracking. WPS should be turned off as a security best practice.

Universal Plug and Play (12.2.5.4)

Universal Plug and Play (UPnP) is a protocol that enables devices to dynamically add themselves to a network without the need for user intervention or configuration. Although convenient, UPnP is not secure. The UPnP protocol has no method for authenticating devices. Therefore, it considers every device trustworthy. In addition, the UPnP protocol has numerous security vulnerabilities. For example, malware can use the UPnP protocol to redirect traffic to different IP addresses outside your network, potentially sending sensitive information to a hacker.

Many home and small office wireless routers have UPnP enabled by default. Therefore, check this configuration and disable it.

Gibson Research Corporation (GRC) provides a variety of free browser-based vulnerability profiling tools. To use GRC's testing tool to determine whether your wireless router is exposed to UPnP vulnerabilities, research Gibson Research Corporation (GRC) testing tools on the Internet or go to 12.2.5.4 in the online course to find a link.

Firmware Updates (12.2.5.5)

Most wireless routers offer upgradable firmware. Firmware releases may contain fixes for common problems reported by customers as well as security vulnerabilities. You should periodically check the manufacturer's website for updated firmware. After it is downloaded, you can often use the GUI to upload the firmware to the wireless router. Users will be disconnected from the WLAN and the Internet until the upgrade finishes. The wireless router may need to reboot several times before normal network operations are restored.

Firewalls (12.2.5.6)

A *hardware firewall* is a physical filtering component that inspects data packets from the network before they reach computers and other devices on a network. A hardware firewall is a freestanding unit that does not use the resources of the computers it is protecting, so there is no impact on processing performance. The firewall can be configured to block multiple individual ports, a range of ports, or even traffic specific to an application. Most wireless routers also include an integrated hardware firewall.

A hardware firewall passes two different types of traffic into your network:

- Responses to traffic that originates from inside your network
- Traffic destined for a port that you have intentionally left open

There are several types of hardware firewall configurations:

- *Packet filter*—Packets cannot pass through the firewall, unless they match the established rule set configured in the firewall. Traffic can be filtered based on different attributes, such as source IP address, source port or destination IP address or port. Traffic can also be filtered based on destination services or protocols such as WWW or FTP.
- *Stateful packet inspection (SPI)*—This is a firewall that keeps track of the state of network connections traveling through the firewall. Packets that are not part of a known connection are dropped.
- **Application layer**—All packets traveling to or from an application are intercepted. All unwanted outside traffic is prevented from reaching protected devices.
- *Proxy*—This is a firewall installed on a proxy server that inspects all traffic and allows or denies packets based on configured rules. A proxy server is a server that is a relay between a client and a destination server on the Internet.

Hardware and software firewalls protect data and equipment on a network from unauthorized access. A firewall should be used in addition to security software.

Table 12-11 compares hardware and software firewalls.

Table 12-11 Hardware and Software Firewall Comparison

Hardware Firewall	Software Firewall
Dedicated hardware component	Available as third-party software, cost varies
Initial cost for hardware and software updates can be expensive	Free version included with Windows operating system
Multiple computers can be protected	Typically protects only the computer on which it is installed
No impact on computer performance	Uses computer resources, having a potential impact on performance

Demilitarized Zone

A *demilitarized zone (DMZ)* is a subnetwork that provides services to an untrusted network. An email, web, or FTP server is often placed into the DMZ so that the traffic using the server does not come inside the local network. This protects the internal network from attacks by this traffic, but does not protect the servers in the DMZ in any way. It is common for a firewall or proxy to manage traffic to and from the DMZ.

On a wireless router, you can create a DMZ for one device by forwarding all traffic ports from the Internet to a specific IP address or MAC address. A server, game machine, or web camera can be in the DMZ so that the device can be accessed by anyone. The device in the DMZ however is exposed to attacks from hackers on the Internet.

Port Forwarding and Port Triggering (12.2.5.7)

Hardware firewalls can be used to block ports to prevent unauthorized access in and out of a LAN. However, there are situations when specific ports must be opened so that certain programs and applications can communicate with devices on different networks. *Port forwarding* is a rule-based method of directing traffic between devices on separate networks.

When traffic reaches the router, the router determines if the traffic should be forwarded to a certain device based on the port number found with the traffic. Port numbers are associated with specific services, such as FTP, HTTP, HTTPS, and POP3. The rules determine which traffic is sent on to the LAN. For example, a router might be configured to forward port 80, which is associated with HTTP. When the router receives a packet with the destination port of 80, the router forwards the traffic to the server inside the network that serves web pages.

Figure 12-18 shows that port forwarding is enabled for port 80 and is associated with the web server at IP address 192.168.1.254.

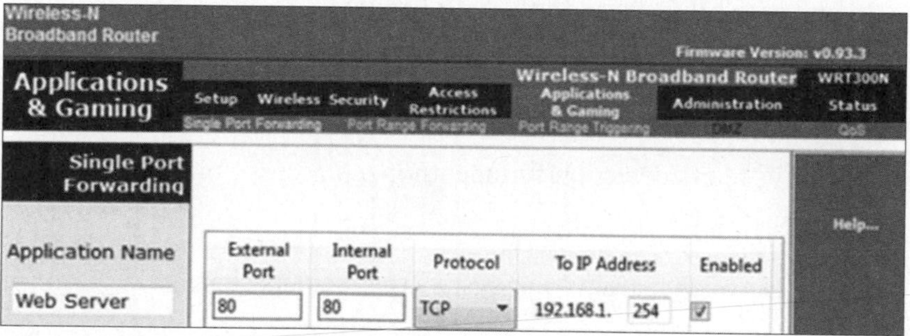

Figure 12-18 Port Forwarding to a Web Server

Port triggering allows the router to temporarily forward data through inbound ports to a specific device. You can use port triggering to forward data to a computer only when a designated port range is used to make an outbound request. For example, a video game might use ports 27000 to 27100 for connecting with other players. These are the trigger ports. A chat client might use port 56 for connecting the same players so that they can interact with each other. In this instance, if there is gaming traffic on an outbound port within the triggered port range, inbound chat traffic on port 56 is forwarded to the computer that is being used to play the video game and chat with friends. When the game is over and the triggered ports are no longer in use, port 56 is no longer allowed to send traffic of any type to this computer.

Packet Tracer
☐ Activity

Packet Tracer—Configure Wireless Security (12.2.5.8)

In this Packet Tracer activity, you configure a wireless router to use WPA2 personal as a security method, rely on MAC filtering to increase security, and support single port forwarding.

To access the activities found in this book, please refer to the instructions found in the introduction.

Protecting Physical Equipment (12.2.6)

Just as important as the logical protection of data through means such as encryption and firewalling so is the physical protection of equipment which is vulnerable to data and revenue loss.

Physical Equipment Protection Methods (12.2.6.1)

Physical security is as important as data security. When a computer is taken, the data is also stolen. It is important to restrict access to premises using fences, door locks, and gates. For example, a mantrap is often used to prevent tailgating, it is a small room with two doors, one of which must be closed before the other can be opened. Protect the network infrastructure, such as cabling, telecommunication equipment, and network devices, with the following:

- Secured telecommunications rooms, equipment cabinets, and cages
- Cable locks and security screws for hardware devices
- Wireless detection for unauthorized access points
- Hardware firewalls
- Network management system that detects changes in wiring and patch panels
- Wireless devices to prevent physical resets

BIOS/UEFI Passwords

Your Windows, Linux, or Mac user password for logging into your computer does not prevent someone from booting your computer from a CD or flash drive with a different operating system. After it is booted, the malicious user could access or erase your files. You can prevent someone from booting your PC or laptop by entering a BIOS or UEFI password. Although encrypting your hard drive is a better solution, there are situations where you may consider configuring a BIOS or UEFI password. For example, computers that are regularly used by the public or in a public workspace would be candidates for a BIOS or UEFI password. After it is configured, a BIOS or UEFI password is relatively difficult to reset. Therefore, be sure you remember it.

AutoRun and AutoPlay

AutoRun is a Windows feature that automatically follows the instructions in a special file called **autorun.inf** when new media, such as a CD, DVD, or flash drive, is inserted into the computer. *AutoPlay* is different from AutoRun. The AutoPlay feature is a convenient way to automatically identify when new media, such as optical disks, external hard drives, or thumb drives, are inserted or connected to the computer. AutoPlay prompts the user to choose an action based on the content of the new media, such as run a program, play music, or explore the media.

On Windows, AutoRun is executed first, unless it is disabled. If AutoRun is not disabled, it follows the instructions in the autorun.inf file. Beginning with Windows Vista, AutoRun is not allowed to bypass AutoPlay. However, you are still just one click away from unknowingly running malware through the AutoPlay dialog. Therefore, it is a security best practice to determine what programs will use AutoPlay. AutoPlay is found in **Control Panel > AutoPlay** in all versions of Windows from starting with Vista.

The most secure solution is to turn off AutoPlay, as shown in Figure 12-19.

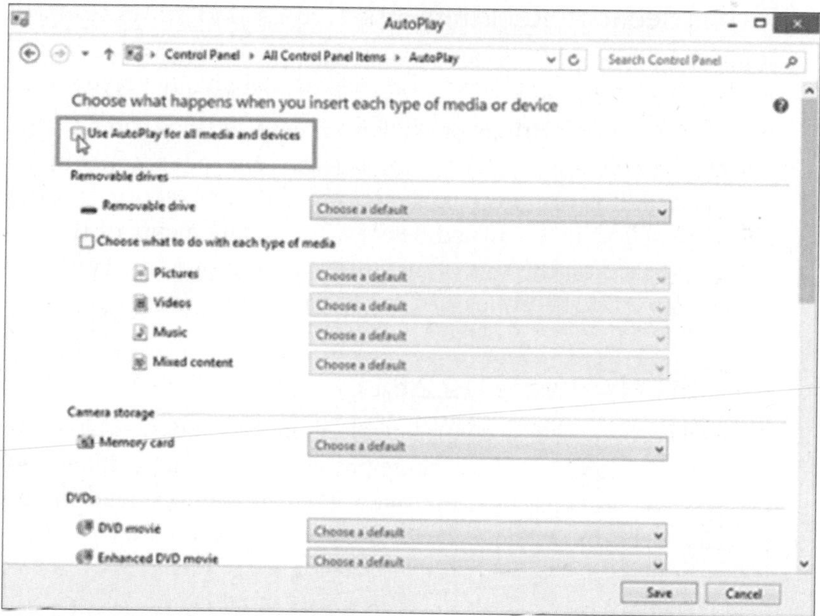

Figure 12-19 Disable AutoPlay

Multifactor Authentication

Earlier, we discussed two-factor authentication using a security key fob. The two factors are something you know, such as a password, and something you have, such as a security key fob. *Multifactor authentication* adds something you *are*, such as a fingerprint scan. When considering a security program, the cost of the implementation has to be balanced against the value of the data or the equipment to be protected.

Bring Your Own Device (BYOD)

Personal and corporate-owned mobile devices must also be protected. It used to be that the only devices that were allowed to be used within the corporate infrastructure were the ones that the company owned. With the drastic increase in personal devices, almost all companies now must create and follow a ***bring your own device (BYOD)*** policy. One of the biggest challenges to the company is to what degree the company can control the device. Sensitive, confidential, or privileged information must be protected, no matter who owns the device. A BYOD policy can save a company a lot of money, but the user must agree to and follow the policy. Another challenge to this arrangement is employee privacy. When the employee gives up some control of their device, they may also be giving up some of their own privacy along with it.

Profile Security Requirements

A good security practice is to create and apply security profiles to mobile devices. A ***security profile*** is usually a text file that defines the security settings and specifies configuration settings on a device. These settings can be applied directly to a device, a specific user, or a group of users. Multiply profiles may apply at the same time as well. It is common for there to be different security profiles for devices in a BYOD than corporate-owned devices. The requirements of these security profiles will vary based on the role of an individual or group, the type of device or operating system, and also the policies of the organization.

Security Hardware (12.2.6.2)

Physical security access control measures include locks, video surveillance, and security guards. ***Card keys*** secure physical areas. If a card key is lost or stolen, only the missing card must be deactivated. The card key system is more expensive than security locks, but when a conventional key is lost the lock must be replaced or rekeyed.

Network equipment should be mounted in secured areas. All cabling should be enclosed within conduits or routed inside walls to prevent unauthorized access or tampering. ***Conduit*** is a casing that protects the infrastructure media from damage and unauthorized access. Network ports that are not in use should be disabled.

Biometric devices, which measure physical information about a user, are ideal for highly secure areas. However, for most small organizations, this type of solution is expensive. The security policy should identify hardware and equipment that can be used to prevent theft, vandalism, and data loss. Physical security involves four interrelated aspects: access, data, infrastructure, and the physical computer.

There are several methods of physically protecting computer equipment:

- Use cable locks with equipment
- Keep telecommunication rooms locked
- Fit equipment with security screws
- Use security cages around equipment
- Label and install sensors, such as radio-frequency identification (RFID) tags, on equipment
- Install physical alarms triggered by motion-detection sensors
- Use webcams with motion-detection and surveillance software

For access to facilities, there are several means of protection:

- Card keys that store user data, including level of access
- Identification badges with photographs
- Biometric sensors that identify physical characteristics of the user, such as fingerprints
- Posted security guard
- Sensors, such as RFID badges, to monitor location and access

Use locking cases, cable locks, and laptop docking station locks to protect computers from being moved. Use lockable hard drive carriers and secure storage and transport of backup media to protect data and media theft.

Protecting Data While in Use

The information on computer screens can be protected from prying eyes with a privacy screen. A *privacy screen* is a panel that is often made of plastic. It prevents light from projecting at low angles, so that only the user looking straight on can see what is on the screen. For example, on an airplane, a user can prevent the person sitting in the next seat from seeing what is on a laptop screen.

The Right Security Mix

Factors that determine the most effective security equipment to use to secure equipment and data include:

- How the equipment is used
- Where the computer equipment is located
- What type of user access to data is required

For instance, a computer in a busy public place, such as a library, requires additional protection from theft and vandalism. In a busy call center, a server may need to be secured in a locked equipment room. Where it is necessary to use a laptop computer in a public place, a security dongle and key fob ensures that the system locks if the user and laptop are separated.

Packet Tracer ☐ Activity

Activity—Identify the Physical Security Device (12.2.6.3)

Go to the online course to perform this practice activity.

Common Preventive Maintenance Techniques for Security (12.3)

Preventive maintenance plans should include detailed information about the maintenance of all aspects of computers and networks, including security practices.

Security Maintenance (12.3.1)

Maintaining proactive security practices is essential to keeping your devices and network running smoothly and properly. Security maintenance is an ongoing process that requires planning and scheduling.

Operating System Service Packs and Security Patches (12.3.1.1)

Patches are code updates that manufacturers provide to prevent a newly discovered virus or worm from making a successful attack. From time to time, manufacturers combine patches and upgrades into a comprehensive update application called a *service pack*. Many devastating virus attacks could have been much less severe if more users had downloaded and installed the latest service pack.

Windows routinely checks the Windows Update website for high-priority updates that can help protect a computer from the latest security threats. These updates include security updates, critical updates, and service packs. Depending on the setting you choose, Windows automatically downloads and installs any high-priority updates that your computer needs or notifies you as these updates become available. Procedures for updating Windows were covered in a previous chapter.

Data Backups (12.3.1.2)

You can make a Windows backup manually or schedule how often the backup takes place automatically. To successfully back up and restore data in Windows, the appropriate user rights and permissions are required.

- All users can back up their own files and folders. They can also back up files for which they have the Read permission.
- All users can restore files and folders for which they have the Write permission.
- Members of the Administrators, Backup Operators, and Server Operators (if joined to a domain) can back up and restore all files, regardless of the assigned permissions. By default, members of these groups have the Backup Files and Directories and Restore Files and Directories user rights.

To start the Windows 7 Backup Files Wizard for the first time, use the following path:

Control Panel > Backup and Restore > Set up backup

To start the Windows Vista Backup Files Wizard, use the following path:

Control Panel > Backup and Restore Center > Back up files

Beginning with Windows 8, backup and restore became part of the File History utility. In Windows 8.1 and 8.0, use the following path:

Control Panel > File History > Turn on

You will need to designate a backup location for File History. A network location or another internal or external physical drive can be used. Backing up data can take time, so it is preferable to do backups when computer and network utilization requirements are low. Click the **Advanced settings** to change backup parameters.

Lab—Configure Data Backup and Recovery in Windows (12.3.1.3)

In this lab, you back up data. You also perform a recovery of the data. Refer to the lab in *IT Essentials v6 Lab Manual*.

Windows Firewall (12.3.1.4)

A firewall selectively denies traffic to a computer or network segment. Firewalls generally work by opening and closing the ports used by various applications.

By opening only the required ports on a firewall, you are implementing a restrictive security policy. Any packet not explicitly permitted is denied. In contrast, a permissive security policy permits access through all ports, except those explicitly denied. In the past, software and hardware were shipped with permissive settings. As users neglected to configure their equipment, the default permissive settings left many devices exposed to attackers. Most devices now ship with settings that are as restrictive as possible while still allowing easy setup.

Configuring the Windows firewall can be completed in two ways:

- **Automatically**—The user is prompted to Keep Blocking, Unblock, or Ask Me Later for unsolicited requests. These requests might be from legitimate applications that have not been configured previously or from a virus or worm that has infected the system.
- **Manage Security Settings**—The user manually adds the program or ports that are required for the applications in use on the network.

To allow program access through the Windows Firewall in Windows 7, use the following path:

Control Panel > Windows Firewall > Allow a program or feature through Windows Firewall > Change settings > Allow another program ...

To allow program access through the Windows Firewall in Windows Vista, use the following path:

Control Panel > Security Center > Windows Firewall > Change Settings > Continue > Exceptions > Add Program

To allow program access through the Windows Firewall in Windows 8.1 and 8.0, use the following path:

Control Panel > Windows Firewall > Allow an app or feature through Windows Firewall > Change settings > Allow another app ...

If you wish to use a different software firewall, you will need to disable Windows Firewall.

To disable the Windows Firewall in Windows 7, use the following path:

Control Panel > Windows Firewall > Turn Windows Firewall on or off > Turn off Windows Firewall (not recommended) > OK

To disable the Windows Firewall in Windows Vista, use the following path:

Control Panel > Security Center > Windows Firewall > Turn Windows Firewall on or off > Continue > Off (not recommended) > OK

To disable the Windows Firewall in Windows 8.1 and 8.0 use the following path:

Control Panel > Windows Firewall > Turn Windows Firewall on or off > Turn off Windows Firewall (not recommended) > OK

Lab—Configure the Firewall in Windows (12.3.1.5)

In this lab, you explore the Windows Firewall and configure some advanced settings. Refer to the lab in *IT Essentials v6 Lab Manual*.

Maintaining Accounts (12.3.1.6)

Employees in an organization often require different levels of access to data. For example, a manager and an accountant might be the only employees in an organization with access to the payroll files.

Employees can be grouped by job requirements and given access to files according to group permissions. This process helps manage employee access to the network. Temporary accounts can be set up for employees who need short-term access. Close management of network access can help to limit areas of vulnerability that might allow a virus or malicious software to enter the network.

Terminating Employee Access

When an employee leaves an organization, access to data and hardware on the network should be terminated immediately. If the former employee has stored files in a personal space on a server, eliminate access by disabling the account. If the employee's replacement requires access to the applications and personal storage space, you can re-enable the account and change the name to the name of the new employee.

Guest Accounts

Temporary employees and guests may need access to the network. For example, visitors might require access to email, the Internet, and a printer on the network. These resources can be made available to a special account called Guest. When guests are present, they can be assigned to the Guest account. When no guests are present, the account can be disabled until the next guest arrives.

Some guest accounts require extensive access to resources, as in the case of a consultant or a financial auditor. This type of access should be granted only for the period of time required to complete the work.

To configure all of the users and groups on a computer, open the **Local Users and Groups Manager**, as shown for Windows 8.1 in Figure 12-20. In all versions of Windows, type **lusrmgr.msc** in the Search box or run line utility.

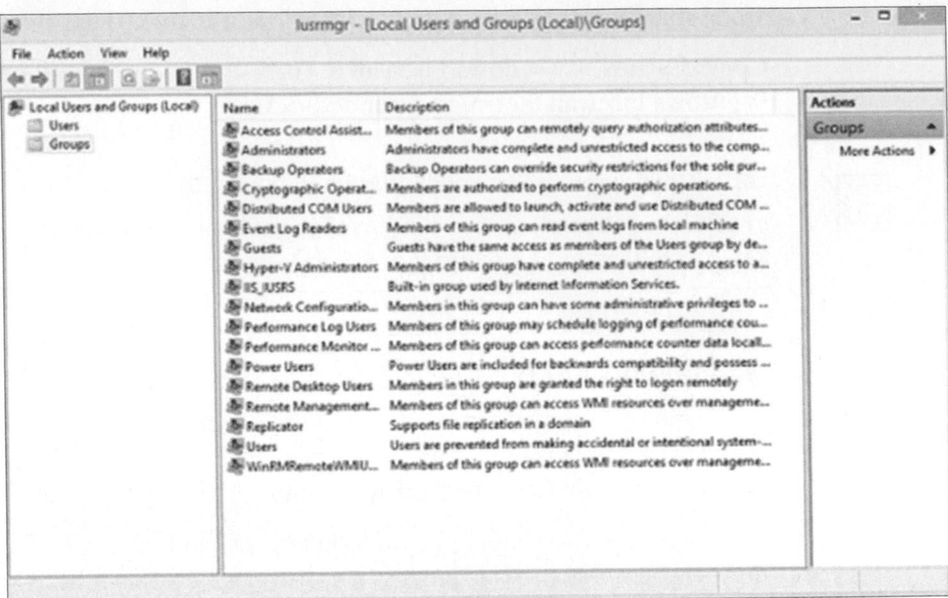

Figure 12-20 Local User and Groups Manager

Login Times

In some situations, you may want employees to only be allowed to login during specific hours, such as 7 a.m. to 6 p.m. Logins would be blocked during other times of the day.

Failed Login Attempts

You may want to configure a threshold for the number of times a user is allowed to attempt a login. By default in Windows, failed login attempts are set to zero, which means that the user will never be locked out until this setting is changed.

Idle Timeout and Screen Lock

Employees may or may not logout of their computer when they leave the workplace. Therefore, it is a security best practice to configure an idle timer that will automatically log the user out and lock the screen after a specified period of time. The user must log back in to unlock the screen.

Managing Users (12.3.1.7)

A regular maintenance task for administrators is to create and remove users from the network, change account passwords, or change user permissions.

The following can be done when managing local user accounts:

- Create a local user account
- Reset the password for a local user account
- Disable or activate a local user account
- Delete a local user account
- Rename a local user account
- Assign a logon script to a local user account
- Assign a home folder to a local user account

There are two tools that can be used to accomplish these tasks:

- **User Account Control (UAC)**—Use this to add, remove, or change attributes of individual users. When logged in as an administrator, use the UAC to configure settings to prevent malicious code from gaining administrative privileges.
- **Local Users and Groups Manager**—Can be used to create and manage users and groups that are stored locally on a computer.

Note

You must have administrator privileges to manage users.

To open the UAC, use the following path:

Control Panel > User Accounts > Manage another account

To open the Local Users and Groups Manager, use the following path:

Control Panel > Administrative Tools > Computer Management > Local Users and Groups

By using Local Users and Groups, you can limit the ability of users and groups to perform certain actions by assigning rights and permissions to them. A right authorizes a user to perform certain actions on a computer, such as backing up files and folders or shutting down a computer. A permission is a rule that is associated with an object (usually a file, folder, or printer), and it regulates which users can have access to the object and in what manner.

From the Local Users and Groups window, double-click **Users**. There are two built-in accounts:

- **Administrator**—This account is disabled by default. When enabled, the account has full control of the computer, and it can assign user rights and access control permissions to users as necessary. The Administrator account is a member of the Administrators group on the computer. The Administrator account can never be deleted or removed from the Administrators group, but it can be renamed or disabled.

- **Guest**—This account is disabled by default. This account is used by users who do not have an account on the computer. By default, the account does not require a password. It is a member of the default Guests group, which allows a user to log on to a computer.

Figure 12-21 shows built-in accounts being accessed through the Local User and Groups manager.

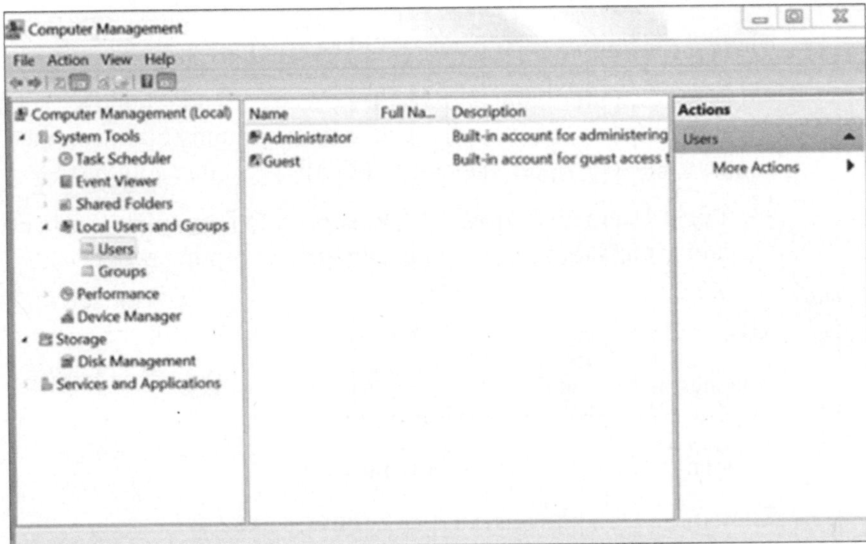

Figure 12-21 Displaying Current Users—Built-in Accounts

To add a user, click the **Action** menu and select **New User**. This opens the New User window. From here you can assign a username, full name, description, and account options.

Double-clicking a user or right-clicking and choosing **Properties** opens the user properties window. This window allows you to change the user options defined when the user was created. Additionally, it permits you to lock an account. The window also lets you assign a user to a group using the **Member of** tab, or controlling which folders the user has access to using the **Profile** tab.

Note

There is also another important type of account called the *Power User*. This account possesses most of the power of an administrator, such as installing programs or changing firewall settings, but it lacks some of the privileges of an administrator, for security reasons.

Managing Groups (12.3.1.8)

Users can be assigned to groups for easier management.

The following can be done when managing local groups:

- Create a local group
- Add a member to a local group
- Identify members of a local group
- Delete a local group
- Create a local user account

To open the Local Users and Groups Manager, use the following path:

Control Panel > Administrative Tools > Computer Management > Local Users and Groups

From the Local Users and Groups window, double-click **Groups**. There are many built-in groups available. However, the three most commonly used groups are:

- **Administrators**—Members of this group have full control of the computer, and they can assign user rights and access control permissions to users as necessary. The Administrator account is a default member of this group. Because this group has full control of the computer, use caution when you add users to this group.
- **Guest**—Members of this group have a temporary profile created at log on, and when the member logs off, the profile is deleted. The Guest account (which is disabled by default) is also a default member of this group.
- **Users**—Members of this group can perform common tasks, such as running applications, using local and network printers, and locking the computer. Members cannot share directories or create local printers.

It is important to note that running your computer as a member of the Administrators group makes the system vulnerable to Trojan horses and other security risks. It is recommended that you add your domain user account only to the Users group (and not to the Administrators group) to perform routine tasks, including running programs and visiting Internet sites. When it becomes necessary to perform administrative tasks on the local computer, use **Run as Administrator** to start a program using administrative credentials.

To create a new group, click the **Action** menu and select **New Group**. Alternatively, you can also right-click **Groups** and select **New Group ...** which opens the **New Group** window. From here you can create new groups and assign users to them.

Lab—Configure Users and Groups in Windows (12.3.1.9)

In this lab, you create users and groups and delete users using the Local Users and Groups Manager. You also assign group and user permission to the folders. Refer to the lab in *IT Essentials v6 Lab Manual*.

Basic Troubleshooting Process for Security (12.4)

Using the troubleshooting process to identify and correct security problems helps technicians maintain a consistent approach to managing and mitigating threats to data and equipment. Knowing some of the common problems and solutions that occur with security can speed the troubleshooting process.

Applying the Troubleshooting Process to Security (12.4.1)

The troubleshooting process is used to help resolve security issues. These problems range from simple, such as preventing someone from watching over your shoulder, to the more complex, such as manually removing infected files from multiple networked computers. Use the troubleshooting steps as a guideline to help you diagnose and repair problems.

Identify the Problem (12.4.1.1)

Computer technicians must be able to analyze a security threat and determine the appropriate method to protect assets and repair damage. The first step in the troubleshooting process is to identify the problem.

Table 12-12 shows a list of open-ended and closed-ended questions to ask the customer.

Table 12-12 Step 1: Identify the Problem

Open-ended questions	■ When did the problem start? ■ What problems are you experiencing? ■ What websites have you visited recently? ■ What security software is installed on your computer? ■ Who else has used your computer recently?

Closed-ended questions	■ Is your security software up to date? ■ Have you scanned your computer recently for viruses? ■ Did you open any attachments from a suspicious email? ■ Have you changed your password recently? ■ Have you shared your password?

Establish a Theory of Probable Cause (12.4.1.2)

After you have talked to the customer, you can begin to establish a theory of probable causes. You may need to conduct additional internal or external research based on the customer's description of the symptoms.

Table 12-13 shows a list of some common probable causes for security problems.

Table 12-13 Step 2. Establish a Theory of Probable Cause

Common causes of security problems	■ Virus ■ Trojan horse ■ Worm ■ Spyware ■ Adware ■ *Grayware* or malware ■ Phishing scheme ■ Password compromised ■ Unprotected equipment rooms ■ Unsecured work environment

Test the Theory to Determine Cause (12.4.1.3)

After you have developed some theories about what is wrong, test your theories to determine the cause of the problem If a quick procedure corrects the problem, you can verify full system functionality. If a quick procedure does not correct the problem, you might need to research the problem further to establish the exact cause.

Table 12-14 shows a list of quick procedures that can determine the exact cause of the problem or even correct the problem.

Table 12-14 Step 3. Test the Theory to Determine Cause

Common steps to determine cause	■ Disconnect from the network ■ Update antivirus and spyware signatures ■ Scan computer with protection software ■ Check computer for the latest OS patches and updates ■ Reboot the computer or network device ■ Login as an administrative user to change a user's password ■ Secure equipment rooms ■ Secure work environment ■ Enforce security policy

Establish a Plan of Action to Resolve the Problem and Implement the Solution (12.4.1.4)

After you have determined the exact cause of the problem, establish a plan of action to resolve the problem and implement the solution.

Table 12-15 shows some sources you can use to gather additional information to resolve an issue.

Table 12-15 Step 4: Establish a Plan of Action to Resolve the Problem and Implement the Solution

If no solution is achieved in the previous step, further research is needed to implement the solution.	■ Helpdesk repair logs ■ Other technicians ■ Manufacturer FAQs ■ Technical websites ■ Newsgroups ■ Computer manuals ■ Device manuals ■ Online forums ■ Internet search

Verify Full System Functionality and, If Applicable, Implement Preventive Measures (12.4.1.5)

After you have corrected the problem, verify full functionality and, if applicable, implement preventive measures.

Table 12-16 shows a list of the steps to verify the solution.

Table 12-16 Step 5: Verify Full System Functionality and, If Applicable, Implement Preventive Measures

Verify full functionality	■ Rescan computer to ensure no viruses remain ■ Rescan computer to ensure no spyware remains ■ Check the security software logs to ensure no problems remain ■ Check computer for the latest OS patches and updates ■ Test network and Internet connectivity ■ Ensure all applications are working ■ Verify access to authorized resources such as shared printers and databases ■ Make sure entries are secured ■ Ensure security policy is enforced

Document Findings, Actions, and Outcomes (12.4.1.6)

In the final step of the troubleshooting process, you must document your findings, actions, and outcomes.

Table 12-17 shows a list of the tasks required to document the problem and the solution.

Table 12-17 Step 6: Document Findings, Actions, and Outcomes

Document your findings, actions, and outcomes	■ Discuss the solution implemented with the customer ■ Ask the customer to verify the problem has been solved ■ Provide the customer with all paperwork ■ Document the steps taken to solve the problem in the work order and technician's journal ■ Document any components used in the repair ■ Document the time spent to solve the problem

Common Problems and Solutions for Security (12.4.2)

Understanding solutions to the more common problems that plague computer and network system enables a technician to be better prepared when the problems arise. Although there is no comprehensive fix for the existing vulnerabilities, a good step in preparing to fixing issues is to have the knowledge and readiness to approach problem-solving.

Identify Common Problems and Solutions (12.4.2.1)

Security problems can be attributed to hardware, software, or connectivity issues, or some combination of the three. You will resolve some types of security problems more often than others.

Table 12-18 is some common security problems and solutions.

Table 12-18 Common Problems and Solutions

Problems Symptom	Problems Causes	Problems Solutions
A wireless network is compromised even though 128-bit WEP encryption is in use.	A hacker issuing commonly available wireless hacking tools to crack the encryption.	■ Upgrade to WPA Encryption ■ Add MAC address filtering for older clients that do not support WPA
A user is receiving hundreds or thousands of junk emails each day.	The network is not providing detection or protection for the email server from spammers.	Install antivirus or an email software program that removes spam from an email inbox
An unknown printer repair person is observed looking under keyboards and on desktops.	Visitors are not being monitored properly or user credentials have been stolen to enter the building.	■ Contact security or police ■ Advise users never to hide passwords near their work area
An unauthorized wireless access point is discovered on the network.	A user has added a wireless access point to increase the wireless range of the company network.	■ Disconnect and confiscate the unauthorized device ■ Enforce security policy by taking action against the person responsible for the security breach
Users with flash drives are infecting computers on the network with viruses.	The flash drive is infected with a virus and is not scanned by virus protection software when a network computer accesses it.	Set virus protection software to scan removable media when data is accessed
A Security Alert is displayed.	■ The Windows Firewall is turned off. ■ Virus definitions are out of date. ■ Malware has been detected.	■ Turn on Windows Firewall ■ Update virus definitions ■ Scan the computer to remove any malware

Problems Symptom	Problems Causes	Problems Solutions
Windows Update fails.	■ The downloaded update is corrupted. ■ The update requires a previous update that is not installed.	■ Download the update manually and install ■ Use System Restore to restore the computer to a time before the attempted update ■ Restore the computer from a backup
System files have been renamed, applications crash, files are disappearing, or file permissions have changed.	The computer has a virus.	■ Remove the virus using antivirus software ■ Restore the computer from a backup
Your email contacts report spam coming from your address.	Your email has been hijacked.	■ Change your email password ■ Contact the email service support to reset the account

Lab—Document Customer Information in a Work Order (12.4.2.2)

In this lab, you document customer information in a work order. Refer to the lab in *IT Essentials v6 Lab Manual*.

Summary (12.5)

This chapter discussed computer security and why it is important to protect computer equipment, networks, and data.

Summary (12.5.1)

Threats, procedures, and preventive maintenance relating to data and physical security were described to help you keep computer equipment and data safe.

Some of the important concepts to remember from this chapter are:

- Security threats can come from inside or outside of an organization.
- Viruses and worms are common threats that attack data.
- Develop and maintain a security plan to protect both data and physical equipment from loss.
- Keep operating systems and applications up to date and secure with patches and service packs.

Summary of Exercises

This is a summary of the Labs and activities associated with this chapter.

Labs

The following labs cover material from this chapter. Refer to the labs in the *IT Essentials v6 Lab Manual*.

Lab—Configure Windows Local Security Policy (12.2.1.8)

Lab—Configure Data Backup and Recovery in Windows (12.3.1.3)

Lab—Configure the Firewall in Windows (12.3.1.5)

Lab—Configure Users and Groups in Windows (12.3.1.9)

Lab—Document Customer Information in a Work Order (12.4.2.2)

Check Your Understanding

You can find the answers to these questions in the appendix, "Answers to 'Check Your Understanding' Questions."

1. Where in Windows would a technician configure a guest account for a temporary employee?
   A. BIOS
   B. Device Manager
   C. Local Users and Groups
   D. Windows Firewall

2. Which three rules increase the level of password strength? (Choose three.)
   A. Passwords should never expire.
   B. Passwords should be a combination of upper and lower case letters, numbers, and special characters.
   C. Passwords should combine user special dates and initials so that they can be alphanumeric.
   D. Passwords should be changed by the user after specific periods of time.
   E. Password reuse and lockout policies should be implemented.
   F. Passwords should be short to reduce the chances of users forgetting them.

3. Which is an example of social engineering?
   A. A computer displaying unauthorized pop-ups and adware
   B. The infection of a computer by a virus carried by a Trojan
   C. An anonymous programmer directing a DDoS attack on a data center
   D. An unidentified person claiming to be a technician collecting user information from employees

4. What is an example of the implementation of physical security?
   A. Establishing personal firewalls on each computer
   B. Encrypting all sensitive data that is stored on the servers
   C. Requiring employees to use a card key when entering a secure area
   D. Ensuring that all operating system and antivirus software is up to date

5. What security technique could provide secure access to a server located in a small office without the expense of implementing a DMZ or purchasing a hardware firewall?
   A. Implement hash encoding for all wireless devices
   B. Implement MAC address filtering
   C. Implement port forwarding
   D. Implement basic security on all wireless access points

6. A technician discovers that an employee has attached an unauthorized wireless router to the company network so that the employee can get WiFi coverage while outside taking a break. The technician immediately reports this to a supervisor. What are two actions that the company should take in response to this situation? (Choose two.)

   A. Create a guest account for the employee to use when outside the building

   B. Add an authorized wireless access point to the network to extend coverage for the employee

   C. Make sure that the wireless router is not broadcasting an SSID

   D. Immediately remove the device from the network

   E. Consult the company security policy to decide on actions to take against the employee

7. Which action could be used to determine if a host is compromised and flooding traffic onto the network?

   A. Unseat and then reconnect the hard drive connectors on the host

   B. Disconnect the host from the network

   C. Check the host hard drive for errors and file system issues

   D. Examine the Device Manager on the host for device conflicts

8. When would a PC repair person want to deploy the idle timeout feature?

   A. When users are inserting media and running applications not sanctioned by the company

   B. When users are leaving their desk but remaining logged on

   C. When users are playing music CDs and leaving them playing even after the users have left for the day

   D. When users are surfing the Internet and not doing their job

9. For security reasons a network administrator needs to ensure that local computers cannot ping each other. Which settings can accomplish this task?

   A. Smartcard settings

   B. Firewall settings

   C. MAC address settings

   D. File system settings

10. What is the best description of Trojan horse malware?

    A. It is the most easily detected form of malware.

    B. It is malware that can only be distributed over the Internet.

C. It is software that causes annoying but not fatal computer problems.
D. It appears as useful software but hides malicious code.

11. When a support technician is troubleshooting a security issue on a system, which action should the technician take just before documenting the findings and closing the ticket?

A. Boot the system in Safe Mode
B. Disconnect the system from the network
C. Ensure that all applications are working
D. Ask what the problem is that the customer is experiencing

12. Which security threat installs on a computer without the knowledge of the user and then monitors computer activity?

A. Adware
B. Viruses
C. Worms
D. Spyware

13. A computer can successfully ping outside the local network, but cannot access any World Wide Web services. What is the most probable cause of this problem?

A. Windows Firewall is blocking port 80.
B. Windows Firewall blocks port 23 by default.
C. The computer network interface card is faulty.
D. The BIOS or CMOS settings are blocking web access.

14. What must be done to ensure that the antivirus software on a computer is able to detect and eradicate the most recent viruses?

A. Download the latest signature files on a regular basis
B. Schedule a scan once a week
C. Schedule antivirus updates using Windows Task Manager
D. Follow the firewall configuration guidelines on the antivirus manufacturer website

15. Which level of Windows security permission is required for a local user to backup files from another user?

A. Write
B. Change
C. Full
D. Read

CHAPTER 13

The IT Professional

Objectives

Upon completion of this chapter, you will be able to answer the following questions:

- Why are good communication skills and professional behavior important?
- Does working with computer technology have ethical and legal aspects?
- What techniques can you use to keep the customer focused on the issue they need to have taken care of?
- What is the relationship between communication and troubleshooting?
- What are good stress and time management techniques?
- What is a call center environment, and what are the technician's responsibilities?

Key Terms

This chapter uses the following key terms. You can find the definitions in the Glossary.

communication skills *Page 731*

closed-ended questions *Page 733*

Netiquette *Page 738*

Workstation Ergonomics *Page 739*

Time Management *Page 739*

Stress Management *Page 740*

service-level agreement (SLA) *Page 740*

Customer Call Rules *Page 741*

cyber law *Page 748*

First response *Page 748*

chain of custody *Page 745*

computer forensics *Page 747*

Call Center Employee Rules *Page 742*

level one technician *Page 752*

level two technician *Page 750*

end user license agreement (EULA) *Page 745*

Persistent data *Page 748*

Volatile data *Page 748*

Introduction (13.0)

The IT professional needs more than just technical skills to be effective. Communication, problem-solving, team work, and planning skills are just as important and, in some instances, even more necessary than just having technical abilities.

Welcome (13.0.1)

Learning the technical knowledge required to work in the IT industry is just one aspect you need to become a successful IT professional; however, it takes more than technical knowledge. An IT professional must be familiar with the legal and ethical issues inherent in this industry. Privacy and confidentiality concerns must also be taken into consideration during every customer encounter in the field, in the office, or over the phone in a call center.

The IT Professional (13.0.1.1)

If you become a bench technician, you might not interact with customers directly, but you will have access to their private and confidential data. This chapter discusses some common legal and ethical issues.

Call center technicians work exclusively over the phone with customers. This chapter covers general call center procedures and the process of working with customers.

As an IT professional, you will troubleshoot and fix computers, and you will frequently communicate with customers and coworkers. In fact, troubleshooting is as much about communicating with the customer as it is about knowing how to fix a computer. In this chapter, you learn to use good communication skills as confidently as you use a screwdriver.

Communication Skills and the IT Professional (13.1)

This section addresses proper communication techniques for working with customers. It is necessary to explore these topics as a technician because it affects customer service. Developing a rapport and establishing a professional relationship with the customer will be beneficial to your information gathering and problem-solving abilities.

Communication Skills, Troubleshooting, and the IT Professional (13.1.1)

The ability to communicate well with people at all levels of an enterprise, from IT personnel to the CEO, is essential, and it is just as important in client-facing roles such as those I help-desk and call centers. Whether you're troubleshooting computer issues or managing a team, it's important to know how to interact and communicate well with others at all levels of the organization. You need to be proficient at explaining issues, talking people through solutions, and managing a team efficiently. This section addresses proper communication techniques for working with customers both internal and external to an organization.

Relationship Between Communication Skills and Troubleshooting (13.1.1.1)

Think of a time when you had to call a repair person to get something fixed. Did it feel like an emergency to you? Perhaps you had a bad experience with a repair person. Are you likely to call that same person to fix a problem again?

Perhaps you had a good experience with a repair person. That person listened to you as you explained your problem and then asked you a few questions to get more information. Are you likely to call that person to fix a problem again?

A technician's good *communication skills* are an aid in the troubleshooting process. Developing a rapport and establishing a professional relationship with the customer will be beneficial to your information gathering and problem solving abilities. It takes time and experience to develop good communication and troubleshooting skills. As your hardware, software, and OS knowledge increases, your ability to quickly determine a problem and find a solution will improve. The same principle applies to developing communication skills. The more you practice good communication skills, the more effective you will become when working with customers. A knowledgeable technician who uses good communication skills will always be in demand in the job market.

To troubleshoot a computer, you need to learn the details of the problem from the customer. Most people who need a computer problem fixed are probably feeling some stress. If you establish a good rapport with the customer, the customer might relax a bit. A relaxed customer is more likely to be able to provide the information that you need to determine the source of the problem so it can be fixed.

Speaking directly with the customer is usually the first step in resolving the computer problem. As a technician, there are several communication and research tools available. All these resources can be used to help gather information for the troubleshooting process.

Relationship Between Communication Skills and Professional Behavior (13.1.1.2)

Whether you are talking with a customer on the phone or in person, it is important to communicate well and to present yourself professionally.

If you are talking with a customer in person, that customer can see your body language. If you are talking with a customer over the phone, that customer can hear your tone and inflection. Customers can also sense whether you are smiling when you are speaking with them on the phone. Many call center technicians use a mirror at their desk to monitor their facial expressions.

Successful technicians control their own reactions and emotions from one customer call to the next. A good rule for all technicians to follow is that a new customer call means a fresh start. Never carry your frustration from one call to the next.

Lab—Technician Resources (13.1.1.3)

In this lab, you use the Internet to find resources for a specific computer component. Search online for resources that can help you troubleshoot the component. Refer to the lab in *IT Essentials: PC Hardware and Software Lab Manual 6.0*.

Working with a Customer (13.1.2)

Customers that seek support from a computer technician are generally doing so because they are experiencing problems with their systems. It is the responsibility of the technician to determine the problem while providing a positive customer experience with consideration, respect, and empathy. Listening is an essential part of communication. Ensure that you listen attentively. This section discusses how to identify customer types and relate to customers to provide quality support.

Using Communication Skills to Determine Customer Problems (13.1.2.1)

One of the first tasks of the technician is to determine the type of computer problem that the customer is experiencing.

Remember these three rules at the beginning of your conversation:

- **Know**—Call your customer by name
- **Relate**—Create a one-to-one connection between you and your customer
- **Understand**—Determine the customer's level of knowledge about the computer to determine how to best communicate with the customer

To accomplish this, practice active listening skills. Allow the customer to tell the whole story. During the time that the customer is explaining the problem, occasionally interject some small word or phrase, such as *I understand*, *Yes*, *I see*, or *Okay*. This behavior lets the customer know that you are there and that you are listening.

However, a technician should not interrupt the customer to ask a question or make a statement. This is rude, disrespectful, and creates tension. Many times in a conversation, you might find yourself thinking of what to say before the other person finishes talking. When you do this, you are not really listening. Instead, listen carefully when your customers speak, and let them finish their thoughts.

After you have listened to the customer explain the whole problem, summarize what the customer has said. This helps convince the customer that you have heard and understand the situation. A good practice for clarification is to paraphrase the customer's explanation by beginning with the words, "Let me see if I understand what you have told me." This is a very effective tool that demonstrates to the customer that you have listened and that you understand.

After you have assured the customer that you understand the problem, you will probably have to ask some follow-up questions. Make sure that these questions are pertinent. Do not ask questions that the customer has already answered while describing the problem. Doing this only irritates the customer and shows that you were not listening.

Follow-up questions should be targeted, *closed-ended questions* based on the information that you have already gathered. Closed-ended questions should focus on obtaining specific information. The customer should be able to answer a closed-ended question with a simple yes or no or with a factual response, such as "Windows 8.1." Use all the information that you have gathered from the customer to complete a work order.

Displaying Professional Behavior with Customers (13.1.2.2)

When dealing with customers, it is necessary to be professional in all aspects of your role. You must handle customers with respect and prompt attention. When on a telephone, make sure that you know how to place a customer on hold, as well as how to transfer a customer without losing the call.

Be positive when communicating with the customer. Tell the customer what you can do. Do not focus on what you cannot do. Be prepared to explain alternative ways that you can help them, such as emailing information and step-by-step instructions, or using remote control software to solve the problem.

Table 13-1 outlines the process to follow before you put a customer on hold.

Table 13-1 How to Place a Call on Hold

Do	Do Not
Let the customer finish explaining the problem.	Interrupt the customer
Explain to the customer you need to put them on hold and why. Ask the customer for permission to put the call on hold.	Put the customer on hold without an explanation
When given consent, thank the customer and tell them that you will be away only a few minutes. Explain what you will be doing during that time.	Put the customer on hold without the customer's consent
If after placing the call on hold it takes longer to return to the call than expected be sure to keep the customer updated on the status and estimate a time again.	Assume your time is more valuable than the customer's time.
Always thank the customer for their patience as you work to fix their problem.	Assume your time is more valuable than the customer's time

Table 13-2 outlines the process for transferring a call.

Table 13-2 How to Transfer a Call

Do	Do Not
Let the customer finish speaking.	Interrupt the customer
Explain that you will have to transfer the call and tell the customer to whom and why.	Abruptly transfer the call Transfer without providing information to the new technician
Ask the customer if it is alright to transfer the call now. When given consent, make the transfer.	Transfer without explanation and the customer's consent
Tell the customer the number you are transferring the call to. Tell the new technician who you are, the ticket number, and the name of the customer.	Transfer without providing information to the new technician

It is similar to placing a call on hold, with a few differences. When dealing with customers, it is sometimes easier to explain what you should not do. The following list describes things that you should not do when talking with a customer:

- Do not minimize a customer's problems.
- Do not use jargon, abbreviations, acronyms, and slang.
- Do not use a negative attitude or tone of voice.
- Do not argue with customers or become defensive.

- Do not say culturally insensitive remarks.
- Do not disclose any experiences with customers on social media.
- Do not be judgmental or insulting or call the customer names.
- Avoid distractions and do not interrupt when talking with customers.
- Do not take personal calls when talking with customers.
- Do not talk to co-workers about unrelated subjects when talking with the customer.
- Avoid unnecessary holds and abrupt holds.
- Do not transfer a call without explaining the purpose of the transfer and getting customer consent.
- Do not use negative remarks about other technicians to the customer.

Packet Tracer
☐ Activity

Activity Professional Behaviors with Customers (13.1.2.3)

Please refer to the Activities in the Cisco Networking Academy IT Essentials 6.0 online course.

Keeping the Customer Focused on the Problem (13.1.2.4)

Part of your job is to keep the customer focused during the phone call. When you focus the customer on the problem, it allows you to control the call. This makes the best use of your time and the customer's time. Do not take any comments personally, and do not retaliate with any comments or criticism. If you stay calm with the customer, finding a solution to the problem will remain the focal point of the call.

Just as there are many different computer problems, there are many different types of customers. There are multiple strategies for dealing with different types of difficult customers. The following tables represent different problem-customer types these are not comprehensive and often a customer can display a combination of traits, but are intended to help the technician to recognize which traits their customer exhibits. Recognizing these traits can help manage the call accordingly.

Talkative Customers

During the call, a talkative customer discusses everything except the problem. The customer often uses the call as an opportunity to socialize. It can be difficult to get a talkative customer to focus on the problem. Table 13-3 outlines how to deal with talkative customers.

Table 13-3 Dealing with Talkative Customers

Do	Do Not
Allow the customer to talk for 1 minute. Gather as much information about the problem as possible. Politely step in to refocus the customer. This is the exception to the rule of never interrupting a customer Ask as many closed-ended questions as you need after you have regained control of the call.	Encourage non-problem-related conversation by asking social questions such as "How are you today?"

Rude Customers

A rude customer complains during the call and often makes negative comments about the product, the service, and the technician. This type of customer is sometimes abusive and uncooperative and gets aggravated very easily. Table 13-4 outlines how to deal with rude customers.

Table 13-4 Dealing with Rude Customers

Do	Do Not
Listen carefully, because you do not want to ask the customer to repeat any information. Follow a step-by-step approach to determining and solving the problem. If the customer has a favorite technician, try to contact that technician to see if he or she can take the call. For example, tell the customer, "I can either help you right now or see if (the preferred technician) is available. He will be available in 2 hours. Is that acceptable?" If the customer wants to wait for the other technician, record this in the ticket. Apologize for the wait time and the inconvenience, even if there has been no wait time. Reiterate that you want to solve the customer's problem as quickly as possible.	Ask the customer to follow any obvious steps if there is any way you can determine the problem without the customer Be rude to the customer

Angry Customers

An angry customer talks loudly and often tries to speak when the technician is talking. Angry customers are usually frustrated that they have a problem and upset that they have to call somebody to fix it.

Table 13-5 outlines how to deal with angry customers.

Table 13-5 Dealing with Angry Customers

Do	Do Not
Let customers tell their problem without interrupting, even if they are angry. This allows customers to release some of their anger before you proceed. Sympathize with the customer's problem. Apologize for the wait time and inconvenience.	Put this customer on hold or transfer the call (if at all possible). Spend call time talking about what caused the problem. (Instead, you should redirect the conversation to solving the problem.)

Knowledgeable Customers

A knowledgeable customer wants to speak with a technician who is equally experienced in computers. This type of customer usually tries to control the call and does not want to speak with a level one technician the starting point for issues to be resolved.

Table 13-6 outlines how to deal with knowledgeable customers.

Table 13-6 Dealing with Knowledgeable Customers

Do	Do Not
If you are a level one technician, you might want to try to set up a call with a level two technician. Give the customer the overall approach to what you are trying to verify.	Follow a step-by-step process with this customer. Ask to check the obvious such as the power cord or the power switch. For example, you could suggest a reboot instead.

Inexperienced Customers

An inexperienced customer has difficulty describing the problem. These customers are sometimes not able to follow directions correctly and not able to communicate the errors that they encounter.

Table 13-7 outlines how to deal with inexperienced customers.

Table 13-7 Dealing with Inexperienced Customers

Do	Do Not
Use a simple step-by-step process of instructions with this customer. Speak in plain terms.	Use industry jargon Be condescending to your customer

Using Proper Netiquette (13.1.2.5)

Have you read an online forum where two or three members have stopped discussing the issue and have begun to insult each other? Have you ever wondered if they would actually say those things to each other in person? Perhaps you have received an email that had no greeting or was written entirely in capital letters. How did this make you feel while you were reading it?

As a technician, you should be professional in all communications with customers. For email and text communications, there is a set of personal and business etiquette rules called *Netiquette*. Here is a list the basic rules of Netiquette:

- Be pleasant and polite.
- Begin each email, even within a thread, with an appropriate greeting.
- Never send chain letters via email.
- Do not send or reply to flames which is a hostile online interaction.
- Use mixed-case. UPPER CASE IS CONSIDERED SHOUTING.
- Check grammar and spelling before you post.
- Be ethical.
- Never mail or post anything you would not say to someone's face.

In addition to email and text Netiquette, there are general rules that apply to all your online interactions with customers and coworkers:

- Respect other people's time.
- Share expert knowledge.
- Respect other people's privacy.
- Be forgiving of other people's mistakes.

Employee Best Practices (13.1.3)

Effective planning makes it possible to anticipate problems and challenges and transform them into positive opportunities. Effective time management is significant to a less stressful life. This section describes in detail various techniques for managing all of these factors.

Time and Stress Management Techniques (13.1.3.1)

As a technician, you are a very busy person. It is important for your own well-being to use proper time and stress management techniques.

Workstation Ergonomics

The ergonomics of your work area can help you do your job or make it more difficult. Because you spend a major portion of your day at your workstation, make sure that the desk layout works well. Have your headset and phone in a position that is both easy to reach and easy to use. Adjust your chair to a height that is comfortable. Adjust your computer screen to a comfortable angle so that you do not have to tilt your head up or down to see it. Make sure your keyboard and mouse are also in a position that is comfortable for you. You should not have to bend your wrist to type. If possible, try to minimize external distractions, such as noise.

Time Management

It is important to prioritize your activities. Make sure that you carefully follow the business policy of your company. The company policy might state that you must take "down" calls first, even though they might be harder to solve. A down call usually means that a server is not working, and the entire office or company is waiting for the problem to be resolved to resume business.

If you have to call a customer back, make sure that you do it as close to the callback time as possible. Keep a list of callback customers and check them off one at a time as you complete these calls. Doing this ensures that you do not forget a customer.

When working with many customers, do not give favorite customers faster or better service. When reviewing the call boards, do not take only the easy customer calls. Do not take the call of another technician, unless you have permission to do so.

See Figure 13-1 for a sample customer call board.

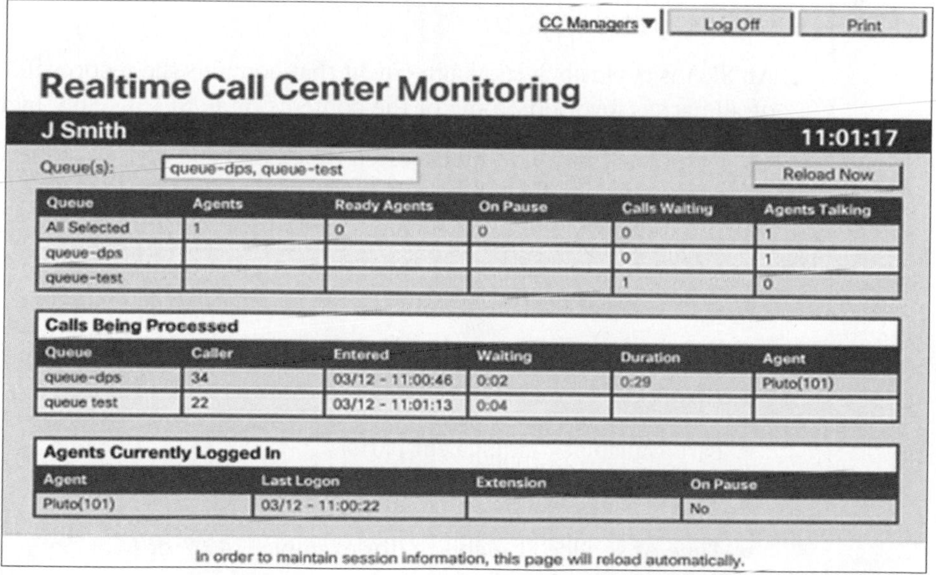

Figure 13-1 Call Board

Stress Management

Take a moment to compose yourself between customer calls. Every call should be independent of other calls. Do not carry any frustrations from one call to the next.

You might have to do some physical activity to relieve stress. Occasionally, stand up and take a short walk. Do a few simple stretch movements or squeeze a tension ball. Take a break if you can, and try to relax. You will then be ready to answer the next customer call effectively. Listed are some ways to relax:

- Practice relaxed breathing: inhale-hold-exhale-repeat.
- Listen to soothing sounds.
- Massage your temples.
- Take a break; go for a quick walk, or climb a flight of stairs.
- Eat a small snack; protein is best.
- Plan your weekend.
- Avoid stimulants like coffee, carbonated drinks, and chocolate if they contain caffeine that can add to stress.

Observing Service-Level Agreements (13.1.3.2)

When dealing with customers, it is important to adhere to that customer's *service-level agreement (SLA)*. An SLA is a contract that defines expectations between an organization and the service vendor to provide an agreed-upon level of support. As an employee of the service company, your job is to honor the SLA that you have with the customer.

An SLA is typically a legal agreement that contains the responsibilities and liabilities of all parties involved. Some of the contents of an SLA usually include the following:

- Response time guarantees (often based on type of call and level of service agreement)
- Equipment and software that is supported
- Where service is provided
- Preventive maintenance
- Diagnostics
- Part availability (equivalent parts)
- Cost and penalties
- Time of service availability (for example, 24×7 or Monday to Friday, 8 a.m. to 5 p.m. EST)

Figure 13-2 shows an example of a service-level agreement and some standard sections.

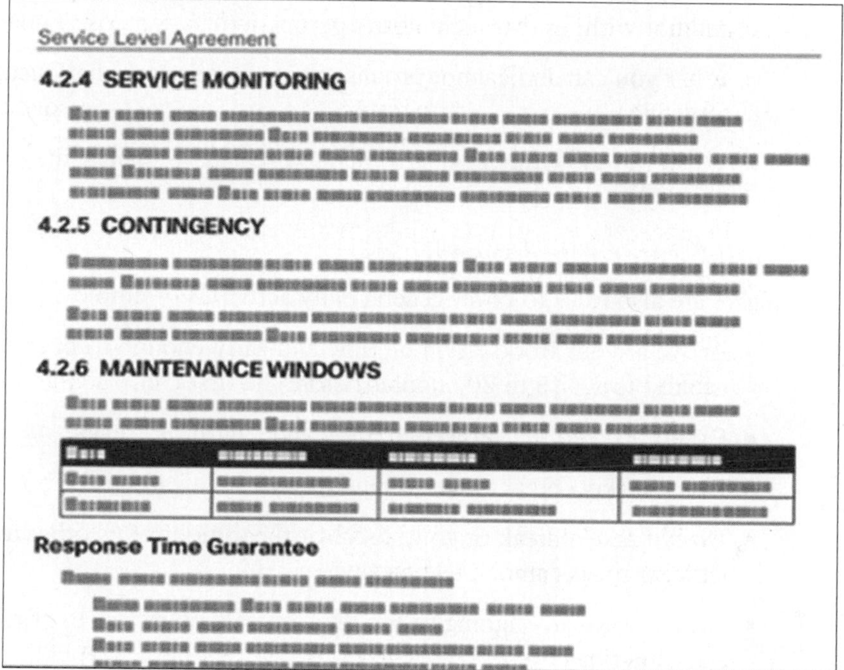

Figure 13-2 Service-Level Agreement

Occasionally, there might be exceptions to the SLA. Some exceptions might include a customer's option to upgrade the level of service or to escalate a problem to management for review. Escalation to management should be reserved for special situations. For example, a long-standing customer or a customer from a large company might have a problem that falls outside the parameters stated in their SLA. In these cases, management might choose to support the customer for customer-relation reasons.

Following Business Policies (13.1.3.3)

As a technician, you should be aware of all business policies related to customer calls. You would not want to make a promise to a customer that you cannot keep. Also have a good understanding of all rules governing employees.

Customer Call Rules

These are examples of rules a call center might use to handle customer calls:

- Maximum time on call (example: 15 minutes)
- Maximum call time in queue (example: 3 minutes)

- Number of calls per day (example: minimum of 30)
- Passing calls on to other technicians (example: only when absolutely necessary and not without that technician's permission)
- What you can and cannot promise the customer (see that customer's SLA fordetails)
- When to follow the SLA and when to escalate to management

Call Center Employee Rules

There are also rules to cover general daily activities of employees:

- Arrive at your workstation on time and early enough to become prepared, usually about 15 to 20 minutes before the first call.
- Do not exceed the allowed number and length of breaks.
- Do not take a break or go to lunch if there is a call on the board.
- Do not take a break or go to lunch at the same time as other technicians (stagger breaks among technicians).
- Do not leave an ongoing call to take a break, go to lunch, or take some personal time.
- Make sure that another technician is available if you have to leave.
- If no other technician is available, check with the customer to see if you can call back later.

Customer Satisfaction

The following rules should be followed by all employees to ensure customer satisfaction:

- Set and meet a reasonable timeline for the call or appointment and communicate this to the customer.
- Communicate service expectations to the customer as early as possible.
- Communicate the repair status with the customer, including explanations for any delays.
- Offer different repair or replacement options to the customer, if applicable.
- Give the customer proper documentation on all services provided.
- Follow up with the customer at a later date to verify satisfaction.

Ethical and Legal Issues in the IT Industry (13.2)

IT personnel often have access to confidential data and knowledge about individuals' and companies' networks and systems. The work of an IT professional puts them in a position facing many ethical decisions and challenges especially involving around privacy issues.

Ethical and Legal Considerations (13.2.1)

As information technology professionals, it is just as important to study ethical and legal concerns as it is technical skills. It is important to recognize the responsibility and ethical obligations that come from having access to customer personal and professional information.

Ethical Considerations in IT (13.2.1.1)

When you are working with customers and their equipment, there are some general ethical customs and legal rules that you should observe. These customs and rules often overlap.

You should always have respect for your customers, as well as for their property. Computers and monitors are property, but property also includes any information or data that might be accessible, for example:

- Emails
- Phone lists
- Records or data on the computer
- Hard copies of files, information, or data left on a desk

Before accessing computer accounts, including the administrator account, get the permission of the customer. From the troubleshooting process, you might have gathered some private information, such as usernames and passwords. If you document this type of private information, you must keep it confidential. Divulging customer information to anyone else is not only unethical, but might be illegal. Legal details of customer information are usually covered under the SLA.

Take particular care to keep personally identifiable information (PII) confidential. PII is any data that could potentially identify a specific individual. NIST Special Publication 800-122 defines PII as, "any information about an individual maintained by an agency, including (1) any information that can be used to distinguish or trace an individual's identity, such as name, social security number, date and place of birth, mother's maiden name, or biometric records; and (2) any other information that is linked or linkable to an individual, such as medical, educational, financial, and employment information."

Examples of PII include, but are not limited to:

- Name, such as full name, maiden name, mother's maiden name, or alias
- Personal identification numbers, such as social security number (SSN), passport number, driver's license number, taxpayer identification number, or financial account or credit card number
- Address information, such as street address or email address
- Personal characteristics, including photographic image (especially of face or other identifying characteristic), fingerprints, handwriting, or other biometric data (e.g., retina scan, voice signature, facial geometry)

Do not send unsolicited messages to a customer. Do not send unsolicited mass mailings or chain letters to customers. Never send forged or anonymous emails. All these activities are considered unethical and, in certain circumstances, might be considered illegal.

Legal Considerations in IT (13.2.1.2)

The laws in different countries and legal jurisdictions vary, but generally actions such as the following are considered to be illegal:

- It is not permissible to make any changes to system software or hardware configurations without customer permission.
- It is not permissible to access a customer's or coworker's accounts, private files, or email messages without permission.
- It is not permissible to install, copy, or share digital content (including software, music, text, images, and video) in violation of copyright and software agreements or the applicable law. Copyright and trademark laws vary between states, countries and regions.
- It is not permissible to use a customer's company IT resources for commercial purposes.
- It is not permissible to make a customer's IT resources available to unauthorized users.
- It is not permissible to knowingly use a customer's company resources for illegal activities. Criminal or illegal use typically includes obscenity, child pornography,

threats, harassment, copyright infringement, Internet piracy, university trademark infringement, defamation, theft, identity theft, and unauthorized access.

- It is not permissible to share sensitive customer information. You are required to maintain confidentiality of this data.

This list is not exhaustive. All businesses and their employees must know and comply with all applicable laws of the jurisdiction in which they operate.

Licensing (13.2.1.3)

As an IT technician, you may encounter customers who are using software illegally. It is important that you understand the purpose and types of common software licenses, should you determine that a crime has been committed. Your responsibilities are usually covered in your company's corporate end-user policy. In all instances, you must follow security best practices, including documentation and *chain of custody* procedures.

A software license is a contract that outlines the legal use, or redistribution, of that software. Most software licenses grant an end-user permission to use one or more copies of software. They also specify the end-user's rights and restrictions. This ensures that the software owner's copyright is maintained. It is illegal to use licensed software without the appropriate license.

Personal License

Most software is licensed rather than sold. Some types of personal software licenses regulate how many computers can run a copy of the software. Other licenses specify the number of users that can access the software. Most personal software licenses allow you to run the program on only one machine. There are personal software licenses that allow you to copy the software onto multiple computers. These licenses usually specify that the copies cannot be used at the same time.

One example of a personal software license is an *end user license agreement (EULA)*. A EULA is a license between the software owner and an individual end-user. The end-user must agree to accept the terms of the EULA. Sometimes, accepting a EULA is as simple as opening the physical package that holds a CD of the software, or by downloading and installing the software. A common example of agreeing to a EULA occurs when updating software on tablets and smartphones. The end-user must agree to accept the EULA when updating the operating system, or installing or updating software found on the device, by clicking "I accept the license terms," as shown in Figure 13-3.

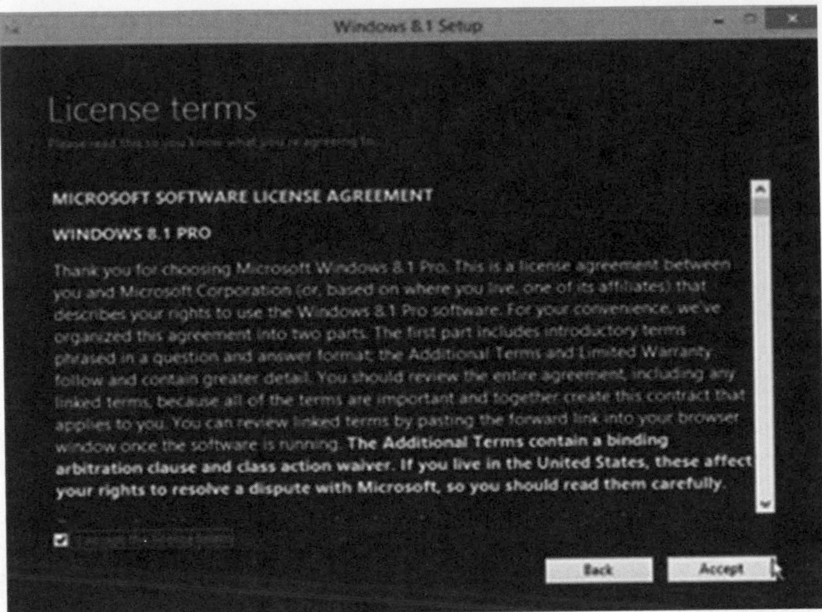

Figure 13-3 End User License Agreement

The end-user can decline a EULA by returning the unopened software package, or by clicking "I do not accept" when prompted.

Enterprise License

An *enterprise license* is a software site license held by a company. Typically, with an enterprise license, the company pays for its employees to use the software. This software does not need to be registered every time it is installed on another employee's computer. In some cases, the employees may need to use a password to activate each copy of the license.

Open Source Licenses and Commercial Licenses

Open source licensing is copyright license for software that allows developers to modify and share the source code that runs the software. In some cases, an open source license means that the software is free to all users. In other cases, it means that the software can be purchased. In both instances, users have access to the source code. Some examples of open source software are Linux, WordPress, and Firefox.

If software is being used by an individual who is not using it to make money, that person would have a personal license for that software. Personal software licenses are often free or low-cost.

If a person uses software to make money, that person would pay a commercial license. Commercial software licenses are usually more expensive than personal licenses.

Digital Rights Management

In addition to licensing, there is also software that helps to control illegal use of software and content. *Digital rights management (DRM)* is software that is designed to prevent illegal access to digital content and devices. DRM is used by hardware and software manufacturers, publishers, copyright holders, and individuals. Their purpose for using DRM is to prevent copyrighted content from being copied freely. This helps the copyright holder to maintain control of the content and to be paid for access to that content.

Legal Procedures Overview (13.2.2)

Many legal and ethical issues arise as companies use computers and computer networks in all aspects of business. All types of data are collected and stored about business processes as well as customers and employees. During criminal investigations, audits, and litigation that data may be required as part of a legal action. This section discusses different ways of handling data for legal purposes.

Computer Forensics (13.2.2.1)

Data from computer systems, networks, wireless communications, and storage devices may need to be collected and analyzed in the course of a criminal investigation. The collection and analysis of data for this purpose is called *computer forensics*. The process of computer forensics encompasses both IT and specific laws to ensure that any data collected is admissible as evidence in court.

Depending on the country, illegal computer or network usage may include:

- Identity theft
- Using a computer to sell counterfeit goods
- Using pirated software on a computer or network
- Using a computer or network to create unauthorized copies of copyrighted materials, such as movies, television programs, music, and video games
- Using a computer or network to sell unauthorized copies of copyrighted materials
- Pornography

This is not an exhaustive list.

Two basic types of data are collected when conducting computer forensics procedures:

- *Persistent data*—Persistent data is stored on a local drive, such as an internal or external hard drive, or an optical drive. When the computer is turned off, this data is preserved.
- *Volatile data*—RAM, cache, and registries contain volatile data. Data in transit between a storage medium and a CPU is also volatile data. It is important to know how to capture this data, because it disappears as soon as the computer is turned off.

Cyber Law and First Response (13.2.2.2)

There is no single law known as a *cyber law*. Cyber law is a term to describe the international, regional, country, and state laws that affect computer security professionals. IT professionals must be aware of cyber law so that they understand their responsibility and their liability as it relates to cybercrimes *First response* is the term used to describe the official procedures employed by those people who are qualified to collect evidence.

Cyber Law

Cyber laws explain the circumstances under which data (evidence) can be collected from computers, data storage devices, networks, and wireless communications. They can also specify the manner in which this data can be collected. In the United States, cyber law has three primary elements:

- Wiretap Act
- Pen/Trap and Trace Statute
- Stored Electronic Communication Act

IT professionals should be aware of the cyber laws in their country, region, or state.

First Response

System administrators, like law enforcement officers, are usually the first responders at potential crime scenes. Computer forensics experts are brought in when it is apparent that there has been illegal activity.

Routine administrative tasks can affect the forensic process. If the forensic process is improperly performed, evidence that has been collected might not be admissible in court.

As a field or a bench technician, you may be the person who discovers illegal computer or network activity. If this happens, do not turn off the computer. Volatile data about the current state of the computer can include programs that are running, network connections that are open, and users who are logged in to the network or to the computer. This data helps to determine a logical timeline of the security incident. It may also help to identify those responsible for the illegal activity. This data could be lost when the computer is powered off.

Be familiar with your company's policy regarding cybercrimes. Know who to call, what to do and, just as importantly, know what not to do.

Documentation and Chain of Custody (13.2.2.3)

Chain of custody is bing able to validate how evidence is collected, protected, and kept track of so that its authenticity can be proven. This is crucial to using the evidence in legal actions. To ensure that the chain of custody is kept intact careful, detailed documenting must be kept.

Documentation

The documentation required by a system administrator and a computer forensics expert is extremely detailed. They must document not only what evidence was gathered, but how it was gathered and with which tools. Incident documentation should use consistent naming conventions for forensic tool output. Stamp logs with the time, date, and identity of the person performing the forensic collection. Document as much information about the security incident as possible. These best practices provide an audit trail for the information collection process.

Even if you are not a system administrator or computer forensics expert, it is a good habit to create detailed documentation of all the work that you do. If you discover illegal activity on a computer or network on which you are working, at a minimum, document the following:

- Initial reason for accessing the computer or network
- Time and date
- Peripherals that are connected to the computer
- All network connections
- Physical area where the computer is located
- Illegal material that you have found
- Illegal activity that you have witnessed (or you suspect has occurred)
- Which procedures you have executed on the computer or network

First responders want to know what you have done and what you have not done. Your documentation may become part of the evidence in the prosecution of a crime. If you make additions or changes to this documentation, it is critical that you inform all interested parties.

Chain of Custody

For evidence to be admitted, it must be authenticated. A system administrator may testify about the evidence that was collected. But he or she must also be able to prove how this evidence was collected, where it has been physically stored, and who has had access to it between the time of collection and its entry into the court proceedings. This is known as the *chain of custody*. To prove the chain of custody, first responders have documentation procedures in place that track the collected evidence. These procedures also prevent evidence tampering so that the integrity of the evidence can be ensured.

Incorporate computer forensics procedures into your approach to computer and network security to ensure the integrity of the data. These procedures help you capture necessary data in the event of a network breach. Ensuring the viability and integrity of the captured data helps you prosecute the intruder.

Call Center Technicians (13.3)

Call center technicians are required to have strong written and verbal communication skills in addition to their technical skills. This section describes the call center environment and the responsibilities of a call center technician.

Call Centers, Level One Technicians, and Level Two Technicians (13.3.1)

Call center technicians answer customer calls then analyze, troubleshoot and resolve technical issues for them. Depending on the type of call, it is handled by different levels of technicians providing a basic to intermediate level of technical support.

Call Centers (13.3.1.1)

A call center environment is usually very professional and fast-paced. Customers call in to receive help for a specific computer-related problem. The typical workflow of a call center is that calls from customers are displayed on a callboard. Level one technicians answer these calls in the order that the calls arrive. If the level one technician cannot solve the problem, it is escalated to a *level two technician*. In all instances, the technician must supply the level of support that is outlined in the customer's SLA.

A call center might exist within a company and offer service to the employees of that company as well as to the customers of that company's products. Alternatively, a call center might be an independent business that sells computer support as a service to outside customers. In either case, a call center is a busy, fast-paced work environment, often operating 24 hours a day.

Call centers tend to have a large number of cubicles. Each cubicle has a chair, at least one computer, a phone, and a headset. The technicians working at these cubicles have varied levels of experience in computers, and some have specialties in certain types of computers, hardware, software, or operating systems.

All the computers in a call center have support software. The technicians use this software to manage many of their job functions.

Table 13-8 shows some of the features of support software.

Table 13-8 Features of Support Software

Log and track incidents	The software may manage call queues, set call priorities, assign calls, and escalate calls.
Record contact information	The software may store, edit, and recall customer names, email addresses, phone numbers, location, websites, fax numbers, and the information in a database.
Research product information	The software may provide technicians with information regarding the products supported, including features, limitations, new versions, configuration constraints, known bugs, product availability, links to online help files, and other information.
Run diagnostic utilities	The software may have several diagnostic utilities including remote diagnostic software, in which the technician can take over a customer's computer while sitting at a desk in the call center.
Research a knowledge base	The software may contain a knowledge database that is preprogrammed with common problems and their solutions. This database may grow as technicians add their own records of problems and solutions.
Collect customer feedback	The software may collect customer feedback regarding satisfaction with the call center's products and services.

Each call center has business policies regarding call priority. Table 13-9 provides a sample chart of how calls can be named, defined, and prioritized.

Table 13-9 Call Prioritization

Name	Definition	Priority
Down	The company cannot operate any of its computer equipment.	1 (Most Urgent)
Hardware	One (or more) of the company's computers is not functioning correctly.	2 (Urgent)
Software	One (or more) of the company's computers is experiencing software or operating system errors.	2 (Urgent)
Network	One (or more) of the company's computers cannot access the network.	2 (Urgent)
Enhancement	There has been a request from the company for additional computer functionality.	3 (Important)

Level One Technician Responsibilities (13.3.1.2)

Call centers sometimes have different names for *level one technicians*. These technicians might be known as level one analysts, dispatchers, or incident screeners. Regardless of the title, the level one technician's responsibilities are fairly similar from one call center to the next.

The primary responsibility of a level one technician is to gather pertinent information from the customer. The technician has to accurately enter all information into the ticket or work order. These are examples of the type of information that the level one technician must obtain:

- Contact information
- The computer's manufacturer and model
- The computer's operating system
- Whether the computer uses AC or DC power
- Whether the computer is on a network and, if so, whether it is a wired or wireless connection
- If a specific application was being used when the problem occurred
- If any new drivers or updates have been installed recently and, if so, what they are
- Description of the problem
- Priority of the problem

Some problems are very simple to resolve, and a level one technician can usually take care of these without escalating the work order to a level two technician.

Often a problem requires the expertise of a level two technician. In these instances, the level one technician must be able to write a customer's problem description into a succinct sentence or two that is entered into the work order. This description is important because it helps other technicians to quickly understand the situation without having to ask the customer the same questions again.

Level Two Technician Responsibilities (13.3.1.3)

As with level one technicians, call centers sometimes have different names for level two technicians. These technicians might be known as product specialists or technical-support personnel. The level two technician's responsibilities are generally the same from one call center to the next.

The level two technician is usually more knowledgeable than the level one technician about technology or has been working for the company for a longer period of time. When a problem cannot be resolved within a predetermined amount of time, the level one technician prepares an escalated work order. The level two technician receives the escalated work order with the description of the problem and then calls the customer back to ask any additional questions and resolve the problem.

Level two technicians can also use remote access software to connect to the customer's computer to update drivers and software, access the operating system, check the BIOS, and gather other diagnostic information to solve the problem.

Summary (13.4)

Summary (13.4.1)

In this chapter, you learned about the relationship between communication skills and troubleshooting skills. You have learned that these two skills need to be combined to make you a successful technician. You also learned about the legal aspects and ethics of dealing with computer technology and the property of the customer.

The following concepts from this chapter are important to remember:

- To be a successful technician, you must practice good communication skills with customers and co-workers. These skills are as important as technical expertise.
- You should always conduct yourself in a professional manner with your customers and co-workers. Professional behavior increases customer confidence and enhances your credibility. You should also learn to recognize the classic signs of a difficult customer and learn what to do and what not to do when you are on a call with this customer.
- There are techniques that you can use to keep a difficult customer focused on the problem during a call. Primarily, you must remain calm and ask pertinent questions in an appropriate fashion. These techniques keep you in control of the call.
- There is a right way and a wrong way to put a customer on hold or transfer a customer to another technician. Learn and use the right way every time. Doing either of these operations incorrectly can negatively affect your company's relationship with its customers.
- Netiquette is a list of rules to use whenever you communicate through email, text messaging, instant messaging, and blogs.
- You must understand and comply with your customer's SLA. If the problem falls outside the parameters of the SLA, find positive ways of telling the customer what you can do to help, rather than what you cannot do. In special circumstances, you might decide to escalate the work order to management.
- In addition to the SLA, you must follow the business policies of the company. These policies include how your company prioritizes calls, how and when to escalate a call to management, and when you are allowed to take breaks and lunch.
- A computer technician's job is stressful. You rarely meet a customer who is having a good day. You can alleviate some of the stress by setting up your workstation in the most ergonomically beneficial way possible. Practice time and stress management techniques every day.

- There are ethical and legal aspects of working in computer technology. You should be aware of your company's policies and practices. In addition, you might need to familiarize yourself with your local or country's trademark and copyright laws.
- A software license is a contract that outlines the legal use, or redistribution, of that software. Most software licenses grant an end-user permission to use one or more copies of software. They also specify the end-user's rights and restrictions. There are many different types of software licenses including Personal, Enterprise, Open Source and Commercial.
- Collecting and analyzing data from computer systems, networks, wireless communications, and storage devices is called computer forensics.
- Cyber laws explain the circumstances under which data (evidence) can be collected from computers, data storage devices, networks, and wireless communications. First response is the term used to describe the official procedures employed by those people who are qualified to collect evidence.
- Even if you are not a system administrator or computer forensics expert, it is a good habit to create detailed documentation of all the work that you do. Being able to prove how evidence was collected and where it has been between the time of collection and its entry into the court proceeding is known as the chain of custody.
- The call center is a fast-paced environment. Level one technicians and level two technicians each have specific responsibilities. These responsibilities might vary slightly from one call center to another.

Summary of Exercises

This is a summary of the labs, Packet Tracer, and videos activities associated with this chapter.

Labs

Lab—Technician Resources (13.1.1.3)

The following labs cover material from this chapter. Refer to the labs in the *IT Essentials v6 Lab Manual*.

Activity Professional Behaviors with Customers (13.1.2.3)

Please refer to the Activities in the Cisco Networking Academy IT Essentials 6.0 online course.

Check Your Understanding

You can find the answers to these questions in the appendix, "Answers to 'Check Your Understanding' Questions."

1. What does it mean when a technician receives a "down" call?

   A. A call that is simpler to solve
   B. A call that has exceeded the maximum response time
   C. A call between a technician and a customer that was abruptly interrupted
   D. A call where a significant part of the IT infrastructure is down, affecting the ability of the company to do business

2. What is the definition of the term SLA?

   A. A contract that defines the expectations of the technician about supporting the customer
   B. A legal agreement that contains the responsibilities and liabilities of the service provider
   C. The responsibilities a customer has with the technician to provide hardware and software support
   D. An acronym for stress level agreement

3. During computer forensics investigations, which type of data is lost when power is removed from the computer?

   A. Data that is stored in RAM
   B. Data that is stored on magnetic disk
   C. Data that is stored to an external drive
   D. Data that is stored on solid state drives

4. What are two sections that are usually included in an SLA? (Choose two.)

   A. Contact information of other clients
   B. Supported equipment and software
   C. Service provider part suppliers
   D. Home contact information of the technician
   E. Time of service availability

5. What is a common responsibility of a level one call center technician?

   A. Receiving escalated work orders from a lower level technician
   B. Calling back customers and asking additional questions to solve the problem

C. Entering a concise description of a customer problem into a ticketing system
D. Remotely connecting to customer devices and implementing driver and software updates

6. What skill is essential for a level one technician to have?
   A. The ability to gather relevant information from the customer and pass it to the level two technician so it can be entered into the work order
   B. The ability to translate a description of a customer problem into a few succinct sentences and enter it into the work order
   C. Ability to take the work order prepared by the level two technician and try to resolve the problem
   D. The ability to ask the customer relevant questions, and as soon as this information is included in the work order, escalate it to the level two technician

7. Which statement best describes a call center?
   A. It is a help desk environment where the customers go with their computers to have them fixed.
   B. It is a place to provide computer support to customers.
   C. It is a help desk used by customers to make an appointment to report their computer problems.
   D. It is a busy, fast-paced work environment that documents computer problems after they have been repaired by technicians.

8. What is considered ethical behavior by a technician when communicating with a customer?
   A. A technician can send mass emails to customers.
   B. It is normal to send chain emails to customers.
   C. A technician can send forged emails to customers.
   D. A technician must only send solicited emails.

9. Which is true regarding the treatment of customer property?
   A. Data left on a customer's PC is not property because it is visible to others.
   B. A customer's phone list is customer property and must be kept private.
   C. Customer property is limited to hardware.
   D. A technician does not have to care about copies of customer files because it is not the original.

10. A technician has copied several commercial movies to a company server to be shared with colleagues. How would this behavior be classified?

    A. Illegal but ethical
    B. Ethically wrong but legal
    C. Acceptable
    D. Ethically wrong and illegal

11. What is considered good communication practice for a technician to use when a customer is explaining a computer problem?

    A. Do not waste time listening to the user.
    B. Ask occasional questions to clarify some points.
    C. Have the customer realize that the problem is unimportant.
    D. When the customer is speaking, interrupt frequently to clarify each point.

12. What two roles or tasks are associated with level two technicians? (Choose two.)

    A. Gathering diagnostic information from a customer computer
    B. Prioritizing incoming calls according to their severity
    C. Escalating a trouble ticket to a higher level technician
    D. Gathering customer information to initiate a work order
    E. Remotely updating drivers and software on customer computers

13. Which two data storage locations contain persistent data that can be used by computer forensics specialists? (Choose two.)

    A. Solid state drives
    B. Cache
    C. RAM
    D. Hard disk drives
    E. CPU registers

14. What name is given to a certain set of general rules that apply to written communication over the Internet?

    A. Netiquette
    B. Internet slang
    C. Flames
    D. Online interactions

15. As a technician, which method should be used with a talkative customer on a phone call?

    A. Use industry jargon to show understanding of computer technology.
    B. Sympathize with the customer regarding the problem.
    C. Politely interrupt the customer to take control of the conversation.
    D. Ask as many open-ended questions as needed after regaining control of the conversation.
    E. Place the customer on hold or transfer the call.

CHAPTER 14

Advanced Troubleshooting

Objectives

Upon completion of this chapter, you will be able to answer the following questions:

- What are the advanced diagnostic questions to ask when gathering information about a computer hardware or software problems?
- What are advanced problems with computer components and peripherals, operating systems, networks, and security?
- What are advanced solutions for solving problems with computer components and peripherals, operating systems, networks, and security?
- How do you talk a customer through diagnosing and fixing a problem, as a call center technician?

Key Terms

This chapter uses the following key terms. You can find the definitions in the Glossary.

blue screen of death (BSOD) 766

auto restart function 766

Introduction (14.0)

In your career as a technician, it is important that you develop advanced skills in troubleshooting techniques and diagnostic methods for computer components, operating systems, networks, and security issues.

Welcome (14.0.1)

Advanced troubleshooting can sometimes mean that the problem is unique or that the solution is difficult to perform. More often, advanced troubleshooting means that the probable cause is difficult to diagnose.

Advanced Troubleshooting (14.0.1.1)

Advanced troubleshooting uses not only your advanced diagnostic skills when working with hardware and software, but also the interaction between technicians and customers or other technicians. The way in which you work with customers and other technicians can determine how quickly and comprehensively the problem gets diagnosed and solved. Take advantage of your resources, other technicians, and the online technician community to get answers to your diagnostic challenges. You might be able to help another technician with a problem.

Six Steps for Troubleshooting Review (14.0.1.2)

Use the troubleshooting steps in Table 14-1 as a guide to help you diagnose and repair problems.

Table 14-1 Six Steps for Troubleshooting

Troubleshooting Steps	
Step 1	Identify the problem.
Step 2	Establish a theory of probable cause.
Step 3	Test your theories to determine the cause of the problem.
Step 4	Establish a plan of action to solve the problem and implement the solution.
Step 5	Verify full functionality and, if applicable, implement preventive measures.
Step 6	Document your findings, actions, and outcomes.

Computer Components and Peripherals (14.1)

The physical component of a computer system are comprised of the main system components internal to the system. Components such as RAM, CPU, and motherboard. There are also peripheral is a devices that are added to the computer to expand its capabilities, such as network card, speakers , an external hard disk for back-up storage and usually a printer. These devices are optional in nature and are not required for the basic functioning of the computer.

Apply Troubleshooting Process to Computer Components and Peripherals (14.1.1)

This section describes how to apply the six-step troubleshooting processes to problems with computer components and peripherals and provides a chart of common problems and solutions that can be used by a technician troubleshooting these issues.

Advanced Problems and Solutions for Components and Peripherals (14.1.1.1)

Computer problems can be attributed to hardware, software, networks, or some combination of the three. You will resolve some types of problems more often than others. Table 14-2 shows with advanced problems and solutions for hardware.

Table 14-2 Advanced Problems and Solutions for Printers

RAID cannot be found.	■ The external RAID controller is not receiving power. ■ The BIOS settings are incorrect. ■ The RAID controller has failed.	■ Check the power connection to the RAID controller. ■ Reconfigure the BIOS settings for the RAID controller. ■ Replace the RAID controller.
RAID stops working.	■ The external RAID controller is not receiving power. ■ The RAID controller has failed.	■ Check the power connection to the RAID controller. ■ Replace the RAID controller.

(Continued)

Table 14-2 *Continued*

A computer exhibits slow performance.	■ The computer does not have enough RAM. ■ The computer is overheating.	■ Install additional RAM. ■ Clean the fans or install additional fans.
The computer does not recognize a removable external drive.	■ The OS does not have the correct drivers for the removable external drive. ■ The USB port has too many attached devices to supply adequate power.	■ Download the correct drivers for the drive. ■ Reduce the number of attached devices or add external power for the USB devices.
After updating the BIOS chip firmware, the computer will not start.	The BIOS chip firmware did not install correctly.	■ Restore the original firmware from the onboard backup if one exists. ■ If the motherboard has a second BIOS chip, the second chip can be used. ■ Contact the motherboard manufacturer to obtain a new BIOS chip.
The computer reboots without warning, locks up, or displays messages or the BSOD.	■ RAM is failing. ■ The front-side bus speed is set too high. ■ The CPU multiplier is set too high. ■ The CPU voltage is set too high.	■ Test the RAM modules to see if they are working properly. ■ Reset the motherboard to the factory default settings. ■ Lower the front-side bus settings. ■ Lower the CPU multiplier settings ■ Lower the CPU voltage settings.
After upgrading from a single core CPU to a multi-core CPU the computer runs slowly and show only one CPU graph in the Task Manager.	■ The BIOS does not recognize the multi-core CPU.	■ Update the BIOS firmware to support the multi-core CPU.

Table 14-3 shows with advanced problems and solutions for printers.

Table 14-3 Advanced Problems and Solutions for Printers

Printer prints unknown characters	■ An incorrect print driver is installed. ■ The printer cables are loose.	■ Uninstall the incorrect print driver and install the correct driver. ■ Secure the printer cables.
The printer will not print large or complex images.	■ The printer does not have enough memory.	■ Add more memory to the printer.
Laser printer prints vertical lines or streaks on each page.	■ The drum is damaged. ■ Toner is not evenly distributed in the cartridge.	■ Replace the drum or replace the toner cartridge if it contains the drum. ■ Remove and shake the toner cartridge.
The toner is not fusing to the paper.	■ The fuser is defective.	■ Replace the fuser.
Paper is creasing after printing.	■ The pickup rollers are obstructed, damaged or dirty.	■ Replace or clean the pickup rollers.
The paper is not being feed into the printer.	■ The pickup rollers are obstructed, damaged or dirty.	■ Replace or clean the pickup rollers.
Each time a network printer is restarted the users receive a "Document failed to print" message.	■ The print IP information is set for DHCP configuration. ■ There is a duplicate IP on the network.	■ Assign static IP address to the printer. ■ Assign a different static IP address to the printer that is unique.

Lab—Troubleshoot Hardware Problems (14.1.1.2)

In this lab, you diagnose the cause of various hardware problems and solve them. Refer to the lab in *IT Essentials v6 Lab Manual.*

Lab—Remote Technician—Fix a Hardware Problem (14.1.1.3)

In this lab, you gather data from the customer, and then instruct the customer to fix a computer that does not boot. Refer to the lab in *IT Essentials v6 Lab Manual.*

Operating Systems (14.2)

Troubleshooting is a skill that is needed in all areas of problem-solving for computer hardware and software.

The operating system acts as an interface between hardware and applications so a problem may not be in the operating system but may actually be caused by a fault in the hardware, application, or the operating system itself. Most computers are also connected to a network, so the problem can be caused by the interaction of the system and the network and other devices. This makes the resolving operating system issues a particularly difficult area of troubleshooting for computer technicians.

Apply Troubleshooting Process to Operating Systems (14.2.1)

Operating system issues are not always obvious and easy to diagnose because the origin of the problem may be hardware or software incompatibilities, driver issues, problems inherent to the OS or some other issue. The solution may not come easily, but with a practical, logical approach finding it becomes easier.

Advanced Problems and Solutions for Operating Systems (14.2.1.1)

Operating system problems can be attributed to hardware, software, networks, or some combination of the three. You will resolve some types of OS problems more often than others. A *stop error* is a hardware or software malfunction that causes the system to lock up. An example of this type of error is known as the *blue screen of death (BSOD)* and appears when the system is unable to recover from an error.

The Event Log and other diagnostic utilities are available to research a stop error or BSOD error. To prevent these types of errors, verify that the hardware and software drivers are compatible. In addition, install the latest patches and updates for Windows. When the system locks up during startup, the computer can automatically reboot. The reboot is caused by the *auto restart function* in Windows and makes it difficult to see the error message.

The auto restart function can be disabled in the Advanced Startup Options menu. Table 14-4 shows advanced operating system problems and solutions.

Table 14-4 Advanced Problems and Solutions for Operating Systems

Identify the Problem	Probable Causes	Possible Solutions
The computer displays an "Invalid Boot Disk" error after POST.	■ Media that does not have an operating system is in a drive. ■ The boot order is not set correctly in the BIOS/UEFI settings. ■ The hard drive is not detected. ■ The hard drive does not have operation system installed. ■ MBR/GPT is corrupted. ■ The computer has a boot sector virus. ■ The hard drive is failing.	■ Remove all media from the drives. ■ Change the boot order in the BIOS/UEFI settings to start with the correct boot device. ■ Reconnect the hard drive cables. ■ Install an OS. ■ Use the *bootrec /fixmbr* command from the System Recovery Options of Windows 7 or Vista. ■ Run virus removal software. ■ Replace the hard drive.
The computer displays an "Inaccessible Boot Device" error after the POST.	■ A recently installed device driver is incompatible with the boot controller. ■ BOOTMGR is corrupted.	■ Use the last known good configuration to boot the computer. ■ Boot the computer in safe mode and load a restore point from before the installation of new hardware.
The computer displays a "BOOTMGR is missing" error after POST.	■ BOOTMGR is missing or damaged. ■ The boot order is not set correctly in the BIOS/UEFI settings. ■ The MBR/GPT is corrupted. ■ The hard drive is failing.	■ Restore BOOTMGR using the Windows Recovery Environment. ■ Change the boot order in the BIOS/UEFI settings to start with the correct boot device. ■ Run *chkdsk /F /R* from the recovery console.
A service failed to start when the computer booted.	■ A service failed to start when the computer booted. ■ The service is not enabled. ■ The service is set to Manual and the failed service requires another service to be enabled.	■ Enable the service. ■ Set the service to Automatic and re-enable the required service.

(*Continued*)

Table 14-4 *Continued*

Identify the Problem	Probable Causes	Possible Solutions
A device failed to start when the computer booted.	■ The device has been disabled in the BIOS settings. ■ The device has a conflict with a newly installed device. ■ The driver is corrupted.	■ Enable the device in the BIOS settings. ■ Remove the newly installed device. ■ Re-install or rollback the device driver.
A program listed in the registry is not found.	■ The uninstall program did not work correctly. ■ The hard drive has become corrupted. ■ The computer has a virus.	■ Re-install the program and run the un-install program again. ■ Run chkdsk /F /R to fix the hard drive file entries. ■ Scan for and remove the virus.
The computer continually restarts without displaying the desktop.	■ The computer is set to restart when there is a failure. ■ A startup file has become corrupted.	■ Press F8 to open the Advanced Options Menu and choose Disable automatic restart on system failure. ■ Run chkdsk /F /R from the Recovery Environment. ■ Run the Automatic Repair from the Recovery Environment in Windows 8.
The computer displays a black or blue screen of death (BSOD).	■ A driver is not compatible with the hardware. ■ There is a hardware failure.	■ Research STOP error and the name of the module that produced the error. ■ Replace any failing devices with known-good device.
The computer locks up without any error messages.	■ The CPU of FSB settings are incorrect on the motherboard or in the BIOS settings. ■ The computer is overheating. ■ An update has corrupted the operating system. ■ There is a hardware failure. ■ The computer has virus.	■ Check and reset the CPU and FSB settings. ■ Check and replace any cooling devices as necessary. ■ Uninstall the software update or perform a System Restore. ■ Run chkdsk /F /R from the Recovery Environment. ■ Replace any failing devices with known-good devices. ■ Scan for and remove the virus.

Identify the Problem	Probable Causes	Possible Solutions
An application does not install.	The installation application is not compatible with the operating system.	Run the application under compatibility mode.
The search feature takes a long time to find results.	■ The index service is not running. ■ The index service is not indexing the correct locations.	■ Start the index services using **services.msc**. ■ Change the settings of the index service in the Advanced Options panel.
The computer is running slowly and has a delayed response.	■ A process is using most of the CPU resources.	■ Restart with **services.msc**. ■ If the process is not needed, end the process with Task Manager. ■ Restart the computer.
When you run a program, a missing or corrupt DLL message is displayed.	■ One of more programs using the DLL file was uninstalled and removed the DLL file that was needed by another program. ■ The DLL file was corrupted during a bad installation.	■ Reinstall the program that has the missing or corrupted DLL file. ■ Reinstall the application that uninstalled the DLL file. ■ Find a copy of the DLL file and reinstall it. ■ Boot the computer in Safe Mode and run **sfc /scannow**.
RAID is not detected during installation.	■ Windows does not include the proper drivers to recognize RAID. ■ RAID settings in BIOS/UEFI are incorrect.	■ Install the proper drivers ■ Change the settings in BIOS/UEFI to enable RAID.
A system file is corrupted.	Computer was shut down improperly.	■ Repair your computer from the advanced startup options menu. ■ Boot the computer in Safe Mode and run **sfc /scannow**.
Computer boots to Safe Mode.	The computer has been configured to boot in Safe Mode.	Use msconfig to adjust the startup settings for the system.
A file fails to open.	■ The computer has a virus. ■ The file is corrupted. ■ The file type is not associated with any program.	■ Run virus removal software. ■ Restore the file from backup. ■ Choose a program to open the file type.

Lab—Troubleshoot Operating System Problems (14.2.1.2)

In this lab, you diagnose the cause of various operating system problems and solve them. Refer to the lab in *IT Essentials v6 Lab Manual.*

Lab—Remote Technician—Fix an Operating System Problem (14.2.1.3)

In this lab, you gather data from the customer, and then instruct the customer to fix a computer that does not connect to the network. Refer to the lab in *IT Essentials v6 Lab Manual*.

Networks (14.3)

Networks are an interaction between several individual systems that are used to share information and resources. They require the use of both hardware and software to function.

Apply Troubleshooting Process to Networks (14.3.1)

Network problems can be attributed to hardware, software, or a combination of the two.

Advanced Problems and Solutions for Networks (14.3.1.1)

You will resolve some types of problems more often than others, whereas other problems may require more in-depth troubleshooting skills.

Network Connection Problems

These types of connection problems are often related to incorrect TCP/IP configurations, firewall settings, or devices that have stopped working, as shown in Table 14-5.

Table 14-5 Advanced Problems and Solutions for Network Connections

Identify the Problem	Probable Causes	Possible Solutions
A computer can connect to a network device by the IP address but not by the host name.	■ Incorrect host name. ■ Incorrect DNS settings. ■ DNS server is not operational.	■ Reenter the host name. ■ Reenter the IP address of the DNS server. ■ Restart the DNS server.

Identify the Problem	Probable Causes	Possible Solutions
The computer does not obtain or renew the IP address on the network.	■ The computer is using a static IP address from a different network. ■ Firewall is blocking DHCP. ■ DHCP server is not operational. ■ Wireless NIC is disabled.	■ Enable the computer to obtain an IP address automatically. ■ Change the firewall settings to allow DHCP traffic. ■ Restart the DHCP server. ■ Enable Wireless NIC.
An IP address conflict message displays when connecting a new computer to the network.	■ The same IP address is assigned to two devices on the network. ■ Another computer has been configured a static IP address that was already assigned by the DHCP server.	■ Configure each device a unique IP address. ■ Configure each device using *ipconfig /release and ipconfig /renew* commands.
A computer has network access but does not Internet access.	■ The gateway IP address is incorrect. ■ A router is configured incorrectly. ■ DNS server is no operational.	■ Reboot the modem. ■ Reboot the router. ■ Reconfigure the router settings. ■ Restart the DNS server.
The computer automatically obtained the IP address 169.254.x.x, but cannot connect to the network.	DHCP service is not operational.	Restart the DHCP service.
Users are experiencing slow transfer speeds, weak signal strength, and intermittent connectivity on the wireless network.	■ Wireless security has not been implemented allowing unauthorized users access. ■ There are too many users connected to the access point. ■ User is too far away from access point. ■ The wireless signal is experiencing interference from outside sources.	■ Implement a wireless security plan. ■ Ensure the access point is centrally located. ■ Restart the access point. ■ Move the access point. ■ Turn off unneeded devices that are connected. ■ Add another access point or a repeater to strengthen signal. ■ Upgrade the access point. ■ Change the channels on the wireless network.

Email Failure

Not being able to send or receive email is often caused by incorrect email software settings, firewall settings, and hardware connectivity issues, as shown in Table 14-6.

Table 14-6 Advanced Problems and Solutions for Email Failures

Identify the Problem	Probable Causes	Possible Solutions
The computer cannot send or receive email.	■ The computer has incorrect email client settings. ■ The email server is down.	■ Reconfigure the email client settings. ■ Reboot the email server of notify your email service provider.
The computer can send but cannot receive email.	■ The inbox is full. ■ The computer has incorrect email client settings.	■ Archive and/or delete emails to create space. ■ The computer has incorrect email client settings.
The computer cannot receive a specific email with an attachment.	■ The email attachment is too large. ■ The email attachment contains a virus and has been blocked by a virus protection program. ■ The email attachment file type is not allowed has been blocked.	■ Ask the sender resend with multiple emails and smaller attachments. ■ Ask the sender to scan the attachment before sending it. ■ Ask the sender to resend the email with the file compressed.

FTP and Secure Internet Connection Problems

File transfer problems between FTP clients and servers are often caused by incorrect IP address and port settings, or security policies. Secure Internet connection problems are often related to incorrect certificate settings and ports blocked by software or hardware, as shown in Table 14-7.

Table 14-7 Advanced Problems and Solutions for FTP and Secure Internet Connections

Identify the Problem	Probable Causes	Possible Solutions
A user cannot access the FTP server.	■ FTP is being blocked by the network and/or host-based firewall. ■ The maximum number of users has been reached.	■ Ensure that ports 20 and 21 are allowed through the firewalls. ■ Increase the maximum number of users on the FTP server.
The FTP client software cannot find the FTP server.	■ The FTP client has an incorrect server/domain name or port setting. ■ The FTP server is not operational or is offline. ■ The DNS server is not operational and is not resolving names.	■ Enter the correct server/domain name and port setting in the FTP client. ■ Restart the FTP server. ■ Restart the DNS server.
A computer cannot access a specific HTTPS site.	The site is not on the browser's list of trusted sites on that system.	Decide if that site is one that should be added to the trusted site list.

Problems Using Network Troubleshooting Tools

Unexpected information reported from CLI commands is often caused by incorrect IP address settings, hardware connection issues, and firewall settings, as shown in Table 14-8.

Table 14-8 Advanced Problems and Solutions when Using Network Troubleshooting

Identify the Problem	Probable Causes	Possible Solutions
Computer can ping an IP address but not a host name.	■ The host name is incorrect. ■ The DNS setting of the computer are incorrect. ■ The DNS server is not operational.	■ Enter the correct host name. ■ Enter the correct DNS settings. ■ Restart the DNS service.

(Continued)

Table 14-8 *Continued*

Identify the Problem	Probable Causes	Possible Solutions
A computer on one network cannot ping a computer on another network.	■ There is a broken link between the two networks. ■ ICMP is blocked at the network and host-based firewall. ■ Default gateway configured incorrectly.	■ Use tracert to locate which link is down and fix the broken link. ■ Configure the firewalls to allow ICMP ping. ■ Correct the default gateway configuration.
Nslookup reports "Can't find server name for 127.0.0.1: timed out."	■ DNS server is not responding ■ No DNS server is configured on the client.	■ Restart the DNS server. ■ Change DNS server settings. ■ Add DNS server address to the client TCP/IP settings.
A computer cannot connect to a shared network folder using the *net use* command.	■ The folder is not shared. ■ The computer is not in the same workgroup.	■ Make sure the network folder is shared using the *net share* command. ■ Set the computer to the same workgroup as the computer with the shared network folder.
When attempting to use the *ipconfig /release or ipconfig /renew* command, you receive the message "No operation can be performed on the adapter while is media is disconnected."	■ The network cable is unplugged. ■ The computer has been configured with a static IP address.	■ Reconnect the network cable. ■ Reconfigure the NIC to obtain IP addressing automatically.
The computer cannot Telnet into a remoter computer.	The remote compute has not been configured to accept Telnet connections or the Telnet service has not been started.	Start the Telnet service on the remoter computer and configure the remote computer to accept Telnet connections.
When attempting to use the *ipconfig /release or ipconfig /renew* command, you receive the message "The operation failed as no adapter is in the state permissible for this operation"	A static IP address has been assigned to the interface.	Reconfigure the NIC to obtain IP addressing automatically.

Lab—Troubleshoot Network Problems (14.3.1.2)

In this lab, you diagnose the causes and solve the network problems. Refer to the lab in *IT Essentials v6 Lab Manual.*

Lab—Remote Technician—Fix a Network Problem (14.3.1.3)

In this lab, you gather data from the customer, and then instruct the customer to fix a computer that does not connect to the network. Refer to the lab in *IT Essentials v6 Lab Manual.*

Security (14.4)

To successfully protect computers and the network from security-related problems a technician must understand the potential problems and solutions to them.

Apply Troubleshooting Process to Security (14.4.1)

This section describes how to apply the troubleshooting process to problems with security and provides a table of common problems and solutions that can be used by a technician troubleshooting these issues.

Advanced Problems and Solutions for Security (14.4.1.1)

Security problems can be attributed to hardware, software, networks, or some combination of the three. You will resolve some types of security problems more often than others.

Malware Settings

Malware protection problems are often related to incorrect software settings or configurations. As a result of these faulty settings, a computer may display one or more of the symptoms caused by malware and boot sector viruses, as shown in Table 14-9.

Table 14-9 Advanced Problems and Solutions for Malware

Identify the Problem	Probable Causes	Possible Solutions
Message "MBR has been changed or modified" appears at boot up.	A boot sector virus has changed the master boot record.	Boot the computer with bootable media and run antivirus software to remove the boot sector virus.
A Windows 7 or windows Vista computer starts with the error message" Caution this hard disk may be infected by a virus!	A virus has damaged the master boot record.	Boot the computer from the installation media. At the Install Windows screen, select **Repair your computer.** At the command prompt, type *bootrec.exe /fixboot*.
A Windows 7 or windows Vista computer starts with the error message" Caution: this hard disk may be infected by a virus!."	A virus has damaged the master boot record.	Boot the computer from the installation media. At the Install Windows screen, select **Repair your computer.** At the command prompt, type *bootrec.exe /fixboot*.
A Windows 7 computer will not boot.	A virus has damaged Windows system files.	Boot the computer from Windows PE media. Access Windows Startup Repair tool to recover corrupted system files.
Your contacts are receiving spam from your email account.	Your email account has been hijacked by a virus or spyware.	Run antivirus software and repair, delete, or quarantine the infected files. Run antispyware software and remove any spyware infections. After the computer is cleaned, change the email account password.

User Accounts and Permissions

Unauthorized access or blocked access is often caused by incorrect user account settings or incorrect permissions, as shown in Table 14-10.

Table 14-10 Advanced Problems and Solutions for User Permissions

Identify the Problem	Probable Causes	Possible Solutions
User can log on but receives an "access denied" message when trying to access some folders and files.	The user is not a member of the group that has access to the folders and files.	Add the user to the correct group. Add the correct user's permissions to the folders and files.
User can locate a file on the server but cannot download the file.	The user permissions are not correct.	Change the user's permissions on the file to read and execute.

Identify the Problem	Probable Causes	Possible Solutions
User is gaining access to a subfolder that should be inaccessible.	The subfolder inherited permissions from the upper level folder.	Change the subfolder permission settings so it does not inherit the permissions from the parent folder. Set proper permissions for the subfolder.
Users of a group cannot see one folder to which they are supposed to have access.	The folder permissions are set deny.	Change the folder permissions to allow.
Encrypted files that are moved over the network to a new computer are no longer encrypted.	The new computer does not have an NTFS partition.	Convert the partition on the new computer to NTDS and re-encrypt the files.

Computer Security

Computer security problems can be caused by incorrect security settings in the BIOS or on the hard drive, as shown in Table 14-11.

Table 14-11 Advanced Problems and Solutions for Computer Security Settings

Identify the Problem	Probable Causes	Possible Solutions
Computer runs slowly at the same time every day.	Antivirus software is set to scan the computer at the same time every day.	Configure the antivirus software to scan the computer when the compute is not in use.
User complains that the computer BIOS settings keep changing.	The BIOS password is not set, allowing others to change the BIOS settings.	Set a password to protect access to the BIOS settings.
Trusted Platform Module (TPM) does not show up in the Device Manager.	The TPM is disabled.	Enable the TPM.

Firewall and Proxy Settings

Blocked connections to networked resources and the Internet are often related to incorrect firewall and proxy rules, and incorrect port settings, as shown in Table 14-12.

Table 14-12 Advanced Problems and Solutions for Firewall or Proxy Settings

Identify the Problem	Probable Causes	Possible Solutions
Computer cannot ping another computer on the network.	■ The Windows Firewall is blocking the requests. ■ A router is blocking ping requests.	■ Configure the Windows Firewall to allow ping requests. ■ configure the router to allow ping requests
Laptop firewall exceptions are allowing unauthorized connections from rogue computers.	■ The Windows Firewall settings are incorrect. ■ The Windows Firewall is disabled.	■ Set the Windows Firewall to "Do not allow exceptions when using a public network." ■ Enable the Windows Firewall
Email program is properly configured but cannot connect to the email server.	■ The email server is down. ■ The Windows Firewall is blocking the email software.	■ Verify that the email server is operational. ■ Create Windows Firewall exception for the email software.
Computer can ping the proxy server, but has no Internet connectivity.	■ The browser proxy server settings are incorrect. ■ The proxy server is offline.	■ Reenter the proxy server settings including the IP address and port of the proxy server, and any exceptions that should be defined. ■ Reboot the proxy server.

Lab—Troubleshoot Security Problems (14.4.1.2)

In this lab, you diagnose the cause of various access security problems and solve them. Refer to the lab in *IT Essentials v6 Lab Manual*.

Lab—Remote Technician—Fix a Security Problem (14.4.1.3)

In this lab, you gather data from the customer and instruct the customer to fix a computer that cannot connect to a workplace wireless network. Refer to the lab in *IT Essentials v6 Lab Manual*.

Summary (14.5)

Troubleshooting and resolving problem can be done both in person and remotely. While a technician is responsible for both it is sometimes necessary to have a remote user actually do the work to fix the problem. A logical and well thought out approach is very important in such situations. This chapter exposure you to many potential problems and solutions to them. It also offered a guideline to troubleshooting steps for a problem solving approach in both an onsite and remote environment.

Summary (14.5.1)

Using a logical troubleshooting methodology and increasing experience improves problem-solving abilities. This chapter provided reference to various computer problems and solutions and a means to practice troubleshooting skills and practice problem resolution with hands-on labs.

In this chapter, you were given multiple opportunities to hone your troubleshooting knowledge and skills.

This chapter covered advanced diagnostic questions to ask when gathering information about a computer hardware or software problem. It also presented more advanced versions of problems and solutions for computer components and peripherals, operating systems, networks, and security.

In labs you fixed a problem. You then talked someone else through diagnosing and fixing a problem, as a call center technician would.

Summary of Exercises

This is a summary of the labs, Packet Tracer, and videos activities associated with this chapter.

Labs

The following labs cover material from this chapter. Refer to the labs in the *IT Essentials v6 Lab Manual*.

Lab—Troubleshoot Hardware Problems (14.1.1.2)

Lab—Remote Technician—Fix a Hardware Problem (14.1.1.3)

Lab—Troubleshoot Operating System Problems (14.2.1.2)

Lab—Remote Technician—Fix an Operating System Problem (14.2.1.3)

Lab—Troubleshoot Network Problems (14.3.1.2)

Lab—Remote Technician—Fix a Network Problem (14.3.1.3)

Lab—Troubleshoot Security Problems (14.4.1.2)

Lab—Remote Technician—Fix a Security Problem (14.4.1.3)

Check Your Understanding

You can find the answers to these questions in the appendix, "Answers to 'Check Your Understanding' Questions."

1. What is a symptom that toner is unevenly distributed in a printer toner cartridge?

   A. Ghost images on the paper

   B. Vertical lines or streaks on the paper

   C. Toner not fused on the paper

   D. Frequent paper jams

2. A user reports that the corporate web server cannot be accessed. A technician verifies that the web server can be accessed by its IP address. What are two possible causes of the problem? (Choose two.)

   A. The default gateway address is misconfigured on the workstation.

   B. The DNS server address is misconfigured on the workstation.

   C. The network connection is down.

   D. The web server information is misconfigured on the DNS server.

   E. The web server is misconfigured.

3. A user needs to open some files that are being shared from a remote computer. However, the user receives an "access denied" message when trying to open some files and folders. What is a probable cause of this?

   A. The TPM must be enabled.

   B. The user is not a member of the group that has permission to access those resources.

   C. A firewall is blocking access to those resources.

   D. The BIOS settings are not configured correctly.

4. When starting a computer running Windows Vista, a technician sees that the error message "BOOTMGR is missing" appears after the POST. What are two possible solutions for this problem? (Choose two.)

   A. Run virus removal software.

   B. Run chkdsk /F /R from the recovery console.

   C. Secure the display adapter on the motherboard.

   D. Run the bootrec /fixboot command.

   E. Restore boot.ini from the installation media.

   F. Restore BOOTMGR using the Windows Recovery Environment.

5. What is an indication that a printer does not have enough memory?

   A. Paper does not feed through the printer correctly.

   B. Unknown characters are printed.

   C. Printed pages have a ghost image.

   D. Large or complex images do not print.

6. A user reports that the workstation CPU and boot settings have been modified. The network administrator suspects that someone may be tampering with the machine. What is a possible solution to prevent this from reoccurring?

   A. Set a Windows account password.

   B. Run the startup repair tool.

   C. Scan the operating system with antivirus software.

   D. Set a BIOS password.

7. Multiple users report that the workstations are assigned a 169.254.x.x IP address. The users are able to communicate only between each other. What is a possible solution?

   A. Verify the network cable on all user machines.

   B. Statically configure a default gateway on each workstation.

   C. Restart the DNS server.

   D. Restart the DHCP server.

8. Why would a computer not recognize an external drive?

   A. Incorrect drivers

   B. Insufficient RAM

   C. A failed CMOS firmware update

   D. Failing RAM

9. What Windows OS utility can be used to identify possible causes of the BSOD?

   A. BIOS boot sequence
   B. Task Manager
   C. Event Log
   D. Disk Management

10. A user reports that a workstation is continually rebooting. What can a technician do to stop the rebooting in order to troubleshoot?

    A. Change the boot sequence in BIOS or UEFI.
    B. Power cycle the workstation.
    C. Disable the auto restart function in the Advanced Startup Options menu.
    D. Replace RAM modules with known good ones.

11. A workstation has been moved from headquarters to a branch office. The user is now reporting that the workstation cannot connect to the network. A technician suspects that the workstation did not correctly obtain an IP address from a DHCP server. What are two possible causes for the problem? (Choose two.)

    A. The DHCP server is misconfigured.
    B. The workstation has been configured with a static IP address.
    C. The default gateway address is misconfigured on the workstation.
    D. A host-based software firewall is blocking DHCP.
    E. An IP address conflict occurred.

12. What is an open-ended question a technician could ask when troubleshooting a suspected malware infection?

    A. Have you scanned the computer for viruses recently?
    B. Have you ever had this problem before?
    C. Do you have a firewall installed on your system?
    D. What security software is installed on your system?

13. What is a symptom of failed RAM in a PC?

    A. Slow performance
    B. Unrecognized drives
    C. Blue screen of death (BSOD)
    D. The display of a BOOTMGR error

APPENDIX A

Answers to "Check Your Understanding" Questions

Chapter 1:

1. B.

   Explanation: The voltage selector switch sets the correct input voltage to the power supply, depending on the country where the power supply is used.

2. B.

   Explanation: FireWire uses the Institute of Electrical and Electronics Engineers (IEEE) 1394 standard and is also known as i.Link. IEEE 1284 is a standard that defines bi-directional parallel communications between computers and other devices. IEEE 1451 is a set of smart transducer interface standards and

3. D.

   Explanation: USB 2.0 allows transmission speeds up to 480 Mb/s. USB 1.1 allowed transmission rates of up to 12 Mb/s in full-speed mode and 1.5 Mb/s in low-speed mode. USB 3.0 allows transmission speeds up to 5 Gb/s.

4. D.

   Explanation: A keyboard, video, mouse (KVM) switch is a hardware device that can be used to control more than one computer using a single keyboard, monitor, and mouse. KVM switches provide cost-efficient access to multiple servers using a single keyboard, monitor, and mouse.

5. A.

   Explanation: Do not open a power supply. Electronic capacitors located inside a power supply can hold a charge for extended periods of time, even after the main power has been disconnected.

6. C.

   Explanation: Overclocking is a technique that is used to make a processor work at a faster speed than its original specification. Overclocking is not a reliable way to improve computer performance and can result in damage to the CPU.

7. D.

   Explanation: A RAID controller controls the expansion of internal and external drives as well as providing drive redundancy and data protection for storage devices.

8. C.

   Explanation: Hot-swappable is the capability of being able to disconnect and connect devices while the computer or another device is on and have those devices be detected without having to reboot the computer or device. For example, eSATA.

9. A.

   Explanation: These are some other functions of virtual computing:

   - Browse the Internet without harmful software hurting your main installation.

- Test software or software upgrades in an environment that does not hurt your current operating system environment.
- Use more than one type of operating system on one computer, such as Linux or Mac OS X.
- Run old applications that are not compatible with modern operating systems.

10. A, B, E.

    Explanation: The form factor pertains to the shape of the mother board and case. Additionally the case must accommodate the shape of the power supply.

11. A.

    Explanation: Power supplies convert AC input to DC output voltages.

Chapter 2:

1. B.

   Explanation: Cleaning the outside of the computer and the mouse can be done with glass cleaner and a soft cloth.

2. A.

   Explanation: The Safety Data Sheet (SSD) summarizes information about materials, including hazardous ingredients, fire hazards, and first-aid requirements.

3. D.

   Explanation: Multimeter—A device that measures AC/DC voltage, electric current, and other electrical characteristics.

   Power supply tester—A device that checks whether the computer power supply is working properly.

   Cable tester—A device that checks for wiring shorts, faults, or wires connected to the wrong pins.

   Loopback plug—A device that connects to a computer, switch, or router port to perform a diagnostic procedure called a loopback test.

4. C.

   Explanation: The Disk Management utility is used to create or delete different types of partitions on a hard disk. The partitions are then formatted with an appropriate file system using the format tool. Chkdsk, Defrag, and SFC are tools used to perform other disk management tasks.

5. D.

   Explanation:Electromagnetic Interference (EMI) is a type of interference that can be caused by motors. A device that supplies a constant level of electrical power to a computer is called an uninterruptible power supply (UPS). ESD is the buildup of static electricity and it can cause damage to electronic components when it is discharged through them.

6. C.

   Explanation: An antistatic wrist strap equalizes the electrical charge between the technician and the equipment and protects the equipment from electrostatic discharge.

7. A.

   Explanation: Use the correct size hex driver to loosen and tighten bolts with a six-sided head.

8. B.

   Explanation: Any cans or bottles that contain solvents used in computer cleaning or repair should be handled with care and treated as hazardous waste.

9. C.

Explanation: The Windows System File Checker (SFC) can scan and automatically repair corrupted system files. Chkdsk is used to verify the integrity of the file system on a hard drive. Fdisk is used to create and delete partitions on the disk. Defrag is used to optimize the space on a hard drive for faster access.

10. C.

Explanation: A crimper is used to attach wires to an RJ-45 connector. A punch down tool is used when terminating network cabling. A toner probe has one part that connects to a cable at one end and the toner probe is used to determine which jack or port terminates the cable at the other end. A loopback adapter would be used to check the functionality of a computer port such as the RJ-45 NIC.

11. C.

Explanation: Surge suppressor—Helps protect against damage from surges and spikes.

Uninterruptible power supply (UPS)—Helps protect against potential electrical power problems by supplying a consistent level of electrical power to a computer or other device. The battery is constantly recharging while the UPS is in use.

Standby power supply (SPS)—Helps protect against potential electrical power problems by providing a backup battery to supply power when the incoming voltage drops below the normal level. The battery is on standby during normal operation.

12. A.

Explanation: A technician should keep a journal that documents upgrades and repairs. This is a valuable resource for future situations as well as providing reference when providing the formal documentation and invoice.

13. B.

Explanation: Documentation can be paper-based or stored electronically. It is important that a technician document all services and repairs so that technicians will have this documentation as a reference for similar problems in the future.

14. A, C.

Explanation: Radio Frequency Interference (RFI) is the interference that is caused by radio transmitters and other devices that are transmitting in the same frequency.

15. A, E.

Explanation: Laser printers require high voltage when initially powered on and to charge the drum in preparation for writing data to the drum. This high voltage requirement is why most laser printers are not normally connected to a UPS. A laser printer also has a fuser assembly used to apply heat and pressure to the toner to permanently attach it to the paper. The laser printer must be unplugged and the fuser assembly must be allowed to cool before working inside the printer.

16. A, B, G.

Explanation: Basic safety procedures to use while fixing a computer include the following: 1) Remove all jewelry and secure clothing such as ties and ID badge. 2) Turn off the power to all devices. 3) Cover sharp edges with tape. 4) Never open a power supply. 5) Know where the fire extinguisher is and how to use it. 6) Keep your workspace clean and free of clutter. 7) Bend your knees when lifting heavy objects.

17. D.

    Explanation: When using compressed air to clean inside the computer, blow the air around the components with a minimum distance of 4 inches (10 cm) from the nozzle. Clean the power supply and the fan from the back of the case.

Chapter 3:

1. A.

   Explanation: None of the incorrect answers are mounting hardware.

2. C.

   Explanation: Rubbing alcohol may contain a higher content of water than a higher percentage of isopropyl alcohol.

   When reinstalling the heat sink, clean the base of the heat sink with isopropyl alcohol. This removes all traces of old thermal compound so the newly applied thermal compound works properly.

   Thermal compound helps to conduct heat away from the CPU.

3. A.

   Explanation: Before you install a memory module, it is important to verify that there are no compatibility issues. A DDR3 RAM module will not fit in a DDR2 slot. Verification is best done by consulting the motherboard documentation or by checking the website of the manufacturer.

4. D.

   Explanation: The Advanced Technology Extended (ATX) main power connector will have either 20 or 24 pins. The power supply may also have a 4-pin or 6-pin Auxiliary (AUX) power connector that connects to the motherboard. A 20-pin connector will work in a motherboard with a 24-pin socket.

   None of the incorrect answers are real options for pin counts on the ATX motherboard power connector.

5. C.

   Explanation: Go to the motherboard manufacturer site to get the correct software to update the BIOS program located on the BIOS chip.

6. B.

   Explanation: CPUs are installed into the processor socket and secured by lowering and securing the load lever. The other answers are part of the motherboard and memory installation steps.

7. A.

   Explanation: Standoffs keep the motherboard from grounding to the case. The holes in the motherboard should align to the standoffs. Each standoff screws into the case. Then, screws are used to securely attach the motherboard to the case (via the standoffs). The other answers are part of the CPU, CPU cooling, and memory installations steps.

8. B.

   Explanation: Cases, motherboards, and power supplies all come in the ATX form factor, but only cases have drive bays.

9. C.

   Explanation: A power supply. Power supplies have fans that provide proper air flow through the interior of the computer case. Power supplies should be tightly screwed to the case (but not overtightened) so that the fan vibrations do not loosen it.

10. C, E.

    Explanation: The BIOS contains a power-on self-test (POST) program that tests hardware during computer startup. One beep is a common indication that all is well. Several beeps indicate a hardware issue. BIOS is built into the motherboard, so it is the motherboard documentation that should be consulted to resolve this issue.

11. C.

    Explanation: The BIOS configuration data is saved to a special memory chip called a complementary metal oxide semiconductor (CMOS).

12. A, E.

    Explanation: The BIOS setup program is used to change settings if memory modules, storage devices, and adaptor cards are added. Most manufacturers provide the ability to modify boot device options, security and power settings, and adjustments for voltage and clock settings.

13. C.

    Explanation: Increasing the CPU clock speed makes the computer run faster, but it also generates more heat and causes overheating issues.

14. C.

    Explanation: A signed driver is a driver that has passed the Windows hardware quality lab test and has been given a driver signature by Microsoft. Installing an unsigned driver can cause system instability, error messages, and boot problems.

15. A.

    Explanation: After the new motherboard is in place and cables are connected, you should install and secure all expansion cards. Finally, connect the keyboard, mouse, and monitor, then power on the computer to check for problems.

16. C.

    Explanation: The computer time and date are held in CMOS. This requires power from a small battery. If the battery is getting low, the system time and date may become incorrect.

Chapter 4:

1. C.

   Explanation: Each light on the front of the case is powered by the motherboard through a cable that attaches somewhere on the board. If this cable comes loose, a particular light on the front of the case will not work.

2. B.

   Explanation: The steps of the troubleshooting process:

   Step 1. Identify the problem.

   Step 2. Establish a theory of probable cause.

   Step 3. Test the theory to determine the cause.

   Step 4. Establish a plan of action to resolve the problem and implement the solution.

   Step 5. Verify full system functionality and, if applicable, implement preventive measures.

   Step 6. Document findings, actions, and outcomes.

3. A.

   Explanation: Spinning the fan blades with the power off, especially by using compressed air, can damage the fan. The best way to ensure the fan is working is to visually inspect it with the power on.

4. C.

   Explanation After the repairs have been completed, continue the troubleshooting process by verifying full system functionality.

5. B.

   Explanation: A failing power supply could also cause a computer to reboot unexpectedly. If the power cord does not attach properly, then it is likely that the wrong type of power cord is being used.

6. D.

   Explanation: Always perform a backup before beginning any troubleshooting.

7. D.

   Explanation: To remove dust inside a computer, use a can of compressed air.

8. A.

   Explanation: A power supply. A burning electronics smell is often detected when a power supply is overloaded and damaged.

9. C.

   Explanation: When the cause of the problem is determined, a technician should research possible solutions, sometimes by visiting various websites and consulting with manuals.

10. A.

    Explanation: Storage device problems are often related to loose or incorrect cable connections.

11. B.

    Explanation: Preventive maintenance helps reduce software and hardware problems by preventing undue wear on components, thereby extending the life of those components. It also assists in identifying failed components that require replacement, such as cooling fans.

12. B.

    Explanation: Some CPU settings such as speed and voltage can be changed through the system BIOS.

13. B.

    Explanation: A technician should seek to determine the exact cause of a computer problem by testing theories of probable cause one at a time, beginning with the quickest and easiest to eliminate.

14. B.

    Explanation: Hold the fan blades in place when you clean the inside of the computer with compressed air to prevent overspinning the rotor or moving the fan in the wrong direction.

15. A, D.

    Explanation: RAM problems are often caused by faulty RAM modules, loosely seated modules, an inadequate amount of RAM, or compatibility issues.

16. A.

    Explanation: When all repairs have been made, the last step of the troubleshooting process is to verify to the customer the problem and the solutions and demonstrate how the solution corrected the problem.

Chapter 5:

1. C, E.

   Explanation: Network operating systems, sometimes called server operating systems, are designed to support many users who connect to a server over a network. Many network users can access storage and printer resources and can run multiuser applications at the same time. Desktop operating systems can support a limited number of users who access shared resources. However, security and user management functionality is limited. So, although desktop operating systems have limited network sharing capabilities, most businesses will require the use of a network operating system for serious business use.

2. A.

   Explanation: NFS (Network File System) is used to access files on other computers across a network. Windows operating systems support several file systems. FAT, NTFS, and CDFS are used to access files stored on drives installed in the computer.

3. A.

   Explanation: When cloning an operating system to be installed on multiple computers, a technician can use Sysprep to remove undesirable settings that should not be included in the cloned image.

4. B, E.

   Explanation: Two types of computer operating system user interfaces are CLI and GUI. CLI stands for command-line interface. In a command-line interface, a user enters commands at a prompt using a keyboard. The second type is the GUI, or graphical user interface. With this type of user interface, a user interacts with the operating system by working with icons and menus. A mouse, finger, or stylus can be used to interact with a GUI. PnP is the name of a process by which an OS assigns resources to different hardware components of a computer. The other answers are examples of application programming interfaces, or APIs.

5. C.

   Explanation: The registry contains information about applications, users, hardware, network settings, and file types. The registry also contains a unique section for every user, which contains the settings configured by that particular user.

6. B.

   Explanation: Master boot record (MBR) is the boot sector standard that supports a maximum primary partition size of 2TB. MBR allows four primary partitions per drive. The globally unique identifier (GUID) partition table standard (GPT) can support enormous partitions with a theoretical maximum size of 9.4ZB (9.4×10^{24} bytes). GPT supports a maximum of 128 primary partitions per drive.

7. A.

   Explanation: Hard disk drives are organized by several physical and logical structures. Partitions are logical portions of the disk that can be formatted to store data. Partitions consist of tracks, sectors, and clusters. Tracks are concentric rings on the disk surface. Tracks are divided into sectors and multiple sectors are combined logically to form clusters

8. A, B

   Explanation: The Windows Upgrade Advisor is used to run a scan on a system to detect incompatible software and hardware.

Windows Easy Transfer allows a technician to migrate personal files and settings from one computer to another. The Microsoft System Preparation tool is used to prepare an operating system created on a base system to be copied onto multiple computers.

9. C.

   Explanation: A RAID 5 volume creates partitions on multiple redundant hard disk drives. Data is stored in stripes across those disks and a parity check is provided for each stripe. RAID 5 volumes are fault tolerant.

10. C.

   Explanation: Thread is a small piece of a program in execution. Multiprocessing is related to a system with more than one processor. Multiuser is related to a system that supports more than one user at the same time. Multitask is a system that can perform more than one task at the same time.

11. B.

   Explanation: The tracks of a hard drive form complete circles on the disk platter surfaces. The tracks are divided into multiple sectors, and the sectors are grouped into clusters.

12. C.

   Explanation: Pressing the F8 key during the boot process allows the user to choose to start the computer in Safe Mode.

13. A.

   Explanation: Multiprocessing allows an operating system to use two or more CPUs. Support for two or more users is provided by the multiuser feature. Multitasking allows multiple applications to run at the same time. Multithreading allows different parts of the same program to run at the same time.

14. A.

   Explanation: Master boot record (MBR) is the boot sector standard that supports a maximum primary partition size of 2TB. MBR allows four primary partitions per drive.

Chapter 6:

1. B.

   Explanation: The **AT** command is used from a Windows command prompt to schedule commands and programs to run at a specific date and time. Any command followed by **/?** lists the options associated with a particular command.

2. D.

   Explanation: The Windows Task Manager utility includes a Users tab from which the system resources consumed by each user can be displayed.

3. D.

   Explanation: General—Configure basic Internet settings, such as selecting the Internet Explorer (IE) home page, viewing and deleting browsing history, adjusting search settings, and customizing the browser appearance.

   Security—Adjust the security settings for the Internet, local intranet, trusted sites, and restricted sites. Security levels for each zone can range from low (minimal security) to high (maximum security).

   Privacy—Configure privacy settings for the Internet zone, manage location services, and enable the pop-up blocker.

Advanced—Adjust advanced settings, and reset IE's settings to the default state.

4. D.

Explanation: Because the video capture card worked before the OS upgrade, it is most likely that the driver for Windows 7 does not work in Windows 8.1. Because the video card is a third-party product, upgrading the OS or video editing software will not resolve the problem. Instead, updating the driver to a Windows 8.1 version should fix the problem.

5. C.

Explanation: Virtual PC is a Type 2 (Hosted) hypervisor because it is hosted by an operating system and does not run directly on the hardware.

6. A.

Explanation: Each virtual machine runs its own operating system. The number of virtual machines that can be made available depends on the hardware resources of the host machine. Virtual machines are susceptible to threats and malicious attacks, like physical computers. To connect to the Internet, a virtual machine uses a virtual network adapter that acts like a physical adapter in a physical computer, connecting through the physical adapter on the host to establish a connection to the Internet.

7. A.

Explanation: Running Hyper-V on Windows 8 requires a minimum of 4GB of system RAM.

8. C.

Explanation: The Services console in Windows OS allows for the management of all the services on the local and remote computers. The setting of Automatic in the Services console enables the chosen service to start when the computer is started.

9. B, C.

Explanation: Close-ended questions generally have a fixed or limited set of possible responses, such as "yes" or "no." Open-ended questions imply no limited or fixed set of replies but rather generally prompt the responder to provide more meaningful feedback.

10. A, C.

Explanation: Restore points contain information about the system and registry settings that can be used to restore a Windows system back to a previous configuration. Restore points should be created before software is installed or updated. Because restore points do not back up user data, a dedicated backup system should also be implemented to back up data.

11. C, D.

Explanation: During the troubleshooting process, if a quick procedure does not correct the problem, further research should be conducted to identify the exact cause of the problem.

12. C.

Explanation: A PC that shows signs of being slow and having delayed input responses is normally associated with a process or processes using up most of the CPU resources. An incompatible driver would result in an unresponsive device. A recently installed driver incompatible with a boot controller would probably cause the PC to display an "Inaccessible Boot Device" error after the POST.

13. A.

    Explanation: The master boot record (MBR) locates the operating system boot loader. If the MBR is missing or corrupt, then the operating system cannot start.

14. C.

    Explanation: ReadyBoost allows an external flash drive or hard drive to be used as hard drive cache. This is particularly beneficial when the maximum amount of RAM has been installed and performance is suffering.

15. B.

    Explanation: The System Information tool shows the status of various hardware, software, and other computer components on both local and remote computers. Chkdsk is a tool for verifying that the file system is not corrupt. The System Configuration utility allows you to modify the Windows startup process to diagnose problems. Component Services allows you to modify COM components, and Performance Monitor is used to monitor the use of system resources and to troubleshoot performance issues.

16. B.

    Explanation: Task Scheduler allows you to create all kinds of automated tasks in Windows in a graphical user environment

Chapter 7:

1. A.

   Explanation: The IEEE standards describe current Ethernet features. The IEEE standard for Ethernet is 802.3.

2. D.

   Explanation: The color sequence for the wires in the T568B standard are as follows:

   Orange/white
   Orange
   Green/white
   Blue
   Blue/white
   Green
   Brown/white
   Brown

3. C.

   Explanation: A switch maintains a switching table that contains a list of available MAC addresses on the network. The switching table records MAC addresses by inspecting the source MAC address of every incoming frame.

4. B.

   Explanation: When a PC does not have a static IP address or cannot pick one up from a DHCP server, using APIPA Windows automatically assigns the PC an IP address within the range of addresses 169.254.0.0 to 169.254.255.255.

5. C.

   Explanation: Virtual PC is a Type 2 (Hosted) hypervisor because it is hosted by an operating system and does not run directly on the hardware.

6. B.

   Explanation: The OSI model divides network communications into seven layers. It is used to ensure that equipment and applications that are developed by one vendor are compatible with equipment and applications developed by other vendors.

7. B.

   Explanation: Hubs are sometimes called repeaters because they regenerate the signal. All devices connected to the hub share the same bandwidth (unlike a switch, which gives each device dedicated bandwidth).

8. B, D.

   Explanation: The TCP/IP model includes four layers: the application layer, the transport layer, the internet layer, and the network access layer. The functions at each layer include different protocols. The transport layer includes both the TCP and the UDP protocols.

9. B.

   Explanation: The TCP/IP model includes four layers: the application layer, the transport layer, the internet layer, and the network access layer. Each layer supports different protocols and functions. The internet layer supports routing and routing protocols.

10. D.

    Explanation: The proper CIDR notation for a subnet mask of 255.0.0.0 is /8. This is because the /8 indicates that the first eight bits of the subnet mask are set to binary 1.

11. E.

    Explanation: Host is a general term for any device on a network that can send and receive data.

12. C.

    Explanation: A subnet mask of 255.255.0.0 represents sixteen bits in the host portion of the address identified by zeros. Sixteen bits allows for 2^{16} possible host addresses that can used on a network. When calculating USABLE addresses in a subnet for hosts, you subtract 2 (for the network address and the broadcast address).

13. D.

    Explanation: A WAN connects multiple LANs that are in geographically separated locations. A MAN connects multiple LANs in a large campus or in a city. WLAN is a wireless LAN that covers a rather small geographic area.

14. D.

    Explanation: A personal area network (PAN) connects devices, such as mice, keyboards, printers, smartphones, and tablets. These devices are often connected with Bluetooth technology. Bluetooth allows devices to communicate over short distances.

15. B.

    Explanation: There are two rules for IPv6 address compression: Rule 1: leading zeros in any hextet can be removed. Rule 2: contiguous hextets of all zeros can be compressed to a double colon. Rule two can only be applied once.

16. A.

    Explanation: The protocols are associated with the following TCP/IP layers:

    HTTP > application layer
    TCP > transport layer
    IP and ICMP > internet layer

17. D.

    Explanation: Cable television companies and satellite communication systems both use copper or aluminum coaxial cable for connections between devices.

Chapter 8:

1. D.

   Explanation: Dynamic Host Configuration Protocol (DHCP) can be used to allow end devices to automatically configure IP information, such as their IP addresses, subnet masks, DNS servers, and default gateways. The DNS service is used to provide domain name resolution, mapping hostnames to IP addresses. Telnet is a method for remotely accessing a CLI session of a switch or router. Traceroute is a command used to determine the path a packet takes as it traverses the network.

2. D.

   Explanation: The closer to the CO the connection is located, the higher the possible DSL speed.

3. B.

   Explanation: Network preventive maintenance procedures include checking the condition of cables, network devices, servers, and computers to make sure that they are kept clean and are in good working order.

4. D.

   Explanation: A dollar sign ($) at the end of a folder name identifies that folder as an administrative share.

5. B.

   Explanation: Cloud service providers use one or more data centers for services and resources such as data storage. A data center is a data storage facility located inside the company and maintained by the IT staff or leased from a co-location provider where the maintenance can be done by the provider or the corporate IT staff.

6. C.

   Explanation: An IDS system is implemented to passively monitor the traffic on a network. Both IPSs and firewalls actively monitor network traffic and take immediate actions when previously defined security criteria match. A proxy server, when it functions as a firewall, also actively monitors the traffic that travels through it and takes immediate actions.

7. C.

   Explanation: The **nslookup** command was created to allow a user to manually query a DNS server to resolve a given host name. The **ipconfig /displaydns** command only displays previously resolved DNS entries. The **tracert** command was created to examine the path that packets take as they cross a network and can resolve a hostname by automatically querying a DNS server. The **net** command is used to manage network computers, servers, printers, and network drives.

8. A.

   Explanation: The manufacturer maintains up-to-date drivers.

9. B.

   Explanation: Wireless routers use network address translation to translate internal or private addresses into Internet-routable or public addresses.

10. C.

    Explanation: If the LEDs are unlit, it could mean that either the NIC, the switch port, or the cable is faulty. It might also indicate an issue with the NIC configuration. Green or amber lights typically mean that the NIC is functioning correctly. A flashing green or amber light often indicates network activity.

11. A.

    Explanation: This item is based on information contained in the presentation. Routers, switches, and firewalls are infrastructure devices that can be provided in the cloud.

12. C.

    Explanation: Broadband technology uses different frequencies divided into different channels to allow simultaneous transmission of multiple different signals on the same cable. DSL, cable, and satellite are examples of broadband network connections.

13. A, E.

Explanation: In troubleshooting, after data is gathered from the user, the technician must identify the problem.

14. B.

Explanation: Windows Remote Desktop allows a technician to log in to a remote computer through an existing user account. The technician can run programs and view and manipulate files within the system of the remote computer.

15. B, E.

Explanation: Normally, the closer a wireless NIC is to an access point, the faster the connectivity. This problem does not require the network password to be reissued. The combination of the low bandwidth and the intermittent connectivity is pointing towards a weak signal or interference from outside sources.

Chapter 9:

1. B.

Explanation: Some functionality can be added to mobile devices through the use of built-in ports and docking stations.

2. A.

Explanation: AGP, ISA, and EISA are not laptop slots. USB is a port, and PCI is an internal slot, not external. Some laptops contain a PC Card or ExpressCard slots.

3. A, B, E.

Explanation: Laptop computers are more likely to be used in hostile conditions than are desktop computers. Laptop computers are more likely to be dropped or to be a target of spills and other accidents. Having a virus, performance issues, or outdated drivers are failures that are common to both desktop and laptop computers.

4. B.

Explanation: A closed-ended question is one that is used to determine the exact cause of a problem. It focuses on a specific aspect of the problem and is used to establish a theory of probable cause.

5. C.

Explanation: SRAM is not used for desktops or laptops as a RAM module but as L1 cache inside the CPU. SIMMs were replaced by DIMMs on desktops as RAM modules.

6. D.

Explanation: The S4 ACPI state is defined as existing when the CPU and RAM are off and the contents of RAM have been saved to a temporary file on the hard disk. This state is also known as the hibernate mode.

7. B.

Explanation: A Bluetooth Class 1 network has a maximum distance of 100 meters. A Bluetooth Class 2 network has a maximum distance of 10 meters, and a Bluetooth Class 3 network has a maximum distance of 1 meter.

8. C.

Explanation: Some common problems related to the keyboard are caused by having the Num Lock key on. None of the incorrect options are related to the keyboard.

9. B.

Explanation: When the battery does not hold a charge, a battery replacement is needed.

Even though the battery is not good, the peripherals such as hard disks and the screen will turn on as long as the laptop is on.

10. D.

    Explanation: Being proactive in keeping the laptop clean is to anticipate possible accidents such as fluid spills or food drops over the equipment. The incorrect options are scheduled tasks to clean the computer after it gets dirty.

11. D.

    Explanation: At this stage, you are just identifying the problem and not yet in the position to establish a theory of probable causes.

12. A.

    Explanation: Laptop computers use proprietary form factors and therefore they are different from one manufacturer to another.

13. A.

    Explanation: Solid state drives store data in flash memory chips and do not have moving parts found in conventional hard drives, such as a drive head, disk platter, or spindle.

14. C.

    Explanation: CMOS chips and SODIMM memory modules are volatile in nature and will lose information when removed from a power source. An external hard drive has mechanical moving parts.

Chapter 10:

1. C, D, F.

   Explanation: The physical Home button on an iOS device can perform many functions depending on how it is used. Pressing the button while the device screen is turned off wakes the device. While an app is in use, pressing the Home button returns the user to the Home screen. Double-pressing the Home button while the screen is locked shows the audio controls, which makes it possible to adjust music volume without entering a passcode to enter the system.

2. C, D.

   Explanation: Rooting and jailbreaking are the terms that describe unlocking Android and iOS mobile devices to grant users full access to the file system and full access to kernel modules. Remote wipe, sandboxing, and patching are examples of mobile operating system features and functions that are related to device security.

3. A, C.

   Explanation: Mobile devices are frequently fitted with GPS radio receivers, enabling them to calculate their position. Some devices do not have a GPS receiver. Instead, they use information from WiFi and cellular networks.

4. D.

   Explanation: In the Windows Phone interface, apps are represented by tiles. Tiles are not only short cuts to an app. They can display active content and they can be resized to unclutter and visually organize screens.

5. True.

   Explanation: Both the OS X and Android operating systems use the Unix operating software as a base.

6. B, C.

   Explanation: To avoid the loss of irreplaceable information, it is critical that regular backups be executed and that the hard drives be checked regularly. The signature files are scanned constantly by antimalware software. Updating the OS should happen when necessary but should not occur automatically. Because the factory reset of a device deletes all settings and user data, a factory reset should only be done if a major issue requires it.

7. A.

   Explanation: If a problem occurs with an Android device that cannot be solved with a normal power-off and -on, a user can try a reset of the device. Holding the power button and the volume-down key until the device powers off and then powering it back on is one way to reset most Android devices.

8. C, E.

   Explanation: Locator apps and remote backup are two types of cloud-enabled services for mobile devices. Passcode configuration, screen calibration, and screen app locking are performed on the device directly by the user, not as a cloud-enabled service.

9. D.

   Explanation: During the pairing process, a Bluetooth device is set to discoverable mode so as to be detected by another Bluetooth device. Also, a PIN may be requested as part of the pairing process.

10. B.

    Explanation: Because mobile device apps do run in a sandbox (an isolated location) it is difficult for malicious programs to infect the device. The passcode and remote lock features secure the device against unauthorized use. The carrier may disable access to some features and programs based on the service contract, but this a commercial, not a security, function.

11. D.

    Explanation: Most airlines do not permit wireless devices to be used during take-off and landing in case it interferes with airplane systems. Most mobile devices have a setting called Airplane Mode that turns off the WiFi, cellular, and Bluetooth radios while leaving all other functions enabled. This allows a mobile device to be used on an airplane or anywhere else where data transmissions are not permitted.

12. A.

    Explanation: The IMAP protocol allows email data to be synchronized between a client and server. Changes made in one location, such as marking an email as read, are automatically applied to the other location. POP3 is also an email protocol. However, the data is not synchronized between the client and the server. SMTP is used for sending email and is typically used in conjunction with the POP3 protocol. Multipurpose Internet Mail Extension (MIME) is an email standard that is used to define attachment types, and it allows extra content like pictures and documents to be attached to email messages.

13. A, C.

    Explanation: As an open source operating system, Android allows anyone to contribute to the development and evolution of compatible software. Android has been implemented on a wide range of devices and platforms including cameras, smart TVs, and e-book readers. Royalties are not payable to Google, and Google has not tested and approved all available Android applications. Android applications are available from a range of sources.

14. A.

Explanation:

man—displays the documentation for a specific command

ls—displays the files inside a directory

cd—changes the current directory

mkdir—creates a directory under the current directory

cp—copies files from source to destination

mv—moves files to a different directory

rm—removes files

15. B.

Explanation:

man—displays the documentation for a specific command

ls—displays the files inside a directory

cd—changes the current directory

mkdir—creates a directory under the current directory

cp—copies files from source to destination

mv—moves files to a different directory

rm—removes files

16. C.

Explanation:

man—displays the documentation for a specific command

ls—displays the files inside a directory

cd—changes the current directory

mkdir—creates a directory under the current directory

cp—copies files from source to destination

mv— moves files to a different directory

rm—removes files

17. D.

Explanation:

man—displays the documentation for a specific command

ls—displays the files inside a directory

cd—changes the current directory

mkdir—creates a directory under the current directory

cp—copies files from source to destination

mv—moves files to a different directory

rm—removes files

18. E.

Explanation:

man—displays the documentation for a specific command

ls—displays the files inside a directory

cd—changes the current directory

mkdir—creates a directory under the current directory

cp—copies files from source to destination

mv—moves files to a different directory

rm—removes files

Chapter 11:

1. C.

Explanation: Some printers have the capability to perform duplex printing, which is printing on both sides of the paper. IR printing is a form of wireless printing using infrared technology. Buffering is the process of using printer memory to store print jobs. Spooling puts print jobs into a print queue.

2. D.

Explanation: Because multiple jobs can be received by a printer while it is busy printing other documents, these jobs must temporarily be stored until the printer is free to print them. This process is called print buffering.

3. C, E.

Explanation: Using components not recommended by the manufacturer may result in poor print quality and may void the manufacturer warranty. The price and availability of nonrecommended parts may be advantageous, and the cleaning requirements may vary.

4. A.

Explanation: Enabling print sharing allows a computer to share the printer over the network. Installing a USB hub allows a number of peripheral connections to the same computer. Print drivers do not provide the ability to share printers.

5. A.

Explanation: Hardware print servers permit several users to connect to a single printer without the need for a computer to share the printer. USB hubs, LAN switches, and docking stations are incapable of sharing printers.

6. B.

7. B.

Explanation: Before performing maintenance on a printer, or on any computer or peripheral, always disconnect the power source to prevent exposure to dangerous electrical voltages.

8. D.

Explanation: If the printer is connected to the wrong computer port, then the print jobs will appear on the print queue, but documents will not be printed by the printer.

9. A.

Explanation: Inkjet print heads cannot usually be effectively cleaned by physical means. The vendor supplied printer software utility is recommended.

10. B, D.

Explanation: Closed-ended questions require only a yes or no answer that can confirm a fact. Open-ended questions require the user to describe the problem symptoms in detail.

11. A.

Explanation: The more complex the structure of the printout, the more time it takes to print. Photo-quality pictures, high-quality text, and draft text are less complex than digital color photographs.

12. D.

Explanation: Virtual printing sends the print job to a file (.pm, .pdf, .XPS, or an image file) or to a remote destination in the cloud. Connecting a printer to the web using an application such as Google Cloud Print allows virtual printing from any location.

13. C.

Explanation: A printer driver is software that allows a computer and a printer to communicate with each other. Configuration software enables users to set and change printer options. Firmware is a set of instructions stored on the printer that controls how the printer operates. Word processing applications are used to create text documents.

14. D, E.

    Explanation: That other computers are not required to be cabled directly to the printer is an advantage of printer sharing. To share a printer, computers do not need to be running the same operating system, and more than one computer can send print jobs to the shared printer at the same time. However, the computer directly connected to the printer needs to be powered on, even if it's not in use. It uses its own resources to manage all the print jobs coming to the printer.

15. D.

    Explanation: The greater the number of dots per inch, the better the resolution of the picture and therefore the quality of printing.

Chapter 12:

1. C.

   Explanation: The guest account should be used sparingly. Also, restrictions should be applied to the guest account so that the user cannot access data or resources not needed.

2. B, D, E.

   Explanation: Passwords should include both upper- and lowercase letters, numbers, and special characters. They should be at least eight characters in length. In addition, passwords should expire after a period time, such as 90 days, and the reuse of passwords should be limited. In addition, computers should be configured to lock a user out after a series of failed attempts.

3. D.

   Explanation: A social engineer attempts to gain the confidence of an employee and convince that person to divulge confidential and sensitive information, such as usernames and passwords. DDoS attacks, pop-ups, and viruses are all examples of software-based security threats, not social engineering.

4. C.

   Explanation: Encrypting data, keeping software up to date, and the use of personal firewalls are all security precautions, but they will not restrict physical access to secure areas by only authorized people.

5. C.

   Explanation: Port forwarding provides a rule-based method to direct traffic between devices on separate networks. This method provides access to devices across the Internet in a less expensive way than using a DMZ.

6. D, E.

   Explanation: Adding an unauthorized wireless router or access point to a company network is a serious potential security threat. The device should be removed from the network immediately in order to mitigate the threat. In addition, the employee should be disciplined. The company security policy, which employees agree to, should describe penalties for behavior that threatens the security of the company.

7. B.

   Explanation: If a network is experiencing an extremely high volume of traffic, disconnecting a host from the network may confirm that the host is compromised and is flooding traffic onto the network. The other issues are hardware issues and are not typically security-related.

8. B.

   Explanation: The idle timeout and screen lock feature is a great security measure that protects the computer and data accessible through it if the user steps away from the desk for a specified period of time and forgets to lock the computer or log off.

9. B.

Explanation: Smartcard and file system settings do not affect network operation. MAC address settings and filtering may be used to control device network access, but they cannot be used to filter different data traffic types.

10. D.

Explanation: The best description of Trojan horse malware, and what distinguishes it from viruses and worms, is that it appears to be useful software, but it hides malicious code. Trojan horse malware may cause annoying computer problems, but it can also cause fatal problems. Some Trojan horses may be distributed over the Internet, but they can also be distributed by USB memory sticks and other means. Specifically targeted Trojan horse malware can be some of the most difficult malware to detect.

11. C.

Explanation: The last step before documenting findings is to verify full system functionality. Ensuring that all of the applications are working would be an example of verifying functionality. Asking what problem the user is experiencing is part of the first step: identifying the problem. Disconnecting from the network and rebooting in Safe Mode are both examples of the third step: determining an exact cause.

12. D.

Explanation: Spyware normally installs on a system without end-user knowledge and monitors activity on a computer, which can then be sent to the source of spyware. Viruses infect systems and execute malicious code. Worms self-replicate and propagate across networks from a singular host, consuming a lot of bandwidth. Adware is normally distributed through downloaded software and results in the exhibition of several pop-up windows on the system.

13. A.

Explanation: The World Wide Web (HTTP) protocol uses port 80; port 23 is used by Telnet. Successful pings to other devices indicate that the network interface card is working correctly. BIOS and CMOS settings control system hardware functions, not network applications such as the World Wide Web.

14. A.

Explanation: Having an antivirus program on a computer does not protect a PC from virus attacks unless the signature updates are done regularly in order to detect newer and emerging threats. It should be noted that if the signature update lacks a signature for a new threat, the software will be unable to protect against that threat.

15. D.

Explanation: A local user requires the Read permission to backup files, but the Write permission is required to restore files.

Chapter 13:

1. D.

Explanation: A "down" call usually means that a server is not working and the entire office or company is waiting for the problem to be resolved to resume business.

2. B.

   Explanation: A service-level agreement (SLA) defines the level of service that a technician or service provider is obligated to provide to a customer. It outlines responsibilities and liabilities such as when and where service is to be provided, response time guarantees, and the penalties that are applied if the agreement is broken.

3. A.

   Explanation: Volatile data that is contained in cache, RAM, and CPU registers is lost when power is removed from the computer.

4. B, E.

   Explanation: The contents of an SLA usually include the following:

   - response time guarantees (often based on type of call and level of service agreement)
   - equipment and software that is supported
   - where service is provided
   - preventive maintenance
   - diagnostics
   - part availability (equivalent parts)
   - cost and penalties
   - time of service availability (for example, 24×7; Monday to Friday, 8 a.m. to 5 p.m. EST; etc.)

5. C.

   Explanation: The primary responsibility of a level one technician is to gather pertinent information from a customer and to enter that information into a work order or ticket system.

6. B.

   Explanation: The level one technician must be able to translate the description of a customer problem into a succinct sentence or two that is entered into the work order.

7. B.

   Explanation: A call center might exist within a company and offer service to the employees of that company as well as to the customers of that company. Alternatively, a call center might be an independent business that sells computer support as a service to outside customers. In either case, a call center is a busy, fast-paced work environment, often operating 24 hours a day.

8. D.

   Explanation: Unsolicited, chain, and forged emails are unethical, and maybe illegal, and they must not be sent by a technician to a customer.

9. B.

   Explanation: All customer property is important, including files, phone lists, hardware, and other data, and it should be treated with respect. Any data should be considered as private and confidential.

10. D.

    Explanation: It is not permissible to install, copy, or share digital content (including software, music, text, images, and video) in violation of copyright and software agreements or applicable laws. This is legally and ethically wrong.

11. B.

    Explanation: The technician must ask a few questions but without interrupting the customer. It is important that the technician listens patiently and that the customer realizes that the problem is considered important.

12. A, E.

Explanation: Level two technicians are primarily tasked with receiving and working on escalated work orders. Their tasks involve using remote access software to connect to the computer of a customer to perform maintenance and fixes.

13. A, D.

Explanation: Persistent data is data stored on an internal or external hard drive or an optical drive. Data is preserved when the computer is turned off.

14. A.

Explanation: Netiquette is a set of general rules used when communicating with other people over the Internet to ensure that the communications stay professional. Avoiding flames, spam, and writing in capital letters, as well as respecting the privacy of others, are examples of good netiquette.

15. C.

Explanation: The only exception to the rule of interrupting a customer is when the customer is identified as a talkative customer. When a talkative customer is identified, the technician may politely step in and refocus the customer. The customer should not be placed on hold or transferred in an effort to take control. Open-ended questions should be avoided and close-ended questions should be used. Sympathizing with the customer or using industry jargon is not recommended as a method to take control with a talkative customer.

Chapter 14:

1. B.

Explanation: A printer that produces pages with vertical lines or streaks can indicate that the toner is not distributed evenly in the cartridge.

2. B, D.

Explanation: The fact that the web server can be accessed by its IP address indicates that the web server is working and that there is connectivity between the workstation and the web server. However, the web server domain name is not resolving correctly to its IP address. This could be caused by a misconfiguration of the DNS server IP address on the workstation or the wrong entry of the web server in the DNS server.

3. B.

Explanation: An access-denied message occurs when a user lacks the privileges that are required to access a resource. An improperly configured BIOS setting would not block access to files. A firewall has nothing to do with file system access, and TPM is used for secure access to a system.

4. B, F.

Explanation: The message "BOOTMGR is missing" could be a symptom of a missing or damaged BOOTMGR, a boot configuration data file missing or damaged, a boot order not set correctly in BIOS, a corrupted MBR, or a failing hard drive. The fix cannot be done using a regular command because the OS cannot be located to start. The fact that the screen displays an error message indicates that the display card can perform at least basic functions and the error is not related to the display.

5. D.

   Explanation: The failure of a printer to print large or complex images can be an indication that more memory needs to be installed.

6. D.

   Explanation: A password should be used to prevent tampering with the settings within the BIOS of a workstation.

7. D.

   Explanation: When a network device automatically obtains the IP address 169.254.x.x, it is unable to receive an IP address from a DHCP server. The DHCP server should be restarted to ensure that it is operational.

8. A.

   Explanation: A computer that does not recognize an external drive can be an indication that incorrect drivers are installed.

9. C.

   Explanation: The Event Log can be used to research BSOD errors because it records alerts and notifications that occur during OS operations. The BIOS boot sequence indicates the sequence of devices to be searched for booting the OS. Disk Management is used to format and manage storage partitions. The Task Manager monitors and shows the programs, processes, and services that are currently running on the PC.

10. C.

    Explanation: An automatic reboot can occur if a workstation locks up during startup. The continual reboot makes it difficult to see any error messages. To stop the workstation from rebooting, go to the Advanced Startup Options menu and disable the auto restart function. Modifying the boot sequence in BIOS or UEFI changes the search sequence of the devices used to find a bootable partition. Executing a power cycle on the workstation will not help because the problem happens during the startup process. Bad RAM causes POST to fail during startup.

11. B, D.

    Explanation: In most cases, when a computer is moved from one place to another, it needs a new IP address to connect to the network. When the computer is configured with a static IP address, it will not initiate the process of obtaining a new IP address from DHCP servers. Also if a firewall is misconfigured, it may block the DHCP messages. The default gateway being misconfigured would not cause a problem for the workstation trying to connect to the network only when it tries to connect to a device on another network or the Internet. An IP address needs to be unique, and an error would prevent the device from being configured with a duplicate.

12. D.

    Explanation: Open-ended questions are supposed to elicit longer, more detailed responses as opposed to closed-ended questions that can be answered with a yes or no.

13. C.

    Explanation: When RAM fails in a computer, the computer can reboot, lockup, or display error messages such as the blue screen of death (BSOD).

Glossary

This glossary defines many of the terms and abbreviations related to PC hardware and operating systems. It includes the key terms used throughout the book. As with any growing technical field, some terms evolve and take on several meanings. Where necessary, multiple definitions and abbreviation expansions are presented.

10BASE-T A 10-Mb/s baseband Ethernet specification that uses two pairs of Category 3, 4, or 5 twisted-pair cabling. One pair of wires is used to receive data and the other pair is used to transmit data. 10BASE-T, which is part of the IEEE 802.3 specification, has a distance limit of approximately 328 feet (100 m) per segment.

100BASE-T IEEE 802.3 standard that has transfer rate of 100 Mb/s and distance limit of approximately 328 feet (100 m) per segment.

1000BASE-T IEEE 802.3 standard that has transfer rate of 1000 Mb/s or 1 Gb/s and distance limit of approximately 328 feet (100 m) per segment.

10GBASE-T IEEE 802.3 standard that has transfer rate of 10 Gb/s and distance limit of approximately 328 feet (100 m) per segment. It operates in full-duplex only.

A

AC power connector A socket that is used to connect the AC power adapter to a computer or docking station.

accelerometer A sensor in a mobile device that detects the orientation of the device. An example of this technology at work is the auto rotate screen mode.

active partition The operating system uses the active partition to boot the computer.

adapter card An expansion card that increases the number of controllers and ports available on a computer.

address bus The address portion of the collection of wires known as the bus, the address bus carries the memory addresses of the locations where data is read or written by the CPU.

Address Resolution Protocol Provides dynamic address mapping between an IP address and a hardware address.

ad-hoc A WLAN mode that is temporary and created when the WLAN is not using an access point an wireless devices directly communicate with each other. Operating in ad-hoc mode allows all wireless devices within range of each to communicate in peer-to-peer network.

Advanced Configuration and Power Interface (ACPI) An interface that allows the operating system to control power management. Replaces Advanced Power Management (APM).

Advanced Technology (AT) power supply This is the original power supply for legacy computer systems now considered obsolete.

AT Extended (ATX) The updated version of the AT; still considered to be obsolete.

ATX12V This is the most common power supply on the market today. It includes a second motherboard connector to provide dedicated power to the CPU. There are several versions of ATX12V available.

airplane mode A setting on a mobile device that turns off all cellular, WiFi, and Bluetooth radios. Airplane mode is useful when traveling on an airplane or when located where accessing data is prohibited or expensive.

alert badge Apple iOS uses badges displayed as small icons above an application to show that the application needs attending such as a new text message or an application is ready for update.

alternating current (AC) A current that changes direction at a uniformly repetitious rate. This type of electricity typically is provided by a utility company and is accessed by wall sockets.

Android An open source mobile operating system developed by Google.

Android Application Package (APK) An archive format in which Android, applications are packaged.

Android launcher Defines the format of the home screens, the look and feel of its icons, buttons, color scheme, and animations.

Android Studio A Google Software Development Kit (SDK) for Android development. The Android SDK supports several development platforms which include computers running Linux, Mac OS X 10.5.8 or later, and Windows XP or later.

antistatic mat A surface that provides a safe environment for computer components by dissipating ESD.

antistatic wrist strap A device worn on the wrist to dissipate electrostatic discharge (ESD) between a person and electronic equipment.

Apple OS X A proprietary operating system used by Apple computers.

Apps Programs that are executed on mobile devices. Mobile devices come with a number of different apps preinstalled to provide basic functionality.

application programming interface (API) A set of guidelines to ensure a new application is compatible with an OS.

Aero a Windows 7 and Vista theme with translucent window borders, numerous animations, and icons that are thumbnail images of the contents of a file.

aspect ratio The horizontal to vertical measurement of the viewing area of a monitor.

asymmetric DSL (ADSL) Currently the most common DSL implementation. Speeds vary from 384 Kb/s to more than 6 Mb/s downstream. The upstream speed is usually lower.

audio and video editing workstation This type of workstation is used during many stages of development when creating audio and video material.

authentication A means used to verify the identity of the users. Authentication occurs when users enter a username and password to access a user account.

authentication services (AAA) Access to network devices is typically controlled through authentication, authorization, and accounting services. Referred to as AAA or "triple A," these services provide the primary framework to set up access control on a network device.

auto restart function When the system locks up during startup, the computer can automatically reboot. The reboot is caused by the auto restart function in Windows.

Automatic Repair This tool scans the system and tries to automatically repair issues that can prevent Windows from booting properly.

B

backlight Supplies the main source of light to the screen of the laptop display. Without it the image on the screen would not be visible. The backlight shines through the screen and illuminates the display. Two common types of backlights are cold cathode fluorescent lamp (CCFL) and LED.

backoff algorithm Calculates random times in which the end station tries transmitting again. This random time is typically in 1 or 2 milliseconds (ms). This sequence occurs every time there is a collision on the network and can reduce Ethernet transmission by up to 40 percent.

Backup and Restore A Windows 7 and earlier tool that allows you to back up your files, or create and use a system image backup, or repair disc.

backup app An application used for data and system backups. Mobile devices provide a means to centrally store information through the use of backup client software that stores data remotely on the cloud.

Backup utility Allows users to access backup settings and create schedules for backups.

Bad Sector Check Using a disk utilities tool to search, detect, flag bad sectors, and attempt to salvage data stored in bad sectors by moving it to healthy disk sectors.

bandwidth The amount of data that can be transmitted within a fixed amount of time.

base station A device that attaches a laptop to AC power and to desktop peripherals.

basic disk Contains primary and extended partitions, in addition to logical drives.

basic input/output system (BIOS) A program stored in a ROM chip in the computer that provides the basic code to control the computer's hardware and to perform diagnostics on it. The BIOS prepares the computer to load the operating system.

battery Allows the laptop to function when it is disconnected from an external power source.

battery latch A tool used to insert, remove, and secure the laptop battery.

beep codes An audible reporting system for errors that are found by the BIOS during the POST, represented by a series of beeps.

blackout A complete loss of AC power.

blue screen of death (BSOD) A stop error that causes the system to lock up because of a hardware or software malfunction. The BSOD appears when the system is unable to recover from an error.

Bluetooth A wireless industry standard that uses an unlicensed radio frequency for short-range communication, enabling portable devices to communicate over short distances.

Bluetooth pairing When two Bluetooth devices establish a connection to share resources. For the devices to pair, the Bluetooth radios are turned on, and one device begins searching for other devices. Other devices must be set to discoverable mode, also called visible, so that they can be detected.

boot order Shortly after completing POST, the computer attempts to load the operating system. The boot order list, or boot sequence, is an ordered list of devices from which the computer is allowed to boot.

BOOTP Enables a diskless workstation to discover its own IP address, the IP address of a BOOTP server on the network, and a file to be loaded into memory to boot the machine

bridge Segments network traffic by filtering and forwarding packets based on MAC addresses.

broadband Multiple signals using multiple frequencies over one cable.

brownout A temporary drop in AC power.

built-in LCD Similar to a desktop LCD monitor, except that you can adjust the resolution, brightness, and contrast settings using software or button controls. You cannot adjust the laptop monitor for height and distance because it is integrated into the lid of the case.

C

cable Connects one computer to the next.

cable Internet connection This does not use does not use telephone lines. Cable uses coaxial cable lines originally designed to carry cable television. A cable modem connects your computer to the cable company.

cable tester A device that checks for wiring shorts or faults, such as wires connected to the wrong pin.

cache A data storage area that provides high-speed access for the system.

capture card Capture cards send a video signal to a computer so that the signal can be recorded to the computer hard drive with Video Capture software.

card key Secures physical areas. Card keys can be easily activated and deactivated.

carrier sense multiple access collision detect (CSMA/CD) An access control method that allows any end station to send a message at any time, assuming it first listened and heard no other end station transmitting. If two end stations send at the same time and the collision is detected, a jam signal is sent and every host stops sending. Each end station must wait a number of milliseconds before it can transmit again. That wait time can be randomly assigned or based on the MAC address, depending on the specific protocols.

carrier sense multiple access with collision avoidance (CSMA/CA) An access control method that does not detect collisions but attempts to avoid them by waiting before transmitting. Each device that transmits includes in the frame the time duration that it needs for the transmission. All other wireless devices receive this information and know how long the medium will be unavailable.

cathode ray tube (CRT) An older display technology that uses electron beams to light up colored phosphor dots on the screen. The combination of light and dark areas on the screen creates the image.

CAx workstation A workstation used to design products and control the manufacturing process.

cellular data network A wide-area network that has the technology for the use of a cell phone or laptop for voice and data communications.

cellular technology Enables the transfer of voice, video, and data. With a cellular WAN adapter installed, a user can access the Internet over the cellular network.

cellular WAN A wide-area network that has the technology for the use of a cell phone or laptop for voice and data communications.

central processing unit (CPU) Interprets and processes software instructions and data. Located on the motherboard, the CPU is a chip contained on a single integrated circuit called the microprocessor. Most calculations take place in the CPU.

Charms bar A GUI element in Windows 8.x that is a vertical bar with a set of shortcuts to common tasks: Search, Start, Share, Devices, and Settings.

chipset Chips on a motherboard that enable the CPU to communicate and interact with the computer's other components.

chkdsk A command used to check the integrity of files and folders on a hard drive by scanning the disk surface for physical errors.

Classless Inter-Domain Router (CIDR) CIDR also called *supernetting*, a way to aggregate multiple Internet addresses of the same class.

client-server network The client requests information or services from the server. The server provides the requested information or service to the client

clock speed The speed at which data travels through the bus. This is measured in megahertz (MHz) or gigahertz (GHz).

closed source The source code is not released to the public.

closed-ended questions Questions that generally require a yes or no answer. These questions are intended to get the most relevant information in the shortest time.

Cloud computing Typically, an off-premise service that offers on-demand access to a shared pool of configurable computing resources. These resources can be rapidly provisioned and released with minimal management effort.

cloud services model National Institute of Standards and Technology (NIST) Special Publication 800-145 defines a model that consists of five characteristics, three service models and four deployment models.

cloud storage Online storage that is accessed via the Internet.

cluster Also called a *file allocation unit*. Smallest unit of space used for storing data and made up of one or more sectors.

coaxial cable Copper-cored cable surrounded by a heavy shielding. Used to connect computers in a network.

cold boot To turn on the computer from a powered-down state.

command-line interface (CLI) An interface, such as a DOS prompt, that requires commands to be entered manually on the command line.

compact disc file system (CDFS) A file system created specifically for optical disk media.

complementary metal-oxide semiconductor (CMOS) A type of semiconductor, or low-power memory firmware, that stores basic configuration information.

complex instruction set computer (CISC) This CPU architecture uses a broad set of instructions, which requires fewer steps per operation.

Component Services An administrative tool in Windows used by administrators and developers to deploy, configure, and administer Component Object Model (COM) components.

computer case The enclosure that contains and protects the computer components.

Computer Management A management console utility that allows a user to manage many aspects of a computer.

conduit A casing that protects the infrastructure media from damage and unauthorized access.

contrast ratio The measurement of difference in intensity of light between the brightest point (white) and the darkest point (black).

Control Panel The centralized configuration area in Windows and is where settings for the system can be modified. It is used to make modifications and control tasks for almost every aspect of the hardware and software including OS functions.

Control Panel applets A collection of programs and utilities that can be used to configure the operating system.

Converter This performs the same function as an adapter but also translates the signals from one technology to the other. For example, a USB 3.0 to SATA converter enables a hard disk drive to be used as a flash drive.

Cortana Windows Phone 8.1 and later digital assistant, a program that can understand natural conversational language and perform tasks for the end user.

CPU throttling Manually setting the CPU to run slower, usually to conserve power or reduce heat.

critical battery level Low battery warning with an alarm that is set to warn the user to connect the portable device to a power source very soon or risk a shutdown and potentially the loss of data. The default for critical battery level is 5 percent. You can also set the type of notification and the action to take, such as whether to sleep, hibernate, or shut down the laptop when the battery capacity reaches the specified level.

cron service Responsible for scheduled tasks in Linux and OS X operating systems As a service, cron runs in the background and executes tasks at specific dates and times as determined by the administrator.

crossover cable Uses both wiring schemes, T568A on one end of the cable and T568B on the other end of the same cable.

crosstalk Interfering energy, such as electromagnetic interference (EMI), that is transferred from one circuit to another.

current The movement of electrons.

customer-replaceable unit (CRU) A component that customers may install at their location.

cylinder A stack of tracks lined up one on top of another to form a cylinder shape.

D

data backup Information on a computer stored on removable backup media that can be kept in a safe place or cloud storage. If the computer hardware fails, the data backup can be restored so that processing can continue.

data bus The data portion of the collection of wires known as the bus. The data bus carries data between the computer components.

data center Areas located on premise of an organization used to manage the storage and data access needs of the organization. In these single tenant data centers, the enterprise is the only customer or tenant using the data center services.

data object A program element that allows you to make manual changes to a program so that it works better, or in a different way.

data migration The process of transferring data between data storage systems, data formats or computer systems. When a new installation is required, user data must be migrated from the old OS to the new one.

data synchronization The exchange of data between two or more devices while maintaining consistent data on those devices.

DC jack Receives power from a laptop's AC/DC power converter and supplies the power to the system board.

default gateway A node or router on a network that provides access to another network or the Internet.

Defrag Disk Defragmenter gathers fragmented data that is spread over the clusters in the hard drive and puts them in one place on the drive, increasing speed and efficiency.

defragmentation Consolidates files for faster access, and disk error checking, which scans the hard drive for file structure errors.

Déjà Dup A backup tool available for Linux.

destination port number UDP or TCP port number associated with the destination application on the remote device.

desktop operating system Intended for use in a small office, home office (SOHO) environment with a limited number of users.

device driver A program that allows the operating system to access and communicate with a hardware component.

Device Manager An application that displays a list of all the hardware that is installed on the system.

device tracking Locates the device on a map if it is lost or stolen.

digital assistant (virtual assistant) A program that can understand natural conversational language and perform tasks for the end user.

Digital Light Processing (DLP) A technology used in projectors that uses a spinning color wheel and an array of mirrors to project an image.

digital multimeter A device that can take many types of measurements. It tests the integrity of circuits and the quality of electricity in computer components.

digital subscriber line (DSL) A public network technology that delivers high bandwidth over conventional copper wiring at limited distances. Always-on technology that allows users to connect to the Internet.

Digital Visual Interface (DVI) port A digital video port that allows backward compatibility to analog video signals. It can transmit very large amounts of data and is often used for applications that require a large monitor resolution.

direct current (DC) Current flowing in one direction, as used in a battery.

DirectX A collection of APIs related to multimedia tasks for Microsoft Windows.

disk cloning Copying the contents of an entire hard drive to another hard drive, thereby decreasing the time it takes to install drivers, applications, updates, and so forth on the second drive.

Disk Error-Checking tool Checks the integrity of files and folders by scanning the hard disk surface for physical errors.

Disk Format Before a partition can be used by the user or the system, it must be formatted.

Disk Management A system utility used to manage hard drives and partitions, such as initializing disks, creating partitions, and formatting partitions.

display colors Specifies the number of colors visible on the screen at one time. The more bits, the greater the number of colors.

DisplayPort An interface for digital displays, particularly computer monitors. as a high-performance replacement for other display modes such as VGA (Video Graphics Array) and DVI (Digital Visual Interface).

docking station A device that attaches a laptop to AC power and desktop peripherals.

docking station connector The port through which a laptop connects to a docking station. Details regarding the shape and design of docking station connectors vary widely among manufacturers.

domain A logical group of computers and electronic devices with a common set of rules and procedures administered as a unit.

Domain Name System (DNS) A system that provides a way to map friendly hostnames, or URLs, to IP addresses.

dot pitch The distance between pixels on the screen.

Double Data Rate (DDR) RAM that reads on the rising and on the falling side of the clock cycle, thereby doubling the access speed. Normal SDRAM is read once per clock cycle.

Double Data Rate 2 (DDR2) DDR RAM with a modified bus speed that allows RAM to be read four times every clock cycle.

Double Data Rate 3 (DDR3) DDR RAM that expands memory bandwidth by doubling the clock rate of DDR2.

Double Data Rate 4 SDRAM (DDR4 SDRAM) This memory technology quadruples DDR3 maximum storage capacity, requires 40 percent less power due to it using a lower voltage and has advanced error correction features.

double touch Mobile devices can detect when two or more points of contact are made on the screen. For example, for zoom items such as photographs, maps, and text, touch the screen twice quickly to zoom in, and touch the screen twice quickly again to zoom out.

drive mapping Assigning letter names to physical or logical drives in Windows.

dual channel This memory technology adds a second channel to single channel to be able to access a second RAM module at the same time.

dual in-line memory module (DIMM) A circuit board that holds SDRAM, DDR SDRAM, DDR2 SDRAM, and DDR3 SDRAM chips.

dual voltage power supply A power supply that has a small switch on the back that allows input voltage to be selected it can be set to either 110/115v or 220/230v.

Duplex Multimode LC Connector A fiber optical cable connector that Is a duplex connector

DxDiag A tool used to test video and sound cards as well as the functionality of DirectX.

dynamic disk The ability to create volumes instead of partitions that can span across more than one disk.

Dynamic Host Configuration Protocol (DHCP) A software utility that automatically assigns IP addresses to client devices in a large network.

dynamic link library (DLL) Consists of program code that can be used by different programs to perform common functions.

dynamic RAM (DRAM) RAM that stores information in capacitors that must be periodically refreshed with pulses of electricity in order to maintain the data stored on the chip.

E

electromagnetic interference (EMI) The intrusion of outside electromagnetic signals in a transmission media, such as copper cabling. In a network environment, EMI distorts the signals so that the receiving devices have difficulty interpreting them.

Electronic capacitors electrical components found inside a power supply that can hold a charge for extended periods of time.

electronic reader (e-reader) A device optimized for reading electronic books, e-books, newspapers, and other documents. They have WiFi or cellular connectivity to download content. An e-reader has a similar form factor as a tablet, but the screen provides much better readability, especially in sunlight.

electronically erasable programmable read-only memory (EEPROM) Also called *flash ROM*, an EEPROM chip can be erased and rewritten without having to remove the chip from the computer.

electrostatic discharge (ESD) The discharge of static electricity from one conductor to another conductor of a different potential.

email clients Utilized by users to compose, read and manage their messages. Email clients can be web-based or standalone applications. Standalone email clients are platform dependent.

email protocol Interactions between email servers and clients are governed by email protocols and different protocols provide different email services.

email server Responsible for forwarding email messages sent by their users.

Embedded MultiMediaCard (eMMC) Although slower and less expensive than SSD, eMMC is very popular in cell phones, PDAs, and digital cameras.

encapsulation Source data has header control information from successive layers added to it before transmission across a network.

EPS12V A type of power supply that was originally designed for network servers but is now commonly used in high-end desktop models.

erasable programmable read-only memory. (EPROM) Information is written to an EPROM chip after it is manufactured and the chip can be erased with exposure to UV light by using special equipment.

error-correcting code (ECC) Technology that can detect multiple bit errors in memory and correct single bit errors in memory.

Ethernet A baseband LAN specification invented by Xerox Corporation and developed jointly by Xerox, Intel, and Digital Equipment Corporation. Ethernet networks use CSMA/CD and run on a variety of cable types at 10 Mb/s or more. Ethernet is similar to the IEEE 802.3 series of standards.

Ethernet port An RJ-45 socket that is used to connect a computer to a cabled LAN.

EUCIP (European Certification of Informatics Professionals) IT Administrator program that offers a recognized certification of competence in IT. The certification covers the standards prescribed by the Council of European Professional Informatics Societies (CEPIS).

Event Viewer An application that monitors system events, application events, and security events.

exFAT (FAT 64) A file system created to address some of the limitations of FAT, FAT32, and NTFS when formatting USB flash drives, such as file size and directory size.

expansion slots Slots on the motherboard where a PC adapter card can be inserted to add capabilities to the computer.

extended partition The second partition on a hard drive. This partition can be separated into logical drives.

external diskette drive connector A port that connects older laptops to floppy disk drives.

External Serial ATA (eSATA) Provides a hot-swappable external interface for SATA drives.

F

factory recovery partition A partition that contains an image of the bootable partition created when the computer was built.

fiber broadband Delivers faster connection speeds and bandwidth than cable modems, DSL, and ISDN. Fiber broadband can deliver a multitude of digital services, such as telephone, video, data, and video conferencing simultaneously.

field-replaceable unit (FRU) A component that should be replaced rather than repaired, by the user or a trained service technician, rather than sending the entire device back to the manufacturer.

File Allocation Table, 32-bit (FAT32) A table that the operating system uses to store information about the location of the files stored on a disk. Used by Windows XP and earlier OS versions.

File Explorer A file management application in Windows 8. It allows you to navigate the file system and manage the folders, subfolders, and applications on your storage media.

file system Provides the directory structure that organizes the user's operating system, application, configuration, and data files.

File Transport Protocol A reliable, connection-oriented, and acknowledged file delivery protocol. Sets rules that enable a user on one host to access and transfer files to and from another host over a network

File Transfer Protocol Secure (FTPS) An FTP client can request the file transfer session be encrypted using Transport Layer Security (TLS). The file server can accept or deny the request.

Finder The default file manager and graphical user interface shell used on all Macintosh operating systems.

FireWire (i.LINK or IEEE 1394) A high-speed hot-swappable interface that connects peripheral devices to a computer flash drive.

firmware A type of software designed to provide low-level functionality for a device.

fitness monitors Designed to clip onto clothing or be worn on the wrist. They are used for tracking a person's daily activity and body metrics as they work toward their fitness goals. These devices measure and collect activity data. They can also connect with other Internet-connected devices to upload the data for later review. Some fitness monitors may also have basic smartwatch capabilities, such as displaying caller ID and text messages.

flash card A data storage device that uses flash memory to store information. Flash cards are small, portable, and require no power to maintain data.

flash card reader A device that reads flash cards. Most modern laptops feature a flash card reader for Secure Digital (SD) and Secure Digital High Capacity (SDHC) flash cards.

flash drive Also known as a *thumb drive*, is a removable storage device that connects to a USB port. An external flash drive uses the same type of nonvolatile memory chips as a solid state drive (SSD).

flash memory chips A rewritable memory chip that retains data after the power is turned off.

form-factor The physical size and shape of computer components.

format To prepare a hard drive to store information.

frame rate The frame rate refers to how often a video source can feed an entire frame of new data to a display. A monitor's refresh rate in Hz directly equates to the maximum frame per second (FPS) of that monitor. For example, a monitor with a refresh rate of 144 Hz will display a maximum of 144 frames per second.

front-side bus (FSB) The front-side bus is the path between the CPU and the Northbridge. It is used to connect various components, such as the chipset and expansion cards.

full-duplex transmission Data transmission that can go two ways at the same time. An Internet connection using DSL service is an example.

full format Removes files from the partition while scanning the disk for bad sectors.

function key (Fn key) A modifier key usually found on laptop computers. It is used in combination with other keys to perform specific functions.

G

geocaching A mapping app that shows the location of geocaches (hidden containers) around the world. Users find them and often sign a logbook to show that they found it.

geotagging Embeds location information into a digital object, like a photograph or a video, to record where it was taken.

gestures Using the multi-touch function on a mobile device touchscreen to perform certain function such as slide, double touch, long touch, and scroll.

global positioning system (GPS) A navigation system that determines the time and location on Earth using messages from satellites in space and a receiver on Earth.

Gnome-keyring A security credentials manager for Ubuntu Linux.

Google Now Launcher Created by Google, this launcher comes installed by default in Nexus devices, which are one of Android's digital assistants.

globally unique identifier (GUID) partition table (GPT) Designed as a partition table scheme standard for hard drives makes use of a number of modern techniques to expand on the older MBR partitioning scheme. GPT is commonly used in computers with UEFI firmware.

graphical user interface (GUI) An interface that allows the user to navigate through the operating system using icons and menus.

grub A popular boot manager for Linux.

H

half-duplex transmission Data transmission that can go two ways, but not at the same time. A two-way radio is an example.

hard disk drive (HDD) A device that stores and retrieves data from magnetic-coated platters that rotate at high speeds. The HDD is the primary storage medium on a computer.

hard drive access panel The panel that allows access to a hard drive in a laptop.

hardware Physical electronic components that make up a computer system.

hardware firewall A freestanding hardware device that inspects data packets from the network before they reach computers and other network devices.

headphone connector Also called a *headphone jack*. Allows audio output for headphones.

hibernate A power level in which the computer is essentially off. RAM is copied to the hard drive so the computer does not need send power to RAM. It is very efficient but takes longer to recover from hibernate than from standby.

hidden shares Created by Windows XP, 7, 8 and later operating systems that allow remote access to every disk volume on a network-connected system are identified with a dollar sign ($) at the end of the share name. You must have administrative privileges to access.

history of repairs A detailed list of problems and repairs, including the date, replacement parts, and customer information. The history allows a technician to determine what work has been performed on a specific computer in the past.

home screen Multiple screens organized for easy access to icons and widgets. These screens can be customized to user preference.

HomeGroup Allows computers on the same home network to automatically share files and printers.

Home Network One of three windows network location profiles. Choose this network location for home networks or when you trust the people and devices on the network.

home theater personal computer A specialized PC system used to control high-quality video and audio systems.

horizontal, vertical, and color resolution The number of pixels in a line is the horizontal resolution. The number of lines in a screen is the vertical resolution. The number of colors that can be reproduced is the color resolution.

host A computer system on a network. Similar to the term node, except that host usually implies a computer system. Node generally applies to any networked system, including access servers and routers.

hot-swappable A device peripheral or component that can be removed or added while a computer is running.

hub Extends the range of a network by receiving data on one port and then regenerating the data and sending it out to all other ports.

Hypertext Transport Protocol (HTTP) A set of rules for exchanging text, graphic images, sound, video, and other multimedia files on the World Wide Web. HTTP operates on port 80.

secure HTTP (HTTPS) HTTP is a set of rules for exchanging text, graphic images, sound, and video on the World Wide Web. HTTPS adds encryption and authentication services using Secure Sockets Layer (SSL) protocol or the newer Transport Layer Security (TLS) protocol. HTTPS operates on port 443.

hyperthreading When multiple pieces of code (threads) are executed simultaneously in the CPU.

hypertransport Used to enhance CPU performance, a high-speed, low-latency connection between the CPU and the Northbridge chip.

hypervisor The software that creates and manages a virtual machine on a host.

I

iOS A closed-source OS developed by Apple.

Intermediate Distribution Facility (IDF) The network drop locations on each floor connect to the IDF and this is where you can connect your networking equipment and feed it back to your MDF when the cable exceeds the distance limitation of cable segment.

In-Plane switching (IPS) A common technology used in the manufacturing of LCD displays. IPS displays offer better color reproduction and better viewing angles.

infrared port A line-of-sight wireless transceiver that is used for data transmission.

infrared (IR) wireless technology Electromagnetic waves whose frequency range is above that of microwaves but below that of the visible spectrum. LAN systems based on this technology represent an emerging technology.

infrastructure as a service (IaaS) The cloud provider is responsible for access to the network equipment, virtualized network services, and supporting network infrastructure.

infrastructure mode One of the modes that WLANs operate requires wireless clients to connect to a wireless router or access point, which provides access to the rest of the network.

input devices An input device enters data or instructions into a computer. Typical input devices are keyboards and mice.

input/output (I/O) ports Connects peripheral devices, such as displays, printers, scanners, portable drives, and audio devices. They also connect the computer to network resources, such as modems or external network drives.

Integrated Services Digital Network (ISDN) A communication protocol, offered by telephone companies, that permits telephone networks to carry data, voice, and other source traffic.

Interlace/Non-Interlace Interlaced monitors create the image by scanning the screen two times. The first scan covers the odd lines, top to bottom, and the second scan covers the even lines. Non-interlaced monitors create the image by scanning the screen, one line at a time from top to bottom.

Interface Drivers Provides instruction to a machine for the control of a specific interface on a network device.

Internet Control Message Protocol (ICMP) Used for network testing and troubleshooting, ICMP enables diagnostic and error messages. The ping utility uses ICMP echo messages to determine whether a remote device can be reached.

Internet Message Access Protocol (IMAP) Used by local email clients to synchronize and retrieve email from a server and leave email on the server.

Internet email Refers to an email service that is hosted somewhere on the Internet and controlled by a third-party team of administrators.

Internet port An Ethernet port that is used to connect the router to a service provider device such as a broadband DSL or cable modem.

IT as a service (ITaaS) The cloud provider is responsible for IT support for IaaS, PaaS, and

SaaS service models. In the ITaaS model, an organization contracts with the Cloud provider for individual or bundled services.

Intrusion detection systems (IDSs) Passively monitor traffic on the network. Standalone.

intrusion prevention system Actively monitors traffic on the network identifies potential threats, and responds to them swiftly.

inverter Converts DC power to the higher voltage AC power that is required by the backlight.

iOS Home button Apple iOS navigation button that allows a user to perform a variety of functions such as, wake the device, start Siri, open Search, and more.

ipconfig A command-line utility used to verify that a NIC has a valid IP address.

IPv4 Fourth version of development of Internet Protocol (IP) consists of a series of 32 binary bits (1s and 0s).

IPv6 Latest revision of the Internet Protocol (IP), it is a three-part hierarchy consisting of 128 bits. It is intended to replace IPv4.

International Mobile Equipment Identity (IMEI) Every mobile device has a unique 15-digit number. This number identifies the device to a carrier's network. The numbers come from a family of devices called the Global System for Mobile Communications (GSM).

J

jailbreaking A hack that involves unlocking the bootloader and giving iPhone users access to the underlying operating system of iOS and opens the phone to customization that is not normally available to the user.

Java APIs A collection of APIs related to the development of Java programming.

K

kernel Responsible for allocating CPU time and memory to processes. It also manages the file system and communications in response to system calls.

keyboard port A PS/2 socket used to connect older keyboards to the computer.

keyed connectors Connectors that are designed to be inserted in one direction only.

KVM switch A hardware device that can be used to control more than one computer while using a single keyboard, monitor, and mouse.

L

L1 cache Internal cache; is integrated into the CPU.

L2 cache External cache; was originally mounted on the motherboard near the CPU. L2 cache is now integrated into the CPU.

L3 cache Used on some high-end workstations and server CPUs.

Land Grid Array (LGA) In LGA architecture, the pins are in the CPU socket instead of on the processor.

LAN A network that encompasses a small geographical area typically owned by an individual, such as in a home or small business, or wholly managed by an IT department, such as in a school or corporation. This individual or group enforces the security and access control policies of the network.

laptop A small form-factor computer designed to be mobile. Operates much the same as a desktop computer. Laptop hardware is proprietary and usually is more expensive than desktop hardware.

laptop latch A lever used to open the laptop lid.

Last Known Good Configuration Loads the configuration settings that were used the last time that Windows started successfully. It does this by accessing a copy of the registry that is created for this purpose.

latency The amount of time it takes data to travel from source to destination.

LC connector A snap-in connector that latches with a simple push-pull motion.

LCD cutoff switch A small pin on the laptop cover contacts a switch when the case is closed and helps conserve power by extinguishing the backlight and turning off the LCD when the laptop is closed.

LCD monitor An output device that passes polarized light through liquid crystals using cold cathode fluorescent lamp (CCFL) backlighting to produce images on the screen.

light-emitting diode (LED) An LCD display that uses LED backlighting to light the display.

Lightning connector Allows Apple mobile devices to connect to host computers and other peripherals, such as USB battery chargers, monitors, and cameras.

liquid crystal display (LCD) Commonly used in flat panel monitors, laptops, and some projectors, it consists of two polarizing filters with a liquid crystal solution between them.

LED monitors An output device that uses light emitting diodes replacing the cold cathode fluorescent lamps (CCFL) for the backlighting while using an LCD screen.

line-in connector Allows audio input from pre-amplified sources like iPods.

line of sight A characteristic of certain transmission systems such as laser, microwave, and infrared systems in which no obstructions in a direct path between transmitter and receiver can exist.

Linux A popular open source version of UNIX that offers a much more user-friendly GUI than previous versions of UNIX offered.

lithium-ion (Li-Ion) battery A lightweight battery for the power that has no memory effect so the battery can be recharged before completing discharging. Li-Ion batteries can easily overheat, so should be kept cool, and can degrade quickly, so they have a short lifespan of two to three years.

lithium-polymer (Li-Poly or LiPo) A battery that can charge quickly and hold the charge for long period. A LiPo battery has no memory effect, so the battery can be recharged before completing discharging it.

locator app An app used for remotely locating a mobile device.

logical drive A logical drive is a section of an extended partition.

LoJack A security feature that consists of two programs: the Persistence Module, which is embedded in the BIOS, and the Application Agent, installed by the user.

Long-Term Evolution (LTE) A 4G wireless broadband technology that supports mixed data, voice, video, and messaging traffic.

long touch A gesture used on Android mobile devices; when a user presses on an application icon for a few seconds, that allows the application to be moved to the desktop, and long touches on the desktop clock allow you to remove it.

loopback adapter Also called a *loopback plug*, tests the basic functionality of computer ports. The adapter is specific to the port that you want to test.

low battery warning An alarm warning the user to connect the portable device to a power source.

M

MAC address A physical address that is hard coded onto the network interface card (NIC) by the manufacturer. The address stays with the device regardless of what network the device is connected to. A MAC address is 48 bits and represented in hexadecimal format.

magic packet Wake on LAN message that is sent to the NIC, it contains the MAC address of the NIC it intends to wake.

main distribution facility (MDF) A building's primary communications room. Also, the central point of a star networking topology, where patch panels, hubs, and routers are located. Can connect to an IDF, or intermediate distribution facility.

master boot record (MBR) Contains information on how the hard drive partitions are organized.

material safety data sheet (MSDS) A fact sheet that summarizes information about material identification, including hazardous ingredients that can affect personal health, fire hazards, and first-aid requirements.

media reader A device that reads and writes to different types of media cards.

medium (media) Provides the channel over which the message travels from source to destination.

memory modules Special circuit boards with memory chips soldered on to them.

memory card A memory card (sometimes called a *flash memory card* or a *storage card*) is a small storage medium used to store data such as text, pictures, audio, and video, for use on small, portable or remote computing devices.

Messaging Application Programming Interface (MAPI) A proprietary messaging MAPI is used by Microsoft Office Outlook to connect to Exchange servers, to provide email, calendar, and contact management.

metropolitan-area network (MAN) A network that spans across a large campus or a city. The network consists of various buildings interconnected through wireless or fiber-optic backbones.

Metro-style apps (Windows Store) Microsoft launched its application store in 2012. Starting with Windows 8 and Windows Server 2012, the Windows Store allows Windows users to search, download, and install Windows Store Apps.

microphone jack A socket used to connect a microphone used for audio input.

Micro/Mini universal serial bus (USB) connectors USB connectors that can charge a device and transfer data between devices.

microsegmenting Switches filter and segment network traffic by sending data only to the device to which it is sent. This provides higher dedicated bandwidth to each device on the network.

Microsoft Exchange A mail server, contact manager, and calendaring software created by Microsoft.

Microsoft System Preparation (Sysprep) A tool to install and configure the same OS on multiple computers. *See* disk cloning.

Mini-PCI Commonly used by older laptops. Mini-PCI cards have 124 pins and are capable of 802.11a, 802.11b, and 802.11g wireless LAN connection standards.

Mini-PCIe Most common type of wireless card in laptops. Mini-PCIe cards have 54 pins and support all wireless LAN standards.

mirroring RAID method that duplicates data on a second drive.

mobile device Any device that is hand-held, lightweight, and typically has a touchscreen for input.

mobile hotspot A hotspot is where devices connect using WiFi to share a cellular data connection.

Mobile WiMAX A wireless standard that provides ultra-broadband Internet access. Even though Mobile WiMAX and LTE fall short of the data rate to be compliant with 4G (128 Mb/s and 100 Mb/s, respectively), they are still considered 4G standards because they offer so much improvement over the performance of 3G.

modem A device that converts digital computer signals into a format that is sent and received over an analog telephone line.

modem port An RJ-11 jack that connects a computer to a standard telephone line. The modem port can be used to connect the computer to the Internet to send and receive fax documents and to answer incoming calls.

monitor resolution Refers to the level of image detail that can be reproduced.

mounted drive Mapping an empty folder to a volume. These are assigned drive paths instead of a drive letter.

mount or unmount disk partitions On Unix-like systems, mounting a partition relates to the process of binding a partition of a disk or a disk image file (usually an .iso) to a folder location. This is a common task in Unix-like systems.

mouse port A PS/2 socket that is used to attach an external mouse.

Msconfig A Windows utility designed to aid in troubleshooting the operating system. Allows the user to edit start-up applications and access the BOOT.INI, SYSTEM.INI, and WIN.INI files.

Msinfo32 The filename of System Information utility. It provides very detailed information about the hardware, OS, and key applications.

multiboot The capability for installing two or more operating system.

Multicore processors Two or more processors on the same integrated circuit is recommended for applications such as video editing, gaming, and photo manipulation. They conserve power and produce less heat than multiple single-core processors, thus increasing performance and efficiency.

Multimedia Messaging Service (MMS) The protocol used in picture or video text messaging.

multimode Optical fiber that has a thicker core than single-mode. It is easier to make, can use simpler light sources (such as LEDs), and works well over short distances. This type of fiber allows light waves to be dispersed into many paths as they travel through the fiber.

multiprocessing To enable programs to share two or more CPUs.

Multipurpose Internet Mail Extensions (MIME) A standard that extends the email format to include text in ASCII standard format, as well as other formats, such as pictures and word processor documents. Normally used in conjunction with SMTP.

Multi rail A power supply that has a separate printed circuit board for each connector.

multitasking Capable of operating multiple applications at the same time.

multithreading To divide a program into smaller parts that can be loaded as needed by the operating system. Multithreading allows individual programs to be multitasked.

multi-touch Mobile devices have the ability to recognize when two or more points of contact are made on the screen.

N

native resolution The best-quality resolution setting for an LCD monitor.

navigation A mapping app that provides turn-by-turn directions to a place, address, or coordinates.

navigation icons Android OS uses navigation icons on the home screen to perform functions such as returning to the home screen, accessing recently opened apps, context screen menu, and a back button.

nbtstat The command is used to show statistics, current connections, and services running on local and remote computers.

near-field communication (NFC) Enables mobile devices to establish radio communications with other devices by placing the devices close together or by touching them together.

netboot A special tool built-in to OS X allows some unique installation configurations. It can boot multiple OS X machines remotely.

net commands Commands used to manage network computers, servers, and resources like drives and printers.

netdom The command is used to manage computer accounts, join computers to a domain, and perform other domain-specific tasks.

Netiquette Being polite in email, text, forums, and all Internet-based interactions.

Network Address Translation (NAT) The process used to convert private addresses to Internet-routable addresses. With NAT, a private (local) source IP address is translated to a public (global) IP address. The process is reversed for incoming packets.

network interface card (NIC) A computer interface with the LAN. This card typically is inserted into an expansion slot in a computer and connects to the network medium.

network LED A light that shows the status of the network connection. The green link light indicates network connectivity. The other LED indicates traffic.

network location profile Computers running Windows 7 and Windows Vista can detect different types of network locations called profiles, based on these profiles the firewall and security setting are made.

network operating system (NOS) An operating system designed specifically to provide additional network features.

networks Systems that are formed by links.

Network and Sharing Center Allows an administrator to configure and review nearly all network operations in a Windows computer. It also shows how your computer connects to a network.

New Technology File System (NTFS) A type of file system that provides improved fault tolerance over traditional file systems, and also provides file-level security.

nickel-cadmium "Ni-Cad" (NiCd) battery First type of battery commonly used in laptop computers. It is heavy and has a short charge life; memory effect can be a problem so the battery must be completely discharged before it can be recharged to prevent the problem.

nickel-metal hydride (NiMH) battery Older type of laptop battery, not expensive, moderate capacity, and memory effect can be a problem so the battery must be completely discharged before it can be recharged to prevent problems.

noise Interference, such as EMI or RFI, that causes unclean power and may cause errors in a computer system.

nonparity A type of memory that does not check for errors in memory.

nonvolatile memory A type of memory that does not need power to retain data.

Northbridge Although the functions may vary depending on the manufacturer, the Northbridge usually controls access to the RAM, video card, and the speeds at which the CPU can communicate with them.

Nslookup A command that returns the IP address of a given hostname. This command can also do the reverse and find the hostname for a specified IP address.

NTOSKRNL.EXE A Windows kernel file that starts the login file called WINLOGON.EXE and displays the Windows Welcome screen.

O

on-body detection An extended Android unlock option. This feature uses the device's accelerometer to detect if the user has the device on his possession. By detecting some specific pattern of movement, Android assumes the device is in the user's hands, pocket or bag and will not require unlocking until it is set down by the user.

OLED An organic LED display uses a layer of organic material that responds to electrical stimulus to emit light.

OneDrive Microsoft cloud storage for synchronizing data between devices OneDrive is also able to synchronize data between mobile devices and PCs.

Open Graphics Library (OpenGL) Cross-platform standard specification for multimedia graphics.

Open Shortest Path First (OSPF) A link-state routing protocol.

open source The developer's programming code, known as source code, is published when it is released. The public can change, copy, or redistribute the code without paying royalty fees to the software developer.

open system authentication An authentication method in which any wireless device can connect to the wireless network. This should only be used in situations where security is of no concern.

Open Systems Interconnect (OSI) A reference model to standardize the way devices communicate on a network. This model was a major step toward ensuring interoperability between network devices. The OSI model divides network communications into seven distinct layers.

open-ended questions Questions that allow customers to explain the details of a problem in their own words.

operating system (OS) Software program that performs general system tasks, such as controlling RAM, prioritizing the processing, controlling input and output devices, and managing files.

optical drive A disk drive that uses a laser to read and/or write CDs and DVDs.

optical fiber A glass or plastic medium that transmits information using light. Fiber-optic cable has one or more optical fibers enclosed in a sheath or jacket.

optical media Refers to discs read by a laser. This includes CD-ROMs, DVD-ROMs, and all the variations of the two formats—CD-R, CD-RW, DVD-R, DVD+R, Blu-ray, and many others.

orientation Determines whether the display of a mobile device appears in Landscape, Portrait, flipped Landscape, or flipped Portrait orientations.

OS X boot camp A common boot manager for OS X.

OS X Mission Control A quick way to see everything that is currently open on your Mac. It allows you to organize your apps on multiple desktops and to navigate the file system.

output device Presents information to the user from a computer. Typical output devices are monitors and printers.

overclocking A technique used to make a processor work at a faster speed than its original specification.

P

packet A logical grouping of information that includes a header that contains control information and usually user data. The term packet is most often used to refer to network layer units of data.

paging file A space where data is stored until enough RAM is available to process the data.

parallel port A standard Type A DB-25 female connector, usually used to connect a printer or scanner.

parity Parity memory contains eight bits for data and one bit for error checking. The error-checking bit is called a parity bit.

partition A logical storage area that hard drives are divided into and can be formatted to store data.

Partition management When working with computer disks, partitions may need to be created, deleted or resized. If the OS is running off a partition that needs attention, the computer should be booted from an external disk before any work is done in the system partition.

passcode lock Locks a device and puts it in a power-saving state. The lock can also be delayed to engage after a specified amount of time passes after the device goes into the power-saving state.

patches Code updates that manufacturers provide to prevent a newly discovered virus or worm from making a successful attack.

patch panel A place to collect incoming cable runs from the various networking devices throughout a facility.

Pattern Android passcode type that locks the device when the user slides a finger over the screen in a certain pattern. To unlock the device, the exact pattern must be repeated on the screen.

PC Card/ExpressCard slot Two legacy laptop expansion slots that allowed early laptops to install wireless NICs, external hard drives, and other devices that typically connect through USB ports today.

PC combo expansion slot Receives expansion cards like PCMCIA and PC Card/ExpressCard.

PCI Express (PCIe) PCIe is a serial bus expansion slot. It is replacing AGP as an expansion slot for video adapters and can be used for other types of adapters.

PCI Express Micro Commonly found in newer and smaller laptops, such as Ultrabooks, because they are half the size of Mini-PCIe cards. PCI Express Micro cards have 54 pins and support all wireless LAN standards.

PCI Extended (PCI-X) A 32-bit bus with higher bandwidth than the PCI bus.

peer-to-peer network Each network device runs both client and server portions of an application. Also describes communication between implementations of the same OSI reference model layer in two different network devices.

Peek A feature of Windows that makes the open windows transparent.

Performance Monitor A tool that shows the real-time levels of CPU and RAM usage.

Peripheral Component Interconnect (PCI) slot A 32-bit or 64-bit expansion slot. PCI is the standard slot currently used in most computers.

permission levels Configured to limit individual or group user access to specific data.

Personalization A tool in Windows 8 where you can change the desktop appearance, display settings, and sound settings.

phablet A mobile device with a size between a typical smartphone and a typical tablet.

pinch A gesture used on touchscreens and tablets to zoom out from objects, such as photographs, maps, and text. Touch the screen with two fingers and pinch them together to zoom out from the object.

ping A simple but highly useful command-line utility that is included in most implementations of TCP/IP. Ping can be used with either the hostname or the IP address to test IP connectivity. Determines whether a specific IP address is accessible by sending an ICMP echo request to a destination computer or other network device. The receiving device then sends back an ICMP echo reply message.

Pin Grid Array (PGA) PGA architecture, the pins are on the underside of the processor. The CPU is inserted into the motherboard CPU socket using zero insertion force (ZIF).

pixel An abbreviation for *picture element*. Pixels are the tiny dots that comprise a screen. Each pixel consists of red, green, and blue.

plain old telephone service (POTS) The regular phone system, which typically uses analog signals to transmit voice and data. Sometimes called the public switched telephone network (PSTN).

plasma A type of flat-panel monitor that uses tiny cells of ionized gas that light up when stimulated by electricity.

plasma displays Rarely found in laptops because they consume a large amount of power made up of tiny fluorescent lights to create the image.

platform as a service (PaaS) The cloud provider is responsible for access to the development tools and services used to deliver the applications.

plenum Any area that is used for ventilation, such as the area between the ceiling and a dropped ceiling.

plenum cable A cable that is safe for installation between a dropped ceiling and the structural ceiling of a building where air circulation takes place. Plenum-rated cables are made from a special plastic that retards fire and produces less smoke than other cable types.

plug-and-play (PnP) Technology that allows a computer to automatically configure the devices that connect to it.

Point-to-Point Protocol Provides a means of encapsulating packets for transmission over a serial link.

Power over Ethernet (PoE) switch A device that transfers small amounts of DC current over Ethernet cable, along with data, to power PoE devices.

port number A numeric identifier used to keep track of specific conversations. Every message that a host sends contains both a source and destination port.

port replicator A fixed-base unit in which a laptop is inserted and can connect to peripheral devices.

Post Office Protocol Version 3 (POP3) An application layer protocol used to allow clients to communicate with email servers.

Power A measure of the pressure required to push electrons through a circuit (voltage), multiplied by the number of electrons going through that circuit (current). The measurement is called watts (W). Computer power supplies are rated in watts.

Power Options A utility in Windows allows you to change the power consumption of certain devices or the entire computer.

power supply Converts AC (alternating current) into the lower voltages of DC (direct current), which powers all the computer's components. Power supplies are rated in watts.

power The measurement of power. Computer power supplies are rated in watts.

power supply tester A device that checks whether the computer power supply is working properly. A simple power supply tester might just have indicator lights; more advanced versions show the amount of voltage and amperage.

power surge Dramatic increase in voltage above the normal flow of electrical current. A power surge lasts for a few nanoseconds, or one-billionth of a second.

power-on self-test (POST) A diagnostic test of memory and hardware when the system is powered up.

Preboot Execution Environment (PXE) installation Uses a PXE boot program and a client's network card to access the setup files from the network server.

Preferred Roaming List (PRL) Configuration information that a cellular phone needs to communicate on networks other than its own, so that a call can be made outside of the carrier's network.

prefix notation An alternate way to express the value of a subnet mask different than the dotted decimal format.

preventive maintenance A detailed program that determines maintenance timing, the type of maintenance performed, and the specifics of how the maintenance plan is carried out.

primary partition The first partition on a hard drive. A primary partition usually contains the operating system and cannot be subdivided into smaller sections.

Primary Rate ISDN (PRI) Consists of 23 B-channels and one 64 Kpbs D-channel if using a T-1 line or 30 B-channels and 1 D-channel if using an E1 line. A Primary Rate Interface user on a T-1 line can have up to 1.544 Mbps service or up to 2.048 Mbps service on an E1 line.

printed circuit board (PCB) The board base for physically supporting and wiring the surface-mounted and socketed components in most electronics.

print server The device that interfaces between a computer and a printer.

privacy screen A plastic panel that attaches to a computer screen and keeps light from projecting at low angles, so that only the user looking straight at the screen can see the contents.

programmable read-only memory (PROM) Information is written to a PROM chip after it is manufactured, and the chip cannot be erased or rewritten.

Programs and Features utility Used when removing, changing, or repairing applications in Windows. The utility guides you through the software removal process and removes every file that was installed.

proprietary vendor specific ports Proprietary vendor specific ports can be found on some mobile devices. These ports are not compatible with other vendors, but often compatibles with other products from the same vendor. These ports are used to charge the device and communicate with other devices.

protocol A formal description of a set of rules and conventions that govern how devices on a network exchange information.

protocol data unit (PDU) A unit of data that is specified in a protocol of a layer of the OSI reference model. For example, the PDU for Layer 1 is bits or the data stream, Layer 2 is framing, Layer 3 is the packet, and Layer 4 is the segment.

proximity sensor Turns off the touchscreen when the phone is up to your ear and turns it on when you pull the device away from your ear on some smartphones. This prevents icons or numbers from being activated by contact with your face or ear, and also saves power.

proxy servers Proxy servers have the authority to act as another computer and can effectively hide the IP addresses of internal hosts because all requests going out to the Internet are sourced from the proxy server's IP address.

Public Network One of three windows network location profiles. Choose this network location for airports, coffee shops, and other public places. Network discovery is turned off. This network location provides the most protection. Also choose this network location if you connect directly to the Internet without using a router, or if you have a mobile broadband connection.

push and pull When a user runs the Google Play app or the Apple App Store app from a mobile device, apps and content that are downloaded are pulled from a server to the device. With Android devices, a user can browse Google Play using any desktop or laptop computer and purchase content. The content is pushed to the Android device from the server. iOS users are able to purchase content from iTunes on a desktop or laptop computer that is then pushed to an iOS device.

Q

quality of service (QoS) Also called 802.1q. QoS, is a variety of techniques that control the flow of network traffic, improve transmission speeds, and improve real-time communications traffic.

quick format A means of removing files from the partition; does not scan the disk for bad sectors.

Quick Response (QR) code A type of bar code that is designed to be scanned by the camera of a mobile device. It is similar to a bar code but can contain much more information.

R

RAID-5 Volume RAID 5 is a dynamic partition that stores data in stripes on more than one physical disk, while also storing recovery information for each stripe. Called parity data, this recovery information can be used to rebuild the data on a disk that has failed. The creation of parity information makes the data on a RAID-5 volume fault tolerant.

radio frequency interference (RFI) Radio frequencies that create noise that interferes with information being transmitted across unshielded copper cabling.

Rail The printed circuit board (PCB) inside the power supply to which the external cables are connected.

RAM access panel The panel that grants easy access to RAM on a laptop.

random-access memory (RAM) The temporary storage for data and programs that are being accessed by the CPU. RAM is volatile memory, which means that the contents will be erased when the power is turned off.

read-only memory (ROM) Memory that permanently stores prerecorded configuration settings and data on a chip that can only be read. This type of memory retains its contents when power is not being supplied to the chip.

ReadyBoost Enables Windows to treat an external flash device, such as a USB drive, as hard drive cache.

repeater A device that regenerates weak signals sent across a network medium.

reduced instruction set computer (RISC) A CPU architecture that uses a small set of instructions and executes them very rapidly.

redundant array of independent disks (RAID) Provides a way to store data across multiple hard disks for redundancy.

refresh rate The refresh rate is how often per second the image on a monitor is rebuilt. A higher refresh rate produces a better image.

Regedit A Windows application that allows users to edit the registry.

registers Storage areas used by the CPU when performing calculations.

Registry A systemwide database used by the Windows operating system to store information and settings for hardware, software, users, and preferences on a system.

remote assistance Allows technicians to assist customers with problems from a remote location.

remote backup A backup method by which a device copies its data to a website using a backup app.

Remote Desktop A utility that can be used to remotely control one networked computer from another networked computer via a graphical interface.

remote installation Downloads the installation across the network. The installation can be requested by the user or forced on to a computer by an administrator.

Remote Installation Services (RIS) A software package used to communicate with the client, store the setup files, and provide the necessary instructions for the client to access the setup files, download them, and begin the operation system installation.

remote lock Allows a user to lock a mobile device with a passcode.

remote wipe Deletes all data from the device and returns it to a factory state. To restore data to the device, Android users must set up the device using a Gmail account, and iOS users must synchronize their devices to iTunes.

resistance The opposition to the flow of current in a circuit, Lower resistance allows more current, and therefore more power, to flow through a circuit. It is measured in ohms.

restore point A system restore point is a set system date and time. A user can "roll back" to this restore point when troubleshooting problems with the operating system.

RJ-45 connector Registered jack (RJ) is a standardized physical network interface for connecting telecommunications or data equipment. The most common twisted-pair connector is an 8-position, 8-contact (8P8C) modular plug and jack.

Roll back a driver Changing the currently installed driver to the previously installed driver.

root An elevated user level that has the highest level of rights and permissions.

rooting A hack that involves unlocking the bootloader and giving Android users access to the root directory and the OS, which opens the phone to customization that is not normally available to the user.

router A network layer device that forwards packets from one network to another based on network layer information.

S

Safe Mode A diagnostic mode used to troubleshoot Windows and Windows startup issues. Functionality is limited as many device drivers are not loaded.

Safe Mode with Networking Starts Windows in Safe Mode with networking support.

Safe Mode with Command Prompt Starts Windows and loads the command prompt instead of the GUI.

sandbox A location of the OS that keeps code isolated from other resources or code.

SATA data cable The cable that connects the motherboard and the SATA drive. Most commonly they have seven pins. Some cables can also provide power to the drive as well as data.

satellite The use of orbiting satellites to relay data between multiple Earth-based stations. Satellite communications offer high bandwidth and broadcast capability at a cost that is unrelated to the distance between Earth stations. Because of the satellite's altitude, satellite communications can be subject to long propagation delays.

screen resolution Specifies the number of pixels. A higher number of pixels provides better resolution.

scroll A gesture for navigating touchscreens or tablets When items are too large for the display screen viewing area, touch and hold the screen, moving your finger in the direction you want to move the item so that an area you want to examine comes into view.

sector A hard drive area that contains a fixed number of bytes, generally at least 512.

Secure Boot Secure Boot is a UEFI security standard that ensures that a computer only boots an OS that is trusted by the motherboard manufacturer. Secure Boot prevents an "unauthorized" OS from loading during startup.

Secure Copy (SCP) SCP uses SSH to secure file transfers.

secure sockets layer (SSL) Developed to transmit files securely across the Internet.

security key fob A small radio system that communicates with the computer over a short range. The computer must sense the signal from the key fob before it accepts the user login name and password.

security keyhole A hard point in the case that is used to attach a security cable.

segment A portion of a computer network in which every device communicates using the physical layer of the OSI reference model. Hubs and repeaters extend and become part of a network segment, whereas switches and routers define and separate network segments.

Self-Monitoring, Analysis, and Reporting Technology (S.M.A.R.T.) Included in the disk's controller itself, S.M.A.R.T. can detect and report a number of attributes about the disk's health. The goal of S.M.A.R.T. is to anticipate disk failure, allowing the user to move the data to a healthy disk before the failing disk becomes inaccessible.

Serial ATA (SATA) SATA hard drives use 7-pin, 4-conductor cables. SATA is replacing IDE and EIDE as the standard interface for hard drives and SSDs serial port.

serial port Connects a computer to a peripheral device such as a mouse or trackball.

service-level agreement (SLA) A contract that defines expectations between an organization and the service vendor to provide an agreed-upon level of support.

service pack System patches and upgrades that are combined into a comprehensive update application.

service set identifier (SSID) The broadcast name of a wireless network.

Shadow Copy A feature of Windows operating system that automatically creates backup copies of files and data on a hard drive.

Shake A method of minimizing all windows that are not being used; click and hold the title bar of one window and shake it with the mouse.

shared key authentication A type of authentication that provides mechanisms to authenticate and encrypt data between a wireless client and AP or wireless router.

shell A program that interprets the commands from the keyboard and passes them to the operating system.

shielded twisted-pair (STP) A two-pair wiring medium used primarily with Token Ring networks. STP cabling has a layer of shielded insulation to reduce electromagnetic interference (EMI). Compare with UTP.

Short Message Service (SMS) The protocol used in text messaging.

Sidebar A Windows Vista graphical pane on the desktop that keeps gadgets organized.

sideloading Another way to install apps on mobile devices. Apps can be downloaded from different sources on the Internet and transferred to a mobile device through WiFi, Bluetooth, data cable, or other methods. Sideloading is not recommended because many sources for apps cannot be trusted; it is best to only install apps from trusted sources and developers.

signatures The list of known virus code patterns to which antivirus software compares files to determine if the file is infected with a virus.

Simple Mail Transfer Protocol (SMTP) An email protocol servers use to send ASCII text messages. When augmented by the MIME protocol, SMTP can carry email with pictures and documents. Email clients sometimes use SMTP to retrieve messages from an email server. However, because of the limited capability to queue messages at the receiving end, other protocols such as POP or IMAP are typically used to receive email.

Simple Passcode A passcode type for iOS devices only. When this option is set to On, the passcode must be a four-digit number. When set to Off, more complex passwords using characters, numbers, and symbols can be used.

simplex The capability for data transmission in only one direction between a sending station and a receiving station.

single channel With this technology, all of the RAM slots are addressed at the same time.

single-mode A fiber cable that has a very thin core. Uses a high-energy laser as a light source. Can transmit signals over longer distances than multimode fiber-optic cable.

single rail A power supply that has all of the connectors connected to the printed circuit board.

single sign-on (SSO) authentication An authentication method that allows users to log in once to access all system features versus requiring them to log in each time they need to access an individual resource.

Siri Special software that understands advanced voice controls.

sleep A power-saving state of a computer in which documents, applications, and the state of the operating system are saved in RAM. This allows the computer to power on quickly, but uses power to retain the information in RAM.

slide/swipe The user slides an icon, such as a lock or an arrow, to unlock the device. This option is the least secure.

small outline DIMM (SODIMM) A SODIMM is a smaller version of DIMM that is ideal for use in laptops printers and in other devices where conserving space is necessary. SODIMM has 72-pin and 100-pin configurations for support of 32-bit transfers and 144-pin, 200-pin, and 204-pin configurations for support of 64-bit transfers.

smart card A credit-card-sized device that includes a processor and memory. Used to store information and authenticate network users.

smart headsets Headsets designed to be worn like a pair of eyeglasses. The headset has a small screen built into the frame or projected onto glass. The headset is often connected to a smartphone for network connectivity.

smartphone A cellular phone that performs many of the functions of a computer, typically having a touchscreen interface, Internet access, and an operating system capable of running downloaded applications.

smart watches Watches that combine the functions of a watch and some of the functions of mobile devices.

Snap Resize a window by dragging it to one of the edges of the screen.

software The operating system and programs used by a computer.

software as a service (SaaS) The cloud provider is responsible for access to services, such as email, communication, and virtual desktops that are delivered over the Internet.

software development kit (SDK) Contains a number of software tools designed to allow external programs to be written for a specific software package.

software firewall A program that runs on a computer to allow or deny traffic between the computer and other computers to which it is connected.

solid state drives (SSD) A solid state drive has no moving parts and uses semiconductors to store data. Nonvolatile flash memory chips manage all storage on an SSD.

solid state hybrid disks (SSHDs) A popular and less expensive option than SSDs, SSHD devices combine the speed of SSDs with the lower price of HDDs by packing both technologies in the same enclosure. In SSHDs, data is stored in an HDD, but a small flash memory is used to cache frequently used data.

source code The sequence of instructions that is written in human readable language, before it is turned into machine language (zeroes and ones).

source port number A UDP or TCP port number associated with origination application on the local device. It is dynamically generated by the sending device.

sound adapter These provide audio capability to computers.

Southbridge Usually allows the CPU to communicate with the hard drive, sound card, USB ports, and other I/O ports.

spanned volume Creates a disk partition that consists of disk space from more than one physical disk. The data on a spanned volume is not fault tolerant.

specialized search results For example, search results based on proximity,

spike A sudden increase in voltage that lasts for a short period and exceeds 100 percent of the normal voltage on a line. Spikes can be caused by lightning strikes, but can also occur when the electrical system comes back on after a blackout.

Spotlight Apple iOS search feature.

spread A tablet or touchscreen gesture used to zoom in on objects, such as photographs, maps, and text. Touch the screen with two fingers and spread them apart to zoom in on the object.

SSH File Transfer Protocol (SFTP) As an extension to Secure Shell (SSH) protocol, SFTP can be used to establish a secure file transfer session.

standby power supply (SPS) Battery backup that is enabled when voltage levels fall below normal.

standoff A barrier/screw used to physically separate parts (in particular, the system board) from the case.

Startup Repair This tool scans the hard drive for problems and automatically fixes missing or corrupt system files that prevent Windows from starting.

stateful packet inspection A firewall that keeps track of the state of network connections traveling through the firewall. Packets that are not part of a known connection are dropped.

static IP addressing An IP address is manually assigned to each node on the same network. The IP address must be unique for each node.

static RAM (SRAM) A type of RAM that retains its contents for as long as power is supplied, and is usually used as cache memory. SRAM does not require constant refreshing, like dynamic RAM (DRAM).

stereo headphone jack A small round plug that uses cylindrical bands as contacts. Two audio signal wires (right and left) transmit analog audio signals.

Straight-Tip (ST) Connectors The first type of fiber optic cable connector used. The connector locks securely with a "twist-on/twist-off" bayonet style mechanism.

straight-through cable The most common cable type. It maps a wire to the same pins on both ends of the cable. In other words, if T568A is on one end of the cable, T568A is also on the other. If T568B is on one end of the cable, T568B is on the other. This means that the order of connections (the pinout) for each color is the exact same on both ends.

Striping RAID method that writes data across multiple drives.

subnet mask The second group of numbers used when configuring an IP address on a device.

End devices use the subnet mask to determine the network portion of an IP address.

Subscriber Connector An optical fiber cable connector sometimes referred to as a *square connector* or *standard connector*. It is a widely adopted LAN and WAN connector that uses a push-pull mechanism to ensure positive insertion. This connector type is used with multimode and single-mode fiber.

subscriber identity module (SIM) card This small card contains information used to authenticate a device to mobile telephone and data services. SIM cards can also hold user data such as contacts and text messages.

surge suppressor A device that ensures that the voltage going to another device stays below a certain level.

S-Video A display cable that carries analog video signals.

S-Video connector A 4-pin mini-DIN connector that is used to output video signals to a compatible device. S-Video separates the brightness and color portions of a video signal.

switch A Layer 2 network device; also known as a *multiport bridge*.

switching table A table that contains a list of all MAC addresses on the network and a list of switch ports that can be used to reach a device with a given MAC address. The switching table records MAC addresses by inspecting the source MAC address of every incoming frame, as well as the port on which the frame arrives. The switch then creates a switching table that maps MAC addresses to outgoing ports.

Sync process on Android Synchronizes user data to services, including Facebook, Google, and Twitter. As a result, all devices associated to that Google account have access to the same data, making it easier to replace a damaged device without data loss.

System File Checker (SFC) Enables you to check all the protected system files, such as krnl386.exe, and to replace them with known good versions if they have become corrupted or deleted.

System Image Recovery This tool restores the computer using a system image file.

System Utility Allows all users to view basic system information, access tools, and configure advanced settings. Found in the Control Panel.

System Restore This tool restores a computer to an earlier restore point.

T

T568A/T568B Two standards for connecting Category 3, Category 5, and Category 6 wire to connectors. Both are appropriate for high-speed data.

Type 1 hypervisor Runs directly on the hardware of a host and manages the allocation of system resources to virtual operating systems.

Type 2 hypervisor Like a type1 hypervisor but hosted by an OS.

tablet A portable PC that can be folded back on the keyboard or, more commonly, a PC that has no moving parts and is read and handled like a piece of paper. Tablets often use touchscreen technology in place of a mouse and keyboard.

Task Manager Displays active applications and identifies those that are not responding so that they can be shut down.

tethering A mobile device can connect to another mobile device or computer to share a network connection.

terminal emulator application One way to access the command-line interface in a GUI-based operating system. These applications provide user access to the command-line interface and are often named as some variation of the word *terminal*.

thermal compound A substance that increases thermal conductivity between the surface of two of more objects. Used between the CPU and heat sink/fan assembly.

thicknet Coaxial cable that was used in older networks and operated at 10 Mb/s with a maximum length of 500 meters. Also called *10BASE5*.

thinnet Coaxial cable that was used in older networks and operated at 10 Mb/s with a maximum length of 185 meters. Also called *10BASE2*.

Thunderbolt card These connect a computer to peripheral devices.

Time Machine An OS X backup tool.

toner probe A two-part tool in which the toner part is connected to a cable at one end using specific adapters, such as an RJ-45, coaxial, or metal clips and generates a tone that travels the length of the cable. The probe part traces the cable.

Touch ID A passcode type for iOS devices only. Starting with the iPhone 5S, it is also possible to unlock an iOS device based on the user's fingerprints. The Home button in selected iPhone devices contain a fingerprint scanner that can be used to unlock the device, authorize payments, and access to apps.

touchscreen An interactive LCD or CRT monitor that detects when something is pressed on it.

touchpad An input device considered to be a field-replaceable unit.

Tracert A Windows utility that traces the route that a packet takes from source computer to destination host.

track A complete circle around a hard-drive platter; made up of groups of 512-byte sectors.

TCP A reliable, full-featured transport layer protocol, which ensures that all of the data arrives at the destination.

Transport Layer Specifies which application requested or is receiving data through specific ports.

Trivial File Transport Protocol A simple, connectionless file transfer protocol.

troubleshooting A systematic approach to locating the cause of a fault in a computer system or network.

Trusted Devices An extended Android unlock option. This feature unlocks the Android phone or tablet whenever it is paired with a specific Bluetooth device or NFC tag of the user's choice. For example, it is convenient to be able to keep the Android phone or tablet unlocked when paired to a car's Bluetooth.

Trusted Face An extended Android unlock option that when activated, Trusted Face allows Android to unlock itself based on a preregistered image of the user's face.

Trusted Platform Module (TPM) A specialized chip installed on the motherboard of a computer to be used for hardware and software authentication.

Trusted Places An extended Android unlock option, which, by using the GPS chip built into the device, allows the user to define home and work locations. The device will no longer require unlocking when it is in either one of those locations.

Trusted Voice An extended Android unlock option. This feature relies on the user's unique voiceprint to unlock the Android device when a registered user says "Okay Google."

TV tuners and cable cards A TV tuner converts analog and digital television signals into audio and video signals the computer can use and store. Cable cards can be used to receive television signals from a cable company.

twisted nematic (TN) The most common and the oldest technology used in the manufacturing of LCD displays. TN displays offer high brightness, uses less power than IPS, and are inexpensive to manufacture.

twisted pair A pair of insulated wires wrapped together in a regular spiral pattern to control the effects of electrical noise.

U

Ubuntu Linux A Linux distribution that uses Unity as its default GUI.

UDP A very simple transport layer protocol that does not provide for any reliability.

unattended installation A custom installation of an operating system with minimal user intervention. Windows performs unattended installations by using an answer file called unattend.txt.

Unified Extensible Firmware Interface (UEFI) Recently, the BIOS has been enhanced by UEFI. UEFI specifies a different software interface for boot and runtime services but still relies on the traditional BIOS for system configuration, power-on self-test (POST), and setup.

uninterruptible power supply (UPS) A device that maintains a continuous supply of electric power to connected equipment by supplying power from a separate source when utility power is unavailable.

Universal Serial Bus (USB) port An external, hot-swappable, bidirectional connection for USB cables connecting to peripheral devices.

universal threat management (UTM) A generic name for an all-in-one security appliance. UTMs include all the functionality of an IDS/IPS as well as stateful firewall services.

UNIX A non-proprietary operating system based on the C programming language and featuring a user command interface.

unshielded twisted-pair (UTP) A four-pair wire medium used in a variety of networks. UTP is rated in categories, with higher categories providing the best performance and highest bandwidth. The most popular categories are Category 3, Category 5, Category 5e, Category 6, and Category 6A.

Upgrade Advisor Windows 7 and Upgrade Assistant (Windows 8.x) A Microsoft tool to advise customers on what hardware is compatible with an OS. It is used to determine whether an OS upgrade will be successful.

USB ports Standard interfaces that connect peripheral devices to a computer. A single USB port can support up to 127 separate devices with the use of multiple USB hubs.

User Account Control The User Account Control monitors programs on a computer and warns users when an action might present a threat to the system. Users can adjust the level of monitoring by using the User Account Control settings.

User Accounts utility provides options to help you manage passwords, change account pictures, change account names and types, and change User Account Control (UAC) settings.

User State Migration Tool This downloadable tool migrates all user files and settings to a new operating system.

V

ventilation A series of vents that allow hot air to be expelled from the interior of the device.

video adapter card An integrated circuit board that stores digital data in VRAM and converts it to analog data. The interface between a computer and a display monitor.

video port Connects a monitor cable to a computer. There are several video ports and connector types.

Virtual Desktop Infrastructure (VDI) Allows users to log in to a server to access their own virtual computers. Input from the mouse and keyboard is sent to the server to manipulate the virtual computer.

virtual memory An area on the hard drive that can be used when a computer does not have enough RAM available to run a program.

virtual private network (VPN) An encryption system that protects data as it travels, or tunnels, over the Internet or another unsecured public network.

virtualization Simultaneously running two or more operating systems on one computer.

volatile memory With volatile memory, the contents are erased when the computer is powered off. RAM is an example of volatile memory.

voltage A measurement of the work required to move a charge from one location to another. Voltage is measured in volts (V). A computer power supply usually produces several different voltages.

voltage selector switch This switch sets the input voltage to the power supply to either 110V/115V or 220V/230V.

W

Wake on LAN (WoL) Settings used to wake up a networked computer from a very low power mode state. Very low power mode means that the computer is turned off but is still connected to a power source. To support WoL, the computer must have an ATX-compatible power supply and a WoL-compatible NIC.

wearable devices Clothing or accessories that have miniature computing devices.

wide-area network (WAN) A data communications network that serves users across a broad geographic area and often uses transmission devices provided by common carriers.

widget A small program that runs to launch larger programs.

WiFi Brand originally licensed by the WiFi Alliance to define the embedded technology of a wireless network (based on the IEEE 802.11 specifications).

WiFi calling Instead of using the cellular carrier's network, modern smartphones can use the Internet to transport voice calls by taking advantage of a local WiFi hotspot.

WiFi networks Any type of computer network that is not connected by cables of any kind.

WiFi Protected Access (WPA) A security standard for WiFi wireless technology. Provides better encryption and authentication than the earlier WEP system.

WiFi Protected Access 2 (WPA2) Wireless encryption that uses 128-bit AES block ciphering to encrypt data. WPA2 can be enabled in two versions: Personal (password authentication) and Enterprise (server authentication). It is not backward compatible with WEP.

WiFi Protected Setup (WPS) Commonly uses a PIN method to allow users to set up a wireless network quickly, easily, and with security enabled.

WiFi Sync A wireless sync between an iPad or iPhone and PC, allowing a user to keep files in sync without having to connect their devices to a PC via the sync/charge cable.

Windows Action Center Checks the status of essential security settings. The Action Center continuously checks to make sure that the software firewall and antivirus programs are running. It also ensures that automatic updates download and install automatically.

Windows Firewall Runs continuously to protect against unauthorized communications to and from your computer.

Windows application programming interface (API) Also known as *WinAPI*. Allows applications from older versions of Windows to operate on newer versions.

Windows Automatic Updates The Automatic Updates utility scans the system for needed updates, and then, depending on the user settings, downloads and installs the updates or recommends the updates be installed. This ensures the OS and applications are constantly updated for security purposes and added functionality.

Windows Boot Manager (BOOTMGR) Controls several installation steps during the startup process, depending on the system configuration.

Windows Easy Transfer Migrates personal files and settings from an old computer to a new one.

Windows Explorer The file management application in Windows 7 and earlier.

Windows Hyper-V A virtualization platform for Windows 8.

Windows Libraries A means to organize content from various storage devices on your computer and network locations, including removable media, without moving the files. A library presents content from different locations in the same folder.

Windows Memory Diagnostic This tool examines computer memory to detect malfunctions and diagnose problems.

Windows Startup Settings The Startup Settings option allows you to enable Safe Mode. You can also disable automatic restart after failure and allow you to see the error message shown on blue screen.

Windows Recovery Environment (WinRE) A recovery platform based on the Windows Preinstallation Environment, which helps users troubleshoot operating system failures.

Windows Task Scheduler A GUI-based scheduling tool that allows you to run a command at a specific time, or on an ongoing basis on selected days or times.

Windows Virtual PC The virtualization platform for Windows 7.

WinLoad A part of the boot process that locates the boot partition and loads two files that make up the core of Windows: NTOSKRNL.EXE and HAL.DLL. It also reads the Registry files, chooses a hardware profile, and loads the device drivers.

Wired Equivalent Privacy (WEP) A first-generation security standard for wireless technology.

wireless access point (WAP) A device that connects wireless devices to form a wireless network. An access point usually connects to a wired network, and it can relay data between wired and wireless devices. Connectivity distances can range from several feet or meters to several miles or kilometers.

wireless adapters A device to add wireless connectivity to a laptop. Adapters can be built-in to the laptop or attached to the laptop through a laptop expansion port. Three major types of wireless adapters used in laptops are Mini-PCI, PCI Express Micro, and Mini-PCIe.

wireless channel Wireless devices communicate over specific frequency ranges.

Wireless Emergency Alerts (WEA) Emergency messages sent by authorities through mobile carriers. In the U.S.A., government partners include: local and state public safety agencies, FEMA, the FCC, the Department of Homeland Security, and the National Weather Service. Mobile carriers do not charge for WEA messages.

wireless LAN (WLAN) A network that uses radio signals instead of cables to connect computers to access points and wireless routers.

wireless router A device that connects multiple wireless devices to the network; similar to an AP but with more features.

workgroup A collection of workstations and servers on a LAN that are designed to communicate and exchange data with one another.

Work One of three windows network location profiles. Choose this network location for a small office or other workplace network.

Worldwide Interoperability for Microwave Access (WiMAX) An IP-based wireless 4G broadband technology that offers high-speed mobile Internet access for mobile devices. WiMAX is a standard called IEEE 802.16e.

X

Xcode Apple's official integrated development environment (IDE). Xcode can be downloaded at no cost and allows developers to write and test their iOS apps in an iPhone simulator.

Y-Z

zero insertion force (ZIF) A chip socket that permits the insertion and removal of a chip without using tools or force. This is common for delicate chips such as a CPU.

Index

Symbols

: (colon), 367
– (dash), 582
1G, 421, 559
1Mobile, 523
2G, 421, 559
2.5G, 421
3DES (Triple Data Encryption Algorithm), 699
3G, 421, 560
3.5G, 421
4G, 421, 560
4-pin to 8-pin auxiliary power connectors, 9
10BASE2, 353
10BASE5, 353
10BASE-T, 344
10GBASE-T, 345
20-pin connectors, 9
24-pin connectors, 9
32-bit architecture, 192
64-bit architecture, 192
100BASE-TX, 344
802.1q QoS (Quality of Service), 392
802.11 standard (WiFi)
  antenna connectors, 462–463
  configuration, 471–472
  hotspots, 560–561
  mobile device connectivity, 557–559
  overview, 343–346
  WiFi analyzers, 87
  WiFi calling, 541
  WiFi Sync, 577
  WPA (WiFi Protected Access), 344, 402, 702
  WPA2 (WiFi Protected Access 2), 344, 402, 702
  WPS (WiFi Protected Setup), 702
802.15.1 standard (Bluetooth)
  characteristics of, 468–469
  configuration, 470
  definition of, 496
  installation, 470
  for mobile devices, 563
  overview, 328–329, 644
  pairing, 564–566
  specifications, 469–470
802.3 standard, 318, 342–345
1000BASE-T, 344
1284 standard, 622–623
1394 standard
  capabilities, 39
  FireWire 400, 31
  FireWire 800, 31
  overview, 39
  printers, 623

A

AAA, 431
AC (alternating current)
  definition of, 7
  power fluctuations, 78
accelerometers, 539
Access Control Lists (ACLs), 349–350
"access denied" message, 777
access points (APs), 323
accessories (mobile), 496–498
accounts
  administrator
    definition of, 715–716
    Run as Administrator option, 258
  creating, 210–212
  email accounts
    Android, 568–570
    Internet email, 571–572
    iOS, 570–571
  guest accounts, 713–714, 716
  maintaining, 713–714
  policies
    lockout policy, 678
    password policy, 677–678
  troubleshooting, 776–777
ACLs (Access Control Lists), 349–350
ACPI (Advanced Configuration and Power Interface), 464–465
Acqua GUI, 580–582
action, plan of
  Linux issues, 602–607
  mobile operating system issues, 602–607
  network issues, 436

operating system issues, 304–307
OS X issues, 602–607
preventive maintenance issues, 170–172
printer issues, 653–654
security issues, 720

Action Center, 267
Action Launcher, 527
active cooling, 18
active listening, 733
active partitions, 205
ActiveX controls, 681
ActiveX filtering, 681
ad hoc mode (WLANs), 327
adapter cards
inspecting, 162
installation
video adapter cards, 120–121
wireless NICs, 119–120
selecting, 56–57
types of, 118–119

adapters, 40–41
Adaptive Frequency Hopping (AFH), 328–329
Add Hardware utility, 274
Add Printer wizard, 642–643
Address Resolution Protocol (ARP), 340
addresses
IP (Internet Protocol) addressing
classful and classless IPv4 addressing, 365–366
configuration, 389
dynamic addressing, 370–371
ICMP (Internet Control Message Protocol), 371–373
IPv6 address format, 367–370
number of IPv6 addresses, 366–369
static addressing, 368–370
MAC (Media Access Control) addressing, 347, 361–364
NAT (network address translation), 337, 399

administrative shares, 412–414
Administrative Tools (Windows)
Component Services, 279–280, 283
Computer Management, 277–278
Data Sources (ODBC), 280–281, 284
definition of, 277
Event Viewer, 279
Performance Monitor, 282–283
Services console, 281
System Configuration, 281–282
Windows Memory Diagnostic, 246–283

administrator accounts
Administrators group, 717
definition of, 715–716
Run as Administrator option, 258

Administrators group, 717
Adobe PostScript, 633
ADSL (asymmetric digital subscriber line), 384–420
Advanced Configuration and Power Interface (ACPI), 464–465
Advanced Encryption Standard (AES), 344, 402, 699
Advanced Mode (UEFI), 144
advanced problems and solutions
internal components, 763–764
networks
connection problems, 770–771
email failure, 772
FTP (File Transfer Protocol) problems, 772–773
network troubleshooting tools, 773–775
secure Internet connections, 772–773
operating systems, 766–769
printers, 765
security
computer security, 777–778
firewall settings, 778–779
malware settings, 775–776
proxy settings, 778–779
user accounts and permissions, 776–777

Advanced Startup Options, 220–221
Advanced tab (Internet Options), 265
AT (Advanced Technology), 7
Advanced Technology (AT), 7
Advanced Technology Extended (ATX), 7, 13
advanced troubleshooting
networks
connection problems, 770–771
email failure, 772
FTP (File Transfer Protocol) problems, 772–773
network troubleshooting tools, 773–775
secure Internet connections, 772–773
operating systems
advanced problems and solutions, 766–769
overview, 766
preventive maintenance
advanced problems and solutions, 763–764
review, 762
printers, 765
security
computer security, 777–778
firewall settings, 778–779
malware settings, 775–776
proxy settings, 778–779
user accounts and permissions, 776–777

adware, 668
Aero theme, 245–249
aerosol cans, disposal of, 81–82
AES (Advanced Encryption Standard), 344, 402, 699
AFH (Adaptive Frequency Hopping), 328–329
AIK (Windows Automated Installation Kit), 219
Airplane Mode, 561–562
AirPort Extreme, 645
alert badges, 534
alerts
alert badges, 534
WEAs (Wireless Emergency Alerts), 544–545
All Apps screen (Android), 529–530
all-in-one cases, 5
alternating current (AC)
definition of, 7
power fluctuation, 78
Amazon App Store, 523
AMBER alerts, 545
amps (A), 10
analog modems, 344–345
Android. *See also* **mobile devices**
apps
development, 521–522
installation, 524–525
sources for, 522–524
email configuration
account setup, 568–570
Exchange, 568
Internet email, 571–572
protocols, 566–568
factory reset, 609
GPS (global positioning system), 540
mobile device synchronization, 573–574
mobile payments, 542
network connectivity
Bluetooth, 563–566
cellular communications, 559–562
wireless data networks, 557–559
open source licensing, 520–521
screen calibration, 539–540
screen orientation, 538–539
security
antivirus protection, 553–556
locator apps, 551–552
passcode locks, 545–550
patches, 556–557
remote backup, 551
remote lock, 518–552
remote wipe, 518–552
rooting, 554–556
updates, 556–557
touch interface
All Apps screen, 529–530
app management, 527–528
folders, 528–529
home screen items, 525–527
widget management, 528
WiFi calling, 541
Android Application Package (APK), 523
Androidzoom, 523
angry customers, 736–737
antimalware software
for Linux and OS X, 596
overview, 694–695
antistatic mats, 73, 92
antistatic wrist straps, 73, 91–92
antivirus protection
Linux and OS X, 596
mobile devices, 553–556
APIPA (Automatic Private IP Addressing), 370
APIs (application programming interfaces), 191
APK (Android Application Package), 523
App History tab (Task Manager), 254
Apple
AirPort Extreme, 645
App Store, 523
Bonjour Printer Server, 645
iOS. *See* iOS
OS X. *See* OS X
Apple menu, 585
applets, 245
application layer firewalls, 704
Application menu (OS X), 585
application programming interfaces (APIs), 191
applications
application management, 191–192
definition of, 4
installation, 259
mobile apps
app management, 527–538
definition of, 521
development, 521–522
GPS (global positioning system)-related apps, 540
locator apps, 551–552
push versus pull installation, 524–525
sources for, 522–524
pinned applications, 253
uninstallation, 259–260
Applications tab (Task Manager), 255
applied networking. *See also* **networks**
cloud computing
characteristics of, 425–426
compared to data centers, 425

IaaS (Infrastructure as a Service), 426
ITaaS (IT as a Service), 426
PaaS (Platform as a Service), 426
SaaS (Software as a Service), 426
types of, 426–427
data centers, 425
host services
authentication services, 431
DHCP (Dynamic Host Configuration Protocol), 427
DNS (Domain Name System), 427–428
email services, 430
FTP (File Transfer Protocol), 428–429
IDSs (intrusion detection systems), 431
IPSs (intrusion prevention systems), 431
print services, 429
proxy servers, 430–431
UTM (Universal Threat Management), 431–432
web services, 428
ISPs (Internet Service Providers)
broadband technology, 384–418
selecting, 423–424
network sharing
administrative shares, 412–414
domains, 406–407
drive mapping, 414
network file sharing, 410–411
Windows homegroups, 408–409
Windows Vista, 409–410
workgroups, 406–407
NICs (network interface cards)
configuration, 389–393
connecting, 393–394
installation, 388–389
network installation completion list, 386–387
overview, 385–386
selecting, 386–387
updating, 388–389
preventive maintenance, 432–433
remote access
definition of, 415
Remote Assistance, 415–416
Remote Desktop, 415–416
VPNs (virtual private networks), 415–416
routers
Internet connections, 394–395
logging in to, 397–398
network location profiles, 395–397
network setup, 398–399
NIC connections, 393–394
testing connectivity of, 402–405
wireless settings, 399–402
troubleshooting
common problems and solutions, 437–439
documentation of outcomes, 437
full system functionality verification, 436–437
plan of action, 436
problem identification, 434
testing, 435
theory of probable cause, 434–435
apps (mobile)
app management
Android, 527–528
iOS, 533
Windows Phone, 537–538
definition of, 521
development, 521–522
GPS (global positioning system)-related apps, 540
locator apps, 551–552
push versus pull installation, 524–525
sources for, 522–524
AppsAPK, 523
APs (access points), 323
architecture
CPUs, 14–15, 192
sockets, 108
ARP (Address Resolution Protocol), 340
arrangement of Windows Phone tiles, 537
aspect ratio, 47
assembly of computers. *See* computer assembly
ASUS Advanced Mode (UEFI), 144
asymmetric digital subscriber line (ADSL), 384–420
at command, 298
attacks. *See* threats
ATX (Advanced Technology Extended), 7, 13
audio
audio ports, 37, 129
audio/video (A/V) drives, 68
audio/video editing workstations, 64–65
sound adapters, 23
sound cards, 56–57
Sound utility, 274
audio/video editing workstations, 64–65
authentication
authentication services, 431
definition of, 210
multifactor authentication, 707–708
open system authentication, 344

auto restart function, 766
Automated Installation Kit (AIK), 219
Automatic (delayed) setting (services), 281
Automatic Private IP Addressing (APIPA), 370
Automatic Repair, 221
Automatic setting (services), 281
AutoPlay, 706
AutoRun, 706
autorun.inf, 707
A/V (audio/video) drives, 68

B

B (bytes), 20, 325
backlights, 461–462
backoff algorithm, 342
Backup and Restore utility, 300
Backup Files Wizard, 711
Backup process (iOS), 575–576
backups
 configuration, 686–687
 definition of, 585
 hard disk drives, 299–300
 importance of, 164
 Linux, 585–587
 OS X, 588–589
 remote backup for mobile devices, 551
 utilities
  Backup and Restore utility, 300
  Backup Files Wizard, 711
  iOS Backup process, 575–576
 Windows, 711
bad sector checks (Linux/OS X), 589
baiting, 673
bandwidth, 325
basic disks, 205–206
basic input/output system. *See* BIOS (basic input/output system)
batteries
 battery latches, 453
 battery warnings, 468
 disposal of, 81
 laptop batteries
  replacing, 480–481
  types of, 450–451
 mobile devices, 492, 497
battery latches, 453
BD (Blu-ray disc), 27–28
beep codes (BIOS), 133–134, 165–166, 222
Berg keyed connectors, 9
biometric identification devices, 46, 685–686, 709
BIOS (basic input/output system)
 beep codes, 133–134, 165–166, 222
 CMOS (complementary metal oxide semiconductor) chip, 135–136
 component information, 138
 definition of, 12
 hardware diagnostics and monitoring, 141–143
 main configurations, 138–139
 passwords, 706
 security configurations, 140–141
 settings, 139–140
 Setup program, 137–138
 troubleshooting, 166
 upgrades, 147–148
BitLocker, 689–691
BitLocker To Go, 691
bits per second (b/s), 325
blackouts, 78
blue screen of death (BSOD), 764, 766, 768
Bluetooth
 characteristics of, 468–469
 configuration, 470
 definition of, 496
 installation, 470
 for mobile devices, 563
 overview, 328–329, 644
 pairing, 564–566
 specifications, 469–470
Blu-ray disc (BD), 27–28
On-body detection feature (Android), 547
Bonjour Printer Server, 645
Boot Camp, 591
boot loaders, 204
boot managers (Linux/OS X), 591
boot process
 BIOS (basic input/output system)
  beep codes, 133–134
  BIOS Setup program, 137–138
  CMOS (complementary metal oxide semiconductor) chip, 135–136
  component information, 138
  hardware diagnostics and monitoring, 141–143
  main configurations, 138–139
  security configurations, 140–141
  settings, 139–140
  UEFI Setup program, 103–138
 boot loaders, 204
 boot managers (Linux/OS X), 591
 overview, 222
 POST (power-on self-test), 103–134

startup modes, 223–224
UEFI (Unified Extensible Firmware Interface)
ASUS Advanced Mode, 144
EZ Mode, 143–144
Windows boot process, 222–223
Windows Registry, 224–225
Boot tab (System Configuration), 283
BOOTMGR, 223
"BOOTMGR is missing" error, 311, 767
bootrec command, 288, 289, 311, 767
box. *See* cases
bridges, 346
bring your own device (BYOD), 708
broadband technology
ADSL (asymmetric digital subscriber line), 384–420
cable, 383–422
capabilities, 317
cellular, 421–422
DSL (digital subscriber line), 420
fiber broadband, 384–422
history of, 419
line of sight wireless Internet, 384–420
satellite, 383–422
WiMAX (Worldwide Interoperability for Microwave Access), 420–421
brownouts, 78
browser security
ActiveX filtering, 681
InPrivate Browsing, 682–683
overview, 679–680
pop-up blockers, 681
SmartScreen Filter, 682
b/s (bits per second), 325
BSOD (blue screen of death), 764, 766, 768
buffered memory, 55–56
building PCs (personal computer systems), 49–50
built-in diagnostics, 142–143
business policies, 741–742
busses
bus speed, monitoring, 142
FSB (front-side bus), 16
buying tips. *See* selecting
BYOD (bring your own device), 708
bytes (B), 20, 325

C

cabinets. *See* cases
cable Internet connections, 383–422, 424
cable testers, 94
cable tools, 85
cables
cable testers, 94
cable tools, 85
coaxial cables, 351–353
copper cabling, 323
eSATA data cables, 39
Ethernet standards, 342–343
fiber-optic cabling, 323, 358–360
FireWire
capabilities, 39
FireWire 400, 31
FireWire 800, 31
overview, 39
printer connections, 623
inspecting, 162
installation
case fan connections, 124–126
eternal cables, 131–133
front panel cables, 127–131
internal data cables, 126–127
internal drive connections, 124–126
motherboard power connections, 122–124
twisted-pair cables
category ratings, 319–355
definition of, 318
STP (shielded twisted-pair), 319–355
UTP (unshielded twisted-pair), 318–354
wiring schemes, 356–357
USB (Universal Serial Bus) cables, 39
video cables, 33–38
cache
definition of, 15
levels of, 23
CAD (computer-aided design), 64
calibration
mobile device screens, 539–540
printers, 640
call center environments, 750–752
call center technicians
call center environments, 750–752
call prioritization, 751–752
levels of technicians
level one technicians, 739–753
level two technicians, 753
support software, 751
calls
placing on hold, 733–734
prioritization, 751–752
transferring, 734
WiFi calling, 541
CAM (computer-aided manufacturing), 64

"Can't find server name for 127.0.0.1: timed out" message, 774
capture cards, 23, 57
card keys, 708
Carrier Sense Multiple Access with Collision Avoidance (CSMA/CA), 318–343
Carrier Sense Multiple Access with Collision Detection (CSMA/CD), 341–342
cases
- cleaning, 95, 160–161
- opening, 104–105
- reassembly, 131
- selecting, 51–52
- types of, 5–7

cat command, 602
category ratings for twisted-pair cables, 319–355
"Caution this hard disk may be infected by a virus!" message, 776
CAx workstations, 64
CCFL (cold cathode fluorescent lamp), 461–462
cd command, 288, 602
CDFS (Compact Disc File System), 207
CDs (compact discs), 27–28
cellular communications
- cellular technology, 421–422, 424
- cellular towers, 552
- cellular WAN, 471
- mobile device connectivity
  - *Airplane Mode, 561–562*
  - *hotspots, 560–561*
  - *industry standards, 559–562*
  - *LTE, 560–561*
  - *Mobile WiMAX, 560*

Central Processing Units. *See* CPUs
chain of custody, 745, 750
change permissions, 411
channels, 401
charging process (laser printing), 626
Charms bar, 245
chassis. *See* cases
Check for Update button (iOS), 557
chemical solvents, disposal of, 81–82
chipsets, 12
chkdsk command, 88, 289, 311
choosing. *See* selecting
CIDR (Classless Inter-Domain Router), 365–366
CISC (complex instruction set computer), 15
cladding (optical fiber), 361
classful IPv4 addressing, 365–366
Classless Inter-Domain Router (CIDR), 365–366
classless IPv4 addressing, 365–366
cleaning
- cases, 160–161
- cleaning process (laser printing), 627
- cleaning tools, 85, 94–96
- internal components, 160–161
- printers, 649–651

cleaning process (laser printing), 627
CLI (command-line interface). *See also* commands
- definition of, 190–191, 286
- Linux and OS X
  - *administrative commands, 598–599*
  - *file/folder commands, 597–598*
  - *overview, 582–584*
- Run Line utility, 289–290
- Windows, 286–288

clients
- client-server networks, 331–332
- email clients, 566
- thick clients, 63
- thin clients, 63

client-server networks, 331–332
client-side virtualization
- hypervisors
  - *definition of, 291*
  - *Type 1 hypervisors, 246–292*
  - *Type 2 hypervisors, 246–292*
  - *Windows Hyper-V, 292–293*
  - *Windows Virtual PC, 246–293*
  - *Windows XP Mode, 293–294*
- logical virtual machine diagram, 291
- purpose of, 290–291
- virtual machine requirements, 294

climate, effect on equipment, 77
clock speed, monitoring, 142
Clock widget, 528
cloning disks, 214–215
closed source licensing, 520–521
closed-ended questions
- definition of, 157–165, 733
- laptop/mobile device issues, 503–506
- network issues, 434
- operating system issues, 305
- security issues, 718–719

cloud computing
- characteristics of, 425–426
- cloud-enabled services for mobile devices
  - *locator apps, 551–552*
  - *remote backup, 551*
  - *remote lock, 518–552*
  - *remote wipe, 518–552*
- compared to data centers, 425
- definition of, 324

IaaS (Infrastructure as a Service), 426
ITaaS (IT as a Service), 426
OneDrive, 577
PaaS (Platform as a Service), 426
printing, 631
SaaS (Software as a Service), 426
types of, 426–427

clusters, 202

CMOS (complementary metal oxide semiconductor) chip, 135–136

CMY, 621

CMYK, 621

coaxial cables, 351–353

cold boots, 222

cold cathode fluorescent lamp (CCFL), 461–462

collated printing, 635

colon (:), 367

color

color codes for power supply voltages, 9–10
color resolution, 47
display colors, 266

COM (Component Object Model) components, 246

COMMAND command, 289

Command Prompt, 221

command-line interface. *See* CLI (command-line interface)

command-line tools. *See* CLI (command-line interface)

commands. *See also* utilities

at, 298
bootrec, 288, 289, 311, 767
cat, 602
cd, 288, 602
chkdsk, 289, 311
COMMAND, 289
COPY, 289
cp, 602
crontab, 592–594
DEFRAG, 289
defrag, 289
DEL, 288
DIR, 289
DXDIAG, 289
EXIT, 289
EXPAND, 289
EXPLORER, 289
FORMAT, 288
GPRESULT, 289
GPUPDATE, 289
grep, 602
help, 288
imageX, 215–216
ipconfig, 397, 404, 774
ls, 598, 602
man, 602
MD, 288
mkdir, 602
MMC, 289
MSINFO32, 290
MSTSC, 290
mv, 602
nbtstat, 404
net, 404, 774, 778
netdom, 404
netstat, 556
NOTEPAD, 290
nslookup, 405
ping, 371, 404
RD, 288
REGEDIT, 290
rm, 602
ROBOCOPY, 289
RSTRUI, 289
RUNAS, 289
sfc, 289, 769
shutdown, 288
taskkill, 288
tasklist, 288
tracert, 404–405
uname, 556
XCOPY, 289

commercial licenses, 746–747

common problems and solutions

CPUs, 176–179
internal components, 174–176
Linux, 608–609
memory, 176–179
mobile devices, 604–610
mobile operating systems, 606–612
monitors, 177–181
motherboards, 174–176
networks, 437–439
operating systems, 305–314
OS X, 608–609
power supplies, 175–177
printers, 655–657
security, 721–723
storage devices, 172–175

Commonly Used Settings menu (iOS), 531–532

communication encryption types, 698–701

communication skills

challenges
angry customers, 736–737
customer focus, maintaining, 735–737

inexperienced customers, 737
knowledgeable customers, 737
rude customers, 736
talkative customers, 735–736
netiquette, 738
overview, 732–733
problem identification
beep codes, 165–166
BIOS settings, 166
closed-ended questions, 157–165
conversation etiquette, 164–165
Device Manager, 167
diagnostic tools, 168
documentation of outcomes, 165
Event Viewer, 166
open-ended questions, 157–165
Task Manager, 167–168
professional behavior, 732, 733–735
troubleshooting and, 731
community clouds, 427
Compact Disc File System (CDFS), 207
compact discs (CDs), 27–28
compact tower cases, 5
CompactFlash, 60
complementary metal oxide semiconductor (CMOS) chip, 135–136
complex instruction set computer (CISC), 15
component contacts, cleaning, 95
Component Object Model (COM) components, 246
Component Services, 279–280, 283
component-retrieving tools, 94
compressed air, 95
computer assembly. *See also* boot process
adapter card installation
video adapter cards, 120–121
wireless NICs, 119–120
BIOS (basic input/output system), 147–148
cable connections
case fan connections, 124–126
eternal cables, 131–133
front panel cables, 127–131
internal data cables, 126–127
internal drive connections, 124–126
motherboard power connections, 122–124
reassembly, 131
cases, 104–105
cooling systems, 148
CPUs
installation, 107–112
upgrades, 148
hard drive installation, 116–117
motherboards
installation, 114–116
upgrades, 145–147
optical drive installation, 117
peripheral devices, 150–152
power supply connections, 105–106
RAM (random-access memory)
installation, 112–114
upgrades, 149
storage drives, 149–150
Computer feature, 257
computer forensics, 747–748
Computer Management utility, 277–278
computer networks. *See* networks
computer-aided design (CAD), 64
computer-aided manufacturing (CAM), 64
computer-to-network connections. *See also* networks
network sharing
administrative shares, 412–414
domains, 406–407
drive mapping, 414
network file sharing, 410–411
Windows homegroups, 408–409
Windows Vista, 409–410
workgroups, 406–407
NICs (network interface cards)
configuration, 389–393
connecting, 393–394
installation, 388–389
network installation completion list, 386–387
overview, 385–386
selecting, 386–387
updating, 388–389
remote access
definition of, 415
Remote Assistance, 415–416
Remote Desktop, 415–416
VPNs (virtual private networks), 415–416
routers
Internet connections, 394–395
logging in to, 397–398
network location profiles, 395–397
network setup, 398–399
NIC connections, 393–394
testing connectivity of, 402–405
wireless settings, 399–402
conduits, 708
configuration. *See also* installation
backups

Linux, 587
OS X, 588–589
overview, 686–687
BIOS (basic input/output system)
hardware diagnostics and monitoring, 141–143
main configurations, 138–139
security configurations, 140–141
settings, 139–140
Bluetooth, 470
browser security
ActiveX filtering, 681
InPrivate Browsing, 683
pop-up blockers, 681
SmartScreen Filter, 682
firewalls
software firewalls, 683–685
Windows Firewall, 268
GPS (global positioning system), 540
hardware firewalls, 703–705
IP (Internet Protocol) addressing
dynamic addressing, 370–371
static addressing, 368–370
laptops
power settings, 464–468
wireless configuration, 468–472
mobile device connectivity
Bluetooth, 563–566
cellular communications, 559–562
wireless data networks, 557–559
networks. *See* applied networking
NICs (network interface cards), 389–393
passcode locks, 547–548
permissions, 687
printers
common settings, 637–638
global configuration, 638–639
per-document configuration, 640
Remote Assistance, 417–418
Remote Desktop, 417
routers
network setup, 398–399
testing connectivity of, 402–405
wireless settings, 399–402
shared printers, 641–642
UEFI (Unified Extensible Firmware Interface)
ASUS Advanced Mode, 144
EZ Mode, 140–141
VPN connections
from mobile devices, 543
in Windows, 416
Windows BitLocker, 689–691

connections. *See also* connectors
adapters, 40–41
computer-to-network. *See* computer-to-network connections
converters, 40–41
domains, 406–407
drive connections, 28–32
ISPs (Internet Service Providers)
broadband technology, 384–418
selecting, 423–424
mobile devices, 495–496
motherboards, 12–13, 122–124
printer connections, 622–623
secure Internet connections, troubleshooting, 772–773
shared printers, 642–643
VPNs (virtual private networks), 543
workgroups, 406–407
Connections tab (Internet Options), 264
connectors
fiber-optic cabling, 359–360
Lightning connectors, 495
Micro/Mini USB connectors, 447
power supplies, 8–9
RJ-11 connectors, 356
RJ-45 connectors, 355
storage device connectors, 28–31
S-Video connectors, 451
video ports and cables, 33–38
WiFi antenna connectors, 462–463
contactless NFC (near field communication), 542
Content tab (Internet Options), 264
contrast ratio, 47
Control Panel utilities
Action Center, 267
Add Hardware, 274
Device Manager, 272–273
Devices and Printers, 273–274
Display Settings, 265–266
Folder Options, 266–267
HomeGroup, 276–277
Internet Options, 264–265
Network and Sharing Center, 277
overview, 260–262
Power Options, 269–270
Program and Features, 275–276
Region, 275
Region and Language, 275
Security Center, 267
Sound, 274
System, 270–272

Troubleshooting, 275–276
User Accounts, 262–264
Windows Firewall, 268
controls (ActiveX), 681
conversations
customer conversations. *See* communication skills
network conversations, 373
converters, 40–41
cooling systems
cleaning, 161
connecting power to, 124–126
fans
cleaning, 161
monitoring, 142
selecting, 51–52
selecting
CPU cooling systems, 53–55
fans, 51–52
types of, 17–20
upgrades, 148
copper cabling, 323
COPY command, 289
corona, primary, 626
Cortana, 544
cost of printers, 621–622
covers for mobile devices, 496
cp command, 602
CPUs
architecture of, 14–15
common problems and solutions, 176–179
CPU throttling, 16
installation, 107–112
laptop CPUs, 456
performance-enhancing features, 15–17
processor architecture, 192
replacing, 488–490
selecting, 53–55
socket architecture, 108
upgrades, 148
credit card readers, 498
cron service, 592–594
cron table, 592–594
crontab command, 592–594
crosstalk, 319
CRUs (customer-replaceable units), 478
CSMA/CA (Carrier Sense Multiple Access with Collision Avoidance), 318–343
CSMA/CD (Carrier Sense Multiple Access with Collision Detection), 341–342
current, electrical, 10, 78
custody, chain of, 745, 750
custom operating system installation methods
disk cloning, 214–215
network installations, 217–218
recovery partitions, 220
system images, 215–217
system recovery options, 220–221
System Restore, 219
customer call rules, 741–742
customer center employee rules, 742
customer satisfaction, 742
customer service
challenges
angry customers, 736–737
customer focus, maintaining, 735–737
inexperienced customers, 737
knowledgeable customers, 737
rude customers, 736
talkative customers, 735–736
definition of customers, 163
netiquette, 738
overview, 732–733
problem identification
beep codes, 165–166
BIOS settings, 166
closed-ended questions, 157–165
conversation etiquette, 164–165
Device Manager, 167
diagnostic tools, 168
documentation of outcomes, 165
Event Viewer, 166
open-ended questions, 157–165
Task Manager, 167–168
professional behavior, 732, 733–735
troubleshooting and, 731
customer-replaceable units (CRUs), 478
customization
libraries, 258
Start menu, 252–253
Windows desktop, 250–251
cyber law, 748
cylinders, 202

D

daily wheel printers, 629
dash (-), 582
data backups. ***See*** **backups**
data centers, 425
data migration, 198–208

data persistence, 748
data protection
backups
Backup and Restore utility, 300
Backup Files Wizard, 711
configuration, 686–687
definition of, 585
hard disk drives, 299–300
importance of, 164
iOS Backup process, 575–576
Linux, 585–587
OS X, 588–589
remote backup for mobile devices, 551
Windows, 711
biometric identification devices, 685–686
data wiping
mobile devices, 518–552
tools for, 691–693
encryption
drive encryption, 141
EFS (Encrypting File System), 689
types of, 698–701
hard drive recycling and destruction, 693–694
permissions, 687–689
smart cards, 685–686
software firewalls, 683–685
Windows BitLocker, 689–691
Data Sources (ODBC), 280–281, 284
data synchronization. *See* synchronization
data threats, 666
data transmission, 317–325
data volatility, 748
data wiping
mobile devices, 518–552
tools for, 691–693
DC (direct current), 7
DC jacks, replacing, 481–482
DDoS (distributed DoS), 670
DDR SDRAM (Double Data Rate SDRAM), 21
DDR2 SDRAM (Double Data Rate 2 SDRAM), 21
DDR3 SDRAM (Double Data Rate 3 SDRAM), 21
DDR4 SDRAM (Double Data Rate 4 SDRAM), 21
dedicated print servers, 646
de-encapsulation, 340
Defrag, 88, 289
degaussing wand, 692–693
Déjà Dup, 585–587
DEL command, 288
demilitarized zone (DMZ), 704–705
denial of service (DoS), 670
desktop (Windows), 247–251
desktop operating systems, 193. *See also* Windows 7; Windows 8/8.1; Windows Vista
destination port numbers, 376–380
destroying hard disk drives, 693–694
Details tab (Task Manager), 255
developing process (laser printing), 626
device drivers. *See* drivers
Device Manager
Android, 551–552
overview, 167
Windows, 213–214, 272–273
devices
Devices and Printers utility, 273–274
host devices, 321–322
intermediary devices, 322–323
mobile. *See* mobile devices
Devices and Printers, 273–274
DHCP (Dynamic Host Configuration Protocol), 338, 427
DHCPDISCOVER, 427
DHCPOFFER, 427
diagnostic tools
BIOS hardware diagnostics, 141–143
overview, 85–88, 168
dialog boxes, Printer Properties, 642
dialup connections, 384
digital assistants, 543–544
digital cameras, 45
Digital Light Processing (DLP), 46
digital micromirror device (DMD), 46
digital multimeters (DMMs), 85, 94
digital rights management (DRM), 747
digital signatures, 700
digital subscriber line (DSL), 317, 344–345, 420, 423–424
digital versatile discs (DVDs), 27–28
Digital Visual Interface (DVI), 34, 446
digitizers, 46
DIMMs (dual inline memory modules), 22
Din-6, 37
DIP (dual inline package) chips, 22
DIR command, 289
direct current (DC), 7
direct mobile billing, 542
directories
definition of, 190
file extensions, 237–239
file locations, 236–237
file/folder properties, 239–240
DirectX, 192
Disabled setting (services), 281

discovering Bluetooth devices, 470
Disk Cleanup, 88
disk cloning, 214–215
Disk Defragmenter, 284–285
disk drives. *See* drives
Disk Error-Checking tool, 285
disk format (Linux/OS X), 589
disk management tools
- Disk Management utility, 88, 227–229, 233–234
- Linux/OS X, 589–591
- overview, 88

Disk Management utility, 88, 227–229, 233–234
disk utilities (Linux/OS X), 589–591
Disk Utility, 590–591
DISKPART command, 289
Display Settings utility, 265–266
DisplayPort connectors, 35
displays. *See* monitors
disposal of equipment, 80–82
distributed DoS (DDOS), 670
DLL (Dynamic Link Library) files, 225
DLP (Digital Light Processing), 46
DMD (digital micromirror device), 46
DMMs (digital multimeters), 85, 94
DMZ (demilitarized zone), 704–705
DNS (Domain Name System)
- DNS poisoning, 672
- overview, 337, 427–428

docking station connectors, 446
docking stations, 457–459, 497
documentation
- chain of custody, 750
- laptops/mobile devices, 506–509
- Linux, 603–608
- mobile operating systems, 603–608
- networks, 437
- operating systems, 305–308
- OS X, 603–608
- overview, 165, 749–750
- preventive maintenance, 172
- printers, 654–655
- security, 721

Domain Name System. *See* DNS (Domain Name System)
Domain Network location profile, 396
domains, 210, 406–407
DoS (denial of service), 670
dot matrix printers, 629–630
dot pitch, 47
dots per inch (dpi), 621
double colon (::), 367
Double Data Rate 2 SDRAM (DDR2 SDRAM), 21
Double Data Rate 3 SDRAM (DDR3 SDRAM), 21
Double Data Rate 4 SDRAM (DDR4 SDRAM), 21
Double Data Rate SDRAM (DDR SDRAM), 21
double touch, 447
dpi (dots per inch), 621
DRAM (dynamic RAM), 21
drive activity LEDs, 129
drive bays, 116
drive letter assignment, 231–233
drivers
- definition of, 190
- interface drivers, 340
- printer drivers
  - *installation, 633–634*
  - *types of, 632–633*
- signed drivers, 151–152
- updates, 296–297

drives
- adding, 231
- connections, 28–32
- data wiping, 691–693
- drive letter assignment, 231–233
- encryption, 141
- external storage, 61–62
- flash drives
  - *definition of, 474*
  - *structure of, 202–203*
- hard disk drives
  - *backups, 299–300*
  - *connecting power to, 124–126*
  - *data wiping, 691–693*
  - *definition of, 26*
  - *encryption, 141*
  - *laptop hard disk drives, 485–486*
  - *overview, 57–58*
  - *partitioning, 203–206*
  - *partitions, 230–231*
  - *RAID (redundant display of independent disks), 24, 31–33, 232, 763*
  - *recycling and destruction, 693–694*
  - *selecting, 57–58*
  - *structure of, 200–202*
  - *troubleshooting, 172–175*
  - *upgrades, 149–150*
- laptops
  - *overview, 456*
  - *replacing, 485–486*
- mapping, 231–233, 414
- mirroring, 234

mobile devices, 494–495
mounted drives, 235–236
optical drives, 61
overview, 26–28, 200
partitions
configuration, 203–206
extending, 230
Linux/OS X partition management, 589
recovery partitions, 220
shrinking, 230–231
recycling and destruction, 693–694
troubleshooting, 172–175
DRM (digital rights management), 747
DSL (digital subscriber line), 317, 344–345, 420, 423–424
dual core CPUs, 16
dual inline memory modules (DIMMs), 22
dual inline package (DIP) chips, 22
dual rail power supplies, 10
dual voltage power supplies, 11
dual-channel RAM, 22
Duplex Multimode LC connectors, 363
Duplex setting (NIC), 390
DVDs (digital versatile discs), 27–28
DVI (Digital Visual Interface), 34, 446
DXDIAG command, 289
dynamic addressing, 370–371
dynamic disks, 206
Dynamic Host Configuration Protocol (DHCP), 338, 427
Dynamic Link Library (DLL) files, 225
dynamic RAM (DRAM), 21

E

ear buds, 497
ECP (Enhanced Capabilities Port), 623
EDGE (Enhanced Data Rates for GSM Evolution), 422
EEPROM (electrically erasable programmable read-only memory), 20
EFS (Encrypting File System), 689
EIDE (enhanced integrated drive electronics), 29
EIGRP (Enhanced Interior Gateway Routing Protocol), 340
electrical safety, 75
electrically erasable programmable read-only memory (EEPROM), 20
electromagnetic degaussing wand, 692–693
electromagnetic interference (EMI), 77, 319
electronic readers, 499
electrostatic discharge (ESD)
damage from, 76–77, 108
tools for preventing, 83–84, 91–92
email
clients, 566
configuration for mobile devices
Android, 568–570
Exchange, 568
Internet email, 571–572
iOS, 570–571
protocols, 566–568
email services, 430
servers, 566
spam, 670, 673
troubleshooting, 772
Embedded MultiMediaCard (eMMC), 60, 203, 492
emergency notifications, 544–545
EMI (electromagnetic interference), 77, 319
eMMC (Embedded MultiMediaCard), 60, 203, 492
employee best practices
customer call rules, 741–742
customer center employee rules, 742
customer satisfaction, 742
SLAs (service level agreements), 740–741
stress management, 740
time management, 739
workstation ergonomics, 739
enabling. *See* configuration
encapsulation
encapsulation process, 338
example of, 339–340
Encrypting File System (EFS), 689
encryption
drive encryption, 141
EFS (Encrypting File System), 689
types of, 698–701
end user license agreement (EULA), 745–746
Enhanced Capabilities Port (ECP), 623
Enhanced Data Rates for GSM Evolution (EDGE), 422
enhanced integrated drive electronics (EIDE), 29
Enhanced Interior Gateway Routing Protocol (EIGRP), 340
Enhanced Parallel Port (EPP), 623
enterprise licenses, 746
environment, effect on computer performance, 162
environmental protection
equipment disposal, 80–82
SDSs (safety data sheets), 79–80
EPP (Enhanced Parallel Port), 623
EPROM (erasable programmable read-only memory), 20
EPS12V, 7
equations, Ohm's Law, 10

equipment disposal, 80–82
equipment protection
AutoPlay, 706
AutoRun, 706
BIOS/UEFI passwords, 706
BYOD (bring your own device), 708
climate concerns, 77
EMI (electromagnetic interference), 77
ESD (electrostatic discharge), 76–77
multifactor authentication, 707–708
overview, 706
power fluctuation, 78
power-protection devices, 78–79
security hardware, 708–710
security profiles, 708
erasable programmable read-only memory (EPROM), 20
Erase feature (Android), 518
Erase Phone option (iOS), 518
e-readers, 499
ergonomics, 739
error-correcting code memory, 23
errors. *See also* troubleshooting
BOOTMGR is missing, 311, 767
Can't find server name for 127.0.0.1: timed out, 774
Caution this hard disk may be infected by a virus! 776
Inaccessible Boot Device, 767
Invalid Boot Disk, 767
Invalid Boot Disk Error, 311
MBR has been changed or modified, 776
Missing GRUB, 613
Missing LILO, 613
missing or corrupt DLL, 769
eSATA (external SATA), 29–32, 39
ESD (electrostatic discharge)
damage from, 76–77, 108
tools for preventing, 83–84, 91–92
eterm, 583
eternal cable installation, 131–133
Ethernet
ports, 38, 451
printer connections, 623
standards
cable standards, 342–343
CSMA/CA, 318–343
CSMA/CD, 341–342
definition of, 340
PoE (Power over Ethernet), 351
wireless security, 344–345, 401–402
wireless standards, 343–346
Windows 8/8.1, 403
ethical considerations, 743–744
etiquette
conversation etiquette, 164–165
online interactions, 738
EULA (end user license agreement), 745–746
EV-DO (Evolution-Data Optimized), 422
Event Viewer, 166, 279
Evolution-Data Optimized (EV-DO), 422
Exchange, 568
execute disable bits, 17
executing Android apps, 527
exFAT (FAT 64), 206
EXIT command, 289
EXPAND command, 289
expanding Ribbon, 245
expansion cards
installation, 472–473
selecting, 56–57
expansion ports
expansion cards
installation, 472–473
selecting, 56–57
flash memory, 474–475
smart card readers, 475–476
SODIMM (small outline DIMM), 476–478
expiration of passwords, 677
EXPLORER command, 289
exporting local security policy, 679
exposure process (laser printing), 626
ExpressCards, 472–473
ext3 file system, 585
ext4 file system, 585
extended partitions, 205, 230
extensions (file), 237–239
external flash drives. *See* flash drives
external SATA (eSATA), 29–32, 39
external storage, selecting, 61–62
EZ Mode (UEFI), 140–141

F

factory reset (mobile devices), 609
failed login attempts, 714
failed passcode attempts, 549–550
fans
cleaning, 161
connecting power to, 124–126
installation, 107–112
monitoring, 142
overview, 17
selecting, 51–52
upgrades, 148

FAT 64 (exFAT), 206
fat clients, 63
FAT32, 206
fiber broadband, 384–422
fiber-optic cabling, 323, 358–360
field-replaceable units (FRUs), 478
File Allocation Table, 32 bt (FAT32), 206
File Explorer, 245–256
File History, 299–300
file systems
Linux and OS X, 585
Windows, 206–207
File Transfer Protocol (FTP)
definition of, 338, 428–429
FTPS (File Transfer Protocol Secure), 429
troubleshooting, 772–773
File Transfer Protocol Secure (FTPS), 429
files
adding to libraries, 258
autorun.inf, 707
definition of, 190
DLL (Dynamic Link Library) files, 225
encryption, 689
extensions, 237–239
File History, 299–300
file locations, 236–237
file systems, 206–207
HAL.DLL, 223
management
Linux and OS X file commands, 597–598
Windows, 190
network file sharing, 410–411
NTOSKRNL.EXE, 223
opening, 257–258
paging files, 246
PDF (Portable Document Format), 631
permissions, 411, 687–689
program files, 237
properties of, 239–240
signature file updates, 697
temporary files, 237
XPS (XML Paper Specification), 631
filtering, ActiveX, 681
finalizing operating system installation, 212–214
Find My iPhone, 551–552
Finder, 582
finding shared printers on network, 643–644
findings, documenting. ***See*** **documentation**
fingerprint readers, 453, 683
fire extinguisher operation, 75
fire safety, 75–76
firewalls
hardware firewalls, 349–350, 703–705
software firewalls
compared to hardware firewalls, 704
configuration, 683–685
troubleshooting, 778–779
Windows Firewall
configuration, 268
preventive maintenance, 711–713
FireWire
capabilities, 39
FireWire 400, 31
FireWire 800, 31
overview, 39
printer connections, 623
firmware
definition of, 20
printer firmware, 640
updates, 297, 703
first response, 748–749
fitness monitors, 498
Fixed WiMAX, 421
flash card readers, 474–475
flash cards, 474–475
flash drives
definition of, 474
overview, 27
structure of, 202–203
flash memory
flash ROMs, 20
installing, 474–475
flash ROMs, 20
flashing the BIOS, 147
flathead screwdrivers, 93
Fn (Function) key, 456–457
Folder Options utility, 266–267
folders
adding to libraries, 258
definition of, 190
encryption, 689
Folder Options utility, 266–267
iOS, 534–535
management
Android, 528–529
Linux and OS X folder commands, 597–598
Windows, 190
permissions, 411, 687–689
Program Files, 237
properties of, 239–240
Temporary Files, 237
Windows Phone, 537–538

fonts, 236
forensics (computer), 747–748
form factors
  definition of, 5
  motherboards, 13–14
  power supplies, 7
Format, 88, 288
formatting, 206
forwarding, port, 705
frame rate, 47
front panel cables, 127–131
front-side bus (FSB), 16, 54
FRUs (field-replaceable units), 478
FSB (front-side bus), 16, 54
FTP (File Transfer Protocol)
  definition of, 338, 428–429
  FTPS (File Transfer Protocol Secure), 429
  troubleshooting, 772–773
FTPS (File Transfer Protocol Secure), 429
full control permissions, 411, 688
full format, 207
full system functionality verification
  laptops/mobile devices, 505–508
  Linux, 603–608
  mobile operating systems, 603–608
  networks, 436–437
  operating systems, 304–308
  OS X, 603–608
  preventive maintenance, 171–172
  printers, 654
  security, 720–721
full-duplex mode, 317–326
full-size HDMI, 35
full-size tower cases, 5
Function (Fn) key, 456–457
fusing process (laser printing), 627

G

gadgets, 245–249
game ports, 37
gamepads, 44, 498
gaming PCs, 66–67
Gb/s (gigabits per second), 325
General Packet Radio Service (GPRS), 422
General tab
  Folder Options, 266
  Internet Options, 264
  System Configuration, 283
general tool use, 82–83
geocaching, 540
geotagging, 540
gestures, 493
GET requests, 428
GHz (gigahertz), 16
Gibson Research Corporation (GRC), 700
gigabits per second (Gb/s), 325
gigahertz (GHz), 16
global positioning system (GPS), 447–499, 540
global printer configuration, 638–639
Global System for Mobile Communications (GSM), 421, 545
gnome-terminal, 583–584
Google
  Google Cloud Print, 631
  Google Now, 544
  Google Now Launcher, 527
  Google Play, 523
  Google search, 526
GPRESULT command, 289
GPRS (General Packet Radio Service), 422
GPS (global positioning system), 447–499, 540
GPT (GUID partition table), 204–206
GPUPDATE command, 289
GPUs (graphics-processing units), 19
graphical user interface. *See* GUI (graphical user interface)
graphics cards, 56
graphics-processing units (GPUs), 19
GRC (Gibson Research Corporation), 703
grep command, 602
group management, 717
grub, 591
GSM (Global System for Mobile Communications), 421, 545
guest accounts, 713–714, 716
guest computers. *See* virtual machines
Guest group, 717
GUI (graphical user interface)
  definition of, 190–191
  Linux, 579–584
  OS X, 580–582
  Windows
    Action Center, 267
    Add Hardware, 274
    application installation, 259
    application uninstallation, 259–260
    CLI (command-line interface) commands, 286–288
    Component Services, 279–280, 283
    Computer feature, 257
    Computer Management, 277–278
    Control Panel, 260–262

Data Sources (ODBC), 280–281, 284
Device Manager, 272–273
Devices and Printers, 273–274
Disk Defragmenter, 284–285
Disk Error-Checking tool, 285
Display Settings, 265–266
Event Viewer, 279
File Explorer, 245–256
Folder Options, 266–267
HomeGroup, 276–277
Internet Options, 264–265
Network and Sharing Center, 277
Performance Monitor, 282–283
Power Options, 269–270
Program and Features, 275–276
Region, 275
Region and Language, 275
Run as Administrator option, 258
Run Line utility, 289–290
Security Center, 267
Services console, 281
Sound, 274
Start menu, 251–253
System Configuration, 281–282
System Information, 285–286
System utility, 270–272
Task Manager, 253–256
taskbar, 253
This PC feature, 257
Troubleshooting, 275–276
User Accounts, 262–264
Windows desktop, 247–251
Windows Explorer, 245
Windows Firewall, 268
Windows libraries, 258
Windows Memory Diagnostic, 246–283
GUID partition table (GPT), 204–206

H

HAL.DLL, 223
half-duplex mode, 326
hand tools, 84, 93–94
hands-free headsets, 569
hard disk drives
backups, 299–300
connecting power to, 124–126
data wiping, 691–693
definition of, 26
encryption, 141
laptops
overview, 456
replacing, 485–486
mapping, 231–233
mounted drives, 235–236
partitioning, 203–206
partitions
configuration, 203–206
extending, 230
Linux/OS X partition management, 589
recovery partitions, 220
shrinking, 230–231
RAID (redundant display of independent disks), 24, 31–33, 232, 763
recycling and destruction, 693–694
selecting, 57–58
structure of, 200–202
troubleshooting, 172–175
upgrades, 149–150
hard drive access panel (laptops), 453
hardware, definition of, 4
hardware access, 190
hardware firewalls, 349–350, 703–705
hardware maintenance tasks, 159
hardware print servers, 645–646
hardware requirements for operating systems, 195–196, 248
hardware tools
cable tools, 85
cleaning tools, 85, 94–96
diagnostic tools, 85–88
ESD (electrostatic discharge) tools, 83–84, 91–92
general tool use, 82–83
hand tools, 84, 93–94
hash encoding, 698
hashing, 698
HDDs. ***See*** **hard disk drives**
HDMI (High Definition Multimedia Interface), 35
headphones, 46
headsets, 497–499
heat sinks
installation, 107–112
overview, 18
upgrades, 148
help command, 288
HEPA (high efficiency particulate air) filtration, 650–651
hex drivers, 93
hexa-core CPUs, 16
HFC (hybrid fiber coax), 344–345
HFS+ (Hierarchical File System Plus), 585
Hibernate setting, 446
hidden shares, 412–414
Hierarchical File System Plus (HFS+), 585

High Definition Multimedia Interface was (HDMI), 35
high efficiency particulate air (HEPA) filtration, 650–651
High Speed Downlink Packet Access (HSDPA), 422
high-level formatting, 694
history of repairs, documenting, 90
HKEY_ Registry keys, 224–225
hold, placing calls on, 733–734
Home button (iOS), 531
Home Network location profile, 395
home screen items
  Android, 525–527
  iOS, 530–532
  Windows Phone, 535–537
home theater personal computers (HTPCs), 67–68
HomeGroup utility, 276–277
homegroups
  definition of, 210
  joining, 276–277
  network sharing, 408–409
horizontal cases, 5
horizontal resolution, 47
host devices, 246, 321–322
host services
  authentication services, 431
  DHCP (Dynamic Host Configuration Protocol), 427
  DNS (Domain Name System), 427–428
  email services, 430
  FTP (File Transfer Protocol), 428–429
  IDSs (intrusion detection systems), 431
  IPSs (intrusion prevention systems), 431
  print services, 429
  proxy servers, 430–431
  UTM (Universal Threat Management), 431–432
  web services, 428
hotspots, 471, 496, 552, 560–561
hot-swappable, 29–30
housing. *See* cases
HSDPA (High Speed Downlink Packet Access), 422
HTPCs (home theater personal computers), 67–68
HTTP (Hypertext Transfer Protocol), 339, 428
HTTPS (secure HTTP), 428
hubs, 345–346
hybrid clouds, 427
hybrid drives, 26
hybrid fiber coax (HFC), 344–345
Hypertext Transfer Protocol (HTTP), 339, 428
Hyper-Threading, 15–16
HyperTransport, 15–16
hypervisors
  definition of, 291
  Type 1 hypervisors, 246–292
  Type 2 hypervisors, 246–292
  virtual machine requirements, 294
  Windows Hyper-V, 292–293
  Windows Virtual PC, 246–293
  Windows XP Mode, 293–294

I

IaaS (Infrastructure as a Service), 426
IANA (Internet Assigned Numbers Authority), 335
ICANN (Internet Corporation for Assigned Names and Numbers), 335
ICMP (Internet Control Message Protocol), 339, 371–373
IDE (integrated development environment), 521
IDE (integrated drive electronics), 29
IDF (independent distribution facility), 356
idle timeout, 714
IDSs (intrusion detection systems), 142, 431
IEEE (Institute of Electrical and Electronics Engineers)
  802.11 standard (WiFi)
    antenna connectors, 462–463
    configuration, 471–472
    hotspots, 552, 560–561
    mobile device connectivity, 557–559
    overview, 343–346
    WiFi analyzers, 87
    WiFi calling, 541
    WiFi Sync, 577
    WPA (WiFi Protected Access), 344, 402, 702
    WPA2 (WiFi Protected Access 2), 344, 402, 702
    WPS (WiFi Protected Setup), 702
  802.11 standards, 343–346
  802.15.1 standard (Bluetooth)
    characteristics of, 468–469
    configuration, 470
    definition of, 496
    installation, 470
    for mobile devices, 563
    overview, 328–329, 644
    pairing, 564–566
    specifications, 469–470
  802.3 standard, 342–345
  1284 standard, 622–623
  1394 standard
    capabilities, 39
    FireWire 400, 31
    FireWire 800, 31
    overview, 39
    printers, 623
  definition of, 335

IETF® (Internet Engineering Task Force), 335, 362
i.Link. *See* FireWire
image-based installation, 215–216
imageX, 215–216
imaging drums, 625
IMAP (Internet Message Access Protocol), 338, 430, 567
IMEI (International Mobile Equipment Identity), 545
Imminent Threat alerts, 545
impact printers, 629–630
"Inaccessible Boot Device" error, 767
independent distribution facility (IDF), 356
Industrial, Scientific, and Medical (ISM) band, 328–329
inexperienced customers, 737
infected systems, remediation for, 695–696
infrared (IR), 496
Infrastructure as a Service (IaaS), 426
infrastructure mode (WLANs), 327
ink (printer), 648–649
inkjet printers, 623–625
InPrivate Browsing, 682–683
input devices
  cleaning
    keyboards, 96
    mice, 96
  laptop input devices, 453–454
  overview, 41–45
  selecting, 62
  upgrades, 150–152
inspecting internal components, 161–162
installation. *See also* configuration
  adapter cards
    video adapter cards, 120–121
    wireless NICs, 119–120
  applications, 259
  apps, push versus pull installation, 524–525
  Bluetooth, 470
  cables
    case fan connections, 124–126
    eternal cables, 131–133
    front panel cables, 127–131
    internal data cables, 126–127
    internal drive connections, 124–126
    motherboard power connections, 122–124
  CPUs, 107–112
  hard disk drives, 116–117
  laptop expansion devices
    expansion cards, 472–473
    flash memory, 474–475
    smart card readers, 475–476
    SODIMM (small outline DIMM), 476–478
  laptop hardware
    batteries, 480–481
    CPUs, 488–490
    DC jacks, 481–482
    internal drives, 485–486
    keyboards, 483
    motherboards, 490–491
    screens, 485
    speakers, 488
    touchpads, 483–484
    wireless cards, 487
  Linux/OS X updates, 594–596
  motherboards, 114–116
  NICs (network interface cards), 388–389
  operating systems
    account creation, 210–212
    default settings, 208–210
    disk cloning, 214–215
    file systems, 206–207
    finalizing, 212–214
    hard drive partitioning, 203–206
    network installations, 217–218
    recovery partitions, 220
    Refresh Your PC tool, 219
    storage device types, 200–203
    system images, 215–217
    system recovery options, 220–221
    System Restore, 219
    Windows 8/8.1, 208–210
  optical drives, 117
  power supplies, 105–106
  printer drivers, 633–634
  printers, 631–632
  RAM (random-access memory), 112–114
installer programs, 203
Institute of Electrical and Electronics Engineers. *See* IEEE (Institute of Electrical and Electronics Engineers)
integrated development environment (IDE), 521
integrated drive electronics (IDE), 29
integrated routers, 348
Integrated Services Digital Network (ISDN), 419, 423
interface drivers, 340
interlaced monitors, 47
intermediary devices, 322–323
internal components
  cleaning, 160–161
  inspecting, 161–162
  troubleshooting
    advanced problems and solutions, 763–764
    common problems and solutions, 174–176

International Mobile Equipment Identity (IMEI), 545
International Organization for Standardization (ISO), 334
Internet Assigned Numbers Authority (IANA), 335
Internet connections
mobile devices, 496
routers, 394–395
Internet Control Message Protocol (ICMP), 339, 371–373
Internet Corporation for Assigned Names and Numbers (ICANN), 335
Internet email, 571–572
Internet Engineering Task Force (IETF®), 335, 362
Internet Explorer security
ActiveX filtering, 681
InPrivate Browsing, 682–683
overview, 679–680
pop-up blockers, 681
SmartScreen Filter, 682
Internet Message Access Protocol (IMAP), 338, 430, 567
Internet Options utility, 264–265
Internet Protocol. *See* IP (Internet Protocol) addressing
Internet protocols, 334
Internet reference tools, 90
Internet Service Providers. *See* ISPs (Internet Service Providers)
intrusion detection systems (IDSs), 142, 431
intrusion prevention systems (IPSs), 431
"Invalid Boot Disk" error, 767
Invalid Boot Disk Error message, 311
inverters, 461–462
I/O cards, 57
iOS. *See also* mobile devices
apps
app management, 533
development, 521–522
installation, 524–525
sources for, 522–524
closed source licensing, 520–521
email configuration
account setup, 570–571
Exchange, 568
Internet email, 571–572
protocols, 566–568
factory reset, 609
GPS (global positioning system), 540
mobile device synchronization, 575–576
mobile payments, 542
network connectivity
Bluetooth, 563–566
cellular communications, 559–562
wireless data networks, 557–559
screen calibration, 539–540
screen orientation, 538–539
security
antivirus protection, 553–556
jailbreaking, 554–556
locator apps, 551–552
passcode locks, 545–550
patches, 556–557
remote backup, 551
remote lock, 518–552
remote wipe, 518–552
updates, 556–557
touch interface
app management, 533
folders, 534–535
home screen items, 530–532
multitasking bar, 533
WiFi calling, 541
IP (Internet Protocol) addressing
configuration, 389
dynamic addressing, 370–371
ICMP (Internet Control Message Protocol), 371–373
IPv4
address format, 363–365
classful and classless IPv4 addressing, 365–366
IPv6
IPv6 address format, 367–370
number of IPv6 addresses, 366–369
overview, 339, 362–363
static addressing, 368–370
ipconfig command, 397, 404, 774
IPS (in-plane switching), 446
IPSs (intrusion prevention systems), 431
IR (infrared), 496
ISDN (Integrated Services Digital Network), 419, 423
ISM (Industrial, Scientific, and Medical) band, 328–329
ISO (International Organization for Standardization), 334
isopropyl alcohol, 95
ISPs (Internet Service Providers)
broadband technology
ADSL (asymmetric digital subscriber line), 384–420
cable, 383–422
cellular, 421–422
DSL (digital subscriber line), 420
fiber broadband, 384–422
history of, 419
line of sight wireless Internet, 384–420
satellite, 383–422
WiMAX (Worldwide Interoperability for Microwave Access), 420–421
dialup connections, 345
selecting, 423–424

IT professionals
call center technicians
call center environments, 750–752
call prioritization, 751–752
levels of technicians, 739–753
support software, 751
challenges
angry customers, 736–737
customer focus, maintaining, 735–737
inexperienced customers, 737
knowledgeable customers, 737
rude customers, 736
talkative customers, 735–736
employee best practices
customer call rules, 741–742
customer center employee rules, 742
customer satisfaction, 742
SLAs (service level agreements), 740–741
stress management, 740
time management, 739
workstation ergonomics, 739
ethical considerations, 743–744
legal considerations
chain of custody, 750
computer forensics, 747–748
cyber law, 748
documentation, 749–750
first response, 748–749
licensing, 745–747
overview, 744–745
netiquette, 738
overview, 730, 731, 732–733
problem identification
beep codes, 165–166
BIOS settings, 166
closed-ended questions, 157–165
conversation etiquette, 164–165
Device Manager, 167
diagnostic tools, 168
documentation of outcomes, 165
Event Viewer, 166
open-ended questions, 157–165
Task Manager, 167–168
professional behavior, 732, 733–735
ITaaS (IT as a Service), 426
ITU, 334
ITX, 14

J

jackets (optical fiber), 360
jailbreaking, 554–556
Java APIs, 192
joining
homegroups, 276–277
workgroups, 277
journaled file systems, 585
journals, 90
joysticks, 44
Jump list, 253
junk mail, 670

K

kb/s (kilobits per second), 325
kernels
Linux, 582
Windows, 223
keyboard, video, mouse (KVM) switches, 45
keyboards
cleaning, 96, 162
overview, 43
replacing, 483
keyloggers, 694
keys
card keys, 708
public/private keys, 700
Registry keys, 224–225
kilobits per second (kb/s), 325
knowledgeable customers, 737
konsole, 583
KVM (keyboard, video, mouse) switches, 45

L

L1 cache, 23
L2 cache, 23
L3 cache, 23
laboratories
environmental protection
equipment disposal, 80–82
SDSs (safety data sheets), 79–80
equipment protection
climate concerns, 77
EMI (electromagnetic interference), 77
ESD (electrostatic discharge), 76–77
power fluctuation, 78
power-protection devices, 78–79
human safety
electrical safety, 75
fire safety, 75–76
general safety, 74–75
personal safety, 74
proper use of tools. *See also* utilities

cable tools, 85
cleaning tools, 85, 94–96
diagnostic tools, 85–88
ESD (electrostatic discharge) tools, 83–84, 91–92
general tool use, 82–83
hand tools, 84, 93–94
magnetic tools, 93
miscellaneous tools, 90–91
organizational tools, 89–91
land grid array (LGA), 14, 108
LANs (local area networks), 326–327
laptops. ***See also*** **mobile devices**
components
backlights, 461–462
CPUs, 456
docking stations, 457–459
external features, 449–453
input devices, 453–454
inverters, 461–462
LCD (liquid crystal display), 446–460
LED (light-emitting diode) displays, 446–460
LED (light-emitting diode) lights, 454
microphone, 463
motherboards, 454–455
OLED (organic LED), 446–460
port replicators, 460
RAM (random-access memory), 455
special function keys, 456–457
storage devices, 456
webcam, 463
WiFi antenna connectors, 462–463
configuration
power settings, 464–468
wireless configuration, 468–472
expansion ports
expansion cards, 472–473
flash memory, 474–475
smart card readers, 475–476
SODIMM (small outline DIMM), 476–478
hardware replacement
CPUs, 488–490
internal drives, 485–486
keyboards, 483
motherboards, 490–491
overview, 478–480
power, 480–482
screens, 485
speakers, 488
touchpads, 483–484
wireless cards, 487
preventive maintenance, 500–501
troubleshooting
common problems and solutions, 506–512
documentation of outcomes, 506–509
full system functionality verification, 505–508
problem identification, 503–506
testing, 504–507
theory of probable cause, 503–506
laser printers, 620, 625–627
Last Known Good Configuration, 224
latency, 325
Launcher
Android, 527
Linux, 584
LC (Lucent Connectors), 362
LCD (liquid crystal display)
cleaning, 95
cutoff switches, 446
definition of, 45–46
laptops, 446–460
least privilege, principle of, 688
LED (light-emitting diode), 46, 454, 446–460
legal considerations
chain of custody, 750
computer forensics, 747–748
cyber law, 748
documentation, 749–750
first response, 748–749
licensing
importance of, 745–747
open source versus closed source, 520–521
overview, 744–745
lenses (Linux), 584
levels of technicians, 739–753
LGA (land grid array), 14, 108
libraries, 258
licensing
importance of, 745–747
open source versus closed source, 520–521
LIF (low-insertion force), 108
light-emitting diode (LED), 46, 454, 446–460
Lightning connector, 495
Li-Ion (lithium-ion) batteries, 445
line of sight wireless Internet, 384–420
Line Print Terminal (LPT), 623
link lights, 394
Linux
backup and recovery, 585–587
CLI (command-line interface)
administrative commands, 598–599
file/folder commands, 597–598
overview, 582–584

disk utilities, 589–591
file systems, 585
GUI (graphical user interface), 579–584
multiboot procedures, 591
overview, 577–578
scheduled tasks, 592–594
security
antivirus/antimalware, 596
firmware updates, 596
operating system updates, 594–597
security credentials manager, 597
troubleshooting
common problems and solutions, 608–609
documentation of outcomes, 603–608
full system functionality verification, 603–608
plan of action, 602–607
problem identification, 601–605
testing, 602–607
theory of probable cause, 601–606
Li-Po (lithium-polymer) batteries, 445
liquid crystal display. *See* LCD (liquid crystal display)
lithium-ion (Li-Ion) batteries, 445
lithium-polymer (LiPo) batteries, 445
live tiles, 245
local area networks (LANs), 326–327
Local Users and Groups Manager, 713–715
location profiles, 395–397
locator apps, 551–552
Lock feature (Android), 553
locked computers, troubleshooting, 768
locks
locked computers, troubleshooting, 768
passcode locks
configuration, 547–548
definition of, 545–546
restrictions on failed login attempts, 549–550
types of, 546–547
remote lock, 518–552
logging in to routers, 397–398
logical drives, 205
logical virtual machine diagram, 291
login times, 714
LoJack, 141
Long Term Evolution (LTE), 560
long touch, 447
loopback adapters, 86
loopback plugs, 86, 94
Lost mode (iOS), 553
low-insertion force (LIF), 108
low-level formatting, 694
LPT (Line Print Terminal), 623
ls command, 598, 602
LTE (Long Term Evolution), 560
Lucent Connectors (LC), 362

M

MAC (Media Access Control) addressing, 347, 361–364
Mac OS X. *See* OS X
magnetic tools, 93
main boards. *See* motherboards
main distribution facility (MDF), 356
maintenance. *See* preventive maintenance
maintenance tools
Disk Defragmenter, 284–285
Disk Error-Checking tool, 285
System Information, 285–286
malware
adware, 668
antimalware software, 694–695
definition of, 667
malware settings, troubleshooting, 775–776, 777–778
ransomware, 668
remediation for infected systems, 695–696
rootkits, 669
signature file updates, 697
spyware, 668
Trojan horses, 667–668
viruses, 667
worms, 668
man command, 602
management
application management, 191–192
file/folder management, 190
folder management
Android, 528–529
iOS, 534–535
Windows Phone, 537–538
group management, 717
Linux/OS X partition management, 589
local password management, 678–679
mobile app management
Android, 527–528
iOS, 533
Windows Phone, 537–538
power management, 464–465
stress management, 740

time management, 739
user management, 714–716
widget management, 528
man-in-the-middle (MitM) attacks, 671
MANs (metropolitan area networks), 329
Manual setting (services), 281
MAPI (Messaging Application Programming Interface), 568
mapping network drives, 231–233, 414
master boot record (MBR), 204, 776
material safety and data sheet (MSDS), 73
maximum speed rating, 54
MBR (master boot record), 204, 776
"MBR has been changed or modified" message, 776
Mb/s (megabits per second), 325
MD command, 288
MD5 (Message Digest 5) algorithm, 698
MDF (main distribution facility), 356
mean time between failures (MTBF), 621
Media Access Control (MAC) addressing, 347, 361–364
media readers, selecting, 59–60
medium, 323
megabits per second (Mb/s), 325
megahertz (MHz), 16
memory
cache
definition of, 15
levels of, 23
flash memory, 474–475
memory cards, 492
printers, 641
RAM (random-access memory)
inspecting, 161
installation, 112–114
laptops, 455
memory modules, 22–26
types of, 21
upgrades, 149–150
ROM (read-only memory), 20
troubleshooting, 176–179
memory cards, 492
memory modules, 55–56
Memory Stick, 60
Message Digest 5 (MD5) algorithm, 698
message digests, 698
messages
DHCP (Dynamic Host Configuration Protocol), 427
error messages
BOOTMGR is missing, 311, 767
Can't find server name for 127.0.0.1: timed out, 774
Caution this hard disk may be infected by a virus! 776
Inaccessible Boot Device, 767
Invalid Boot Disk, 767
Invalid Boot Disk Error, 311
MBR has been changed or modified, 776
Missing GRUB, 613
Missing LILO, 613
missing or corrupt DLL, 769
Messaging Application Programming Interface (MAPI), 568
metropolitan area networks (MANs), 329
Metro-style apps, 524
MHz (megahertz), 16
mice
cleaning, 96, 162
overview, 43
Micro USB connectors, 447
Micro-ATX, 13–14
microphone jacks, 452
microphones, 463
MicroSD, 60, 498
microsegmenting, 318
Microsoft Management Console (MMC), 289
migrating data, 198–208
MIME (Multipurpose Internet Mail Extensions), 567
Mini DisplayPort, 35
Mini USB connectors, 447
mini-HDMI, 35
Mini-ITX, 14
Mini-PCI cards, 25, 471
Mini-PCIe cards, 471
MiniSD, 60
mini-tower cases, 5
mirroring
mirror sites, 697
mirrored volumes, 31, 232, 234
Missing GRUB message, 613
Missing LILO message, 613
missing or corrupt DLL message, 769
Mission Control, 582
MitM (man-in-the-middle) attack, 671
mkdir command, 602
MMC (Microsoft Management Console), 289
MMC command, 289
MMF (multimode fiber), 359
MMS (Multimedia Messaging Service), 422
mobile devices. *See also* laptops; mobile operating systems
device tracking, 540
electronic readers, 499
fitness monitors, 498

GPS (global positioning system), 447–499
hardware
accessories, 496–498
connection types, 495–496
mobile device parts, 446–492
non-upgradeable hardware, 492–493
SSDs (solid state drives), 494–495
touchscreens, 493–494
phablets, 499
preventive maintenance, 502
resetting, 609
security
antivirus protection, 553–556
locator apps, 551–552
passcode locks, 545–550
patches, 556–557
remote backup, 551
remote wipe, 518–552
rooting/jailbreaking, 554–556
updates, 556–557
smart cameras, 499
smart headsets, 498–499
smart watches, 498
synchronization
Android, 573–574
connection types, 576–577
definition of, 572–573
iOS, 575–576
troubleshooting
common problems and solutions, 509–514, 604–610
documentation of outcomes, 506–509
full system functionality verification, 505–508
problem identification, 503–506
testing, 504–507
theory of probable cause, 503–506
mobile hotspots, 496
mobile operating systems. *See also* **Android; iOS; mobile devices**
apps
development, 521–522
installation, 524–525
sources for, 522–524
definition of, 520
email configuration
Android, 568–570
Exchange, 568
Internet email, 571–572
iOS, 570–571
protocols, 566–568
GPS (global positioning system), 540
mobile device synchronization
Android, 573–574
connection types, 576–577
definition of, 572–573
iOS, 575–576
mobile payments, 542
network connectivity
Bluetooth, 563–566
cellular communications, 559–562
wireless data networks, 557–559
open source versus closed source, 520–521
resetting, 609
screen calibration, 539–540
screen orientation, 538–539
security
antivirus protection, 553–556
locator apps, 551–552
passcode locks, 545–550
patches, 556–557
remote backup, 551
remote lock, 518–552
remote wipe, 518–552
rooting/jailbreaking, 554–556
updates, 556–557
touch interface
Android, 525–530
iOS, 530–535
Windows Phone, 535–538
troubleshooting
common problems and solutions, 606–612
documentation of outcomes, 603–608
full system functionality verification, 603–608
plan of action, 602–607
problem identification, 600–605
testing, 602–607
theory of probable cause, 601–606
virtual assistants, 543–544
VPNs (virtual private networks), 543
WEAs (Wireless Emergency Alerts), 544–545
WiFi calling, 541
mobile payments, 542
mobile speakers, 569
mobile web payments, 542
Mobile WiMAX, 421, 560
modem ports, 445
modems, 344–345
modify permissions, 688
modules (memory), 22–26
Molex keyed connectors, 9
Molex-to-SATA adapters, 125

monitoring, BIOS hardware monitoring, 141–143
monitors
characteristics of, 47–48
cleaning, 95
connecting multiple, 48–49
display colors, 266
disposal of, 81
laptop displays
backlights, 461–462
inverters, 461–462
LCD (liquid crystal display), 446–460
LED (light-emitting diode), 446–460
microphone, 463
OLED (organic LED), 446–460
webcam, 463
WiFi antenna connectors, 462–463
troubleshooting, 177–181
types of, 45–46
motherboards
component connections, 12–13
connecting power to, 122–124
form factors, 13–14
installation, 114–116
laptop motherboards, 454–455
replacing, 490–491
selecting, 50–51
standoffs, 115
troubleshooting, 174–176
upgrades, 145–147
mounted drives
Linux/OS X, 589
Windows, 235–236
moving Android apps, 527
MSCONFIG, 281–282
MSDS (material safety and data sheet), 73
MSINFO32 command, 290
msinfo32.exe, 285–286
MSTSC command, 290
MTBF (mean time between failures), 621
multi rail power supplies, 10
multiboot
definition of, 226
Disk Management utility, 227–229
drive mapping, 231–233
Linux/OS X, 591
multiboot procedures, 226–227
partitions, 230–234
multicore processors, 16
multifactor authentication, 707–708
Multimedia Messaging Service (MMS), 422
multimode fiber (MMF), 359
multiple monitors, 48–49
multiprocessing, 189
multipurpose devices, 386
Multipurpose Internet Mail Extensions (MIME), 567
multitasking, 189
multitasking bar (iOS), 533
multithreading, 189
multi-touch, 493
multiuser, 189
mv command, 602

N

NAT (network address translation), 337, 399
native resolution, 47, 245
navigation apps, 540
navigation icons
Android, 526
Windows Phone, 537
nbtstat command, 404
near field communication (NFC), 496, 542
near letter quality (NLQ), 629–630
net command, 404
net share command, 778
net use command, 774
Netboot, 579
netdom command, 404
netiquette, 738
netstat command, 556
network address translation (NAT), 339, 399
Network and Sharing Center, 277
Network File System (NFS), 207
network installations, 217–218
network interface cards. *See* NICs (network interface cards)
network location profiles, 395–397
network media, 323–325
Network Mode, 399
network operating system (NOS), 194
network troubleshooting tools, problems with, 773–775
networking, definition of, 320. *See also* networks
Networking tab (Task Manager), 256
networks
bandwidth, 325
bridges, 346
cables
coaxial cables, 351–353
fiber-optic cabling, 358–360
twisted-pair cables, 353–357
cloud computing
characteristics of, 425–426
compared to data centers, 425

IaaS (Infrastructure as a Service), 426
ITaaS (IT as a Service), 426
PaaS (Platform as a Service), 426
SaaS (Software as a Service), 426
types of, 426–427
data centers, 425
data transmission, 317–325
definition of, 320–321
Ethernet standards
cable standards, 342–343
CSMA/CA, 318–343
CSMA/CD, 341–342
PoE (Power over Ethernet), 351
wireless security, 343–346
wireless standards, 343–346
firewalls
hardware firewalls, 349–350, 703–705
software firewalls, 683–685, 704
troubleshooting, 778–779
Windows Firewall, 268, 711–713
host devices, 321–322
host services
authentication services, 431
DHCP (Dynamic Host Configuration Protocol), 427
DNS (Domain Name System), 427–428
email services, 430
FTP (File Transfer Protocol), 428–429
IDSs (intrusion detection systems), 431
IPSs (intrusion prevention systems), 431
print services, 429
proxy servers, 430–431
UTM (Universal Threat Management), 431–432
web services, 428
hubs, 345–346
intermediary devices, 322–323
IP (Internet Protocol) addressing
classful and classless IPv4 addressing, 365–366
dynamic addressing, 370–371
ICMP (Internet Control Message Protocol), 371–373
IPv4 address format, 363–365
IPv6 address format, 367–370
number of IPv6 addresses, 366–369
overview, 362–363
static addressing, 368–370
ISPs (Internet Service Providers)
broadband technology, 384–418
dialup connections, 345
selecting, 423–424
latency, 325
Media Access Control (MAC) addressing, 361–364
mobile device connectivity
Bluetooth, 563–566
cellular communications, 559–562
wireless data networks, 557–559
modems, 344–345
network media, 323–325
network sharing
administrative shares, 412–414
domains, 406–407
drive mapping, 414
network file sharing, 410–411
Windows homegroups, 408–409
Windows Vista, 409–410
workgroups, 406–407
NICs (network interface cards)
configuration, 389–393
connecting, 393–394
installation, 388–389
network installation completion list, 386–387
overview, 23, 57, 385–386
selecting, 386–387
updating, 388–389
patch panels, 350
preventive maintenance, 432–433
reference models
comparison of, 341
de-encapsulation example, 340
encapsulation example, 339–340
open standards, 333–335
OSI model, 335–337
protocol data units, 338–339
protocols, 334–336
TCP/IP model, 335–340
remote access
definition of, 415
Remote Assistance, 415–418
Remote Desktop, 415–418
VPNs (virtual private networks), 415–416
repeaters, 351
routers
Internet connections, 394–395
logging in to, 397–398
network location profiles, 395–397
network setup, 398–399
NIC connections, 393–394
overview, 348–349
testing connectivity of, 402–405
wireless settings, 399–402
shared printers
configuration, 641–642

connecting to, 642–643
finding, 643–644
social networking, 317
switches, 346–347
transport layer
definition of, 373
features of, 373–374
port numbers, 376–380
TCP (Transmission Control Protocol), 374–376
UDP (User Datagram Protocol), 376
troubleshooting
common problems and solutions, 437–439
connection problems, 770–771
documentation of outcomes, 437
email failure, 772
FTP (File Transfer Protocol) problems, 772–773
full system functionality verification, 436–437
network troubleshooting tools, 773–775
plan of action, 436
problem identification, 434
secure Internet connections, 772–773
testing, 435
theory of probable cause, 434–435
types of
client-server networks, 331–332
LANs (local area networks), 326–327
MANs (metropolitan area networks), 329
peer-to-peer networks, 330–331
PLANs (personal area networks), 328–329
WANs (wide area networks), 329–330
WLANs (wireless LANs), 327–328
wireless access points, 347–348
New Mirrored Volume option, 232
New Spanned Volume option, 232
New Striped Volume option, 232
New Technology File System (NTFS), 206
NFC (near field communication), 496, 542
NFS (Network File System), 207
nickel-cadmium (NiCd) batteries, 450
nickel-metal hydride (NiMH) batteries, 445
NICs (network interface cards)
configuration, 389–393
connecting, 393–394
installation, 119–120, 388–389
network installation completion list, 386–387
overview, 23, 57, 385–386
selecting, 386–387
updating, 388–389
NiMH (nickel-metal hydride) batteries, 445
NLQ (near letter quality), 629–630
noise, 78
non-interlaced monitors, 47
nonparity memory, 23
non-upgradeable hardware (mobile devices), 492–493
nonvolatile memory, 21
Northbridge chipsets, 12–13
NOS (network operating system), 194
note taking, 89
Notepad, 634
NOTEPAD command, 290
Notification Center
iOS, 531
OS X, 585
notifications
Android, 526–527
iOS, 531
OS X, 585
WEAs (Wireless Emergency Alerts), 544–545
Nova Launcher, 527
nslookup command, 405
NTFS (New Technology File System), 206
NTOSKRNL.EXE, 223
numbers, port, 376–380
NX bits, 17

O

Occupational Safety and Health Administration (OSHA), 80
octa-core CPUs, 16
octets, 363
ODBC (Open Database Connectivity), 246, 284
ohms, 10
Ohm's Law, 10
OLED (organic LED), 46, 446–460
OneDrive, 577
online etiquette, 738
Open Database Connectivity (ODBC), 246, 284
Open Graphics Library (OpenGL), 191
Open Shortest Path First (OSPF), 340
open source licensing, 520–521, 746–747
open standards, 333–335
open system authentication, 344
Open Systems Interconnect (OSI) model, 335–337
open-ended questions
definition of, 157–165
laptop/mobile device issues, 503–506
network issues, 434
operating systems, 304
security issues, 718–719

OpenGL, 191
opening
cases, 104–105
files, 257–258
Task Manager, 255–256
operating systems
Android. *See* Android
boot process
overview, 222
startup modes, 223–224
Windows boot process, 222–223
Windows Registry, 224–225
customer requirements
hardware requirements, 195–196
OS-compatible applications and environments, 194–195
definition of, 4
desktop operating systems, 193
directories
file extensions, 237–239
file locations, 236–237
file/folder properties, 239–240
structure of, 234–236
functions of
application management, 191–192
file/folder management, 190
hardware access, 190
user interface, 190–191
installation
account creation, 210–212
default settings, 208–210
disk cloning, 214–215
file systems, 206–207
finalizing, 212–214
hard drive partitioning, 203–206
network installations, 217–218
recovery partitions, 220
Refresh Your PC tool, 219
storage device types, 200–203
system images, 215–217
system recovery options, 220–221
System Restore, 219
Windows 8/8.1, 208–210
iOS. *See* iOS
Linux
backup and recovery, 585–587
CLI (command-line interface), 582–584, 597–599
disk utilities, 589–591
file systems, 585
GUI (graphical user interface), 579–584
multiboot procedures, 591
overview, 577–578
scheduled tasks, 592–594
security, 594–597
mobile. *See* mobile operating systems
multiboot
definition of, 226
Disk Management utility, 227–229
drive mapping, 231–233
multiboot procedures, 226–227
partitions, 230–231
NOS (network operating system), 194
OS X
backup and recovery, 588–589
CLI (command-line interface), 582–584, 597–599
disk utilities, 589–591
file systems, 585
GUI (graphical user interface), 580–582
multiboot procedures, 591
Netboot, 579
overview, 578–579
scheduled tasks, 592–594
security, 594–597
overview, 188–189
preventive maintenance plans
contents of, 295–296
hard drive backups, 299–300
restore points, 298–299
task scheduling, 297–298
updates, 296–297
printer-sharing settings, 641–642
processor architecture, 192
security packs, 710–711
security patches, 710–711
troubleshooting
advanced problems and solutions, 766–769
common problems and solutions, 305–314
documentation of outcomes, 305–308
full system functionality verification, 304–308
overview, 766
plan of action, 304–307
problem identification, 302–305
testing, 303–306
theory of probable cause, 302–305
updates, 246–297
upgrades
data migration, 198–208
OS compatibility, 196–197
reasons for, 196
Windows OS upgrades, 197–198
Windows. *See* Windows 7; Windows 8/8.1; Windows Vista

operational environment of printers, 651
optical drives
connecting power to, 124–126
laptop optical drives, replacing, 486
selecting, 61
troubleshooting, 172–175
types of, 27–28
optical fiber, 358–360
optimization
drive optimization, 88, 284–285
Linux and OS X, 598–599
printer performance, 640–641
Optimize Drives, 88
organic LED (OLED), 46, 446–460
organizational tools, 89–91
orientation
Android, 538–539
Windows, 266
orientation, mobile device screens, 538–539
OS X
backup and recovery, 588–589
CLI (command-line interface)
administrative commands, 598–599
file/folder commands, 597–598
overview, 582–584
disk utilities, 589–591
file systems, 585
GUI (graphical user interface), 580–582
multiboot procedures, 591
Netboot, 579
overview, 578–579
scheduled tasks, 592–594
security
antivirus/antimalware, 596
firmware updates, 596
operating system updates, 594–596
security credentials manager, 597
troubleshooting
common problems and solutions, 608–609
full system functionality verification, 603–608
plan of action, 602–607
problem identification, 601–605
testing, 602–607
theory of probable cause, 601–606
OSHA (Occupational Safety and Health Administration), 80
OSI (Open Systems Interconnect) model, 335–337
OSPF (Open Shortest Path First), 340
OSs. *See* operating systems
outcomes, documenting. *See* documentation
output devices
headphones, 46
monitors
characteristics of, 47–48
cleaning, 95
connecting multiple, 48–49
disposal of, 81
troubleshooting, 177–181
types of, 45–46
printers
capabilities of, 619–622
characteristics of, 619–622
troubleshooting, 765
types of, 46
selecting, 62
speakers, 46
upgrades, 150–152
overclocking, 16
overheating
cooling systems
connecting power to, 124–126
fans, 142
selecting, 51–52
types of, 17–20
fire safety, 75–76
safety procedures, 76

P

PaaS (Platform as a Service), 426
packet filters, 704
packets, 317
Page Description Language (PDL), 632–633
pages, test, 634
pages per minute (ppm), 620
paging files, 246
pairing (Bluetooth), 564–566
parallel ATA, 29
parallel data transfer, 622–623
parity, 23, 31
partitions
Linux/OS X partition management, 589
Windows partition management
configuration, 203–206
extending, 230
recovery partitions, 220
shrinking, 230–231
passcode locks
configuration, 547–548
definition of, 545–546
restrictions on failed login attempts, 549–550
types of, 546–547

passwords
BIOS/UEFI passwords, 140, 706
with passcode locks, 546
Windows Local Security Policy
guidelines for, 677
levels of password protection, 676–677
management, 678–679
password policy, 677–678
patch panels, 350
patches
Linux and OS X
antivirus/antimalware, 596
firmware updates, 596
operating system updates, 594–596
security credentials manager, 597
mobile devices, 556–557
overview, 710–711
Pattern passcode locks, 546
payments, mobile, 542
PC Combo Card slot, 452
PCBs (printed circuit boards), 10
PCI (peripheral component interconnect)
overview, 25, 118
PCI Express Micro, 471
PCI Express (PCIe), 26, 118
PCI-Extended, 25
PCL (Printer Command Language), 633
PCs (personal computer systems). ***See also*** **computer assembly**
building, 49–50
definition of, 4
specialized systems
audio/video editing workstations, 64–65
CAx workstations, 64
gaming PCs, 66–67
home theater PCs, 67–68
thick clients, 63
thin clients, 63
virtualized workstations, 65–66
PDF (Portable Document Format), 631
PDL (Page Description Language), 632–633
PDUs (protocol data units), 338–339
PE (Preinstallation Environment), 220
Peek feature, 249
peer-to-peer networks, 330–331
pencils, 94
per-document printer configuration, 640
Performance Monitor, 282–283
performance optimization
drive optimization, 88, 284–285
Linux and OS X, 598–599
printer performance, 640–641
printers, 640–641
Performance tab (Task Manager), 254–256
peripheral component interconnect (PCI), 25, 118
permissions
file/folder permissions, 687–689
troubleshooting, 776–777
types of, 411
persistent data, 748
personal area networks (PLANs), 328–329
personal computer systems. ***See*** **PCs (personal computer systems)**
personal identification number (PIN), 546, 686
personal licenses, 745–746
personal reference tools, 89–90
personalization
Start menu, 252–253
Windows desktop, 250–251
Personalization window (Windows), 250–251
personally identifiable information (PII), 743–744
PGA (pin grid array), 14, 108
phablets, 499
Phillips head screwdrivers, 93
phishing, 669, 673
physical equipment protection
AutoPlay, 706
AutoRun, 706
BIOS/UEFI passwords, 706
BYOD (bring your own device), 708
multifactor authentication, 707–708
overview, 706
security hardware, 708–710
security profiles, 708
physical threats, 666
piezaelectric crystals, 624
PII (personally identifiable information), 743–744
PIN (personal identification number), 546, 686
pin grid array (PGA), 14, 108
pinching, 494
ping command, 371, 404
pinned applications, 253
pinning content to Start screen (Windows Phone), 536–537
pixels, 47
placing calls on hold, 733–734
plain old telephone service (POTS), 384–419, 423
in-plane switching (IPS), 446
plans
plan of action, establishing
Linux issues, 602–607
mobile operating system issues, 602–607
network issues, 436

operating system issues, 304–307
OS X issues, 602–607
preventive maintenance issues, 170–172
printer issues, 653–654
security issues, 720
power plans, 245
preventive maintenance plans
contents of, 295–296
hard drive backups, 299–300
restore points, 298–299
task scheduling, 297–298
updates, 296–297
PLANs (personal area networks), 328–329
plasma displays, 46
Platform as a Service (PaaS), 426
plenum, 319
plenum-rated cables, 319
PoE (Power over Ethernet), 351
pointing sticks, 453
Point-to-Point Protocol (PPP), 340
poisoning (DNS), 672
policies
business policies, 741–742
BYOD (bring your own device), 708
lockout policy, 678
password policy, 677–678
security policy
accessing, 675–676
definition of, 674–675
exporting, 679
passwords, 676–679
usernames, 676–677
Windows Local Security Policy
accessing, 675–676
definition of, 674–675
exporting, 679
passwords, 676–679
usernames, 676–677
POP (Post Office Protocol), 338, 430
POP3 (Post Office Protocol version 3), 567
pop-up blockers, 681
port forwarding, 705
port replicators, 460
port triggering, 705
portable chargers, 497
Portable Document Format (PDF), 631
ports
audio ports, 129
expansion ports, 472–473
other ports, 36–39
port forwarding, 705
port numbers, 376–380
port replicators, 460
port triggering, 705
USB (Universal Serial Bus), 23, 129
video ports and cables, 33–38
POST (power-on self-test), 103–134, 222
Post Office Protocol (POP), 338, 430
Post Office Protocol version 3 (POP3), 567
PostScript, 633
POTS (plain old telephone service), 384–419, 423
power button, 128
Power Control widget, 528
power fluctuation, 78
power LED, 129
power management (laptops)
ACPI (Advanced Configuration and Power Interface), 464–465
Power Options utility, 465–468
Power Options utility, 269–270, 465–468
Power over Ethernet (PoE), 351
power plans, 245
power supplies
case fan connections, 124–126
connectors, 8–9
definition of, 10
electrical safety, 75
form factors, 7
installation, 105–106
internal drive connections, 124–126
mobile devices, 497
motherboards, 122–124
power fluctuation, 78
Power Options utility, 269–270
power supply testers, 94
power surges, 78
power-protection devices, 78–79
selecting, 53
troubleshooting, 175–177
voltages, 9–10, 78
wattages, 10–12
power surges, 78
power-on self-test (POST), 103–134, 222
power-protection devices, 78–79
ppm (pages per minute), 620
PPP (Point-to-Point Protocol), 340
preboot execution environment (PXE), 217
Preferred Roaming List (PRL), 557
prefix notation, 365
Preinstallation Environment (PE), 220
Presidential alerts, 545

pretexting, 673
preventive maintenance. *See also* **troubleshooting**
benefits of, 159
cases, cleaning, 160–161
definition of, 157
Disk Defragmenter, 284–285
Disk Error-Checking tool, 285
environmental concerns, 162
hardware maintenance tasks, 159
implementing, 171–172
internal components
cleaning, 160–161
inspecting, 161–162
laptops, 500–501
mobile devices, 502
networks, 432–433
operating systems
hard drive backups, 299–300
preventive maintenance plan contents, 295–296
restore points, 298–299
task scheduling, 297–298
updates, 296–297
printers
cleaning methods, 649–651
consumables, replacing, 648–649
operational environment, 651
vendor guidelines, 647–648
security
account maintenance, 713–714
data backups, 711
group management, 717
implementing, 720–721
operating system security packs, 710–711
security patches, 710–711
user management, 714–716
Windows Firewall, 711–713
software maintenance tasks, 160
System Information, 285–286
PreviousVersions, 301
PRI (Primary Rate ISDN), 557
primary corona, 626
primary partitions, 205
Primary Rate ISDN (PRI), 557
principle of least privilege, 688
print job buffering, 640
print servers, 644–646
print services, 429
printed circuit boards (PCBs), 10
printer cartridges, disposal of, 81
Printer Command Language (PCL), 633
printer drivers
installation, 633–634
types of, 632–633
Printer Properties dialog box, 642
printers
calibration, 640
capabilities of, 619–622
characteristics of, 619–622
configuration
common settings, 637–638
global configuration, 638–639
per-document configuration, 640
connection types, 622–623
Devices and Printers utility, 273–274
firmware, 640
impact printers, 629–630
inkjet printers, 623–625
installation, 631–632
laser printers, 625–627
memory, 641
overview, 46
performance optimization, 640–641
preventive maintenance
cleaning methods, 649–651
consumables, replacing, 648–649
operational environment, 651
vendor guidelines, 647–648
print servers, 644–646
printer cartridges, disposal of, 81
printer drivers
installation, 633–634
types of, 632–633
shared printers
configuration, 641–642
connecting to, 642–643
finding on network, 643–644
wireless printers, 644
testing
printer functions, 635–636
test pages, 634
thermal printers, 628
troubleshooting
advanced problems and solutions, 765
common problems and solutions, 655–657
documentation of outcomes, 654–655
full system functionality verification, 654
plan of action, 653–654
problem identification, 652
testing, 653
theory of probable cause, 652–653
virtual printers, 630–631

prioritization of calls, 751–752
privacy screens, 709
Privacy tab (Internet Options), 264
private clouds, 426
private keys, 700
PRL (Preferred Roaming List), 557
problem identification
closed-ended questions, 157–165
conversation etiquette, 164–165
documentation of customer responses, 165
laptop/mobile device issues, 503–506
Linux issues, 601–605
mobile operating system issues, 600–605
network issues, 434
open-ended questions, 157–165
operating system issues, 302–305
OS X issues, 601–605
preventive maintenance
beep codes, 165–166
BIOS settings, 166
Device Manager, 167
diagnostic tools, 168
Event Viewer, 166
Task Manager, 167–168
printer issues, 652
security issues, 718–719
theory of probable cause
establishing, 168–169
testing, 169–170
problems and solutions. *See also* **troubleshooting**
CPUs, 176–179
internal components
advanced problems and solutions, 763–764
common problems and solutions, 174–176
Linux, 608–609
memory, 176–179
mobile devices, 604–610
mobile operating systems, 606–612
monitors, 177–181
motherboards, 174–176
networks
common problems and solutions, 437–439
connection problems, 770–771
email failure, 772
FTP (File Transfer Protocol) problems, 772–773
network troubleshooting tools, 773–775
secure Internet connections, 772–773
operating systems
advanced problems and solutions, 766–769
common problems and solutions, 305–314
OS X, 608–609
power supplies, 175–177
printers
advanced problems and solutions, 765
common problems and solutions, 655–657
security
common problems and solutions, 721–723
computer security, 777–778
firewall settings, 778–779
malware settings, 775–776
proxy settings, 778–779
user accounts and permissions, 776–777
storage devices, 172–175
processes, 254
Processes tab (Task Manager), 254–255
processing step (laser printing), 626
processor data bus, 16
professional behavior, 732
professionalism, 733–735
professionals (IT). *See* **IT professionals**
profiles
definition of, 683
network location profiles, 395–397
security profiles, 708
Program and Features utility, 275–276
program files, 237
programmable read-only memory (PROM), 20
programming tools (Windows)
Component Services, 283
Data Sources (ODBC), 284
programs. *See* **applications**
Programs tab (Internet Options), 265
PROM (programmable read-only memory), 20
protection. *See* **security**
protocol data units, 338–339
protocols, 334–336
proxy firewalls, 704
proxy servers, 430–431
proxy settings, troubleshooting, 778–779
PS/2 ports, 37
public clouds, 426
public key encryption, 700
public keys, 700
Public Network location profile, 396
pull installation, 524–525
purchasing. *See* **selecting**
push installation, 524–525
PXE (preboot execution environment), 217

Q

QoS (Quality of Service), 392
QR (Quick Response) codes, 523

quad-band, 422
quad-core CPUs, 16
quality of printers, 621
Quality of Service (QoS), 392
quick format, 207
Quick Response (QR) codes, 523
quid pro quo, 673

R

radio frequency interference (RFI), 77, 319
RAID (redundant display of independent disks), 24, 31–33, 232, 763
rails, 10
RAM (random-access memory)
  adapter cards, 56–57
  inspecting, 161
  installation, 112–114
  laptops, 455
  memory modules, 22–26
  printers, 641
  RAM access panel (laptops), 446
  selecting, 55–56
  types of, 21
  upgrades, 149
randomware, 668
RD command, 288
REACH (Registration, Evaluation, Authorization and restriction of Chemicals), 80
read and execute permissions, 688
read permissions, 411, 688
read-only memory (ROM), 20
rearranging Windows Phone tiles, 537
reassembling cases, 131
recovery
  Linux, 585–587
  OS X, 588–589
  recovery partitions, 220
  system recovery options, 220–221
recycling hard disk drives, 693–694
reduced instruction set computer (RISC), 15, 24
redundant display of independent disks (RAID), 31–33, 232, 763
reference models
  comparison of, 341
  de-encapsulation example, 340
  encapsulation example, 339–340
  open standards, 333–335
  OSI model, 335–337
  protocol data units, 338–339
  protocols, 334–336
  TCP/IP model, 335–340
reference tools, 89–90
refresh rate, 47, 266
Refresh Your PC tool, 219
REGEDIT command, 290
Region and Language utility, 275
Region utility, 275
registering DLL (Dynamic Link Library) files, 225
Registration, Evaluation, Authorization and restriction of Chemicals (REACH), 80
Registry, 224–225
reliability of printers, 621
remediation for infected systems, 695–696
remote access
  definition of, 415
  Remote Assistance, 415–416
  remote backup for mobile devices, 551
  Remote Desktop, 415–416
  remote lock, 518–552
  remote network installation, 217–218
  remote wipe, 518–552
  RIS (Remote Installation Services), 217
  VPNs (virtual private networks), 415–416
Remote Assistance, 415–416
Remote Desktop, 415–416
Remote Installation Services (RIS), 217
renaming folders, 538
repeaters, 351
replay attacks, 672
reset button, 129
resetting mobile devices, 609
resistance, 10
resizing tiles, 537
resolution
  monitors, 47
  native resolution, 245
  screen resolution, 266
restore points, 298–299
restricting permissions, 688–689
RFI (radio frequency interference), 77, 319
RG-6, 353
RG-59, 353
RGA connectors, 37
Ribbon, 245
RIS (Remote Installation Services), 217
RISC (reduced instruction set computer), 15
RJ-11 connectors, 356
RJ-45 connectors, 355, 623
rm command, 602

ROBOCOPY command, 289
rogue antivirus products, 695
ROM (read-only memory), 20
rooting, 554–556
rootkits, 669
routers
  configuration, 393–394
  definition of, 323
  Internet connections, 394–395
  logging in to, 397–398
  network location profiles, 395–397
  network setup, 398–399
  overview, 348–349
  testing connectivity of
    with Windows CLI, 403–405
    with Windows GUI, 402–403
  wireless settings, 399–402
RSA, 700
RSTRUI command, 289
rude customers, 736
Run as Administrator option, 258
Run Line utility, 289–290
RUNAS command, 289

S

SaaS (Software as a Service), 426
Safe Mode, 224
safety
  electrical safety, 75
  environmental protection
    equipment disposal, 80–82
    SDSs (safety data sheets), 79–80
  equipment protection
    climate concerns, 77
    EMI (electromagnetic interference), 77
    ESD (electrostatic discharge), 76–77
    power fluctuation, 78
    power-protection devices, 78–79
  fire safety, 75–76
  general safety, 74
  importance of, 74
safety data sheets (SDSs), 79–80
sandboxes, 553
SATA (Serial AT Attachment) connections
  installation, 124–126
  overview, 28–29
satellite Internet connections, 383–422, 424
SC (Subscriber Connector) connectors, 362
Scandisk, 88
scanners, 45
scheduled servicing (printers), 621
scheduled tasks
  Linux and OS X, 592–594
  Windows, 297–298
SCP (Secure Copy), 429
screen calibration (mobile devices), 539–540
screen lock, 714
screen orientation (mobile devices), 538–539
screen resolution, 266
screen sharing (OS X), 582
screens, replacing, 485
screwdrivers, 93
screws, 93
scrolling, 493
SD (secure digital) cards, 60, 474
SDHC (Secure Digital High Capacity), 474
SDKs (software development kits), 517
SDRAM (Synchronous DRAM), 21
SDSs (safety data sheets), 79–80
search feature, troubleshooting, 769
Search tab (Folder Options), 266
SEC (single-edge connector), 108
sectors, 202
Secure Boot, 141
Secure Copy (SCP), 429
Secure Digital High Capacity (SDHC), 474
secure digital (SD) cards, 60, 474
secure erase, 691–693
Secure Hash Algorithm (SHA), 698
secure HTTP (HTTPS), 428
secure Internet connections, troubleshooting, 772–773
Secure Sockets Layer (SSL), 384, 568
security
  BIOS (basic input/output system), 140–141
  data protection
    biometric identification devices, 685–686
    data backups, 686–687
    data wiping, 691–693
    encryption, 689
    hard drive recycling and destruction, 691–693
    permissions, 687–689
    smart cards, 685–686
    software firewalls, 683–685
    Windows BitLocker, 689–691

firewalls
hardware firewalls, 349–350, 703–705
software firewalls, 683–685, 704
troubleshooting, 778–779
Windows Firewall, 268, 711–713
Linux and OS X
antivirus/antimalware, 596
firmware updates, 596
operating system updates, 594–596
security credentials manager, 597
malware protection
antimalware software, 694–695
remediation for infected systems, 695–696
signature file updates, 697
mobile devices
antivirus protection, 553–556
common problems and solutions, 606–612
locator apps, 551–552
passcode locks, 545–550
patches, 556–557
remote backup, 551
remote wipe, 518–552
rooting/jailbreaking, 554–556
updates, 556–557
operating systems, 296
overview, 666
physical equipment protection
AutoPlay, 707
AutoRun, 707
BIOS/UEFI passwords, 706
BYOD (bring your own device), 708
multifactor authentication, 707–708
overview, 706
security hardware, 708–710
security profiles, 708
preventive maintenance
account maintenance, 713–714
data backups, 711
group management, 717
operating system security packs, 710–711
security patches, 710–711
user management, 714–716
Windows Firewall, 711–713
protection software tools, 88–89
security policy
accessing, 675–676
definition of, 674–675
exporting, 679
passwords, 676–679
usernames, 676–677
techniques
communication encryption types, 698–701
DMZ (demilitarized zone), 704–705
firewalls, 349–350, 703–705
firmware updates, 703
port forwarding, 705
port triggering, 705
SSIDs (service set identifiers), 701–702
UPnP (Universal Plug and Play), 702
wireless security modes, 702
threats
data threats, 666
malware, 667–669, 694–697
phishing, 669
physical threats, 666
social engineering, 673–674
spam, 670
TCP/IP attacks, 670–672
zero-day attacks, 672–673
troubleshooting
common problems and solutions, 721–723
computer security, 777–778
documentation of outcomes, 721
firewall settings, 778–779
full system functionality verification, 720–721
malware settings, 775–776
plan of action, 720
preventive measures, 720–721
problem identification, 718–719
proxy settings, 778–779
testing, 719–720
theory of probable cause, 719
user accounts and permissions, 776–777
web security
ActiveX filtering, 681
InPrivate Browsing, 682–683
overview, 679–680
pop-up blockers, 681
SmartScreen Filter, 682
Windows Local Security Policy
accessing, 675–676
definition of, 674–675
exporting, 679
passwords, 676–677
usernames, 676–677
wireless security, 344–345, 401–402
Security Center, 267
security credentials manager, 597
security hardware, 708–710
security key fobs, 686

security keyhole, 445
security policy
accessing, 675–676
definition of, 674–675
exporting, 679
passwords
guidelines for, 677
levels of password protection, 676–677
management, 678–679
password policy, 677–678
usernames, 676–677
security profiles, 708
Security tab (Internet Options), 264
selecting
ISPs (Internet Service Providers), 423–424
PC components
adapter cards, 56–57
cases, 51–52
CPUs, 53–55
external storage, 61–62
fans, 51–52
hard disk drives, 57–58
input/output devices, 62
media readers, 59–60
motherboards, 50–51
NICs (network interface cards), 386–387
optical drives, 61
power supplies, 53
RAM (random-access memory), 55–56
Self-Monitoring, Analysis and Reporting Technology (S.M.A.R.T.), 589
serial AT Attachment (SATA) connections, 28–29
serial data transfer, 622
servers
email servers, 566
print servers, 644–646
proxy servers, 430–431
service level agreements (SLAs), 740–741
service set identifiers (SSIDs), 400, 701–702
services, 246
Services console, 281
Services tab
System Configuration, 283
Task Manager, 255
services.msc, 281, 769
settings. ***See also*** **configuration**
BIOS (basic input/output system), 139–140
Control Panel utilities
Action Center, 267
Device Manager, 272–273
Devices and Printers, 273–274
Display Settings, 265–266
Folder Options, 266–267
HomeGroup, 276–277
Internet Options, 264–265
Network and Sharing Center, 277
overview, 260–262
Power Options, 269–270
Program and Features, 275–276
Region, 275
Region and Language, 275
Sound, 274
System utility, 270–272
Troubleshooting, 275–276
User Accounts, 262–264
Windows Firewall, 268
firewalls, 778–779
malware settings, 775–776
NICs (network interface cards), 390–393
proxy settings, 778–779
routers, 399–402
Setup programs
BIOS (basic input/output system), 137–138
UEFI (Unified Extensible Firmware Interface), 103–138
SFC (System File Checker), 88
sfc command, 289, 769
SFF (small form factor) cases, 5
SFTP (SSH File Transfer Protocol), 429
SHA (Secure Hash Algorithm), 698
shadow copies, 301
Shake feature, 249
shared key authentication, 344
sharing
network sharing
administrative shares, 412–414
domains, 406–407
drive mapping, 414
network file sharing, 410–411
Windows homegroups, 408–409
Windows Vista, 409–410
workgroups, 406–407
printer sharing
configuration, 641–642
connecting to, 642–643
finding on network, 643–644
wireless printers, 644
shells, 582
shielded twisted-pair (STP) cables, 319–355
Short Message Service (SMS)
mobile payments, 542
overview, 422
shrinking partitions, 230–231

shutdown command, 288
Shutdown option (laptops), 466
Sidebar (Windows Vista), 245
sideloading apps, 525
signature files
overview, 596
updates, 697
signatures, 596, 697
signed drivers, 151–152
SIM (subscriber identity module) cards, 446, 545
SIM (System Image Manager), 218
SIMMs (single inline memory modules), 22
Simple Mail Transfer Protocol (SMTP), 338, 430, 567
simple passcode locks, 547
simplex mode, 317
single inline memory modules (SIMMs), 22
single rail power supplies, 10
single sign-on (SSO), 210
single-channel RAM, 22
single-core CPUs, 16
single-edge connector (SEC), 108
single-mode fiber (SMF), 359
S-IPS (Super-IPS), 446
Siri, 544
SLAs (service level agreements), 740–741
Sleep setting, 466
sleep timers, 467–468
sliding, 447
small form factor (SFF) cases, 5
small outline DIMM (SODIMM), 22, 455, 476–478
S.M.A.R.T. (Self-Monitoring, Analysis and Reporting Technology), 589
smart cameras, 499
smart card readers, 46, 475–476
smart cards, 475–476, 685–686
smart headsets, 498–499
Smart Lock (Android), 547
smart watches, 498
smartphones, 492
SmartScreen Filter, 682
SMF (single-mode fiber), 359
SMS (Short Message Service)
mobile payments, 542
overview, 422
SMTP (Simple Mail Transfer Protocol), 338, 430, 567
Snap feature, 249
snap-ins, 289
social engineering, 673–674
social networking sites, 317
socket architecture, 108
SODIMM (small outline DIMM), 22, 455, 476–478
software. *See* applications; apps (mobile)
Software as a Service (SaaS), 426
software development kits (SDKs), 517
software firewalls
compared to hardware firewalls, 704
configuration, 683–685
software maintenance tasks, 160
software optimization. *See* optimization
software print servers, 645
software tools, 88–89
solid state drives (SSDs)
mobile devices, 494–495
overview, 26, 202, 284
solid state hybrid drives (SSHD)
data wiping, 693
overview, 26, 202, 284
something for something, 673
sound. *See* audio
sound adapters, 23
sound cards, 56–57
Sound utility, 274
source port numbers, 376–380
Southbridge chipsets, 13
spam, 670, 673
spanned volumes, 232
speakers
Bluetooth speakers, 569
for mobile devices, 497
overview, 46
replacing, 488
spear phishing, 669, 673
special function keys, 456–457
specialized computer systems
audio/video editing workstations, 64–65
CAx workstations, 64
gaming PCs, 66–67
home theater PCs, 67–68
thick clients, 63
thin clients, 63
virtualized workstations, 65–66
specialized search results, GPS (global positioning system) and, 540
speed of printers, 620
Speed setting (NIC), 390
SPI (stateful packet inspection), 704
spikes (AC), 78
spoofing, 671

Spotlight, 532, 585
spreading, 494
SPS (standby power supply), 78–79
SRAM (static RAM), 21
SSDs (solid state drives)
data wiping, 693
mobile devices, 494–495
overview, 26, 202, 284
SSH File Transfer Protocol (SFTP), 429
SSHD (solid state hybrid drives)
data wiping, 693
overview, 26, 202, 284
SSIDs (service set identifiers), 400, 701–702
SSL (Secure Sockets Layer), 384, 568
SSO (single sign-on), 210
ST (Straight-Tip) connectors, 362
standards
802.11 standard (WiFi)
antenna connectors, 462–463
configuration, 471–472
hotspots, 552, 560–561
mobile device connectivity, 557–559
overview, 343–346
WiFi analyzers, 87
WiFi calling, 541
WiFi Sync, 577
WPA (WiFi Protected Access), 344, 402, 702
WPA2 (WiFi Protected Access 2), 344, 402, 702
WPS (WiFi Protected Setup), 702
802.11 standards, 343–346
802.15.1 standard (Bluetooth)
characteristics of, 468–469
configuration, 470
definition of, 496
installation, 470
for mobile devices, 563
overview, 328–329, 644
pairing, 564–566
specifications, 469–470
802.3 standard, 342–345
1284 standard, 622–623
1394 standard
capabilities, 39
FireWire 400, 31
FireWire 800, 31
overview, 39
printers, 623
definition of, 335
Ethernet standards
cable standards, 342–343
CSMA/CA, 318–343
CSMA/CD, 341–342
wireless standards, 343–346
reference models
comparison of, 341
de-encapsulation example, 340
encapsulation example, 339–340
open standards, 333–335
OSI model, 335–337
protocol data units, 338–339
protocols, 334–336
TCP/IP model, 335–340
standby power supply (SPS), 78–79
standoffs, 115
Start menu, 251–253
Start screen items (Windows Phone), 535–537
startup modes, 223–224
startup programs, 296
Startup Repair, 221
Startup tab
System Configuration, 283
Task Manager, 254
stateful packet inspection (SPI), 704
static IP addressing, 368–370
static RAM (SRAM), 21
stereo headphone jacks, 452
stop errors, 766
Stopped setting (services), 281
storage controllers, 57
storage drives
adding, 231
connecting power to, 124–126
connections, 28–32
data wiping, 691–693
drive letter assignment, 231–233
external storage, selecting, 61–62
flash drives
definition of, 474
structure of, 202–203
hard disk drives
backups, 299–300
connecting power to, 124–126
data wiping, 691–693
definition of, 26
encryption, 141
installation, 116–117
laptop hard disk drives, 485–486
partitioning, 203–206
partitions, 230–231
RAID (redundant display of independent disks), 24, 31–33, 232, 763
recycling and destruction, 693–694

selecting, 57–58
structure of, 200–202
troubleshooting, 172–175
upgrades, 149–150
inspecting, 162
laptops
overview, 456
replacing, 485–486
mapping, 231–233, 414
media readers, 59–60
mirroring, 234
mobile devices, 494–495
mounted drives, 235–236
optical drives
installation, 117
selecting, 61
overview, 26–28, 200
partitions
configuration, 203–206
extending, 230
Linux/OS X partition management, 589
recovery partitions, 220
shrinking, 230–231
recycling and destruction, 693–694
troubleshooting, 172–175
upgrades, 149–150
STP (shielded twisted-pair), 319–355
straight-through cables, 357
Straight-Tip (ST) connectors, 362
stress management, 740
striped volumes, 232
striping, 31
subdirectories, 190
subfolders, 190
subnet masks, 364, 368
Subscriber Connector (SC) connectors, 362
subscriber identity module (SIM) card, 446, 545
Super-IPS (S-IPS), 446
supernets, 365–366
support software, 751
surge supressors, 78
S-Video connector, 451
Swipe passcode locks, 546
swiping, 447
switches, 323, 346–347
switching tables, 347
symmetric encryption, 699
SYN flood, 671
Sync process
Android, 573–574
iOS, 575–576
synchronization
mobile devices
Android, 573–574
connection types, 576–577
definition of, 572–573
iOS, 575–576
WiFi Sync, 577
synchronous DRAM (SDRAM), 21
Sysprep, 215
system boards. *See* motherboards
System Configuration, 281–282
System File Checker (SFC), 88
system folder, 236
system functionality, verifying. *See* full system functionality verification
system icons (Android), 526–527
System Image Manager (SIM), 218
System Image Recovery, 220, 221
System Information, 285–286
System Preparation (Sysprep), 215
System Recovery Options, 220–221
System Restore, 219–221
System utility, 270–272

T

T568A, 356–357
T568B, 356–357
tables
cron table, 592–594
GPT (GUID partition table), 204–206
switching tables, 347
tablets, 492
tailgating, 673
talkative customers, 735–736
tape drives, 26
Task Manager, 167–168, 253–256
Task Scheduler, 297–298
task scheduling
Linux and OS X, 592–594
Windows, 297–298
taskbar, 253
taskkill command, 288
tasklist command, 288
TCO (total cost of ownership), 621–622
TCP (Transmission Control Protocol), 339, 374–376
TCP/IP (Transmission Control Protocol/ Internet Protocol)
attacks, 670–672
network model, 335–340

Telecommunications Industry Association, 335
temperature control. *See* **cooling systems**
Temporal Key Integrity Protocol (TKIP), 344, 401
temporary files, 237
terminal, 583
terminal emulators, 583
Terminal utility, 583
terminating employee access, 713
Terminator, 583
test pages, printing, 634
testing
  printers, 634
  router connectivity
    with Windows CLI, 403–405
    with Windows GUI, 402–403
  theory of probable cause
    laptop/mobile device issues, 504–507
    network issues, 435
    operating system issues, 303–306
    OS X issues, 602–607
    preventive maintenance issues, 169–170
    printer issues, 653
    security issues, 719–720
tethering, 471, 496, 559, 569
TFT (thin film transistor), 45–46
TFTP (Trivial File Transfer Protocol), 338
themes, 245
theory of probable cause
  establishing
    laptop/mobile device issues, 503–506
    Linux, 601–606
    mobile operating systems, 601–606
    networks, 434–435
    operating systems, 302–305
    OS X, 601–606
    overview, 168–169
    printer issues, 652–653
    security issues, 719
  testing
    laptop/mobile device issues, 504–507
    Linux issues, 602–607
    mobile operating system issues, 602–607
    networks, 435
    operating systems, 303–306
    OS X, 602–607
    preventive maintenance issues, 169–170
    printer issues, 653
    security issues, 719–720
thermal inkjet nozzles, 624
thermal printers, 628
thick clients, 63
Thicknet, 353
thin clients, 63
thin film transistor (TFT), 45–46
Thinnet, 353
This PC feature, 257
threats. *See also* **security**
  data threats, 666
  malware
    adware, 668
    antimalware software, 694–695
    definition of, 667
    ransomware, 668
    remediation for infected systems, 695–696
    rootkits, 669
    signature file updates, 697
    spyware, 668
    Trojan horses, 667–668
    viruses, 667
    worms, 668
  phishing, 669
  physical threats, 666
  social engineering, 673–674
  spam, 670
  TCP/IP attacks, 670–672
  zero-day attacks, 672–673
throttling (CPUs), 16
thumb drives, 61–62
thunbnail previews, 253
Thunderbolt, 24, 36
tiles, live, 245
Time Machine, 588–589
time management, 739
time shifting, 67
TKIP (Temporal Key Integrity Protocol), 344, 401
TLS (Transport Layer Security), 384
TN (twisted nematic), 446
tone generator and probe, 73
toner kits, disposal of, 81
tools (hardware). *See also* **utilities**
  cable tools, 85
  cleaning tools, 85, 94–96
  diagnostic tools, 85–88
  ESD (electrostatic discharge) tools, 83–84, 91–92
  general tool use, 82–83
  hand tools, 84, 93–94
  magnetic tools, 93
  miscellaneous tools, 90–91
  organizational tools, 89–91
Tools tab (System Configuration), 283
total cost of ownership (TCO), 621–622

touch ID passcode locks, 547
touch interface
Android
All Apps screen, 529–530
app management, 527–528
folders, 528–529
home screen items, 525–527
widget management, 528
iOS
app management, 533
folders, 534–535
home screen items, 530–532
multitasking bar, 533
Windows Phone
app and folder management, 537–538
Start screen items, 535–537
touchpads
overview, 453
replacing, 483–484
touchscreens
mobile devices, 493–494
PCs (personal computer systems), 44
tower cases, 5
TPM (Trusted Platform Module), 141, 689, 778
tracert command, 404–405
tracking mobile devices, 540
tracks, 202
tractor feeds, 630
transferring calls, 734
transferring process (laser printing), 626
Transmission Control Protocol (TCP), 339, 374–376
transmission of data, 317–325
transport layer
definition of, 373
features of, 373–374
port numbers, 376–380
TCP (Transmission Control Protocol), 374–376
UDP (User Datagram Protocol), 376
Transport Layer Security (TLS), 384
triggering (port), 705
triple A, 431
triple core CPUs, 16
Triple Data Encryption Algorithm (3DES), 699
triple-channel RAM, 22
Trivial File Transfer Protocol (TFTP), 338
Trojan horses, 667–668
troubleshooting. *See also* **preventive maintenance**
backing up data before, 164
communication skills and, 731
CPUs, 176–179
definition of, 158, 302
internal components, 174–176
laptops
common problems and solutions, 506–512
documentation of outcomes, 506–509
full system functionality verification, 505–508
problem identification, 503–506
testing, 504–507
theory of probable cause, 503–506
Linux
common problems and solutions, 608–609
documentation of outcomes, 603–608
full system functionality verification, 603–608
plan of action, 602–607
problem identification, 601–605
testing, 602–607
theory of probable cause, 601–606
memory, 176–179
mobile devices
common problems and solutions, 509–514
documentation of outcomes, 506–509
full system functionality verification, 505–508
problem identification, 503–506
testing, 504–507
theory of probable cause, 503–506
mobile operating systems
Android problems and solutions, 604–610
documentation of outcomes, 603–608
factory resets, 609
full system functionality verification, 603–608
iOS problems and solutions, 604–610
mobile OS security problems and solutions, 606–612
plan of action, 602–607
problem identification, 600–605
testing, 602–607
theory of probable cause, 601–606
monitors, 177–181
motherboards, 174–176
networks
common problems and solutions, 437–439
connection problems, 770–771
email failure, 772
FTP (File Transfer Protocol) problems, 772–773
network troubleshooting tools, 773–775
problem identification, 434
secure Internet connections, 772–773
operating systems
advanced problems and solutions, 766–769
overview, 766
problem identification, 302–305
testing, 303–307
theory of probable cause, 302–305

OS X
  common problems and solutions, 608–609
  documentation of outcomes, 603–608
  full system functionality verification, 603–608
  plan of action, 602–607
  problem identification, 601–605
  testing, 602–607
  theory of probable cause, 601–606
overview, 163
power supplies, 175–177
preventive maintenance
  advanced problems and solutions, 763–764
  documentation of outcomes, 172
  full system functionality verification, 171–172
  plan of action, 170–172
  preventive measures, 171–172
  problem identification, 164–168
  review, 762
  theory of probable cause, 168–170
printers
  advanced problems and solutions, 765
  common problems and solutions, 655–657
  documentation of outcomes, 654–655
  full system functionality verification, 654
  plan of action, 653–654
  preventive maintenance, 647–651
  problem identification, 652
  testing, 653
  theory of probable cause, 652–653
security
  common problems and solutions, 721–723
  computer security, 777–778
  documentation of outcomes, 721
  firewall settings, 778–779
  full system functionality verification, 720–721
  malware settings, 775–776
  plan of action, 720
  preventive measures, 720–721
  problem identification, 718–719
  proxy settings, 778–779
  testing, 719–720
  theory of probable cause, 719
  user accounts and permissions, 776–777
storage devices, 172–175
Troubleshooting utility, 275–276
Trusted Devices feature (Android), 547
Trusted Faces feature (Android), 547
Trusted Places feature (Android), 547
Trusted Platform Module (TPM), 141, 689, 778
trusted sources, 695
Trusted Voice feature (Android), 547
turning on. *See* configuration
TV tuner cards, 23
twisted nematic (TN), 446
twisted-pair cables
  category ratings, 319–355
  definition of, 318
  STP (shielded twisted-pair), 319–355
  UTP (unshielded twisted-pair), 318–354
  wiring schemes, 356–357
Type 1 hypervisors, 246–292
Type 2 hypervisors, 246–292

U

UAC (User Account Control), 245–264, 715
Ubuntu Linux. *See* Linux
UDP (User Datagram Protocol), 339, 376
UEFI (Unified Extensible Firmware Interface)
  ASUS Advanced Mode, 144
  chips, 12
  EZ Mode, 140–141
  passwords, 706
  Setup program, 103–138
UEFI Firmware Settings, 221
uname command, 556
unattended installations, 218
unbuffered memory, 55
Unified Extensible Firmware Interface. *See* UEFI (Unified Extensible Firmware Interface)
uninstalling applications, 259–260
uninterruptible power supply (UPS), 78
Unity GUI, 579–584
Universal Plug and Play (UPnP), 702
Universal Serial Bus. *See* USB (Universal Serial Bus)
Universal Threat Management (UTM), 431–432
UNIX, 577, 599
unlisted printers, finding on network, 643–644
unmounting drives (Linux/OS X), 589
unshielded twisted-pair (UTP), 318–354
untrusted sources, 695
updates. *See also* upgrades
  device drivers, 296–297
  firmware, 297, 703
  Linux and OS X
    antivirus/antimalware, 596
    firmware updates, 596
    operating system updates, 594–596
    security credentials manager, 597

mobile devices, 556–557
NICs (network interface cards), 388–389
operating systems, 246–297
printer drivers, 633–634
signature file updates, 697
Windows, 296–297

Upgrade Advisor, 196

Upgrade Assistant, 196

upgrades. *See also* **updates**
BIOS (basic input/output system), 147–148
CPUs, 147–148
fans, 148
heat sinks, 148
motherboards, 145–147
operating systems
data migration, 198–208
OS compatibility, 196–197
reasons for, 196
Windows OS upgrades, 197–198
peripheral devices, 150–152
RAM (random-access memory), 149
storage drives, 149–150

UPnP (Universal Plug and Play), 702

uppercase, 738

UPS (uninterruptible power supply), 78

USB (Universal Serial Bus)
capabilities, 39
connectors, 30–32
flash drives, 202
ports, 23, 39, 129
printers, 623

User Account Control (UAC), 245–264, 715

user accounts. *See* **accounts**

User Accounts utility, 262–264

User Datagram Protocol (UDP), 339, 376

user interfaces (OS), 190–191

user management, 714–716

User State Migration Tool (USMT), 198

usernames, Windows Local Security Policy, 676–677

Users group, 717

Users tab (Task Manager), 255–256

USMT (User State Migration Tool), 198

utilities. *See also* **commands**
Administrative Tools
Component Services, 279–280, 283
Computer Management, 277–278
Data Sources (ODBC), 280–281, 284
definition of, 277
Event Viewer, 279
Performance Monitor, 282–283
Services console, 281
System Configuration, 281–282
Windows Memory Diagnostic, 246–283
command-line tools
CLI (command-line interface) commands, 286–288
definition of, 286
Run Line utility, 289–290
Control Panel utilities
Action Center, 267
Device Manager, 272–273
Devices and Printers, 273–274
Display Settings, 265–266
Folder Options, 266–267
HomeGroup, 276–277
Internet Options, 264–265
Network and Sharing Center, 277
overview, 260–262
Power Options, 269–270
Program and Features, 275–276
Region, 275
Region and Language, 275
Sound, 274
System utility, 270–272
Troubleshooting, 275–276
User Accounts, 262–264
Windows Firewall, 268
maintenance tools
Disk Defragmenter, 284–285
Disk Error-Checking tool, 285
System Information, 285–286
software tools, 88–89

UTM (Universal Threat Management), 431–432

UTP (unshielded twisted-pair), 318–354

V

V (volts), 10

validating backups, 687

VDI (virtual desktop infrastructure), 65

ventilation (laptops), 452

verification of system functionality
laptops/mobile devices, 505–508
Linux, 603–608
mobile operating systems, 603–608
networks, 436–437
operating systems, 304–308
preventive maintenance, 171–172
printers, 654
security, 720–721

vertical resolution, 47
VGA connectors, 36
video
  audio/video editing workstations, 64–65
  video adapter cards, 120–121
  video ports and cables, 33–38
View tab (Folder Options), 266
virtual assistants, 543–544
virtual desktop infrastructure (VDI), 65
virtual machine managers (VMMs). *See* hypervisors
virtual machines
  definition of, 246
  hypervisors
    definition of, 291
    Type 1 hypervisors, 246–292
    Type 2 hypervisors, 246–292
    Windows Hyper-V, 292–293
    Windows Virtual PC, 246–293
    Windows XP Mode, 293–294
  logical virtual machine diagram, 291
  virtual machine requirements, 294
virtual printers, 630–631
virtual private networks. *See* VPNs (virtual private networks)
virtualization
  definition of, 62
  hypervisors
    definition of, 291
    Type 1 hypervisors, 246–292
    Type 2 hypervisors, 246–292
    Windows Hyper-V, 292–293
    Windows Virtual PC, 246–293
    Windows XP Mode, 293–294
  logical virtual machine diagram, 291
  purpose of, 290–291
  virtual machine requirements, 294
  virtualized workstations, 65–66
viruses, 667
VMMs (virtual machine managers). *See* hypervisors
volatile data, 748
volatile memory, 21
voltage regulator module (VRM), 54
voltage selector switches, 11
voltages, 9–10, 78, 142
volts (V), 10
VPNs (virtual private networks)
  configuration
    from mobile devices, 543
    in Windows, 415–416
  connecting from mobile devices, 543
VRM (voltage regulator module), 54

W

W (watts), 10
Wake on LAN setting (NIC), 391
WANs (wide area networks), 329–330, 471
WAP (Wireless Application Protocol), 542
warranties for printers, 621
watches, smart watches, 498
wattages, 10–12
watts (W), 10
wearable devices
  fitness monitors, 498
  smart headsets, 498–499
  smart watches, 498
WEAs (Wireless Emergency Alerts), 544–545
Weather widget, 528
web security
  ActiveX filtering, 681
  InPrivate Browsing, 682–683
  overview, 679–680
  pop-up blockers, 681
  SmartScreen Filter, 682
web services, 428
web slices, 264
webcams, 453, 463
websites, social networking, 317
well-known port numbers, 376–380
WEP (Wired Equivalent Privacy), 344, 401, 702
What You See Is What You Get (WYSIWYG), 632–633
wide area networks (WANs), 329–330
widgets, 528
WiFi. *See* 802.11 standard (WiFi)
WiFi analyzers, 87
WiFi calling, 541
WiFi On/Off widget, 528
WiFi Protected Access 2 (WPA2), 344, 402, 702
WiFi Protected Access (WPA), 344, 402, 702
WiFi Protected Setup (WPS), 702
WiFi Sync, 577
WiMAX (Worldwide Interoperability for Microwave Access), 420–421, 560
Windows 7
  account creation, 210–212
  Administrative Tools
    Component Services, 279–280, 283
    Computer Management, 277–278
    Data Sources (ODBC), 280–281, 284
    definition of, 277

Event Viewer, 279
Performance Monitor, 282–283
Services console, 281
System Configuration, 281–282
Windows Memory Diagnostic, 246–283
backups, 711
Bluetooth devices, discovering, 470
boot process, 222–223
client-side virtualization
hypervisors, 291–294
logical virtual machine diagram, 291
purpose of, 290–291
virtual machine requirements, 294
command-line tools
CLI (command-line interface) commands, 286–288
definition of, 286
Run Line utility, 289–290
Control Panel utilities
Action Center, 267
Device Manager, 272–273
Devices and Printers, 273–274
Display Settings, 265–266
Folder Options, 266–267
HomeGroup, 276–277
Internet Options, 264–265
Network and Sharing Center, 277
overview, 260–262
Power Options, 269–270
Program and Features, 275–276
Region and Language, 275
Sound, 274
System utility, 270–272
Troubleshooting, 275–276
User Accounts, 262–264
Windows Firewall, 268
Device Manager, 213–214
directories
file locations, 236–237
structure of, 234–236
Disk Management utility, 227–229
GUI (graphical user interface)
application installation, 259
application uninstallation, 259–260
Computer feature, 257
Run as Administrator option, 258
Start menu, 252–253
Task Manager, 253–256
taskbar, 253
Windows desktop, 247–251
Windows Explorer, 245
Windows libraries, 258
hardware requirements, 245–249
IP address configuration
dynamic addressing, 370
static addressing, 369
maintenance tools
Disk Defragmenter, 284–285
Disk Error-Checking tool, 285
System Information, 285–286
network connections, testing, 402–403
network sharing
administrative shares, 412–414
drive mapping, 414
homegroups, 408–409
NICs (network interface cards)
configuration, 389
installation, 388–389
overview, 193
Power Options utility, 465–468
preventive maintenance plans
contents of, 295–296
hard drive backups, 299–300
restore points, 298–299
task scheduling, 297–298
updates, 296–297
PreviousVersions, 301
printer sharing, 641–642
Remote Desktop, 417
System Recovery Options, 221
test pages, printing, 634
troubleshooting
common problems and solutions, 305–314
documentation of outcomes, 305–308
full system functionality verification, 304–308
plan of action, 304–307
problem identification, 302–305
testing, 303–306
theory of probable cause, 302–305
Upgrade Advisor, 196
VPN (virtual private network) configuration, 416
Windows Easy Transfer, 198–199
Windows Registry, 224–225
Windows Update, 212–213
Windows 8/8.1
account creation, 210–212
Administrative Tools
Component Services, 279–280, 283
Computer Management, 277–278
Data Sources (ODBC), 280–281, 284
definition of, 277
Event Viewer, 279
Performance Monitor, 282–283

Services console, 281
System Configuration, 281–282
Windows Memory Diagnostic, 246–283
Advanced Startup Options, 220–221
backups, 711
Bluetooth devices, discovering, 470
boot process, 222–223
client-side virtualization
hypervisors, 291–294
logical virtual machine diagram, 291
purpose of, 290–291
virtual machine requirements, 294
command-line tools
CLI (command-line interface) commands, 286–288
definition of, 286
Run Line utility, 289–290
Control Panel utilities
Action Center, 267
Device Manager, 272–273
Devices and Printers, 273–274
Display Settings, 265–266
Folder Options, 265–267
HomeGroup, 276–277
Internet Options, 264–265
Network and Sharing Center, 277
overview, 260–262
Power Options, 269–270
Program and Features, 275–276
Region, 275
Sound, 274
System utility, 270–272
Troubleshooting, 275–276
User Accounts, 262–264
Windows Firewall, 268
Device Manager, 213–214
directories
file locations, 236–237
structure of, 234–236
Disk Management utility, 227–229
GUI (graphical user interface)
application installation, 259
application uninstallation, 259–260
File Explorer, 245–256
Run as Administrator option, 258
Start menu, 251–252
Task Manager, 253–256
taskbar, 253
This PC feature, 257
Windows desktop, 247–251
Windows libraries, 258
hardware requirements, 248
installation
with default settings, 208–210
Windows Update, 212–213
IP address configuration
dynamic addressing, 371
static addressing, 370
maintenance tools
Disk Defragmenter, 284–285
Disk Error-Checking tool, 285
System Information, 285–286
network connections, testing, 402–403
network sharing
administrative shares, 412–414
drive mapping, 414
NICs (network interface cards)
configuration, 389
installation, 388–389
overview, 193
Power Options utility, 465–468
preventive maintenance plans
contents of, 295–296
hard drive backups, 299–300
restore points, 298–299
task scheduling, 297–298
updates, 296–297
printer sharing, 642
Refresh Your PC tool, 219
Remote Assistance, 417–418
test pages, printing, 634
troubleshooting
common problems and solutions, 305–314
documentation of outcomes, 305–308
full system functionality verification, 304–308
plan of action, 304–307
problem identification, 302–305
testing, 303–306
theory of probable cause, 302–305
Upgrade Assistant, 196
upgrading to, 197–198
VPN (virtual private network) configuration, 416
Windows Easy Transfer, 198–199
Windows Registry, 224–225
Windows Action Center, 89
Windows API, 192
Windows Automated Installation Kit (AIK), 219
Windows BitLocker, 689–691
Windows Boot Manager, 223
Windows Defender, 89
Windows Easy Transfer, 198–199

Windows Explorer, 245
Windows Firewall
configuration, 683–685
overview, 89, 268
preventive maintenance, 711–713
Windows Hyper-V, 292–293
Windows kernel, 223
Windows Local Security Policy
accessing, 675–676
definition of, 674–675
exporting, 679
passwords
guidelines for, 677
levels of password protection, 676–677
management, 678–679
password policy, 677–678
usernames, 676–677
Windows Memory Diagnostic, 221, 246–283
Windows Phones touch interface
app and folder management, 537–538
Start screen items, 535–537
Windows Preinstallation Environment (PE), 220
Windows Recovery Environment (WinRE), 220
Windows Registry, 223–224
Windows Startup Settings, 221
Windows Task Scheduler, 297–298
Windows Update, 212–213
Windows Virtual PC, 246–293
Windows Vista
account creation, 210–212
Administrative Tools
Component Services, 279–280, 283
Computer Management, 277–278
Data Sources (ODBC), 280–281, 284
definition of, 277
Event Viewer, 279
Performance Monitor, 282–283
Services console, 281
System Configuration, 281–282
Windows Memory Diagnostic, 246–283
backups, 711
Bluetooth devices, discovering, 470
boot process, 222–223
client-side virtualization
hypervisors, 291–294
logical virtual machine diagram, 291
purpose of, 290–291
virtual machine requirements, 294
command-line tools
CLI (command-line interface) commands, 286–288
definition of, 286
Run Line utility, 289–290
Control Panel utilities
Add Hardware, 274
Device Manager, 272–273
Display Settings, 265–266
Folder Options, 266–267
Internet Options, 264–265
Network and Sharing Center, 277
overview, 260–262
Power Options, 269–270
Program and Features, 275–276
Region and Language, 275
Security Center, 267
Sound, 274
System utility, 270–272
Troubleshooting, 275–276
User Accounts, 262–264
Windows Firewall, 268
Device Manager, 213–214
directories
file locations, 236–237
structure of, 234–236
Disk Management utility, 227–229
GUI (graphical user interface)
application installation, 259
application uninstallation, 259–260
Computer feature, 257
Run as Administrator option, 258
Start menu, 252–253
Task Manager, 253–256
taskbar, 253
Windows desktop, 247–251
Windows Explorer, 245
hardware requirements, 245–249
maintenance tools
Disk Defragmenter, 284–285
Disk Error-Checking tool, 285
System Information, 285–286
network connections, testing, 402
network sharing
administrative shares, 412–414
drive mapping, 414
overview, 409–410
NICs (network interface cards)
configuration, 389
installation, 388–389
overview, 193
Power Options utility, 465–468
preventive maintenance plans
contents of, 295–296
hard drive backups, 299–300

restore points, 298–299
task scheduling, 297–298
updates, 296–297
Remote Desktop, 417
System Recovery Options, 221
test pages, printing, 634
troubleshooting
common problems and solutions, 305–314
documentation of outcomes, 305–308
full system functionality verification, 304–308
plan of action, 304–307
problem identification, 302–305
testing, 303–306
theory of probable cause, 302–305
Upgrade Advisor, 196
VPN (virtual private network) configuration, 416
Windows Easy Transfer, 198–199
Windows Registry, 224–225
Windows Update, 212–213
Windows XP Mode, 293–294
WinLoad, 223
WinRE (Windows Recovery Environment), 220
wiping data
remote wipe, 518–552
tools for, 691–693
wired connections, mobile devices and, 495–496
Wired Equivalent Privacy (WEP), 344, 401, 702
wireless access points, 347–348
Wireless Application Protocol (WAP), 542
wireless cards, replacing, 487
wireless configuration
laptops
Bluetooth, 468–470
cellular WAN, 471
WiFi, 471–472
mobile devices, 496
Wireless Emergency Alerts (WEAs), 544–545
wireless Ethernet standards, 343–346
wireless LANs (WLANs), 327–328, 644
wireless NICs
installation, 119–120
overview, 23
wireless printers, 623, 644
wireless routers, 323, 399–402
wireless security, 344–345, 401–402, 702
wiring schemes (twisted-pair cables), 356–357
wizards
Add Printer wizard, 642–643
Backup Files Wizard, 711
WLANs (wireless LANs), 327–328, 644
Work Network location profile, 396
workgroups, 210, 277, 406–407
workspace safety
electrical safety, 75
environmental protection
equipment disposal, 80–82
SDSs (safety data sheets), 79–80
equipment protection
climate concerns, 77
EMI (electromagnetic interference), 77
ESD (electrostatic discharge), 76–77
power fluctuation, 78
power-protection devices, 78–79
fire safety, 75–76
general safety, 74–75
importance of, 74
workstations
audio/video editing workstations, 64–65
CAx workstations, 64
ergonomics, 739
Worldwide Interoperability for Microwave Access (WiMAX), 420–421, 560
worms, 668
WPA (WiFi Protected Access), 344, 402, 702
WPA2 (WiFi Protected Access 2), 344, 402, 702
WPS (WiFi Protected Setup), 702
write permissions, 688
WYSIWYG (What You See Is What You Get), 632–633

X

Xcode, 521
XCOPY command, 289
xD, 60
XPS (XML Paper Specification), 631
xterm, 583

Y-Z

Yosemite. *See* OS X
zero-day attacks, 672–673
zero-hour, 672–673
ZIF (zero-insertion force), 108

PEARSON IT CERTIFICATION

Save 10% on CompTIA Exam Voucher

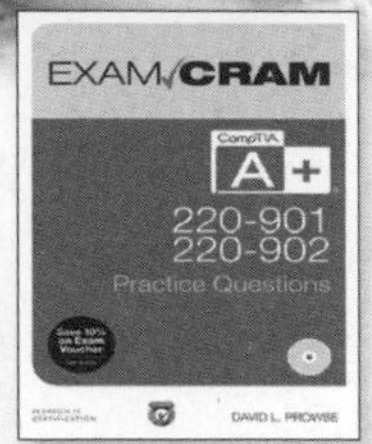

Complete Exam Preparation

CompTIA A+ (220-901) Complete Video Course
9780134499307
18+ hours of personal visual instruction with dynamic and interactive exercises, quizzes, and practice exams.

CompTIA A+ (220-902) Complete Video Course
9780134494128
12+ hours of personal visual instruction with dynamic and interactive exercises, quizzes, and practice exams.

CompTIA A+ 220-901 and 220-902 Complete Video Course Library
9780789758095
A library combining the 220-901 and 220-902 Complete Video Courses providing 30+ hours of instruction. Perfect as complete training or to reinforce other learning.

CompTIA A+ 220-901 and 220-902 Cert Guide
9780789756527
A complete and comprehensive A+ exam prep with two full practice exams.

CompTIA A+ 220-901 and 220-902 Cert Guide Premium Edition and Practice Tests
9780134400594
An enhanced digital version of the *CompTIA A+ 220-901 and 220-902 Cert Guide* with four full practice exams.

Late-Stage Exam Preparation

CompTIA A+ 220-901 and 220-902 Exam Cram
9780789756312
The long-time proven Exam Cram method of study that has helped thousands prepare for and pass their certification exams.

CompTIA A+ 220-901 and 220-902 Practice Questions Exam Cram
9780789756305
700+ practice test questions and complete answer explanations giving readers the perfect complementary tool for their A+ studies.

31 Days Before Your CompTIA A+ Certification Exam
9780789758163
All the exam topics broken up into 31 daily review sessions using short summaries, lists, tables, examples, and graphics.

31 Days Before Your CompTIA A+ Certification Exam (Digital Study Guide)
9780134540030
A self-paced online resource that integrates text, graphics, video screencasts, dynamic exercises, and interactive quizzes into a complete study resource.

SAVE UP TO 45% ON ALL NEW
CompTIA A+ 220-901 and 220-902 Training Materials
PearsonITCertification.com/CompTIA